Panama

Comarca de Guna Yala
p227

Bocas del Toro Province
p181

Colón Province
p212

Panamá Province
p73

Panama City
p44

Chiriquí Province
p153

Coclé Province
p94

Darién Province
p242

Veraguas Province
p135

Península de Azuero
p112

Regis St Louis, Steve Fallon, Carolyn McCarthy

PLAN YOUR TRIP

SUE BISHOP / SHUTTERSTOCK ©

HUMMINGBIRD, BOQUETE P164

RUBICO / SHUTTERSTOCK ©

BOCAS DEL TORO PROVINCE P181

ON THE ROAD

Contents

Welcome to Panama

From clear turquoise seas to the coffee farms and cloud forests of Chiriquí, Panama can be as chilled out or as thrilling as you wish.

Endless Summer

With a plethora of deserted islands, chilled Caribbean vibes on one side and monster Pacific swells on the other, Panama sits poised to deliver the best of beach life. And a whole other world begins at the water's edge. Seize it by scuba diving with whale sharks in the Pacific, snorkeling the rainbow reefs of Bocas del Toro or setting sail in the indigenous territory of Guna Yala, where virgin isles sport nary a footprint. Meanwhile surfers will be psyched to have world-class breaks all to themselves. Hello, paradise.

Cosmopolitan Panama

The dazzling blue coastline and shimmering skyscrapers say Miami, though many joke that you hear more English spoken in Panama. Panama City is culturally diverse and driven, rough-edged yet sophisticated. And there's much that's new or improved. Central America's first subway is operating, the historic Casco district has been beautifully restored and a massive canal expansion completed. Take in the city's funky particulars. Pedal the coastal green space, explore the Casco or attend an avant-garde performance and you will realize this tropical capital isn't only about salsa: that's just the backbeat.

The Great Outdoors

In Panama, nature is all about discovery. Explore the ruins of Spanish forts on the Caribbean coast or boat deep into indigenous territories in a dugout canoe. Wildlife is incidental: a resplendent quetzal on the highland trail, an unruly troupe of screeching howler monkeys outside your cabin or a breaching whale that turns your ferry ride into an adrenaline-filled event. Adventure tourism means zipping through rainforest canopies, swimming alongside sea turtles or trekking to sublime cloud-forest vistas. One small tropical country with two long coasts makes for a pretty big playground.

Lost-World Adventure

You don't have to make it all the way to the Darién to get off the beaten path – though if you do, you've hit one of the most biodiverse spots on the planet. Go where the wild things are. Soak in the spray of towering waterfalls near highland Santa Fé. Visit one of Panama's seven indigenous groups through community tourism. Live out your castaway fantasies in the Guna Yala or idle on a wilderness beach in Península de Azuero. Howl back at the creatures sharing the canopy. Panama is as wild as you want it to be.

Why I Love Panama

By Carolyn McCarthy, Writer

In a world where wilderness and native cultures are disappearing, Panama – against all odds – continues with its essence intact. Trekking through rainforests, watching Congo drumming and paddling between pristine tropical islands offer pure wonder. The wildlife viewing is astounding – both in expected places, like the waters of Isla de Coiba, and in patches of preserved forest just outside the capital. For me Panama is a confluence – an explosion of nature, cultures and beliefs in that messy, musical arrangement that's everyday life in Latin America. All that energy feeds you, and you see the world in new ways.

For more about our writers, see p320

Above: El Valle (p96)

Panama

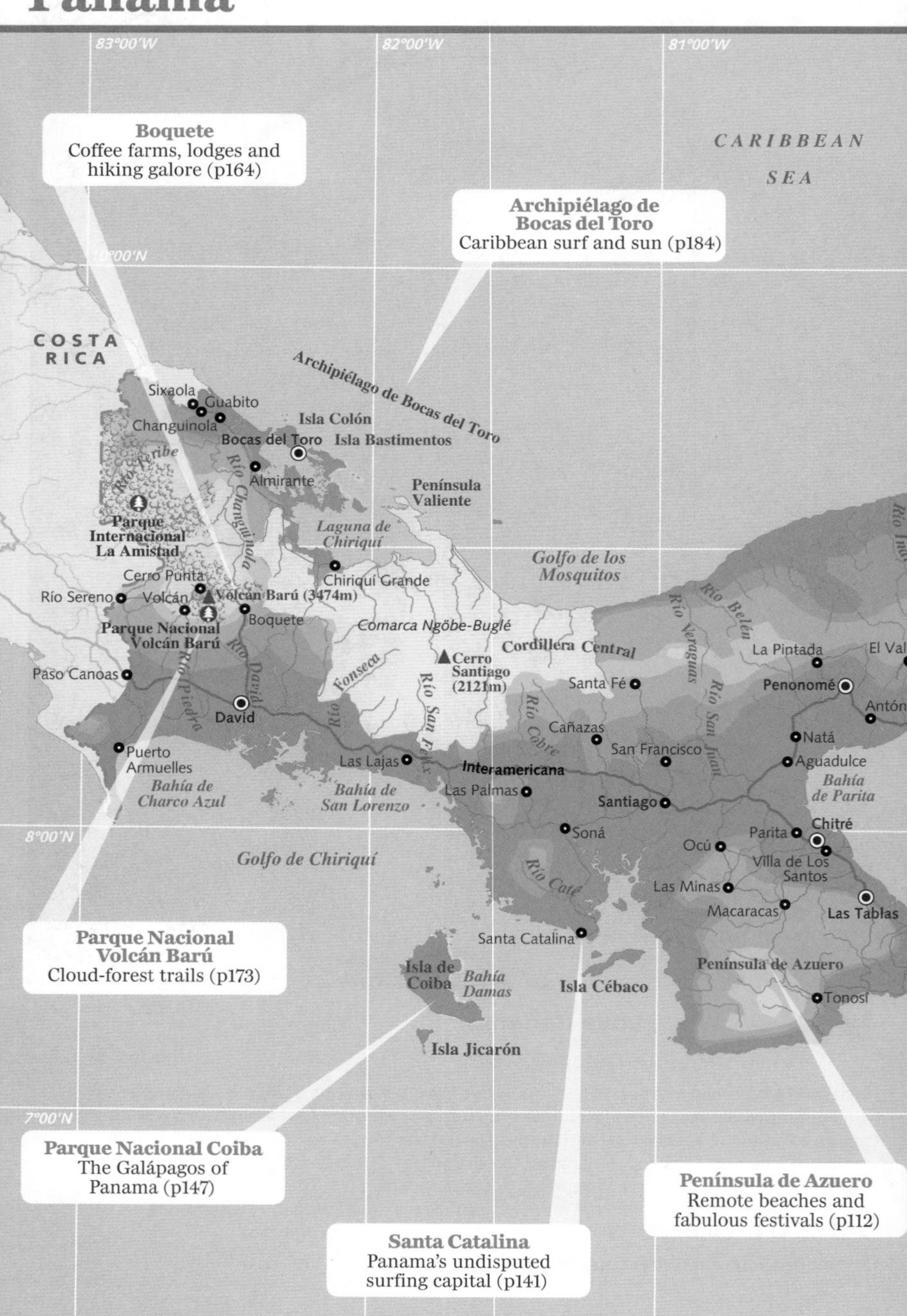

Boquete
Coffee farms, lodges and hiking galore (p164)
Archipiélago de Bocas del Toro
Caribbean surf and sun (p184)
Parque Nacional Volcán Barú
Cloud-forest trails (p173)
Parque Nacional Coiba
The Galápagos of Panama (p147)
Santa Catalina
Panama's undisputed surfing capital (p141)
Península de Azuero
Remote beaches and fabulous festivals (p112)
CARIBBEAN SEA
COSTA RICA
83°00'W
82°00'W
81°00'W
10°00'N
8°00'N
7°00'N
Archipiélago de Bocas del Toro
Sixaola
Guabito
Changuinola
Isla Colón
Bocas del Toro
Isla Bastimentos
Río Teribe
Río Changuinola
Almirante
Península Valiente
Parque Internacional La Amistad
Laguna de Chiriquí
Golfo de los Mosquitos
Chiriquí Grande
Cerro Punta
Río Sereno
Volcán
Volcán Barú (3474m)
Boquete
Parque Nacional Volcán Barú
Comarca Ngöbe-Buglé
Río Indio
Río Belén
Río Veraguas
Cordillera Central
La Pintada
El Valle
Cerro Santiago (2121m)
Paso Canoas
Río David
Río Piedra
Río Fonseca
Río San Félix
Santa Fé
Penonomé
Río Cobre
Río San Juan
Antón
David
Cañazas
Natá
Puerto Armuelles
Las Lajas
San Francisco
Aguadulce
Interamericana
Bahía de Charco Azul
Bahía de San Lorenzo
Las Palmas
Bahía de Parita
Santiago
Chitré
Parita
Soná
Ocú
Villa de Los Santos
Golfo de Chiriquí
Río Caté
Las Minas
Macaracas
Las Tablas
Santa Catalina
Península de Azuero
Isla de Coiba
Bahía Damas
Isla Cébaco
Tonosí
Isla Jicarón

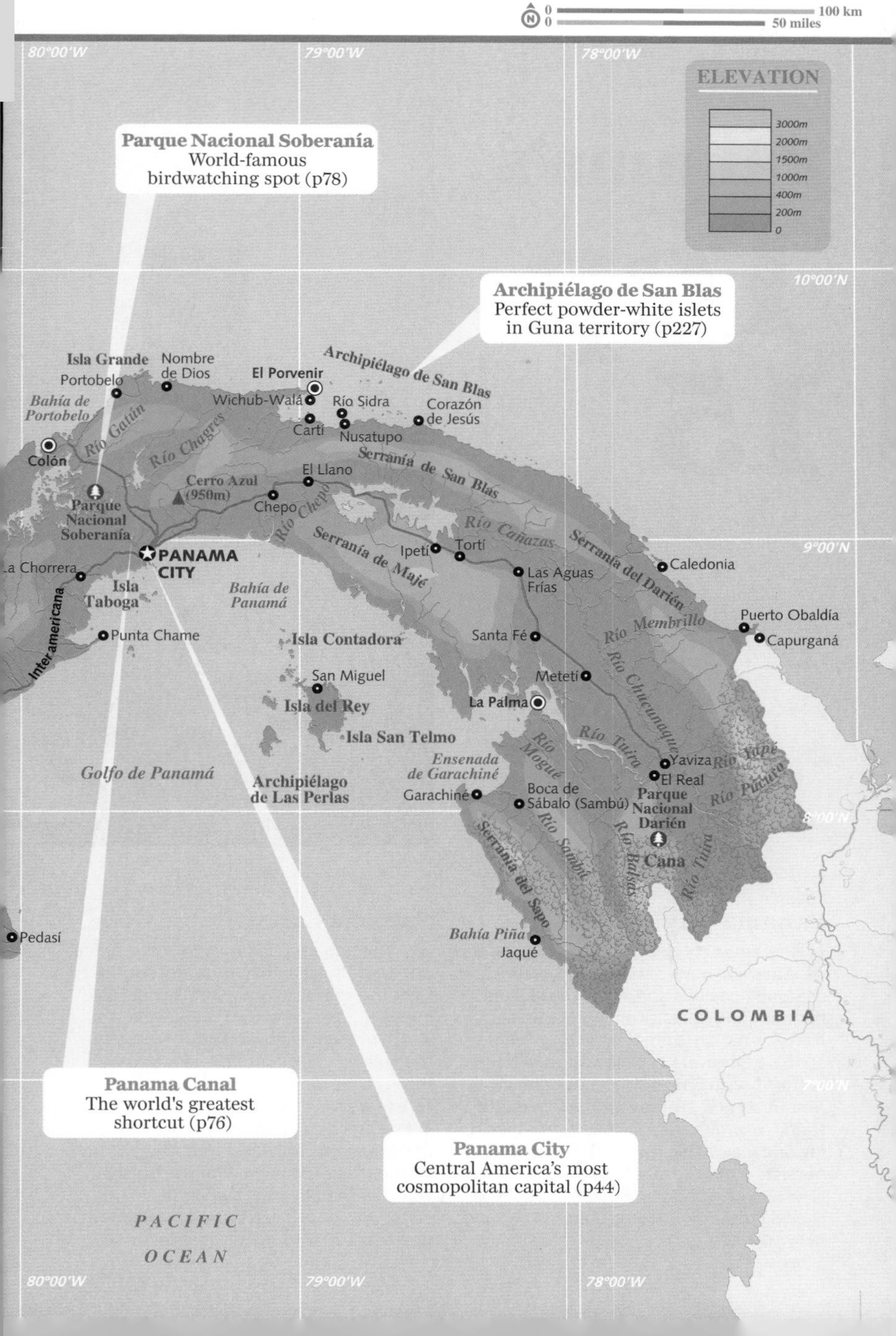

0 100 km
0 50 miles

ELEVATION
3000m
2000m
1500m
1000m
400m
200m
0

Parque Nacional Soberanía
World-famous birdwatching spot (p78)

Archipiélago de San Blas
Perfect powder-white islets in Guna territory (p227)

Panama Canal
The world's greatest shortcut (p76)

Panama City
Central America's most cosmopolitan capital (p44)

80°00'W
79°00'W
78°00'W
10°00'N
9°00'N
8°00'N
7°00'N

Isla Grande
Nombre de Dios
Portobelo
Bahía de Portobelo
El Porvenir
Wichub-Walá
Río Sidra
Corazón de Jesús
Cartí
Nusatupo
Archipiélago de San Blas
Colón
Río Gatún
Río Chagres
Serranía de San Blas
El Llano
Cerro Azul (950m)
Chepo
Río Chepo
Parque Nacional Soberanía
Río Cañazas
Serranía de Majé
Ipetí
Tortí
Serranía del Darién
Caledonia
PANAMA CITY
La Chorrera
Las Aguas Frías
Isla Taboga
Bahía de Panamá
Interamericana
Río Membrillo
Puerto Obaldía
Capurganá
Punta Chame
Isla Contadora
Santa Fé
Río Chucunaque
San Miguel
Metetí
Isla del Rey
La Palma
Isla San Telmo
Río Moguê
Río Tuira
Río Yapé
Golfo de Panamá
Ensenada de Garachiné
Yaviza
El Real
Archipiélago de Las Perlas
Garachiné
Boca de Sábalo (Sambú)
Parque Nacional Darién
Río Pucuro
Río Sambú
Río Balsas
Serranía del Sapo
Cana
Río Tuira
Pedasí
Bahía Piña
Jaqué
COLOMBIA
PACIFIC OCEAN

Panama's Top 15

Panama City

1 Panama City (p44) is high-octane Latin America: think *ceviche* (citrus-cured seafood), casinos and a stacked skyline. For this sparkling city of nearly a million, transformation is afoot: coastal green space, a biodiversity museum, colonial restoration in Casco Viejo and Central America's first subway system. Sure, the traffic resembles a boa constrictor digesting one megalithic meal, but its appeal persists. People are real here and nature is never very far away. Beauty lives in the skewed rhythms, incongruous visions and fiery sunsets.

Panama Canal

2 The Panama Canal (p76) is one of the world's greatest shortcuts, cutting right through the continental divide, linking the Atlantic and the Pacific. And it's worth marveling at. Just as stunning as the hulking steel container ships passing through the locks are the legions of creatures watching from the jungle fringes. Two visitor centers offer viewing platforms and museums that lay bare the construction and its expansion. There are also worthwhile boat and kayak trips on the waterway, or you can book a partial transit and squeeze through the locks yourself.

MAREK POPLAWSKI / SHUTTERSTOCK ©

DANNY LEHMAN / GETTY IMAGES ©

3

SHARPAIKA / GETTY IMAGES ©

4

DAMSEA / SHUTTERSTOCK ©

Casco Viejo

3 Casco Viejo (p47) is Panama City's most historical living neighborhood, full of crumbling convents and cobblestones. The colonial architecture may hark back to Havana, but this is not a spot where time stands still. It's as much about today's urban mix as the eclectic, easygoing vibe. The Cinta Costera, a recently completed green space, takes walkers and bikers from downtown past Casco Viejo. On sticky evenings artists' booths line the promenade, couples dine under parasols and live music fills the plazas.

Water Sports

4 Water sports (p34) in Panama range from diving with a rare whale shark, ocean kayaking around uninhabited islands or getting soaked while rafting in the highlands. Clear and cool, the Pacific is the best place to spot a wide variety of marine mammals, including whales, in spots such as Parque Nacional Coiba and the Golfo de Chiriquí, while the Caribbean is known for its colorful corals and starfish around Bocas del Toro and the powdery white-sand beaches of the Archipiélago de San Blas.

HALFEGMOON / SHUTTERSTOCK ©

SL-PHOTOGRAPHY / SHUTTERSTOCK ©

Parque Nacional Coiba

5 Parque Nacional Coiba (p147), often compared to the Galápagos, is a veritable lost world of pristine ecosystems and unique fauna. Spy flocks of scarlet macaws, enormous schools of fish, migrating humpback whales with calves, and manta rays scuffing the ocean floor. Scuba divers might glimpse a hammerhead or whale shark. Most importantly, it's still wild, with few visitors and little infrastructure. Not long ago an infamous prison operated on the main island, but now everyone comes here by choice.

Festivals

6 Festivals (p23) are a window into the country's wilder side. Panama's many fetes also reveal the breadth of cultures packed into this small nation. From Caribbean Congo celebrations in Portobelo to the vibrant folkloric traditions of the Península de Azuero, the three-day Guna stomp that is Nogapope or Panama City's open-air jazz festival, all of Panama loves a good rum-soaked time. When it's all over, a replenishing bowl of 'Get Up Lazarus' (a potent seafood soup) at Mercado de Mariscos in the capital is in order. Congo celebrations in Portobelo (p222)

ANGEL DIBILIO / SHUTTERSTOCK ©

Boquete

7 Boquete (p164) is equal parts adventure hub and mountain retreat, plus a magnet for expats, retirees and travelers of all stripes. Birdwatchers come for a glimpse of the resplendent quetzal, while adventurers come to climb a mountain, ride a zipline or raft white water. But what really moves this small town is one of the world's most important export crops: coffee. Coffee farms dot the countryside, with tours showing the process from leaf to cup. Fuel up, and you're ready for the next adventure.

Coffee plant

Península de Azuero

8 Península de Azuero (p112) has sweet landscapes of sculpted hills, lonely beaches and crashing surf: this rural peninsula has become today's hot getaway. Yet the strongest impression is one of tradition. Spanish culture has deep roots here, evident in the charm of tiled colonials, country hospitality, religious festivals and elaborate *polleras* (embroidered lace dresses). Playa Venao is a major surf destination, while the delightfully untrammeled Sunset Coast has quiet beaches, great surfing and community turtle tours.

Girl in a *pollera*

Archipiélago de Bocas del Toro

9 Archipiélago de Bocas del Toro (p184) is Panama's number one vacation spot. 'It's all good,' say the laid-back locals of this Caribbean island chain. Pedal to the beach on a cruiser bike, hum to improvised calypso on Isla Bastimentos and laze over dinner in a thatched hut on the waterfront. Lodgings range from cheap backpacker digs to stunning jungle lodges and luxury resorts located on outer islands. Surfers hit the breaks, but there's also snorkeling with varied sea life or volunteering opportunities to help nesting sea turtles.

The Highlands

10 Panama's highlands are the equivalent of a breath of fresh air in the steamy tropics. The topography ranges from lush forest with tiny golden frogs to mist-covered coffee plantations. From Panama City, weekenders take to El Valle (p96) and Parque Nacional Omar Torrijos (p109). Boquete (p164) is the classic mountain town, but if you are looking to get off the beaten path, the hamlet of Santa Fé (p138) has true mountain tranquility, with local-led horse rides and hikes to waterfalls with swimming holes. Paradise is not lost.

Hiking in El Valle (p97)

Parque Nacional Volcán Barú

11 Parque Nacional Volcán Barú (p173) features Panama's only volcano. It dominates the landscape of the Chiriquí highlands, and at 3474m, it is also the highest point in the country. Enthusiasts can make the predawn climb, steep and usually muddy, to view the Atlantic and Pacific Oceans at the same time – if it's clear. Another, perhaps saner, option is the Sendero Los Quetzales, a stunning trail that traverses the park, crossing over the Caldera River, with the possibility of seeing exotic orchids, tapirs and resplendent quetzals.

Archipiélago de San Blas

12 Archipiélago de San Blas could be your definition of paradise. There's little to do but negotiate the price of a coconut, sway in a hammock or snorkel turquoise waters. Locally known as Guna Yala (p227), this 400-plus island archipelago in the Caribbean is an independent indigenous territory steeped in tradition. Get around by speedboat, sailboat or dugout canoe. Most guest lodges are remote palm-fringed islets surrounded by clear waters. The Guna residents mostly live on community islands teeming with livestock, commerce, and thatched or concrete homes.

SHUTTERSTOCK ©

BGREMLER / SHUTTERSTOCK ©

ROB CRANDALL / SHUTTERSTOCK ©

KRISTINA VACKOVA / SHUTTERSTOCK ©

ONDREJ PROSICKY / SHUTTERSTOCK ©

Parque Nacional Soberanía

13 Parque Nacional Soberanía (p78), a quick day trip from the glass towers of Panama City, is one of the most accessible tropical rainforests in Panama. It's also one of the premier birdwatching sites in the world: on Pipeline Rd over 500 bird species – from toucans to motmots – have been sighted. While out on the trail also look for sloths, howler monkeys and white-faced capuchins. For an alternative view of the canopy, climb the towers at Rainforest Discovery Center or visit the neighboring Emberá and Wounaan communities. Capuchin monkey

Santa Catalina

14 Santa Catalina (p141) is a surf village that's all small town, with wave-front *hotelitos* and hostels far off the one paved road. Here nature is a delight and 'resort' is still a foreign word. The biggest draws are the world-class waves that roll in year-round but peak in February and March. The town is also the launching pad for excursions and diving trips into the wildlife-rich Parque Nacional Coiba, an island where nature and marine life flourish. With roads now paved, day trips here are easier than ever.

Wildlife-Watching

15 Wildlife-watching (p278) in Panama, with over 220 mammal and 978 bird species, is crack for naturalists. Scarlet macaws, toucans, sloths and squirrel monkeys are just a few of the local stars. As a spectator sport, this activity is nothing short of thrilling. The calls, cries and rumbles of the rainforest will be stamped on your memory forever. Serious birders might head to the highlands to spot a quetzal or brave the Darién for a glimpse of the legendary harpy eagle. Bring your binoculars. Toucan

Need to Know

For more information, see Survival Guide (p287)

Currency
US dollar (balboa; $)

Language
Spanish, English

Visas
Visas are generally not required for stays of up to 90 days.

Money
ATMs are readily available except in Darién Province, on Islas Contadora and Tobago and in the Archipiélago de San Blas. Credit cards are accepted at restaurants and hotels but may be problematic elsewhere.

Cell Phones
Local SIM cards can be used in unlocked phones. Choose your carrier carefully, as only certain operators have coverage in the San Blás islands and Darién Province.

Time
Eastern Standard Time (GMT/UTC minus five hours, or minus six hours early April to late Oct)

When to Go

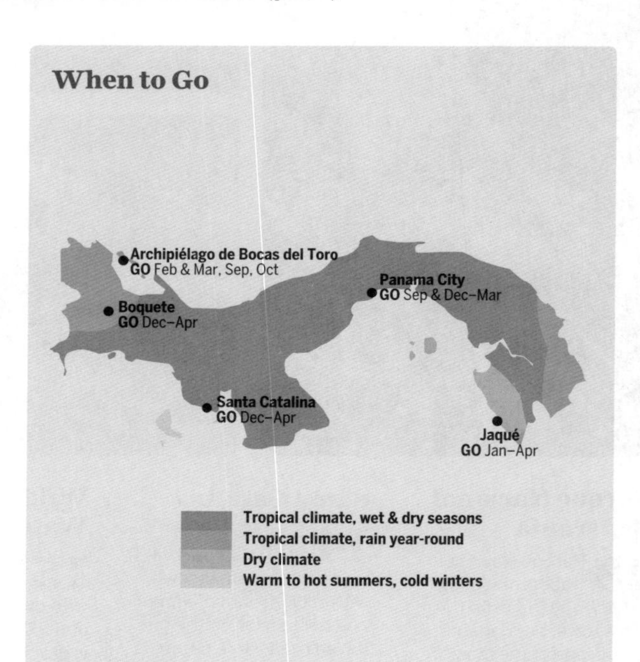

High-Season Peak
(public holidays)

- Includes November festivals, Christmas and New Year, plus Easter.
- Hotel rates may be up to double that of normal rates.
- Resorts, festival towns and beaches are crowded with Panamanian vacationers.

Shoulder Season
(mid-Dec–mid-Apr)

- Corresponds with the Pacific-side dry season.
- Little rain in Panama City and elsewhere south of the continental divide.

Low Season
(mid-Apr–early Dec)

- Corresponds with rainy season in most of the country.
- Rain is sporadic: check regional climate guides, as many destinations can still be enjoyed.
- Lodging rates and resorts are better priced.

Useful Websites

Visit Panama (www.visitpanama.com) The English-language official national tourism website.

Lonely Planet (www.lonelyplanet.com/panama) The popular Thorn Tree forum, travel news and links to other useful sites.

Casco Viejo (www.cascoviejo.org) Panama City information.

Degusta Panama (www.degustapanama.com) Website and app with locals' restaurant picks.

Panama Today (www.panamatoday.com) English-language news site useful for culture and local politics.

Lanic (http://lanic.utexas.edu/la/ca/panama) Academic links from the University of Texas Latin American Information Center.

Important Numbers

Panama has no regional dialing codes.

Panama country code	507
International operator	106
Directory assistance	102
Ambulance	455 & 107
Police	104

Exchange Rates

Australia	A$1	US$0.71
Canada	C$1	US$0.75
Euro zone	€1	US$1.13
Japan	¥100	US$0.90
New Zealand	NZ$1	US$0.68
UK	£1	US$1.30

For current exchange rates, see www.xe.com.

Daily Costs

Budget: Less than US$70

- Dorm bed: US$18
- Dine on *comida corriente* (set meals; US$7), visit markets and street stalls
- Plan sightseeing via bus, DIY visits to beaches and waterfall hikes

Midrange: US$70–150

- Double room at a midrange hotel: US$60–130
- Some fine dining, activities (snorkel rental or surf lessons) and regional flights
- Car rental: per day US$50

Top end: More than US$150

- Double room at a high-end hotel, resort or lodge: from US$130
- Meal at a fine-dining restaurant: US$50
- Guided trips with bilingual naturalist guides
- Internal flights and 4WD rental

Opening Hours

Opening hours vary throughout the year. The following are high-season hours.

Banks 8am–3pm Monday to Friday, 9am–noon Saturday

Bars & clubs Bars from 9pm; clubs 11pm–3am or 4am

Government offices 8am–4pm Monday to Friday

Malls & shops 10am–9pm or 10pm

Offices 8am–noon and 1:30–5pm Monday to Friday

Restaurants 7–10am, noon–3pm and 6–10pm (later in Panama City); often closed Sunday

Supermarkets 8am–9pm; some open 24 hours

Arriving in Panama

Tocumen International Airport Most international flights arrive at this airport in Panama City. Hire taxis (from around US$30) at the transport desk near baggage claim. It's a 40-minute ride to downtown. In daylight hours local buses (US$1.25) depart every 15 minutes for Albrook Bus Terminal, near Albrook regional airport (one hour), and other destinations.

Panamá Pacífico International Airport Located 12km southwest of Panama City. Viva Air Colombia airline began using this small airport, the former US Howard Air Force Base, in 2014. A taxi will cost about US$6.

Aeropuerto Enrique Malek (David) This airport handles flights to and from San José (Costa Rica). It's about 5km from town; take a taxi (US$5).

Getting Around

As most Panamanians use public transportation, it's reasonably priced and connections are frequent.

Bus Most cities have a terminal with frequent regional departures and connections to Panama City and often to Costa Rica.

Car Rentals are not cheap, but roads are generally in decent condition. Some areas, including Panama City and many rural parts of the country, are very poorly signposted.

Train Mostly a novelty for tourists, a rail service runs between Panama City and Colón.

Air Domestic flights depart Panama City's Albrook Airport to certain destinations within the country.

For much more on **getting around**, see p300

First Time Panama

For more information, see Survival Guide (p287)

Checklist

➡ Check passport validity

➡ Check visa situation and government travel advisories

➡ Organize travel insurance

➡ Check luggage restrictions

➡ Check your immunization history

➡ Contact your credit-card provider to see if there's car-rental insurance coverage

➡ Put in a travel notice with credit or debit card companies

What to Pack

➡ Passport

➡ Phrasebook or language app

➡ Swimsuit

➡ Camera and battery charger

➡ Flip-flops

➡ Sun protection

➡ Poncho or rain jacket

➡ Binoculars

➡ Strong insect repellent (30% to 50% DEET)

➡ Refillable water bottle

➡ Driver's license, if you plan to rent a car

➡ Field guide

➡ Flashlight or headlamp

➡ Offline map app

Top Tips for Your Trip

➡ Don't flag a taxi in front of a high-end hotel if you don't want to be charged tourist rates off the bat; taxis aren't metered, so walk a block – it pays!

➡ Outside the cities, many perfectly good lodgings don't have a handle on email and websites. Don't get frustrated if no one sees your reservation – the hotel email might have been created by a precocious nephew who never checks it. If you have even basic Spanish, call ahead.

➡ Panamanians are used to foreigners dissing local idiosyncrasies – like drivers not using signals, or crowds that can't form lines. But, instead, ask *why* it is the way it is and you'll have a lively conversation.

What to Wear

Locals rarely wear shorts if not at the beach. Bring lightweight pants or skirts and short-sleeved shirts or tops. Dining and nightlife can be formal in the capital: bring proper dress shoes or sandals and a skirt or dress for women, pants and a dress shirt for men. Pack a light sweater for over-air-conditioned restaurants and bus rides. A fleece and lightweight shell are necessary for the highlands. For hiking, long sleeves and (quick-drying) pants help keep the bugs away.

Sleeping

Book accommodations two to six months ahead for Semana Santa ('Holy Week'; the week preceding Easter), the November festivals and the week between Christmas and New Year. Most lodgings require reservations in high season.

Hotels In abundance in the midrange and high-end categories.

B&Bs A midrange phenomenon most common in the capital as well as Boquete and Bocas del Toro.

Hostels Cheap and spreading in Panama, ranging from quiet budget digs to party central.

Lodges From rustic to high end, found mostly in the highlands.

Etiquette

Asking for help Say *discúlpame* to get someone's attention; *perdón* to say 'excuse me.'

Personal space Don't be surprised if locals have fewer boundaries about personal space than what's customary in North America and Europe.

Visiting indigenous communities Ask permission to take photos, particularly of children, and dress modestly. Some bargaining may be appropriate for buying crafts but not for lodging and food. The best gifts for children are those that are useful (pens, paper, notebooks, games or books), not sweets.

Surfing Novice surfers should be aware of 'dropping in' on more experienced surfers and of swimmers in their path.

Money

Panama uses the US dollar as its currency. The official name for it is the balboa, but it's exactly the same bill. People use the terms *dólar* and balboa interchangeably.

Panamanian coins are of the same value, size and metal as US ones, though both are used interchangeably. Coins include one, five, 10, 25 and 50 *centavos* – 100 *centavos* equal one balboa (dollar). Most businesses won't break US$50 and US$100 bills.

Bargaining

It's OK but not common to bargain at markets and street stalls, but first ask around for an idea of the price of different items, particularly handmade goods, and the factors that contribute to quality. Rather than intensive negotiations, ask for a *descuento* (discount).

Guna *molas* for sale (p233)

Tipping

Restaurants Tipping should be 10%. Check if it's included in the bill.

Taxis Tipping is optional, but you can round up a dollar or two, especially at night.

Guides It is customary to tip US$7 to US$10 per person for day tours; tip on the high end for naturalist guides.

Language

Knowing some basic Spanish phrases (p303) is not only courteous but often essential, particularly when navigating through rural areas, interacting with park rangers and shopping at local markets. That said, English speakers are easier to find here than in any other part of Latin America. Not only did the US occupation leave its stamp, but many Panamanians have lived abroad or have family in the USA. Some restaurants feature English menus, and it's certainly the standard for guides. If you visit Guna Yala, learning a few words of Guna (p232) beforehand is a great way to warm relations but is hardly essential.

What's New

National Parks Free
Panama's national parks no longer charge an entrance fee, with the exception of Parque Nacional Coiba.

Sloth Refuge
Excellent for families, a new sloth rescue center at the Gamboa Rainforest Resort offers sanctuary to these handsome creatures and prepares them for reintroduction into the wild. (p81)

Panama City Metro
Central America's first subway system is an efficient way to get around Panama City. In the works are extensions to the suburbs and Tocumen International Airport. (p301)

Tocumen International Airport Expansion
The finishing touches are being put on the US$800 million dollar expansion of Panama's main airport, set for 2019, strengthening its status as a regional hub. (p298)

Budget Gourmet in Panama City
Panama's best chefs now have casual eateries turning out some of their finest fare. Try Lo Que Hay (p63) by José Carles, or Mario Castrellon's Botanica (p65).

Amador Convention Center
Located on the Amador Causeway, this ultramodern event center opening at the end of 2018 will draw international fairs and exhibitions.

Papal Visit
Pope Francisco's July 2019 visit for World Youth Day will bring tens of thousands to El Santuario de Atalaya near Santiago, Veraguas. (p137)

Improvements on the Interamericana
Motorists can enjoy smooth highway on the Interamericana between David and Santiago, while near Panama City, the new Atlantic Bridge crosses over the canal.

Dorms fit for a Queen
Just outside Boquete, the new Bambuda Castle brings hostel living to a modern-day castle in coffee country. (p168)

Alternative Access to Coiba
Divers heading to Parque Nacional Coiba have an excellent new option. Ecofriendly Dive Base Coiba operates out of the tiny village of Pixvae, cutting boating time to dive sites in half. (p149)

Casco Viejo Nightlife
As real estate in Panama City's hottest neighborhood gets more precious, the best nightlife creeps toward the fringe, where you will find new favorites like The Stranger's Club (p66) and Casa Jaguar (p66).

W Hotel Panama City
Opened in 2018, this sleek highrise is not your parents' luxury hotel. In a playful-modern design, the new W Hotel uses colorful shipping containers reminiscent of the Panama Canal. (p61)

San Blas Sailing Ban
After the congress of Guna Yala banned foreign-owned charters in the *comarca,* sailboats to Colombia now depart from Puerto Lindo.

For more recommendations and reviews, see lonelyplanet.com/Panama

If You Like...

Beaches

Guna Yala Known for perfect postage-stamp-size islets with turquoise waters. (p227)

Golfo de Chiriquí The national marine park boasts islands of monkeys, nesting turtles and plenty of isolated beaches. (p160)

Farallón Within reach of the capital, this wide, brilliantly white resort beach is a natural beauty perfect for long strolls. (p104)

Isla Bastimentos From the eco resorts of Punta Vieja to the sparkling sands of Wizard Beach. (p202)

Nightlife

Casco Viejo Dart across the cobblestones between underground bars, brewpubs and wine bars and live-music venues. (p66)

Bocas del Toro With Aqua Lounge's deckside swings and La Iguana partying hard, it's the scene of the young and the restless. (p185)

Tántalo Bar The best exotic cocktails and rooftop bar rolled into one – you could only do better booking its dominatrix-themed suite. (p66)

Boquete Comfort and *cervezas* draw expats and locals alike to places like Boquete Brewing Company. (p164)

Romantic Getaways

Los Quetzales Cabins Cabins tucked into the rainforest canopy, with fireplaces and the mountain air buzzing with hummingbirds. (p179)

Casco Viejo B&Bs A hefty dose of pampering with this vibrant old-world neighborhood right out the door. (p56)

Archipiélago de Bocas del Toro From secluded ecolodges to thatched beach huts, these resorts can erase the world beyond. (p184)

Villa Távida Lodge Luxury summit villas surrounded by a waterfall, gardens and shrouded peaks. (p109)

Art Lodge On the remote Isla Gobernadora, this inspired Pacific getaway is romance incarnate. (p142)

Surfing

Santa Catalina It's all about world-class waves here, and hostels boast front-row seats. (p142)

Playa Venao Gorgeous stretches of dark volcanic sand and consistent waves for all abilities. (p130)

Playa Bluff Powerful barrels rush this wilderness beach; avoid May to September, when turtles nest. (p198)

Playa El Palmar A Panama City weekend break with two surf schools and a white-sand beach as your campus. (p93)

Wildlife

Isla Barro Colorado Nature geeks shouldn't miss this rainforest, the most intensely studied area in the neotropics. (p80)

Parque Nacional Coiba Dive with a whale shark, spy scarlet macaws or search for endemic howlers. Wildlife is epic here. (p147)

San San Pond Sak Sloths, river otters and the occasional manatee inhabit this little-known Caribbean wetland near Changuinola. (p208)

Isla Bastimentos From July to August, loggerhead, hawksbill, green and leatherback turtles hatch on the north shore. (p202)

Parque Nacional Darién A world of mysterious wildlife lives within this lush, remote park that lies at the end of the road. (p250)

Parque Natural Metropolitano A patch of rainforest amid Panama City. Don't mind the *tití* monkeys on the trail! (p51)

Off-the-Beaten-Track Destinations

Soposo Rainforest Adventures Step off the gringo trail to sleep in stilted huts and explore remote Naso villages. (p210)

Sante Fé Dancing butterflies, swimming holes and giant waterfalls grace this humble mountain town. (p138)

The Darién Steeped in indigenous culture and exotic wildlife; with permits required, checkpoints and delays, the only hassle is getting here. (p242)

Isla Gobernadora Home to locals and artists, this seldom-visited island offers an original crowd-free retreat. (p142)

The Sunset Coast At this surfer's paradise with little development, unadulterated nature takes center stage. (p150)

Outdoor Adventures

Nivida Bat Cave Trek to this massive Caribbean cavern rife with nectar bats; perfect for a subterranean swim. (p202)

Parque Internacional La Amistad True wilderness hiking without the drama of the Darién; access via the highlands or the Caribbean coast. (p179)

Volcán Barú Terribly steep, hard, and invariably foggy and muddy, but how else can you view Atlantic and Pacific at once? (p173)

Jungle Treks Panama's best trekking outfitter will take you from the jungles to the wildest coastlines. (p302)

Top: Green vine snake, Isla Barro Colorado (p80)

Bottom: Comarca de Guna Yala (p227)

Month by Month

TOP EVENTS

Panama Jazz Festival, January

Carnaval, February–March

Festival de Diablos y Congos, February–March

Festival of Nogagope, October

January

With dry season and tourist season at their peaks, this is a big month for travel in Panama. It's prime time for kitesurfing and swimming, with Pacific temperatures at their warmest and the wind blowing.

☆ Panama Jazz Festival

The weeklong jazz festival (www.panamajazzfestival.com) is one of the biggest musical events in Panama, drawing top-caliber international musicians from jazz, blues, salsa and other genres. Held throughout the city, the open-air events are usually free.

Fiesta del Mar

At the end of the month on tiny Isla Taboga, a boat ride away from Panama City, this new tradition revives island culture with a weekend festival (www.fiestadelmarpanama.com) of calypso music, dancing and food events.

March

It's prime time for surfing on both Pacific and Caribbean swells. High season is winding down. Events related to the religious calendar may take place in February or March.

Carnaval

On the four days preceding Ash Wednesday, general merriment prevails in Panama City and the Península de Azuero. This anything-goes, multi-event period features street parades, water fights, costumes and live music till the wee hours. (p55)

Festival de Diablos y Congos

Held every other year two weeks after Carnaval, this Congo festival celebrates rebellious slave ancestors with spirited public dancing featuring beautiful masks and costumes. Participants assume the role of escaped slaves and take captives on the street. (p222)

Semana Santa

During Holy Week (the week before Easter), the country hosts many special events, including a re-enactment of the crucifixion and resurrection of Christ. On Good Friday, religious processions are held in towns across the country.

May

With sporadic, refreshing rain showers, the weather is generally pleasant throughout the country. May begins a five- to six-month nesting season for both loggerhead and green sea turtles on the Caribbean coast.

Fiesta de Corpus Christi

Forty days after Easter, this religious holiday features colorful celebrations in Villa de Los Santos. Masked and costumed dancers representing angels, devils, imps and other mythological figures perform dances, acrobatics and dramas. In May or June.

July

Though it's the middle of rainy season, the weather is relatively dry on the Caribbean side. It's also off-peak for visitors, and hotels offer better rates.

Nuestra Señora del Carmen

Celebrating the patron saint of Isla Taboga, this event on July 16 starts with a procession parading the Virgin statue, followed by fire-breathing, games and dance.

Virgen del Carmen

Every July 16, the Veraguas coast celebrates the Festival of Virgen del Carmen. Decorated boats tour the islands and gulf around Santa Catalina. Singing and celebrations invoke long life and the protection of the fishing boats.

Fiesta de Santa Librada

Celebrating the patron saint of Las Tablas and incorporating the Festival de la Pollera, this July 19 event stretches over four days, with huge street celebrations and solemn religious services and processions in Península de Azuero.

August

Breeding humpback whales can be observed in the Archipiélago de Las Perlas. Mid-month Panama City celebrates its founding in 1519 with

Top: Día de Independencia celebrations

Bottom: Masked dancers, Fiesta de Corpus Christi (p23)

a stream of events. Rainy season continues.

Festival del Manito Ocueño

Among the country's best folkloric events, this three-day bash features traditional music and dancing, and culminates in a country wedding. Held the third week of August in the rural village of Ocú.

September

The rain usually lets up a little, particularly around Panama City. Still low season, it's a good time to travel around the country, with no need for reservations.

Feria de la Mejorana

In late September, Panama's largest folkloric festival draws musicians and traditional dancers from all over the country to tiny Guararé on the Península de Azuero. Party with oxcart parades and *seco* cocktails.

October

October 12 is Día de la Raza (Colombus Day); a dubious legacy nonetheless celebrated by every high-school brass band letting loose. Throughout Panama, some very different yet excellent festivals are well worth attending.

Festival of Nogagope

Guna converge on Isla Tigre for three days of tireless traditional dancing. It's visually engaging and fully authentic. Held from October 10 to 12, it's followed by a four-day fair with art shows and canoe races. (p240)

Festival of the Black Christ

On October 21, thousands honor the black Christ in Portobelo. Many make the pilgrimage on foot from the capital to honor this maker of miracles. After a nighttime procession there's dancing and drinking till late.

Toro Guapo

One of the best street parties in the country, the 'Handsome Bull' festival takes place in the Coclé town of Antón for three days during the second week of October.

November

Don't come to Panama for business between November and December, as the whole country takes off to celebrate multiple independence-related holidays in November, and then there's the Christmas holiday. Panama City empties out and beaches are full.

Día de Independencia

On November 28 Panama celebrates its independence from Spain with parties and revelry throughout the country. Most locals head to the beach and enjoy a drink or 10. Book any travel well ahead.

DIEGO GRANDI / SHUTTERSTOCK ©

Plan Your Trip
Itineraries

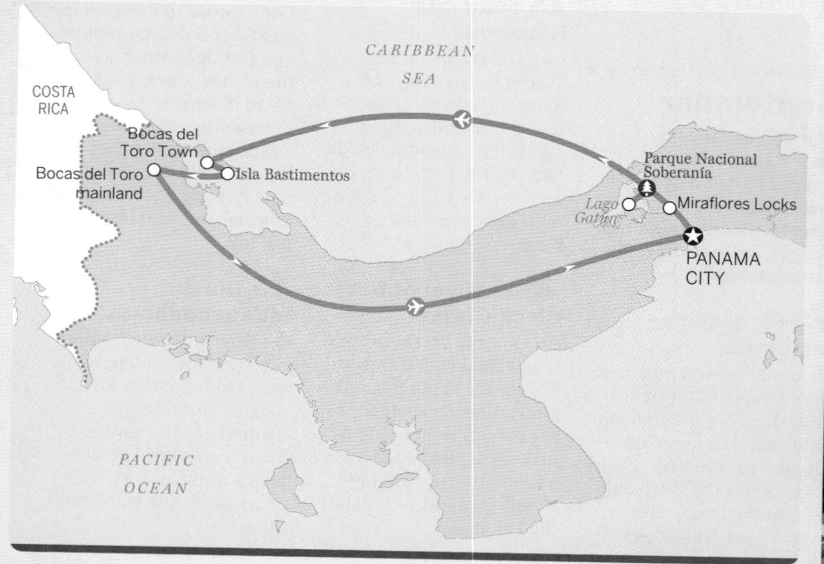

Essential Panama

For a taste of tropical Panama, start with the hyper-charged capital. Explore the city and see colonial ruins and landmarks such as the famous Panama Canal while getting a dose of rainforest adventure. Top it off with a chilled Caribbean getaway.

Imbibe the rush of **Panama City**. In Panamá Viejo, admire Spain's first Pacific settlement, laid waste in a massive pirate raid. Pedal along the coastal beltway Cinta Costera to historic Casco Viejo, with hip plaza restaurants, rooftop bars, galleries and 18th-century cathedrals.

Take a day trip to **Miraflores Locks** to watch mammoth ships make their way through the canal. Visit nearby rainforest in the wildlife-rich **Parque Nacional Soberanía**, a favorite of birdwatchers. Or kayak on **Lago Gatún** alongside howler monkeys and sunbathing crocodiles.

From Panama City, fly to **Bocas del Toro Town** for four days of Caribbean relaxation and snorkeling among colorful coral reefs. Explore Isla Colón by cruiser

bike and go on a pub crawl in quirky Bocas Town.

Boat out to the idyllic thatched resorts at **Isla Bastimentos**, take a chocolate tour on the **Bocas del Toro mainland** or visit indigenous groups on other islands through a community-tourism initiative.

Fly back to the capital for a last call in the city's sleek bars and clubs.

VILAINECREVETTE / GETTY IMAGES ©

Above: Panamá Viejo (p51)
Right: Cacao pods, Bocas del Toro Province (p181)

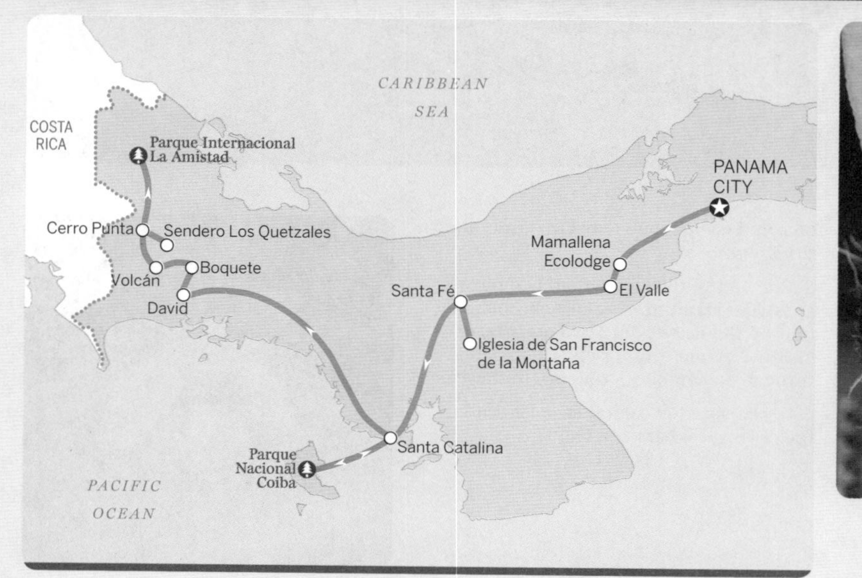
CARIBBEAN
SEA
COSTA
RICA
Parque Internacional
La Amistad
Cerro Punta
Sendero Los Quetzales
Boquete
Volcán
David
Santa Fé
Iglesia de San Francisco
de la Montaña
Mamallena
Ecolodge
El Valle
PANAMA
CITY
Santa Catalina
Parque
Nacional
Coiba
PACIFIC
OCEAN

Pacific Coast & Highlands

Whether you're traveling on buses or with your own wheels, hit the Interamericana for a route that alternates between scenic beaches and highland cloud forests.

Spend your first few days exploring **Panama City**. Then head west along the Interamericana, where you can stop for a leisurely seafood lunch and explore the string of beaches along the Pacific coast. Overnight at **Mamallena Ecolodge** in the cool, sculpted foothills. The next stop is **El Valle**, a mountain retreat surrounded by lush cloud forests and green peaks. Return to the Interamericana, visiting Coclé's roadside attractions, then detour for **Santa Fé**, a tiny highland town amid sparkling rivers and gorgeous waterfalls. On your way out, browse the gorgeous **Iglesia de San Francisco de la Montaña** outside Santa Fé.

For surf time, backtrack to the Interamericana and detour to **Santa Catalina**. Soak up the laid-back vibe at thatched restaurants and join the local surfing kids nailing the waves on the town beach. Another very good reason to stop here is to connect to **Parque Nacional Coiba**, a far-flung, pristine island in a vast marine park. Snorkeling, diving and hiking are all top notch; although there's minimal infrastructure, it's worth staying a few days.

Head via **David** to the popular highland retreat of **Boquete** in Chiriquí. Go hiking or rafting or take a canopy tour and fill up on mountain-grown coffee. Birdwatchers can stalk the resplendent quetzal. Choose from one of the fine-dining options and sleep soundly in clean mountain air.

If you have your own wheels, take the paved road to **Volcán**, a very scenic shortcut. Those without wheels can bus via David to **Cerro Punta**. Retreat to a charming rainforest cabin before hitting the trail to hike the **Sendero Los Quetzales**, a stunning trail through wildlife-rich cloud forest. If traveling by bus, you can loop back to Boquete on this hike. If adventure *still* calls, from Cerro Punta you can access the trails of **Parque Internacional La Amistad**. Take a guide – the Panamanian side of this international park is virtually undeveloped and largely unexplored.

To save time, you can fly back to Panama City from David.

Top: Hawksbill turtle, Parque Nacional Coiba (p147)
Bottom: *Ceviche*

12 DAYS Bicoastal Explorer

If you're itching to get off the beaten path, this seafarer route will bring you to the less touristed Península de Azuero on the Pacific coast, and on to the Afro-Caribbean heartland and the furthest reaches of Guna Yala (and possibly even Colombia).

Start in the capital of **Panama City**. From there, take a ride in the luxury train along the historical Panama Railroad through the Canal Zone to **Colón** to admire the Unesco World Heritage Site of **Fuerte San Lorenzo**. While in the area, check out the Panama Canal expansion at the nearby **Agua Clara Visitors Center**. Using **Portobelo** as your base, explore 16th-century Spanish forts, boat out to deserted island beaches, scuba dive or attend a festival.

Return to Panama City to travel to the **Península de Azuero** by bus. From time to time traditional festivals take over the streets of these tiny colonial towns. If your visit coincides, join the revelers! Otherwise, check out workshops where regional artisans craft Panama hats, lace dresses and colorful *diablo* (devil) masks. Make your base **Pedasí** for leisurely trips to the beach and a friendly village atmosphere. Move on to the more remote **Playa Venao** to enjoy a pretty half-moon bay, meet other travelers and ride some waves without the crowds. If turtles are hatching, it's worth making the pilgrimage to **Isla Cañas**.

When you're ready, return to the capital and take a 4WD or flight to **Guna Yala**, a string of hundreds of pristine islands ruled by Guna. Thatched huts on dozens of islands run the gamut, from bare bones to creature comforts, with meals and excursions always included. Snorkel and swim to your heart's content, or charter a sailboat for the grand tour. Highlights include snorkeling the reefs and wrecks of the **Cayos Holandeses** and meeting locals on the tiny community islands. If you are heading on to South America – and bent on adventure – consider a three- to four-day sailing or boat trip to Colombia.

Otherwise, end your trip by returning to Panama City, where you can check out the world-class BioMuseo and have a night out in Casco Viejo.

Top: BioMuseo (p52), Panama City
Bottom: Fortifications near Portobelo (p219)

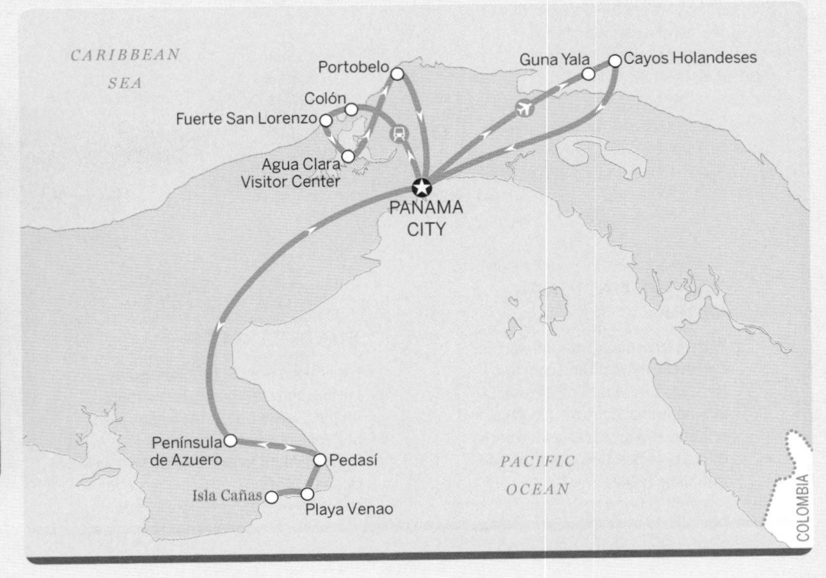
CARIBBEAN
SEA
Portobelo
Colón
Fuerte San Lorenzo
Agua Clara
Visitor Center
Guna Yala
Cayos Holandeses
PANAMA
CITY
Península
de Azuero
Pedasí
Isla Cañas
Playa Venao
PACIFIC
OCEAN
COLOMBIA

Off the Beaten Track: Panama

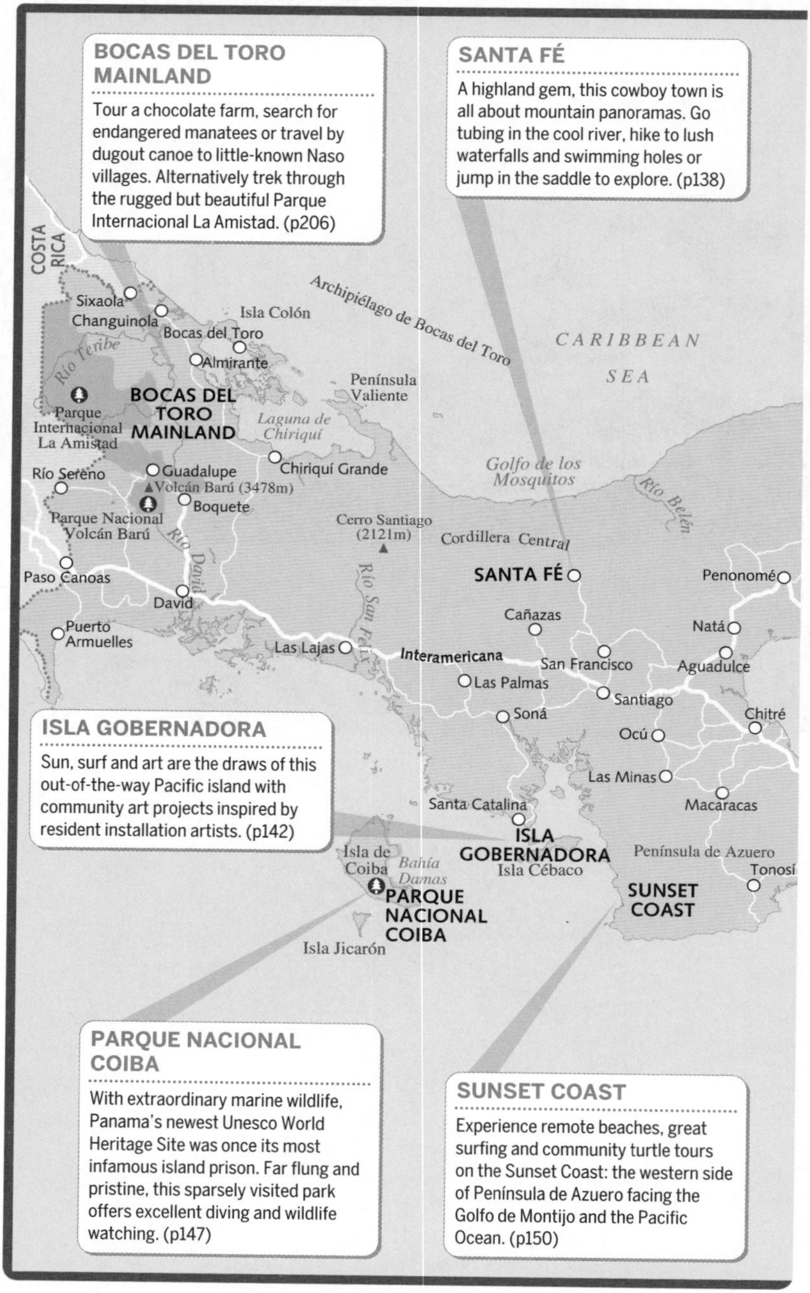

BOCAS DEL TORO MAINLAND

Tour a chocolate farm, search for endangered manatees or travel by dugout canoe to little-known Naso villages. Alternatively trek through the rugged but beautiful Parque Internacional La Amistad. (p206)

SANTA FÉ

A highland gem, this cowboy town is all about mountain panoramas. Go tubing in the cool river, hike to lush waterfalls and swimming holes or jump in the saddle to explore. (p138)

COSTA RICA
Sixaola
Changuinola
Isla Colón
Bocas del Toro
Almirante
Río Teribe
Archipiélago de Bocas del Toro
CARIBBEAN SEA
Península Valiente
Parque Internacional La Amistad
BOCAS DEL TORO MAINLAND
Laguna de Chiriquí
Río Sereno
Guadalupe
Volcán Barú (3478m)
Chiriquí Grande
Golfo de los Mosquitos
Río Belén
Boquete
Parque Nacional Volcán Barú
Río David
Cerro Santiago (2121m)
Cordillera Central
Paso Canoas
Río San Félix
SANTA FÉ
Penonomé
David
Cañazas
Natá
Puerto Armuelles
Las Lajas
Interamericana
San Francisco
Aguadulce
Las Palmas
Santiago
Soná
Chitré
Ocú
Las Minas
Santa Catalina
Macaracas
ISLA GOBERNADORA
Isla Cébaco
Península de Azuero
Isla de Coiba
Bahía Damas
Tonosí
PARQUE NACIONAL COIBA
SUNSET COAST
Isla Jicarón

ISLA GOBERNADORA

Sun, surf and art are the draws of this out-of-the-way Pacific island with community art projects inspired by resident installation artists. (p142)

PARQUE NACIONAL COIBA

With extraordinary marine wildlife, Panama's newest Unesco World Heritage Site was once its most infamous island prison. Far flung and pristine, this sparsely visited park offers excellent diving and wildlife watching. (p147)

SUNSET COAST

Experience remote beaches, great surfing and community turtle tours on the Sunset Coast: the western side of Península de Azuero facing the Golfo de Montijo and the Pacific Ocean. (p150)

PARQUE NACIONAL DARIÉN

Call it the ultimate adventure. A visit to Central America's most biodiverse park requires authorization and an experienced guide, but no self-respecting adventurer can forgo the jungles of the Darién. (p250)

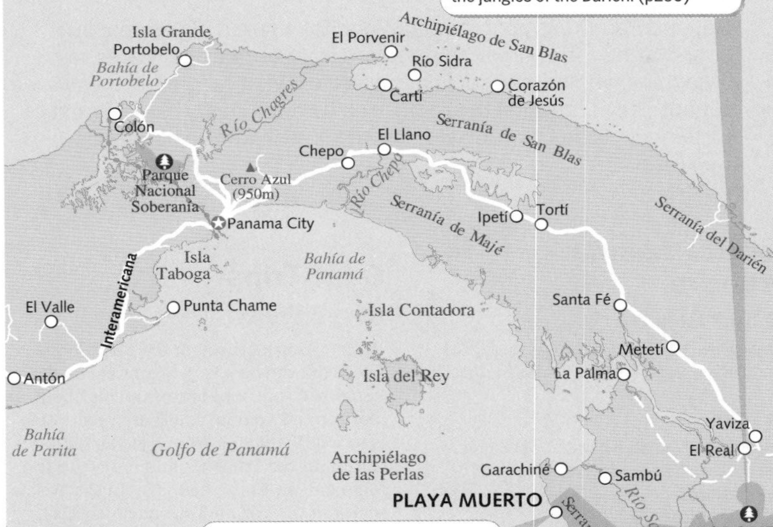

PLAYA MUERTO

On the seldom visited Pacific coast of Darién Province, with pounding waves and empty beaches, this non-tourist destination has a vibrant Emberá community and offers the chance to spot the elusive harpy eagle. (p254)

ISLA CAÑAS

Hop into a *lancha* that will ferry you through the mangrove to the island that time forgot and where olive ridley sea turtles nest in droves from July to November. (p133)

Plan Your Trip

Panama Outdoors

Beyond Panama's cosmopolitan capital, there's big appeal outdoors. Start with wildlife that ranges from curious primates to breaching whales and darting butterflies. Visit jungle waterways via dugout canoe, snorkel the reefs, trek through misty cloud forest or surf Pacific tubes. Refuel with fresh coffee from the highlands, and then repeat.

Best of Panama Outdoors

Best Surf Beach

Laid-back vibes, access to Parque Nacional Coiba and world-class waves: it's all at Santa Catalina.

Best Hike

Sendero Los Quetzales is a beautiful 8km route, running between Cerro Punta and Boquete in Chiriquí Province.

Best Sportfishing

If you want to break a sportfishing world record, your chances are high at Bahía Piña.

Best Dive Site

Parque Nacional Coiba has extraordinary marine wildlife; you might spot hammerheads or a whale shark.

Best Accessible Wildlife-Watching

More than 500 bird species have been sighted along Pipeline Rd in Parque Nacional Soberanía – hit the trail and start counting!

Best White-Water Rafting

Tackle the white water of Río Chiriquí May through December.

Boat Trips

River Trips

Partial transits through the Miraflores Locks are the best way to appreciate the Panama Canal, and one of the highlights of any trip to Panama. Another great option is to wildlife-watch from a kayak on Lago Gatún. In the Darién, tours cruise up Río Mogué to an Emberá village. In the Wekso sector of the Parque Internacional La Amistad, travelers can explore indigenous villages while heading upriver on motorized dugouts.

Ocean Trips

The 226km-long Archipiélago de San Blas is a thrill for ocean explorers. Run as an autonomous region by the Guna people, it features hundreds of coconut-fringed islands and islets surrounded by turquoise waters. Independent travelers can travel by small boat between the islands, or charter sailboats through the area and even on to Colombia.

Hiking

Panama offers everything from dry tropical rainforests and highland cloud forests to humid jungles and blustery mountain peaks.

Starting near the capital on the shores of the canal, Parque Nacional Soberanía contains a section of the historic Sendero Las Cruces. Closer to Panama City, Parque Natural Metropolitano boasts a number of short but rewarding hikes in plush rainforest that skirts the capital.

Popular highland retreats include Boquete; El Valle, nestled into the extinct volcano now known as Valle de Antón; and Santa Fé, surrounded by rivers, waterfalls and cloud forests. All feature hikes in a pristine mountain setting.

Chiriquí is home to two of Panama's most famous hikes: Volcán Barú and Sendero Los Quetzales in Parque Nacional Volcán Barú. While Los Quetzales is more scenic in poor weather, ascents up Barú, which is Panama's highest peak, can offer views of both oceans on a clear day.

Recommended remote destinations include the Las Nubes sector of the Parque Internacional La Amistad. With trails only accessible with a guide, it is as rugged and uncharted as Central America gets.

THE TRANSPANAMA TRAIL

This cross-country circuit (www.transpanama.org) runs from the border of Costa Rica toward Panama City, but you can hike any three-day stretch for a good taste of Panama's rugged backcountry. More information is available on the website, where you can also download GPS tracks for free.

The best diving in Panama is around Isla de Coiba, the centerpiece of a national marine park accessed via Santa Catalina. Divers here scout for enormous sharks including schools of hammerheads, blacktips and whitetips as well as the occasional tiger or whale shark.

The Guna prohibit dive operators from working in the Comarca de Guna Yala, but the snorkeling is some of the best in Panama.

Diving & Snorkeling

Panama's underwater world spans two great oceans, and abounds with colorful coral gardens, towering rock shelves, sunken wrecks and a rich diversity of marine life. Fans of multicolored reef fish and bathtub-warm water should head for the Caribbean, while more advanced divers in search of enormous pelagic animals and remote dive sites should head to the Pacific. Three major spots in Panama that have a deserved reputation for fine scuba diving are the Archipiélago de Bocas del Toro, the Caribbean town of Portobelo and the Pacific-coast Isla de Coiba.

The Caribbean islands of Bocas del Toro have a thriving dive community. During the rainy season (mid-April to mid-December) underwater visibility is extremely poor – nearly 40 rivers deposit silt into the seas around the islands, which turns the water a murky green.

Near historic Portobelo, 16 major dive sites feature underwater attractions including a 110ft cargo ship, a C-45 twin-engine plane, soft-coral-laden walls, offshore reefs and rock gardens.

Surfing

Although the joy of Panama is riding some of the lesser-known surf breaks – or even discovering your own – the country has two world-class spots in Santa Catalina and the Archipiélago de Bocas del Toro. Even these are significantly less crowded than similar places in neighboring Costa Rica.

The face of a typical wave at Santa Catalina is 2m, though during February and March, 4m waves are fairly common. Waves are at their best during medium to high tide, when rides approaching 150m are possible. On the Caribbean side, the islands of Bocas del Toro offer some of the best and most varied surfing in Panama, especially from December to March.

Surfing spots are also found in the provinces of Panamá, Veraguas (Playa Morillo), Los Santos, Colón and Chiriquí.

Cycling

Owing to its compact size and modern infrastructure, Panama is the perfect country to unleash a little pedal power.

DIVING RESPONSIBLY

- Never anchor on the reef and take care not to ground boats on coral.
- Avoid touching or standing on living marine organisms. Polyps can be damaged by even the most gentle contact. If you must hold on, only touch exposed rock or dead coral.
- Watch your fins. The surge from fin strokes can damage delicate reef organisms and clouds of sand can smother organisms.
- Make visits quick to underwater caves, as trapped air bubbles damage organisms.
- Resist the temptation to collect or buy corals or shells or to loot marine archaeological sites.
- Do not feed fish and never ride on the backs of turtles.

As with all long-distance cycling, you need to prepare yourself both physically and mentally for the rigors of the road. The major factor when considering a lengthy bike ride is the weather. With heat a serious factor, riding in the early morning and resting in the heat of the day is a good strategy. Also, it's not entirely safe to ride in the rain. Throughout much of the country, the rains come from mid-April to mid-December, though the Caribbean has rain virtually year-round. Beyond the capital, you're essentially on your own, but never underestimate the prowess of the village mechanic.

Wildlife-Watching

Unlike in the savannahs of Africa, wildlife-watching in the neotropical rainforest is an exercise in patience and stealth – a little luck doesn't hurt, either. Although it's unlikely you'll come across top predators such as jaguars and pumas, primates and lesser mammals are commonly sighted. Top national parks for watching wildlife include La Amistad, Volcán Barú and the Darién. Closer to the capital, Parque Natural Metropolitano and Parque Nacional Soberanía are easily accessible and quite good.

Highlights

Nowhere else in the world are rainforests as easily accessible as they are in this tiny sliver of a country. To make the most of your wildlife-watching experience, pick up a good field guide. Some highlights include the following:

Two- and three-toed sloths Found only in neotropical rainforests, these ancient mammals came into being when South America was isolated. Curled up high on a branch, they are hard to spot. They spend 16 hours a day asleep or inactive but busy with digestion.

Mantled howlers Greeting sunrise and sunset with booming calls that resonate for kilometers, howlers are incredibly vocal. Their antics are also good storm indicators.

Jaguars The largest cat in the Americas, jaguars are extremely rare and elusive, though their evidence is all around, from dried spoor to fresh tracks.

Parrots and macaws Panama has over 20 species, including five macaws. Big macaws can be identified by their huge bills, bare facial patch and long, tapered tails.

Toucans The spectacular multicolored bill is a giveaway. This powerful tool is full of air cavities and quite lightweight. A serrated upper mandible helps grip slippery fruits and intimidate other birds.

Birdwatching

With more than 900 bird species in Panama, all you need to do to spot feathered friends is get a good pair of binoculars and hit the trails. Two popular spots include Pipeline Rd in Parque Nacional Soberanía and Burbayar Lodge in Panamá Province. Panama Audubon Society (p54), located in Panama City, organizes the annual Christmas bird count on Pipeline Rd, and runs birdwatching expeditions throughout the country.

PHOTOCECHCZ / SHUTTERSTOCK ©

Top: Surfing in Bocas del Toro province (p197)
Bottom: Jaguar

SURVIVING A RIPTIDE

Rip currents are formed when excess water brought to shore by waves returns to the sea in a rapidly moving depression in the ocean floor. They are comprised of three parts: the feeder current, the neck and the head.

The feeder current consists of rapidly moving water that parallels the shore but isn't always visible from the beach. When this water reaches a channel, it switches direction and flows out to sea, forming the neck of the rip. This is the fastest-moving part of the riptide, moving with a speed of up to 10km/h. The head of the riptide current occurs past the breakers where the current quickly dissipates.

If caught in a riptide, immediately call or signal for help. Conserve your energy and do not fight the current – this is the principal cause of drownings as it's almost impossible to swim directly back to shore. Instead, try one of two methods. The first is to float or tread water and let yourself be swept out past the breakers; once you're in the head of the rip, you can swim out of the channel and ride the waves back to shore. Alternatively you can swim parallel to shore until the current weakens.

Rip currents usually occur on beaches with strong surf, but temporary rips can occur anywhere, especially when there is an offshore storm or during low tide. Indicators include a brownish color to the surface of the water caused by swept-up sand and debris. Also look for surface flattening, which occurs when the water enters a depression in the ocean floor and rushes back out to sea. If you're ever in doubt, it's best to inquire locally about swimming conditions. And never ever swim alone.

White-Water Sports

Whether you take to the water by raft or kayak, Panama boasts some excellent opportunities for river running. The best-known white-water runs are on the Ríos Chiriquí and Chiriquí Viejo, with Class III-plus rapids. The unofficial river-running capital of Panama is the highland town of Boquete. Sea-kayaking centers are Bocas del Toro and Chiriquí Provinces.

Fishing

Panamá means 'abundance of fish,' and with 2988km of coastline, there's no problem finding a fishing spot. Freshwater anglers usually set their sights on trout and bass, while serious sportfishers ply the seas for trophy fish including tarpon, sailfish and marlin. Freshwater angling can be pursued independently, especially in the highland rivers of Chiriquí and Veraguas. In the Canal Zone you can fish for peacock bass in Lago Gatún and the Río Chagres.

For deep-sea fishing, Panama offers three world-class areas – Bahía Piña, the Archipiélago de Las Perlas and Isla de Coiba – all served by extremely professional fishing outfits. In the Darién's Bahía Piña, more International Game Fish Association world records have been broken than anywhere else on the planet. This top spot is served exclusively by Tropic Star Lodge (p254). The seas around Isla de Coiba are home to several species of sport fish including yellowfin tuna, wahoo, dolphinfish, Spanish mackerel, jacks and rooster fish. The Veraguas coast is another good option.

Regions at a Glance

Located at the heart of the Americas, Panama is the narrow but crucial link between Central and South America. The Panama Canal joins the Atlantic to the Pacific, wedding east to west in global commerce. In the last century, the canal defined Panama, but it's what lies just beyond that may define the next. Pristine beaches, lush rainforest and big-city nightlife are major assets. English is widely spoken, yet the lost world of rainforests and dugout canoes is never too far off. The canal expansion will translate to further growth and glitz. But, for now, you can still pick an empty islet and play survivor for a day.

Panama City

History
Cuisine
Nightlife

Colonial Echoes

Wander the cobblestone streets of the Casco Viejo, admire the 16th-century ruins of Panamá Viejo or pedal the greenbelt Cinta Costera for the long view. Admire the treasures privateers forgot. History's most notorious explorers, pirates and marauders came before you.

Tropical Tastes

Panama chefs are reinventing traditional ingredients and refining tropical tastes, and the capital's lively dining scene is finally reflecting its cultural plurality, with more options than ever reflecting its global citizenship. *Provecho!*

La Rumba

From rooftop cocktails with city views to live salsa bands and open-air bars under crumbling colonial walls, Panama City nightlife is dynamic, daring and ever hip. While anything goes, locals usually dress to the nines.

p44

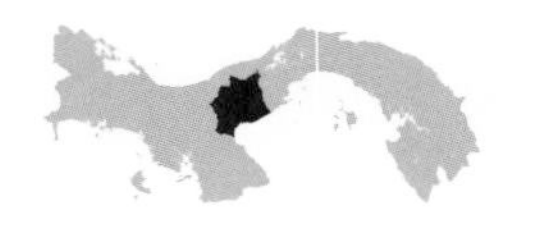

Panamá Province

Human-Made Marvels
Rainforests
Island Getaways

Panama Canal

The expansion of this 80km cross-continental shortcut is even more reason to set your sights on the impressive Panama Canal. Yet few know that, off the shipping lanes, there are also fishing, kayaking and wildlife-watching opportunities in these tropical waterways.

Wildlife-Watching

Rainforest adventures and some of the best wildlife-watching in Central America sit just outside Panama City. For nature on steroids, reserve ahead for the exclusive Smithsonian Tropical Research Institute tour, or explore the leafy stillness of Parque Nacional Soberanía.

Beaches

Isla Contadora makes a great city escape, with pristine beaches and deserted shores on this underpopulated island – for a price. On a budget? Flee to lively Isla Taboga for the day for beach time. Both now have frequent ferry services.

p73

Coclé Province

Highlands
Culture
Beaches

Mountain Time

Coclé's highland retreats are prime weekend getaways. El Valle is an established resort town with boutique hotels and charming waterfall walks. For something wilder, seek replenishment in the deep forests of Reserva Privada Távida or Parque Nacional Omar Torrijos.

Latin Tradition

Pick up the signature product of Coclé: a Panama hat (a striped sombrero woven from natural fibers) at a streetside stand, or take an up-close look at the production of fine cigars and cane sugar on a factory tour.

Resort Life

Wide, pearly beaches are a Coclé signature. With an airport at Río Hato near Farallón and resorts popping up, the area is poised to boom. Day trippers can stop in Farallón or Santa Clara to kick back for a couple days.

p94

Península de Azuero

Festivals
Beaches
Turtles

Street Parties

If the peninsula is the heart and soul of Panama, then festivals are its pulse. Villa de Los Santos, Las Tablas and Guararé are the places to get your groove on; Panama's biggest festival, La Mejorana, happens here in September.

Deserted Beaches

With access improving, the rugged Azuero coast may not remain solitary for long. Yet today its essence is still wild, especially further down, towards the end of the fabulous Sunset Coast in Veraguas Province.

The Moonlight Hatch

Late August through November, thousands of olive ridley turtles land on remote Isla de Cañas in the wee hours to lay eggs which hatch later in the season. Visitors come with guides to bear witness to the stirring nighttime spectacles.

p112

Veraguas Province

Surfing
Diving
Country Roads

Riding Waves

With some of the biggest breaks in Central America, Santa Catalina is deliriously fun. Big tubes and long rides attract the experts (especially December through April); beginners have their own sandy-bottom spot at Playa El Estero, a 15-minute walk away.

Marine Life

Pure delight for divers and snorkelers, Parque Nacional Coiba hosts amazing biodiversity. With whale sharks and sea horses, it's not your average plunge. Though out of the way, it's very worthwhile, especially if you overnight and double your time underwater.

Off the Beaten Track

Brave the winding lanes to the rugged and relatively undiscovered landscapes of the highlands. The village of Santa Fé makes an ideal base for waterfall hikes with swimming holes, river tubing, horseback riding and hiking Santa Fé National Park.

p135

Chiriquí Province

Rafting & Kayaking
Hiking
Highland Lodges

White Water

Adrenaline addicts head to Boquete, the highland coffee-farm town that has become a major hub for rafting and kayaking. You can paddle year-round on the Río Chiriquí (though it's best from May to December) or on Chiriquí Viejo.

Highland Trails

The iconic Quetzal Trail weaves through gorgeous highland forest in search of its exquisite namesake. Brave Volcán Barú or set out expedition-style to Parque Internacional La Amistad from Las Nubes, located just 10km northwest of highland village Cerro Punta.

Coffee with a View

A delicious treat in high country, cabin lodges in the coffee farms of Boquete and in the cloud forests of Cerro Punta and Buena Vista take the chill off with fireplaces, bottles of wine and hot tubs, with porch views of dancing hummingbirds.

p153

Bocas del Toro Province

Beaches
Surfing
Culture

Idyllic Shores

Many an idyllic palm-fringed crescent is a bicycle or boat-taxi ride away from Bocas town. Take care of the many starfish on its namesake beach as well as on Red Frog Beach and its neighbors, Playas Wizard, Polo and Larga.

Waves for All

While second to Santa Catalina, Bocas offers the most varied waves in Panama, with plenty of options to get beginners on board, especially at Old Man's and Black Rock on Isla Carenero. Then a cool Caribbean vibe reels you in.

Community Tourism

Connect with local and indigenous culture through the popular Oreba chocolate-farm tour, a visit to the Ngöbe-Buglé community on Isla San Cristóbal, or a real adventure to little-known Naso country, where ecotourism projects provide adventure and insight.

p181

Colón Province

History
Diving
Culture

Essential Sites

Old Spanish fortresses, the Panama Railroad and the canal expansion seen from Agua Clara Visitor Center: the tumultuous history of Colón is Panama's most compelling. Visit on a day tour from Panama City or spend a few days around Portobelo.

Underwater Treasures

While it doesn't quite rival the clear waters of the Pacific, there's enjoyable diving to soft coral walls, offshore reefs and Atlantic wrecks with storied pasts. Keep an eye out for eagle rays, nurse sharks and reef sharks.

Caribbean Culture

The Caribbean province of Colón marches to its own beat. To get a sense of this vibrant Congo culture, it's worth checking out the artist workshop in Portobelo, attending a lively, color-spattered festival and wandering the forts.

p212

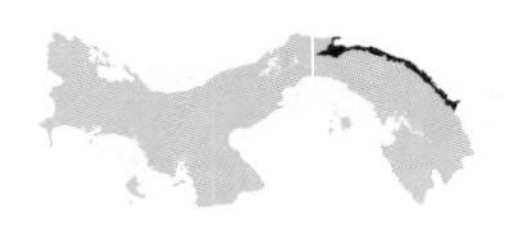

Comarca de Guna Yala

Islands
Culture
Arts

Back to Basics

With hundreds of idyllic islands and waters of technicolor turquoise, you could indeed do much worse. Resort islands consist of little more than thatched huts with sandy floors and a few hammocks, but what more do you need in paradise?

Guna Culture

The world of the strong, self-governing Guna is very different from mainland Panama, and it's well worth engaging a local guide or host to learn about their crafts and everyday lives. Community islands further your cultural understanding, especially at festival time.

Molas

Beautiful and often exquisitely crafted, *molas* (colorful panels of intricate embroidery) are the signature of Guna culture and Panama's most beloved craft. Designs range from abstract, with traditional maroon, white and black, to modern, adorned with cats or Santa.

p227

Darién Province

Nature
Culture
Fishing

Remote Wilderness

Beyond the last kilometer of the fabled Interamericana, the lush rainforest of Parque Nacional Darién is the most ecologically diverse park in Central America. Search for jaguars and harpy eagles and bathe in chilly waterfalls. Just arriving is an adventure.

Indigenous Culture

Remote pockets of Emberá and Wounaan peoples have inhabited the Darién's ancient forests and paddled its labyrinthine waterways for centuries. With a guided expedition to villages promoting community tourism, the most intrepid of travelers can learn about real jungle survival.

Sportfishing

Bahía Piña is the granddaddy of sportfishing destinations, reeling in mammoth marlin and sailfish. More world records have been set here than anywhere else. An exclusive fishing lodge is fitted with all the trimmings on this windswept Pacific coast.

p242

On the Road

Panama City

POP 880,700 / ELEV 6FT

Includes ➡

Best Places to Eat

- Donde José (p63)
- Mercado de Mariscos (p62)
- Lo Que Hay (p63)
- Avatar (p64)
- Super Gourmet (p62)

Best Places to Stay

- American Trade Hotel (p58)
- Magnolia Inn (p57)
- W Hotel (p61)
- Bristol Panama (p61)
- El Machico (p59)

Why Go?

The most cosmopolitan capital in Central America, Panama City is both vibrant metropolis and gateway to tropical escapes. Many worlds coexist here. Welcoming both east and west, Panama is a regional hub of trade and immigration. The resulting cultural cocktail mix leads to a refreshing 'anything goes' attitude, more dynamic and fluid than that of its neighbors.

Unflinchingly urban, the capital rides the rails of chaos, with traffic jams, wayward taxis and casinos stacked between chic clubs and construction sites. A center of international banking and trade, it has a sultry skyline of shimmering glass and steel towers that is reminiscent of Miami. In contrast, the colonial peninsula of Casco Viejo has become a hip neighborhood where cobblestones link boutique hotels with rooftop bars and crumbled ruins with pirate lore.

Escape is never far away. Day-trip to sandy beaches (Pacific or Caribbean), admire the canal, or explore lush rainforests of howler monkeys, toucans and sloths.

When to Go

Jan In the peak of high season, the weeklong Panama Jazz Festival features open-air concerts and events held mostly in the historic neighborhood of Casco Viejo.

Dec–mid-Mar High season is dry season, with sunnier weather for outdoor cafe dining and day trips to the beach; hotel rates are up and travelers should book ahead.

Apr–Nov Low-season prices and occasional showers, though a rain reprieve usually comes in October. A slew of public holidays in November means ubiquitous parades, party events and closures. It can also be hard to book hotels.

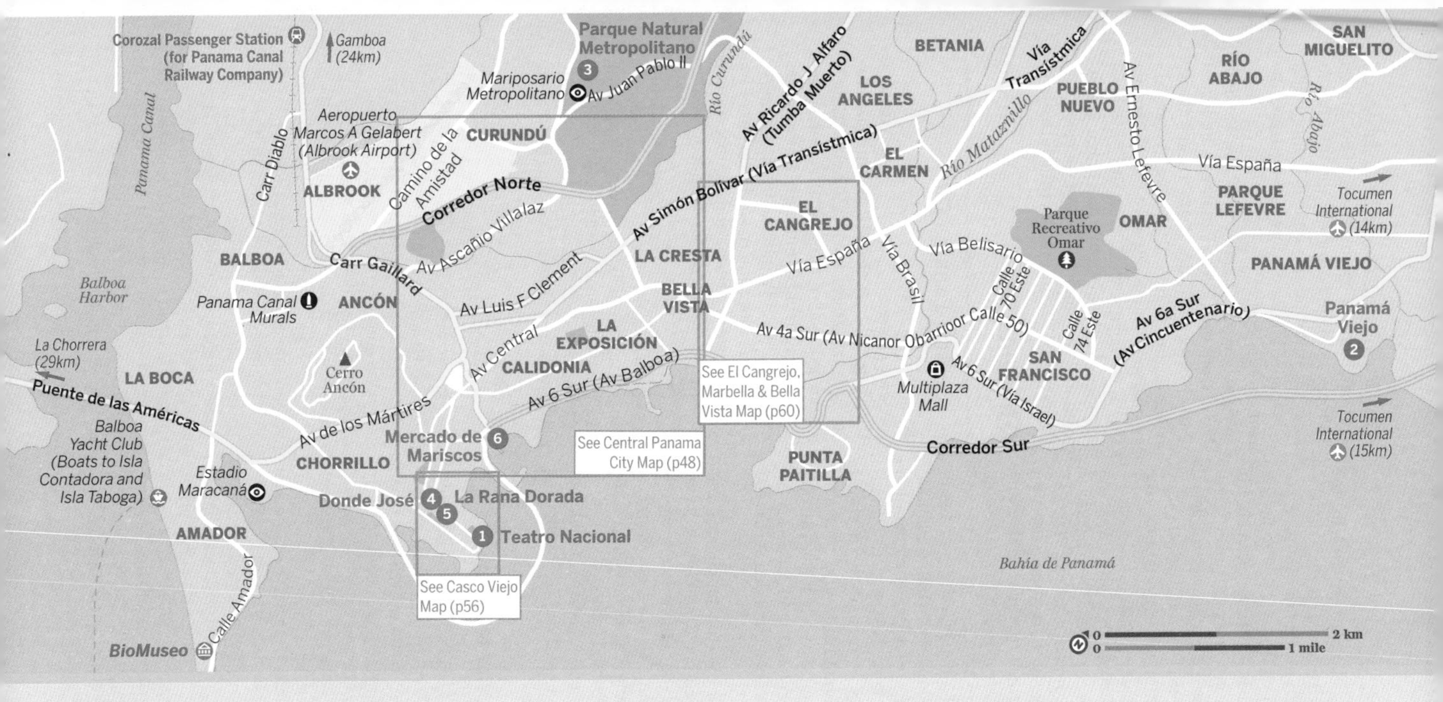

Panama City Highlights

1 **Teatro Nacional** (p49) Catching a performance at one of historic Casco Viejo's most striking venues, nestled among crumbling colonials, soaring churches and grand plazas.

2 **Panamá Viejo** (p51) Reconnecting with the past at the ruins of the original city.

3 **Parque Natural Metropolitano** (p51) Hiking through 265 hectares of rainforest, just 10 minutes from downtown.

4 **Donde José** (p63) Feasting on new tropical fusion cuisine in Casco Viejo at one of Panama City's hottest restaurants.

5 **La Rana Dorada** (p66) Sampling craft beers at one of the city's best microbreweries.

6 **Mercado de Mariscos** (p62) Treating your hangover by pedaling along the Cinta Costera to for cheap *ceviche* (citrus-cured seafood) and the freshest fish around.

History

Panama City was founded in 1519 by the Spanish governor Pedro Arias de Ávila (Pedrarias), not long after conquistador Vasco Núñez de Balboa first saw the Pacific. Although the Spanish settlement quickly became an important center of government and church authority, the city was ransacked and destroyed in 1671 by the English pirate Captain Henry Morgan, leaving only the stone ruins of Panamá Viejo.

Three years later, the city was reestablished about 8km to the southwest in the area now known as Casco Viejo. Although the peninsular location was well defended, the Spanish overland trade route faded upon the destruction of the Caribbean port at Portobelo in 1746.

Panama gained independence from Spain in 1821 and became part of Gran Colombia; a decade later the regional confederation dissolved and Panama belonged to Colombia. Panama City subsequently declined in importance, though it would return to prominence in the 1850s when the Panama Railroad was completed, and gold seekers on their way to California flooded across the isthmus by train.

Panama declared its independence from Colombia on November 3, 1903, and Panama City was firmly established as the capital. After the Panama Canal was completed in 1914, the city emerged as a center for international business and trade.

The city's greatest modern setback occurred in 1989, when the USA invaded to oust dictator (and former US collaborator) Manuel Noriega from power. The capital suffered damage both from the invasion itself and from the subsequent looting, with residential blocks of Chorrillo destroyed by combat-ignited fire.

Following the handover of the Panama Canal from the USA to Panama in 1999, and the subsequent closure of American military bases in the country, Panama City has taken charge of its own destiny. Today Panama City is by far the wealthiest city in Central America. With an influx of foreign investment and the Panama Canal expansion, the city is poised to continue its transformation.

Sights

Central Panama City

★Museo de Arte Contemporáneo MUSEUM

(MAC; Map p48; 262-8012; www.macpanama.org; Av de los Mártires, Ancón; adult/child US$5/3; 10am-5pm Tue-Sun, to 8pm Thu) This wonderful privately owned museum features the best collection of Panamanian art anywhere, an excellent collection of works on paper by Latin American artists, and the occasional temporary exhibition by a foreign or national artist.

Museo Afro-Antilleano MUSEUM

(Map p48; 501-4130; cnr Av Justo Arosemena & Calle 24 Este, Ancón; adult/child US$1/0.25; 9am-4pm Tue-Sat) The small Afro-Antillean museum has exhibits on the history of

CAPTAIN HENRY MORGAN

After sacking the original Panama City settlement (now known as Panamá Viejo) in 1671, Captain Henry Morgan burnt the place to the ground, massacred its inhabitants and made off with the richest booty in the Americas. Because his actions violated a peace treaty between England and Spain, Morgan was arrested and conducted to England the following year, but he was acquitted because he supposedly had no prior knowledge of the treaty. In 1674 Morgan was knighted before departing for Jamaica to take up the post of lieutenant governor.

Although Captain Morgan is best remembered for his nefarious exploits at sea, the last several years of his life in Port Royal (the 'Sodom of the New World') are the stuff of legend. Here, he lived out his life spending the riches of Panama.

The events surrounding his death remain a mystery. He died in 1688, at the age of 53, leaving behind an immense personal fortune. Although his death has been attributed to tuberculosis and dropsy (edema), local lore has it that the world's most infamous pirate simply drank himself to death. Now his name lives on in the form of spiced rum.

To see the legacy left by Captain Morgan, visit the ruins of Panamá Viejo (p51), or check out Casco Viejo's Iglesia de San José, which houses a golden altar – the only item salvaged after Morgan's raid.

Panama's West Indian community, particularly their work building the railroad and later the canal.

Museo de Ciencias Naturales MUSEUM
(Map p48; ☎ info 225-0645; Av Cuba btwn Calles 29 Este & 30 Este, Calidonia; admission US$1; ⊗ 8am-4pm Tue-Sat) Museo de Ciencias Naturales has sections on geology, paleontology, entomology and marine biology, as well as an impressive display of taxidermy.

Casco Viejo

Following the destruction of the old city by Captain Henry Morgan in 1671, the Spanish moved their city 8km southwest to a rocky peninsula at the foot of Cerro Ancón. The new location was easier to defend as the reefs prevented ships from approaching the city except at high tide. The new city was also easy to defend, as a massive wall surrounded it, which is how Casco Viejo (Old Compound) got its name.

In 1904, when construction began on the Panama Canal, all of Panama City existed where Casco Viejo stands today. However, as population growth and urban expansion pushed the boundaries of Panama City further east, the city's elite abandoned Casco Viejo and the neighborhood rapidly deteriorated into a slum.

Today Casco Viejo's crumbling facades have been mostly replaced by immaculate renovations. Declared a Unesco World Heritage Site in 2003, the area is getting international recognition. The newly restored architecture gives a sense of how magnificent the neighborhood must have looked in past years. Some developers, committed to mitigating the effects of gentrification here, are creating one affordable unit for each high-end one constructed, and working on interesting local cultural initiatives. Yet the consensus is that most of the neighborhood's former occupants have already been relegated to the periphery.

Change continues to prove tricky for the Casco. The expansion of the Cinta Costera, a coastal beltway, has ringed the peninsula with an elevated highway built some 8m above the sea and 200m offshore. With little regard for environmental concerns, the project threatened the area's World Heritage status. Worst of all, the US$189 million project, created to fix city traffic problems by providing an alternative route, has not been effective as it does not bypass the worst bottleneck areas.

Museo del Canal Interoceánico MUSEUM
(Panama Canal Museum; Map p56; ☎ 211-1649; www.museodelcanal.com; Calle 6a Oeste; adult/child US$10/5; ⊗ 9am-5pm Tue-Sun) This impressive museum is housed in a beautifully restored building that once served as the headquarters for the original French canal company. The Panama Canal Museum (as it's more commonly known) presents excellent exhibits on the famous waterway, framed in their historical and political context. Signs are in Spanish, but English-speaking guides and audio guides (US$5) are available.

Iglesia de San José CHURCH
(Map p56; Av A) This church protects the famous Altar de Oro (Golden Altar), the sole relic salvaged after privateer Henry Morgan sacked Panamá Viejo.

According to local legend, when word came of Morgan's impending attack, a priest attempted to disguise the altar by painting it black. The priest told Morgan that the famous altar had been stolen by another pirate, and even convinced Morgan to donate handsomely for its replacement. Morgan is said to have told the priest, 'I don't know why, but I think you are more of a pirate than I am.' Whatever the truth, the baroque altar was later moved from the old city to the present site.

Plaza de Francia PLAZA
(Map p56) At the tip of the southern point of Casco Viejo, this beautiful plaza pays homage to the French role in the construction of the canal. Its large stone tablets and statues are dedicated to the memory of the 22,000 workers who died trying to create the canal.

Most of the workers died from yellow fever and malaria. Among the busts is a monument to Cuban doctor Carlos J Finlay, whose discovery of how mosquitoes transmit yellow fever led to the eradication of the disease.

On one side of the plaza are nine restored dungeons that were used by the Spaniards and later by the Colombians. Although they're now home to some rather upscale art galleries and shops, you can still see the original stonework. Also on the plaza are the Teatro Anita Villalaz (p68) and the Instituto Nacional de Cultura (p51).

Central Panama City

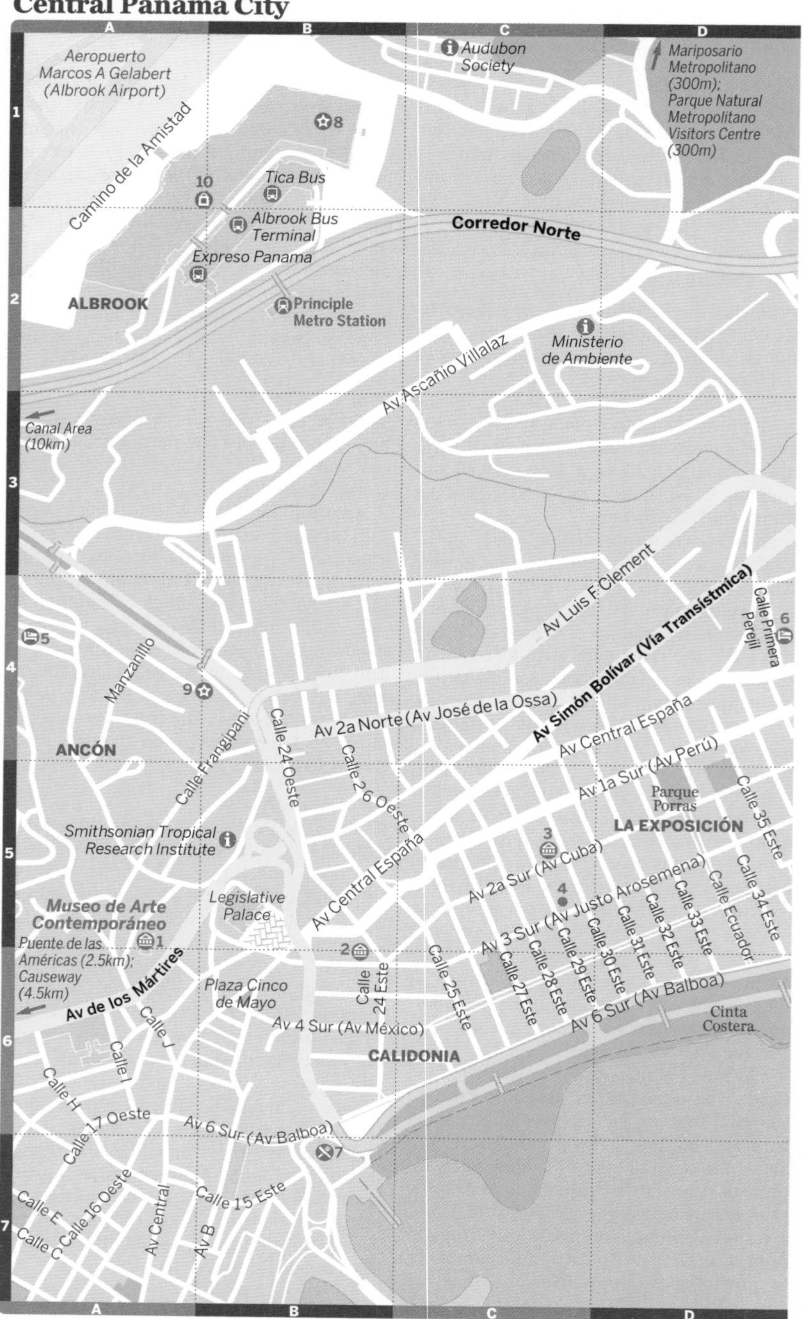

Central Panama City

Top Sights
1 Museo de Arte Contemporáneo......... A5

Sights
2 Museo Afro-Antilleano......... B6
3 Museo de Ciencias Naturales......... C5

Activities, Courses & Tours
4 City Sightseeing Panama......... C5
Panama Travel Unlimited......... (see 6)

Sleeping
5 Dos Palmitos......... A4
6 Mamallena......... D4

Eating
7 Mercado de Mariscos......... B7

Entertainment
8 Albrook Cinemark......... B1
9 Ancon Guild Theater......... B4

Shopping
10 Albrook Mall......... A1

Teatro Nacional THEATER
(Map p56; ☎501-4107; www.inac.gob.pa/teatros/73-teatro-nacional; Av B) Built in 1907, the interior of this ornate theater has been completely restored. It boasts red and gold decorations, a once-magnificent ceiling mural by Roberto Lewis (one of Panama's finest painters) and an impressive crystal chandelier. Performances are still held here. For information visit the office at the side of the building.

Iglesia y Convento de Santo Domingo CHURCH
(Map p56) Built in 1678, these gorgeous ruins are what remain after two major fires brought down the church's tower and interior areas. Left are the walls and arches, including a notable flat arch meant to aid in the acoustics of the choir.

Iglesia de la Compañía de Jesús CHURCH
(Map p56; Av A s/n) These days only a shell, this 1741 convent and church was destroyed in a fire and further damaged in an earthquake but remains a thing of beauty. It has numerous seashell niches that represent the marine riches of Panama.

Iglesia de La Merced CHURCH
(Map p56; Calle Central s/n) An example of the baroque style in Panama, this church was built in 1673 with a facade transferred from Panamá Viejo.

Paseo las Bóvedas WATERFRONT
(Map p56) This esplanade runs along the top of the sea wall built by the Spanish to protect the city. From here, you can see the Puente de las Américas arching over the waterway and the ships lining up to enter the canal.

Parque Bolívar PLAZA
(Map p56) In 1826, in a schoolroom opposite this park, Simón Bolívar held a meeting urging the union of the Latin American countries. Bolívar eventually succeeded in liberating Bolivia, Colombia, Ecuador, Peru and Venezuela from Spanish rule and uniting them as Gran Colombia. Although he was unable to keep Gran Colombia together, he is venerated as a hero throughout Latin America.

Museo de Arte Religioso Colonial MUSEUM
(Museum of Colonial Religious Art; Map p56; 519-9915; www.inac.gob.pa/museos; cnr Av A & Calle 3a Este; US$1; 8am-4pm Mon-Fri) Housed beside the ruins of the Iglesia y Convento de Santo Domingo, the Museo de Arte Religioso Colonial has a collection of colonial-era religious artifacts, some dating from the 16th century.

Just inside the ruins' doorway, the Arco Chato is a long arch that stood here unsupported for centuries. It even played a part in the selection of Panama over Nicaragua as the site for the canal, since its survival was taken as proof that the area was not subject to earthquakes. It collapsed in 2003 but has since been rebuilt.

Museo de Historia de Panamá MUSEUM
(Map p56; 501-4128; www.inac.gob.pa/museos; Palacio Municipal, Calle 6a Oeste; adult/child US$1/0.50; 8am-4pm Mon-Fri) FREE The modest Museo de Historia de Panamá has a small selection of exhibits covering Panamanian history from the colonial period to the modern era.

Plaza de la Independencia PLAZA
(Map p56) In this plaza, in the heart of Casco Viejo, Panama declared its independence from Colombia on November 3, 1903.

Palacio de las Garzas HISTORIC BUILDING
(Presidential Palace; Map p56; Av Alfaro) The Palacio de las Garzas is named after the great *garzas blancas* (white herons) that reside here. The president of Panama lives on the upper floor.

PANAMA CITY FOR CHILDREN

Panama City has a variety of attractions to enthrall and entertain kids. The city's Cinta Costera has waterfront paths and a playground. The setting also hosts sporting events and occasional fairs. Another park option is Parque Recreativo Omar (p54), the local answer to New York City's Central Park, with greens that were once a golf course.

A perfect reward for a day well spent is ice cream, and Casco Viejo's Granclement (p62) is a parlor that even mom and dad would beg to visit.

Great rainforest excursions abound. At the **Rainforest Discovery Center** (314-9386, 6588-0697; www.pipelineroad.org; adult/child US$30/5, night walk US$30; 6am-4pm), kids can walk short paths and check out the wildlife from the top of a 32m tower. Alongside huge canal boats, jungle boats cruise along Lago Gatún, fishing for peacock bass or just spotting troupes of monkeys, birds and other animals.

Isla Taboga (p82) is another interesting day trip, with plenty of sand to play in and a cool ferry ride that's a blast for small travelers.

For more adventure, families can visit an Emberá village in the Parque Nacional Soberanía (p78), tour the old cannon-lined forts in Portobelo, or take a moderate hike through Parque Nacional Soberanía or even just in town at Parque Natural Metropolitano, where the chances of spotting a monkey or toucan are pretty good.

The Panama Canal Railway Company (p71), which links the two oceans, provides a lovely journey along the canal and through rainforest. Kids might also enjoy a visit to the Miraflores Locks (p76), especially since the new museum there has lots of eye-catching multimedia exhibitions and is hands-on in parts.

If you need a respite from the heat (or the rain), head to Centro Natural Punta Culebra (p52) to get close to Panama's amazing underwater world. Or if all else fails, stroll down to Multicentro Mall (p68), which has dozens of shops and restaurants, a movie theater and an internet cafe.

American Trade Hall HISTORIC BUILDING
(Map p56; ☎211-2000; www.americantradehotel.com/american-trade-hall.html; Av Central & Calle 10 Oeste; P ♿) Once the headquarters of the First National City Bank of New York, this is where much of the financing of the Panama Canal took place. Today the American Trade Hall opens for cultural events only, but it's worth passing by to admire its beautiful art deco architecture that has been lovingly restored.

Instituto Nacional de Cultura GALLERY
(INAC; Map p56; ☎501-4000; www.inac.gob.pa; Plaza de Francia; ⏰8am-4pm Mon-Fri) INAC is responsible for maintaining the country's museums and other cultural institutions. There is a small gallery on the 1st floor that displays works by Panamanian artists.

Parque Natural Metropolitano

On a hill north of downtown, the 265-hectare **Parque Natural Metropolitano** (☎info 232-5516; www.parquemetropolitano.org; Av Juan Pablo II; US$5; ⏰8am-5pm Mon-Fri, to 1pm Sat) protects vast expanses of tropical semideciduous forest within the city limits. It serves as an incredible wilderness escape from the trappings of the capital. Two main **walking trails**, the Nature Trail and the Tití Monkey Trail, join to form one long loop, with a 150m-high *mirador* (lookout) offering panoramic views of Panama City, the bay and the canal, all the way to the Miraflores Locks.

Mammals in the park include *tití* monkeys, anteaters, sloths and white-tailed deer, while reptiles include iguanas, turtles and tortoises. More than 250 bird species have been spotted here. Fish and shrimp inhabit the Río Curundú along the eastern side of the park.

The park was the site of an important battle during the US invasion to oust Noriega. Also of historical significance, concrete structures just past the park entrance were used during WWII as a testing and assembly plant for aircraft engines.

The park is bordered to the west and north by Camino de la Amistad and to the south and east by Corredor Norte; Av Juan Pablo II runs right through the park.

Pick up a pamphlet for a self-guided tour in Spanish and English at the **visitors center** (⏰8am-4:30pm Mon-Fri, to 1pm Sat), 40m north of the park entrance.

Mariposario Metropolitano NATURE CENTER
(Butterfly Garden; https://mariposariometropolitano.com; adult/child US$5/1.25; ⏰9:30am-4:30pm Tue-Sun) With 1600 species, Panama City's butterfly garden is a worthy stop for nature lovers. Fifteen-minute guided tours explain the life cycle of butterflies and point out their favorite plants. Panama itself is home to 30 native butterfly species. Note that the butterflies themselves are most active on hot and sunny days.

Panamá Viejo

Founded on August 15, 1519, by Spanish conquistador Pedro Arias de Ávila, the city of Panamá was the first European settlement along the Pacific. For the next 150 years it profited mainly from Spain's famed bullion pipeline, which ran from Peru's gold and silver mines to Europe via Panamá. Because of the amount of wealth that passed through the city, the Spaniards kept many soldiers here, and their presence kept the buccaneers away.

In 1671, 1200 pirates led by Captain Henry Morgan ascended the Río Chagres and proceeded overland to Panamá. Although the city was not fortified, it was protected on three sides by the sea and marshes, and on the land side was a causeway with a bridge to allow tidal water to pass underneath. But to the bewilderment of historians, when Morgan and his men neared the city, the Spanish soldiers left this natural stronghold and confronted the buccaneers in a hilly area outside town.

It was the first of many mistakes in battle. After the Spanish force fell to pieces nearly everything of value was either plundered and divvied up or destroyed by fire.

For the next three centuries, the abandoned city served as a convenient source of building materials. By the time the government declared the ruins a protected site in 1976 (Unesco followed suit in 1997), most of the old city had already been dismantled and overrun.

So little of the original city remains that its size, layout and appearance are the subject of much conjecture. Today much of Panamá Viejo lies buried under a poor residential neighborhood, though the **ruins** (Map p53; ☎226-8915; www.panamaviejo.org; Vía Cincuentenario s/n; adult/child US$15/5; ⏰9am-5pm Tue-Sun) are a must-see, even if only to stand on the hallowed grounds of one of Central America's greatest cities.

For safety reasons, explore the area only during daylight hours.

Panamá Viejo buses will drop you off at the Mercado Nacional de Artesanías (p69) behind the first remnants of the old city as you approach from Panama City.

See opposite page for a walking tour of this historic area.

The Causeway

At the Pacific entrance to the Panama Canal, a 2km palm tree-lined *calzada* (causeway) connects the four small islands of Naos, Culebra, Perico and Flamenco to the mainland. The Causeway is popular in the early morning and late afternoon, when residents walk, jog, skate and cycle its narrow length.

The Causeway also offers sweeping views of the skyline and the old city, with flocks of brown pelicans diving into the sea. Some people come here simply to savor the pleasant breeze at one of the many restaurants and bars.

If you don't have your own vehicle, it's most convenient to take a taxi to the Causeway (US$4 to US$8). Any of the restaurants or bars can call one for you.

★**BioMuseo** MUSEUM
(Museum of Biodiversity; www.biomuseopanama.org; adult/child US$18/11; ⌚10am-4pm Tue-Fri, to 5pm Sat & Sun) Celebrating Panama as the land bridge that has permitted astonishing biodiversity in the region, this world-class museum is a visual feast. Exhibits tell the story of Panama's rich biodiversity through engaging, oversized visuals, examining human presence throughout time, how the Atlantic and Pacific evolved differently, and the interconnectedness of all species. A more abstract than literal approach creates a fresh view. World-renowned architect Frank Gehry, who created the Guggenheim Museum in Bilbao (Spain), designed this landmark museum of crumpled multicolor forms.

Centro Natural Punta Culebra MUSEUM
(CEM; ☎212-8793; https://stri.si.edu/visit/punta-culebra; Amador Causeway, Punta Culebra; adult/child US$7/4; ⌚1-5pm Tue-Fri, 10am-6pm Sat & Sun) Ideal for families, CEM is operated by the Smithsonian Tropical Research Institute (STRI). This informative marine museum features two small aquariums and a nature trail with three-toed sloths and iguanas in a surviving patch of dry forest, once prolific

City Walk Panamá Viejo

START PUENTE DEL MATADERO
END PUENTE DEL REY
LENGTH 3.5KM; 1½ TO 2 HOURS

Panamá Viejo was founded on a coastal bar alongside a shallow cove. The primary government buildings were at the mouth of the cove, also a port. All of the major Catholic religious orders – the Franciscans, Dominicans, Jesuits and Augustines – were established here. The best houses and most of the convents were built on the narrow strip of land along the beachfront.

Buildings in the ruins are open 9am to 5pm, Tuesday to Sunday. Visitors enter the sector over a modern bridge parallel to 1 **Puente del Matadero** (Bridge of the Slaughterhouse), an awkwardly over-restored stone bridge that took its name from a nearby slaughterhouse. It marked the beginning of the Camino Real to Portobelo.

Continuing two blocks east along Av Cincuentenario are the ruins of 2 **Iglesia y Convento de La Merced**. Erected by the Mercedarian friars in the early 17th century, the buildings survived the fire that swept the city following the assault of privateer Henry Morgan. However the church's facade was dismantled by friars and moved to Casco Viejo, where it can be seen today.

Churches were Panamá Viejo's most outstanding buildings. Bordering the avenue are the remains of 3 **Iglesia y Convento de San Francisco**, erected by the Franciscans. The church faced the sea and stood on a massive base. The The adjoining convents had inner courts surrounded by wooden galleries, and the larger ones had enclosed gardens and orchards.

The colonial city followed a grid plan with a main square. The lots tended to be narrow, and the houses often consisted of two or three stories. There's not much left of the city's sole hospital, 4 **Hospital de San Juan de Dios**. Much of the remains were scattered when Av Cincuentenario and a side road were laid not long ago.

Just north are the spacious ruins of a church and convent, 5 **Iglesia y Convento de la Concepción**, erected by the

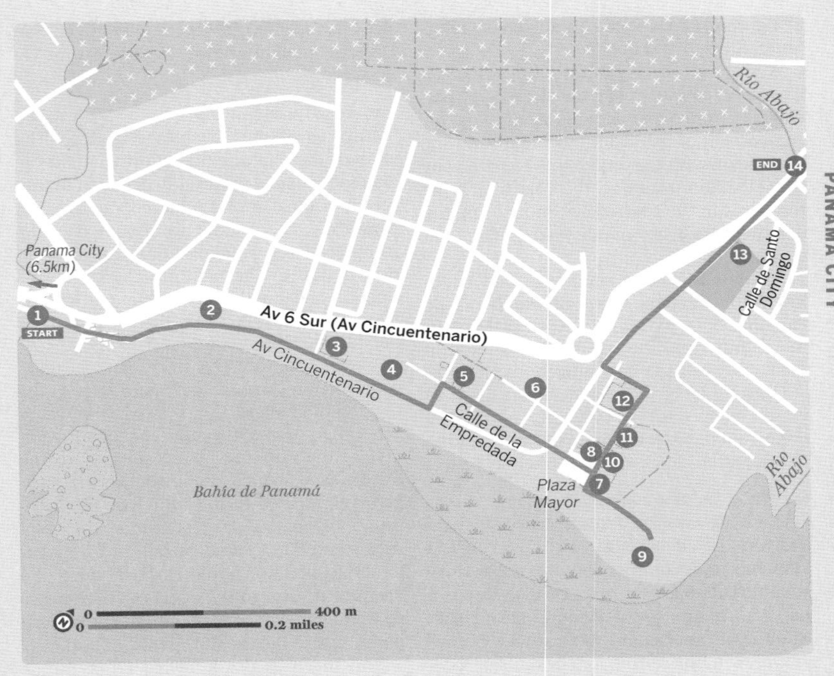

nuns of Nuestra Señora de la Concepción. Most of the ruins, which cover the better part of two blocks, were part of the church – little remains of the convent.

The Jesuits built 6 **Iglesia y Convento de la Compañía de Jesús** (Church & Covenant of the Company of Jesus), whose stone ruins are visible today.

Facing the Plaza Mayor are the 7 **Cabildo de la Ciudad** (City Hall) and the 8 **Casas de Terrín**, houses built by one of the city's wealthiest citizens, Francisco Terrín. Most of the better houses were built from timber and placed wall to wall, with small inner courts, open-air kitchens and separate wings for the servants. Some had ground-floor galleries and balconies, and most had plain exterior walls. A few of the fancier homes were built from stone and their ruins remain. The poor had far simpler dwellings, usually thatched huts built with inexpensive materials such as reeds.

The center of power resided at 9 **Casas Reales** (Royal Houses), a complex ringed by timber ramparts and separated from the city proper by a moat. Within the complex were the customs house, the royal treasury, a prison and the governor's house. Only scattered walls remain of the once impressive structures.

10 **Catedral de Nuestra Señora de la Asunción** (Cathedral of Our Lady of Asunción), built between 1619 and 1626, is the best-preserved building of the ruins. In traditional fashion, it was designed so that its two side chapels gave it a cross-like shape when viewed from the heavens.

Immediately north of the cathedral are the ruins of 11 **Casa Alarcón**, the town's best-preserved and largest known private residence, which dates from the 1640s. Just north of that, 12 **Iglesia y Convento de Santo Domingo** (Church & Convent of St Dominic) is the best-preserved church of the ruins. The convent dates from the 1570s, though the church was built 20 or more years later.

13 **Iglesia de San José** (Church of St Joseph) belonged to the Augustine order. Of special interest here are the building's vaulted side chapels, an architectural feature seldom seen in Panama.

14 **Puente del Rey** (Bridge of the King) is visible from Av Cincuentenario near the northern edge of town. Built in 1617, it may be the oldest standing bridge in the Americas.

along Central America's Pacific coast. Signs are in English and Spanish.

A tropical frogs exhibit brings you up close with creatures like the strawberry poison dart frog. Separate aquariums allow for comparison of fish from the Pacific and the Caribbean, with the differences explained by staff. Exhibits examine the role of marine resources in the country's economy, and the destructive effects of harvesting fish and shrimp by net.

Exhibits include a small six-sided building with sweeping views of the Bahía de Panamá, built by Manuel Noriega for intimate gatherings. Today it has exhibits on the history of Panama's indigenous cultures.

Outside, large, intelligent illustrations of vessels allow visitors to glance out at the ocean and identify the types of ships waiting to transit the canal, aided by a telescope.

Fuerte Amador Resort & Marina MARINA
(☎314-1980; www.fuerteamador.com; Isla Flamenco s/n; ⊙8am-midnight) At the end of Isla Flamenco, this complex contains a two-story shopping center, a marina, a cruise-ship terminal and a number of restaurants and bars. At night, these open-air spots are a big draw, providing a fine setting for cocktails or a decent meal. Daily boats depart the marina for the nearby resort island of Isla Taboga.

Greater Panama City

Explora Center of Science & Arts MUSEUM
(Science Museum; ☎230-3066; http://explorapanama.org; Condado del Rey Urbanization, off Ave Ricardo J Alfaro; adult/child under 12 yr US$3/2; ⊙9am-5pm Tue-Fri, 10am-6pm Sat & Sun; P ♿) Mini travelers (and those young at heart) will love this museum dedicated to interactive learning. Six exhibition rooms explore such themes as electricity, sound, natural phenomena, the Panama Canal and more. Don't miss the gravity room, a tilted room of optical illusions that will leave you feeling disoriented…and maybe a little sick! Guided tours available in English and Spanish.

Estadio Maracaná STADIUM
(☎6423-2455; Cinta Costera 3, Chorrillo) Inaugurated in April 2014, this is the home stadium of Chorrillo FC and Club Deportivo Plaza Amador. It was named after the legendary Maracanã Stadium in Rio de Janeiro, Brazil.

Parque Recreativo Omar PARK
The biggest park in the city is filled with children, joggers and the occasional salsa class. It's located in Omar, behind the San Francisco neighborhood. Access is from Vía Belisario.

Panama Canal Murals PUBLIC ART
(Balboa; ⊙7:30am-4:15pm Mon-Fri) FREE The story of the monumental effort to build the Panama Canal is powerfully depicted in murals by notable artist William B Van Ingen of New York. The murals are mounted in the rotunda of the Panama Canal Administration Building. The paintings have the distinction of being the largest group of murals by an American artist on display anywhere outside the USA.

The murals tell the story of the canal's construction through four main scenes: the digging of Gaillard Cut at Gold Hill, where the canal passes through the continental divide; the building of the spillway of the Gatún Dam, which dammed the Río Chagres and created Lago Gatún; the construction of one of the giant lock gates (the canal uses some 80 of these gates); and the construction of the Miraflores Locks near the Pacific entrance to the canal. A frieze located immediately below the murals presents a panorama of the excavation of Gaillard Cut.

Van Ingen is also known for his murals in the Library of Congress and the US Mint.

It's closed on weekends, but guards may allow visits between 10am and 2:30pm if you ask politely.

Baha'i House of Worship TEMPLE
(☎231-1191; ⊙10am-6pm) On the northeastern outskirts of Panama City, the white-domed Baha'i House of Worship is the mother temple for all of Latin America. It looms like a giant egg atop the crest of a hill, with a beautiful, breezy interior. Readings from the Baha'i writings (in English and Spanish) are held Sunday morning at 10am. Any bus to Colón can let you off on the highway, but it's a long walk up the hill. It's 11km from the city center on Vía Transístmica.

Activities & Courses

Panama Audubon Society OUTDOORS
(☎232-5977; www.audubonpanama.org; Parque Natural Metropolitano visitors center) Organises birding walks and monthly meetings with interesting speakers at the Parque Natural Metropolitano visitors center (p51). It's a good opportunity to get to know some Panamanian birdwatchers and to learn more about tropical bird species. Both English and Spanish are spoken.

Casco Antiguo Spanish School LANGUAGE
(Map p56; ☎228-3258; www.cascospanish.com; Av A s/n; 1-week 20hr intensive US$250; ⏲7am-7pm Mon-Fri, 8am-noon Sat) This recommended Spanish school sits in the heart of Casco Viejo. Group lessons have only four students and private classes are available with excellent instructors. Also offers accommodations and activities.

Casco Yoga YOGA
(Map p56; ☎6265-5588; www.cascoyogapanama.com; Calle José de Obaldía s/n, Casco Viejo) Offers a variety of quality yoga classes in a 2nd-floor studio, with English-speaking instruction. Check the website for special events and schedules.

Bicicletas Moses CYCLING
(☎211-2718; Amador Causeway; per hour from US$4; ⏲9am-7pm) This bike tent has mountain bikes as well as reclining bikes, tandems, bicycle carts and options for kids. See the Facebook page for more details.

Scubapanama DIVING
(☎261-3841; www.scubapanama.com; Calle 52c Oeste, Vista Hermosa; ⏲8am-6pm Mon-Fri, to 4pm Sat) Panama's oldest dive operator, offering a variety of trips throughout the country.

Tours

Ancon Expeditions TOURS
(Map p60; ☎269-9415; www.anconexpeditions.com; Edificio Dorado, 2nd fl, Calle 49a Este, El Cangrejo; ⏲9am-5pm Mon-Fri, to 1pm Sat) A pioneer in Panamanian tour operations, Ancon Expeditions offers city and nationwide tours as well as regularly scheduled canal transits. Try to book in advance as this is one of the company's most popular offerings.

Panama Road Trips TOURS
(☎6800-7727; www.panamaroadtrips.com; tours from US$25) This small enterprise runs affordable day trips to Portobelo or an Emberá village in addition to popular canal and city tours. Also works with interesting rural tourism options throughout Panama.

Barefoot Panama TOURS
(Map p56; ☎211-3700; www.barefootpanama.com; cnr Av A & Calle 7; city tour per person US$90; ⏲9:30am-6:30pm) Prompt and professional, this American-run agency based in Casco Viejo does a great tour of Panama City that takes in everything from the history to the flora and fauna. They offer 14 different tours, including day trips to San Lorenzo and Gamboa, with visits to a Wounaan indigenous village, and trips throughout the country.

Diablo Cyclo CYCLING
(☎6670-4934; www.barracudapartybike.com; Shopping Plaza Isla Flamenco, Amador Causeway; ⏲9am-7pm; 👪) This 14-seat pedal-powered bus is modeled on the colorful Diablo Rojos buses that act as public transportation by day and party buses by night. Tours run along the Amador Causeway; a bar sits in the middle so you can enjoy a cold beer while you pedal.

City Sightseeing Panama BUS
(Map p48; ☎392-6000; www.city-sightseeing.com; Av Justo Arosemena & Calle 29 Este, Calidonia; 24hr ticket adult/child US$35/20) These red double-deckers loop the city and are a good way to get your bearings. Stops include Multicentro Mall, Calle Uruguay, Casco Viejo and the Amador Causeway. Service is hop-on, hop-off, so you can explore the sights all you want with hourly pickups. Departures run between 9am and 4pm, except for the night tour. Tickets are good for 24 or 48 hours.

Festivals & Events

Carnaval CULTURAL
Carnaval in Panama City is celebrated with merriment and wild abandon in the days preceding Ash Wednesday, between February and March. From Saturday until the following Tuesday, work is put away and masks, costumes and confetti come out, and for 96 hours almost anything goes.

Ciclovía Panama SPORTS
(Cycle Sunday; Cinta Costera; ⏲6am-noon Sun) FREE Every week, the Cinta Costera (Ave Balboa), the main avenue that follows the city's seafront, shuts for Ciclovía Panama. Join the pedalling masses as they cycle, skate, jog and walk their dogs in this car-free zone. Bikes, rollerblades and cyclo carts can be hired from pop-up stalls opposite the Hilton Hotel. Free bikes (including helmets and kids' bikes) are also available from an on-site Rali sports tent (photo ID required) set up for the event.

Panama Jazz Festival MUSIC
(☎317-1466; www.panamajazzfestival.com) A real blast, the Panama Jazz Festival is gaining momentum as one of the biggest musical events in Panama, drawing hundreds of thousands of spectators. Events are held in theaters around the city for a week in

Casco Viejo

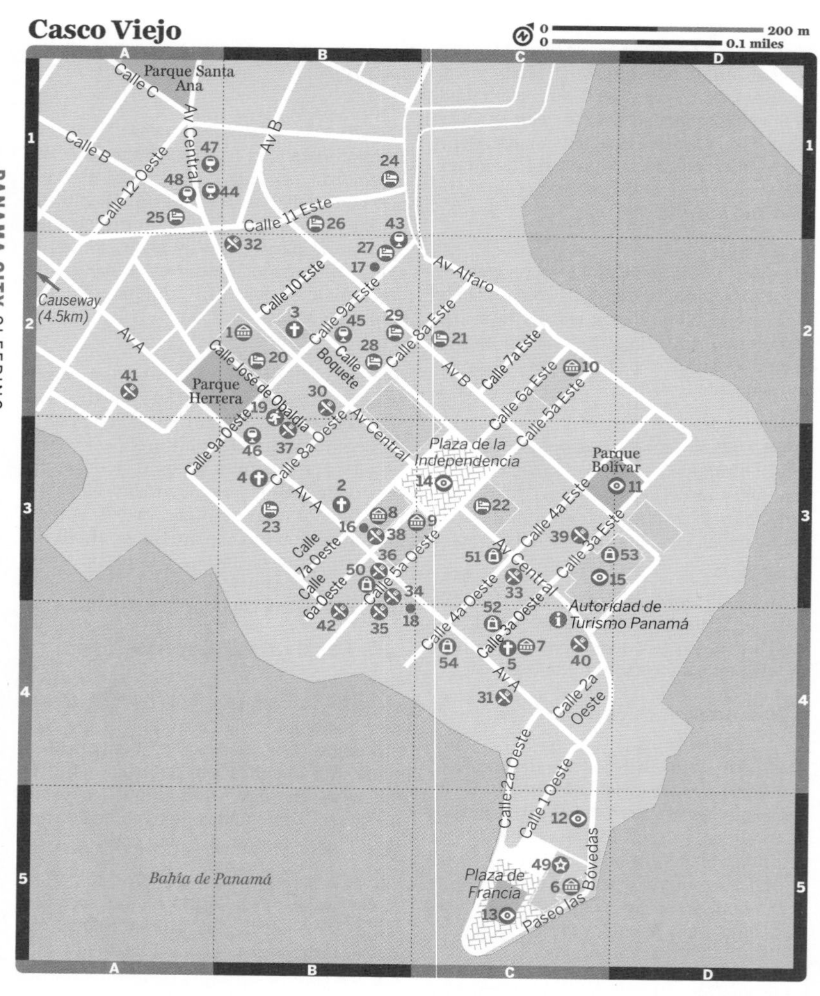

mid-January, ending with a free concert in the Plaza de la Independencia. Open-air events are usually free, while big-draw theater spectacles require tickets.

Sleeping

Panama City offers every kind of accommodation you could want. A glut of options means that many charge bargain rates for their category. For those who prefer the quiet life, outlying neighborhoods have excellent B&B options. These include the former US-occupied neighborhoods of Albrook, Ancón and Amador, located in the Canal Zone.

Casco Viejo

Luna's Castle HOSTEL $

(Map p56; 262-1540; www.lunascastlehostel.com; Calle 9a Este; dm/d/tr incl breakfast US$16/37/55;) Housed in a creaky, colonial mansion, Luna's masterfully blends Spanish-colonial architecture with funky, laid-back backpacker vibes and great service. Cavernous dorms feature curtained bunks and air-conditioning. Perks include hammocks, house guitars, free bikes and laundry service. It has long been an iconic meeting point for budget travelers.

Casco Viejo

Sights

1 American Trade Hall B2
2 Iglesia de la Compañía de Jesús B3
3 Iglesia de La Merced B2
4 Iglesia de San José B3
5 Iglesia y Convento de Santo Domingo C4
6 Instituto Nacional de Cultura C5
7 Museo de Arte Religioso Colonial C4
8 Museo de Historia de Panamá B3
9 Museo del Canal Interoceánico C3
10 Palacio de las Garzas C2
11 Parque Bolívar D3
12 Paseo las Bóvedas C5
13 Plaza de Francia C5
14 Plaza de la Independencia C3
15 Teatro Nacional C3

Activities, Courses & Tours

16 Barefoot Panama B3
17 Cacique Cruiser B2
18 Casco Antiguo Spanish School B4
19 Casco Yoga B2

Sleeping

20 American Trade Hotel B2
21 Casa Sucre C2
22 Central Hotel C3
23 Hospedaje Casco Viejo B3
24 Hotel Casa Panama B1
25 La Concordia A1
26 Las Clementinas B1
27 Luna's Castle B2
28 Magnolia Inn B2
29 Tántalo B2

Eating

30 Barrio Pizza B2
Cafe Unido (see 20)
31 Caffe Per Due C4
32 Donde José B2
33 Granclement C3
34 Laboratorio Madrigal B3
35 Lo Que Hay B4
36 Mahalo B3
37 Ochoymedio B3
38 Super Gourmet B3
39 Tacos la Neta C3
40 Tío Navaja C4
41 Tomillo A2
42 Tropical Chocolate Cafe B4

Drinking & Nightlife

43 Bar Relic B2
44 Casa Jaguar A1
45 La Rana Dorada B2
46 Pedro Mandinga Rum Bar B3
Tántalo Bar (see 29)
47 Teatro Amador A1
48 The Stranger's Club A1

Entertainment

49 Teatro Anita Villalaz C5
Teatro Nacional (see 15)

Shopping

50 Casa Latina B3
51 El Palacio del Sombrero C3
52 Karavan C4
53 Mercadito Artesanías Catedral C3
54 No Me Olvides C4

Hospedaje Casco Viejo HOSTEL $
(Map p56; 211-2027; www.hospedajecascoviejo.hostel.com; Calle 8a Oeste; dm/d incl breakfast without bathroom US$10/25, d US$30; P @ wi-fi) This renovated hostel offers triple-decker bunks and plain, pleasant rooms at great prices. Showers are temperate. There's a lovely rooftop with city views, a communal kitchen and an open-air courtyard. It's on a quiet side street near the Iglesia de San José.

★ **Magnolia Inn** INN $$
(Map p56; 202-0872, USA 1-786-375-9633; www.magnoliapanama.com; cnr Calle Boquete & Calle 8a Este; dm US$15, r US$90-135; air-con wi-fi) Details speak to the thoughtfulness of this cool inn, a restored three-story colonial run by American expats whose service and travel advice excels. Ample top-floor doubles with skyline views rank among the city's best, with coffee makers, mini-fridges and flat-screen TVs. Grown-ups like the air-conditioned dorm with single beds, orthopedic mattresses, quality bedding, individual lamps and numerous outlets. Very family-friendly.

Tántalo BOUTIQUE HOTEL $$
(Map p56; 262-4030; www.tantalohotel.com; cnr Calle 8a Este & Av B; d incl breakfast from US$125) Industrial chic has hit Casco hard. Do oversized spikes on the ceilings work for you? Various artists were commissioned to decorate the 12 rooms of this boutique hotel with oversized murals, stenciled Bukowski quotes and stripped-down decor. On the downside, rooms are sandwiched between a lively restaurant and rooftop bar not so conducive to resting.

Hotel Casa Panama BOUTIQUE HOTEL $$
(Map p56; 303-0992; www.hotelcasapanama.com; cnr Av Alfaro & Calle 11 Este; d from US$100; air-con wi-fi pool) With a good location and dark, modern rooms featuring polished concrete and tropical decor, this boutique offering

DAY TRIPS FROM PANAMA CITY

Looking to get out of the city for the day? Take our author-tested suggestions:

- Laying eyes on the awe-inspiring Panama Canal (p76).
- Spotting feathered friends along Pipeline Rd in Parque Nacional Soberanía (p78).
- Visiting the world-famous tropical biology center on Isla Barro Colorado (p80).
- Escaping to the flower-dotted island of Isla Taboga (p82).
- Surfing gnarly breaks along the Pacific coast (p92).

has appeal. However, service seems a bit indifferent, especially given the price tag. Still, some will come for the rooftop pool alone. Some rooms are tiny – ask to see a few before choosing. Those with sea views are considerably higher in price.

★ American Trade Hotel HISTORIC HOTEL **$$$**
(Map p56; ☎831-2051; www.americantradehotel.com; Plaza Herrera s/n; d incl breakfast from US$350; P❄︎📶🏊) Evoking old-time tropical grandeur, the refurbished Trade Hotel reinvests Plaza Herrera with a prosperous feel. With recycled floors from the canal expansion, a pool and a library, it's gorgeous, with many pleasant nooks. It's hard to believe that it long sat abandoned and trolled by gangs (though their graffiti still decorates an interior staircase). Upper floors offer views of the Causeway.

Also has a restaurant, a fair-trade cafe serving excellent coffee and a notable jazz club.

Las Clementinas BOUTIQUE HOTEL **$$$**
(Map p56; ☎228-7613; www.lasclementinas.com; cnr Calle 11 Este & Av B; d US$130-150, apt US$195; ❄︎@📶) 🍃 With its antique regional maps, recycled hardwood floors from the canal, and unusual relics from the original house, this is a slice of authentic Panama. The restored colonial has airy suites and much smaller doubles alongside a leafy courtyard. When first opened, this boutique hotel was at the vanguard, but since then it has unfortunately lost some shine.

Casa Sucre B&B **$$$**
(Map p56; ☎393-6130, 6982-2504; www.casasucreboutiquehotel.com; cnr Calle 8a Este & Av B; d/apt incl breakfast US$140/150; ❄︎📶) Set in an 1873 convent, this American-run B&B features plush lodgings amid family heirlooms and period furniture. The setting is serene, with a wraparound balcony overlooking the action of Casco Viejo. Watch for the friendly ghost rumored to dwell on the entrance staircase. There's also a downstairs cafe with great coffee, run by California natives Alyce and Rich.

La Concordia BOUTIQUE HOTEL **$$$**
(Map p56; ☎300-1125; https://laconcordiapanama.com; cnr Av Central & Calle B; r incl breakfast US$240; ❄︎📶) Once the home of the Mexican embassy, this refurbished 19th-century flatiron-style building at the base of Casco Viejo has some simply stunning details, from the chandeliers to clawfoot tubs and colonial-style headboards. There are just 10 rooms and a gorgeous rooftop bar and restaurant. Perhaps it's the price tag or noisy location, but it's yet to find its adoring public.

Central Hotel HOTEL **$$$**
(Map p56; ☎309-0300; www.centralhotelpanama.com; Calle 5a Este; d/ste incl breakfast US$169/250; ❄︎📶🏊) On the Plaza Independencia, the former Grand Hotel Central was Panama's first hotel when it opened in 1874. Its renovation was a massive undertaking years in the making, but the final results underwhelm. It does remain a busy hub for travelers with attentive service, but the rooms are small and cookie-cutter. On the plus side, it has a rooftop pool.

Calidonia

Calidonia is central to city highlights but is a very working-class area not frequented by outsiders. Given that foot traffic dwindles in the evening, it's best to take taxis at night.

Mamallena HOSTEL **$**
(Map p48; ☎393-6611, 6676-6163; www.mamallena.com; Calle Primera Perejil; dm/d incl breakfast US$13/33; ❄︎@📶) On a residential street that's somehow survived the wrecking ball, this small, homey hostel nails the mark on service. Amenities include 24-hour desk service, pancake breakfasts, a guest kitchen and DVD library. High-ceilinged dorms have air-con at night and

the cute motel-style doubles offer considerable privacy. The on-site travel agency offers sailing to San Blas and popular day trips.

El Cangrejo, Marbella & Bella Vista

Fast-paced modern Panama is best experienced in the overlapping neighborhoods of Bella Vista, Marbella and El Cangrejo. As central as it gets, these neighborhoods have no lack of restaurants or bars within walking distance. However, this area is one of the noisier spots in town, with snaking traffic and honking horns dominating the daytime hours.

★El Machico HOSTEL **$**
(Map p60; ☎203-9430, 6473-5905; www.elmachicohostel.com; Calle 47 Este 2, Marbella; dm/d US$16/50;) In a suburban two-story, this stylish and popular Italian-run hostel indulges your inner kid with projected movies in the swimming pool, a PlayStation and foldable bikes for rent (US$10 per day). Also offers cheap tours, including to San Blas. Dorms sleep six to 12 people with blessed air-conditioning that runs at night. Doubles are relatively bare for the price tag.

La Milonga HOSTEL **$**
(Map p60; ☎269-3315, 6949-4509; www.la-milonga.com; Av 5a B Sur s/n, Bella Vista; dm/d incl breakfast US$15/50;) This tiny retro-cute hostel has only six rooms, including two dorms. Though conveniently located, there's little in the way of shared spaces, beyond a small living room and guest kitchen. Rooms are sparkling, and it's pretty quiet as far as dorms go. When we visited last it had just changed ownership.

Metro Hotel HOTEL **$**
(Map p60; ☎202-5050; www.metrohotelpanama.com; Calle D, El Cangrejo; d/tr incl breakfast US$55/70;) Cute and convenient in a busy part of town, Metro feels like a chain hotel with an extra ounce of cool (witness the crashed-out party boys in the lobby). Rooms feature tile floors, safe boxes, flat-screen TVs and minifridges. Those with two beds have better decor.

Coral Suites Aparthotel APARTMENT **$**
(Map p60; ☎269-2727; www.coralsuitespanama.com; Calle D, El Cangrejo; d/tr US$60/80;) This all-suites hotel is serviceable for traveling executives wanting amenities, or long-term visitors in need of more than a hotel room. Suites are unremarkable yet functional, with spacious bathrooms, bouncy mattresses and fully equipped kitchens. The staff are pleasant and guests have use of a full gym, business center and 24-hour rooftop pool.

Riande Granada Hotel DESIGN HOTEL **$$**
(Map p60; ☎204-4444, 291-9000; http://riandehoteles.com; Av Eusebio A Morales, El Cangrejo; d US$90;) With a chic look and feel, good-value Riande is popular with the millennial crowd. Spare and modern, it's clad in dripping foliage and a curtain of cascading water. There's a reputable restaurant and beer garden with an enormous wooden lounge deck set around the outdoor pool. The rooms feature minifridges and flat-screen TVs.

Saba Hotel HOTEL **$$**
(Map p60; ☎201-6100; www.thesabahotel.com; Vía Argentina s/n, Bella Vista; s/d US$48/60;) Modern and cheerful, the Saba is great value in Bella Vista. With lots of glass and bamboo, there's a sustainable theme that's probably more stylish than substantial. Amenities like iPod docks and flat-screen TVs are appreciated. Under new administration, service is attentive.

Baru Lodge B&B **$$**
(☎393-2340; www.barulodge.com; Calle 2a Norte H-7, El Carmen; s/d incl breakfast US$70/80;) Tasteful and cordial, this inn sits on a central residential street. Rooms are sleek and modern, with subdued colors and soft lighting. The English-speaking owner makes guests right at home. Cable TV, fast wi-fi and air purifiers are among the perks. Continental breakfasts are served on a garden patio with wicker seating.

Executive Hotel HOTEL **$$**
(Map p60; ☎265-8011; www.executivehotelpanama.com; cnr Calles 52 & Aquilino de la Guardia, El Cangrejo; s/d/tr incl breakfast US$70/80/90;) Bustling and efficient, this revamped business hotel is centrally located in El Cangrejo with an array of prim white rooms with tropical accents. Service is friendly and caring. There are flat-screen TVs, in-room coffee and safe boxes. The cafe is the secret spot in the city for outstanding American breakfasts (24-hour service Thursday to Saturday).

El Cangrejo, Marbella & Bella Vista

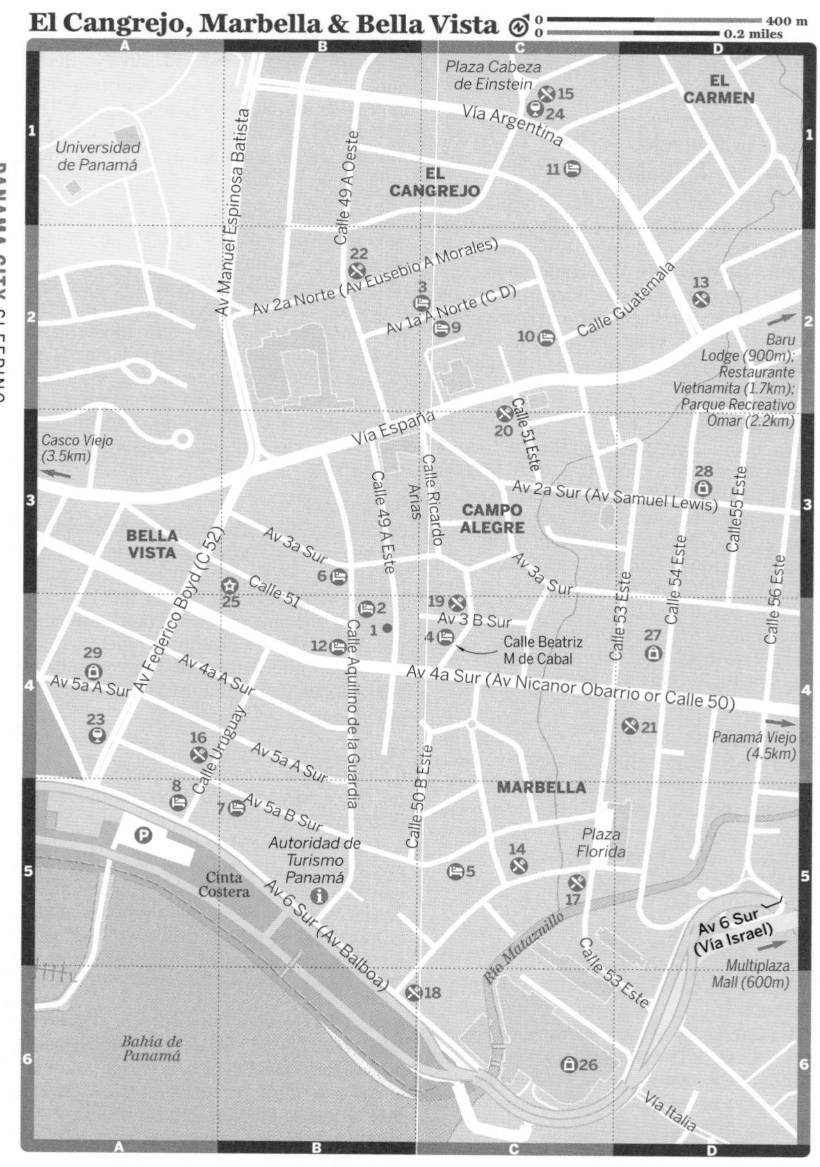

DeVille Hotel BOUTIQUE HOTEL **$$**
(Map p60; ☎206-3100; www.devillehotel.com.pa; Calle Beatriz M de Cabal, Bella Vista; d/ste incl breakfast US$65/80; P ❄ @ ☎) Overshadowed by newer, bigger hotels, the sleepy DeVille remains a sweetheart option with 33 classy, tasteful rooms and sterling service. Rooms feature antique Thai dressers, glistening with inlaid mother-of-pearl, and marble-topped antique tables set with Louis XV chairs. Guests sleep on US-made mattresses, dressed with custom Egyptian-cotton bed linen and goose-feather pillows.

El Cangrejo, Marbella & Bella Vista

Activities, Courses & Tours
1 Ancon Expeditions ... B4

Sleeping
2 Bristol Panama ... B4
3 Coral Suites Aparthotel ... C2
4 DeVille Hotel ... C4
5 El Machico ... C5
6 Executive Hotel ... B3
7 La Milonga ... B5
8 Le Meridien ... A5
9 Metro Hotel ... C2
10 Riande Granada Hotel ... C2
11 Saba Hotel ... C1
12 W Hotel ... B4

Eating
13 Avatar ... D2
14 Hikaru ... C5
15 New York Bagel Café ... C1
16 Ozone Cafe ... A4
17 Petit Paris ... C5
18 Segundo Muelle ... B6
19 Sukhi ... C4
20 Supermercado Rey ... C3
21 Suvla's ... D4
22 Wine Bar ... B2

Drinking & Nightlife
23 El Apartamento ... A4
24 La Rana Dorada ... C1

Entertainment
Multicentro Cinemark ... (see 26)
25 Restaurante-Bar Tinajas ... B3

Shopping
26 Multicentro Mall ... C6
27 Nina Concept Store ... D4
28 Reprosa ... D3
29 Weil Art Gallery ... A4

★ **Bristol Panama** HOTEL $$$
(Map p60; ☎265-7844; www.thebristol.com; Calle Aquilino de la Guardia, Bella Vista; d incl breakfast from US$270; P ❄ @ ☎ ≋) The elegant Bristol features oriental carpets, flamboyant orchids and precious woods, and that's just the lobby. Rooms are refined and lovely. No more do-not-disturb tags here: heat sensors determine if rooms are occupied. Other five-star amenities include a spa, 24-hour butler service and free cell-phone loan. The restaurant is run by an award-winning Panamanian chef.

★ **W Hotel** LUXURY HOTEL $$$
(Map p60; ☎309-7500; www.starwoodhotels.com/whotels; cnr Calle 50 & Calle Aquilino de la Guardia, Bella Vista; d/ste US$200/400; P ❄ ☎ ≋) Opened in 2018, this 203-room downtown high rise takes inspiration from the Panama Canal and the country's diverse cultures. Not your parents' luxury hotel, it's playful-modern, with colorful shipping containers, chairs upholstered in Congo dress 'rags' patterns and wall displays of woven hats. Bright rooms feature floor-to-ceiling windows and floating beds rimmed with LED lighting underneath. Staff aim to please.

Le Meridien HOTEL $$$
(Map p60; ☎297-3200; www.starwoodhotels.com; cnr Calle Uruguay & Av Balboa, Bella Vista; d incl breakfast from US$160; P ❄ @ ☎ ≋) Created by 100 artists, Le Meridien features cool digital art and even birdsong in the elevator. Yet, while innovative, some details here are simply off. Rooms have laminated-wood walls and the furniture seems a bit cheap given the all-out setting. The effect is a little Le Mediocre. The rooftop pool, however, offers a delicious city-skyline view.

Canal Zone

Hostal Amador Familiar INN $
(☎314-1251; www.hostalamadorfamiliar.com; Casa 1519, Calle Akee, Balboa; dm incl breakfast US$17, d US$35-55; P ❄ @ ☎) If you like quiet, this big, red canal house offers cheap and reliable accommodations. The pleasant dining patio and open-air kitchen offer respite from the city. Worn high-ceilinged rooms with rod-iron beds have been updated with with fresh, bright bedding. Dorms feature single beds, no bunks. Guests must take a taxi to the center (US$5); it's just off the Causeway.

Dos Palmitos B&B $$
(Map p48; ☎6051-4723; www.panamabedandbreakfast.com; Calle Victor Hugo 0532B, Cerro Ancón; s/d incl breakfast US$80/85; ❄ @ ☎) If your attraction to Panama is more about wildlife than wild life, check out this tucked-away French B&B. There are just four rooms, decorated with retro posters and vintage newsclips and featuring immaculate wooden floors, king-size beds and wicker furniture. The backyard terrace offers birdwatching and abundant breakfasts featuring homemade bread and fresh juice. Also offers transportation and tours.

It's on the quiet Cerro Ancón – a good place to take a walk, but for everything else you'll need a taxi.

Albrook Inn INN $$

(315-1789; www.albrookinn.com; Calle Las Magnolias 14, Albrook; s/d/ste incl breakfast US$65/75/90;) Set amid lush greenery and removed from city chaos, this lodging near Albrook airport aspires to country inn but feels a bit lackluster and impersonal. Motel-style rooms have modern decor and flat-screen TVs but could be roomier. A small kidney-shaped pool spruces up the garden. Ideal for an early-morning domestic flight.

Country Inn & Suites HOTEL $$

(211-4500; www.countryinns.com/panamacanalpan; cnr Avs Amador & Pelicano, Amador; d US$100;) They say there are only two lodgings overlooking the canal: one is the prison that once held Noriega, the other is this chain hotel. Though reminiscent of a retirement community in Panama City, Florida, it's well run and good value, with causeway access and a huge swimming pool. Rooms boast private balconies overlooking the Puente de las Américas.

Eating

Boasting the most innovative contemporary cuisine of Central America, Panama City is a fun place to dine out. There are literally hundreds of places to eat and – thanks to a big immigrant population – cuisine from every corner of the globe.

Casco Viejo

★ **Granclement** GELATO $

(Map p56; www.granclement.com; Av Central; gelato US$3.50-5; 12:30pm-9pm Mon-Fri, to 10pm Sat, 10am-8pm Sun) Pure pleasure defines these intense tropical-fruit gelatos and rich, creamy flavors such as coffee, orange-chocolate and ginger. A few scoops of these fussy French creations will sweeten a leisurely stroll through the Casco.

★ **Super Gourmet** DELI $

(Map p56; 212-3487; www.supergourmetcascoviejo.com; Av A; mains US$3-9; 8am-5pm Mon-Sat, 10am-4pm Sun;) With the cheeriest staff around, Super Gourmet is a favorite of both locals and travelers. Stop by the air-conditioned cafe for traditional soups, fresh tropical juices or a baguette deli sandwich done American style. For breakfast, eggs on English muffins with cheese, bacon or vegetables or *arepas* (savory corn cakes) with an espresso drink hit the spot.

Also stocks a variety of quality goods ranging from wine to local chocolate and natural repellents.

★ **Mercado de Mariscos** MARKET $

(Map p48; 506-5741; Av Balboa; mains US$3-14; 6am-5pm) Get your seafood fix above a bustling fish market. Come early, as service at peak time is painfully slow. Gems include whole fried fish and cavernous bowls of 'Get Up Lazarus' soup (a sure hangover cure). Outside, stands ladle out delicious US$3 plastic cups of *ceviche,* including classic concoctions, Mediterranean style (with olives) and curry.

Tropical Chocolate Cafe CAFE $

(Map p56; 388-6843; www.facebook.com/tropicalchocolatecafe; Calle 6; bonbons US$2-10; 10am-7pm; ; Mercado de Mariscos) With red velvet chairs and lush tropical-themed wallpaper, this button-cute chocolate shop and cafe serves beautifully adorned natural bonbons: 100% Panamanian chocolate meets local pineapple, chili and cilantro. Coinciding with Sunday brunch, the cafe hosts story time for children at 10am and chocolate tastings by reservation (US$30 per person, two participants).

Tacos la Neta TACOS $

(Map p56; 387-5279; www.tacoslaneta.com; Calle 3era 5-48; mains US$10; noon-midnight Tue-Sat, 11am-8pm Sun) While Panama has never had much in the way of Mexican cuisine, dive-ish Tacos la Neta wrestles to turn the tide. The scrumptious soft-corn tacos come in a half-dozen varieties, including crisp sea bass and *cochinita pibil* (sweet, seasoned pork). Top with homemade hot sauces like the superb smoked *ají chombo.* Service is swift and slushy fruit cocktails oversized.

Mahalo CAFE $

(Map p56; 6356-0500; www.mahalopanama.com; cnr Av A & Calle 5; mains $8-14; 9:15am-10pm Mon-Sun;) If you miss your cold-pressed juices, quinoa bowls and avocado toast, rush to this casual, plant-filled cafe run by two Canadian sisters. Set lunches are particularly good value. There's also an enjoyable shady courtyard where weekend barbecues and brunches take place.

DINING 101

Casco Viejo is home to a number of boutique eateries and European-inspired cafes. Bella Vista has a good concentration of satisfying restaurants. San Francisco and Marbella also have some good options.

With so many salaried earners on their lunch break, the banking district of El Cangrejo is home to a number of pricey eateries. These tend to be slightly more conservative and less trendy.

Owing to the wealth of city denizens and the popularity of dining out, reservations are a good idea. Although you can probably get a table most days of the week, don't even think about just showing up on Friday or Saturday night without calling ahead.

For groceries and self-catering, stop by the 24-hour Supermercado Rey, which has several locations throughout the city, including one in **El Cangrejo** (Map p60; ☎223-4981; Plaza Concordia, Via España s/n; ⏲24hr) and another inside the **El Dorado Mall** (☎394-3080; Av Ricardo J Alfaro, El Dorado; ⏲9am-8pm Mon-Fri, to 7pm Sat & Sun).

Cafe Unido CAFE $
(Map p56; ☎399-2408; http://cafeunido.com; American Trade Hotel; ⏲7:30am-9pm Mon-Sun; 📶) This small, local chain of chic coffee houses boasts branches around the city, but our favorite is in Casco Viejo. Stop by for a great caffeine kick or splurge on a steaming cup of the geisha coffee, otherwise known as the champagne of coffees.

Caffe Per Due ITALIAN $
(Map p56; ☎228-0547; Av A; mains US$5-12; ⏲9am-10pm Tue-Sun; 🖉) Our pick for a quick bite, this never-fail Italian-run eatery serves scrumptious thin-crust pizzas. Check out the award-winning pizza bianca, with roasted garlic, brie, truffle oil, mushrooms and sun-dried tomatoes. For privacy, try the tiny brick courtyard with a couple of tables.

Barrio Pizza PIZZA $
(Map p56; ☎393-4444; www.barriopizza.com; Av Central s/n; mains US$8-13; ⏲11am-11pm; ❄📶) Happiness is blistering wood-fired pizza cooked to order and topped with truffle oil, roasted eggplant or meatballs. The simple menu also has Caesar salads, wine and beer. Come early for a seat.

★**Lo Que Hay** PANAMANIAN $$
(Map p56; Calle 5 Oeste s/n; mains US$12-20; ⏲noon-3pm & 6:30-10pm Thu-Sat, 11am-4:30pm Sun) Neighborhood *fondas* (cheap restaurants) serve cheap Panamanian classics, but this one – by Panama's top chef – delivers a massive twist. Sexy rice *(concolón)* has a crust of crisp perfection, served with smoked tomatoes or fragrant clams. There's also tender whole fish, yucca tostadas with carpaccio and mango kimchee served as streetside *encurtido*. It's overpacked, not air-conditioned and good fun. End with a massive *raspado* (shaved ice flavored with fruit).

Chef José Carles is a big proponent of Panamanian street food and local ingredients, both taken to new and thrilling heights. If you can't get a reservation for Donde José or afford it, come here. You will be happy.

Tío Navaja PANAMANIAN $$
(Map p56; ☎395-1749; www.facebook.com/tioNavaja; Av Central s/n; mains US$11-26; ⏲10am-10:30pm Tue-Sun) In the most touristy of locations, step into this narrow colonial for Panamanian comfort food done right. Think fried yucca or crunchy *concolón* (a Caribbean tradition of rice cooked crisp on the bottom of the pan) topped with fresh tuna poke and sesame seeds. With a backbeat of Panamanian rap.

★**Donde José** PANAMANIAN $$$
(Map p56; ☎262-1682; www.dondejose.com; Av Central s/n; 8-course meal US$80, chef bar US$90; ⏲7pm & 9:30pm seatings Tue-Sat) Elevating humble Panamanian staples to haute cuisine, this 16-seat eatery is Panama's hottest reservation. Chef Jose prepares *ñandu* beans (native black beans), crisp, tender pork and *ñame* (an indigenous tuber) in playful, revelatory fashion. Servers have an intimate, casual rapport through a cascade of eight courses. Reservations are best made months in advance. Drinks are extra.

For an additional US$10, get a seat at the chef's table for behind-the-scenes glimpses.

★**Ochoymedio** FUSION $$$
(Map p56; ☎209-4185; www.ochoymediopanama.com; Calle José de Obaldía, btwn Calles 8 & 9; ⏲7-11pm Mon-Sun) Under hanging vines and fairy lights, this gastronomical garden by Michelin-starred chef Andres Madrigal is

romance incarnate. Start with a tropical-style lychee *ceviche*. Keep it fresh and light with an arugula salad or spicy langostino yakitori. Opt for a table in the inner courtyard and kick-start your evening with an excellent cocktail named for a Beatles song. Service is great.

Laboratorio Madrigal INTERNATIONAL **$$$**
(Map p56; ☎211-1956; http://laboratoriomadrigal.com; Av A; mains US$12-25; ⊙noon-2:30pm Mon-Fri, 6:30-11:30pm Mon-Sat) Subdued and upscale, this stylish, sometimes fussy eatery uses seasonal produce (much of it coming all the way from Britain) to bring you asparagus and delicate watercress alongside French classics like chicken cordon bleu, duck confit and Cornish mackerel. Presentation is excellent.

Tomillo PANAMANIAN **$$$**
(Map p56; ☎202-6881; www.tomillopanama.com; Calle Victoriano Lorenzo s/n; mains US$12-35; ⊙7pm-midnight Tue-Sat) With an open-air dining room awash in violet light and set in a shell of Casco ruins, Tomillo's bare, beautiful ambience reigns supreme. Generating a lot of hype, it delivers best with hearty meat preparations of grilled rib eye, smoked pork and lamb ribs. End with a featherlight deconstructed lemon pie. It's by Felipe Milanes, one of Panama's top creative chefs.

El Cangrejo, Marbella & Bella Vista

Suvla's GREEK **$**
(Map p60; ☎302-2727; www.suvlas.com; Calle 53 Este, Plaza New York; mains US$6-11; ⊙11am-midnight) For fresh fast food, this modern Greek eatery does delicious Angus beef or chicken gyros and Greek salads, as well as burgers and fries and syrupy baklava for dessert. It's a local chain with a few other outlets.

Wine Bar ITALIAN **$**
(Map p60; Av Eusebio A Morales, El Cangrejo; mains US$7-17, pizzas US$6-8; ⊙noon-1am) Some say this Italian bistro with an encyclopedic wine list is the best dinner value in town. It's certainly popular among the local cognoscenti. You can order off two menus: Wine Bar for a bite with wine, or Pomodoro (open for lunch) for pizza and satisfying pasta. Or grab a plate of soft and hard cheeses and enjoy the patio.

Petit Paris BAKERY **$**
(Map p60; ☎391-8778; http://petitparispanama.com; Calle 50e Este, Galeria Marbella, Marbella; mains US$7-19; ⊙6:30am-8:30pm) Get your fresh croissants and baguettes at this French bakery and cafe, also serving handsome meals of baguette sandwiches, pâté, couscous, meats and quiches.

New York Bagel Café CAFE **$**
(Map p60; ☎390-6050; www.newyorkbagelcafe.com; Plaza Cabeza de Einstein, El Cangrejo; mains US$3-9; ⊙7am-8pm Mon-Fri, 8am-8pm Sat, 8am-3pm Sun; ❄📶) More San Francisco than Brooklyn, this fully American creation near Vía Argentina nonetheless packs in expats with freshly baked bagels, lox and oversized breakfasts. It also serves handsome burgers. The setting offers jazz, soft sofas and an assortment of laptop geeks.

★**Hikaru** JAPANESE **$$**
(Map p60; ☎203-5087; www.hikaru.restaurant; Calle 50 Este Alley, Marbella; mains US$10-16; ⊙noon-2:30pm & 6-11pm Mon-Sat) For authentic Japanese food prepared by a Tokyo chef, this unassuming alleyside restaurant is pay dirt. While Hikaru serves good sushi and sashimi, you would be amiss not to sample the ramen noodles, prepared in a complex, buttery broth, or *takoyaki* (melt-in-your-mouth octopus fritters). Start with a cold Sapporo beer and some edamame in rock salt. Reservations recommended for dinner.

Avatar INDIAN **$$**
(Map p60; ☎393-9006; www.avatarindiancuisine.com; cnr Vías Argentina & España, El Cangrejo; mains US$9-16; ⊙11am-11pm) Serving rich kormas, fragrant rice and complex curries in a swanky piano bar, Canadian-run Avatar is sheer delight for spice enthusiasts. Southern Indian cuisine is the house specialty, though if you want it really hot you will have to insist. On weekdays, lunch is 25% off.

Ozone Cafe INTERNATIONAL **$$**
(Map p60; ☎214-9616; www.ozonecafepanama.com; Calle Uruguay, Bella Vista; mains US$10-22; ⊙noon-3pm & 6-10pm) Packed with worker bees at midday, Ozone is a local fixture serving enormous, fragrant portions of good food from 110 countries. There are even kosher and halal options. It's too bad the ambience is wanting – the dark location was once a garage. It's also hard to find – look closely for the sign.

Segundo Muelle PERUVIAN $$
(Map p60; ☎387-7755; http://segundomuelle.com/inicio-panama; Ave Balboa, Balboa Boutiques; mains US$14-26; ⏰noon-11pm Tue-Sun) Part of an upscale Peruvian chain, Segundo Muelle knows seafood. You would do well to sample the *causas* (creamy potato dishes served stacked) alongside *ceviche* prepared Peruvian-style with sweet potato, fiery pepper and sometimes crisp tempura. Also try the *tiradito* (slices of fresh fish bathed in fragrant *leche de tigre* broth). It has cool modern decor and fantastic views over the bay.

Sukhi THAI $$
(Map p60; ☎395-6081; Calle Beatriz M de Cabal, Bella Vista; mains US$10-14; ⏰11:30am-10pm Mon-Sat) A casual and cheerful cafe offering lovely – though not the most authentic – Southeast Asian food. Start with the fried calamari with ginger-cilantro dipping sauce. Flavors pop in the green-bean green curry, while ladna (noodles in gravy) comes in fragrant beef broth with broccoli rabe. Service is good and the price is right, though portions run small.

Lung Fung CHINESE $$
(☎260-4011; www.facebook.com/Lungfungpanama; cnr Av Periodista & Vía Transístmica, Los Angeles; mains US$5-21; ⏰7am-11pm) Locals swear by this longtime Chinese restaurant, one of the best in a city with good Chinese fare. Stop by on the weekend for dim sum or succulent roast duck.

San Francisco & Punta Paitilla

Miranda Bakery & Cafe CAFE $
(☎226-4014; www.facebook.com/mirandabakery; cnr Calle 75 Este & Calle Andres Mojíca, San Francisco; mains US$10-14; ⏰9am-6:45pm Mon-Fri, to 5pm Sat) This wonderful homestyle bakery and cafe gets packed with locals hungry for sourdough, fresh bagels and amazing fat burgers with crispy french fries, homemade hot sauce optional. There's also a velvety lava cake worth trying, plus good espresso and artisanal beer. The baked goods run out before noon.

Athanasiou BAKERY $
(☎203-1010; www.athanasioupastry.net; Ocean Mall, Av de la Rotonda, Costa del Este; pastries US$3-5; ⏰7am-10pm Mon-Sun) Indulge your sweet tooth at Athanasiou, an airy Greek-style bakery and cafe in Costa del Este. There's a bread corner filled with freshly baked goods, a patisserie with rows of pastries and homemade chocolates stacked high, plus a deli counter with fresh salads and ciabatta sandwiches. Take your treat away or grab a table for afternoon coffee and cake.

Restaurante Vietnamita VIETNAMESE $
(☎394-6923; Casa 7a, Calle 68 Este, San Francisco; mains US$7-9; ⏰11am-10pm) Fragrant *pho* (broth with noodles) with brisket, garlicky sea bass with gangalal, and barbecued pork over rice noodles are some of the mouthwatering specialties at this authentic eatery with friendly owners from Hanoi. A cold beer or avocado smoothie and you're all set.

Botanica CAFE $$
(☎270-1111; http://botanicapanama.com; 6 Calle Esther Neira de Calvo, San Francisco; mains US$14-19; ⏰noon-10:30pm Tue-Sat, to 9pm Sun; 🖉) An Instagram darling, this clean-style eatery from Mario Castrellon caters to gourmet tastes on a budget. Think bubbly pizza topped with lobster or manchego cheese and greens, tropical salads from the house garden and more. Tries to source quality ingredients from regional providers. Indoor and outdoor seating and delivery.

★**Maito** PANAMANIAN $$$
(☎391-4657; www.maitopanama.com; Av 3m Sur, San Francisco; mains US$16-25; ⏰noon-10:30pm Mon-Sat) With style and pedigree, Maito toys with the classics, folding in everyday Caribbean, Latin and Chinese influences. While results are mixed, it's still worthwhile. Start with a watermelon Waldorf salad. Ribs glazed in passionfruit are tender but lack the crispness of the duck chow mein. Seafood risotto in squid ink proves divine. There's garden seating and impeccable service.

Canal Zone & Around

Saint Honoré BAKERY $
(☎387-7935; www.facebook.com/sainthonorepanama; Clayton Plaza, local 13, Clayton; pastries US$3-5; ⏰6am-9pm; P❄👪) Saint Honoré, a French-run bakery and patisserie, has locals going weak at the knees for its fluffy pastries, rich cakes and colorful macaroons. Also for sale are freshly baked baguettes and loaves, homemade quiches and a range of sandwiches. You can eat in

or take away, but make sure to order one of its top-notch coffees.

Saint Honoré is just a short detour away from Miraflores Locks and well positioned for a morning or afternoon pick-me-up.

Mika CAFE $

(394-1414; www.mikabazarcafe.com; Hospital Rd, Clayton Mall, Clayton; 8am-8pm Mon-Sat, to 4pm Sun;) Channeling a NYC vibe, this cool coffee shop is a great place for a morning caffeine kick and croissant, or a fill-you-up brunch. Later in the day, the menu switches to burgers, pastas and healthier main dishes such as the Plant Powered Quinoa. It's popular with creative types who park up for the morning with their laptops.

Drinking & Nightlife

Bars and clubs open and close with alarming frequency in Panama City, though generally speaking, nightlife is stylish, sophisticated and fairly pricey. The well-to-do denizens of the capital love a good scene, so it's worth scrubbing up and donning some nice threads. Remember to bring ID. Most clubs have a cover charge of US$10 to US$25.

Big areas for nightlife include Casco Viejo and San Francisco. The current boom in craft beer has people hitting small breweries.

DJs usually pull from a broad repertoire, from salsa and merengue to UK and US '80s classics, with electronic music (house, drum 'n' bass) liberally added to the mix. The scene is young and you can expect to pay to play here. Moreover, clubs change hands quickly in this neighborhood, so it's best to ask locals about the latest and greatest additions.

The district of Bella Vista is home to Calle Uruguay, a strip of trendy bars and clubs reminiscent of Miami's South Beach. At the time of writing it was undergoing massive renovation, so few venues were open. It should be fully operative sometime in 2019.

Casco Viejo

★ **La Rana Dorada** MICROBREWERY

(Map p56; 392-0660; www.laranadorada.com; cnr Calle 9 & Calle Boquete; noon-12:30am Sun-Wed, to 3am Thu-Sat) Replete with brass fixtures and polished wood bars, this gorgeous low-lit brewpub serves its own award-winning small craft beers, alongside tasty thin-crust pizzas or bratwursts (mains US$3 to US$9). After-work happy hour is just catching on, but it goes gangbusters here in indoor and outdoor spaces. A second location is located on Vía Argentina.

Tántalo Bar COCKTAIL BAR

(Map p56; http://tantalohotel.com/roofbar; cnr Calle 8a Este & Av B; cover US$5-10; rooftop deck 5pm-2am) Though it serves casual lunches, this ultra-hip cafe-bar is best known for sunset happy hours on its rooftop deck. Pair your cocktail with fusion-style tapas. Cover is charged after 10pm, but to get a spot on the tiny roof deck, show up around 7pm. Wednesday is salsa night.

Bar Relic BAR

(Map p56; www.relicbar.com; Calle 9a Este; 9pm-2am Tue-Sat) Wildly popular with travelers and hip young Panamanians, this cavernous hostel bar is a hit. Service is friendly and patrons easily mingle in the ample courtyard with shared picnic tables. Not only are you partying outside (a rarity in Panama City) but you're also next to the historical wall of the city.

Upstairs in the hostel there's a calmer, more grown-up option for cocktails.

Casa Jaguar CLUB

(Map p56; 6866-8483; http://casajaguarpanama.com; Av Central s/n; 8pm-2am Tue-Thu, to 4am Fri & Sat) Don your stilettos and glitter for a night out at the Casco's hottest club, located on the 2nd floor next to Teatro Amador. There's no hurry, though, as things don't heat up until late at night, with dedicated reggaetón and electronica rooms in addition to smaller nooks and crannies. Check the website for theme nights.

The Stranger's Club COCKTAIL BAR

(Map p56; 282-0064; www.facebook.com/strangersclubpanama; Av Central s/n; 6pm-2am Mon-Wed, to 4am Thu-Sat, noon-4pm & 6pm-midnight Sun) For a buzzy scene of 20- to 40-somethings, duck into this dimly lit cocktail bar. The Consuelo, a revelation of muddled cucumber, gin and elderflower liqueur, is worth the trip in itself.

Teatro Amador CLUB

(Map p56; 212-1565; www.teatroamador.com; Av Central, btwn Calles 11 & 13; 10pm-4am Thu-Sun) When Teatro Amador first opened its doors in 1912, it was one of the city's first movie theaters. It was abandoned in the 1990s and only reopened after careful restoration in 2013. Today it serves as a popular weekend nightclub and hosts a variety of events from jazz and salsa to electronic and reggaetón. It also boasts one of the most beautiful facades in Casco Viejo.

Pedro Mandinga Rum Bar BAR
(Map p56; ☎391-5596; http://pedromandinga.com; Av A, btwn Plaza Herrera & Calle 8a; ⊙4pm-1am Mon-Thu, from noon Fri-Sun) The first dedicated rum bar to call Casco Viejo home offers a laid-back Caribbean vibe, an extensive rum-based cocktail menu, and a six-hour-long happy hour. You may never leave. Make sure to sample the spiced and silver house rums, traditionally made from *raspadura* (pure cane sugar), before ordering your drink.

Around the City

El Apartamento BAR
(The Apartment; Map p60; ☎6617-3038; www.facebook.com/elapartamentopanama; Av Federico Boyd; ⊙7pm-4am Tue-Sat) At any given time there's three floors of mischief going on at the Apartment, a yellow villa with a *discoteca,* live music floor and great bar with bottle service.

La Rana Dorada PUB
(Map p60; ☎269-2989; www.laranadorada.com; Vía Argentina 20, El Cangrejo; ⊙noon-2am) The sister outlet to a Casco Viejo microbrewery, with good pub food and a congenial, relaxed atmosphere.

Cayucos CAFE
(Isla Flamenco s/n, Causeway; ⊙noon-midnight) This open-air resto-bar sits on the water with excellent views of the city. While not exactly a bar, it has the perfect ambience for the first cold beer of the evening or a leisurely drink on the weekend.

☆ Entertainment

Panamanians have an enduring love affair with Hollywood and there are many air-conditioned cinemas in and around the city. Panamanians also love to gamble, and there are quite a few flashy casinos where you can get in on the action. There are also opportunities in the capital to see traditional folk dancing and live performances of music and theater.

Cinemas

Multicentro Cinemark CINEMA
(Map p60; ☎6944-6987; www.cinemarkca.com; Multicentro Mall) Mainstream cinema with some dubbed films and some with subtitles. Near Punta Paitilla.

Albrook Cinemark CINEMA
(Map p48; Albrook Mall) Next to the Albrook bus terminal. There's also a Cinemark in the Multiplaza Mall.

Traditional Dance

Restaurante-Bar Tinajas DANCE
(Map p60; ☎263-7890; Av 3a A Sur, Bella Vista; entry US$5; ⊙noon-10:30pm Mon-Sat) A good opportunity to see traditional Panamanian folk dancing, this dinner show is a classic. Sure it's touristy, but it's nicely done just the same. Shows are held Wednesday to Saturday at 9pm with a US$12 minimum per person for drinks and food. Reservations recommended.

Theater

Teatro Nacional THEATER
(Map p56; ☎262-3525; Av B, Casco Viejo) Casco Viejo's lovely 19th-century playhouse stages ballet, concerts and plays.

Ancon Guild Theater THEATER
(Map p48; http://anconguild.com; Av Gaillard, Ancon; ⊙6:30pm-11pm Mon-Sun) Broadway it is not, but this character-filled wooden building houses a charming 166-seat theater. Founded in 1950 by a group of Panamanian and American artists, it now serves as Panama's longest-running theater and stages a range of good English-language performances from improvisational comedy to classic dramas such as *Clue*. During the interval a makeshift bar is erected on the veranda and beers and spirits are served.

Athenaeum THEATER
(Ateneo; ☎306-3700; www.ciudaddelsaber.org/en/services/athenaeum; Calle Maritza Alabarca, Clayton; 👪) Located within the **City of Knowledge** (Ciudad del Saber; ☎306-3700; www.ciudaddelsaber.org; Edificio No 104; P 👪 🐾), the old Clayton cinema is one of the city's best examples of 'Bellavistina' architecture, a Hispanic neo-classical style popular in the Bella Vista (p59) neighborhood of the capital. Originally built in 1935 by the US Army, it was restored in 2010 and is now a cultural center with occasional film showings and performance-art projects.

Teatro Anita Villalaz THEATER
(Map p56; ☎501-4020; www.inac.gob.pa/teatros/75-teatro-anita-villalaz; Plaza de Francia, Paseo las Bóvedas, Casco Viejo) A historical spot in Casco Viejo to see live performances. Diverse events include opera, theater and film festivals.

Teatro En Círculo THEATER
(☎261-5375; www.teatroencirculo.org; Av 6, Calle Norte, El Carmen) Plays and musicals are scheduled regularly at this theater near Vía Transístmica.

Shopping

The city has a number of markets where you can purchase handicrafts native to regions throughout the country. Here you'll find a range of handmade goods, from baskets made in Emberá villages to *molas* (p233; colorful hand-stitched appliqué textiles) from Guna Yala.

Casco Viejo

★**Karavan** ART
(Map p56; ☎228-7177; www.karavan-gallery.com; Calle 3a Oeste; ⏲10am-6pm Mon-Sat, 11am-3:30pm Sun) An excellent place to find original Guna embroidery with modern designs and Congo art from Portobelo, Karavan commissions local artists, works closely to develop new talent and recovers endangered culture and arts through nonprofit Fundación Mua Mua. Artisans work on-site.

Mercadito Artesanías Catedral GIFTS & SOUVENIRS
(Map p56; Calle 5; ⏲10am-6pm Mon-Sat; Mercado de Mariscos) You may not notice the Mercadito Artesanías Catedral if it wasn't for the resellers who sometimes pop out to invite you in. Spread along an indoor gallery, colorful stands display the best of Panamanian traditional crafts. From Guna indigenous fabrics to hand-woven masks and Afro-Caribbean arts, you will find unique and affordable items to take home.

El Palacio del Sombrero HATS
(Map p56; ☎389-8544; Calle 4; ⏲9am-9:30pm) For a Panama hat with a twist, head to this shop with a small selection of traditional hats dwarfed by other bright, bold designs. Choose from a rainbow of colors or make a statement with checks and stripes.

Casa Latina ARTS & CRAFTS
(Map p56; ☎228-9828; cnr Av A & Calle 5; ⏲10am-7pm) Colorful Casa Latina has a large selection of beautiful handicrafts, ranging from the affordable to a Panama hat on sale for US$2500! Some of the items on collectors' lists include the detailed animal masks made by the Embera people and the handmade baskets created by women of the Waunaan communities.

No Me Olvides CLOTHING
(Map p56; ☎211-1209; cnr Calle 4a Oeste & Av A; ⏲10am-6pm Mon-Fri, 9am-5pm Sat) Featuring the classic Panamanian-made *guayaberas* (tropical dress shirts) made popular in the 1950s, in all colors and patterns, with a few selections for women as well.

MALLS

A number of shopping malls, some quite luxe, highlight the increasing love of Americana in Panama. Consumerism aside, these air-conditioned spots can be a good place to escape the heat or catch a movie.

Multicentro Mall (Map p60; ☎208-2500; www.multicentropanama.com.pa; Av Balboa, Paitilla; ⏲10am-8pm Mon-Thu, to 9pm Fri & Sat, 11am-7pm Sun) Has a cinema and shops, along with many outdoor restaurants.

Albrook Mall (Map p48; ☎303-6255; www.albrookmall.com; Albrook; ⏲10am-8pm Mon-Thu, to 9pm Fri & Sat, 10:30am-7pm Sun) Next to the bus terminal, this mall has a cinema, a supermarket and dozens of stores, including American and European chains. If you need it, there's also an upscale chain hotel here.

Multiplaza Mall (☎833-9991; www.multiplaza.com; cnr Vía Israel & Vía Brasil, Punta Pacifica; ⏲10am-8pm Mon-Sat, 11am-7pm Sun) The biggest downtown mall, with designer shops, restaurants and a cinema. It's east of downtown, on the way to Panamá Viejo.

Isla Flamenco Shopping Center (Amador Causeway, Isla Flamenco; ⏲10am-10pm) A collection of shops surrounded by a concentration of pleasant open-air restaurants.

Around the City

Weil Art Gallery ART
(Map p60; ☎264-9697; www.weilgallery.com; Calle 48, Bella Vista; ⏰9am-6pm Mon-Sat) If you're looking for Panamanian art, then you should visit one of the three branches of the Weil Art Gallery. Each space stocks a selection of paintings by well-known local artists, including some of Rolo de Sedas' distinctive 'Mamis.' You'll also find lots of Panama Canal memorabilia including stock certificates issued in 1880 to finance the building of the Panama Canal.

Nina Concept Store HOMEWARES
(Map p60; ☎390-5671; http://ninaconceptstore.com; Calle 54 Este, Obarrio; ⏰9:30am-6:30pm Mon-Sat, 10am-5pm Sun) This fanciful lifestyle store is filled with a curated selection of homewares and curios. There's also a cafe-restaurant serving light bites and decent espresso.

Reprosa JEWELRY
(Map p60; ☎269-0457; www.reprosa.com; cnr Av 2 Sur & Calle 54 Este, Campo Alegre; ⏰9am-7pm Mon-Sat) Sells quality *huacas* (replicas of pre-Columbian gold pendants) and necklaces made of black onyx and other gemstones.

El Hombre de la Mancha Bookstore BOOKS
(☎396-0756; http://hombredelamancha.com; La Plaza, Ciudad del Saber; ⏰10am-7pm Mon-Sat, to 6pm Sun; 🚸) Located in La Plaza in Ciudad de Saber, this small but well-stocked bookstore is an ideal spot to find kids' books and toys. Books are in Spanish and English. Additional branches can also be found in Altaplaza, Santiago, Albrook Mall, Chiriqui Mall, Multiplaza and Metro Mall.

Mercado Nacional de Artesanías MARKET
(National Artisans Market; Panamá Viejo; ⏰9am-4pm Mon-Sat, to 1pm Sun) A great place to shop for memorable souvenirs.

Information

DANGERS & ANNOYANCES

- Generally speaking, the tip of Casco Viejo southeast of Calle 12 Este and Calle 13 Este is safe for tourists and patrolled by police officers. Inland (north of Parque Herrera and Parque Santa Ana), there are high-density slums.
- Other high-crime areas to avoid include Curundú, Chorrillo, Santa Ana, San Miguelito and Río Abajo.
- Calle Uruguay, a clubbing hub, attracts opportunists. Don't take your full wallet out at night and avoid too-friendly strangers, specifically women, who are known to grope for wallets.
- Taxis generally allow unrelated passengers to share the cab, but robberies do occasionally occur. It's best to avoid taxis that already have a passenger. If you speak Spanish, you can offer a slightly higher fare to keep your taxi to yourself. Evaluate any taxi you hail before getting in (check for door handles and taxi licensing numbers). It's very common for taxi drivers to refuse fares to destinations simply for their own convenience.
- There are occasional reports of robbery near the ruins of Panamá Viejo – don't go after sunset, and always keep an eye out.
- When walking the streets of Panama City, be aware that drivers do not yield to pedestrians. Sometimes it's best to approach intersections like Panamanians – look both ways, then run like hell.

For police, call ☎104.

MAPS

Instituto Geográfico Nacional (Tommy Guardia; Map p48; ☎236-2444; http://ignpanama.anati.gob.pa; La Cresta; ⏰8am-4pm Mon-Fri) Has an excellent collection of maps for sale. Just off Av Simón Bolívar near Av Arturo del Valle, opposite the Universidad de Panamá.

MEDICAL SERVICES

Medical care in Panama, especially in Panama City, is of a high standard.

Centro Médico Paitilla (☎265-8800; http://centromedicopaitilla.com; cnr Calle 53 Este & Av Balboa, Paitilla; ⏰24hr) This medical center has well-trained physicians who speak both Spanish and English.

Centro Metropolitano de Salud (☎512-9100; www.minsa.gob.pa/region-de-salud/region-metropolitana-de-salud; Calle Principal 237, Los Ríos; ⏰8am-noon & 1-3pm Mon-Fri) Offers yellow-fever vaccinations with international certificate (required for travel to Colombia if returning) for a minimal charge. Located in the Canal Zone.

MONEY

ATMs are abundant throughout the city. The Banco Nacional de Panamá counter at Tocumen International Airport is one of the few places in Panama City that exchanges foreign currency.

Panacambios (☎223-1800; ground fl, Plaza Regency Bldg, Vía España, El Cangrejo; ⏰8am-5pm Mon-Fri) Buys and sells international currencies.

POST

Many hotels sell stamps and some will mail guests' letters.

TELEPHONE

Purchase SIM cards at any cell-phone shop or kiosk. They come with minimal credit that can be topped up at the same shop.

TOURIST INFORMATION

Autoridad de Turismo Panamá (ATP) offices give out free maps. The usefulness of a given office depends on the employees; few speak English.

Autoridad de Turismo Panamá (ATP; Panama Tourism Authority; Map p60; ☎526-7000; www.visitpanama.com; 29th fl, Edificio Bisca, cnr Av Balboa & Aquilino de la Guardia, Bella Vista; ⏲8:30am-3pm Mon-Fri) Panama's tourism bureau is headquartered in a highrise next to the Hilton hotel. Help is limited here; it's mostly geared toward high-end tourism. There's also an ATP booth in **Casco Viejo** (ATP; Map p56; ☎211-3365; www.atp.gob.pa; Av Central s/n; ⏲8:30am-4pm).

Ministero de Ambiente (Map p48; ☎500-0855, 315-0855; www.miambiente.gob.pa; Calle Broberg 804, Cerro Ancón, Albrook; ⏲8am-4pm Mon-Fri) Formerly known as ANAM, the Ministry of the Environment can occasionally provide maps and information on national parks. However, it is not set up to provide much assistance to tourists.

Getting There & Away

AIR

International flights arrive at and depart from **Tocumen International Airport** (☎238-2700; www.tocumenpanama.aero; Av Domingo Díaz, Panama City; ⏲24hr), 35km northeast of the city center. It's in the process of undergoing a major expansion that should expand offerings considerably. Domestic flights and a few international flights depart from **Albrook Airport** (Aeropuerto Marcos A Gelabert; ☎501-9272; Av Canfield, Albrook) in the former Albrook Air Force Station near the canal.

Air Panama (☎316-9000; www.airpanama.com; Albrook Airport) covers domestic routes and has its own travel agency. International carrier **Copa Airlines** (☎217-2672; www.copaair.com; Av Central s/n, Casco Viejo; ⏲8am-6pm Mon-Fri, 9am-1pm Sat) now flies to domestic destinations as well.

Flights within Panama are generally inexpensive and short – few are longer than an hour. However, if traveling to Darién Province, Isla Contadora or the Comarca de Guna Yala, it's quite possible that the plane may make multiple stops. Prices will vary according to season and availability.

Flights From Panama City

Fares listed below are one way.

DESTINATION	COST (US$)	FREQUENCY
Achutupu (San Blas)	87	daily
Bocas del Toro	124	multiple daily
Changuinola	124	multiple daily
Chitre	85	2 daily
David	120	multiple daily
Isla Contadora	75	daily
Jaqué (Darién)	96	2 weekly
Ogobuscum (San Blas)	88	4 weekly
Playón Chico (San Blas)	85	daily

BOAT

There are regular ferries to Islas Taboga and Contadora, leaving from Panama City's Causeway and the Balboa Yacht Club.

Barcos Calypso (☎314-1730; Balboa Yacht Club, Amador Causeway; round trip adult/child US$15/10.50) Departures to Isla Taboga at 8:30am weekdays, plus 3pm Friday, and at 8am, 10:30am and 4pm weekends.

Ferry Taboga (Roka-Nk; ☎6892-4844, 391-6605; https://rokapanama.com/ferry; Balboa Yacht Club, Causeway; adult/child round trip US$20/14) Daily service to Isla Taboga from Balboa Yacht Club at 8:30am, 10am and 3:45pm.

Sea Las Perlas (☎391-1424; www.sealasperlas.com; Brisas de Amador, Perico Island Causeway; adult/child one way US$49/39) This catamaran ferry service departs for Isla Contadora daily at 7:30am, returning at 3:30pm. The journey takes one hour and 40 minutes.

Taboga Express (☎6234-8989; www.tabogaexpress.com; Brisas de Amador, Isla Perico; round trip adult/child US$20/14) This catamaran is your fastest option to Taboga (30 minutes one way). Departs daily from Isla Perico on the Causeway at 8am, 9:30am, 11am, 3pm and 4:30pm. There are four returns daily.

BUS

Albrook Bus Terminal (Gran Terminal; Map p48; ☎303-3030; www.grantnt.com; Albrook; ⏲24hr), near Albrook Airport, is a convenient and modern one-stop location for most buses leaving Panama City. The terminal includes a food court, banks, shops, a sports bar, a storage room, bathrooms and showers. A mall, complete with supermarket and cinema, is located next door.

Both **Expreso Panama** (Map p48; ☎314-6837; www.expresopanama.com; Albrook Bus

Terminal, Office 13-14) and **Tica Bus** (Map p48; ☎314-6385; www.ticabus.com; Albrook Bus Terminal, Stand 32) serve San José (Costa Rica); see their websites for hours.

Canal Zone buses depart from the Albrook terminal for Balboa and Clayton, Miraflores Locks, and Gamboa, leaving every 45 minutes. Those going to Clayton and intermediary stops are run by Metrobus.

CAR

Rental rates start at US$22 per day for the most economical cars, including unlimited kilometers. Insurance is considerably extra.

Tolls are your responsibility and carry heavy fines if unpaid. Make sure your dashboard toll sticker has credit before using it: use the ID number to refill the account in any supermarket.

Budget (☎263-8777; www.budgetpanama.com; Tocumen International Airport; ⊙24hr)

Hertz (☎301-2696; www.hertzpanama.com.pa; Tocumen International Airport; ⊙24hr)

National (☎275-7222; www.nationalpanama.com; Tocumen International Airport; ⊙24hr)

TRAIN

The **Panama Canal Railway Company** (PCRC; ☎317-6070; www.panarail.com; Carretera Gaillard, Corozal; one way adult/child US$25/15) operates a glass-domed train that takes passengers on a lovely ride from Panama City to Colón on weekdays, departing at 7:15am and returning at 5:15pm. The train follows the canal, at times engulfed by dense vine-strewn jungle. If you want to relive the heyday of luxury train travel for an hour or two, this is definitely the way to do it.

Note that Panama City's terminus is actually located in the town of Corozal, a 15-minute cab ride from the capital.

Getting Around

GETTING INTO TOWN

Tocumen International Airport is located 33km northeast of the city center. The cheapest way to get into the city is to exit the terminal, cross the street (to the bus shelter) and catch a bus to the city. The 10-minute walk might seem longer with luggage. Taxis (around US$30) can be hired at the Transportes Turísticos desk at the airport exit; they are much faster than the bus.

Albrook Airport is north of Cerro Ancón and handles domestic flights. A taxi ride to downtown should cost between US$5 and US$8.

All long-distance buses arrive at Albrook Bus Terminal; from here there are connections throughout the city. Routes are displayed in the front window; fares are US$0.35. After

BUSES FROM PANAMA CITY

DESTINATION	COST (US$)	DURATION (HR)	FREQUENCY (DAILY)
Aguadulce	6.35	3	33
Antón	5	2	every 20min
Cañita	3	2½	11
Chame	2.60	1¼	37
Changuinola	29	10	8pm
Chitré	10	4	hourly
Colón	3.50	2	every 20min
David	15-19	7-8	15
El Copé	6	4	9
El Valle	4.25	2½	hourly
Las Tablas	10	4½	hourly
Macaracas	10	5	5
Paso Canoas	17-22	8	5
Penonomé	5.25	2½	48
Pesé	9.65	4½	6
San Carlos	3.25	1½	25
San José (Costa Rica)	40	16	1
Santiago	9	4	20
Soná	10	6	6
Villa de Los Santos	9	4	18
Yaviza	16	6-8	8

dark, take a taxi (US$3 to US$7) to your destination.

BICYCLE

You can rent bicycles in some hostels and at the Causeway. Bicicletas Moses (p55) operates a booth with mountain bikes, tandems, bicycle carts and kids' bikes for rent.

BUS

Panama City has almost finished phasing out its *diablos rojos* (red devils) for modern, safe, air-conditioned **Metrobus** (☎504-7200; www.elmetrodepanama.com; fare US$0.35-1.35; ⏰5am-11pm Mon-Fri, to 10pm Sat, 7am-10pm Sun) buses.

Most local buses are on the Metrobus system with designated bus stops. Rides cost between US$0.35 and $1.35, with the higher cost for *corredor* (highway) routes. Cash is not accepted.

Passengers must buy a Rapi-Pass (http://tarjetametrobus.com; US$2) at a special kiosk in Albrook Bus Terminal or at designated locations (such as supermarkets or main bus stops, all listed on the website). If you don't have one, try offering another passenger reimbursement for swiping their card. It also deducts the terminal tax at Albrook.

Buses run along the three major west–east routes: Av Central–Vía España, Av Balboa–Vía Israel and Av Simón Bolívar–Vía Transístmica. The Av Central–Vía España streets are one way going west for much of the route; eastbound buses use Av Perú and Av 4 Sur – these buses will take you into the banking district of El Cangrejo. Buses also run along Av Ricardo J Alfaro (known as Tumba Muerto).

Metrobuses stop at official bus stops and Albrook Bus Terminal near Albrook Airport.

From Albrook Bus Terminal, airport buses (US$1.25, one to 1½ hours) marked 'Tocumen Corredor' depart every 15 minutes to Tocumen airport.

RIDE SHARING

Companies like Uber and Cabify offer an alternative solution to taking a taxi. They are cheaper and more convenient in off-peak hours. Note that Tocumen International Airport does not allow them to give curbside service.

SUBWAY

Panama City's mostly underground transportation system is known as El Metro. Línea 1 runs west–east from Albrook and then north to San Isidro. There are plans for Línea 2 between Av Cincuentenario until the district of Chepo, with links to Tocumen Airport, and Línea 3 between Albrook and the City of Knowledge. The main terminal is across from Albrook Bus Terminal. Fares are paid with the same swipe card used for the Metrobus system.

TAXI

Taxis are plentiful but can be problematic. Some drivers do not travel (or even know) the whole city, so don't be surprised if they leave you standing on the sidewalk upon hearing your destination.

Taxis are not metered, but there is a list of standard fares that drivers are supposed to charge, measured by zones. One zone runs a minimum of US$3; Canal Zone destinations run up to US$15. An average ride, crossing a couple of zones, would cost US$4 to US$6, and more for additional passengers, holidays or if it's late at night. Always agree on a fare with your driver before you get into the cab, or better yet, ask your hotel to estimate the fare to your destination and then simply hand the driver the money upon arriving. Taxis can also be rented by the hour.

Watch out for unmarked large-model US cars serving hotels as cabs. Their prices are up to four times that of regular street taxis.

America Libre (☎800-8294)

Radio Taxi America (☎221-1932)

Taxi Unico Cooperativa (☎221-8258)

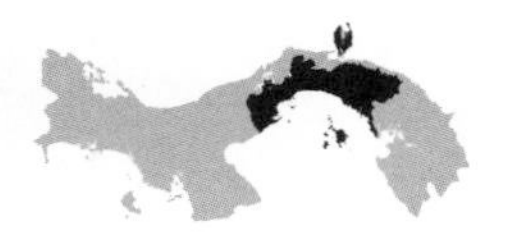

Panamá Province

POP 2.15 MILLION / ELEV SEA LEVEL TO 1026M

Includes ➡

Best Places to Eat

- ➡ La Vista (p84)
- ➡ La Ruina (p92)
- ➡ London's Pier Bar & Grill (p84)
- ➡ Casa Tortuga (p88)
- ➡ Carlitos (p93)

Best Places to Stay

- ➡ Canopy Tower Ecolodge (p80)
- ➡ Hostal Casa Amarilla (p90)
- ➡ Gamboa Rainforest Resort (p81)
- ➡ Mar y Oro (p87)
- ➡ Mamallena Ecolodge (p88)

Why Go?

Panamá Province has a rich history of pirates, plunder and pearls. Although it's the most populous province in the country, Panamá can be as big or as small as you want it to be. Tranquil rainforests and sizzling beaches are yours to explore, and the comforts of the capital are never more than an hour away.

The principal attraction remains the world's most daring engineering achievement. Explore the Panama Canal and its expansion by visiting its locks, boating through its watery recesses or hiking along its jungle-clad shore. It is also the unlikely host of one of the most accessible and best-studied tropical rainforests on the planet.

Day trips from Panama City abound, ranging from beaches and surf breaks to ferry trips to the nearby island village of Taboga. Further flung is the Archipiélago de las Perlas, which attracts everyone from the moneyed elite to, occasionally, *Survivor* contestants.

When to Go

Dec–Apr High season at the Pacific coast beaches when trade winds and dry weather translate to the perfect time to windsurf or kitesurf; beaches are usually full and hotels charge high-season rates.

May–Nov For huge savings, hit the resorts in the low season. Calmer conditions favor wakeboarders.

Aug–Oct A visit to Isla Taboga or Archipiélago de Las Perlas is pleasant year-round, but if you want to see migrating humpback whales come when they put on spectacular displays. It's even possible to spot them on your ferry ride out to the island.

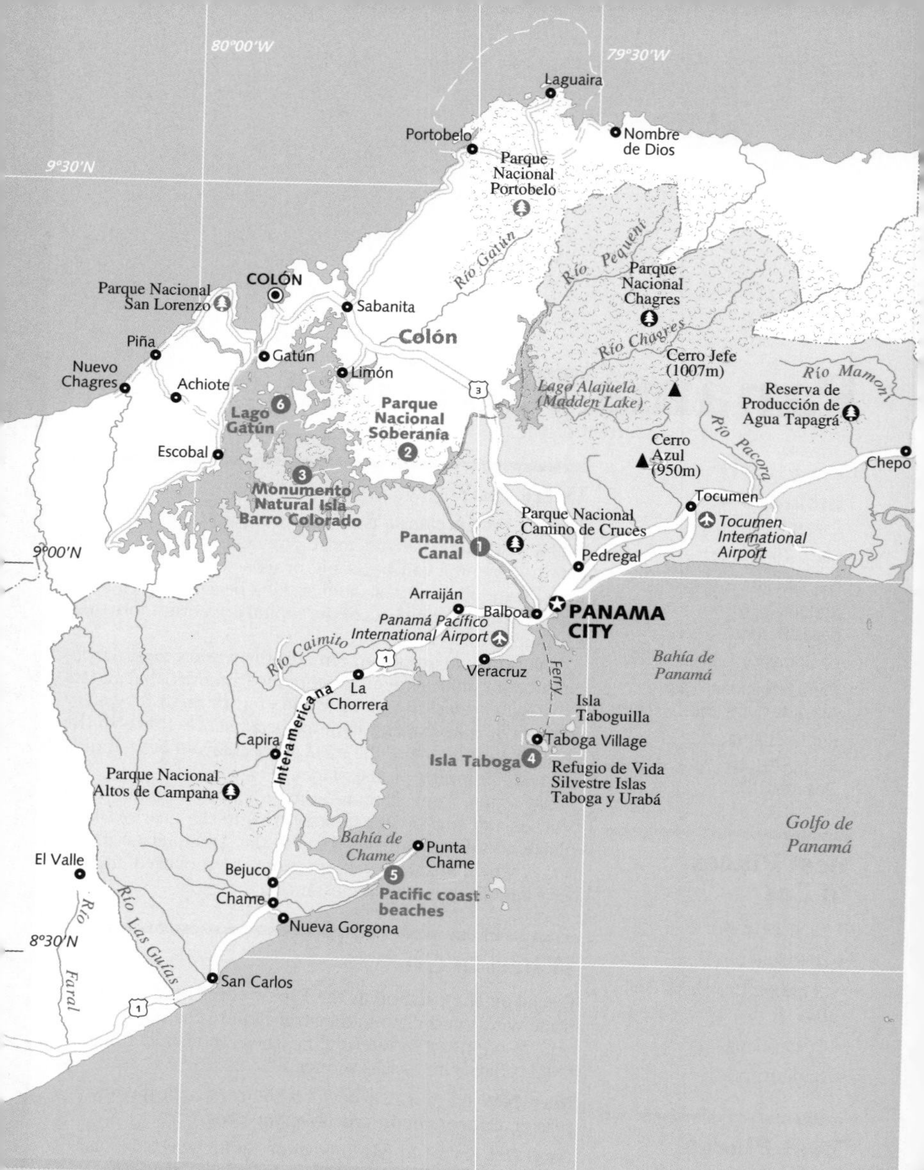

80°00'W
79°30'W
9°30'N
9°00'N
8°30'N
Laguaira
Portobelo
Nombre de Dios
Parque Nacional Portobelo
Río Gatún
Río Pequení
Parque Nacional Chagres
Río Chagres
COLÓN
Parque Nacional San Lorenzo
Sabanita
Colón
Piña
Nuevo Chagres
Gatún
Limón
Achiote
Lago Gatún
6
Parque Nacional Soberanía
2
Escobal
3
Monumento Natural Isla Barro Colorado
Cerro Jefe (1007m)
Lago Alajuela (Madden Lake)
Río Mamoní
Reserva de Producción de Agua Tapagrá
Río Pacora
Cerro Azul (950m)
Chepo
Tocumen
Tocumen International Airport
Parque Nacional Camino de Cruces
Panama Canal
1
Pedregal
Arraiján
Balboa
PANAMA CITY
Panamá Pacífico International Airport
Río Caimito
Veracruz
Ferry
Bahía de Panamá
La Chorrera
Interamericana
Isla Taboguilla
Capira
Taboga Village
Isla Taboga
4
Refugio de Vida Silvestre Islas Taboga y Urabá
Parque Nacional Altos de Campana
Golfo de Panamá
Bahía de Chame
Punta Chame
5
Pacific coast beaches
El Valle
Bejuco
Chame
Nueva Gorgona
Río Faral
Río Las Guías
San Carlos
1
3

Panamá Province Highlights

1 **Panama Canal** (p76) Laying eyes on this awe-inspiring engineering marvel, which has now expanded to triple its former capacity.

2 **Parque Nacional Soberanía** (p78) Spotting feathered friends along Pipeline Rd, one of the world's premier birdwatching sites.

3 **Monumento Natural Isla Barro Colorado** (p80) Visiting the world-famous tropical biology center at the most studied patch of rainforest in the world.

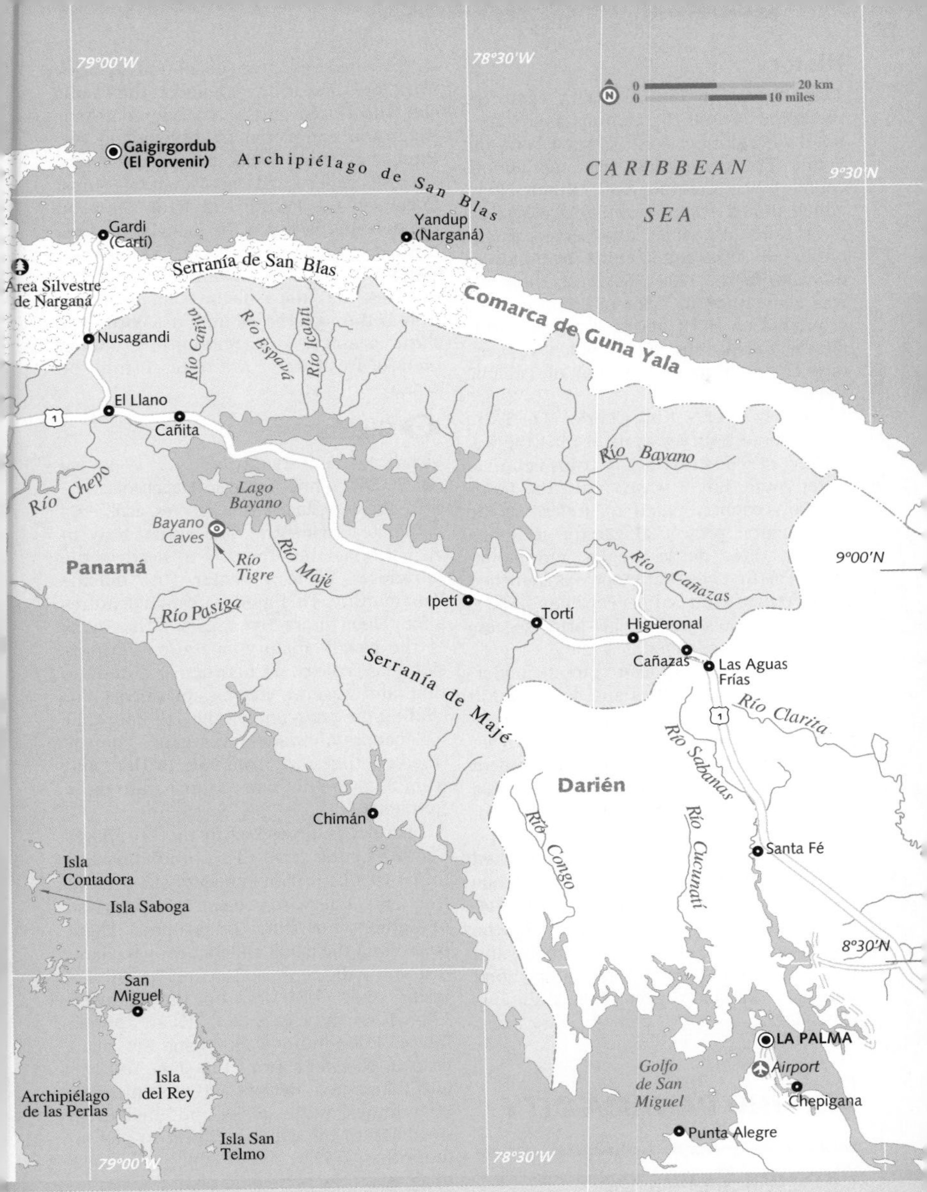

79°00'W
78°30'W
0 20 km
0 10 miles
Gaigirgordub (El Porvenir)
Archipiélago de San Blas
CARIBBEAN SEA
9°30'N
Gardi (Cartí)
Yandup (Narganá)
Área Silvestre de Narganá
Serranía de San Blas
Comarca de Guna Yala
Nusagandi
Río Cañita
Río Espavá
Río Icanti
El Llano
Cañita
Río Bayano
Río Chepo
Lago Bayano
Bayano Caves
Río Tigre
Río Majé
Panamá
Río Cañazas
9°00'N
Ipetí
Tortí
Higueronal
Cañazas
Las Aguas Frías
Río Pasiga
Serranía de Majé
Río Clarita
Río Sabanas
Darién
Chimán
Río Congo
Río Cucunatí
Santa Fé
Isla Contadora
Isla Saboga
8°30'N
San Miguel
LA PALMA
Airport
Golfo de San Miguel
Chepigana
Isla del Rey
Archipiélago de las Perlas
Punta Alegre
Isla San Telmo
79°00'W
78°30'W

4 Isla Taboga (p82)
Escaping the urban grind of the capital on a day trip to this flower-dotted historical island.

5 Pacific coast beaches (p91) Soaking up the sun, surfing gnarly breaks and making the most of the romantic hideaways along this inviting coastline.

6 Lago Gatún (p76)
Paddling a kayak or fishing for peacock bass on the lake, while spotting howler monkeys up above in the canopy.

History

Throughout the 16th and 17th centuries, the Spanish used the isthmus as a transit point for shipping gold between Peru and Spain. The main route was the famous cobblestoned Camino Real (King's Hwy), which linked Panamá to Portobelo in today's Colón Province, and served as the only road across the isthmus for hundreds of years. In the 1700s, however, the route was abandoned in favor of shipping gold around Cape Horn due to repeated pirate attacks, the most famous of which was Captain Henry Morgan's sacking of Panamá Viejo in 1671.

As early as 1524, King Charles V of Spain had ordered a survey to determine the feasibility of constructing a trans-isthmian water route. But it wasn't until the 1880s that any country dared to undertake the monumental project of carving a trench through these dense jungles and mountains. The first canal attempt was launched by a French team led by Ferdinand-Marie de Lesseps, bolstered by his prior success building the Suez Canal.

Sadly, the French team grossly underestimated the difficulties and some 22,000 workers died during the construction attempt. Most lives were lost to yellow fever and malaria, which led to the establishment of an enormous quarantine center on Isla Taboga. It was not then known that mosquitoes were the disease vector.

Several decades later, the USA learned from the mistakes of the French and succeeded in completing the canal in 1914. Today the waterway rests firmly in the hands of the Panamanian government, and the face of the canal is rapidly changing following the completion of an ambitious expansion.

AROUND PANAMA CITY

Panama Canal

One of the world's greatest marvels, the Panama Canal stretches 80km from Panama City on the Pacific side to Colón on the Atlantic side. Around 14,500 vessels pass through each year, and ships worldwide have traditionally been built with the dimensions of the canal's original locks (330m long and 33.5m wide) in mind.

The canal has three sets of double locks: Miraflores and Pedro Miguel on the Pacific side and Gatún on the Atlantic. A 10-year expansion completed in 2016 added two three-chambered locks, allowing the passage of super-sized 'neoPanamax' ships: Cocoli on the Pacific and Agua Clara on the Atlantic. Between the locks, ships pass through a huge artificial lake, **Lago Gatún**, created by the Gatún Dam across the Río Chagres, and the Culebra Cut, a 12.7km trough through the mountains. With each ship's passage, a staggering 197 million liters of fresh water are released into the ocean.

Sights

Miraflores Visitors Center MUSEUM

(☎276-8617; http://visitcanaldepanama.com/en/centro-de-visitantes-de-miraflores; adult/child US$15/10; ⏰8am-6pm) The easiest way to visit the Panama Canal is to head to the Miraflores Visitors Center, just outside Panama City. This modern center features a four-floor interactive museum that looks at the canal's history, operations, expansion and ecology, an instructive 15-minute film and several viewing platforms, including the main one on the 4th floor that has panoramic views over canal transits (the best times are from 9am to 11am and from 3pm to 5pm when transits are more frequent).

There is a direct bus to the Miraflores Visitors Center from the Albrook Bus Terminal (p300) in Panama City, but it is infrequent. Otherwise you can take a Paraíso or Gamboa bus from the terminal. These pass along the canal-side highway to Gamboa and will let you off at the 'Miraflores Locks' sign (US$0.35) on the highway, 12km from the city center. It's an approximately 15-minute walk along the main road to the locks from the sign. You can also take a taxi; drivers will typically wait 30 minutes at the locks and then drive you back to the capital. Expect to pay no more than US$30 round trip, but be sure to agree on the price beforehand.

Pedro Miguel Locks CANAL

FREE North past the Miraflores Locks, the Pedro Miguel Locks can be seen from the highway to Gamboa. One hundred meters beyond the locks there's a parking strip from where onlookers can watch ships transit the canal.

Panama Canal

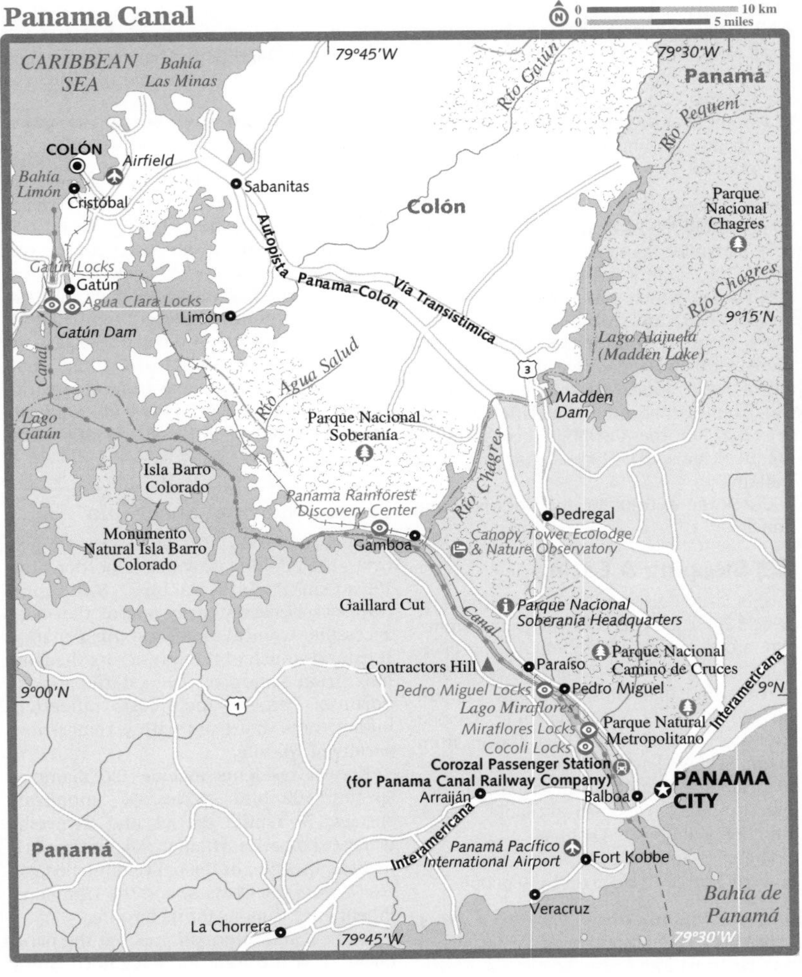

Tours

★Yala Tours ADVENTURE

(☎232-0215, 6641-6676; www.yalatourspanama.com) This small Swiss-run operation provides specialized trips throughout Panama, including day trips to Gamboa and the Canal Zone. A highlight is kayaking Río Chagres and Lago Gatún (US$160) while watching canal ships mow through. Also offers a canal-boat tour in Lago Gatún, wildlife-watching and hiking in Parque Nacional Soberanía (US$70), and cultural visits to an Emberá village.

Manakin Adventures Panama TOURS

(☎6384-4466, 908-9621; www.manakinadventures.com; canal/islands tour per person from US$60/70) This highly recommended agency knows the Panama Canal better than most and leads half-day tours to the Miraflores Visitors Center and Canal Zone. Nature lovers will want to join the boating trip on Lago Gatún to watch container ships in transit, stopping off at one of the lake's islands to meet and feed a colony of Geoffroy's tamarin monkeys.

EcoCircuitos ADVENTURE
(☎315-1488; www.ecocircuitos.com; Albrook Plaza, 2nd fl, No 31, Ancón) A reputable, sustainable operator offering conventional tours to the Panama Canal and canal transits, tours of Parque Nacional Soberanía, birdwatching on Pipeline Rd and fun kayaking trips on Lago Gatún.

Canal & Bay Tours BOATING
(☎6677-1576, 209-2002; www.canalandbaytours.com; partial/full transit adult US$150/195, child US$95/105) Offers partial canal transits (4½ hours), which pass through the Pedro Miguel (p76) and Miraflores (p76) locks every Saturday morning at 8:30am from the Amador ferry pier. On the first Saturday of every month, full transits (10 hours) run from Balboa on the Pacific Coast to Cristóbal on the Caribbean coast, passing all three sets of locks. They depart at 7:30am.

Check the website for dates of upcoming transits.

Sleeping & Eating

Jungle Land Panama HOUSEBOAT $$$
(☎6113-3143, 213-1172; www.junglelandpanama.com; s/d all-inclusive US$250/400) This overnight houseboat offers the novelty of a jungle retreat with canal ships passing by. Captain Carl hosts guests on a charming wooden three-story houseboat on Lago Gatún, from where fishing, kayaking, stand-up paddleboarding and nocturnal safaris are at your fingertips. Day trips also available. Leaves from the boat dock in Gamboa.

There is a total of eight rooms, which can be reconfigured to sleep up to 10 people.

Kotowa Boquete Cafe CAFE $
(☎6844-0889; Miraflores Visitors Center, ground fl; snacks from US$3; ⏲8am-6pm) This branch of a national cafe chain on the ground floor of the Miraflores Visitors Center (p76) serves snacks and light meals throughout the day.

Atlantic & Pacific Co. PANAMANIAN $$$
(☎232-3120; www.atlanticpacificrestaurant.com; Miraflores Visitors Center, 2nd fl; lunch buffet US$55, mains US$16-38; ⏲11:30am-4:30pm daily, 6-11pm Tue-Sat; ❄) This upscale restaurant is worthy of the canal, though prices do reflect the exclusive setting. Serving New Panamanian cuisine and using local produce, it provides distinctive choices, and plenty of them, at the sumptuous lunch buffet. Seafood is a highlight, as well as rich Panamanian coffee and desserts. Ask for balcony seating and watch boats pass the locks.

Canal Zone

The Canal Zone is home to a number of impressive attractions, especially if you're into wildlife-watching, hiking and birding. On a day trip from Panama City, you could visit the Miraflores Locks and finish at the Parque Nacional Soberanía and the Panama Rainforest Discovery Center. With prior arrangements, you could also take an organized tour of Isla Barro Colorado, one of the world's most famous tropical research stations, or visit an Emberá or Wounaan indigenous village on the shores of the Río Chagres.

Parque Nacional Soberanía

Some 27km from Panama City and just over the Colón provincial border, the 195-sq-km **Parque Nacional Soberanía** (www.miambiente.gob.pa) is one of the most accessible tropical rainforests in Panama. It extends much of the way across the isthmus, from Limón on Lago Gatún to just north of Paraíso, and boasts numerous hiking trails that brim with a remarkable variety of wildlife.

Known residents include 125 mammal species, 402 bird species, 55 amphibian species, 79 reptile species and 34 freshwater fish species. Hiking trails in the park include a section of the old Camino de Cruces (Way of the Crosses) and the 17km-long Pipeline Rd, famous for its birdlife.

Leaflets and information about the park, including a brochure for self-guided walks along the nature trail, are available from **park headquarters** (☎232-4192; ⏲7am-5pm) near Gamboa.

Activities

Hiking

If you plan on hiking, note that the trailheads are quite far from the Soberanía park headquarters. Hire a guide to fully appreciate the diversity of wildlife here.

Sendero Las Cruces HIKING
The park has a short 10km-long section of the old Camino de Cruces (Way of the Crosses), which was famously used by the Spanish

to transport gold by mule train between Panama City and Nombre de Dios in today's Colón Province.

Sendero El Charco HIKING

A very easy 800m *sendero natural interpretivo* (interpretive nature trail), El Charco is signposted from Carretera Omar Torrijos, about 3km past the Summit Botanical Gardens & Zoo.

Birdwatching

Pipeline Road BIRDWATCHING

Pipeline Rd is considered to be one of the world's premier birdwatching sites. Unsurprisingly, it is intensely popular with birders, especially in the early morning. More than 400 different species of birds have been spotted on the trail, and it's fairly likely you will spot everything from toucans to trogons.

Also known as the Camino del Oleoducto, the 17km-long dirt track was built to service an oil pipeline constructed (and never used) by the USA during WWII.

A healthy cluster of golden-collared manakins is usually found at the end of the first 100m of the road, on the left-hand side. Other typical sounds along the first 2km of the road come from white-bellied antbirds, black-bellied wrens, collared aracaris, keel-billed toucans and buff-throated woodcreepers. Also keep an eye out for rarities such as the tiny hawk, the hook-billed kite, the great jacamar and the black-tailed trogon.

It's wise to hire a guide to fully appreciate the wildlife.

Fishing

Fishing is permitted on the Río Chagres and Lago Gatún. If you're interested in arranging

VISITING EMBERÁ & WOUNAAN COMMUNITIES

The Río Chagres, which flows through Parque Nacional Soberanía and supplies most of the water for the Panama Canal, is home to several Emberá and Wounaan communities. Although the Darién is the ancestral home of these two indigenous groups, a wave of migration to the shores of the Río Chagres commenced in the 1950s. Following the establishment of the national park in the 1980s, however, the government banned the practice of slash-and-burn agriculture, which has severely affected their livelihood. Today several villages are turning to tourism for survival.

Before visiting these communities, it's important to realize that over the past 50 years the Emberá and the Wounaan communities have had a turbulent history of land grabs, legal battles and political misrepresentation. Both groups have been forced to modernize, though the Emberá and the Wounaan still maintain their incredibly rich cultural heritage. If you arrive expecting to see villagers living traditional lifestyles in harmony with the land, then you will be disappointed. However, the Emberá and the Wounaan still have a lot to show to visitors, especially their traditional dances, music, handicrafts and the surrounding national park that has become their de facto home.

The Emberá communities of **Ella Puru** (☎6537-7223, 6704-0380; http://ellapuruembera.weebly.com; tours per person US$25, entry US$5) and **Katuma** (☎6963-7432) and the Wounaan community of **San Antonio** (☎6637-9503; tours per person US$25) regularly receive tourists. With prior notice you can arrange a pickup from the docks in Gamboa. Tour prices depend on the activities you arrange. There is no shortage of possible excursions, ranging from guided rainforest walks to watching traditional dances. Communities also sell traditional handicrafts.

Visitors praise **Emberá Village Tours** (☎848-4072, 6758-7600; www.emberavillagetours.com), the agency of Anne Gordon de Barrigón, a former animal trainer who married into this warm Emberá community. The tour is well done and provides loads of cultural insight.

Getting There

Take a taxi (US$20 to US$30) or any Gamboa-bound bus (US$0.65) from Albrook Bus Terminal (p300) in Panama City.

To access indigenous communities, head to the boat dock (p81) in Gamboa. Boat trips usually take 10 minutes and cost US$15 per person round trip. The dock at Puerto Corotú is another springboard for indigenous villages.

a private tour, contact **Panama Canal Fishing** (☎399-1537, 6678-2653; www.panamacanalfishing.com; Gamboa; 6hr trips per 1/2 anglers all-inclusive from US$375/495).

Sleeping

★**Canopy Tower Ecolodge** LODGE $$$
(☎Panama City 264-5720; www.canopytower.com/canopy-tower; per person incl meals US$199-320; P) Located in Parque Nacional Soberanía, this former US Air Force radar station now serves a very different function, namely ecotourism. It's an ecologically minded three-story, cylindrical lodge and observatory that offers a full immersion in the sights and sounds of the rainforest as well as accommodations. Rates drop substantially (US$139 to US$220) mid-April to mid-December.

The birdwatching in the surrounding area is top-notch and there's no shortage of other tropical wildlife, including howler monkeys, sloths and a slew of frogs and lizards. From the 3rd and rooftop levels, you have a 360-degree view over the national park and you can even see ships passing through the Panama Canal, some 2km to the west.

In addition to the viewing platforms, there is also a small ground-floor exhibition area, a tropical biology library, a cozy sitting area and a dozen guest rooms, ranging from postage-stamp singles to luxurious four-person suites. Each room is awash in tropical hues, natural hardwoods and firm beds; some rooms share bathrooms. Rates include three meals. Even if you're not spending the night, a day visit will allow you to visit the viewing platforms and partake in a few guided walks (US$70 to US$90) through the park.

To reach the Canopy Tower, pass the entrance to Summit Botanical Gardens & Zoo on your way to Gamboa, and take the second road to the right; the turnoff is marked with a Canopy Tower sign. Follow the road for 1.6km until you reach the top of Semaphore Hill and the entrance to the hotel.

Getting There & Away

From Panama City take any Gamboa-bound bus from Albrook Bus Terminal (p300 ;US$0.65) between 7am and 7pm, or a taxi (US$20 to US$30). If arriving by taxi, have the driver wait for you while you register at park headquarters and then take you to the trailheads, as they are quite far from the entrance station and office.

Panama Rainforest Discovery Center

Geared toward ecotourism and environmental education, this is an excellent facility for birdwatchers and nature-lovers. Since you are probably here to watch wildlife, it's worth making an effort to roll out of bed early – 6am to 8am are the best times. With advance reservations, groups can set up special night tours.

A 32m-high observation tower (172 steps) made of recycled material from the canal is great for spotting blue cotinga and toucans; during premium hours, just 25 visitors are admitted at one time to minimize the impact on wildlife. The sustainably built visitor center provides information and has 15 species of hummingbirds (of Panama's 57) feeding nearby. A new sloth-rescue center offers sanctuary to these shy creatures and prepares them for reintroduction into the wild.

Guides at the visitor center and tower can point out wildlife. Currently, a 1.2km circuit of two forest trails offers options that range from easy to difficult. Lake-side you can view aquatic birds such as wattled jacanas, least grebes, herons and snail kites. Other animals around include monkeys, crocodiles, coatis, butterflies and two- and three-toed sloths.

Contact the center if you'd like to participate in its bird migration counts. These are organized by the **Fundación Avifauna Eugene Eisenmann** (☎306-3133; www.avifauna.org.pa), a nonprofit organization with the mission of protecting Panama's bird fauna and rainforest habitat. Within the center, scientific research includes studies of migratory birds, green macaws and raptors as well as investigations into carbon capture.

There's no bus access to the park. It's best to book a taxi, rent a car or go with an organized tour. The center is located 2km from the entrance to Pipeline Rd. Pass the town of Gamboa, at the end of Gaillard Rd, and follow the signs.

Monumento Natural Isla Barro Colorado

This lush island in the middle of **Lago Gatún** is the most intensively studied area in the neotropics. Formed by the damming of the Río Chagres and the creation of the lake, in 1923 Isla Barro Colorado became one of the first biological reserves in the New World. Home to 1316 recorded plant species, including 500 tree species, 381 bird species and 120 mammal species, the island also contains a 59km network of marked and protected trails. It is managed by the Smithsonian Tropical Research Institute (STRI), which administers a world-renowned research facility on the island.

Isla Barro Colorado is only open to a limited number of visitors participating in guided tours.

Tours

Isla Barro Colorado Tour ECOTOUR
(www.stri.org; tour per adult/student incl lunch US$100/70; 7am-4pm Tue, Wed & Fri, 8am-3pm Sat & Sun) Once restricted to scientists, this 15-sq-km tropical research island is now open to a limited number of visitors on guided tours. The trip includes a boat ride down an attractive part of the canal, from Gamboa across the lake to the island. Hikes are demanding and last two to three hours. Reservations essential; book as far in advance as possible.

The entire trip lasts between seven and nine hours, depending on the size of the group and on the weather.

Information

There are no public visits on certain holidays. For reservations and detailed visitor information, visit the **Smithsonian Tropical Research Institute** (STRI; Map p48; 212-8000; www.stri.org; Tupper Bldg, Av Roosevelt, Ancón; 8:30am-4:30pm Mon-Fri) website.

Getting There & Away

Access is by guided tour only. Boats leave Gamboa at 7am on weekdays and at 8am on weekends for the 45-minute trip to the reserve and you are asked to arrive a half-hour ahead of departure.

Frequent buses link Albrook Bus Terminal (Gran Terminal; Map p48; 303-3030; www.grantnt.com; Albrook; 24hr) in Panama City with Gamboa (US$0.65).

Gamboa

A pleasant community of leafy streets and old wooden canal houses, Gamboa is an ideal base for wildlife-watchers who want some quiet. The small town is the base for many foreign scientists working for the Smithsonian Tropical Research Institute (STRI).

Sleeping & Eating

Ivan's Bed & Breakfast B&B $$
(314-9436, 6981-4583; www.gamboaecotours.com; Av Jadwin 111; r per person US$50, 4-person apt US$210;) Decked out with memorabilia, this comfortable canal house tends to draw birdwatchers and hikers keen on quick access to Pipeline Rd, which is minutes away. The two 3rd-floor rooms with shared bathrooms are fresher than the pair at ground level. A 2nd-floor living area is cozy and tasteful, while the gazebo is ideal for an afternoon beer.

Reserve ahead for the large-portioned dinners (US$17), which include salad and dessert courses. English-speaking Ivan and his wife Gladys can arrange birdwatching and fishing tours, as well as airport transfers. The Casa de los Abuelos (Grandparents' House), a two-bedroom apartment on the ground floor of the lodge, is also available.

★**Gamboa Rainforest Resort** RESORT $$$
(314-5000; www.gamboaresort.com; d from US$215;) Near the Panama Canal and Río Chagres junction, 9km past the turnoff for Canopy Tower on the road to Colón, is this US$30 million spot. It's not an ecolodge but a resort located in a rainforest; nevertheless, it's hard to deny its grandeur. All 166 luxurious guest rooms and the lobby offer sweeping vistas of the jungle-flanked Río Chagres.

Canopy B&B B&B $$$
(833-5929, reservations 264-5720; www.canopytower.com; Av Jadwin 114; s/d incl breakfast standard US$95/140, deluxe US$111/158;) In an old canal house dating from 1937, this lovely B&B with five rooms has a clean design of classic features mixed in with bold patterns. The heated towel racks and hair dryers add a nice touch. Note that the three deluxe rooms upstairs are a significant upgrade. In the morning, pancakes, eggs and wheat toast are served at the huge breakfast table.

Getting There & Away

Gamboa is 35km from Panama City. Take a frequent Gamboa-bound bus (US$0.65) from the Albrook Bus Terminal (p300) in Panama City or a taxi (US$20 to US$30).

PACIFIC ISLANDS

Isla Taboga

POP 1650

A tropical island with just one road and no traffic, Isla Taboga is a pleasant escape from the rush of Panama City, only 20km offshore. With the addition of some decent restaurants and boutique lodgings in the town of San Pedro and plenty of activities, it's growing as a destination. Named the 'Island of Flowers,' it is covered with sweet-smelling blossoms much of the year. First settled by the Spanish in 1515, the quaint village is also home to the western hemisphere's second-oldest church. While there are better beaches elsewhere, this quick, almost Caribbean getaway is a salve for city living.

History

Taboga is part of a chain of islands that were inhabited by indigenous peoples who lived in thatched huts and fished. In 1515 Spanish soldiers led by conquistador Vasco Núñez de Balboa announced their arrival by killing or enslaving the islanders and establishing a small colony. It then became a favorite haunt of English pirates.

In August 1686, the ship of an English buccaneer named Captain Townley was moored off Taboga when it was attacked by three Spanish ships armed with cannons. During the ensuing battle, Townley destroyed one of the ships and took captive the two other vessels as well as a fourth ship that had arrived as reinforcement. Townley sent a messenger to authorities in Casco Viejo demanding supplies, the release of five pirates being held prisoner and ransom for the Spanish captives. When they refused, a standoff ensued, with Townley sending the officials a canoe with the heads of 20 Spaniards. The pirate's demands were soon met.

For years, peace eluded the little island that lay in such a strategic location. During the 1880s, when the French attempted to build a canal, Taboga became the site of an enormous sanatorium for workers who had contracted malaria or yellow fever. It was later turned into a posh club and recreation center for Canal employees.

The US Navy used the broad hill facing the town for artillery practice during WWII and even installed a number of anti-aircraft guns and a machine-gun bunker atop the island. Abandoned in 1960, these ruins can still be visited today.

Sights

Fine sand beaches lie in either direction from the ferry dock. Walk north (right) from the pier to **Playa Restinga** and south (left) along the island's narrow main road to San Pedro and the more urban **Playa Honda**. After a fork, a high road leads to the church and a simple square. Further down the road, a pretty 307m-tall public garden displays the statue of the island's patron, the Virgen del Carmen; nearby is the supposed home of 16th-century conquistador Francisco Pizzaro, who led the expedition that conquered the Inca Empire. The road meanders a total of 5.2km, ending at the old US military installation and bunker atop the island's highest point, **Cerro Vigía**.

Refugio de Vida Silvestre Islas Taboga y Urabá WILDLIFE RESERVE

This 258-hectare wildlife reserve was established in 1984 to protect a key avian habitat. Taboga and nearby Urabá are home to one of the world's largest breeding colonies of brown pelicans, with up to 10,000 here at any one time. The reserve covers about a third of Taboga as well as the entire island of Urabá, just off Taboga's southeast coast. May is the height of nesting season, but pelicans can be seen from January to April.

Iglesia de San Pedro CHURCH

Founded in 1550, the Church of St Peter is the second-oldest church in the western hemisphere after the one in Natá in Coclé Province. Inside there is lovely artwork and a handsome altar featuring a seated San Pedro with an Orthodox-style cross and holding his signature keys.

Isla El Morro ISLAND

This island off Tobago's northeast coast contains an English cemetery and a monument erected by the Pacific Steamship Company, which had its headquarters here in the 19th century. It is connected to Playa Restinga by a sandbar, which disappears at high tide.

Activities

★**Taboga Tour Center** TOURS

(☎6704-4028; www.tabogatourcenter.com; 1½hr tours US$25-35; ⏲9am-4pm) Taboga Tour

LA PEREGRINA

The Archipiélago de las Perlas has produced some of the world's finest pearls. However, none is as celebrated or well documented as La Peregrina (Pilgrim Pearl). Enormous and pear-shaped, this white pearl weighs 203.84 grains or 31 carats. More than 450 years ago, it earned the slave who discovered it his freedom.

In the mid-16th century, the pearl was given to King Phillip II of Spain, who later presented it as a wedding gift to his wife, Queen Mary I (Bloody Mary) of England. Later the British Duke of Abercorn acquired it from the son of French emperor Napoleon III.

In 1969 actor Richard Burton purchased the pearl for US$37,000 for his wife, Elizabeth Taylor. La Peregrina was briefly lost when Taylor's puppy scampered away with the pearl in its mouth. In 2011 the pearl was auctioned at Christie's as part of Taylor's estate and fetched US$11 million.

Center, just to the right as you leave the ferry pier, is your one-stop shop for all activities on the island – from hiking and boating to snorkeling and butterfly-watching. The 45-minute Historical Walking Tour (US$5) is a great way to get your bearings. For rent are towels (US$3), lockers (US$4) and snorkeling gear (US$5). Showers cost US$1.

Snorkeling

On weekends, fishers at the pier take visitors around the island to good snorkeling spots and caves on the western side, which are rumored to hold pirate treasure. During the week you can snorkel around Isla El Morro, which doesn't have coral but attracts some large fish.

Diving

The Pacific-style diving here has rocky formations, schools of fish and a wide variety of marine life. On a good dive you can see jack, snapper, jewfish, eels, rays, lobsters and octopuses. With a little luck, you may also come across old bottles, spent WWII-era shells and artifacts from pirate days (remember: look but don't take). Dive outfitters in Panama City occasionally make the trip; check with the Taboga Tour Center.

Whale-Watching

Keep an eye out for whales while on the ferry over to the island. In August and September migrating humpback and sei whales can be seen leaping from the water near Taboga in spectacular displays.

Festivals & Events

Día de San Pedro FIESTA
(Jun 29) This holiday marks the founding of the town of San Pedro in 1524.

Festival de la Virgen del Carmen FIESTA
The island's patron, the Virgen del Carmen, is honored with a seafaring procession each year on July 16. Seemingly everyone then participates in games, fire-eating and/or dancing on the beach.

Sleeping

Hostal Zoraida's Cool GUESTHOUSE $
(6615-0977, 6471-1123; d US$40-50;) Overlooking the bay, this turquoise-and-yellow guesthouse run by affable Rafael has three small rooms – one looking to the sea, one in the center and one facing the hills; two of them have air-conditioning. The nicest feature is the hammock deck with Pacific views that's ideal for a snooze. There's a kitchen too.

To get here, turn left (south) as you exit the dock and walk for a few minutes until you see a sign leading you up the hill.

★ **Vereda Tropical Hotel** HOTEL $$
(250-2154; www.hotelveredatropical.com; d with fan/air-con incl breakfast US$65/80;) Atop a hill with commanding views, this pretty hotel charms with tropical tones, Mexican-style mosaic tiles, rod-iron railings and a caged parrot. Choose room 4 for its superb sea views. The dining patio (mains US$9 to US$18) also has sweeping views and music serenading from the speakers, but service can be a little slow.

The Vereda Tropical is about 100m up a winding path off the main road.

Cerrito Tropical B&B $$
(6489-0074, 390-8999; www.cerritotropicalpanama.com; d incl breakfast US$80, 2-person apt US$130;) This smart Canadian- and Dutch-owned B&B occupies a quiet spot atop a steep road. The three ground-floor rooms are stylish but small; go instead

for one of the three apartments with one or two bedrooms, kitchens and terrace with sea views. Management can arrange activities such as fishing, hiking and whale-watching.

Get here from the pier by taxi (US$1.50) or make the steep walk uphill at the end of Calle Francisco Pizarro.

Eating

Calaloo Fishbar & Grill SEAFOOD $
(6000-5172, 6489-0074; www.facebook.com/CalalooPanama; mains US$8-12; 8:30am-6pm Mon-Thu, to 8pm Fri-Sun;) This cute, colorful eatery above Playa Honda offers the standard fare of fish and chips in addition to veggie options. It's a great place to have a beer and watch the village hubbub. Service is notably slow, and crazy weekend crowds way outnumber the cooks. Just be patient. It's run by the folks from Cerrito Tropical B&B (p83).

★ **London's Pier Bar & Grill** SEAFOOD $$
(6456-0484; www.facebook.com/londonPBG; mains US$7-16; 8am-5pm Mon-Fri, to 9pm Sat & Sun) Our favorite new place for a bite and a sip, this English-owned seafront bar-restaurant with balcony seating serves excellent *ceviche, cazuela de mariscos* (seafood casserole) and cocktails. On Fridays, there's fish and chips for just US$8. Expect a very warm welcome.

Restaurante Playa Honda SEAFOOD $$
(6844-6308; www.facebook.com/Restaurante-Playa-Honda-Isla-de-Taboga-1559909694241428; mains US$12-17; 9am-4:30pm Mon-Fri, to 7:30pm Sat & Sun) The seafood is fresher than fresh, and you couldn't get any closer to the beach at the Restaurante Playa Honda. Bank-like opening hours here and elsewhere reflect the arrival and departure times of day-trippers. If spending the night, expect an early dinner. Go for the *pulpo al ajillo* (octopus in garlic sauce).

★ **La Vista** INTERNATIONAL $$$
(6767-9710, 6671-2028; www.lavistapty.com; mains US$16-32; noon-2pm & 6-10pm) Taking pride of place just below the **Villa Caprichosa** (6632-1725; www.villacaprichosa.com; r from US$130, poolside ste from US$350;), this top-notch eatery with an open kitchen is Isla Taboga's swankiest and priciest. Dining packages (US$150), including a six-course meal with wine, live music and boat transport to and from Panama City, are available Thursday to Saturday nights.

Information

There are no ATMS on the island, so bring sufficient cash with you.

For more information, visit the excellent English-language site www.taboga.panamanow.com, which is kept fairly up to date.

Getting There & Away

The scenic boat trip to Isla Taboga is part of the island's attraction. Ferries land at **Muelle de Taboga** (Taboga Pier), the pier near the northern end of the island. Schedules can change, so check online for updates. Note that the police check ferry passengers for drugs upon arrival. Make sure you bring your passport with you.

Barcos Calypso (314-1730; www.facebook.com/BarcosCalypso; one way/round-trip adult US$9/15, child US$6/10.50) ferries depart from Isla Naos on the Amador Causeway in Panama City. The easiest way to reach the dock is by taxi (US$7). Trips take 45 minutes and depart Panama City at the following times:

DAY	TIME
Mon-Thu	8:30am
Fri	8:30am, 3pm
Sat & Sun	8am, 10:30am, 4pm

Round-trip ferries from Isla Taboga:

DAY	TIME
Mon-Thu	4:30pm
Fri	9:30am, 4:30pm
Sat & Sun	9am, 3pm, 5pm

The faster **Taboga Express** (6234-8989, 6261-1740; www.tabogaexpress.com; one way/round trip adult US$10/20, child US$7/14;) catamaran makes the journey to and from the island in just 30 minutes. It leaves daily from the Brisas de Amador pier on Isla Perico on the Amador Causeway in Panama City at 8am, 9:30am, 11am and 3pm, with an additional departure at 4:30pm at the weekend. It returns from Isla Taboga at 8:45am, 10:15am, 2:30pm and 4pm, with an extra sailing at 5pm on Saturday and Sunday.

Getting Around

At the Taboga pier, **local taxis** (6579-4485) wait to take passengers to their hotels. Unless you enjoy walking up steep hills with luggage and finding your way through unmarked streets, it's well worth taking one.

Archipiélago de las Perlas

Named for the large black-lipped pearl oysters once abundant in its waters, the Archipiélago de las Perlas comprises 39 islands and more than 100 unnamed (and mostly uninhabited) islets, each surrounded by postcard-worthy white-sand beaches and turquoise waters. Home to the palatial mansions of the rich and powerful, Isla Contadora is the best known island (though Isla del Rey is by far the largest). Popular US TV show *Survivor* filmed three seasons (2003–05) on several islands in the chain and versions in other languages continue to film here.

Visitors mostly head to four islands: Isla Contadora, the most accessible, developed and touristed; Isla San José, the site of an exclusive resort; and neighboring Islas Casaya and Casayeta, frequented by shoppers in search of pearls. Uninhabited islets offer ample opportunity for independent exploration, especially if you have a sense of adventure and the help of a local guide.

History

Vasco Núñez de Balboa, within days of discovering the Pacific Ocean in 1513, learned from a local guide of nearby islands rich with pearls. Balboa was anxious to visit, but he was told that a hostile chief ruled them and cautiously decided to postpone the trip. Nonetheless, Balboa named the archipelago 'Islas de las Perlas,' and declared it and all its undiscovered riches the property of Spain. He vowed to return one day to kill the chief and claim his pearls for the king of Spain.

Before he could fulfill his vow, Spanish governor Pedro Arias de Ávila dispatched his cousin Gaspar de Morales to the islands for the pearls. Morales captured 20 chieftains and gave them to his dogs. The purportedly hostile chief, a man named Dites, saw the futility of resisting these conquistadors so instead presented Morales with a basket of large and lustrous pearls. With their greed unappeased, however, the Spanish took just two years to exterminate the indigenous population.

In 1517, the same year that Morales raided Las Perlas, Pedrarias (as the governor was often called) falsely charged Balboa with treason and had him and four of his closest friends beheaded.

In the years that followed, the Spaniards harvested the islands' oyster beds. Having slain the entire native population, they imported slaves from Africa to pearl-dive. Their descendants live on the islands today.

PIRATES IN THE BAY

From the late 17th century Golfo de Panamá (Panama Bay) was the scene of pirate exploits unsurpassed anywhere in the New World. It served as both hideout and springboard for attacks. After Captain Henry Morgan's successful sacking of Panama City in 1671, other buccaneers flooded in to pillage and plunder along the Pacific coast.

In May 1685 the largest number of fighters ever assembled under a buccaneer flag in the Pacific played cat and mouse with a Spanish armada of 18 ships. English captain Edward Blake's French and English pirate fleet was deficient in cannons but had plenty of muskets on board, so avoided long-range fighting. Despite inferior numbers, Blake itched for a close encounter with the Spaniards.

When the two great forces crossed paths on May 28, Blake ordered two of his principal ships to attack the Spanish fleet. Fearing the cannons, both refused to obey. The forces exchanged fire, but with the odds stacked against Blake he ordered the slower ships to flee while his ship and another fast vessel delayed the conquistadors.

The pirates managed some risky evasive maneuvers between rocky islets and anchored that night, expecting the Spanish armada to engage them the next day. Instead the Spanish fleet fled to Panamá. Soon dissent arose among the buccaneers, and the short-lived, French–English pirate confederacy dissolved.

Today almost the only evidence of pirates in the Archipiélago de las Perlas are distant descendants of the Spaniards and their slaves. Forests once felled to build ships have grown back. Storms, termites and woodworm have destroyed the old Spanish structures, though a church and a stone dam on Isla Taboga testify to the Spaniards' erstwhile presence.

Isla Contadora

POP 250

Isla Contadora (Counting House Island) was once the accounting center for pearls before they were shipped to Spain. In more recent times, multimillionaires have made the island their refuge; when ousted Shah Mohammed Reza Pahlavi fled Iran in 1979, he removed his large fortune to Isla Contadora. However, a government crackdown on tax evasion has been embittering the previously sweet deal. Many empty mansions are abandoned or rented to vacationers.

With frequent air and sea connections to Panama City, Isla Contadora is the only island in the archipelago with a developed tourist infrastructure. A prestigious destination, it caters to its wealthy residents and moneyed visitors from the mainland. In low season it's more accessible for all. Beaches are spectacular, the snorkeling is excellent and the island is a great jumping-off point for independent exploration of the archipelago.

Sights

Half of the island's 12 beaches are sand; the rest are rocky. Most are virtually abandoned except during major holidays. Five are particularly lovely: Playa Larga, Playa de las Suecas, Playa Cacique, Playa Ejecutiva and Playa Galeón. Although spread around the island, all can be visited in as little as 20 minutes in a rented ATV (all-terrain vehicle).

Playa Larga (Long Beach) occupies the longest stretch of sand on the island; the only eyesores are a beached ferry and an abandoned hotel behind it. Over the hill to the south and accessible via a well-worn path is **Playa de las Suecas** (Swedish Women's Beach), where you can sunbathe in the buff; it's Panama's only legal naturist beach. Continuing west for 400m, you'll find **Playa Cacique**, a fairly large and unvisited beach ideal for a little peace and quiet. On the northern side of the island, **Playa Ejecutiva** (Executive Beach) is another intimate escape – the large house on the bluff to the east is where the Shah of Iran once lived. **Playa Galeón** (Galleon Beach), to the northeast, is a good spot for snorkeling when the surf is small.

Activities

Snorkeling & Diving

The snorkeling and diving around Contadora is fantastic. In five nearby coral fields you can see schools of angelfish, damselfish, moray eels, parrot fish, puffer fish, butterfly fish, white-tip reef sharks and much more. Even off Playa Larga, the most popular of Isla Contadora's beaches, you can often spot sea turtles and manta rays. There is also a lot of marine life among the rocks in front of and east of Playa Roca.

The coral fields are located offshore from the eastern end of Playa de las Suecas; at Punta Verde, near the southern end of Playa Larga; at both ends of Playa Galeón; and at the western end of Playa Ejecutiva.

Coral Dreams DIVING

(☎6536-1776; www.coral-dreams.com; 2-tank dive US$120, snorkeling US$50; ⏰9am-5pm) This small PADI-certified outfit with experienced instructors is up the hill from Contadora Airport next to the Welcome Center (p88), but it doesn't always keep to its posted hours. Snorkeling tours go to Isla Mogo (Survivor Island). It also runs whale-watching trips (July to October; US$60) with a hydrophone to hear whale calls, and rents out snorkel equipment.

Whale-Watching

Migrating humpback whales can be seen from July to September. Fishers take tourists out on their boats (and you might see whales while out on another excursion), but it's worth going with a naturalist guide.

Whale Watching Panama WILDLIFE

(☎6758-7600; www.whalewatchingpanama.com; day trip adult/child US$160/130; ⏰Jul-Oct) To see humpback whales and dolphin pods in the Islas de Las Perlas, these day and multiday trips are led by expert biologist guides. Some trips have a spiritual focus (ie animal communication or shamanic whale-watching with yoga). The company adheres to international guidelines for whale-watching.

Sleeping

Most places to stay will meet you at the airport or Playa Galeón where the ferry moors and transfer you via golf cart to their resort or hotel.

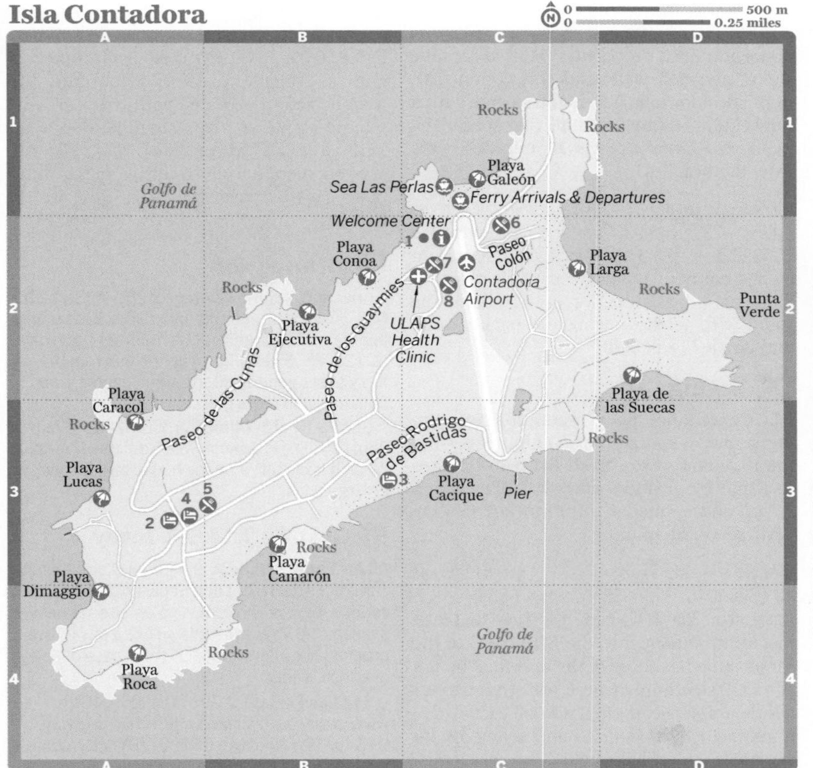

★ Gerald's B&B B&B **$$**
(☎6588-1046, 250-4159; www.island-contadora.com; d incl breakfast US$96-108; ❄📶🏊) With a good location near the ferry landing and an easy walk to Playa de las Suecas, Gerald's is central, clean and comfortable, with consistently good service. The nine rooms may lack views, but are large, modern and well equipped, with flat-screen TVs and air-con. The roof terrace with pool is delightful.

★ Mar y Oro HOTEL **$$**
(Hotel Playa Cacique; ☎6349-0528, 202-7426; www.facebook.com/maryorohotel; Playa Cacique; d garden/sea view incl breakfast from US$95/120, ste US$160; ❄📶) Overlooking lovely Playa Cacique, this delightful property caters for romantic escapes. If you want to be right on the beach, it's your best option. The 14 rooms – half with sea views – and suites have flat-screen TVs, lock boxes and mini-fridges; suites feature full kitchens. The stunning Bella Vista suite offers just that from its own large terrace.

Isla Contadora

Activities, Courses & Tours
1 Coral Dreams ... C2

Sleeping
Gerald's B&B ... (see 6)
2 La Romántica ... A3
3 Mar y Oro ... B3
4 Perla Real ... A3

Eating
5 Casa Tortuga ... B3
6 Gerald's Restaurant ... C2
7 Mini Market ... C2
8 Supermercado Contadora ... C2

Perla Real B&B **$$**
(☎6513-9064, 6982-0962; www.perlareal.com; d/tr/ste incl breakfast US$127/145/165; ❄📶) Looking more Santa Fé than tropical, this

comfortable inn is one of the island's best options. Eight spacious rooms have French doors and prim decor, with painted ceramic sinks, stenciled walls and soft cotton bedding. Ideal for long stays, suites come with a fully equipped kitchen and living space. The quiet residential area is 10 minutes' walk from the beaches.

La Romántica BOUTIQUE HOTEL **$$**
(☎250-4223, 6424-3000; karlpree@web.de; d US$95-125; ❄📶) This very stylish, Austrian-owned boutique hotel has just four rooms in a quiet residential section of the island. The room with terrace facing the back garden and jungle is a delight.

Eating

Isla Contadora's poor reputation for dining is due to sporadic food shipments from the mainland. Even fresh fish can be hard to come by. A **supermarket** (⏲8am-1pm & 2-7pm) and a smaller **mini market** (⏲7am-11pm) serve the island.

Gerald's Restaurant INTERNATIONAL **$$**
(☎6588-1046, 250-4159; mains US$8-24; ⏲7-10am, noon-3pm & 6-10pm; 📶) This thatched restaurant attached to the B&B (p87) of the same name has some of the best food on the island. It's certainly where you would go for a little ambience, though it's still casual. Options include good pizza and seafood with vegetable sides, all cooked by a friendly eponymous German.

★ **Casa Tortuga** ITALIAN **$$$**
(☎250-4061; 3-course set menu US$35, pizza US$12.50-25; ⏲7-9:30pm Wed-Sun) Touted as one of Contadora's best restaurants, this frenetic place decorated with street art with seating inside and in a small garden is the kind of place where your *spaghetti alle vongole* metamorphoses into a pizza, which takes ages to reach the table. Still, it's the real deal.

Information

A private **Welcome Center** (☎250-4081, 6278-0587; www.contadorapanama.com; boat tours per hour US$40, golf cart rentals per hour/day US$25/75; ⏲8am-5pm) up the hill from the ferry offers general information, handles tour bookings and rents golf carts.

ULAPS Health Clinic (☎250-4209; ⏲7am-3pm Mon-Fri) is a short walk from the airstrip. When it is closed, visit the house out the back for emergencies.

Getting There & Away

All **Air Panama** (☎316-9000; www.airpanama.com) flights arrive at and depart from tiny **Contadora Airport**, which has no on-site services available. Always schedule an extra day or two around your international flight in case of delays or cancellations.

Sea Las Perlas (☎391-1424, 209-4010; www.sealasperlas.com; adult/child one way US$49/39, round trip US$90/70) catamaran ferries depart daily from the Brisas de Amador pier on Isla Perico on the Amador Causeway in Panama City at 7:30am, returning from Isla

DON'T MISS

MAMALLENA ECOLODGE

Ever dreamed of creating your own private utopia but haven't got the time? Trek out to the mellow **Mamallena Ecolodge** (☎6673-0752, 6379-8267; http://mamallenaecolodge.com; Camino a la Laguna; dm/d without bathroom US$11/39, 2-person cabins with/without bathroom US$55/44, all incl breakfast; 📶) 🌿, where folks are living off the land, making kombucha health drinks and spreading general good will. Get your kicks hiking around and swimming in a pleasing river pool. Lodgings are in a comfortable Swiss-style home and riverfront cabins, all in a stunning highland setting. In total there are seven rooms plus a dorm sleeping eight.

For sustainable living, this is the real deal. The owners recycle and use organic permaculture to revitalize once-abandoned fruit orchards on the sprawling 174-hectare farm. Guests can cook for themselves or sign up for good-value shared dinners with vegetarian and fish (US$7.50/10) options. Pancake breakfasts are included. For a cooked breakfast, add US$4.50. There's a full bar too.

Mamallena Ecolodge is a 1½-hour drive from Panama City and 30 minutes from El Valle in Coclé Province via a direct new road obviating the need to return to the Interamericana. From Panama City, coordinate a transfer or bus to Coronado where you can catch the La Laguna *collectivo* (US$3, 45 minutes), which will drop you off at the lodge.

Contadora at 3:30pm; arrive for check-in, with ticket and passport, 45 minutes ahead of departure. The journey takes 1½ hours. Oddly there is no pier on Isla Contadora; passengers are decanted from the ferry into smaller boats, from where they disembark on **Playa Galeón**.

Getting Around

Because the island is not even 1.5 sq km in size, it's easy to walk everywhere, but it is hilly; a golf-cart taxi will take you where you need to go for US$5. Most tourist facilities are at the northern end of the island, within walking distance of the airstrip and Playa Galeón; hotels shuttle guests to and from those locations for free via golf cart. Golf carts and ATVs can be rented at hotels for getting around the island.

Isla San José

Home to the most exclusive resort in the Pearl Islands, Isla San José has a sinister history as a US chemical-weapons testing ground. During a 2001 inspection, the entire island was placed under temporary quarantine following the recovery of unexploded ordnance, which led to a tiff between Panama and the USA over who should pick up the cleaning bill.

Most of the 44-sq-km island is covered in a bank of rainforest networked by all-weather roads installed by the US military decades ago. Beyond the roads, the only development on the island is the cliffside resort.

Sleeping

Hacienda del Mar LUXURY HOTEL **$$$**
(832-5439, Panama City 269-6634; www.haciendadelmar.net; cabins from US$375;) Isla San José has 57 tan-sand beaches, nine year-round rivers and seven accessible waterfalls – and Hacienda del Mar has them all to itself. Its 17 stand-alone luxury cabins overflow with amenities and offer views to a picture-perfect sweep of beach. Plunge into the lengthy list of tours or just soak up your exclusive slice of paradise.

Getting There & Away

Flights between Panama City and Isla San José (US$140 round trip) are arranged through Hacienda del Mar. Departures are at 8:30am Monday to Saturday with an additional flight at 4:30pm on Friday and Saturday. The daily return flight leaves Isla San José at 9:25am. Allow a few days between your visit and international flights, as there can be weather delays.

WORTH A TRIP

QUESOS CHELA

The nondescript town of Campana, located 65km from Panama City, is home to the famous **Quesos Chela** (248-5983, 248-5457; Interamericana; snacks $1-3, cheese US$3.50-6; 7:30am-9pm), an institution that few Panamanian drivers can pass by without stopping in. It's a simple shop that usually sells fresh cheese (string, mozzarella, farmers, ricotta) and homemade meat and fruit *empanadas* (turnovers).

The cheese shop is right next door to a large parking lot on the right-hand side of the road, if you're heading west from Panama City.

Islas Casaya & Casayeta

Oysters are still harvested throughout the Archipiélago de las Perlas, and their pearls are just as legendary as they were when Spanish explorer Vasco Núñez de Balboa first arrived in the early 16th century. Although pearls are sometimes offered for sale on other islands, the best places to shop for them are Isla Casaya and neighboring Isla Casayeta, which lie about 12km to the south of Isla Contadora.

When you're looking at pearls, you should know that pearl sellers tend to keep their goods in oil, so that they'll have a lovely shine when presented – always dry the pearl that intrigues you before you buy. Prices are generally very reasonable, and there's always room for bargaining.

As tourist infrastructure is minimal here, eating options are better on nearby Isla Contadora.

PACIFIC COAST

La Chorrera

POP 198,600

One of the first major towns you hit along the Interamericana heading west from Panama City, La Chorrera is famous throughout Panama for its *chicheme* (a sweet nonalcoholic drink made from milk, mashed corn, cinnamon and vanilla). It's not really worth a stop, though.

Festivals & Events

Feria de La Chorrera FERIA

This annual fair, held over 10 days from late January into early February, includes parades, a rodeo, the odd cockfight and drum dances, which have their origin in African music brought to the New World by slaves.

Eating

El Chichemito PANAMANIAN $

(Calle Eusebio Marades; chicheme drinks US$0.50-1.25; 6am-10pm) Join what looks like a Friday bank line at El Chichemito to sample the homemade *chicheme*. It goes nicely with *bollos chorrenanos* (tamales filled with marinated chicken and spice; US$1.35).

Getting There & Away

East- and west-bound buses stop at the gas station on the Interamericana. Buses for Panama City (US$2, one hour) leave every 15 minutes; take the express to avoid frequent stops.

Parque Nacional Altos de Campana

This relatively unknown national park, the first in Panama when it was created in 1966, is a favorite of birdwatchers. Common sightings include the scale-crested pygmy-tyrant, orange-bellied trogon and chestnut-capped brush-finch; rarer birds, including the slaty antwren, the white-tipped sicklebill and the purplish-backed quail-dove, are occasionally spotted here.

The 49-sq-km park is best viewed on foot and requires at least several hours to appreciate fully. Starting at the road's end, beyond the microwave tower, trails will take you into some lovely forest, which is on the much greener Atlantic slope. Nowhere else is the difference between the deforested Pacific and the lush Atlantic sides more evident than here.

Visitors can camp by the ranger station. There's access to water but no other facilities here.

Information

Pay camping fees at the **ranger station** (254-2848; www.miambiente.gob.pa; campsite per night US$5) at the entrance to the park.

Getting There & Away

The park is 77km – a drive of 1½ hours – from Panama City. To reach the park it's best to go with your own vehicle or contract a guide. Buses along the Interamericana can drop you at the turnoff, but it's a very long hike into the park.

The easy-to-miss turnoff is about 25km southwest of La Chorrera, on the western side of the Interamericana, at the top of a steep and windy section known locally as the Loma Campana. From the turnoff, a rocky road winds 4.6km to the ranger station at the entrance to the park, which is located on Cerro Campana (1007m).

Punta Chame

POP 450

Just before the Interamericana reaches the coastline, a turnoff immediately east of the town of Bejuco leads to the tiny sliver of peninsula known as Punta Chame. The 28km-long road out to the sea winds past rolling hills before opening up to flat land that consists mainly of shrimp farms and mangroves. The brackish water makes farming near impossible, though the environment here is unique to this region, and well worth a detour.

Punta Chame is receiving more vacation homes and weekenders since the single road in to the long, 300m-wide peninsula was paved. To the north of the peninsula, a scenic but muddy bay is popular with windsurfers and kitesurfers from December to April, during the trade-wind season. Outside of those months wakeboarding and stand-up paddling takes over.

Sights

Playa Chame BEACH

The beach on the southern side of the peninsula has lovely tan sand and a wilderness backdrop. The area is notorious for stingrays, though, so swim with caution and shuffle your feet while walking out.

Sleeping

★**Hostal Casa Amarilla** B&B $$

(345-3679, 6138-6738; www.hostalcasaamarilla.com; d US$75-115, s/d cabins without bathroom US$25/35; late Oct-late Apr;) Guests adore the 'Yellow House,' a French-run B&B with manicured gardens and a sparkling pool. The 10 rooms in two buildings vary in size and style; the three cute yellow cabins share immaculate bathrooms and outside showers. There's also a pool table and hammocks. Enjoy exquisite Mediterranean cuisine in an open-air restaurant (two-course meals US$17) that draws people from outside.

Nitro City RESORT **$$$**
(202-6875; www.nitrocityresort.com; d/ste incl breakfast from US$130/220;) The world's first 'action sports resort' when it opened in 2010, Nitro City comes alive on weekends. It's pretty much what you'd expect in a beach haven bankrolled by energy drinks and Corona beer. The 36 rooms have sleek decor, which has begun to look a bit tired, while suites have outdoor hot tubs. On weekdays, prices fall by half.

The real draw is a circus of adrenaline-pumping offerings also open to day-trippers (adult/child day passes US$30/20), ranging from a skate park to mountain and motorbike courses, wakeboarding, stand-up paddleboarding and kitesurfing (lessons available). The tamer offerings include a soccer field, games and video rooms, as well as a stunning pool complete with island bar. Hyperactive teens do well here, and young Panama City weekenders don't seem to mind the US$17 burgers with a backing track of live Rasta-rock.

Getting There & Away

From Panama City, take any bus heading south on the Interamericana to the Plaza Imperial shopping center in Bejuco (US$3, 1½ hours), slightly past the crossroads. From here, buses to Punta Chame (US$1.25) leave hourly between 6am and 6pm daily.

Taxis from Panama City cost anywhere between US$70 and US$120.

Pacific Coast Beaches

Starting at the town of Chame and continuing along the Pacific coast for the next 40km or so are dozens of beautiful beaches that are popular weekend retreats for Panama City residents. About half of these beaches are in Panamá Province, while the remainder – and the far superior beaches – are in Coclé Province.

Nueva Gorgona

This small oceanside community fronts a curving beach of mostly black sand. Bring your sandals – the beach gets very hot.

SURFING IN PANAMÁ PROVINCE

The beaches to the southwest of Panama City are a popular destination for Panamanian surfers, especially since they're easy to access and offer relatively consistent surf year-round. The following list will help you get started, though don't be afraid to ask local surfers to let you in on their hidden spots.

Playa Malibú Near Gorgona. Sand-bottom right and left break. Best during medium to low tide. Consistent, good tubes and long rides when there is a strong swell.

Frente de Teta Rock- and sand-bottom break at the mouth of the Río Teta. Long lefts at low tide, and rights and lefts at medium to high tide.

Punta Teta Point break over rocks to the south of the Río Teta river mouth. Lefts and rights with good tubes, especially at medium tide going up.

Rinconcito Rock-bottom point south of Punta Teta with a long, right break on a good swell. Named after California's famous Rincón break.

Frente Palmar South of San Carlos. Beach break, partial rock bottom that is popular with beginners.

Punta Palmar South of San Carlos. Rock-bottom point break. Right peeling waves at medium to high tide when there is a good swell.

Hawaiisito South of San Carlos. Rock-bottom point break. Lefts at full high tide. Closes out if there is a strong swell.

Frente Río Mar Somewhat rocky beach break in front of Río Mar. Rights and lefts at medium to high tide.

Punta Río Mar South of the Río Mar, near jutting rocks. Walk and paddle at low tide. Rights best. Breaks only at low tide.

Pacific Coast Beaches

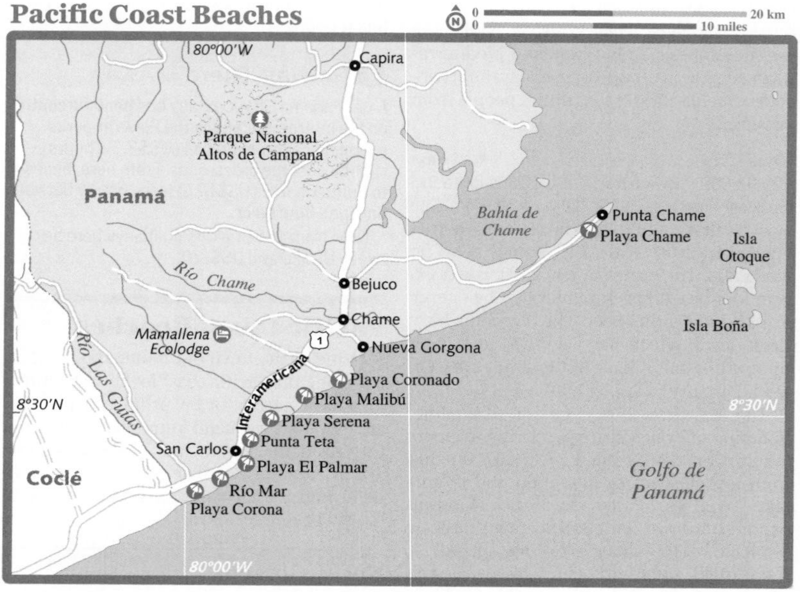

For a leisurely bite, **La Ruina** (☎6527-8462; www.facebook.com/laruina.gorgona; mains US$5-16; ⊙noon-midnight Thu-Sun) serves stem glasses of *ceviche* (citrus-cured seafood) and authentic chicken curries accompanied by coconut rice *bocatoreño*-style. Sit outside at the leatherette booths and pass the time by chatting with the owner or tapping along to the country tunes. There's a pool (US$5) should you feel the need to cool off.

Getting There & Away

Best accessed by car, Gorgona is 85km from Panama City via the Interamericana. The turnoff is 5km south of the exit for the Punta Chame road.

Playa Coronado

International retirees flock to this affluent gated beachside community, which is also a haven for water-sports lovers. A sprawling mall, US chain restaurants and a hospital confirms its growing status among retired gringos. The salt-and-pepper beach here is one of the most developed strips of sand along the coast and is also extremely popular with well-heeled Panama City residents.

Sleeping & Eating

El Litoral B&B B&B $$
(☎6658-1143; www.litoralpanama.com; d incl breakfast from US$95; ❄@🛜🏊) El Litoral B&B is a cute red-and-yellow house with four smart air-conditioned rooms (best is the corner Delicious room). The kicker is a sumptuous patio breakfast with choices such as cappuccino, crêpes, waffles and juice. The lovely French-speaking owners offer yoga and Pilates sessions as well as massage at the on-site holistic center. They rent bikes as well.

Coronado Golf & Beach Resort RESORT $$$
(☎240-4444; www.coronadohotelpanama.com; Av Punta Prieta; d from US$208; P❄@🏊) If you're keen to live it up in unchecked luxury, look no further than the Coronado Golf & Beach Resort. With 105 amenity-laden rooms, a top-notch beachside golf course, swimming pools, tennis courts, day spa, gym and a whole slew of bars and restaurants, you may not actually be able to find the time to visit its own private beach.

El Rincón del Chef INTERNATIONAL $$
(☎6676-4834, 345-2072; cheffernando@elrincondelchefpanama.com; mains US$9-17; ⊙noon-9pm Tue-Fri, from 9am Sat & Sun) A good bet for lunch (set lunch US$6, sandwiches from

US$8) and dinner, the 'Chef's Corner' serves grilled meats, pastas and Panamanian classics. It's located 300m from the Interamericana on the right (south) side.

Getting There & Away

The turnoff for Playa Coronado is 85km from Panama City and 3km south of the turnoff for Gorgona. Access is easiest by private vehicle.

Buses to and from Panama City (US$3.25, 1½ hours) run along the Interamericana, stopping at the turnoff; look for taxis at the intersection to take you into town.

Playa El Palmar

The lovely, white-sand beach of Playa El Palmar lies 14km southwest of Playa Coronado, near the village of San Carlos. Although much less developed than Coronado, El Palmar is popular with weekending families from the capital, but the atmosphere remains low-key.

Run by a well-known local surfer, **Panama Surf School** (6673-0820; www.panamasurfschool.com; Calle 4ta Sur s/n; 1½hr lessons US$40) gives group and private (US$10 extra) lessons, and also rents stand-up paddleboards and bodyboards (per hour/day US$10/20).

Sleeping & Eating

★ Manglar Lodge INN $$
(345-4014; www.manglarlodge.com; d US$88-99;) The area's most stylish digs, Manglar Lodge is professionally run by surfer Ivan, who can also share tips. Outdoor showers will help you rinse off the sand. Manglar has pleasant manicured grounds, a good on-site restaurant serving burgers (US$8.50 to US$12.50) and craft beer, and four good-sized rooms with contemporary styles. Rooms 3 and 4 have windows on two sides.

Palmar Surf Camp HOTEL $$
(240-8004; www.palmarsurfschool.com; campsite per person US$10, d/q US$60/80;) The wave-front Palmar Surf Camp is aimed at surfers or those who want to learn the ropes. Motel-style rooms feature cool murals, cable TV and free coffee. Campers can stake their tents under a thatched roof. Check for midweek discounts. An open-air restaurant serves simple preparations of fresh seafood. Three-hour surf lessons are US$40; an intensive five-lesson package is US$175.

★ Carlitos INTERNATIONAL $
(240-8526; www.carlitospizzas.com; Interamericana; mains US$9-14, pizza US$7-12; 11am-8pm Mon, Tue & Thu, to 9pm Fri-Sun) On the Interamericana opposite the turnoff for Playa El Palmar, Carlitos cooks delicious Argentine-style *empanadas* (turnovers stuffed with meat, cheese or veggie mixes) as well as more elaborate main courses and thin-crust pizzas with a great selection of toppings (whole-wheat crust also available). A very friendly destination.

Getting There & Away

The turnoff for El Palmar is 96km from Panama City and 10km from the turnoff for Playa Coronado along the Interamericana. Buses (US$3.50, 1½ hours) stop at the turnoff, from where the beach is a US$3 taxi ride.

Río Mar

Río Mar is a small, rocky inlet where a few high-rises cast a shadow. If you're a surfer, you've reached near-heaven. Otherwise, you might opt to visit some of the other Pacific beach communities instead.

A right turn on the road in from the Interamericana, **Hotel Rio Mar** (345-4010, 6212-0707; http://panamasurfing.academy; d/q US$60/90;) offers seven bargain-rate rooms that are pleasant and sit on immaculate green grounds with a pea-sized pool. There are basic offerings from the on-site restaurant. The attached surfing academy offers surf lessons and rents boards. Two-hour lessons cost US$45.

Getting There & Away

Río Mar is five minutes along the road from Playa El Palmar. Frequent buses along the Interamericana head northeast to Panama City (US$3.50, 1½ hours) and southwest up the coast. It's a 15-minute walk from the Interamericana to the surf academy at Hotel Río Mar.

Coclé Province

POP 261,310 / ELEV SEA LEVEL TO 1626M

Includes ➡

Best Places to Eat

- La Casa de Lourdes (p102)
- Pipa's Beach Restaurant (p105)
- Xoko (p103)
- Da Vinci Deli Pastas Gourmet (p102)
- La Fogata (p105)

Best Places to Stay

- Park Eden (p100)
- Villa Távida Lodge (p109)
- Togo Bed & Breakfast (p104)
- Cabañas Potosí (p100)
- La Casa de Lourdes (p101)
- La Pintada Inn (p108)

Why Go?

Coclé is known to Panamanians as the land of salt, sugar and presidents. More salt has been reclaimed from the sea, more sugar refined and more Panamanian presidents born here than in any other province. These facts are the source of great civic pride, but Coclé offers a lot more than table condiments and political legacies.

Coclé boasts a wide variety of landscapes, from all-but-abandoned coastline to towering cloud forests, with vast agricultural land in between. With its southern side stretching along the Pacific Ocean for upwards of 100km, the province claims some of the country's most beautiful beaches, which are a magnet at the weekend for day-trippers from nearby Panama City. Up in the highlands, the magnificently situated mountain town of El Valle is another popular retreat. And shoppers take note: the sprawling provincial capital of Penonomé is the best place to pick up a 'real' Panama hat.

When to Go

Dec–Apr High season on the Pacific coast is a party scene,with Panamanians arriving in droves after Christmas. A wild pre-Lenten carnival takes place around Mardi Gras (February or March) in Penonomé.

Jul–Oct Rain means muddy trails but highland waterfalls are in full flow. It's the only season to see Panama's national flower, the ghost orchid, in bloom.

Oct–Dec Bring on the noise: the city of Antón's rowdy Toro Guapo festival in October is followed by at least four days of *fiestas patrias* (national holidays) in November and celebrations of Penonomé's patron in early December.

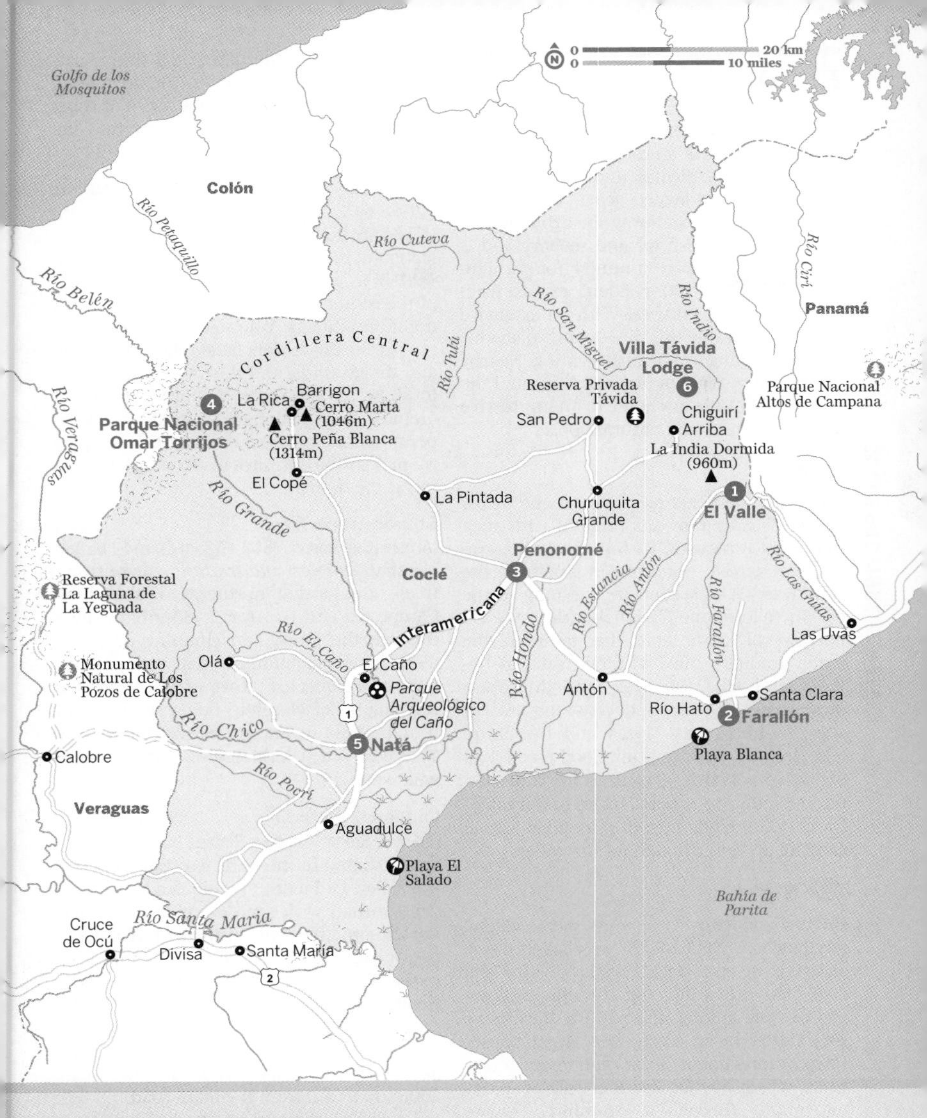

Coclé Province Highlights

❶ **El Valle** (p96) Climbing up to waterfalls, calling on the uber-rare golden frog and browsing the handicrafts market in this lovely town.

❷ **Farallón** (p104) Feasting by the sea on fresh fish with *patacones* (fried plantains) and strolling along the endless sands around this beach town.

❸ **Penonomé** (p106) Shopping for an authentic Panama hat or getting caught up in the madness of one of the regional capital's festivals.

❹ **Parque Nacional Omar Torrijos** (p109) Hiking in dense rainforest and camping in utter solitude in this lesser-known national park.

❺ **Natá** (p110) Enjoying this historic town's tranquility and visiting the splendid altar carvings at Panama's oldest church.

❻ **Villa Távida Lodge** (p109) Observing wildlife from one of Panama's most beautiful mountain lodges and pampering yourself at its spa.

El Valle

POP 7600

Officially known as El Valle de Antón, this picturesque town is nestled in the crater of a huge extinct volcano, and ringed by verdant forests and jagged peaks. El Valle is a popular weekend getaway for urban dwellers in need of fresh air and scenery and is also a retirement community for foreigners, with some 200 resident expats from more than 40 countries. With an extensive network of trails, this is a superb place for walking, hiking or horseback riding. Nearby forests offer excellent birdwatching, and the valleys of El Valle are home to an impressive set of waterfalls and natural pools.

History

Three million years ago, the volcano below where El Valle now sits erupted with such force that it blew off its top, creating a crater 6km across – one of the largest in the Americas. (It is second in size only to the one in Yellowstone National Park in the US northwest.) In the eons that followed, the crater gradually filled with rainwater to create a large lake. However, through erosion or collapse, a breach opened at the present site of Chorro Las Mozas and the entire lake drained. The resulting flood created an extensive network of waterways, which attracted indigenous populations to the valley. Early petroglyphs attesting to their arrival can still be seen throughout the valley.

Sights

Butterfly Haven WILDLIFE RESERVE

(Mariposario; 6062-3131; www.butterflyhavenpanama.com; adult/child US$5/1.50; 9:30am-4pm) One of El Valle's top attractions allows you to walk among up to 250 butterflies as they flutter by in a screened 'flight house.' Learn more about these ephemeral creatures, which live for just a couple of weeks maximum, through a 15-minute video, life-cycle exhibits and a rearing lab, where you'll see lepidoptera in various stages of development.

Chorro El Macho WATERFALL

(Male Waterfall; adult/child US$5/2.50; 8am-5pm) The most famous waterfall in the El Valle region is 35m-high Chorro El Macho, one of four cascades located about 2km north of town; it's a 15-minute walk from the road and the entrance to the Canopy Adventure tour. Below the falls you'll find a natural swimming pool (US$2.50) surrounded by rainforest. There is also a series of short hiking trails that wend their way into the surrounding jungle.

Aprovaca GARDENS

(983-6472; www.aprovaca.com; adult/child US$2/1; 8:30am-4:30pm) For the largest selection of *orquídeas* (orchids) in the region, visit this idyllic, not-for-profit garden east of the center, run by the local association of orchid producers. Volunteers work to maintain the lovely flowers inside the greenhouse and the grounds, and they welcome visitors to show off the more than 100 species of orchids cultivated here. Orchids are temperamental bloomers; check out the display room near the entrance to see what's flowering at the moment.

Square-Trunk Trees FOREST

(Árboles Cuadrados; US$2; 8am-5pm) El Valle's peculiar *árboles cuadrados* (square-trunk trees) are located northeast of the Hotel Campestre (p101). After a 30-minute hike through the forest and climbing over two footbridges (including a scary suspension one), you'll reach a grove of trees that are certainly a lot closer to being square than round. These geometric formations are the source of much local pride; make of them what you will.

La Piedra Pintada ARCHAEOLOGICAL SITE

(Painted Stone; Calle La Pintada; US$3; 8am-4pm) Located in the northwestern corner of the valley, La Piedra Pintada is a huge boulder adorned with pre-Columbian carvings. Locals sometimes fill in the grooves of the petroglyphs with chalk to make them easier to see. The meaning of the petroglyphs isn't clear; some think it is an early map of the area. That doesn't prevent children from giving their interpretation of the petroglyphs for US$2 in Spanish. The stone is about 300m up a trail from the main road.

La Piedra Pintada can be reached by a colorful bus with 'Pintada' above the windshield. It passes along Av Central every 30 minutes or so from 6am to 6pm (US$0.25 one way).

Chorro Las Mozas WATERFALL

(Young Girls Waterfall; adult/child US$1/0.50; 10am-4pm Mon-Fri, 8am-5pm Sat & Sun) The most accessible of the waterfalls around El Valle is Chorro Las Mozas, located about 2km southwest of town; you can reach it on foot from the center in about half an hour. This is the original site where the prehistoric lake breached its banks to form the area's scenic cascades and deep pools. It's popular with locals enjoying El Valle's year-round, near-perfect spring weather.

Museo Histórico Padre José Noto MUSEUM
(Museo de El Valle de Antón; ☎6415-7019, 6592-5577; Av Central; US$2; ⏲8am-4pm Thu-Sun) The most interesting exhibits in this small, very central museum divided into seven sections are the ones focusing on petroglyphs and ceramics produced by indigenous peoples who lived in the area hundreds of years ago. There is also some religious art – the museum is run by the Iglesia de San José (Church of St Joseph) next door – as well as historical and geological information on El Valle's extinct volcano.

Activities

Canopy Adventure ADVENTURE SPORTS
(☎264-5720, 6613-7220; www.canopytower.com/canopy-adventure; canopy rides 1/4 lines US$20/75; ⏲8am-4pm) Canopy Adventure uses cable ziplines to send harnessed riders whizzing through the rainforest high above the jungle floor. You'll ride from one platform to another (there are four lines in all), at times gliding over 35m-high waterfall Chorro El Macho.

Pozos Termales El Valle HOT SPRINGS
(☎6621-3846; Calle Los Pozos; adult/child US$4/2; ⏲8am-4:30pm) This thermal bath complex features three pools of varying temperatures – up to 38°C, or 100.4°F – the waters of which have alleged curative properties. Post-soak, you can have a massage or apply healing mud to your skin from buckets. The baths are a 10-minute walk southwest of the center at the end of Calle Los Pozos, near Río Antón.

Alquiler de Caballo HORSEBACK RIDING
(Horse Rentals; ☎6646-5813; Calle El Hato; per hr US$15; ⏲8am-6pm) This stable northeast of the center of town rents out two dozen horses, which provide an excellent way to explore the nearby mountains. Guides speak limited English only. Call ahead for free transportation from your hotel.

Hiking

Surrounded by humid cloud forest and peaks that rise more than 1000m, El Valle is a hiker's paradise. From the town center, an extensive network of trails radiates out into the valley and up the hills, and there are possibilities for anything from short day hikes to excursions of several days.

Serious trekkers should consider excursions to the tops of Cerro Cara Coral, Cerro Gaital and Cerro Pajita to the north, Cerro Guacamayo to the south and Cerro Tagua to the east. For the most part, the valley floor has been cleared for human habitation while the peaks remain covered in dense forest. For these hikes you will require a guide as trails are not well marked and cloud cover can descend quickly.

On a clear day it's possible to make an ascent to the top of **La India Dormida** (The

GOLDEN FROG REFUGE

A symbol of good fortune since pre-Columbian times, the golden frog *(Atelopus zeteki)*, or *rana dorada* in Spanish, is also a symbol of Panama's incredibly varied wildlife. Unfortunately in the 1990s, a deadly fungus called chytridiomycosis began decimating these uniquely colored toads. The problem was not just local – the fungus soon reached epidemic levels on five continents, killing frogs, toads and salamanders too.

The chytrid fungus, which infects amphibians' skin cells, kills more than 90% of the creatures that it comes into contact with. Though such a percentage would appear to be insurmountable, scientists have found that, while it cannot be prevented in the wild, the fungus is effectively treated in captivity.

In 2006, with support from the Houston Zoo, El Valle's **Panama Amphibian Rescue & Conservation Project Center** (EVACC; ☎983-6142, 212-8222; http://amphibianrescue.org; ⏲9am-5pm Wed-Mon) set about collecting all the golden frogs they could find in the El Valle area in order to protect those that weren't already infected with chytridiomycosis. It also treated the ones in captivity. At one stage, while the conservation center was being built, a room at the Hotel Campestre was used to house the frogs. It was the biggest amphibian rescue mission in history and helped to bring the golden frog back from the brink of extinction.

El Valle

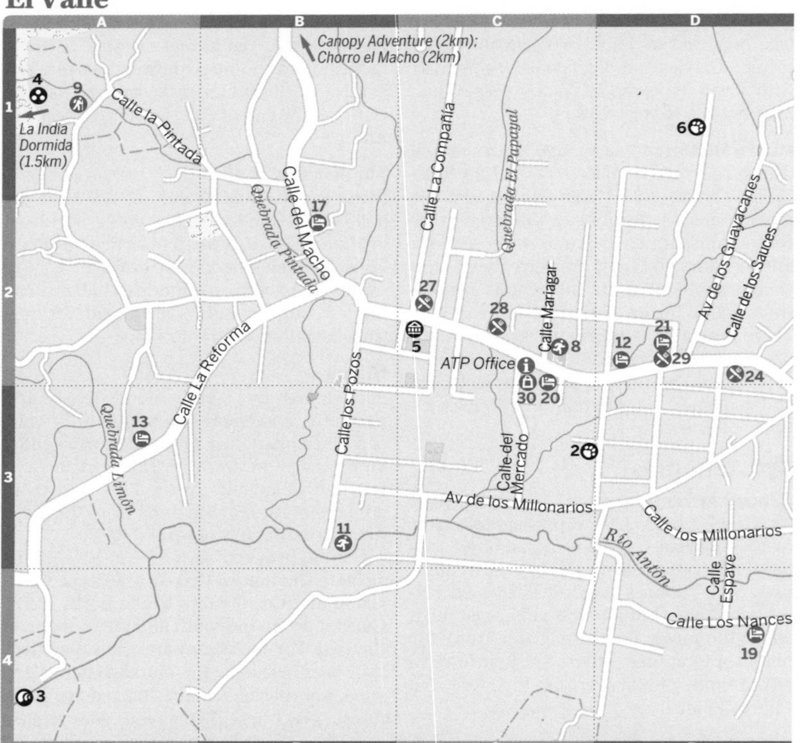

El Valle

Sights
1 Aprovaca.....E3
2 Butterfly Haven.....C3
3 Chorro Las Mozas.....A4
4 La Piedra Pintada.....A1
5 Museo Histórico Padre José Noto.....C2
6 Panama Amphibian Rescue & Conservation Project Center.....D1

Activities, Courses & Tours
7 Alquiler de Caballo.....F2
8 El Valle Mountain Tours.....C2
9 La India Dormida.....A1
10 Panama Explorer Tours.....F3
11 Pozos Termales El Valle.....B3

Sleeping
12 Bodhi Hostel.....D2
13 Cabañas Potosí.....A3
Crater Valley Boutique Hotel.....(see 10)
14 Golden Frog Inn.....F1
Hostal Orquídea.....(see 1)
15 Hotel Campestre.....F1
16 Hotel Valle Verde.....E2
17 La Casa de Juan.....B2
La Casa de Lourdes.....(see 25)
18 Los Mandarinos Boutique Spa & Hotel.....E1
19 Park Eden.....D4
20 Residencial El Valle.....C2
21 Windmill Hostel.....D2

Eating
22 Da Vinci Deli Pastas Gourmet.....E3
23 Don Quijote.....E2
24 El Valle Gourmet & Coffee Shop.....D2
25 La Casa de Lourdes.....E1
26 L'Italiano.....E3
27 Restaurante Bruschetta.....C2
28 Restaurante Massiel.....C2
Restaurante Valle Verde.....(see 16)
29 Restaurante Zapote.....D2

Shopping
30 Mercado Artesanal.....C2

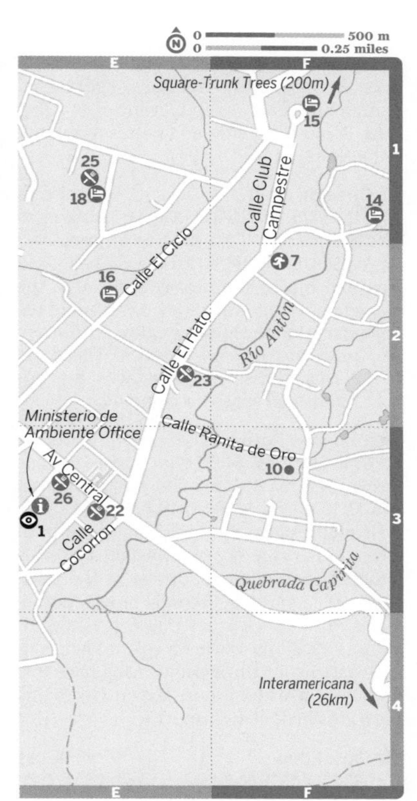

Sleeping Indian) on your own; there are well-defined, safe trails here. The most direct route is to follow the path up past La Piedra Pintada (p96), staying close to the stream till you reach the top. If the weather looks variable, hire a guide – or at least seek out local advice – before hitting the trails.

According to local mythology, the 'Sleeping Indian' was a local maiden who fell in love with a conquistador. When her father refused to allow their marriage, she took her own life. She was buried in the hills, with the mountains taking on her shape as they rise over the valley; the outline of her forehead, nose, chin and breast is easily discernible. Legend has it that she is awaiting the day when her forbidden lover can claim her.

Birdwatching

The forests around El Valle offer numerous opportunities for birdwatching, with some 339 (at last count) species spotted. The area is especially rich in hummingbirds – commonly spotted species include the green hermit, the violet-headed hummingbird and the white-tailed emerald.

Rates for a bilingual naturalist guide are around US$60 per person per day.

Tours

Manakin Adventures Panama WILDLIFE
(☎908-9621, 6384-4466; www.manakinadventures.com; 6hr tour from US$100) Juan José Calvache, one of the finest naturalist guides in Panama, will show you El Valle and surrounds like few others can, with jungle trekking, birdwatching and (his specialty) butterfly photo safaris. Juan José knows the Parque Nacional Omar Torrijos like the back of his hand.

El Valle Mountain Tours ADVENTURE SPORTS
(☎908-7344, 6863-6670; http://elvallemountaintours.com; waterfall tour US$90-110, ride-and-hike tours US$35-60; ⏰8:30am-3:30pm) This agency in the Pekin Plaza shopping center offers tours of three to four hours of the Slot Canyon and Reserva Privada Távida waterfalls, as well as shorter ride-and-hike trips of about an hour and a half. Prices depend on the number of participants.

Mario Bernal BIRDWATCHING
(☎6494-9987; mariobernalg@gmail.com; birdwatching half/full day US$65/100) Mario is an English- and Spanish-speaking birdwatching guide from El Valle who has a very high reputation internationally.

Mario Urriola WILDLIFE
(☎6568-7499, 6569-2676; serpentariomaravillastropicales@hotmail.com) Mario is a reputable, locally based naturalist guide specializing in wildlife-watching, especially reptiles and birds.

Panama Explorer Tours ADVENTURE
(☎6697-0583; www.panamaexplorertours.com; Crater Valley Boutique Hotel, Calle Ranita de Oro) Panama Explorer Tours is an adventure-tourism outfit that offers a wide range of activities. Tours include hiking La India Dormida (p97; US$25, three to four hours) and mountain-biking (from US$25 per hour); prices are per person. There's also a kid-friendly ropes course (from US$40).

Sleeping

Although reservations are generally not necessary, note that El Valle can get busy on weekends and national holidays as urban dwellers head for the hills.

Windmill Hostel HOSTEL $
(☎6344-1199; https://en-gb.facebook.com/windmillhostel/; Av de los Guyacanes; campsite US$10, dm from US$16.50, d with/without bathroom US$66/44;) A welcome addition, this American-run hostelry has 25 rooms in two buildings spread over a large grassy tract of land backed by a stream. Two dormitories have 12 beds each; the one with air-conditioning costs US$22.50. Larger doubles such as No 22 (US$88) include a separate kitchen, though there's a large common kitchen and outdoor barbecue area.

Bodhi Hostel HOSTEL $
(☎6429-4143; http://bodhihostels.com; Av Central; dm/d incl breakfast US$15/40;) Looking a bit worn around the edges but still voted tops in Panama, this central hostel counts six private rooms with shared showers, and a massive, bright and airy dorm with 27 beds in triple-deck bunks. Dorms are curtained and have lockers; the artwork is by volunteers. The Buddha theme, bafflingly prevalent in Panama, is present here.

The Shisha loft lounge above the lobby is full of books and is very cool, as is the 'tree' of Polaroids, which features everyone who's ever stayed at the hostel. Bicycle rentals are available for US$2/8/12 per hour/half day/full day.

Hostal Orquídea HOSTEL $
(☎983-6472; http://aprovaca.com/l_en/hostal.php; dm US$13, s/d from US$27/33;) How often do you get to spend the night in an orchid garden? This rather simple hostel, with two private rooms for up to four people and another two with between four and seven beds, is on the edge of the Aprovaca (p96) orchid garden and a stay overnight includes a free tour. Rooms have fans and there's a communal kitchen.

La Casa de Juan GUESTHOUSE $
(☎6453-9775, 6502-2970; www.lacasadejuanpanama.blogspot.com; Calle del Macho; campsites/dm/d US$8/10/35;) Now in a new location and run by the next generation of the same family, this scaled-down version of the legendary 'John's House' is aglow with street art, mini-mirrors and mosaics. There are two dorms with six and nine beds, five private rooms and space for camping.

★ **Cabañas Potosí** CABIN $$
(☎6946-6148, 983-6181; www.elvallepotosi.com; Calle La Reforma 84; campsites with/without tent US$20/10, d & tr US$59-69;) A very welcoming place and good for a peaceful sleep, American-owned Cabañas Potosí is situated about 1km southwest of the town center. The parklike grounds provide lovely views of the peaks that ring the valley, including La India Dormida (p97). Four concrete cabins for three people each have two beds and a fridge; more expensive rooms have attached kitchen and TV.

★ **Park Eden** B&B $$
(☎983-6167, 6695-6190; www.parkeden.com; Calle Espave 7; d/ste incl breakfast from US$100/140, 4-person house US$260;) A beautiful country retreat run by a North American–trained Panamanian designer and his Ecuadorian wife, this gorgeous property has two rooms and two suites, plus a two-story house with living room and kitchen. Decor is a little bit Laura Ashley, with lots of powder blue, lace doilies and quilting, but the friendly couple and their gardens are simply a delight.

Golden Frog Inn INN $$
(☎6565-8307, 983-6117; www.goldenfroginn.com; d/ste incl breakfast from US$90/135;) Attentive and relaxing, this deluxe Canadian-Panamanian–owned lodge with 11 very different rooms and suites is the perfect place to laze after a long day of play. Start with the swimming pool and migrate to the open-air living spaces and library. The expansive grounds include orchids and fruit trees; adjoining trails mean you can hike from right out the door.

THE HOLY GHOST ORCHID

While hiking though the forests around El Valle, be sure to keep an eye out for a terrestrial orchid known as *la flor del Espíritu Santo*, or the 'Holy Ghost orchid' *(Peristeria elata)*, which was awarded the title of 'national flower of Panama' in 1936. Named by Spanish missionaries during the colonial period, the flower is shaped like a red-spotted dove emerging from ivory petals.

The flower is most commonly found along the forest floor beside trails, but it also grows on the branches of large trees. It blooms from July to October and has an unforgettable aroma. The orchids are under threat from overharvesting and should not be picked.

Residencial El Valle HOTEL $$
(☎983-6536, 6615-9616; www.hotelresidencialelvalle.com; Av Central; d/tr/q US$60/71/93; P 📶) Visitors become loyalists, given the high level of service provided at this friendly motel-style lodging. The longstanding hotel has 17 clean and airy rooms and an enormous veranda with hammocks on the top floor overlooking Av Central with views to the hills. Room 4 has lovely wooden floors and two windows. Enter through the ground-floor shop.

Hotel Campestre HOTEL $$
(☎983-6146, 6365-1545; www.hotelcampestre.com; Calle Club Campestre; s/d incl breakfast US$76/89; P ❄ 📶) Dating back to 1939, El Valle's oldest hotel features enormous grounds, forested walking paths, and a large and comfortable restaurant and bar. Its 20 large, tastefully decorated rooms include heavy wooden 'sleigh' beds and stone-faced bathrooms. The welcoming staff are keen to please, and day trips to the beach at Farallón are available.

Hotel Valle Verde HOTEL $$
(☎983-6080, 6471-8250; www.hotel-valleverde.com; Calle La Cooperativa; s/d/tr from US$66/99/132; P ❄ 📶 🏊) This spick-and-span property with lovely grounds and excellent valley views boasts 18 quite different (and somewhat dated) rooms with firm mattresses, leatherwork tables and spacious bathrooms. Amenities include a capacious terrace in the main building, a newly built swimming pool and a highly recommended Peruvian restaurant (p102).

★**La Casa de Lourdes** BOUTIQUE HOTEL $$$
(☎983-6450,6114-0117;www.lacasadelourdes.com; d US$175-250; P ❄ 📶) About the most luxurious place to stay in El Valle, this secluded and quiet villa counts just four rooms in total. Two of them sit above the hotel's much-acclaimed restaurant (p102), while a larger pair occupy a cottage with a mini stone tower in the garden. The decor is country, with flower-print bedspreads and large carved-wood wardrobes. Bathrooms feature bathtubs.

Los Mandarinos Boutique Spa & Hotel HOTEL $$$
(☎983-6645, 6808-2743; www.losmandarinos.com; d incl breakfast from US$189, ste US$299; P ❄ 📶 🏊) In El Valle's lush countryside, this 70-room fortresslike property contained in four stone 'towers' is way too big to be boutique but it's sumptuous nevertheless. Winding walkways link imposing Spanish-style tile lodgings, which look slightly better at a distance. Large modern rooms are decked in finery, some with king-sized beds and stone baths. There are two pools; one is heated.

Crater Valley Boutique Hotel RESORT $$$
(☎6620-5818, 983-6942; www.crater-valley.com; cnr Calles Capirita & Ranita de Oro; d incl breakfast US$213-230; P ❄ 📶 🏊) Surrounded by beautifully tended gardens, Crater Valley's eight guest rooms are all different and executed with varying degrees of care. All feature stone floors, glass-brick showers and patios with hammocks. The honeymoon suite (US$230 to US$260) has a private garden and is a delight. You won't have to travel far to view wildlife: the fish and frog ponds are teeming.

Eating

★**Don Quijote** SPANISH $
(☎6095-0124, 983-6210; www.facebook.com/LosGabirros; Calle El Hato 1; mains US$8-12; ⊙8am-9pm Tue-Sun) This 'spit' (ie grill) restaurant is a local favorite and noted for well-prepared Spanish dishes like *pulpo a la gallega* (octopus grilled with paprika), paella and the unusual *migas:* herbed breadcrumbs often served with ribs. The Quijote is a simple affair, almost like a *fonda* (cheap restaurant), with an incongruous little fountain in the center adding a dash of color. There's a warm welcome.

Restaurante Massiel PANAMANIAN $
(☎6281-8410, 6214-4480; Av Central; mains US$6-9; ⊙6am-6pm Tue-Thu, to 9:30pm Fri-Sun) The best Panamanian restaurant in El Valle is quite a simple affair – a *fonda*, really – that serves up *pollo asado* (grilled chicken), mixed seafood, meatballs and *ropa vieja* (a spicy shredded beef combination served over rice). It's a friendly place, with a colorful carved toucan at the door wishing you a warm welcome.

El Valle Gourmet & Coffee Shop CAFE $
(Av Central; sandwiches US$4-7; ⊙10am-4pm Tue-Fri, 8:30am-8:30pm Sat, 8am-6pm Sun) Selling gourmet sandwiches and smoothies, this landmark cafe is a good place to stock up on picnic fare before heading for the trails. You can also find a decent selection of cheeses, cured meats and olives here. Lovely garden seating, too.

Restaurante Zapote INTERNATIONAL **$$**
(☎983-6922; Av Central; mains US$9-15; ⏱11am-9pm Wed-Mon) This eclectic restaurant in pleasant surrounds serves up quite a mix of dishes – from Colombian *empanadas* (dough stuffed with meat or cheese and fried) and Panama's national dish, *sancocho* (rich chicken soup), to ribs and pizza. It's one of the restaurants of choice among El Valle's ever-growing expat community.

L'Italiano PIZZA **$$**
(☎983-6883, 6682-9398; www.facebook.com/L-italiano-660035177397679; Calle de Anam; mains US$12-14; ⏱11am-9pm Wed & Thu, to 10pm Fri & Sat, to 8pm Sun) They say that this tiny restaurant and pizzeria just up from the orchid garden has the best pizza in El Valle. With an Italian owner and chef at the oven it certainly tastes like the real thing. Along with some 15 pizzas (US$6.50 to US$13), there are several pasta dishes (US$11 to US$14) and more complex mains too.

Restaurante Bruschetta CAFE **$$**
(☎6518-4416, 983-5118; www.facebook.com/pages/Restaurante-Bruschetta-El-Valle-de-Anton/237616059663192; Av Central; mains US$9-17; ⏱11am-8:45pm) The anchor restaurant of El Valle's main street, Bruschetta features generous versions of its namesake (US$6.50 to US$8) as well as salads, tacos and sandwiches. Unusual treats include the carrot-and-orange juice. It's one of the more atmospheric cafe-restaurants in town and always packed.

★**La Casa de Lourdes** INTERNATIONAL **$$$**
(☎6114-0117, 983-6450; www.lacasadelourdes.com; mains US$12-30; ⏱noon-3:30pm & 7-9pm) The creation of renowned Panamanian chef Lourdes Fábrega de Ward, this place has a nationwide reputation and an elegant setting around a garden patio in a lovely country villa. And the menu? Sea bass Thai curry, blackened chicken in a tamarind sauce and desserts from both sides of 'the pond': sticky toffee pudding and pecan pie.

Restaurante Valle Verde PERUVIAN **$$$**
(☎983-6080, 6471-8250; www.hotel-valleverde.com/restaurante; Calle La Cooperativa; mains US$10-30; ⏱8am-8pm) This upmarket Peruvian restaurant in the Hotel Valle Verde (p101) serves Inca-inspired favorites such as *lomo saltado* (stir-fried beef with vegetables and potatoes) and *jalea de mariscos* (fried seafood platter with yucca and plantains), preceded, of course, by Peruvian *ceviche* (citrus-cured seafood) and the requisite pisco sour.

★**Da Vinci Deli Pastas Gourmet** ITALIAN **$$$**
(☎983-6685, 6215-2497; www.facebook.com/Da-Vinci-Deli-Pastas-Gourmet-509330165758426; Plaza Paseo El Valle; mains US$12-26; ⏱11am-10pm Thu-Sun) OK, its location in the Plaza Paseo El Valle mall east of the center may not be the sexiest, but it's a nice mall (as malls go) and this place has its own pasta machine. Feast on any number of pastas (US$11 to US$16), pizza or more complex meat or fish dishes.

Shopping

Mercado Artesanal MARKET
(Artisan Market; ☎983-6474; Av Central; ⏱7am-5pm) El Valle is home to one of Panama's largest handicrafts market. Indigenous Ngöbe-Buglé people, along with a sprinkling of Emberá and Wounaan, bring a variety of handicrafts to sell to tourists (most of whom are Panamanians from the capital). If you're self-catering, the market also stocks a good selection of fresh produce. Sunday is the busiest day.

A popular item sold here is the *batea,* a tray carved from a local hardwood and used by the Ngöbe-Buglé people for tossing rice and corn. You can also find figurines, colorful baskets woven from palms, gourds painted in brilliant colors, 'real' Panama hats and birdcages made from cane.

Information

ATP Office (☎983-6474; cocle@atp.gob.pa; Av Central; ⏱9:30am-5:30pm Wed-Sun) This small information kiosk next to the handicrafts market is among the most helpful in Panama. Can help with information on bicycle rentals and local guides, too.

Banco Nacional de Panamá (Av Central; ⏱8am-3pm Mon-Fri, 9am-noon Sat) In the center; has one of the five ATMs in El Valle.

Centro de Salud de El Valle (El Valle Health Center; ☎983-6112; Av Central; ⏱24hr) For health needs, turn to this clinic at the western end of Av Central.

Ministerio de Ambiente Office (☎997-7538, 997-9805; off Av Central; ⏱8:30am-3:30pm Mon-Fri) Next to the Aprovaca orchid garden; can answer questions about national parks and protected areas

Getting There & Away

To leave El Valle, hop aboard a bus traveling east along Av Central; on average, buses depart every

30 minutes. Final destinations are marked on the windshield of the bus. If your next destination isn't posted, catch a bus going in the same direction and transfer.

To reach El Valle from the Interamericana, disembark from any bus at San Carlos, about 3km east of Las Uvas, the turning for El Valle. Minibuses collect passengers at the station here and travel to El Valle (US$1.50, 35 minutes, every half-hour). Last departure is 4pm weekdays and 7pm at weekends. From Panama City the trip to El Valle takes just over two hours (US$4.50).

Getting Around

A colorful bus passes along Av Central every 30 minutes or so from 6am to 6pm (US$0.25 one way). Taxis ply Av Central all day long as well, though they are hard to find after 7pm. You can go anywhere in town for US$2 or US$3.

Many hotels offer bike rentals (from US$2/12 per hour/day).

Santa Clara

POP 2150

With a long white-sand beach and towering coconut palms, Santa Clara, the first of three settlements on the so-called Costa Blanca (White Coast), is a great destination if you want to lounge about for a few days without having to worry about someone invading your stretch of sand.

Santa Clara itself was once little more than a sparsely populated fishing village edged between patches of dry tropical forest and the vast blue expanse of the Pacific, though the opening of a US military base nearby during WWII to help safeguard the canal livened things up a bit. These days upscale beach villas and apartment blocks dot the landscape, but there's still plenty of local flavor here to soak up in between beach sessions, which makes a nice change from some of the country's more popular destinations.

Sleeping

A short distance south of the Interamericana you'll come to a fork in the road. Go left for about 1km and you'll see signs directing you to Cabañas Las Sirenas. Going to the right for the same distance leads to the beach and Cabañas Las Veraneras.

XS Memories MOTEL **$**
(993-3096, 6729-1201; www.xsmemories.com; campsites per person US$8, RV hookups from US$20, d from US$55; P) You won't find many RV resorts with sports bars in rural Panama, so this friendly US outfit definitely has the market cornered. Three spacious guest rooms – ask for the studio in a separate cottage – feature one, two or three beds, air-con and fridges. There are also more than 20 hookups for motor homes, providing water, sewers and electricity. Book by phone.

Cabañas Las Veraneras CABIN **$$**
(993-3313; http://veraneraspanama.com; 2-/5-person cabins from US$88/100; P) The *cabañas* here come in three styles. A total of 20 cabins – some in concrete (called Las Palmeras), others thatched huts on two levels (Las Tradicionales) – cling to a slope set away from the beach. The loveliest are the five built on stilts (Las Playeras), which overlook the crashing waves. Cabins 00 and 01 have the best views. There's a large circular pool.

Cabañas Las Sirenas RESORT **$$$**
(6973-7567, 236-1385; www.lassirenasdesantaclara.com; 2-/4-person cottages from US$165/200; P) A resort with a lot of history, Cabañas Las Sirenas is set over a terraced garden, with five concrete structures constructed in the 1950s at the top of the hill and a half-dozen newer huts set at an angle along the beach. All 11 of the cottages have fully equipped kitchens and patios with barbecue and hammocks, but they need renovating.

Eating

Delicias del Mar FAST FOOD **$**
(6711-9975, 908-8508; mains US$7-12; 8am-8pm) Serving better-than-average fast-food fare such as burgers, deep-fried shrimp and chicken with rice or *patacones* (fried plantains), this Chinese-owned beachside eatery is a very convenient (and picturesque) spot for lunch. The *pipa fría* (cold coconut water) goes down a treat. You can rent Jet Skis here too.

★ **Xoko** SPANISH **$$**
(908-8219, 6525-6163; www.facebook.com/pages/Restaurante-xoko/427120730652157; Interamericana s/n; dishes US$13-26; 11:30am-10pm Mon-Thu, to 10:30pm Fri & Sat, 11am-10pm Sun) With its mustard-yellow exterior and oddly shaped columns within, this hangar-like eatery (which was once a US-military social club) offers an excellent selection of tapas (US$4.50 to US$10.50), paella,

BUSES FROM SANTA CLARA

DESTINATION	COST (US$)	DURATION	FREQUENCY
Antón	1	30min	every 30min
Chame	1.75	45min	every 20min
David	12	5½hr	hourly
Panama City	4	1¾hr	every 20min
Penonomé	1.35	1hr	every 30min
San Carlos	1.25	30min	every 20min

delicious clams in white wine and a catch of the day cooked Basque-style (with tomatoes and sweet or hot red peppers). It's on the Interamericana at the turnoff for Santa Clara.

Restaurante Las Veraneras SEAFOOD **$$**
(☎993-3313; http://veraneraspanama.com; mains US$6.50-20; ⏰7:30am-8:30pm) This small thatched restaurant-bar sits directly on the beach facing the waves. It's the perfect setting for a meal of fresh *ceviche, patacones* topped with baby octopus, or a pasta dish accompanied by a sundowner. Note that service can slow down a bit when the place is full.

Getting There & Around

Santa Clara is well served by buses.

There are usually taxis parked beside the turnoff on the Interamericana for Santa Clara. You can take one for US$1.50 to get to any destination in Santa Clara. The beach is just under 2km from the Interamericana.

Farallón & Playa Blanca

POP 1660

The village of Farallón (Spanish for 'cliff'), about 3km southwest of the Santa Clara turnoff, lies on a picture-perfect stretch of powder-white sand called Playa Blanca (White Beach), one of the most beautiful beaches on the Pacific coast. The main part of Playa Blanca is another 3km further on near the sprawling gated community of Buenaventura.

A decade ago, Farallón was a fishing village with the ruins of the Panamanian military base that was destroyed during the US invasion to oust Noriega. However, resort fever has recast it and the entire stretch of Playa Blanca as one of the hottest beach destinations in Panama. A controversial international airport opened at nearby Río Hato in late 2013 and development continues apace in Buenaventura.

Visitors are urged to venture out beyond the resorts. Much of the original village charm is still here, especially along Farallón's beach.

Activities

If you're just visiting for the day, Royal Decameron Beach Resort & Casino offers day passes (from US$75) that give you full access to the facilities from 8am to 5pm. Of course, beaches are public land in Panama, so as long as you don't get into trouble, no one's going to stop you from lying on the sand.

Sleeping

★**Togo Bed & Breakfast** B&B **$$**
(☎6804-2551, 993-3393; www.togopanama.com; d incl breakfast US$99-110, with kitchenette US$110-132; P ❄ ☜) The perfect seaside destination, Togo occupies a renovated beach house and outbuildings where recycled materials are used to create a sleek and stylish design. The four rooms – one with kitchenette – are spacious and airy, with cool pebble-tile bathrooms, gorgeous original artworks and private terraces. The centerpiece is the lush garden, a controlled jungle strewn with hammocks.

A small path across from the B&B, which is adults-only and gay-friendly, leads to the beach. To reach Togo from the main road, turn left at the National Car Rental and taxi stand. It's another 400m further along the road.

La Casita del Farallón B&B **$$**
(☎6835-2890, 908-8501; www.lacasitadelfarallon.com; d US$65-80; P ❄ ☜) This adorable little bed and breakfast run by a delightful Italian couple is in town but on the way to the beach, and has four compact but colorful rooms sleeping between two and four

people. Should you want to get closer to the water, opt for the **annex** (908-8501, 6835-2890; 2-person ste US$65-80, 5-person ste US$100-120; P ❄ 📶) a short distance away with direct access to the beach.

Royal Decameron Beach Resort & Casino RESORT $$$
(993-2255, 294-1900; www.decameron.com; d all-inclusive US$224-257; P ❄ @ 📶 ≋) Panama's answer to Vegas, the Royal Decameron Beach Resort is a whopper, with 600 rooms and enough pools, bars, clubs and restaurants to count on both hands. Strolling a gated compound affixed with a bracelet ID may not be your idea of travel, but if you like buffet food and Latino nightlife, you'll be *en tu salsa,* as they say.

Eating

★ Pipa's Beach Restaurant SEAFOOD $$
(6252-8430, 6844-0373; http://pipasbeach.com; mains US$10-25; 10am-6pm daily Nov-Apr, closed Tue May-Oct) Love, love, love this mostly outdoor bar and restaurant right by the beach and serving seafood with gourmet touches (such as Thai mussels and crab claws in three sauces). One of the delights of dining here is enjoying a cold beer or tropical cocktail while looking out to sea, feet buried in the sand and sometimes washed by the surf.

Rancho del Mar ITALIAN $$
(993-3001; www.facebook.com/ranchomarfarallon; pizza US$9.50-13, pasta US$10.50-17; noon-10pm Wed-Sun) Situated 200m north of the main road to the beach, the 'Sea Ranch' is a new pizza and pasta place – there are some meat and fish dishes but it mostly serves this tried-and-true combo. Its fare is pretty authentic (one of the owners is Italian); try the *linguine ai frutti di mare* to see what we mean.

Nico's Beach INTERNATIONAL $$
(6201-3837, 908-8501; www.nicosbeach.com; mains US$8-18; 11am-9pm Mon & Wed-Fri, 11am-11pm Sat, 9:30am-9pm Sun) It's gringo city at this Italian-owned bar-restaurant on the beach. Among the menu choices is a holdover from the previous owners, a Quebec dish of French fries, cheese curds and gravy called *poutine*. Other selections include clam linguini, whole sea bass and burgers. Hosts Michela and Filippo charm the punters. There's live music from 8pm on Saturday.

★ La Fogata PANAMANIAN $$$
(908-3975, 6688-2240; www.lafogatapanama.com; mains US$13-26; noon-3pm & 6-10pm Tue-Sun) This colorful and quirky little place run by an affable Panamanian-Swiss couple for almost two decades serves up scrumptious Panamanian food à la Caribbean – meaning lots of seafood with coconut flavors. There are a couple of meat dishes to choose from but we'd go back for the three-course Sexy Lobster Special (US$37). The outside garden seating is coveted.

Getting There & Around

Buses traveling along the Interamericana generally drop you off at the Farallón exit ramp; it's a 2km walk to the center or you might be lucky and find a taxi waiting. An easier way to catch a cab is to be let off at the Santa Clara turnoff, where there are usually taxis waiting.

There's a taxi stand about 2km along the main road to the beach, beyond the police station and National Car Rental office.

Antón

POP 9790

The town of Antón is located 18km northwest of Farallón and the same distance southeast of Penonomé in the center of a lush valley dotted with dry rice fields and cattle ranches. Although it has little to offer visitors beyond its natural beauty, its annual patron's day festival and its folkloric **Toro Guapo** (Handsome Bull National Festival; www.festivaltoroguapo.org; Oct) holiday are the best in the province. It's worth stopping by to partake in the festivities if you find yourself in the area; *los antoneros* (the people from Antón) apparently live for these events.

The 30 rooms at the peach-colored **Hotel Rivera** (6127-7216, 987-2245; www.hotelrivera-panama.com; d/tr/q from US$30/40/47; P ❄ 📶 ≋) have sparse furnishings, but the air-con works and there's plenty of hot water. It's hard to complain at this price, and the inviting pool is a nice amenity, especially when the summer sun is beating down. There's an in-house restaurant and bar.

Getting There & Away

All buses, including those headed for Penonomé, will stop at the Antón bus station a block west of the Hotel Rivera if you ask the driver in advance.

Penonomé

POP 28,000

The capital city of Coclé Province is a bustling crossroads with a rich history. Founded in 1581, Penonomé blossomed so quickly that it served as the temporary capital of the isthmus in 1671 after the destruction of the first Panama City (now known as Panamá Viejo) by Henry Morgan and until Nueva Panamá (today's Casco Viejo) was founded a few years later.

Today, the lifeline of the city is the Interamericana, which bisects Penonomé and ensures a steady stream of goods (and people) flowing in and out. If you're heading west, it's likely that you'll pass through here at some point, though it's worth hopping off the bus for the city's two principal attractions: its annual festivals and its traditional hats, especially in the nearby artisan town of La Pintada.

Sights

Museo de Penonomé MUSEUM

(997-8490; www.facebook.com/museo.penonome; Calle San Antonio; adult/child US$3.50/0.75; 9am-4pm Tue-Sat) This renovated museum housed in a beautiful blue-and-white colonial building is small but does a thorough job examining the history and traditions of Coclé and, by extension, Panama, with a surprisingly good collection of pre-Columbian pottery, religious art and traditional furniture.

Basilica Mayor San Juan Bautista CATHEDRAL

(Plaza Bolívar) Dominating the central plaza, this 'major basilica' (a title bestowed on certain Roman Catholic cathedrals) stands on the site of an original 16th-century church. Most of what you see today, however, including the colorful stained-glass windows in the clerestory, dates from a major rebuilding in 1948.

Festivals & Events

Carnaval CARNIVAL

Held during the four days preceding Ash Wednesday, Carnaval is Penonomé's red-letter event. In addition to traditional festivities such as dancing, dressing up in costumes and masks and crowning a festival queen, floats here are literally floated down a tributary of the Río Zaratí. Plaza Bolívar and every street around it are packed with people.

Sleeping

Hotel Dos Continentes HOTEL $

(997-9325; www.facebook.com/hoteldoscontinentes; Av Juan Demóstenes Arosemena; s/d/tr/q US$42/46/48/57; P ❄ @) At the turning into Penonomé from the Interamericana, this sprawling hotel is secure, spacious and relatively central. The 61 rooms are worn but serviceable. Ask for a room in the back for less highway noise. The on-site restaurant is popular for cheap *comida típica* (regional specialties); locals swear its *filete de pechuga de pollo* (chicken breast fillet) is Panama's best.

Hotel Coclé HOTEL $$

(6418-6901, 908-5039; www.hotelcocle.com; Via Interamericana; s/d/ste incl breakfast from US$70/80/130; P ❄) This large modern hotel along the Interamericana and conveniently located next to the Iguana Mall is in a low-rise building recalling a Spanish hacienda. Its 110 rooms and suites are tastefully done in blond wood and shades of blue; ask for breezy No 307. There's a fully equipped gym, and a kidney-shaped pool in the garden.

Hotel La Pradera HOTEL $$

(991-0106; hotelpradera@cwpanama.net; Via Interamericana; s/d US$66/77; P ❄) This sand-colored hotel with terracotta roof tiles feels ritzy for Penonomé and is excellent value for the price; rates drop to US$55/66 at the weekend. Smart earth-tone rooms (30 in total) include built-in cabinets, cable TV, a lounge chair and a desk. Choose a room overlooking the garden and swimming pool out the back, such as No 212.

Eating

Mercado Público MARKET $

(Public Market; Av Nicanor Rosas; mains US$2.50; 6am-4pm) Penonomé's central market dating back to 1918 serves hearty breakfasts, with such dishes as *hojaldras* (fried dough), *bistec encebollado* (steak and onions) and eggs.

Panadería El Paisa BAKERY $

(www.facebook.com/pages/Panaderia-El-Paisa-Penonomé/258165830888595; Av Juan Demóstenes Arosemena; pizza US$4.75-5.50; 6am-9:30pm Mon-Sat) At the northern end of Av Juan Demóstenes Arosemena, this bakery sells wonderful cakes and sweet breads (US$1.75 to US$2.75) and has started baking pizzas in its ovens as well.

Penonomé

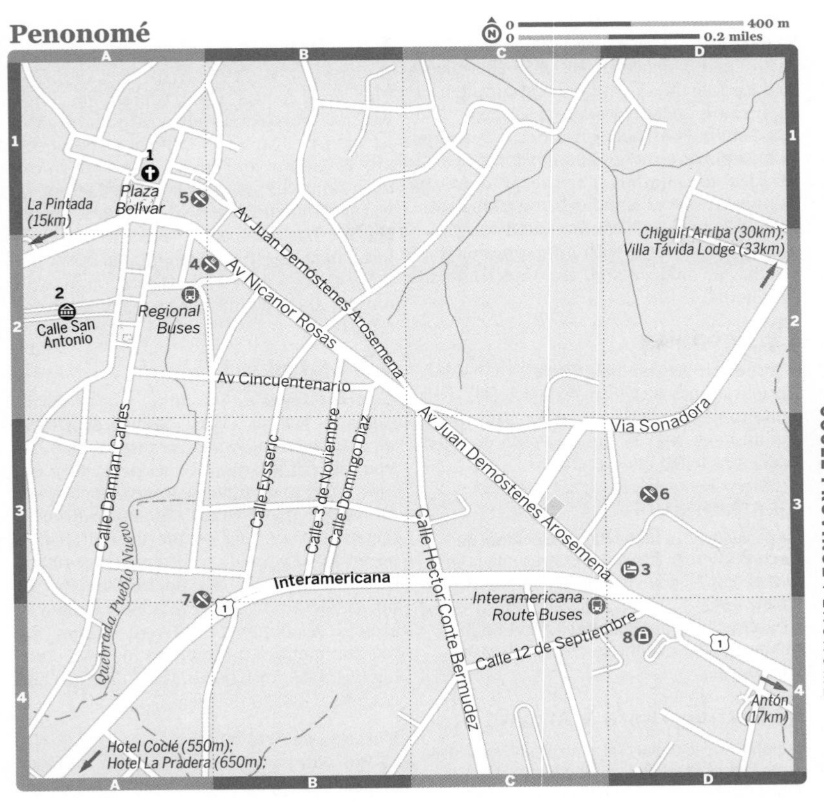

Yukas Grill PANAMANIAN $$
(☎908-6030; www.facebook.com/YukasGrill; Via Interamericana; mains US$8.50-16.50; ⏲10am-10pm) This bar and grill just out of the center on the Interamericana consistently gets rated as Penonomé's top restaurant. It's an *asador* (spit restaurant), so the beef skewers and grilled chicken are the must-orders. Surprisingly for a grill, though, there's a decent range of vegetarian (or near-vegetarian) dishes and great fresh juices. Excellent service and always a warm welcome.

Pits Burgers & Grill BURGERS $$
(☎908-6330; www.facebook.com/pages/Pits-Burguer-Grill/962816170409142?nr; Harinos Mall, Av Juan Demóstenes Arosemena; mains US$8-24; ⏲noon-midnight Mon-Sat, to 10pm Sun) This place in Harinos Mall just off the main drag has a comfortable, well-stocked sports bar with pool table on the ground floor, and a rooftop grill and burger restaurant with open veranda. There's a large selection of steaks, which tends to push prices up, but burgers and pasta dishes come in at between US$9 and US$12.50.

Penonomé

Sights
1 Basilica Mayor San Juan Bautista ... A1
2 Museo de Penonomé ... A2

Sleeping
3 Hotel Dos Continentes ... D3

Eating
4 Mercado Público ... B2
5 Panadería El Paisa ... A1
6 Pits Burgers & Grill ... D3
7 Yukas Grill ... A3

Shopping
8 Mercado de Artesanías Coclé ... D4

Icacos INTERNATIONAL **$$**
(6873-3290; www.icacosadventure.com; Calle Hector Conte Bermudes; mains US$8-20; 9am-8pm Tue-Sun;) A country restaurant in a 6.5-hectare recreational area, Icacos also has fishing, horseback riding, a working farm, a playground and an adventure park. It's ideal for families. The breezy, open-air restaurant serves standards like club sandwiches as well as local fare such as *pernil* (thinly sliced pork) with *patacones* or tilapia fish farmed on-site. It's 4km south of Penonomé.

Shopping

Mercado de Artesanías Coclé MARKET
(Via Interamericana; 8am-4pm Mon-Sat) This market stocks both everyday and high-quality hats from Panama as well as other locally produced handicrafts.

Information

For banking, head to the **Banco Nacional de Panamá** (Av Juan Demóstenes Arosemena; 8am-3pm Mon-Fri, 9am-noon Sat), which has ATMs.

The city's principal **hospital** (997-9386; Interamericana; 24hr) is at the eastern end of town.

Getting There & Around

Regional buses depart from an area two blocks southeast of Plaza Bolívar and behind the public market.

Interamericana route buses use a parking lot on the south side of the highway as a passenger pickup and drop-off point. Buses pass in both directions every 15 minutes or so. From Penonomé there are frequent buses to Panama City (US$5.35, 2½ hours, every 20 minutes) and David (US$12, 4½ hours, every 35 minutes).

The best places to hail a taxi are by the station near the Interamericana route bus area and Plaza Bolívar. The fare for any destination in town won't be more than US$2.

La Pintada

POP 3880

This small foothill town, some 15km northwest of Penonomé, attracts visitors with its natural beauty, its famous artisans selling Panama's very own *sombreros pintados* (painted hats) and its cigar factory. Be warned though: the world's largest copper deposit has been discovered in the hills just 30km north of La Pintada. Visit this delightfully sleepy town before large-scale mining and new money changes it beyond recognition.

Sights

Cigarros Joyas de Panama FACTORY
(Joyas de Panama Cigars; tours 6660-8935; www.facebook.com/joyasde.panama; 8am-2pm Mon-Sat) FREE This local cigar factory enjoys quite a reputation internationally for its unique hand-rolled Cuban-seed *puros* (cigars). Depending on the time of year, a dozen to 40 workers roll as many as 400 cigars a day. Owner Miriam Padilla, who set up the factory in 1982, will gladly show you around. A number of different *vitolas* (the measurement of a cigar) are for sale, starting at US$15 for a box of five Coronitas and reaching US$100 for the #1 Especial.

Mercado de Artesanías La Pintada MARKET
(983-0313; hours vary) La Pintada's artisans' market – specializing in *sombreros pintados,* the 'painted hats' unique to Panama and especially famous in Penonomé and surrounds – is a shadow of its former self. It hosts only a stall or two and their appearance is sporadic, but you might get lucky.

Sleeping & Eating

★**La Pintada Inn** B&B **$$**
(6519-7848, 983-0384; www.lapintadainn.com; d/ste incl breakfast US$75/100;) This delightful inn set in lovely gardens lies just 4km north of La Pintada. Each of the eight

BUSES FROM PENONOMÉ

DESTINATION	COST (US$)	DURATION	FREQUENCY
Aguadulce	2	45min	every 20min
Chiguirí Arriba	2.50	80min	hourly
Churuquita Grande	0.85	45min	every 30min
El Copé	2.50	1hr	hourly
La Pintada	1.05	20min	every 30min

spick-and-span rooms has its own bathroom, cable TV and fridge. There are lovely walks and trails in the area, including one down to the Coclé River. Swim here or in the lovely pool with grand views into the hills.

Shopping

Artesanías Reinaldo Quirós FASHION & ACCESSORIES
(6963-0945; 8:30am-4pm) The workshop and residence of one of La Pintada's most famous hat makers is in the center of town on the west side of the soccer field. He'll gladly show you around his workshop for US$1.50 per person. Hats for sale range in price from US$20 to US$150 but can reach as high as US$1000 for a multi-ring hat.

The materials used in these hats are *bellota* (palm fiber), coarser *junco* dyed black, and *pita,* a fiber related to cactus, used to sew it all together. These plants are growing in Reinaldo's backyard, so you can see what they look like.

In addition to hats, Reinaldo makes and sells dolls wearing folkloric costumes, model Panamanian houses and bottle covers made from palm fiber.

Getting There & Away

Buses costing less than US$1 link La Pintada with Penonomé about every half-hour. The trip takes around 20 minutes.

Reserva Privada Távida

The Reserva Privada Távida is a private mountain reserve that forms part of the Mesoamerican corridor. Once used for livestock, the area is now undergoing reforestation and offers ample trails for hiking or birdwatching and a spectacular waterfall. The springboard for visiting the reserve is the village of Chiguirí Arriba.

Activities

Guided hiking tours (US$15 to US$30 per person) from the Villa Távida Lodge range from easy nature walks to arduous treks, taking in river, forest scenes and the awesome 30m-high **Cascada Távida**. Wildlife to spot includes three-toed sloths, night monkeys, deer and armadillos. Four species of toucan and many species of hummingbird and butterflies also live here and can occasionally be seen from the comfort of the creek-fed swimming pool or the delightful house with circular balcony on a hill above the lodge.

Sleeping & Eating

★**Villa Távida Lodge** LODGE $$$
(6485-0505, 838-6114; www.villatavida.com; Chiguirí Arriba; campsite with/without tent US$25/15, d incl breakfast US$125-175, ste incl breakfast US$175-220; P) This mountain lodge sits within the Reserva Privada Távida atop a summit surrounded by gardens, green valleys and shrouded peaks. Guests have a choice of seven rooms: three in the main lodge and four with views of the Cascada Távida in a luxurious villa. There's also a delightful traditional roundhouse called Casa de David on the hill above the lodge.

Rooms have cable TV, fridges and hot-water showers (except for Casa de David). The lodge restaurant provides quality dining (mains US$12 to US$15) using fresh produce from local organic gardens, with seating both inside and out. Places to relax include a hammock terrace with great views where you'll want to laze away the hours; walks on marked trails are available right outside the door. There's a swimming hole under Cascada Távida, so bring your suit. The lovely spa offers sauna, Jacuzzi, massage (from US$50) and mud therapy (US$30), among other services.

Getting There & Away

To reach Chiguirí Arriba and the Reserva Privada Távida from central Penonomé, follow Av Juan Demóstenes Arosemena to the well-marked turnoff for Churuquita Grande, several hundred meters northwest of the fork in the Interamericana near the landmark Hotel Dos Continentes. Proceed past Churuquita Grande and Caimito and follow the signs to Chiguirí Arriba.

Buses leave for Chiguirí Arriba (US$2.50, 80 minutes) from Penonomé's market every hour between 5:30am and 6:30pm. If you are driving be aware that there are no gas stations on the road between Penonomé and Villa Távida Lodge.

Parque Nacional Omar Torrijos

One of Panama's least visited national parks due to a lack of accessibility, the 252-sq-km Parque Nacional Omar Torrijos encompasses some of the most beautiful forests in Panama, with montane forest on the Pacific side of the continental divide and humid tropical forest on the Caribbean/Atlantic side.

El Copé – a short name for the park taken from a nearby village – is also home to the full complement of Panama's wildlife, including rare bird species such as the golden-olive woodpecker, red-fronted parrotlet, immaculate antbird (which feeds on soldier ants) and white-throated shrike-tanager, as well as all five of Panama's species of big cats, Baird's tapirs and peccaries.

Two great surprises await visitors to El Copé: the condition of the park's trail system is excellent; and the park offers the easiest and surest point from which to see both the Pacific and Atlantic Oceans, from the lookout above the park cabin.

Activities

Next to the **ranger station** (6am-8pm) just inside the park entrance you'll find two side-by-side trails. The left-hand trail follows the ridgeline and summits a nearby mountain in about an hour. From the top, you'll be rewarded with panoramic views of both the Pacific and Atlantic Oceans and the surrounding canopy.

The right-hand trail follows the Caribbean slope of the continental divide. Be advised that this trail should under no circumstances be attempted without a guide organized through the ranger station. It's a fantastic trail that passes several rivers, winds up and down several mountain peaks and penetrates deep into the heart of the forest.

Behind the ranger station, you'll find a visitor center and a 500m-long interpretative loop that points out local species of trees and plants.

As a precaution, inform others of your intentions, always hike in boots and stick to the trails. There are poisonous snakes in the park including the deadly fer-de-lance.

Sleeping & Eating

Park Cabin CABIN **$**

(997-7538; campsite/dm US$5/15) About 200m up the road from the ranger station a cabin run by Ministerio de Ambiente has four bunks, a kitchen with simple cooking facilities, a basic toilet and cold-water shower. There's also a loft and lounge, allowing 10 people to sleep comfortably (bring your own gear). You'll need a sleeping bag and warm clothing – it gets cool at night.

Albergue Navas HOMESTAY **$$**

(Navas Hostel; 983-9130; Barrigon; r per person incl meals & tour guide US$45) The friendly Navas family rents rooms in their house in Barrigon. Accommodations are rustic, but very well maintained and inexpensive, with all meals included. The family – Santos and his sons – work as guides and help to maintain the park and its trails. Their knowledge and love of the area is quite apparent.

Cabaña Navas CABIN **$$**

(Navas Cabin; 983-9130; La Rica; r per person incl meals & tour guide US$45) In addition to Albergue Navas, the Navas family rents rooms in their *cabaña* in La Rica. From here you can take day hikes to the summits of Cerro Marta (1046m) and Cerro Peña Blanca (1314m), visit the impressive waterfalls of Chorros de Tife and hike to the ruins of the plane that crashed here in 1981, killing president Omar Torrijos.

La Rica, a beautiful community inside the park, is remote (no phone, electricity or road) and the hiking is strenuous, but it is a nature-lover's dream and comes highly recommended. All the arrangements can be made through the Navas family (Spanish only). Call ahead or ask around for them when you reach Barrigon.

Getting There & Away

The turnoff to the national park is on the Interamericana, 17km southwest of Penonomé. From the turnoff, it's another 34km to the park entrance. The road, paved for the first 29km or so, winds through rolling countryside dotted with farms and small cattle ranches. The paved road ends at the village of Barrigon. The remaining 4km to the park is on a dirt road that requires a 4WD. Follow the signs directing you to the park entrance (to the right); the ones to the left indicate the park's Sede Administrativa (administrative office).

To reach here by public transportation, catch a bus from Panama City (US$6.50, three hours) or Penonomé (US$2.50, one hour) to El Copé and transfer onto a minibus to Barrigon (US$0.50, 15 minutes), the closest village to the park. From there it's a 4km hike into the park.

Natá

POP 6000

Founded in 1522 by conquistadors in search of gold, Natá is the oldest surviving town in Panama. The town's **Basílica Menor Santiago Apóstol** (Minor Basilica of St James the Apostle; Plaza 19 de Octubre; 6am-8pm), believed to be the oldest church still in use in the Americas, has a dark past. The church was built by the indigenous population who were forced into labor by 60 *caballeros* (knights) who were posted in the region.

Indigenous artisans did all the woodcarving in the church, including the six side altars and the remarkable pulpit. A close look at the altar dedicated to the Virgin Mary to the left of the main one shows the culture's influence in the sculpted fruit, leaves and feathered serpents on its two columns. Behind this altar is the crypt entrance.

The columns in the nave are made of níspero, a hardwood found in Bocas del Toro Province, while the ceiling has been replaced with pine and cedar. The four bells in the belfry date from the 20th century. The originals, made of gold, were stolen years ago. To the left of the entrance is an 18th-century stone baptismal font.

Ecuadorian artist José Samaniego created the Holy Trinity painting to the right of the altar in 1758. For many years it was kept hidden from public view, as it portrays three separate but equal Christ-like individuals and not the usual Father, Son and Holy Spirit – a considerable breach of Roman Catholic dogma. During a 1995 restoration, three skeletons were discovered under the floor beneath the painting. Their identities remain a mystery.

Getting There & Away

Natá can be reached by bus along the Interamericana; they pass in both directions every 15 minutes or so. Natá is 45 minutes from Penonomé (US$1.50) and 15 minutes from Aguadulce (US$0.75). Catch the Penonomé bus on the Interamericana itself; the Aguadulce bus stops in front of the church.

Aguadulce

POP 8700

Hot and flat, the Aguadulce is Panama's sugar capital, surrounded by fields and fields of cane. Oddly enough it is also known for the salt it still claims from the sea. Fans of industrial tourism will think they've died and gone to heaven, for both industries can be viewed up close.

Sights

Playa El Salado BEACH

(Salty Beach) Located 9km southeast of central Aguadulce, this saltworks is a crucial habitat for marsh and shore birds. The area draws local and international birdwatchers to view roseate spoonbills, wood storks and black-necked stilts. When the tide is out, you can walk nearly 2km before reaching the water. But be careful: once the tide turns, it rises quickly.

On a warm day it's fun to loll about in **Las Piscinas**, shallow stone pools that catch the tidal water as it comes in. The surrounding flats are also famous for their jumbo shrimp, which are harvested in abundance and served in restaurants throughout Panama. In the dry season, the heaps of salt look like snow has just fallen on tropical Panama! The best way to reach El Salado is by taxi (US$8) from Aguadulce.

Azucarera Nacional Ingenio Santa Rosa FACTORY

(Santa Rosa National Sugar Refinery; 987-8101; www.azunal.com; 8am-noon Tue-Fri mid-Jan–mid-Mar) FREE From mid-January to mid-March this sugar refinery 15km southwest of Aguadulce processes more than 6500 tons of raw sugarcane daily. The process involves thousands of workers in round-the-clock production. It's a fascinating time to visit the refinery but a tour (in Spanish) requires 24 hours' notice. A taxi costs about US$18 round trip; otherwise take any bus headed west and ask the driver to drop you at the Ingenio de Azúcar Santa Rosa (US$1, 20 minutes, every 15 minutes).

Museo de la Sal y Azúcar MUSEUM

(Museum of Salt & Sugar; 997-4280; www.inac.gob.pa/museos/110-sal-y-azucar; Av Rodolfo Chiari, off Plaza 19 de Octubre; 8:30am-3:30pm Tue-Sat) FREE Officially called the Museo Regional Stella Sierra, but better known by its former title, Museo de la Sal y Azúcar, this museum in the former post office, facing Aguadulce's attractive central plaza, documents the history of the local sea salt and sugar industries. It also displays a number of pre-Columbian artifacts, mostly ceramics and tools found in the nearby cane fields.

Getting There & Around

Aguadulce can be reached by bus from Penonomé (US$2, 45 minutes, every 20 minutes), Chitré (US$3, one hour, every 20 minutes) and Panama City (US$6.25, 2½ hours, every 20 minutes).

Taxis are the best way to get around Aguadulce in the hot weather. Fares rarely exceed US$3, although you can expect to pay more at night.

Península de Azuero

POP 213,300 / ELEV SEA LEVEL TO 1400M

Includes ➡

Best Places to Eat

- Panga (p133)
- Mare Bonita (p117)
- Segreto (p128)
- El Sitio Restaurant (p133)
- El Caserón (p126)

Best Places to Stay

- Casa de Campo (p127)
- Eco Venao (p132)
- Casa Lajagua (p127)
- El Sitio Hotel (p132)
- La Casa del Puerto (p123)
- Hotel Playa Cambutal (p133)

Why Go?

Cherished as Panama's cultural heart and soul, the Península de Azuero is a farming and ranching hub, and the strongest bastion of Spanish colonial influence left in the country. The area's rolling hills are matched by a long and lovely coastline. Over time the peninsula has seen stark transformations – from verdant rainforest to cattle country, from indigenous land to Spanish stronghold and, finally, from sleepy backwater to surf central and one of Panama's travel hot spots.

The passage of time here is a countdown to the next festival, be it Carnaval, La Mejorana or Corpus Christi. Costumes range from swirling devils and dragons to curtsying *reinas* (queens) in traditional lace finery. Joining the throngs for these celebrations is a first-rate introduction to the real Panama.

Península de Azuero consists of three provinces: Herrera, Los Santos and a slice of Veraguas.

When to Go

Jul–Sep Azuero is ground zero for Panama's best traditional festivals, with major celebrations all over the peninsula featuring oxcart parades, *seco* (alcoholic drink made from sugarcane) and live bands.

Aug–Nov Thousands of endangered olive ridley sea turtles come ashore to nest on the broad beach of Isla Cañas; visitors come with guides to watch the nighttime hatchings.

Dec–Mar Dry season is the best time to surf Pacific swells, and options from wilderness beaches to surf villages abound. Also hit Las Tablas' Carnaval – the country's best – in February or March.

History

The Península de Azuero region was one of the first parts of what is now Panama to be settled. Indeed, shell mounds and pottery fragments unearthed at Sarigua (p118) in the northeast of the peninsula have been dated as far back as 11,000 years. The peninsula likes to refer to itself as the *cuna* (cradle) of Panamanian culture and traditions, and rightly so: the colonial Spanish legacy is perhaps felt more strongly here than anywhere else in the country. But there's a dark side to that legacy, too. So efficient were the conquistadors in wiping out the native population that today there are no indigenous communities left on the Península de Azuero, and one of its provinces, Los Santos, is the most deforested in the country.

Chitré

POP 58,400

One of Panama's oldest settlements, the city of Chitré is hardly geared up for travelers, but it's an agreeable stop on the way to the peninsula's famed beaches. The capital of Herrera Province, it's the largest city on the Península de Azuero and the region's cultural and historic capital. A handful of ornate red-tiled row homes hark back to the early days of Spanish settlement as does the main plaza. Colonial records indicate that there was a village here as early as 1558.

For most travelers Chitré serves as a springboard for nearby attractions such as the ceramic shops in La Arena, birdlife at Playa El Agallito, historic Parita, the *seco* factory at Pesé and the wildlife refuge at Cenegón del Mangle. Some of the country's best festivals are just a short bus ride away, and Chitré hosts a few wild parties of its own.

Sights

Museo de Herrera Fabio Rodriquez MUSEUM

(☎996-0077; www.inac.gob.pa/museos/111-museo-de-herrera; Paseo Enrique Geenzier; adult/child US$1/0.25; 8am-4pm Tue-Sat) This small museum, housed in a lovely two-story colonial building, contains many well-preserved pieces of pottery dating from 5000 BC until the Spanish conquest; some of it was found at excavation sites outside Parita. There are also replicas of *huacas* (golden objects placed with indigenous peoples at the time of burial) found on the peninsula – the originals are in the Smithsonian in Washington DC – as well as a recreated chieftain's tomb from the 1st century BC.

Refugio de Vida Silvestre Cenegón del Mangle NATURE RESERVE

This 776-hectare refuge about 25km north of Chitré protects a mangrove forest at the mouth of the Río Santa María. It's an important wildlife area and nesting ground for wading birds. The most commonly sighted species are great egrets, cattle egrets and tricolored herons. The refuge is a 45-minute drive north of Chitré via the Carretera Nacional, easily accessible as a day trip.

The refuge is accessed by a 500m-loop trail that follows a boardwalk through the mangrove forest. Along the way, keep your eyes fixed on the waters below, as the abundance of wading birds also attracts hungry caimans and crocodiles. The herons are here year-round, and opportunistic reptiles tend to congregate during the June-to-September nesting season.

Many of the herons that now inhabit the Palacio de las Garzas (Palace of the Herons), the official residence of the Panamanian president in Casco Viejo, Panama City, hail from this reserve.

The refuge is also home to **La Cueva del Tigre** (The Tiger's Cave), an archaeological site dating back some 12,000 years.

To get here, take the signposted turnoff to the village of Paris. After 1km the road forks at a church; take the right branch and it becomes a dirt road. Proceed 4km on this road, after which you'll come to a sign with an arrow indicating you're 2km from the entrance to the refuge. Expect to pay US$25 for a taxi from Chitré and US$15 from Parita.

Festivals & Events

Carnaval CULTURAL

Chitré's Carnaval festivities, held each year on the four days before Ash Wednesday, are second only to the famed celebrations at Las Tablas and feature parades, folkloric dancing, water fights and lots of drinking.

Fiesta de San Juan Bautista CULTURAL

(Jun 24) Chitré's patron-saint festival starts with a Mass followed by a pair of traditions that could be considered barbaric to some: bullfights, which don't end in the death of the animal, and cockfighting in which roosters with knives strapped to their feet slash each other apart. If you're even moderately

Península de Azuero Highlights

❶ **Playa Venao** (p130) Riding the waves and staying in cool lodgings at this surf destination that is managing to evade the mainstream.

❷ **Pedasí** (p126) Enjoying the down-home ambience of a small town with lovely boutique lodgings, a handful of good eateries and bike rides to the beach.

❸ **Isla Cañas** (p133) Spotting sea turtles as they arrive by the thousands during their annual nesting on this otherworldly island.

❹ **Las Tablas** (p124) Squeezing through the multitudes of revelers dancing in the streets during Carnaval.

❺ **Parita** (p119) Visiting a mask-maker's studio and strolling the colonial center of this historic town.

❻ **Playa Cambutal** (p133) Sunning and surfing on what is arguably Panama's most popular beach.

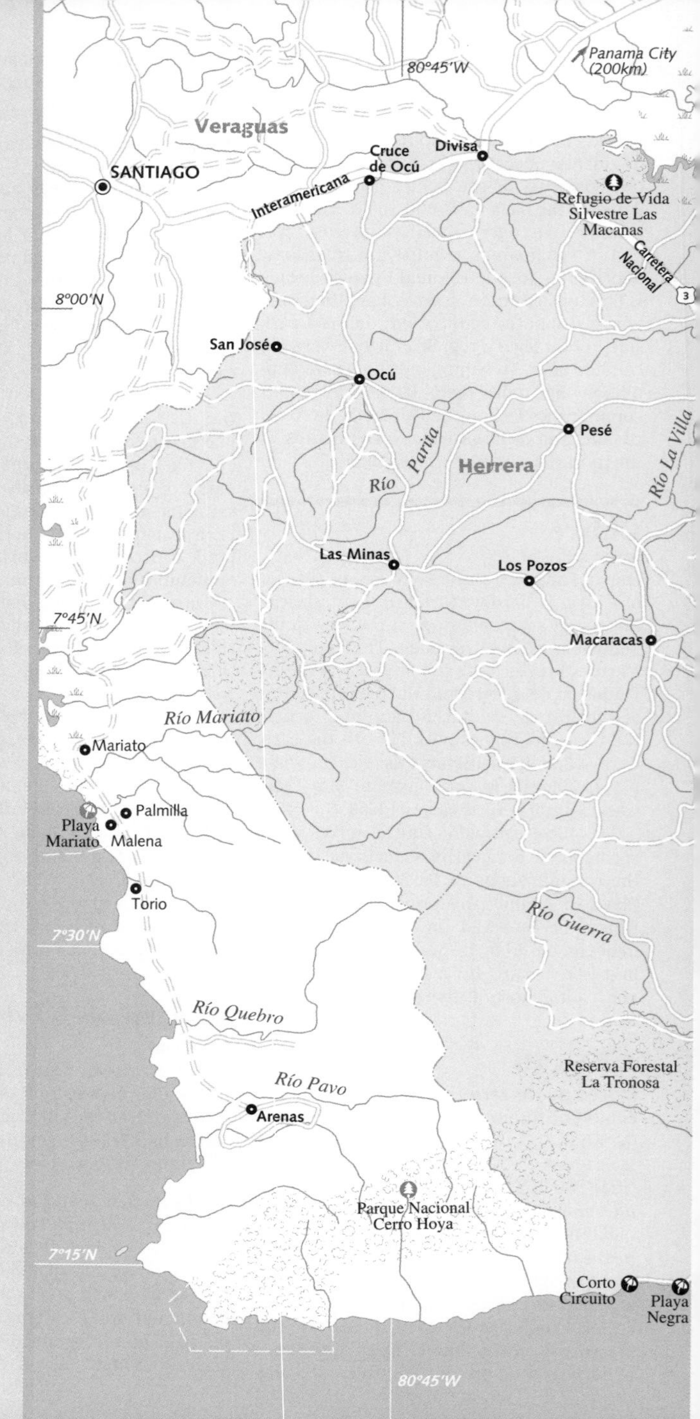

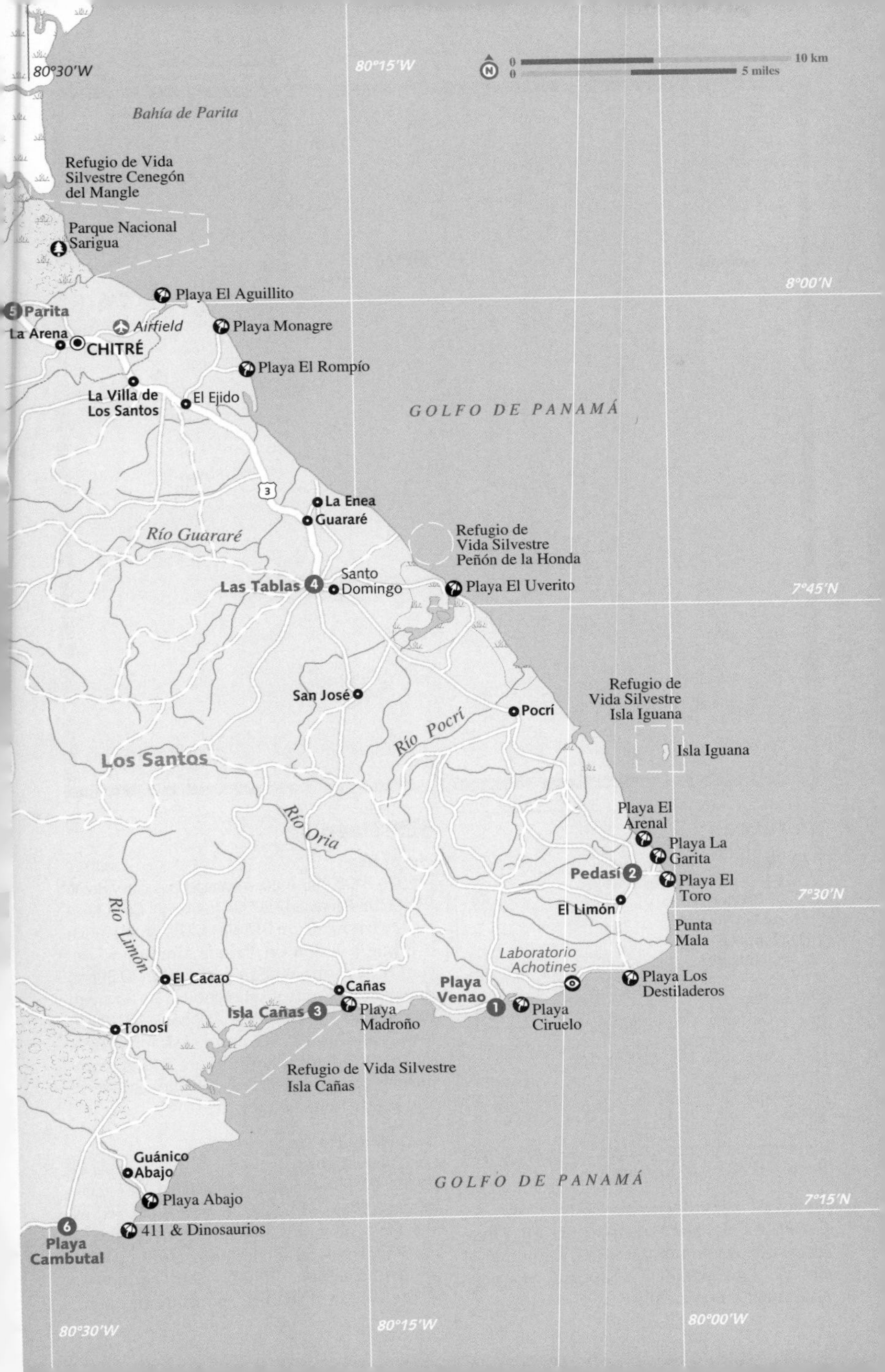
80°30'W
80°15'W
0
10 km
0
5 miles
Bahía de Parita
Refugio de Vida Silvestre Cenegón del Mangle
Parque Nacional Sarigua
8°00'N
Playa El Aguillito
5 Parita
La Arena
Airfield
CHITRÉ
Playa Monagre
Playa El Rompío
La Villa de Los Santos
El Ejido
GOLFO DE PANAMÁ
3
La Enea
Guararé
Río Guararé
Refugio de Vida Silvestre Peñón de la Honda
Santo Domingo
Las Tablas 4
Playa El Uverito
7°45'N
Refugio de Vida Silvestre Isla Iguana
San José
Pocrí
Río Pocrí
Isla Iguana
Los Santos
Río Oria
Playa El Arenal
Playa La Garita
Pedasí 2
Playa El Toro
7°30'N
El Limón
Río Limón
Punta Mala
Laboratorio Achotines
El Cacao
Cañas
Playa Venao
Playa Los Destiladeros
Isla Cañas 3
Playa Madroño
1
Playa Ciruelo
Tonosí
Refugio de Vida Silvestre Isla Cañas
Guánico Abajo
GOLFO DE PANAMÁ
Playa Abajo
7°15'N
6
Playa Cambutal
411 & Dinosaurios
80°30'W
80°15'W
80°00'W

Chitré

Chitré

Sights

1 Museo de Herrera Fabio Rodriquez C2

Sleeping

2 Hotel Rex D2

Eating

3 Ceviches Tio Caimán C1
4 Mare Bonita A2
Restaurante El Meson de Rex .... (see 2)
5 Salsa y Carbon C2

concerned about animal welfare, you might be unsettled by either event.

Fiesta de la Fundación de Chitré CULTURAL
(Foundation of Chitré Holiday; Oct 19) These festivities celebrate the 1848 founding of Chitré, with parades, historical costumes and much merrymaking.

Sleeping

Hotel Rex HOTEL $
(996-2408, 996-4310; www.facebook.com/Hotel-Rex-Chitre-Panama-121877944544889; Calle Melitón Martín s/n; d/tr/q US$44/66/75;) With a prime location on Parque Union and decent **dining** (mains US$7-15; 7:15am-10:30pm) downstairs, Rex is a solid choice. Its 33 clean tiled rooms have brick walls, cable TV, fresh towels and water thermoses. Ask for a room on the 2nd floor where there's a large communal veranda overlooking the cathedral and pretty main square.

Hotel City House Los Guayacanes HOTEL $$
(996-9758; www.losguayacanes.com; Vía Circunvalación; d/ste US$73/138; P) Billed as a resort, this hotel has ample space that is particularly good for families. Built around an artificial lake about 1.5km southwest of the center, it features a swimming pool,

casino and tennis courts. Its 64 rooms are tasteful and bright.

Eating

Ceviches Tio Caimán SEAFOOD $

(996-8040, 6615-0905; www.facebook.com/pages/Restaurante-Boulevar-Tio-Caiman/391111577608369; Calle Independencia; mains US$8-12.50; 8am-9:45pm Mon-Wed, to 10:45pm Thu-Sat, 2-8:30pm Sun) Chitré's favorite seafood restaurant specializes in *ceviche* (citrus-cured seafood, from US$4) but has many more inventive dishes on offer, including those with a Caribbean slant. It's north of the center, next to the public swimming pool.

★**Mare Bonita** FUSION $$

(6200-0124; www.facebook.com/pages/Restaurante-Mare-Bonita/372368832954808; Via Circunvalación; mains US$10-15; noon-10pm) A recent migrant from Pedasí (its loss), this tapas bar and restaurant is considered by many to be the best restaurant in Chitré and it certainly is the most inventive. The Madrid-trained chef keeps the menu in a state of flux, offering teriyaki chicken and Thai-style pork one week, gourmet hamburgers and fried fish *ceviche* the next.

★**Salsa y Carbon** PARRILLA $$

(996-6022; www.salsaycarbon.com; cnr Calles Julio Botello & Francisco Corro; mains US$8-15; 11am-10pm) This open-air Colombian BBQ house grills some of the best steak and ribs in the region. Meat and chicken are exceptionally tender and served with salad and *arepas* (maize flatbread). The covered outside seating catches cool breezes and is a delight on a warm evening. It's opposite Rico Cedeño Stadium and is always heaving.

Information

Banco Nacional de Panamá (970-3300; Paseo Enrique Geenzier; 8am-3pm Mon-Fri, 9am-noon Sat) has an ATM.

Getting There & Away

Chitré is a center for regional bus transportation. Buses arrive and depart from **Terminal de Transportes de Herrera** (996-6426; Via Circunvalación), 1km south of downtown, just off the Vía Circunvalación. The terminal has a 24-hour restaurant. To get there, **Radio Taxi** (996-4442) charges less than US$2. The 'Terminal' bus (US$0.30) leaves from the intersection of Calle Aminta Burgos de Amado and Av Herrera.

Tuasa (996-2661) and **Transportes Inazun** (996-4177) buses head to Panama City (US$9.05, four hours, every 40 minutes from 6am to 6pm).

To get to David (US$9.50), take a bus to Santiago (US$3.25, every half-hour) and then catch a *directo* (direct bus). These *directos* leave from the gas station at the intersection of the Interamericana and the Carretera Nacional.

BUSES FROM CHITRÉ

DESTINATION	COST (US$)	DURATION	FREQUENCY
Aguadulce	3	1hr	every 20min
Divisa	1.50	30min	every 15min
La Arena	0.70	15min	every 15min
La Villa de Los Santos	0.50	5min	every 10min
Las Minas	3	45min	every 30min
Las Tablas	1.50	35min	every 15min
Macaracas	2.50	1hr	hourly
Ocú	2.50	1hr	every 25min
Panama City	9.05	4hr	every 40min
Parita	0.65	15min	every 30min
Pedasí	3.25	1hr	hourly
Pesé	1.10	20min	every 20min
Playa El Agallito	0.50	12min	every 20min
Playas Monagre & El Rompío	1.50	30min	every 20min
Santiago	3.25	1hr	every 30min
Tonosí	5.20	2hr	every 40min

Getting Around

When the Carretera Nacional reaches Chitré from the west, it becomes Paseo Enrique Geenzier, changing its name again a dozen blocks further east to Calle Manuel Maria Correa. The Carretera Nacional re-emerges at the southern end of town.

If you need to travel by vehicle, a taxi is the best way to go. Most fares in town are less than US$3.

Around Chitré

La Arena

POP 7590

The village of La Arena, some 6km west of Chitré, produces some of the highest-quality pottery in the country and is a great place to watch artisans working their craft. The pottery mimics the pre-Columbian designs of the indigenous Ngöbe-Buglé people who once lived nearby. Another product for which the village is noted is bread; *el pan de la Arena* is celebrated (and consumed) nationwide. *Panaderías* line the main drag and stock not just bread but all kinds of pastries and cookies too.

You can buy traditional painted ceramics at wholesale prices at **Ceramica Hermanos Calderón** (910-4076; www.facebook.com/Ceramicas-Hermanos-Calderón-835501223198677; Calle del Río Parita).

Atop a hill in La Arena below the TV tower the restaurant, **El Mirador** (974-4647; www.facebook.com/Restaurante-El-Mirador-955068687866927; mains US$8-15; 4-10pm Mon, noon-10pm Tue-Sat, noon-6pm Sun) is a popular spot where visitors from around Panama congregate to take in the views of the city and the surrounding plains. From downtown Chitré, head west on Paseo Enrique Geenzier for about 2.5km and turn left onto Quintas del Mirador, the road that begins just past the large Paseo Central mall on the right. At the fork, turn right and continue for another 400m until you reach the top of the hill.

Getting There & Away

La Arena can be reached by frequent bus (US$0.70) from Chitré. A taxi ride from Parque Union in central Chitré to La Arena shouldn't cost more than US$3.

Parque Nacional Sarigua

Some 26km northwest of central Chitré, **Parque Nacional Sarigua** (park office 996-8216; 8am-4pm) is arguably the most important pre-Columbian site in Panama. The archaeological site has been dated back 11,000 years, although much of it is yet to be excavated. Created in 1984, it consists of 80

INSIDE AZUERO'S INTRIGUING PAST

Spanish settlements were so effective in wiping out the indigenous populations of Azuero that little is known about these communities. During the 1940s, a major tomb excavation just 10km outside Parita yielded some of the finest pre-Columbian objects ever discovered in Panama.

Artifacts included painted pots in the form of birds and batons shaped like stylized alligators exquisitely carved from manatee bone. Perhaps the most amazing find was a necklace made of more than 800 human teeth.

In the colonial era, the peninsula was covered by dry tropical rainforest and thick mangroves. Early communities subsisted on hunting and fishing, with small-scale agriculture that produced rice, beans and manioc. Several tribes shared the peninsula, though the region was controlled by a powerful Ngöbe-Buglé chief named Parita.

For decades, Parita and his fierce warriors held off Spanish settlement. Yet when Gaspar de Espinosa raided in the early 16th century, Parita was found dead, surrounded by his slaughtered wives, attendants and more than 160kg of gold ornaments. They were presumably killed by another tribe on the peninsula. Also found were 20 native captives lashed to house posts by cords around their necks – about to be buried alive with the late great chieftain.

Following this episode, the Spanish rapidly colonized the Península de Azuero and exterminated its residents. A few Ngöbe-Buglé communities fled to the forested mountains in present-day Chiriquí Province. These same communities were so fearful of further attacks that they placed deadly traps along trails until only a few decades ago.

sq km of wasteland that was once dry tropical rainforest and coastal mangrove patches. Buses do not go all the way to the park. A taxi ride to the park office from Chitré costs about US$15.

To get here from the Carretera Nacional, take the turnoff opposite the unmissable (and bright orange) Super Candy convenience store just before you reach Parita. After going 2.5km, you'll reach a fork with a green-and-yellow sign indicating the park. The ranger's station is another five minutes further on.

Parita

POP 3730

About 13km northwest of downtown Chitré, the colonial town of Parita is one of those little-known places that travelers love to stumble across. Founded in 1556 and named after a Ngöbe-Buglé chief, Parita is full of 18th-century colonial structures, including the delightful Iglesia de Santo Domingo de Guzmán. Buildings have thick walls and solid beams, red-tiled roofs and sweeping arcades. Despite its historic core, Parita is known to few outside the Península de Azuero, so it's unlikely that you will see any tourists here, Panamanian or otherwise.

Sights

★Taller Dario López WORKSHOP
(Dario López Workshop; ☎6534-1958) One of Panama's top artisans, Dario López has been making colorful masks for folkloric dancers since the 1960s. These days most of his masks and satin costumes worn by devil dancers are exported to the USA and Europe. Masks typically cost between US$20 and US$100. To visit his home workshop, look for the gas station near the Parita turnoff on Carretera Nacional. His house is green and on the east side of the highway about 100m north of the station.

Taller de Restauración Macario José Rodriguez WORKSHOP
(Macario José Rodriguez Restoration Workshop; ☎974-2136) Macario José Rodriguez has been restoring the wooden altars and statuary of Panama's colonial churches since the early 1980s, and this is the only such workshop in the country. You'll find it opposite Parita's church on the main square and just behind the green Servicios Médicos building. Visitors are more than welcome.

Iglesia de Santo Domingo de Guzmán CHURCH
(☎6551-5031) This 18th-century churrigueresque (an ornate Spanish baroque style) church has some lovely carvings; check out the pulpit and the retablo (altarpiece). It is the only church in Panama that has its steeple located directly over its entrance rather than over a corner of the structure. This is very unusual as bell towers are always extremely heavy, and therefore are generally built on pillars that rest upon a massive foundation.

Getting There & Away

Parita is about 500m from Carretera Nacional and signposted to the left. Buses run every half-hour to and from Chitré (US$0.60, 15 minutes). A taxi ride from Parque Union in central Chitré to Parita will cost around US$5.

Interior Azuero

Pesé & Ocú

POP 2560 (PESÉ); 7010 (OCÚ)

Interior Azuero towns **Pesé** and **Ocú** west of Chitré offer a glimpse of rural life, with worthwhile traditional festivals, artisans' workshops and liquor production from the endless sea of sugarcane plantations.

Pesé, 23km southwest of Chitré, is home to **Varela Hermanos** (☎974-9401, 6550-4498; www.varelahermanos.com/en; tours US$25-100; ⏲9am-3pm Mon-Fri, to noon Sat), the country's largest *seco* distillery. Four different tours are available, all of which include tastings. Book ahead. Pesé is also famous for its annual Good Friday re-enactment of the Passion of Christ.

About 24km west of Pesé, sleepy Ocú produces its own version of the Panama-style hat called *sombreros ocueños,* the best examples of which cost up to US$100.

Ocú's festivals also have wide notoriety, including **Festival Nacional del Manito Ocueño**, held during the second week in August, and the **Feria de San Sebastián**, celebrating Ocú's patron saint in late January. Both Pesé and Ocú feature folklore programs and an agricultural fair.

Shopping

Ezequela Maure ARTS & CRAFTS
(☎6033-4026; Ocú) Visitors are welcome at the Ocú workshop of this nationally known maker of Panama-style hats. Drive or walk

north about 1km on Av Central; if you come to a fork in the road, you've gone too far. Ezequela's house is the blue one on the left side of the street, about four houses south of the fork.

Elena Montilla ARTS & CRAFTS
(☎974-1365; Ocú) Elena Montilla is a nationally known maker of Panama-style hats based in Ocú; she also makes *polleras* (traditional dresses from the Península de Azuero). To visit her workshop, drive or walk north about 1km on Av Central; if you come to a fork in the road, you've gone too far. Elena's house is the green one south of the fork.

Artesanías Ocueñas ARTS & CRAFTS
(☎6920-2196, 6060-6753; www.facebook.com/artesaniasocuenascarol.ocu; Plaza Sebastián Ocú, Ocú; ⏲8am-4pm) Overlooking the central plaza in Ocú is this outlet of the internationally renowned women's co-op Artesanía Ocueña. The group sells intricate *montunos* (men's folkloric outfits), *polleras* and handmade items such as tablecloths and place mats with exquisite embroidery.

Getting There & Away

From Chitré, frequent buses go to Pesé (US$1.10, 20 minutes) and to Ocú (US$2.50, one hour). The last bus returns sometime around 6pm. Buses also link Ocú with Santiago (US$2, one hour) in Veraguas.

Macaracas

POP 2890

The town of Macaracas, 42km southwest of Chitré and 65km northwest of Tonosí, is the site of the annual **Fiesta de los Reyes Magos** (Feast of the Magis; ⏲Jan 5-10), highlighted by dramatic theater performances including the story of the Epiphany.

Just outside of Macaracas, **Rio La Villa** is ideal for swimming and is very popular on weekends. To get here, turn west from the main road at the San Juan gas station. Continue for 750m until you pass over a bridge, then turn right into the gravel lot.

Above the Farmacia Pinzón on the main road through town, **Pensión Lorena** (☎995-4181; Calle El Comercio s/n; d with shared/private bathroom US$15/25; P❄) has eight spartan rooms with cold-water showers that will do in a pinch.

Getting There & Away

Buses run between Macaracas and Chitré (US$2.50, one hour, hourly) and Macaracas and Tonosí (US$4.50, 1½ hours, hourly) from 7am to 7pm.

La Villa de Los Santos

POP 7990

A quintessential Azuero town, La Villa de Los Santos is where Panama's first move toward independence from Spain began on November 10, 1821. Residents now honor their freedom-fighting forebears by holding truly wild parties on that date. In fact, the local calendar does not skimp on celebrations, making it a very entertaining destination.

Aside from its festivals, Los Santos (as it's usually called) boasts colonial structures dating back to the early days of the Spanish settlement. It is also home to a modest but noteworthy museum dedicated to Panamanian independence as well as one of the country's most magnificent churches.

WORTH A TRIP

PLAYA EL AGALLITO

Playa El Agallito is a mudflat created by silt deposited by the Río Parita and the Río La Villa, 9km north of Chitré. At low tide, it stretches more than 2km from the high-water mark to the surf, supplying a bounty of plankton and small shrimp to thousands of migrating birds. The mudflat is reached from Chitré via Av Herrera just past the airport. A taxi ride from town costs around US$3 one way.

Regular avian visitors to the area include roseate spoonbills, sandpipers, warblers, black-necked stilts, white-winged doves, black-bellied plovers, yellow-crowned amazons, yellowlegs and ospreys. The beach is also home to common ground-doves, which are found only in this one spot in Panama. At high tide, birds congregate around salt ponds to the immediate east of Playa El Agallito. The artificial beach is a failed attempt to create a sunbathing beach by destroying a mangrove forest back in the 1960s.

A bus (US$0.50, 45 minutes) leaves the Chitré station for the beach every 15 minutes or so during daylight hours.

Sights

Iglesia San Atanasio CHURCH

(Plaza Simón Bolívar) On the east side of Plaza Simón Bolívar, this national treasure was consecrated in 1782, although the foundation stone had been laid more than two centuries earlier. It's a wonderful example of the baroque style, with lots of intricately carved and gilded wood depicting cherubs, saints, plants and flowers. Almost everything is original, including the six side altars; some objects predate the church itself.

Museo de la Nacionalidad MUSEUM

(966-8192; www.inac.gob.pa/museos/112-los-santos; Calle José Vallarino; adult/child US$1/0.25; 8am-4pm Tue-Sat) This modest museum, on the north side of Plaza Simón Bolívar, occupies the former house where Panama's Declaration of Independence was signed in 1821. Pre-Columbian ceramics and colonial-era religious art comprise most of the exhibits, though obviously there's a fair amount on Los Santos' role in the independence movement. In an outbuilding in the lovely garden courtyard out the back is a restored *cocina típica* (traditional kitchen).

Taller Carlos Ivan de Leon WORKSHOP

(Carlos Ivan de Leon Workshop; 6938-1330; Calle Tomas Herrera; noon-1pm & 6-10pm) Master mask-maker Carlos Ivan de Leon creates the most elaborate and frightening masks in Panama at his house just after Calle Segundo Villareal. He specializes in devil masks for the famous *baile de los diablos sucios* (dance of the dirty devils).

Festivals & Events

El Grito de La Villa CULTURAL

(Cry of the Village) Also known as El Primer Grito de la Independencia, the anniversary of the historic *grito* (cry) of independence is celebrated in Los Santos on November 10. This patriotic occasion is usually overseen by the president of Panama and is highlighted by a parade, musical and dance performances and a healthy amount of drinking in the streets.

Feria Internacional de Azuero FERIA

(http://atp.gob.pa/eventos/feria-internacional-de-azuero; late Apr/early May) This five-day mainly agricultural fair also features folkloric dancing and competitions among local singers performing regional songs.

Sleeping

Los Santos gets packed to the brim during its many festivals, but with plenty of options in Chitré, just 6km to the north, you need not panic.

Hotel La Villa HOTEL $

(966-8201; www.hotellavillapanama.com; d US$50-55; P ❄ 📶 🏊) About 500m off the Carretera Nacional, this 52-room resort-like property is spread over a large garden and boasts a swimming pool that beckons like a beacon in the dry and dusty Azuero summer. Rooms of varying sizes and shapes have brick-faced walls and folkloric themes, incorporating artisan crafts from Los Santos festivals. The attached bar-restaurant serves up Panamanian favorites.

La Saloma Hostal GUESTHOUSE $

(6782-3438, 923-1399; http://lasalomahostal.wix.com/hostal; Calle Segundo Villareal; dm/d US$15/30; 📶) Located on the south side of the main square, this colorful guesthouse counts some 10 rooms. Five of them are in a building dating to the 1870s; the remainder are in a newer addition in the back courtyard. The rooms are pretty bare-bones – one is a four-bed dorm – and only one has its own bathroom, but the location is great.

Hotel Restaurante Kevin HOTEL $

(966-8276; kevinmoreno@hotmail.com; Vía Dr Belisario Porras; d US$35-45; P ❄ 📶 🏊) Set back from the busy Carretera Nacional, this renovated 20-room hotel features a wide range of nearly identical-looking coral-colored rooms in an L-shaped structure behind the main building. The price is right, with private hot-water bathrooms and satellite TV. Guests get to use the owner's swimming pool behind the hotel.

Paradise Resort HOTEL $$

(923-0630, 6220-8161; www.facebook.com/Paradise-Resort-1349388638437021; Carretera Nacional; s/d incl breakfast US$55/66; P ❄ 📶 🏊) This bright yellow hotel on the Carretera Nacional makes good with 22 deluxe motel-style rooms, some garden-facing. It offers a beautiful pool with covered slide and falls, has solar panels and recycles the pool water for plant watering. It's very family friendly and service is attentive. An on-site restaurant serves fresh juices, burgers and seafood.

FIESTA DE CORPUS CHRISTI

One of the most riotous events in Panama, the **Fiesta de Corpus Christi** has been celebrated ever since Pope Urban IV sanctioned the festival in 1264. Yet the local version coolly incorporates animistic traditions passed down through generations in the Península de Azuero.

As a means of converting the indigenous peoples of the region, Spanish missionaries used the festival to highlight the concept of good versus evil. At the core of the festival is a series of dances including the famous *baile de los diablos sucios* (dance of the dirty devils), which emphasizes the Christian belief in the Apocalypse.

Though God, heaven and the angels predictably win in the end, it doesn't prevent local artisans from creating some truly mind-blowing masks and costumes. Running from Thursday through Sunday, the 40th day after Easter, the festival attracts hundreds of performers, ranging from singers and dancers to theater troops and magicians.

Information

Banco Nacional de Panamá (966-9070; Av 10 de Noviembre; 8am-3pm Mon-Fri, 9am-noon Sat) faces the main square and has an ATM.

Getting There & Around

Buses between Chitré and Las Tablas stop at Los Santos on the Carretera Nacional; buses running from Chitré to Los Santos stop on Calle José Vallarino, half a block from the highway. Fares to these destinations are between US$0.50 and US$2.

Buses to Panama City (US$10, 3½ hours) depart hourly from Calle José Vallarino at Av 10 de Noviembre, and also from Calle Segundo Villarreal, a couple of blocks northeast of Plaza Simón Bolívar.

Taxis are a quick way to get around Los Santos and to and from Chitré. The fare won't exceed US$1.50. Taxis can usually be found near the bus stop on the Carretera Nacional and northwest of Plaza Simón Bolívar.

Road to Las Tablas

The Carretera Nacional from La Villa de Los Santos to Las Tablas runs for about 30km mostly past small farms and cattle ranches, with almost no remaining forest in sight – indeed, Los Santos Province is the most heavily deforested in the country. However, the drive is still scenic, with 'cowboys' on horses aplenty along the way.

About 3km southeast of Los Santos along the Carretera Nacional you'll discover a rustic truck stop, **Kiosco El Ciruelo** (dishes from US$2.50; 6am-10pm Fri-Sun), where everything is cooked on a wood-fire grill. Among the offerings is a traditional specialty of Los Santos Province: tamales made with corn, pork and various spices, and wrapped in plantain leaves.

Getting There & Away

Buses from Los Santos to Las Tablas (US$1.90) are frequent throughout the day. A taxi between the two should cost you about US$12.

Guararé

POP 4520

Tiny Guararé, located on the Carretera Nacional between Los Santos and Las Tablas, is just another sleepy Azuero town until late September, when the comatose town comes to life with **Festival de la Mejorana**, Panama's largest folkloric festival.

Founded by Manuel F Zárate in 1949 to stimulate interest and participation in traditional practices, the festival is the best place to see Panama's folklore in all its manifestations.

Guararé is also the birthplace of four-weight world champion Roberto Durán, one of the greatest boxers of all time and arguably the world's most famous Panamanian.

Sights

Academia de Costumbres y Tradiciones Gabriel Villarreal ARTS CENTER
(994-4581, 6949-6885; www.facebook.com/Academiadefolclor; Edificio Melo; 2-6pm Mon-Fri) A local training ground for young festival artists, the Academy of Customs & Traditions Gabriel Villarreal offers classes in dancing, *mejorana* (a kind of small guitar), accordion, violin and *cantaderas* (folk songs). Visitors are always welcome to watch; contact coordinator Pastor Falconett. It is in the Melo building opposite the Euromax minimarket, just west of the church.

Museo Casa de Manuel F Zárate MUSEUM
(☎994-5644; www.inac.gob.pa/museos/114-museo-zarate; Calle 21 de Enero; ⏰8am-4pm Mon-Sat) FREE Set in the former residence of Manuel F Zárate, the folklorist devoted to conserving the traditions of the Azuero region, this museum is a good introduction to Guararé's festivities. It contains *polleras*, masks, *diablito* (little devil) costumes and other folkloric items. Cultural performances occasionally take place on Monday and Friday afternoons and there are often artisans stitching or carving nearby. The museum is two blocks north of the church and main square.

Festivals & Events

Festival de la Mejorana FIESTA
Dance groups from all over Panama – and even from other Latin American countries – attend this important annual event in late September. Festivities include a colorful procession in which decorated floats parade through the streets in oxcarts.

Folkloric dances that were once part of other celebrations in other places are today sometimes seen only at this event. For example, this is the only festival in which a dance known as La Pajarita (Little Bird) is performed. In contrast to the various exuberant devil dances, a calm, religious quality seems to pervade La Pajarita.

Sleeping

★ **La Casa del Puerto** APARTMENT $
(☎6772-2863, 994-4982; www.panamacasadelpuerto.com; Playa El Puerto; apt US$50; P❄📶) Lovely La Casa del Puerto is located 8km north of Guararé at Playa El Puerto. It has four apartments in two houses that sleep up to three people; two rooms have an outdoor kitchen and a balcony overlooking the ocean. Host Bonnie, a former Peace Corps volunteer, can arrange local excursions and can pick up guests in Guararé or Chitré.

Hotel La Mejorana HOTEL $
(☎994-5794, 994-5796; www.facebook.com/Hotel-Residencial-La-Mejorana-Guararé-135376686524135; Via Nacional; s/d/tr US$28/39/44; P❄📶) Just off the Carretera Nacional, this nondescript hotel has 23 fairly cramped but clean rooms with good storage space, decent bathrooms and chunky carved wooden furniture. It's the only central place to stay; if there's a festival on, you'll need to book well in advance. The in-house restaurant is one of the few places to eat in town.

Shopping

Cooperativa de Artesanos Guararé ARTS & CRAFTS
(☎6767-0866; ⏰9am-2pm Mon-Sat) This mini-shop in the center of Guararé and run by the local artists cooperative is an excellent place to pick up locally produced treasures – from *polleras* and handbags to ceramics and some of the most beautifully worked wooden items we've seen in Panama.

Getting There & Away

Guararé is beside the Carretera Nacional, 16km south of Los Santos and 6km north of Las Tablas. You can hop on any bus that travels the highway in the direction of Guararé; from both Los Santos and Las Tablas the fare is US$1.20. Call ahead for a local **taxi** (☎994-5410, 994-5600); they can be hard to find during the Festival de la Mejorana.

La Enea

POP 1190

This small village 4km north of Guararé produces the finest *polleras* in Panama. Once the daily attire of Spain's lower classes in the 17th and 18th centuries, the *pollera* is today the national costume, distinguished by its stirring beauty and elegance. It is almost entirely handmade, from the attractive embroidery on the blouse and skirt to the delicate filigree ornaments tucked around the gold combs in the hair. The traditional assortment of jewelry worn with a *pollera* can cost upwards of US$10,000.

JUNTA DE EMBARRE

The Spanish cultural heritage of Azuero lives on in various forms, including some bizarre and very ancient traditions. One is *junta de embarre,* which literally translates as 'meeting of mud covering.' After a local wedding, villagers will gather to build a crude mud hut for the newlyweds, getting pretty muddy and having much fun in the process. This practice symbolizes the joining together of two households as well as the beginning of a new family. Although this custom is dying out in larger towns and cities, it continues on in some of the more traditional areas of the peninsula.

By convention, the *pollera* consists of two basic pieces: a *camisola* (blouse) that rests upon the shoulder tops and a *pollerón* (long skirt) divided into two fully gathered tiers. Each dress requires no less than 10m of fine white linen or cotton cloth. Elaborate multicolored needlework contrasts with the white background.

The gold and pearl *tembleques* (hair ornaments) worn with a *pollera* are passed down as heirlooms.

To see how *polleras* are made, particularly the lace trim, visit the **Taller Jaén-Reyes** (☎6529-0650; ⏰7am-4:30pm Mon-Sat, 2-4:30pm Sun), just off the main road, run by husband and wife William Reyes and Belkis Jaén. Belkis is a master lace maker and will give a presentation on how it's done. There's a nice selection of folk craft for sale from all over the peninsula.

Getting There & Away

Buses (US$0.75) link Guararé (4km away) and La Enea about every half-hour. A taxi will cost about US$3.

Las Tablas

POP 8950

Las Tablas is ground zero for the street dancing, booze-soaked celebrations and all-out mayhem associated with the festivals of the Península de Azuero. Home to the country's most famous Carnaval, Las Tablas is the best place in the land to sample *seco* and seriously cut loose.

The capital city of the province of Los Santos, Las Tablas has a fine church and a small museum dedicated to local statesman and three-time president Belisario Porras. The city is also famous for its combined patron-saint and *pollera* festival, which is a colorful mix of religious ceremony, medieval merrymaking and beauty contest.

Sights

Iglesia Santa Librada CHURCH

(Av Belisario Porras) The walls and base of the pulpit in this baroque-style church on Parque Belisario Porras are original, as are the painted faces of cherubs on the ornate gold-leafed altar. Consecrated in 1789, the church suffered through an earthquake in 1802, which destroyed its other tower, and a fire in 1958. Cedar wood was used in the construction of the altar, which was renovated in 2001.

Museo Belisario Porras MUSEUM

(☎994-6326; www.inac.gob.pa/museos/113-museo-belisario-porras; Av Belisario Porras; adult/child US$0.75/0.25; ⏰8am-4pm Tue-Sat, to noon Sun) South of the main square is the former home of three-time president Belisario Porras, during whose administration the Panama Canal opened. The museum contains many artifacts from Porras' life and times and serves as a monument to the achievements of this widely revered man.

Porras was president for all but two years during the period from 1912 to 1924. He is credited with establishing Panama's network of public hospitals, creating a national registry for land titles and constructing scores of bridges and aqueducts.

Festivals & Events

Carnaval CULTURAL

(⏰late Feb/early Mar) Held over the four days preceding Ash Wednesday, Panama's best Carnaval celebration sees floats and musicians parading parallel streets at dusk, and fireworks at night. The queens appear on Saturday night and their coronation is held on Sunday. Monday is masquerade day and on Tuesday townswomen don *polleras*.

The town is divided into two competing groups: *calle arriba* (upper street) and *calle abajo* (lower street). Each street has its own queen, floats and songs; each day, members parade in street clothes and sing songs that poke fun at the rival group. Merrymakers toss blue dye and shaving cream at the opposing side. No one is spared, so dress accordingly.

Fiestas Patronales de Santa Librada CULTURAL

Held for four days from July 19 and incorporating the Festival Nacional de La Pollera. Church services are accompanied by street celebrations that recall a medieval fair, combined with gambling, dancing, singing, and excessive eating and drinking.

Festival Nacional de La Pollera CULTURAL

(⏰Jul 22) This festival features a parade of young women modeling the national costume, while being judged on their grace and on the artisanship, design and authenticity of their costumes.

Las Tablas

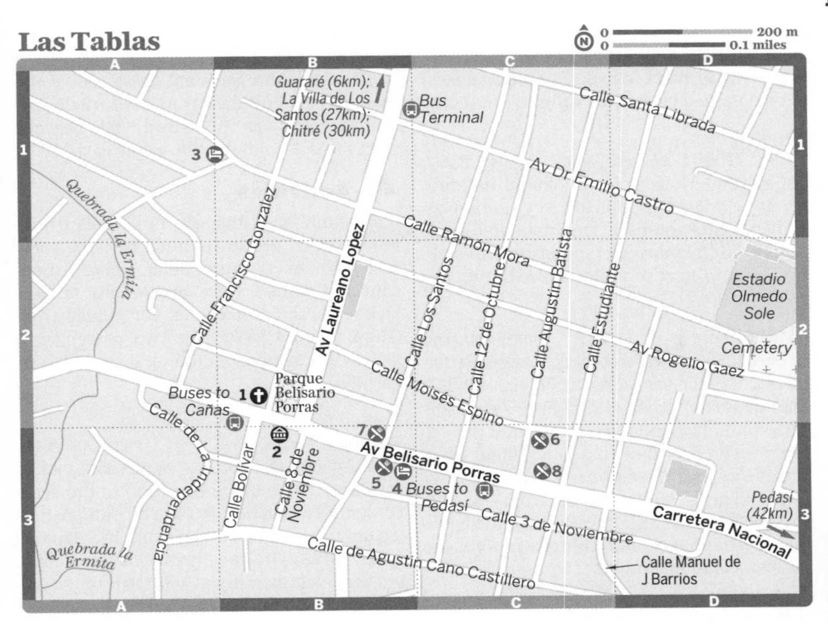

Sleeping

Hotel Piamonte HOTEL $
(923-1603, 923-1903; www.facebook.com/HotelPiamonte; Av Belisario Porras; s/d US$30/39, annex US$27/33; P ❄ 📶) A clean and well-kept place with frilly bedspreads, friendly Piamonte has 44 small-ish rooms; make sure to ask for one with a window. The rooms in the annex across the street are not as nice and thus cheaper. There's a restaurant on the ground floor of the main building.

Hotel Don Jesús HOTEL $$
(6433-9605, 994-6593; www.hoteldonjesus.com; Calle Ramón Mora; d US$60; P ❄ @ 📶 🏊) This 21-room hotel in a converted family home northwest of the main square is beginning to look a bit ramshackle but is still the best centrally located place to stay in Las Tablas. The large communal lounge-balcony with a book exchange is a plus, as is the swimming pool.

Hotel La Luna GUESTHOUSE $$
(6525-9410; www.facebook.com/pages/Hotel-La-Luna/113825222105569; Playa El Uverito; d/tr/q US$75/85/95; P ❄ 📶 🏊) Located 12km east of Las Tablas on the beach, this modern house has four glass-front rooms, modern art and a kidney-shaped pool. It is run by the charming Luca from Milan, who can help organize fishing tours, horseback riding and other activities. A taxi from the center of Las Tablas costs US$7.

Las Tablas

Sights

1 Iglesia Santa Librada B2
2 Museo Belisario Porras B3

Sleeping

3 Hotel Don Jesús B1
4 Hotel Piamonte B3

Eating

5 Boquitas Caseras B3
6 El Caserón C3
7 Los Portales B3
8 Restaurante Aida C3

Eating

Restaurante Aida PANAMANIAN $
(Av Belisario Porras; dishes US$4-6; 24hr) This very basic *fonda* serves *comida típica* (traditional Panamanian dishes) that won't win any culinary awards, but you can't beat the prices or the generous opening hours.

Boquitas Caseras CAFE $
(923-2377; Av Belisario Porras; mains US$2-4; 9am-9pm Mon-Sat) This snack shop is a perfect hunger fix if you have a few minutes

between buses: think marinated meatballs, potato salad and *empanadas* (turnovers stuffed with meat, cheese or veggie mixes) served up in a clean little cafe.

Los Portales PANAMANIAN $
(☎994-7908; Calle Los Santos; mains US$5-7; ⏱6am-2pm) Housed in a colonial building on its very last legs, this low-key spot serves grilled meats and basic Panamanian dishes. Stop by in the morning for a tasty farm-style breakfast to start your day before hitting the road.

★ **El Caserón** INTERNATIONAL $$
(☎994-6066; www.facebook.com/pages/Restaurante-El-Caseron-Las-Tablas/1057814694236037; Calle Moisés Espino; mains US$7-16; ⏱7am-10pm) This pink hacienda-like restaurant has a large covered terrace that is a delight on a warm evening. The emphasis here is on seafood and grills, but the pizzas (from US$4.25 to US$5.50) can also be recommended. It's one of the more comfortable places for a sit-down meal in Las Tablas.

Getting There & Away

The Carretera Nacional becomes Av Laureano Lopez at the northern edge of town and re-emerges as the road to Santo Domingo on the southeastern side of town. From Las Tablas' **bus terminal** (cnr Avs Laureano Lopez & Dr Emilio Castro) there are hourly departures to Santo Domingo (US$0.35, 10 minutes), Cañas (US$3.60, 1½ hours), Chitré (US$1.50, 35 minutes), Tonosí (US$3.50, 1½ hours) and Pedasí (US$2.45, one hour). Buses to **Cañas** and **Pedasí** also stop further south along Av Belisario Porras.

There are frequent buses to Panama City (US$9.70, 4½ hours), with additional departures during the festivals. Buses to Cambutal (US$5, 1¼ hours) via Tonosí depart twice a day at 7am and 2pm.

Pedasí

POP 2410

Unpretentious and laid-back, Pedasí has streets lined with tiled colonials and leafy spaces. For years this sleepy retreat came to life only at festival times. But outsiders are discovering the big appeal of small-town life and relatively unspoiled beaches.

The hometown of erstwhile president Mireya Moscoso, Panama's first female chief executive, Pedasí has become the focus of an intensive push to develop the southwestern coastline. It serves as the gateway to the Azuero coastline and is a convenient base for exploring Refugio de Vida Silvestre Isla Iguana and Isla Cañas.

The Carretera Nacional passes down the western part of Pedasí as Av Belisario Porras (known locally as Av Central). The beaches start just a few kilometers to the east.

Activities

Snorkeling and diving around nearby islands, which are surrounded by large coral reefs, are major attractions. Sport fishers can land wahoo, tuna, mahi-mahi, amberjack and Pacific mackerel. For guided trips (from about US$200 for two passengers), ask at Pedasí Sports Club or Pedasí Nature Paradise Tours.

Pedasí Nature Paradise Tours ADVENTURE SPORTS
(☎452-4560, 6823-8304; www.pedasiparadise.com/tours; Av Central; ⏱8am-5pm) In the dead center of Pedasí, next to Casa de Campo, this agency offers everything from Isla Iguana tours (US$125) and turtle-watching and whale-watching (from US$140) to sportfishing (US$650). It's new and quite keen to please.

Pedasí Sports Club ADVENTURE SPORTS
(☎6749-4308, 995-2894; www.pedasisportsclub.com; Av Central; ⏱7:30am-9pm) This agency has snorkeling trips (US$100) to Isla Iguana as well as sportfishing (US$140), turtle-watching (US$140) in season and horseback riding (US$75).

Festivals & Events

Desfile de Carretas FIESTA
(Cart Parade) This rather unusual festival in late October sees bullock carts and young women dressed in *polleras* parading up and down Av Central. There's lots of merrymaking, with the highlight being the inevitable coronation of Señorita Pedasí. Ensure the festival is taking place before making plans, as it has not been an annual event recently.

Fiestas Patronales de Santa Catalina FERIA
(⏱Nov 24-25) The feast day of St Catherine, patron of Pedasí, is celebrated over two days in late November.

Sleeping

Selina Hostel Pedasí BOUTIQUE HOTEL $
(☎6272-5369; www.selina.com/pedasi; Calle Agustín Moscoso No 2; dm US$11-13, d without bathroom US$22-35, with bathroom US$35-55, deluxe r US$65-100; ❄📶🏊) This branch of a hostel

AZUERO EARTH PROJECT

The most deforested area of Panama, the Península de Azuero has seen generations of cattle ranching degrade what was once dry tropical forest. Gone are the scarlet macaws and most of the spider monkeys. Yet habitat destruction and advancing soil erosion isn't only detrimental to wildlife, it also affects ranchers. Enter **Azuero Earth Project** (☎6773-9127, 995-2995; www.azueroearthproject.org; ⌚8am-5pm Mon-Fri), a nonprofit working to right these wrongs with the help of both volunteers and an elite team of experts collaborating from various fields.

Creating local economic benefits is key to sustainability. Current studies show that locals can win with a greener approach – but it will take time. Ranchers who set aside 10% of their land can double their income by growing hardwoods. The trick is convincing subsistence farmers to wait years for a pay-off when they are used to living day to day.

Currently, the center works closely with the community, promoting organiculture, recycling and conservation education, and working with local elementary schools. Community outreach works with land owners and developers, government agencies and NGOs to make progress toward sustainable solutions.

chain with three other properties elsewhere in Panama has 10 doubles with varying degrees of comfort as well as a 10-bed dorm. There's a wonderful swimming pool and outdoor kitchen, a bar with pool table, US$1 beers at happy hour (6pm to 9pm) and laundry service (US$10). The rough-hewn wood furnishings are fun.

Doña María B&B B&B $
(☎995-2916, 6507-8772; www.donamariabnb.com; Av Central; d/tr incl breakfast US$50/65; P ❄ 📶) Ideal for couples, this caring family-run lodging has six nice rooms above a family home, featuring tiles, firm queen-sized beds with plush quilted covers and cable TV. The upstairs terrace has soft sofas that look out onto the main street. An annex features three additional rooms out the back, one of which has disabled access. Slightly frayed but spotless.

Dim's Hostal GUESTHOUSE $
(☎6274-4156, 995-2303; www.facebook.com/pg/dimshostal/about; Av Central; s/d/tr/q incl breakfast US$30/48/66/84; P ❄ 📶) Dim's has a family atmosphere and a coveted backyard patio, complete with breakfast tables, hammocks and a mango tree. The nine rooms vary in quality – some are quite cramped and have dull tiled floors – but the owners are delightful and service-oriented. A highlight is the huge breakfast spread served on the patio.

★**Casa Lajagua** B&B $$
(☎6303-3848, 995-2912; www.casalajagua.com; d US$77-99, 4-person ste US$129-149; P ❄ 📶 🏊) Set in beautiful leafy grounds away from the hubbub of Av Central, this welcoming place feels more like a resort than the chilled B&B it is. Six individually designed rooms and a suite with orthopedic mattresses and super-strong showers face a huge pool; hammocks swing everywhere, and breakfasts are massive.

Hosts April and Chris are keen water-sports enthusiasts and can organize diving and deep-sea fishing trips on their 25ft Contender Console.

★**Casa de Campo** B&B $$
(☎995-2733, 6780-5280; www.casacampopedasi.com; Av Central s/n; d incl breakfast US$99; ❄ 📶 🏊) Far and away the nicest place to stay in Pedasí, this hospitable and quite chic B&B screams getaway. The seven rooms are named and themed; our favorite is Marina, which has a king-sized bed and measures a full 380 sq meters. The main-street location is deceptive: out back there's a pool and lovely landscaped grounds with thatched *ranchos* and hammocks.

Guests share a family table for big breakfasts with three daily choices. Three-course meals (US$25) are available if prebooked by 1pm, though an in-house restaurant was in the works at the time of research. Hosts Ovidio and Cobi are truly gracious and helpful.

La Rosa de los Vientos B&B $$
(☎6530-4939, 6778-0627; www.bedandbreakfastpedasi.com; Via Playa Toro; d/tr/q incl breakfast US$65/80/90; P 📶) With the feel of a rural hacienda, this lovely red-tile Spanish colonial just up from the beach has three smart rooms with colorful weavings, antique tiles

and ocean views. It's designed to be eco-friendly, so there is no air-con, but fans do the trick. Multilingual owners Isabelle and Robert offer warm hospitality.

The 'Compass Rose' is 2km from town on the road to Playa Toro (taxis cost US$2.50). The beach is a few minutes away on foot.

Casa Loma HOTEL **$$**
(☎6749-4308, 995-2894; www.casalomapedasi.com; Av Central; s/d/tr incl breakfast US$72/83/95; P ❄ 📶 🏊) Sister hotel to the Pedasí Sports Club B&B and sharing the same property, pool and restaurant, the Casa Loma has 10 large and immaculate rooms in a hacienda-like building looking onto a grassy courtyard. There's usually room here when the B&B is full.

Santosha Hostel HOTEL **$$**
(☎6503-0855, 995-2684; www.santoshahostel.com; d/tr US$60/75; P ❄ 📶) What was Pedasí's first hostel has metamorphosed into a budget hotel. Some of its six colorful rooms look out onto the central plaza and behind is a large garden complete with a covered bar and restaurant. A dormitory is apparently on the way.

Pedasí Sports Club B&B **$$**
(☎6749-4308, 995-2894; www.pedasisportsclub.com; Av Central; s/d/tr incl breakfast US$65/77/88; P ❄ 📶 🏊) This property at the northern end of town with 11 motel-style rooms may lack a certain character, but the rooms are impeccably clean and cool, with air-con, wi-fi, satellite TV and hot-water showers. There's a pool that's perfect for dips and a popular restaurant, too.

Pedasí Nature Paradise APARTMENT **$$$**
(☎452-4560, 6216-1236; www.pedasiparadise.com; apt US$180-230; P ❄ 📶 🏊) This new kid on the block is a pricey stunner. It has nine 65-sq-m suites (staff call them apartments) with locally made teak and cedar furniture and fully equipped kitchens on two levels. Four of the suites have their own Jacuzzis and everyone gets to use the lovely pool. The place is very high-tech, with everything controlled by iPhone.

Eating

Fonda Mama Fefa PANAMANIAN **$**
(Calle Los Estudiantes; set meals US$3; ⏲5am-2pm Mon-Sat) Matriarch of Creole cooking, Mama Fefa usually runs out of lunch by noon (though you can linger longer). Cheap and cheerful, these huge *comidas típicas* (regional specialties) include meat or fish, rice, salad and a drink. Devotees share the space at a few outdoor tables. Follow the side street opposite the landmark supermarket for two blocks. It's on the right.

Bakery CAFE **$**
(www.facebook.com/thebakerypedasi; Av Central s/n; mains US$6-14; ⏲7am-8pm; 🌿) Known for exquisite breakfasts (US$4 to US$6.50) with homemade wheat or sourdough bread and organic coffee, this Israeli-run Pedasí institution does a brisk business. In addition to breakfasts, you can order sandwiches (US$5), with vegetarian options, salads (US$4) and lasagna. The shady porch overlooks the main street.

Isla Iguana SEAFOOD **$**
(☎6620-4073; Av Central; mains US$7-12; ⏲11am-10pm Thu-Tue) For filling seafood that won't break the bank, try this roadside restaurant that somehow manages the atmosphere of a friendly truck stop. Try the *ceviche* (a specialty) and the sea bass. It's at the southern end of town next to the gas station.

Pizzeria Tiesto PIZZA **$**
(☎995-2812; Calle Las Tablas; mains US$3-12; ⏲2-10pm Wed-Mon) With brick-oven pizzas topped with local cheese and tasty chicken tacos, this plaza-front Panamanian cafe on the southeast corner of the main square proves a magnet for locals and backpackers alike. Sweets include oatmeal cookies and pineapple cake.

Super Centro El Pueblo SUPERMARKET **$**
(Av Central; ⏲7am-9pm Mon-Thu, 6:30am-10pm Fri-Sun) The town's principal supermarket sits on the corner of Av Central and Calle Los Estudiantes.

★ **Segreto** ITALIAN **$$**
(☎6822-7575; www.facebook.com/pages/Segreto/581448718627827; Av Central; mains US$10-14; ⏲6-9pm Mon-Sat) Pedasí's best (some might stop there) Italian restaurant is set in what feels like a glassed-in conservatory. There are more complex *secondi* (main courses) with usually three meat and three fish dishes, but most come for the delectable pasta dishes. Host Mirko is welcoming and helpful.

Bohemia Pizzeria Restaurante PIZZA **$$**
(☎995-2950, 6214-5163; www.facebook.com/bohemiapedasi; Av Central; pizza US$9-18; ⏲5-10pm Mon, Tue & Thu, from 7am Fri-Sun) Many punters swear by the pasta at this rustic little place at the southern end of town, but we come

here for the pizzas, arguably the best in town. Friendly staff and good service.

Restaurante Smiley's AMERICAN **$$**
(☎6510-9652, 995-2863; www.facebook.com/smileys.restaurante; Av Central; mains US$10-16.50; ⏲noon-late Tue-Sun) Catering largely to expats, this friendly bar-restaurant serves up grilled fish, ribs and deli sandwiches (US$5 to US$7.50), including minced BBQ pork. There's also good live music on Tuesday and Friday nights, sports on the tube, and an extensive drinks menu to match. The daily lunch special is a snip at US$4.

Information

The **ATP** (☎995-2339; azuero@atp.gob.pa; ⏲8am-4pm Mon-Sat) office lies one block past the main road in the north of town. It has a list of boat contacts for Refugio de Vida Silvestre Isla Iguana and Isla Cañas.

Volunteer-friendly NGO Azuero Earth Project (p127) focuses on behind-the-scenes work in conservation and community education. Visitors can check out the research center library, which has naturalist guides and maps for sale. An outdoor information board features a community events calendar. It's on a side street behind the gas station and ATP office by the town entrance.

Banco Nacional de Panama (☎995-2257; Av Central; ⏲8am-3pm Mon-Fri, 9am-noon Sat) in the center has an ATM. It's one of two in town on Av Central.

Getting There & Away

BUS

Buses to Las Tablas leave every hour between 6am and 4pm (US$2.40, one hour) from the **bus stop** next to the El Pueblo supermarket. Buses to Playa Venao (US$2.20, 30 minutes) leave at 7am, noon and 2pm. Buses to Cañas (US$2.40, 45 minutes) depart at 7am and noon.

The Selina Hostel (p126) runs daily vans (one way/round trip US$5/8) to Playa Venao, where it has another hostel. Buses leave Pedasí at 11am, 4pm and 7pm and return from Playa Venao at 9am, noon and 6pm. The hostel also runs buses to Panama City (one way/round trip US$35/70) at 8am on Monday, Wednesday and Friday.

CAR & TAXI

The coastline is easily accessed by private vehicle or **taxi** (☎6847-7535); the taxi stand is on Av Central. Standard one-way fares include Playa El Toro (US$3.50), Playa La Garita (US$5), Playa Los Destiladeros (US$7) and Playa Venao (US$25).

Refugio de Vida Silvestre Isla Iguana

The 53-hectare **Refugio de Vida Silvestre Isla Iguana** (US$10) is centered on a deserted island ringed by corals. The water is shallow enough for snorkeling and, as elsewhere in the Pacific, the reef fish here are enormous. You can get here by boat (US$70) in 40 minutes from Playa El Arenal, a beach 3km northeast of Pedasí's gas station. Stick to the beaten paths on the island as unexploded ordnance is occasionally discovered here (the US Navy used the island for target practice during WWII).

Humpback whales inhabit the waters around Isla Iguana from June to October. These large sea mammals, measuring 15m

THE TUNA COAST

Home to a large population of yellow-fin tuna, the Azuero coastline serves as a benchmark indicator for the health of global stocks.

Among the most sought-after fish in the world, yellow-fin tuna has spawned a billion-dollar industry. Found in subtropical and tropical waters, tuna reach lengths of more than 2m and can weigh upwards of 200kg. Although typically processed and canned, tuna is increasingly flash-frozen and sold in fillets for sushi. Left raw, tuna is blood-red in color, with a smooth texture and a rich buttery taste.

Some 30km southwest of Pedasí, **Laboratorio Achotines** (☎995-8166; www.iattc.org; donation requested) tracks the movement and behavior of these fish, tagging them to study migration patterns. This tuna lab is also the only place in the world where tuna are spawned in captivity to be used for study. Affiliated with the Inter-American Tropical Tuna Commission, a global regulatory consortium on tuna fishing, the lab routinely sets quotas for catches along the Pacific coast of the Americas.

Visitors can tour Laboratorio Achotines by appointment and watch an interesting educational video. Another highlight is to show up for the feeding of their prize-sized tunas.

to 20m long, mate and bear their young here and then teach them to dive. The humpbacks are the famous 'singing whales'; occasionally you can hear their underwater sounds when diving.

Although the island is supposed to be maintained by the Ministerio de Ambiente, Panama's environmental agency, the main beach is often strewn with litter that is washed in with the tide.

The ATP office (p129) in Pedasí has a list of boat operators that can get you to the island.

Azuero Coastline

Gorgeous and somewhat remote, the coast of southeast Azuero offers excellent swimming and surfing possibilities as well as some top accommodations. You can surf here year-round but conditions are best between March and November.

La Playita

Popular among Panamanian day-trippers, the beach at La Playita (day pass adult/child US$7/3) can get pretty crowded at weekends. It's not the prettiest spot on the coast, but the nearby resort and its facilities are an added draw.

Sleeping

Resort La Playita RESORT **$$**
(997-6727, 6615-3898; www.playitaresort.com; d/q US$120/150; P ❄ ☎) More rustic retreat than resort, this place has shady and somewhat dated cabins surrounded by an informal zoo of guacamayas, macaws, emus and howler monkeys. It also has eight rooms with air-con and cold-water showers. The best are rooms 6 to 9, which have oversized furnishings made from driftwood, colorful mosaics, cozy throws and balconies with sea views.

The on-site restaurant (mains US$8 to US$12) serves seafood and typical Panamanian fare.

Getting There & Away

La Playita is about 30km southwest of Pedasí and just 2km east of Playa Venao; from the main road, travel 1.5km down an unsealed road in poor condition to reach the beach and resort. Buses from Pedasí pass the entrance at 7am and return to Pedasí at around 3:30pm.

Playa Ciruelo

Fringing a perfect half-moon bay, Playa Ciruelo retains its fishing-village atmosphere despite the recent spate of building.

The excellent-value **Casa Estrella** (647-3090, 6889-3044; d US$80; P ❄ ☎) has four pristine blue rooms with driftwood beds and sea views. Showers have hot water. The house is inviting and immaculate, with hammocks on a shady deck, great views and a comfortable family living area. Host Pee Wee will take you fishing, and the beach is popular with surfers.

Getting There & Away

The bus heading from the village of Cañas to Las Tablas passes by at around 7:30am and stops on its way back to Cañas at about 4pm. A taxi from Pedasí will cost US$15.

Playa Venao

POP 2500

A long, protected beach, Playa Venao – officially Venado but pronounced and spelled as 'Venao' – recently transformed from a wild beach to a 'go-to' destination. Surfers lay the first claim to its waters; waves are consistent and break in both directions. Depressingly, this gorgeous stretch of blackish volcanic sand looks like a construction site as building continues apace. Venao will hopefully look lovely again when the construction's finished.

Activities

Playa Venao Fishing FISHING
(6246-3651, 6244-5339; www.playavenaofishing.com;) Expat Briton Carlito Crognale offers five-hour fishing trips on Panama's famous Tuna Coast on a fully equipped center console boat (US$350 to US$400 for up to three people) or a more economical *panga* (local flat-bottomed canoe) costing US$250 to US$300 for up to four people. English- and Spanish-speaking guides, and very family friendly. All fishing gear included.

Cañas Jungle Adventure ADVENTURE SPORTS
(838-8751, 6510-2774; www.facebook.com/ZiplinePanama; zipline/swing/hiking US$60/20/10, packages US$75; 8am-3pm) In Cañas, 12km west of Venao, this place has eight cable ziplines spanning some 3km above the jungle, as well as two rappels, a scary suspension bridge and a supercool Tarzan swing. Hiking trails

SURFING THE AZUERO COAST

Though untapped by the international crowd, the Azuero coast boasts some impressive surf. Panamanians mostly hit the coastline near Pedasí, but there is no shortage of wicked spots elsewhere – just a shortage of decent transportation to them.

Playa Lagarto Some 5km southeast of Pedasí. Beach bottom. Breaks at all tides. Good rights and lefts. Closes out when the surf is too big. Popular with boogie boarders.

Playa Toro Near Pedasí. Rock-bottom point break with lefts and rights. Gets big with a strong swell. Best surfed at medium tide, when there's a swell of 1.8m or more.

Playa Los Destiladeros Near Pedasí. Right point over rock bottom, left point over rock bottom, and beach break with pebble bottom. Best at medium tide.

Playa Ciruelo Before Venao. Rock-bottom point break that's rarely surfed. Can get really good left tubes when there is a strong swell and no wind.

Playa Venao Sand-bottom beach break said to be the best year-round one in Panama. This spot catches just about any swell. Best surfed at medium to high tide and in the dry season (November to March). At low tide and swells of over 2.5m to 3m, it tends to close out.

Playa Madroño A 30-minute walk from Playa Venao. Surf can get really good, with hollow tubes at low tide. It's necessary to arrive early in the day before the wind picks up.

Playa Guánico South of Tonosí. Two rock-bottom point breaks with rights and lefts. One beach break with rights and lefts.

Playa Raya A secluded spot just past Playa Madroño. At low tide, you will see miles of secluded beach, with a right point break on the left side of the sand bar, and a left point break on the left side of the sand bar. Waves 4m to 5m on big swells with serious tubes. Many big sea turtles and sharks here as well.

Playa Cambutal Southwest of Tonosí. Perfect beach breaks with rights and lefts. It has several great surf breaks including beach breaks and point breaks and catches just about any swell. Best at medium to high tide.

Playa Negra West of Playa Cambutal, around the first point. Point break over rock bottom. Best during medium to high tide.

411 (Quartro Once) East of Playa Cambutal. Locally famous point break with a long right over a rock ledge bottom. This is one of the most famous breaks in Cambutal and is best during medium to high tide.

Dinosaurios Next to 411, east of Playa Cambutal. Rock-bottom break with rights and lefts at medium to high tide. Can get very big with strong swells.

Horcones Beach Break Down the beach west from Dinosaurios. Sand-bottom beach break with rights and lefts. Good most tides.

Dos Rocas Near Horcones Beach Break. Rock-bottom point break beside two jutting boulders. Can get good rights at medium tide.

Corto Circuito At road's end toward Cerro Hoya, Azuero's southwest corner. Rock-bottom point break with powerful peak. Breaks over a rock ledge and throws a huge tube, then peels for about 100m with a great wall that you can do lots of turns on.

lead to waterfalls and natural pools. Tours depart daily at 8am, 10am and 2pm.

Surf Dojo SURFING
(☎838-3070, 832-5795; www.surfdojo.com) On the beach opposite the landmark Eco Venao (p132) lodge, Surf Dojo is a full-scale training facility dedicated to the sport of surfing. It rents boards (US$20 per day) and other surfing equipment as well as kayaks (US$40 per day). Lessons cost US$40.

Extreme Surf Shop SURFING
(☎6602-0997; www.facebook.com/El-Sitio-Surf-Club-355338711142870; El Sitio Hotel; ⏲8:30am-7pm) This shop at El Sitio Hotel (p132) rents surfboards for US$15/25 for a half/full day; surfing lessons cost US$40.

Sleeping

Selina Hostel Playa Venao HOSTEL $

(☎ 6274-3222, 202-5919; www.selina.com/playa-venao; campsites per person US$10-19, dm US$12-20, d with/without bathroom from US$70/45, d deluxe US$80-119; P 📶 🏊) This beachside branch of a hostel chain consists of 16 colorful thatched bungalows in rows running down to a pool and the beach. The total 41 rooms come in every possible shape and size, from a mixed dorm with 12 beds and a dozen thatched glamping 'tents' to a private double with bathroom and balcony (best: room 204).

The hostel's nerve center is the beachside restaurant (mains US$8 to US$14) and bar, where surfers will regale you with tales of their exploits; escape to the van with the thatched roof opposite or the chilled co-worker space for some net-surfing. Selina rents boards for US$10/75 per day/week and organizes whale-watching and turtle-watching tours to Isla Iguana (US$42 per person) and Isla Cañas (US$38) in season.

★ **Eco Venao** LODGE $

(☎ 6634-4550, 832-0530; www.ecovenao.com; campsite per person US$6, dm/d without bathroom US$11/35, 2-person cabins US$40, 6-person houses US$160; P ❄ 📶) 🌿 North American–owned Eco Venao offers a cool mountain ambience. Perfect for surfers and adventurers, its excellent options range from campsites and hostel dorms to beachside *cabañas* (cabins). The lush 140-hectare property means adventures are close at hand, from howler-monkey visits and a playground to a short waterfall hike.

The Surfers Hostel is a rustic though comfy dormitory with eight beds, mosquito nets and fans. Privates range from the two-person Cabañas Las Escobas huts on stilts with composting toilets, to air-conditioned colonial-style guesthouses with colorful weavings, ovens and wood accents, such as La Casa Mango (sleeping six) and the adorable La Casona for eight high up on the hill. Five thatched *cabañas* on the beach sleep between two and four people (US$95 to US$125). There's a restaurant, **Los Sombreros**, (http://ecovenao.com/restaurant; mains US$8-15; ⏲ 7am-10pm) and a beachfront boat-shaped bar called Barca (open noon to 9:30pm).

Guests can rent horses (US$20) and do yoga. 'Eco' means that trash separation and recycling are practiced, as well as reforestation. It maintains a small footprint, with minimal roads and footpaths leading to the beach; there's a two-hour permaculture tour (US$20) at 9am on Saturday.

Tipi Hostel Panama HOSTEL $

(☎ 832-6532, 6241-8491; www.facebook.com/tipihostelpanama; dm/cabañas/deluxe d US$15/45/65; ❄ 📶 🏊) This new hostel complex in a mini jungle has three dorms with four to six beds, 10 'deluxe' doubles in a flat-roofed, nondescript building and 20 heat-seeking metal-roofed A-frame huts without windows for two or three. Showers are shared. There's a communal kitchen and a good-sized pool, though the ocean is just meters away.

★ **El Sitio Hotel** HOTEL $$

(☎ 6223-6688, 832-1010; www.elsitiohotel.com; d US$99-109, ste US$129-195, apt US$215; P ❄ 📶 🏊) El Sitio's best feature is its location right on Playa Venao; 'You Are Where You Surf' is its motto. But even if you don't surf, the 16 splendid rooms, suites and apartments at this hotel partially built from recycled shipping containers will delight. Choose one of four suites with private sea-facing balconies or the fab new 'lighthouse' sleeping four.

El Sitio has an excellent restaurant as well as a surf shop that sells and rents equipment. Massage is available, as are activities such as jungle tours and seasonal turtle- and whale-watching (from US$38 per person). The welcome from hosts Lira and Assaf is especially warm; service is very attentive and professional.

Villa Marina Lodge HOTEL $$$

(☎ 832-5044; www.villamarinalodge.com; d incl breakfast US$165-195; P ❄ 📶 🏊) At the eastern quieter end of Playa Venao en route to La Playita, Villa Marina Lodge is a stunner. Set amid tranquil gardens, this resort exudes charm, from the spurting fountain to the wide, shady veranda. The nine guest rooms are bright and capture ocean breezes, while the larger master bedroom has French doors opening onto a beachfront terrace.

Guests can spend swim in the stone-bottomed pool, lounge around on hammocks, ride horses on the beach, snorkel and surf in the sea, or take boating excursions and fishing trips (US$255 for four people).

Eating

Coleos Cafe CAFE $

(☎ 6289-2820; www.facebook.com/Coleos-cafe-855109761222106; mains US$8.50-10; ⏲ 11am-1am) This wonderful little place just up from the beach serves Asian noodle dishes such as pad thai, delicious hummus plates, sandwiches (US$4.50 to US$6) and a wide range of delectable breads, brownies and cookies.

★**Panga** PANAMANIAN $$
(☎6787-2146; www.facebook.com/restaurantepanga; mains US$10-18; ⏰noon-3pm Fri-Sun, 6:30-10pm Wed-Sun) When chef Andres Morataya left award-winning Manolo Caracol and Panama City for Playa Venao, he opened this inventive restaurant. He uses products often discarded – deep-fried snapper gills, anyone? – or prepares them in unique ways as in 'Prawns that Want to be Pork' cooked in a sauce usually served with suckling pig.

★**El Sitio Restaurant** INTERNATIONAL $$
(☎832-1010, 6223-6688; mains US$10-22; ⏰7am-9:30pm) This is an excellent choice for sunset dining or just drinks on Playa Venao. Open-air El Sitio offers sesame-crusted tuna and a host of Asian-inspired dishes such as pad thai noodles with octopus, Thai crepes and chicken curry. A dedicated pastry chef prepares lovely desserts like tamarillo sorbet pavlova and chocolate lava cake.

Getting There & Away

The Playa Venao turnoff is 33km southwest of Pedasí, 2km past the turn for Resort La Playita (p130). The Cañas–Tablas bus (US$3.60) passes by about 7am, while Cañas–Pedasí (US$2.20) comes at about 10am. Westbound buses pass by at 1pm or so. Confirm exact times with your hotel. You can also take a taxi from Pedasí (about US$25).

Selina Hostel runs daily vans (one way/round trip US$5/8) to Pedasí, where it has another hostel. Buses leave Playa Venao at 9am, noon and 6pm and return from Pedasí at 11am, 4pm and 7pm. The hostel also runs buses to Panama City (one way/round trip US$40/70) at 7:30am on Monday, Wednesday and Friday.

Playas Cambutal & Guánico

Playas Cambutal and Guánico, 24km southwest and 16km southeast of Tonosí respectively, are two excellent surf beaches along the Azuero coast. Playa Cambutal in particular is expansive and unspoiled. Many people think it is the next Playa Venao.

Tours

Tortuagro TOURS
(☎6264-9124, 6321-4762; www.facebook.com/Tortuagro-778435305562796; Playa Cambutal) This community conservation organization patrols Playa Cambutal with volunteers during turtle season (July to November) and also runs turtle-watching tours during those months.

Sleeping

Hostal Kambutaleko GUESTHOUSE $
(☎6677-0229; www.hostalkambutaleko.com; Playa Cambutal; d US$45-65, f US$85-100; P 📶) This fabulous eyrie-like guesthouse up a steep hill at the western end of Playa Cambutal has 10 very pretty rooms with breathtaking views; the two front ones are particularly awesome. There's a lovely thatched *bohio*-style bar and restaurant (mains US$8 to US$12), hammocks and any number of activities (surfing, fishing, horseback riding) on offer.

★**Hotel Playa Cambutal** RESORT $$
(☎832-0948; www.hotelplayacambutal.net; Playa Cambutal; d incl breakfast US$125-140; P ❄ 📶 🏊) This delightful 10-room hotel surrounded by lush garden and fronting the ocean offers the most comfortable lodgings in the area. Choose one of the half-dozen rooms above with fabulous balconies. It also features a good restaurant (open 8am to 9pm). Surfboards rent for US$6/25 per half/full day; lessons (including board) cost US$45 per hour.

Getting There & Away

Both Playa Cambutal and Playa Guánico are reachable by well-maintained roads. From Las Tablas a bus goes to Cambutal (US$5, 1¼ hours) via Tonosí at 7am and 2pm. From Tonosí's main square, infrequent *chivasa* rural buses, often a 28-seat Toyota coaster bus, go to Playa Guánico.

Isla Cañas

From July through early November, thousands of olive ridley sea turtles come ashore at night to lay eggs on the 14km-long beach of **Isla Cañas**. Peak months are usually September and October.

Once you reach the island in season, you will be approached by a guide. Paying local guides provides a worthy local alternative to inhabitants selling turtle eggs on the black market.

The turtles arrive late at night, so there's no point in hiring a guide during daylight. Instead, agree on a meeting place and an hour when the guide can walk you across the island to the beach. If you're lucky, you'll arrive at the same time as the expectant mothers. Keep in mind that sea turtles are easily frightened, particularly by the bright lights of flashlights, cameras and telephones. Leave these items behind.

Tours

Gisha Samaniego TOURS

(☎6881-3913) If you're looking for a turtle guide on Isla Cañas you can do no better than hiring Gisha, the best on the island. He owns two horse-drawn carts for transport to the nesting sites. You'll need to speak decent Spanish, however.

Isla Cañas Marina ECOTOUR

(☎6673-7472, 6980-0110; www.islacañasmarina.com) This agency, run by tour operator Frederic Lacoste, offers highly recommended turtle and general ecotours of the Isla Cañas reserve by boat, paddle board or sea kayak, the latter two being fun alternatives for exploring the waterways. This is the best choice if you don't speak Spanish. Contact Frederic at the main pier *(muelle)* in Cañas town.

Isla Cañas Tours ECOTOUR

(☎6718-0032; www.facebook.com/islacanastours) Leads turtle-watching tours along the beach and manages the cabins on Isla Cañas.

Sleeping & Eating

Hostal Pachamama HOSTEL $

(☎6957-5918; https://hostal-pachamama.wixsite.com/home; camping/hammock/dm/cabin per person US$10/10/15/20) This remote and very basic hostel with thatched wooden huts is straight out of *Robinson Crusoe*. The French owners will collect you from Puerto de Cañas (the pier in Cañas town) and take you to the island. They also provide mangrove tours by kayak, turtle tours and snorkeling, and can provide meals (US$10).

Isla Cañas Tours Cabañas CABIN $

(☎6718-0032; www.facebook.com/islacanastours; cabañas US$30; ❄) These two *cabañas* (cabins) accommodating up to five people each with two double beds and a single bunk have air-conditioning and their own bathroom. They are just off the island's grassy main square where you'll also find the island's very blue church.

Mama Gita's PANAMANIAN $

(☎6511-5894; meals US$5) This no-frills little family-run restaurant on the way to the beach offers fresh fish and simple Panamanian dishes alongside four very basic double rooms with communal bathroom (US$25). It's very friendly.

Getting There & Away

The turnoff for Isla Cañas is marked by a large green sign beside a bus stop on the south side of the Carretera Nacional, 6km west of the exit for the town of Cañas. From there it's 2.5km to Isla Cañas.

Buses run from Las Tablas to Puerto de Cañas (US$3.60, two hours) at 7am and 1pm, returning from Puerto de Cañas daily at 7am and 11:30am. From Pedasí buses run to Cañas (US$2.20, 45 minutes) at 7am and noon. From Cañas, take an hourly Tonosí-bound bus, which stops in Puerto de Cañas (US$1.50, 30 minutes).

Once at the local *puerto* (port), you'll be able to find a *lancha* (boat) to transport you through the mangrove to the island for about US$1. Be aware that at low tide you'll have to remove your shoes and walk along the very muddy channel to where the water is high enough for the boat to moor.

The other 'port' is Puerto de Cañas, the little boat ramp (or *muelle*) in Cañas town that is signposted. This is the pick-up and drop-off point for most of the tours. Getting here and back in a local fishing boat will cost you US$40.

Playas Toro & La Garita

The two closest beaches to Pedasí serve as a popular day trip for local residents, largely due to the fact that the ocean here is usually safe for swimming. However, the waves can pick up if there's a strong surge coming in. At Playa Toro you can drive close to the beach, but Playa La Garita is flanked by a rocky slope, and a hike of about 100m through light scrub and dirt (which turns to mud if there's been any recent rain) is required to reach the beach. Despite their close proximity to Pedasí, both beaches are quite isolated and private. Neither offers much snorkeling – the water is simply too murky.

There's an open-air restaurant serving seafood and drinks at Playa Toro and a beach club open to the public in a gated community at Playa La Garita.

Getting There & Away

You can reach these beaches by taxi (US$3) from Pedasí. Driving from town, turn east off the Carretera Nacional onto Calle Agustín Moscoso and drive about 250m to the Cantina Hermanos Cedeño bar. Then take the road just past the bar for 1km until the road forks. Playa Toro is 1.5km to the left and Playa La Garita the same distance to the right.

Veraguas Province

POP 227,000 / ELEV SEA LEVEL TO 3478M

Includes ➡

Best Places to Eat

- ➡ Anachoreo Restaurant (p141)
- ➡ Chillinguito (p145)
- ➡ El Encuentro (p146)
- ➡ Cheesecake (p137)
- ➡ Palati Fini (p152)

Best Places to Stay

- ➡ Punta Duarte Garden Inn (p152)
- ➡ Art Lodge (p142)
- ➡ Heliconia Bed & Breakfast (p152)
- ➡ La Buena Vida (p145)
- ➡ Deseo Bamboo (p144)
- ➡ Hotel Anachoreo (p141)

Why Go?

The name of Veraguas province (literally 'see waters') is both descriptive and accurate – it is the only one of Panama's provinces and *comarcas* (indigenous districts) to border both the Pacific Ocean and the Caribbean Sea.

But there's much more here to attract visitors than endless coastline. Unesco World Heritage Site Isla Coiba, the so-called Galápagos of Central America, draws divers, birdwatchers and paradise-seekers. Surfing village Santa Catalina is a destination in its own right. Hikes to waterfalls and swimming holes around the highland village of Santa Fé offer an off-the-beaten-path retreat.

Veraguas' isolated Caribbean coast will one day be accessible on the Carretera de Caribe, an east–west highway that will link Miguel de la Borda in Colón Province with Rambala in Bocas de Toro, some 230km away. This, and tourism, will help this deforested region of ranchers and subsistence farmers redefine itself and recast its fragile fortunes.

When to Go

Feb & Mar The best months to hit the world-class surf breaks in Santa Catalina and at a number of lesser-known spots elsewhere along the Veraguas coast.

Aug & Dec Three species of turtles nest on the beaches of Malena on the Sunset Coast; community volunteers guide visitors on these very off-the-beaten-path trips.

Dec–Apr These months offers up the the best weather for the beach, but the rainy season (May to November) means impressive waterfalls near the highland village of Santa Fé – though trails may be muddy.

Veraguas Province Highlights

1 Parque Nacional Coiba (p147) Exploring the astounding natural beauty of this national park, both above and below the water.

2 Santa Catalina (p141) Riding some serious waves at Panama's top spot for surfing.

3 Santa Fé (p138) Ascending to this highland village, famous for its waterfalls, steep hills and lush forests.

4 Sunset Coast (p150) Adventuring through this delightfully untrampled region, with remote beaches, great surfing and community turtle tours.

5 San Francisco (p138) Visiting the Iglesia de San Francisco de la Montaña, one of the best examples of baroque religious art and architecture in the Americas.

6 Isla Cébaco (p150) Getting inspired off the beaten path with a retreat to this crowd-free island.

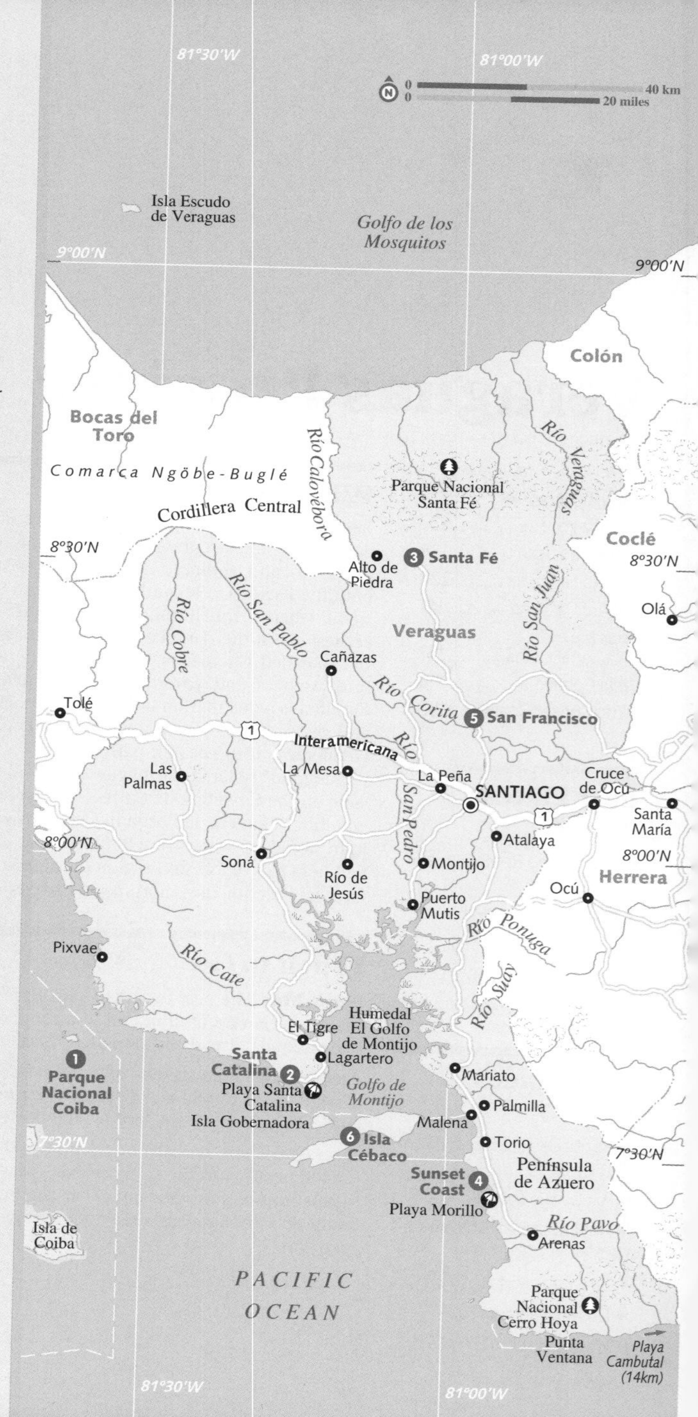

Santiago

POP 41,240

Halfway between Panama City and the Costa Rican border and just north of the Península de Azuero, Santiago is a bustling hub of rural commercial activity. There's no real reason to stop here, though it's a good place to break up a drive and recharge for the night.

Most of Santiago's commerce and services, including stores, banks, gas stations, restaurants and hotels, are along the Interamericana and Av Central, which runs to the west from the highway.

Sleeping & Eating

You'll find most of Santiago's better hotels along the Interamericana. If you're looking to stock up on food, there's a supermarket in front of the bus terminal. Most big hotels in Santiago also have their own restaurant.

Mykonos Hotel HOTEL $$
(933-2000; www.mykonospanama.com; Interamericana s/n; d from US$88;) If overnighting in Santiago but daydreaming of the Mediterranean, this new highway hotel might do the trick. Service is good, rooms are chic and the sprawling swimming pool clinches it. The Greek theme plays out in cobalt and white color schemes, with flat-screen TVs, coffeemakers and safes in rooms. With a good on-site restaurant and bar.

Hotel Plaza HOTEL $$
(6576-5396, 998-3433; hotelplazastgo@gmail.com; Interamericana s/n; d US$66;) Along the Interamericana, but set back opposite a leafy area, the 34-room Hotel Plaza is well regarded locally, mainly because of its swimming pool. Rooms are decked in stucco and tile; some of them are drive-up. Choose a room in the back.

★**Cheesecake** CAFE $
(998-6438; Av Santacoloma; mains US$2-7; 8am-6pm) This bakery and cafe is a popular local lunch spot. Think fast casual, with thick deli sandwiches made to order and healthy Buddha bowls with your choice of grain, protein and veggies. Don't skip dessert. The chocolate-packed *dulce de leche* brownies and passionfruit squares are worth every single calorie.

Cafe Joder CAFE $
(6300-1046; Av Pinzón s/n; mains US$4-8; 1-8pm Mon-Fri) For your latte fix, duck into this sleek hipster coffee shop. For longtime travelers, the grilled sandwiches with plantain chips, cheesy arepas and nachos bring some welcome variety to dining in the provinces.

Shopping

Ceramica La Peña MARKET
(Interamericana s/n; 9am-4:30pm Mon-Fri) A ceramic workshop and artisan market, this place sells wood carvings and baskets made by the Emberá and Wounaan peoples of the Darién, woven purses and soapstone figurines made by local Ngöbe-Buglé people, and masks from the town of Parita. There's also a good selection of pots and sculptures available for purchase, some of which are made on site.

Ceramica La Peña is on the south side of the Interamericana, 8km west of Santiago, just before the turnoff to the town of La Peña.

Information

There are ATMs at the bus terminal and across the street from it. If you are headed for the islands or smaller towns, make sure you take out sufficient funds here.

For regional tourism information, stop by the **ATP tourist office** (998-0929; Av Central, Plaza Catedral; 8:30am-3:30pm Mon-Fri).

The **Ministerio de Ambiente office** (998-4387; Interamericana; 8:30am-3:30pm Mon-Fri) has information on area parks, including Parque Nacional Coiba, and can supply fishing permits.

Getting There & Away

From Santiago's **Veraguas Bus Terminal** (998-4006; Av Pinzón), west of the Interamericana and north of Av Central, buses depart for David (US$9, three hours) hourly from 9am to 3am, Panama City (US$9.50, four hours) hourly from 4am to 9:15pm, and Chitré (US$3, one hour) every 20 minutes.

Buses to Santa Fé (US$3, 1½ hours) depart half-hourly from 5am to 7:30pm. To get to Santa Catalina, you must first take a bus to Soná (US$2.40, one hour, half-hourly from 7am to 6pm), then transfer to Santa Catalina (US$5, 1½ hours, 5am, 11am, 2pm and 4pm). Buses charge extra for surfboards. Up to 10 buses a day link Santiago with Torio (US$5, 1½ hours), via Mariato on the Sunset Coast, between 6am and 5pm.

Express buses to and from Panama City and David also stop at the Centro Piramidal at the eastern end of Av Central on the Interamericana, but at busy times they can often be full.

You can also hire **Radio Taxi** (958-8075) to take you to the Iglesia de San Francisco de la

EL SALTO DE LAS PALMAS

This wonderful 45m-high **waterfall** (Las Palmas Waterfall; daylight hours) located in the town of Las Palmas has a natural pool with refreshing water at its base. The area is surrounded by light forest and you'll probably have this hidden paradise to yourself. Don't forget to take your camera, and be sure to keep your valuables on you.

To get to the El Salto de Las Palmas from the Interamericana, take the Las Palmas turnoff and drive south for 7km. Bypass the first road into town, but turn left at the second one just before the town's cemetery. Follow this dirt road for 200m and then take the fork to the right. This last 1km to the falls, along a much rougher road, requires a 4WD vehicle. If you're not driving one, it's best to play it safe and walk from here to the falls.

Montaña in San Francisco (US$10 one way) or to the towns of Santa Fé (US$30), Soná (US$35) or Santa Catalina (US$80).

Getting Around

Taxis are easy to hail and they go anywhere in town for around US$3.

San Francisco

POP 2220

The small town of San Francisco, 18km north of Santiago on the way to Santa Fé, can lay claim to one of the best and oldest examples of baroque ecclesiastical art and architecture in the Americas. For most, it's an interesting stop on the way to the mountains.

Sights & Activities

Iglesia de San Francisco de la Montaña CHURCH

(9:30am-noon & 1-4pm) This simple stone church, built in 1727, contains nine elaborately carved altarpieces, including the ornate main altar of ash and cedar. Although most colonial altars in the Americas were brought over from Europe, this one was carved by local indigenous people. The eight side altars contain images of the crucifixion and the Virgin Mary with saints as well as portraits of the artisans themselves and prominent indigenous people. Their faces are inserted into religious scenes and onto the bodies of cherubs.

Balneario El Salto SWIMMING

Less than a kilometer from the church, these waterfalls have a fine swimming hole for cooling off on hot days. Follow the road behind the old church and then go left just beyond the more modern magenta-colored one. After a few hundred meters, take the first right; you'll reach the cascades in another several hundred meters or so.

Getting There & Away

To reach the church, head 18km north on the San Francisco turnoff from the Interamericana until you reach the police station near a stop sign. Veer right, proceed 400m and then turn right again at the Supermercado Juan XXIII de San Francisco. Another 100m on, you'll see the church on the left.

A bus leaves the Santiago station for San Francisco (US$1, 30 minutes) every half-hour from 6am to 6pm. An alternative is to hire a taxi in Santiago (about US$20 round trip).

Santa Fé

POP 3050

Santa Fé has fresh, clean air and bucolic surroundings, yet it sees relatively few foreign visitors. With the lush mountainsides, waterfalls, mountain streams and accessible swimming spots of Santa Fé National Park on the town's doorstep, it's a great destination for hikers, birdwatchers and those simply wanting to soak up the beauty of the highlands.

This tiny mountain town 53km north of Santiago lies in the shadow of the continental divide. At an altitude of 500m, Sante Fé is cooler than the lowlands, and much of the surrounding forest is as it was when the Spanish founded the town in 1557. From here, a rough road to the Caribbean coast is under construction, which will eventually bring access to some of Panama's most remote outposts.

Sights

Cerro Tute MOUNTAIN

With excellent open views of the valley, Cerro Tute is home to the area's famed bird life and features a cliff blasted with up-currents that seem to prevent anyone falling off. An extensive trail network winds through primary and secondary rainforest. It's a few

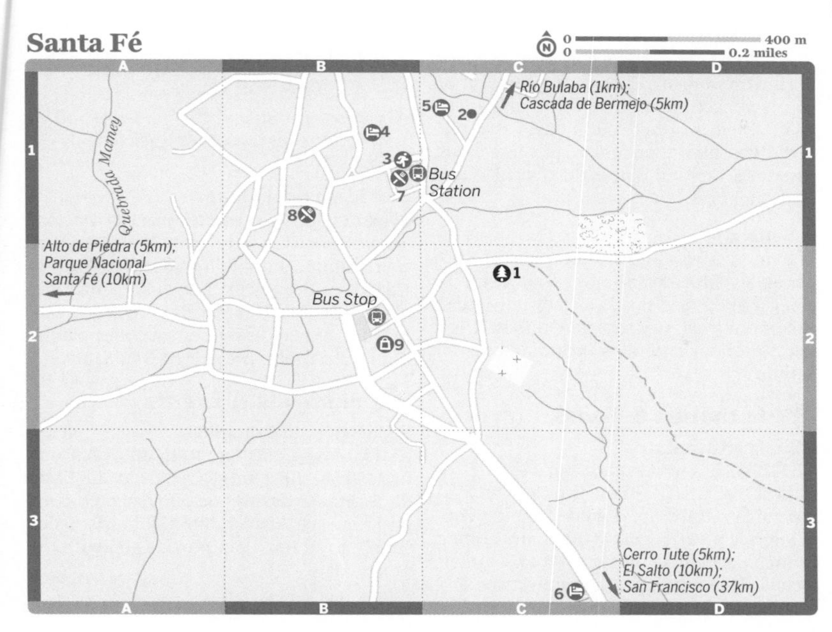

kilometers south of town on the western side of the Santiago–Santa Fé road; count on five hours there and back.

Parque Nacional Santa Fé NATIONAL PARK
(Santa Fé National Park) This vast, mountainous park covers 726 sq km of pristine wilderness, extending from the northern edge of Santa Fé to the Cordillera Central, and includes the rugged area of Alto de Piedra. It's part of the northern portion of the province that remained roadless for so long; a dirt road now penetrates the area as far as El Guabal. It's wise to access this sector with an area guide.

Río Bulaba RIVER
There's a lovely swimming hole on this river about a 20-minute walk from town. Head northeast along the road past the Coffee Mountain Inn on the way to El Pantino. The swimming hole is about 600m from there.

Here a local named William rents out inner tubes (US$8) and life jackets, which allow you to float idly down the river; it eventually merges with Río Santa Maria. He can also arrange a taxi return.

Cascada de Bermejo WATERFALL
An excellent half-day road and trail walk (five hours round trip) leads to this tall waterfall with a delightful swimming hole in the dry season. Follow the road past William's inner-tube rentals; after taking the Bulaba bridge, take your first left where the road continues steeply uphill. Continue until the waterfall, following yellow arrow signs into the trail.

You can return by looping onto the main road (going right leaving the trail and left at every intersection). In rainy season, you should inquire with locals about conditions before going.

Santa Fé

Sights
1 Feria de Santa Fé C2

Activities, Courses & Tours
2 Coffee Mountain Tours C1
3 Isthmian Adventures B1

Sleeping
Coffee Mountain Inn .... (see 2)
4 Hostal La Qhia B1
5 Hotel Anachoreo C1
6 Hotel Santa Fé C3

Eating
Anachoreo Restaurant .... (see 5)
7 Fonda de la Terminal B1
8 Restaurante Hermanos Pineda B1

Shopping
9 Mercado B2

Alto de Piedra WATERFALL

There are three waterfalls in Alto de Piedra northwest of town. Though you can visit on your own, access can be difficult and affected by recent weather conditions; we recommend you hire a guide to visit these areas. Aventuras Cesamo is available for hikes and birdwatching.

El Salto WATERFALL

The impressive waterfall known as El Salto lies about three hours southeast of Santa Fé along a 4WD road that is usually only accessible during the dry season. On foot, it is a full eight-hour excursion including time for bathing.

Activities & Tours

Isthmian Adventures ECOTOUR

(6429-8163; www.isthmianadventures.com; Terminal de Bus, local 3; 8am-4pm Mon-Fri) A reputable outfitter and guide-training entity offering a variety of private tours around Panama, including custom tours. Options include walking, birding, family trips and multisport activities. Guides are certified and English-speaking and travelers who contract guides through an agency have the added bonus of being insured. A member of APTSO (Asociación Panameño de Turismo Sostenible), Panama's sustainable-tourism alliance.

Chon & María Farm Tour TOUR

(6525-4832; half-day tour per person US$10;) To see an organic farm up close, visit with Chon and María, hospitable *campesino* (farmer) hosts happy to show you around their small-scale operation. You can also check out their orchids and sample María's homemade cooking (lunch included). Though they only speak Spanish, this lovely couple finds a way to communicate with non-Spanish-speaking visitors that makes the trip worthwhile.

It's excellent for families too, who can take advantage of the country quiet and a nearby swimming hole. Make sure you book ahead.

Aventuras Cesamo HORSEBACK RIDING

(6792-0571; www.aventurascesamo.blogspot.com) Reputable local guide Cesar Miranda takes visitors on horseback rides using his own horses. He also guides visitors through the Alto de Piedra area and on walks to waterfalls.

> **HIKING SAFETY**
>
> It's best not to go hiking alone. In 2017 a tourist was attacked and assaulted on the trail to Cascada de Bermejo.

Coffee Mountain Tours ADVENTURE

(6988-0921; www.coffeemountaininn.com; 9am-5pm) This very reliable outfit offers everything from hiking tours (US$45 to US$85) of the Parque Nacional Santa Fé to 4WD tours, horseback riding (US$45), tubing and visits to lesser-known coffee plantations. Also runs a popular B&B in Santa Fé.

Festivals & Events

Exposición de Orquídeas EVENT

(Orchid Show) Collectors from all over Panama display their finest orchids at the **Féria de Santa Fé** during the popular orchid exposition each August; the ATP tourist office (p137) in Santiago can provide you with the precise date.

Feria de Agricultura EVENT

(Agricultural Fair) If you're in the area, make sure you don't miss this lively event hosted by the small producers of northern Veraguas in early February. The agricultural fair features traditional dancing, horse races, a multitude of food stands and an occasional boxing match or rodeo competition. It's held at the Feria de Santa Fé in the eastern part of town.

Sleeping

Hostal La Qhia GUESTHOUSE $

(6814-2650; www.panamamountainhouse.com; dm US$12, s/d without bathroom US$35/45, bungalow/cabin US$40/130; P) Surrounded by lush gardens and hammocks, this bamboo-and-stone chalet makes a great base camp for mountain adventures around Santa Fé. There's excellent maps and notes about the area's attractions. Snug rooms feature crisp bedding, while those upstairs are complete charmers. Dorms with six beds and a room with private bathroom occupy a small concrete addition with an outdoor kitchen.

Hotel Santa Fé HOTEL $

(6217-7895, 954-0941; www.hotelsantafepanama.com; s/d US$22/28, deluxe d/tr US$33/39; P) This quiet, motel-style lodging features 16 tidy concrete rooms with cable TV and hot showers; a couple have air-conditioning. They are grouped around a grassy courtyard and shady porch. The attached restaurant serves Panamanian food but isn't always open. The main drawback is that whatever action there is in town is a long walk uphill from here.

★Hotel Anachoreo HOTEL **$$**
(☎6911-4848; www.anachoreo.com; s/d incl breakfast US$55/66; P 📶) Hugging the hillside with panoramic views, this small inn steals your heart with its hammocks strung along fragrant garden beds, warm hospitality and breakfasts that might be the finest in Panama. Ample, high-ceilinged rooms have beds clad in netting, and delightful bathroom mosaics. The vibe is utterly tranquil. Guests can use a shared outdoor kitchen. Offers tours on hiking trails.

Coffee Mountain Inn B&B **$$**
(☎6988-0921; www.coffeemountaininn.com; d US$65-95, tr incl breakfast US$75-105; P ❄ 📶) This cozy inn offers seven rooms in two buildings: the main building has five double rooms while an outbuilding offers two family rooms. All have fine tile floors, queen-sized beds with exceptionally comfortable mattresses and French doors offering direct access to the garden. The main building's long veranda is a delight.

The welcoming Panamanian-American couple also has a travel company offering a full range of tours and excursions.

Eating

Restaurante Hermanos Pineda PANAMANIAN **$**
(☎954-0777; mains US$4-8; ⊙7am-9pm) This welcoming, family-run place just up from the town center serves better food than the plain-Jane menu would have you believe, including worthwhile fish and seafood served with *patacones* (fried plantains), rice or fries. There's also pizza (US$5 to US$12) and burgers. The large veranda overlooking the main road is a plus, as is the wall-sized map of the national park.

Fonda de la Terminal CAFETERIA **$**
(mains US$4; ⊙7am-7pm) This simple, no-nonsense cafeteria next to the bus station offers some of the best *comida típica* (regional specialties) around. It's friendly and very clean.

★Anachoreo Restaurant CAMBODIAN **$$**
(☎6911-4848; www.anachoreo.com; mains US$10-14; ⊙5:30-9pm Wed-Sun) This intimate eatery at the hotel of the same name ranks among the finest eating this side of Panama City. The Cambodian owner-chef is a wonderful cook and a delightful presence. Don't miss the Cambodian chicken curry, her famous spring rolls and the exotic 'Fish Amok' wrapped in banana leaves and steamed in ginger and fresh lemongrass.

Enormous organic salads come from produce grown by the restaurant in their backyard. Book ahead.

Shopping

Mercado MARKET
Just past the entrance to town, this market sells fruits and vegetables, woven handmade bags, a wide range of hats, leather goods and many other interesting items.

Information

Note that Santa Fé has no ATM. Stock up on cash in Santiago.

None of the streets have names in Sante Fé and directions given by locals can be confusing. It's best to confirm that you're on track before you walk right out of town.

Getting There & Away

Buses from Santa Fé to Santiago (US$3, 1½ hours) depart from the bus station every 30 minutes from 4am to 6pm, stopping at the more central bus stop en route. Note that if you are trying to reach the surf town of Santa Catalina in one day, you must leave Santa Fé by 9am to make all the bus connections in time.

The road to the Caribbean coast is planned for completion in 2020. At the time of writing there was a rough section that's drivable with a 4WD.

Santa Catalina

POP 300

Among Central America's top surf spots, little Santa Catalina has right and left breaks comparable to Oahu's Sunset Beach on a good day. Enjoy it while it's still somewhat remote, undeveloped and home to some seriously wicked surf. Life here is pretty tranquil. It's a a fishing village where skateboards rip down main street and kids go barefoot, but clothing is required to walk to and from the beach. Most non-surfers discover the area as the main springboard for day and overnight trips to Isla de Coiba and its national park, where there's outstanding scuba diving and snorkeling to be had.

Activities

There's a variety of superb snorkeling and spear-fishing spots that some locals will divulge. Guiding is an informal business here; look for certified scuba and surf instructors through your lodging. You can also find locals who will lead horseback-riding tours through the nearby forests.

Surfing

The best waves are generally from December to April, though there's surf here year-round. Unlike the Caribbean, the Pacific offers fairly consistent sets, though a good swell will really give a boost to the surfing here. Be advised that many of the breaks in the area are over rocks, and can easily snap your board if you don't know what you're doing. Most of the accommodations in town rent boards and offer surfing lessons.

Santa Catalina Surf Shop SURFING
(6571-4387; www.santacatalinasurfshop.com; Hotel Santa Catalina, Calle Estero; 9am-noon & 3-8pm) In the Hotel Santa Catalina (p145), this surf shop specializes in getting good gear to those who loathe to travel with extra baggage. Sells, rents and buys back quality boards and accessories; also has certified surf instructors.

Surf & Shake SURFING
(6555-4375; www.surfandshake.com; 9am-6pm) On the road to the beach, just 150m in from the main street, Surf & Shake rents out boards and sells leashes, boards and surfwear, as well as tasty fruit shakes. Run by a German surfer, it's also a good spot for surf info.

Diving & Snorkeling

Diving and snorkeling are a great way to see some of the spectacular marine life around Isla de Coiba. There is an incredible variety of fauna and whale sharks have been sighted here. Two-tank dives start at US$135 per person, though diving in the park costs more since the distance is much greater. A rule requiring boats to stay overnight with their diver clients has made multiday trips to Coiba very expensive; an overnight with two days in the water is now US$250. Visitors usually check all shops to see which has a trip visiting their preferred destination.

Snorkelers are better off taking independent snorkel tours as dive companies generally prefer to focus on their deepwater clients.

WORTH A TRIP

ART ISLAND: ISLA GOBERNADORA

If you have ever wanted to watch the moon rise from your thatched hut, head to the **Art Lodge** (6636-5180, 203-4744; www.artlodgepanama.com; bungalow US$60-80) on a small village in the Golfo de Montijo. It's set near a quiet fishing village, with nearby forested trails and a few white-sand beaches.

Run by two hospitable French artists, the six-room retreat defines 'island idyll'. Accommodation is in one of four *ranchos*, open-air bungalows boasting double beds with mosquito nets and showers half-walled with thatch. The more remote *casita* (cottage) has two guest rooms. While the hillside lodge has a beach, there is also a stream perfect for dips and a lovely lounge area with art, games and futons.

To create income for island women, host Valerie has put together community art cooperatives that use natural materials to make gorgeous quality belts, handbags and decorations crafted with design sense. She also works with the community garden and has helped develop a cross-island trail. Guests can tour the village and workshops, talk with locals, snorkel, practice yoga and beachcomb. Set meals incorporate fresh local seafood, fruit and vegetables. Due to its remoteness, the Art Lodge requires a three-night stay (six nights in the cottage). Discounted rates are available for resident artists and there are workshops in ceramics, weaving and woodcarving.

Try to schedule a visit at the end of January when the Feria de Artesanías (Handicrafts Festival) takes place, or on July 16, when the Fiesta de la Virgen del Carmen is marked by the fisherfolk.

Getting There & Away

The only way to reach Isla Gobernadora is by private charter. The Art Lodge charges US$60 for two for a round trip from Santa Catalina.

Dream Diving DIVING
(☎6765-0631; www.dreamdivingpanama.com; ⏰8am-4:30pm) This excellent dive shop just at the turnoff to the beach is run by a very eco-minded Colombian and offers snorkeling trips to Coiba and two- and three-tank dives.

Panama Dive Center DIVING
(☎6665-7879; www.panamadivecenter.com; 3-tank dive US$160; ⏰7am-7pm) Friendly and professional, this PADI-certified dive center is a good local resource for information. It offers all-day two- or three-tank dives and courses. It also has longer dive trips to Coiba (two/three nights US$440/660). It's on the main road, opposite the turnoff to the beach.

MC Diving Coiba DIVING
(☎6442-6922, 6421-3008; www.mcdivingcoiba.com; ⏰9am-7pm) Among the most professional of dive centers in Santa Catalina, this outfit offers a two-tank local dive and the usual two- and three-tank ones to Coiba. It also offers very ambitious three- and five-day diving tours of northern Coiba and Isla Contreras.

Coiba Dive Center DIVING
(☎6774-0808, 6780-1141; www.coibadivecenter.com; ⏰8am-noon & 2-6pm) A reputable PADI-certified dive shop located on the main road. It offers daily day and multiday trips to Isla de Coiba (two nights from US$699, with a minimum of three people), which include entry into the national park, lodging at the Ministerio de Ambiente station on Coiba, and meals. Three-day open-water courses start at US$399.

Fishing

The area is famous for big fish, including yellowfin tuna, wahoo, snapper, Spanish mackerel, jacks and rooster fish. Though there's no major sportfishing operator in town, many locals rent their boat and services for the day. Prices depend on the number of people and the destination, since gasoline is very expensive. Cabañas Rolo (p144) arranges half-day trips to Isla Cébaco with a knowledgeable local captain.

If you'd prefer to go after reef fish (including snapper and grouper), there are some hidden spots along the coast. Plenty of rocky ledges serve as hideouts for lobster, though be sure to only harvest adults – lobster are in danger of being overfished throughout Panama.

If you are sportfishing in Parque Nacional Coiba, you must first obtain a fishing permit (US$50) from any mainland Ministerio de Ambiente office; the nearest is Santiago (p137).

Tours

Watching Dolphin SNORKELING
(☎6666-4272; US$55 without park entrance fee; ⏰7-10am & 3-7pm) For snorkeling in Parque Nacional Coiba, this dedicated snorkeling outfitter is the best bet in Santa Catalina. Trips do three 25-minute snorkel sessions with a picnic lunch on Isla Coiba, with time for a short hike to a lookout. Dolphin viewing on your way to Coiba happens if you're lucky – it can be magical. Friendly and service-oriented.

Bird Coiba ECOTOUR
(☎6544-1806; www.birdcoiba.com; per boat from US$350) A longtime local resident, American Javier Elizondo takes visitors on thoughtful family-friendly trips to Parque Nacional Coiba with a more specialized focus. There's birding trips and options for snorkeling and sightseeing on the main island. Rates depend on the number of participants. There's no office, contact him by phone or email in advance.

Sleeping

Oceans Hotel HOTEL $
(☎6583-8398; per person camping/RV US$7/10, d/q US$50/60; P❄📶) Well-kept and strewn with plants, there's a certain amount of pride in this basic two-story hotel, run by owner Juvenal. It sits on a hilltop with its back to the river. There's eight rooms with flat-screen TVs and deck hammocks, plus access to a guest kitchen. Rents bikes and surfboards.

Oasis Surf Camp CABIN $
(☎6670-5636, 6588-7077; www.oasissurfcamp.com; Playa Estero; camping with/without tent per person US$12/7, dm US$15, d with fan/air-con US$45/55, ste from US$135; P❄📶) This Italian-owned surf camp is a classic, and its beachfront setting is one of the best. Bright, colorful cabins overlooking the black-sand beach have hot showers and ample hammocks. The suite is a two-bedroom wooden house with wicker furniture, a kitchen and great balcony views. It's on Playa Estero, just past a river guests must wade across to reach camp.

Rancho Estero CABAÑAS $
(☎6415-6595; www.ranchoestero.com; beach area; dm US$15, 2-person cabaña US$40-45; P) Perched on a hilltop with soaring ocean views, these family-friendly *cabañas* made of bamboo and thatch are among the most atmospheric places to stay in Santa Catalina. They are surrounded by gardens with decks strewn with hammocks and chaise lounges with the beach just below. Guests have kitchen use. There's quality surf instruction too. It's along the road down to Playa Estero.

Hibiscus Garden RESORT $
(☎6615-6097; www.hibiscusgarden.com; Playa Lagartero; r without bathroom US$22-30, with bathroom US$45-65; P ❄) On Playa Lagartero, 11km northeast of Santa Catalina, these relaxed lodgings, owned by a California-based hip-hop artist, fuse modern with rustic, with stylish installations and minimal fuss. Rooms have recycled driftwood beds and private hammock terraces. There's a recording studio in the works and music festivals planned on-site. The 6km-long beach is calm, secluded and very swimmable.

For some, the distance from town is a drawback, though a shuttle (one way US$5) is available. Hosts can organize horseback riding (US$25), stand-up paddleboarding (SUP), surf lessons and fishing trips. The Hibiscus Restaurant (p146) is a destination in itself (though guests also have use of a fully equipped communal kitchen).

Boarder's Haven GUESTHOUSE $
(☎6572-0664; www.labuenavidahotel.com; s/d without bathroom US$25/30; ❄) The ideal choice for those on a shoestring budget, this tiny guesthouse has just seven single beds in three rooms with real mattresses, shared bathrooms and a petite kitchen that's fully equipped. The brightly colored (and named) rooms have air-con and a ceiling fan. It sits on the main road in the center of town.

Cabañas Rolo CABIN $
(☎6494-3916, 6598-9926; www.rolocabins.net; dm US$15, d/tr without bathroom US$30/45, with bathroom from US$55/66; P ❄) One of Santa Catalina's only hotels owned by lifelong locals, these friendly cabins are a favorite of surfers on a budget. Each has one to three good beds, a fan and a shared cold-water bathroom. Newer cabins include several with waterfront views and ample, more upscale rooms with air-conditioning and bathrooms with hot-water showers.

Hostal Surfers Paradise HOSTEL $
(☎6709-1037; www.facebook.com/surfersparadise.hostal; beach area; incl breakfast dm US$18, s/d US$38/48/66/80, with air-con US$44/55; P ❄) You could watch the tubes roll in all day at this hilltop compound with a box seat to the waves. The eight rooms in a thatched block spread over two floors include two dorms with up to five beds. There is also a restaurant with views, as well as a large outdoor kitchen for self-caterers. With surf instruction and rentals.

Lodge Cool Inside CABAÑAS $
(☎6901-6206; yannatardivenl@gmail.com; dm US$10, d bungalow US$20-35) On the main road in town, these funky, chilled lodgings offer decent value. Simple thatched bungalows sit out back. There's also dining at the in-house restaurant, which serves curries and chicken cordon bleu thanks to the French owner. At the time of writing it was in the process of building a new dorm.

Aguas Verdes CABIN $
(☎6870-7056; www.facebook.com/aguas.verdes.94/about; beach area; s/d US$20/30; ❄) These brightly colored cabins lined up on a hill directly above the beach offer very conveniently located lodgings for surfers on a budget. Rooms have air-conditioning and wi-fi and there are kitchens too.

Hostel Villa Vento Surf HOTEL $
(☎6659-2900; www.villaventohostels.com; dm/d/tr incl breakfast US$13/40/50; P ❄) This branch of a Sunset Coast surf hostel occupies a two-story wooden house on the main road above a minimarket. It features six rooms set around a 2nd-floor veranda. Two are dorms with five and six beds; the rest are doubles and triples with air-conditioning and en-suite bathrooms. There's a very big kitchen and a pool. Offers tours.

★**Deseo Bamboo** CABIN $$
(☎6788-7891, 6951-6671; www.facebook.com/deseobambooecolodge; dm US$18, d/tr cabin US$69/84; P) The crazy dream of a Neapolitan football player, these octagonal thatched huts are a tropical masterpiece. Bamboo huts feature traditional two-tier roofs that offer good ventilation. Rooms, including an attractive dorm, are spare but lovely. There's a congenial atmosphere, plus a yoga deck and a sushi bar, with weekly live music and events such as salsa dancing and movie nights.

It's on a rural property in the process of reforestation. Though the turnoff comes 400m before Santa Catalina (to your left), the property has a hiking shortcut to Playa Estero that's a 10-minute walk. With a shuttle option.

★La Buena Vida CABIN **$$**
(☎6572-0664; www.labuenavidahotel.com; 2-person villa US$66-88, 4-person studio US$110; P ❄ 📶) 🍃 These lovely villas spill down a leafy hillside along the main road. Each is themed and decorated with colorful mosaics and tiles crafted by the American owners. With great service, they have ironed out every little detail here, from local tips to fast internet and quality lunchboxes for tours. There are popular yoga classes on a sprawling deck and professional massages.

Cabins include a fridge, screened windows and air-conditioning. 'Gecko' is the most deluxe, while 'Butterfly' offers the delicious option of showering outdoors. 'Bird' has two floors. One larger group villa (Casa del Mar) features a kitchen and BBQ patio. La Buena Vida composts, recycles and sells local artisan goods.

Hotel Las Hamacas HOTEL **$$**
(☎6849-1796, 6635-1895; www.lashamacashotel.com; r US$49-79; P ❄ 📶) This new courtyard-motel-style lodging offers tiny spotless cabins with porch hammocks and kitchenettes. It's great value. Your host Carolina is a vivacious presence and the high-speed internet on-site is the fastest around. They also manage local properties for long-term stays.

Hotel Santa Catalina HOTEL **$$**
(☎6571-4387; www.hotelsantacatalinapanama.com; d/tr US$90/95; P ❄ 📶 🏊) With manicured grounds strewn with hammocks and Spanish-tile roofs, this 11-room hotel is an excellent midrange option catering to the executive surfer. Tile rooms somewhat crowded with beds feature electric hot-water showers and individual lockers for gear. A big draw is the surf break of La Punta out front. Guests get free use of kayaks, bicycles and foam boards.

There's an on-site restaurant, though the suites have their own kitchenettes. The mix of natural materials – stone, wood, thatch – is commendable and harmonious.

Sol y Mar CABIN **$$**
(☎6920-2631; www.solymarpanama.com; 2-/3-/4-person cabin incl breakfast US$60/75/105; P ❄ 📶 🏊) Surrounded by greenery, these hilltop cabins have hammock porches, lovely wooden furniture, electric hot-water showers, satellite TV and air-con. Guests rave about the special attention that owner, Luis, showers upon them. About 100 steep stairs lead to cabins, with sea views at the highest level. It's 650m to the town center.

The thatched *rancho* with pool table and a lovely pool offers views of Coiba and the Cébaco islands.

Eating & Drinking

La Moncheria Heladería ICE CREAM **$**
(☎6849-1796; cones US$3; ⏲3-10pm) This *gelateria* located on a narrow dirt road on the way to La Punta surfing beach serves some of the best ice cream in Panama.

La Buena Vida AMERICAN **$**
(☎6635-1895, 6572-0664; www.labuenavida.biz; mains from US$7; ⏲6:30am-2pm; 🌶) If you're hitting the water early, this will be the first spot open for a bite and espresso fix. Great options include breakfast burritos and Greek scrambles with feta, olives, tomatoes and eggs. This funky tiled cafe perched above the main street also sells fresh fruit drinks and a lunchtime selection of salads, power bowls and wraps. Vegan friendly.

La Vieja Panaderia BAKERY **$**
(Old Bakery; ☎6900-5776; sandwiches & salads US$5-7.50, pizza US$6.50-8.50; ⏲6:30am-3pm & 6-10pm) This Italian-run local institution is a bakery by day and a pizzeria after dark. Come before 9:30am as bread (US$1.50 to US$2) sells out and breakfasts (think omelets and pancakes) are slow to get served. There's also great coffee, lunchboxes to go, cakes and delectable muffins. Pizzas are tasty and authentic.

Pizzeria Jammin PIZZA **$**
(☎6604-3910; pizzas US$7-12; ⏲from 6:30pm) A Santa Catalina mainstay, this open-air *rancho* offers delicious thin-crust pizzas baked in a stone oven. Nightlife tends to concentrate here – perhaps it's the cheap beer, though there's also good wine and picnic tables conducive to sharing. It gets crowded, so arrive early in the evening. You'll find it on the road to the hotels facing the beach.

★Chillinguito SEAFOOD **$$**
(☎6687-2992; mains US$8-15; ⏲5-9pm Tue-Sat) This thatched restaurant does seafood in slightly different, scrumptious preparations. Try the shrimp in garlic sauce with sautéed vegetables, abundant green salads or fried clam ceviche with yucca. There's also fresh

fruit drinks, kombucha and cocktails. Its signature drink, Tropical Dream, combines gin with frosty watermelon and mint. Service is slow – par for the course in Catalina.

★El Encuentro SEAFOOD **$$**
(☎6377-8909; mains US$12-14; ⊙6:30-11pm) At a converted gas pump, Deivis' popular no-nonsense ceviche stand does superb versions of the citrus-cured seafood on a nest of shoestring fries. The squid version is to die for. There's also a vegetarian option and rum drinks. It's a two-man show with every plate made to order, so plunk down at an outdoor table and enjoy the personal attention.

La Tana Sushi Bar SUSHI **$$**
(☎6788-7891, 6951-6671; rolls US$12-17; ⊙from 6pm Wed-Mon) Run by Francesco, a gregarious Italian chef, this thatched-hut sushi bar uses fresh seafood to create some delightful tropical fare. Think out of the box. Rolls feature fresh fish and tangy homemade soy mayo. There's also mango lobster tempura with organic chocolate. With fine cocktails or beer and weekly live music or events.

It's 400m from the main road, on the left as you drive into Santa Catalina.

Hibiscus Restaurant SEAFOOD **$$**
(☎6615-6097; www.hibiscusgarden.com; mains US$8-20; ⊙7-9am, 11:30am-2pm & 5:30-8:30pm) This fantastic restaurant serves up baked fish, clams and lobster as well as pleasing vegan and vegetarian dishes with fresh fare, quinoa and couscous. It's under the command of Italian chef Matteo, who trained in Michelin-starred restaurants in Italy.

Chano's Point SEAFOOD **$$**
(☎6736-1652; mains US$10-25; ⊙6-10pm) This thatched restaurant offers lovely seafood meals and frozen fruit drinks. Start with fresh local clams or salad with tart passion-fruit dressing. The fish in coconut curry and the lobster are divine. And bring your patience because the wait for food is long and it often runs out. It's off the first right-hand turn en route to Playa Estero.

Pingüino Cafe ITALIAN **$$**
(☎6478-7023; mains US$6-16; ⊙11am-10pm) This thatched Italian-owned restaurant on the public beach is the undisputed spot for a sunset beer. Pasta dishes are a tad pricey given their somewhat reckless preparation. We recommended the whole fried fish with *patacones*. Always a warm welcome.

ℹ Information

Be advised that there are no ATMs in Santa Catalina and very few places take credit cards. Make sure you arrive with cash.

OFF THE BEATEN TRACK

PARQUE NACIONAL CERRO HOYA

On the southwestern side of the Península de Azuero and shared by Veraguas and Los Santos provinces, this 325-sq-km park protects the headwaters of the Ríos Tonosí, Portobelo and Pavo, as well as 30 endemic plant species, and rare fauna including the elusive carato parakeet, Azuero spider monkey, pumas and some jaguars. The country's least-visited national park also contains some of the last remaining dryland rainforest in Azuero, a peninsula that is predominantly agricultural.

The park's terrain is difficult and steep and the trails ill-defined. Visits to the park are reserved for intrepid types truly looking to get away from it all, though they should engage the services of experienced outfitters. Tanager Ecotours (p149) organizes excellent day and multiday trips. The day trip will get you to the lower reaches of the mountains and focuses on wildlife-watching and birding. One of its longer tours, a two-night trek (US$450), reaches the summit of 1559m-tall Cerro Hoya.

Getting There & Away

It's possible to reach the park by a road that winds along the western edge of the Península de Azuero. However, even with a 4WD vehicle (dry season only), visitors are only able to get as far as Restigue, a hamlet south of Arenas, at the edge of the park. That alone requires crossing the Río Varadero three times.

Your best option for getting to the park is to join a guided tour, such as those offered by **Tanager Ecotours** (☎6676-0220, 6679-5504; www.tanagertourism.com; road to Malena; day trip/overnight per person from US$90/400) or Morillo Beach Eco Resort (p151).

Getting There & Away

To reach Santa Catalina from Panama City, take a bus to Santiago, then another to Soná where buses leave for Santa Catalina (US$5, 1½ hours) at 5:30am, 8:40am, 11:20am, 1:30pm, 3:30pm and 4:45pm. Sunday services vary. If you miss the bus, hire a taxi from Soná to Santa Catalina (from US$45). Direct Panama City–Soná buses run every two hours.

From Santa Catalina, seven buses serve Soná daily, leaving at 6:15am, 7am, 8am, 10:45am, 1:30pm, 3:30pm and 6pm. In Santa Catalina, the bus stops at the intersection with the beach road. If you're staying outside the town center, most lodgings are a 1km walk on mostly flat but unshaded terrain. Note that there are never taxis in town, unless, of course, someone is arriving from Soná.

For direct shuttle service to Boquete (four hours), use **Hello Travel! Panama** (757-7004; www.hellotravelpanama.com; one way US$35). These air-conditioned minivans are a good time-saving way to get around Panama without dealing with confusing transfers. You can also go to Las Lajas, Horconcito or David. Departs at noon daily with pick-up on the main road or your hotel. Reserve online.

Parque Nacional Coiba

With the exception of Ecuador's Galápagos Islands and Isla de Coco in Costa Rica, few destinations off the Pacific coast of the Americas are as exotic as this **national park** (Coiba National Park; 998-0615; www.coibanationalpark.com; US$20) covering the 503-sq-km Isla de Coiba. Although just 20km offshore in the Golfo de Chiriquí, Coiba is a veritable lost world of pristine ecosystems and unique fauna.

Isolated for the past century due to its status as a notorious penal colony, Coiba offers travelers the chance to hike through primary rainforest and snorkel and dive in a marine park with increasingly rare wildlife. However, with virtually no tourist infrastructure in place, you're going to have to plan hard (and pay top dollar) to really see it up close.

Coiba was declared a national park in 1991, and in 2005 Unesco made it a World Heritage Site.

Activities

Wildlife-Watching

Over 167 bird species have been identified in Parque Nacional Coiba. While birdwatchers covet sighting the Coiba spinetail, a reddish-brown little bird found only on Coiba, most are awed by the scarlet macaws limited in Panama to Parque Nacional Coiba. The birds nest at Barco Quebrado on the southern tip of Isla Coiba, but are frequently sighted in flight, with distinctive calls that are easy to recognize.

Although a plant survey has been carried out (there are eight ecosystems on the island), Coiba has not had a proper wildlife survey, though it is believed to be home to about 40 different species of mammal. Two rare mammals are endemic to the island – the Coiba agouti and the Coiba howler monkey. While these are difficult to spot, it's common to watch white-faced capuchin monkeys playing on the beach.

Seventeen species of crocodile, turtle and lizard, as well as 15 species of snake – including the dangerous fer-de-lance, coral snakes and boa constrictors – are found here. Enormous crocodiles might inhibit your swim plans at night. Although snakes tend to be extremely shy, you should always walk slowly and carefully through the jungles, stomping occasionally.

The waters surrounding Coiba are home to many large sharks. White-tip reef and bull sharks are the most sighted, though black-tip sharks can also be spotted and hammerheads school in large numbers here as well. Lucky divers may see the occasional tiger and whale shark, especially from December to February.

The marine life in the park is simply astounding. The warm Indo-Pacific current through the Gulf of Chiriquí creates a unique underwater ecosystem atypical of this region, attracting large populations of pelagics and enormous schools of fish. Some two dozen species of dolphins and whales have been identified, and humpback whales and spotted dolphins are frequently seen. Sperm and killer whales are also present, but in much lower numbers. The whale-watching season runs from July to October.

The waters around Coiba are also home to sea turtles (olive ridley, hawksbill and the increasingly rare green). In addition to seriously large fish, you're almost guaranteed to spot schools of snapper and jacks as well as large grouper and barracuda.

Hiking

Coiba boasts a half-dozen trails, four of which are easily accessible from the ranger station. These include a trail up to **Cerro Gambute**, which takes about a half-hour all up, and the short walk to **Playa Tito**. The 5km-long **Sendero de Santa Cruz** to the

Parque Nacional Coiba

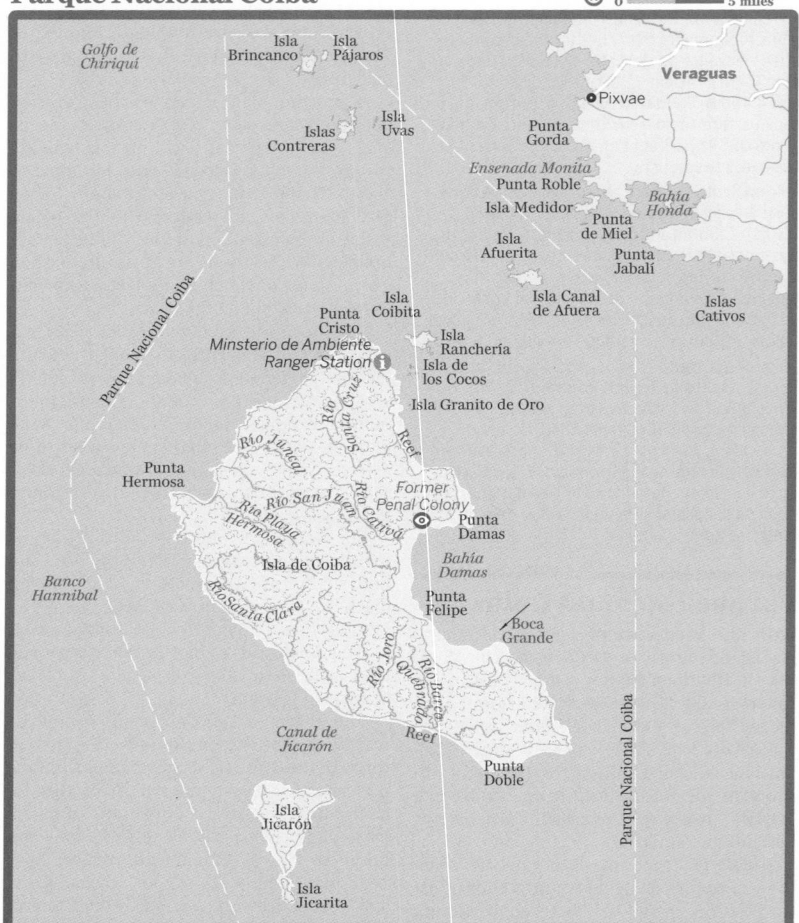

west takes about four hours there and back. Farther afield is **Sendero de los Pozos**, some 45 minutes away by boat. It leads to themal baths built in an old tiled installation. Since there are no markers, you must do longer trails with a guide.

Sendero de Los Monos HIKING

(Monkey Trail) More or less opposite an islet called Granito de Oro, this trail is only accessible by boat. Though it's less than 2km long, it accesses some beaches and is home to several species of monkey. You're most likely to spot howlers and capuchins in the dry season when the foliage isn't as dense.

Scuba Diving, Snorkeling & Swimming

The cove near the ranger station shelters a small island that you can snorkel around during high tide. Be aware that the current on the island's far side is sometimes very strong. If you're a poor swimmer, do not venture outside the cove.

Two other popular spots for swimming and snorkeling are **Isla Granito de Oro** and the mangrove forest close to **Punta Hermosa** in the west. Both can be reached only by boat.

The majority of visitors to Coiba arrange their diving through tour operators or dive centers based in Santa Catalina (p142), though you can also go through the remote village of Pixvae, a 30-minute boat ride away.

★**Dive Base Coiba** DIVING
(☎6948-2240, 6662-4539; www.divebasecoiba.com; Pixvae; ⏲by appointment) PADI instructor Kevan Martell wrote the dive manual for Coiba, so his guided scuba trips could not be more compelling. Moreover, safety is a priority, with well-maintained equipment, radios and first aid. Closer to Isla Coiba than Santa Catalina, the village of Pixvae is rustic (no electricity or internet) and way off the beaten path. Contact the dive center for directions and lodgings.

Options include two-tank dives (US$80) and Coiba trips (US$150 plus equipment and park entry fee), as well as open-water certification. From Sona, Pixvae is one hour and 40 minutes via a rough 4WD road. Transport pickups or public buses are an option.

Tours

Even if you're normally an independent traveler, Coiba is one destination where it's worth joining up with an organized tour. Although you may be able to save a few dollars organizing your own transport to Coiba from Santa Catalina, that's all you'll get; with an operator you'll get to see and experience a whole lot more, especially of the interior. Being part of a chartered expedition also means that you can explore more of the marine park, which is more convenient and ultimately may be cheaper than arranging activities on your own.

★**Tanager Ecotours** ADVENTURE
(☎6676-0220, 6679-5504; www.tanagertourism.com; 3-day all-inclusive per person US$750; 👪) Run by a couple of keen Dutch biologists, these superb guided tours use local fishing boats. Package trips include snorkeling at four to five reefs, hiking on two trails, a boat ride through mangroves, birding and wildlife-watching. More tailored visits are possible in the low season.

Tours depart from Palo Seco, north of Malena on the Sunset Coast, and require a two-guest minimum. Tours include park entry, meals, accommodation at their B&B and in double-occupancy tents on Coiba, avoiding the shared dorm. Book early so they can plan snorkeling to coincide with the best tides. Rates are discounted with larger groups and in low season. Very family-friendly.

Bird Coiba BIRDWATCHING
(☎6544-1806; www.birdcoiba.com; full day per person US$75-320) Responsible local guide Javier Elizondo offers tours of Parque Nacional Coiba, both all-inclusive day trips and several overnight options. Prices decrease with the number of participants, so it's worth getting a group together with other travelers. Options include birding, snorkeling, surfing, hiking and visiting the former penal colony.

Fluid Adventures KAYAKING
(☎6560-6558, in Canada 647-282-8167; www.fluidadventurespanama.com; overnight/3 days & 2 nights per person US$329/519) Run by a team of enthusiastic North Americans, this Santa Catalina–based outfitter offers rentals in Santa Catalina and kayaking trips around Isla de Coiba. Day trips reach Coiba by motorboat for a head start. Camping, guides, all meals and transportation are included and equipment is top-notch.

ARTURIS Coiba ECOTOUR
(Asociación Rural de Turismo Sostenible de la Zona de Amortiguamiento del Parque Nacional Coiba; ☎6529-5802, 933-0325; www.arturiscoiba.blogspot.cl; ⏲day trip per person US$70) Arturis is a network of local providers offering transportation, camping and guides to Coiba for single and multiday trips. Only Spanish is spoken. Boats leave from Puerto Mutis or Santa Catalina; students get discounted rates. For information, contact Faustino Sánchez.

Sleeping & Eating

If traveling as part of a tour, you will not have to worry about meals as everything will be arranged for you. Independent travelers must purchase supplies in advance on the mainland as there is no food available on the island. There is a kitchen but no fuel is provided and utensils are nonexistent.

Ranger Station Cabins CABIN $
(☎333-4570, In Santiago 998-4387, ext 6418 500-0855; campsite/dm per person US$10/20; ❄) At present the only accommodation on the island is at the Ministerio de Ambiente ranger station. There are four cabins (with a total of 40 beds), each with its own common cold shower and toilet. They are clean but spartan; given Coiba's isolation, you shouldn't expect too much. You can also use a tent or a jungle hammock in the dry season.

Electricity is produced by a diesel generator that runs from dusk to dawn; use of the air-conditioning may be restricted. Be sure to pack insect repellent and toilet paper.

Information

Visitors to the island, day-trippers included, register upon arrival at the ranger station run by the Ministry of the Environment. It is very difficult to arrive on the island as an independent traveler, since you must confirm that there is space for lodging and pay in advance at the Ministerio de Ambiente office (p137) in Santiago.

The majority of the island is a restricted area, though there is a large distance between the ranger station and the now-defunct main prison complex (open to tours).

On the northern end of the island, the **ranger station** (Ministerio de Ambiente; ☎333-4570, ext 6418 500-0855, in Santiago 998-4387; park fee US$20) consists of a modest museum, several basic cabins, a camping pitch, showers and toilets. It is located beside an attractive beach alongside a scenic cove.

Getting There & Away

The most common departure point for boats heading to Isla de Coiba is Santa Catalina, though boats also arrive from the Sunset Coast on the Península de Azuero and from Puerto Mutis, a small port about 30km southwest of Santiago. Santa Catalina is about an hour and a half away; it takes about two to three hours from the other two ports. There is an airstrip on Isla de Coiba reserved for private charter flights.

Keep in mind that the open sea can get extremely rough, especially in the dry season and in the afternoon; many fishers have been lost at sea over the years. Boats are required to have as many life jackets as passengers. Make sure you wear one.

Isla Cébaco

POP 650

Panama's third-largest island at 80 sq km (after Isla de Coiba and Isla del Rey), Isla Cébaco in the Gulf of Montijo is very much off the beaten track due to the difficulty of access. No commercial ferries operate there and transportation is by private charter only. As a result there is almost no tourism development and the small population, mostly based around the main settlement of El Jobo to the north, is engaged in agriculture, raising livestock and fishing.

Despite all this, Cébaco's beautiful beaches and breathtaking coastline offer the intrepid traveler a variety of activities: hiking trails of varying degrees of difficultly, fishing, diving, snorkeling and surfing. Indeed, Playa Grande on the island's south side is one of the region's new surfing hot spots.

Sleeping

Cébaco Sunrise CABIN $

(☎6535-4491; www.cebacosunrise.com; camping per person US$20, r per person incl breakfast US$25-35) This property on the east coast of Isla Cébaco, facing the Sunset Coast, is simplicity itself. Guests can camp in tents under the coconut trees on the beach or spread out in cabins (some with shared bathrooms). Perhaps its best feature is the remote location. Snorkeling around the island and hiking are recommended. Meals, tours and transport (one way US$20) are extra.

Be aware, the 30-minute boat ride from Playa Reina can be intense. Ask ahead about sea conditions. Cébaco Sunrise also offers a day tour (US$75 per person) to the island, including transport, lunch, a snack and use of all facilities.

Getting There & Away

You can charter boats to ferry you to Isla Cébaco from Santa Catalina or from Puerto Mutis, 30km southwest of Santiago, but the closest embarkation point (and the one used by Cébaco Sunrise) is Playa Reina. This is about 5km down a paved road west of Mariato, which can be reached by one of 10 daily buses from Santiago (US$4.25, 1¼ hours). Board the boat at the Puerto de los Flojos located at the mouth of the Río Negro or Playa Reina. The journey to Cébaco Sunrise takes a half-hour. Be aware, there are big waves here and at times the sea can be wild.

The Sunset Coast

The Sunset Coast is the name given to the west side of Península de Azuero facing the Golfo de Montijo and Pacific Ocean. The sobriquet is accurate for it is the only place in Panama from which you can watch the sun set into the sea from a beach.

Stretching for about 50km from Mariato in the north to Parque Nacional Cerro Hoya in the south, the Sunset Coast is *terra incognita* for most travelers. That's a shame, for it offers some amazing off-the-beaten-path attractions.

Here you'll find long, sandy beaches virtually empty of holiday-makers, excellent surfing and the chance to see three species of turtles hatching. There are nature walks in the mangroves and Parque Nacional Cerro Hoya is just down the road.

The gateway to the Sunset Coast is Santiago, about 60km north of Mariato. Other important settlements include Malena and Torio, 11km and 15km south of Mariato respectively.

Activities

Surfing

Two of the best surfing beaches in Veraguas can be found on the Sunset Coast: **Playa Reina** near Mariato, and **Playa Morillo**, the latest hot spot south of Torio.

Wildlife-Watching

Local organizations involved in the protection of turtles can help you see these endangered creatures up close. On the Pacific coast, the main season is from July to January, though green turtles can show up until mid-April near Morillo and Mata Oscuro.

Malena Beach Conservation Association WILDLIFE WATCHING
(Asociación Conservacionista de Playa Malena; ☎6865-8908; Playa Malena; donation US$15) The volunteers of the Malena Beach Conservation Association work toward the preservation of three species of turtles on the beaches of Malena. Chairperson Ana González and her community volunteers take visitors on turtle watches; peak season for laying and hatching is September through November. The organization also offers accommodations, horseback riding, boat tours, whale-watching and nature walks.

Outside peak season, there's green turtles from December through February and Carey turtles in July and August. The organization always needs enthusiastic volunteers with basic Spanish skills. To volunteer, contact **Hostal Iguana Verde** (☎6865-8908; anag27154@gmail.com; s/d US$20/30; ❄).

Centro AAPEQ WILDLIFE WATCHING
(☎6491-9365, 6389-5249; www.playamataoscura.blogspot.cl; Rusia de Quebro; ⊙hours vary) This association based near Morillo focuses its attention on the conservation of turtles and reforestation of the Mata Oscura mangrove. For a small fee, the affable couple in charge can take you on a tour through the mangroves or through the forest up to a waterfall, where you can see strawberry poison dart frogs. Kayaks are available as well.

AAPEQ also accepts volunteers for turtle conservation and path maintenance. As staff are often out of range of cell service, have patience in making contact.

Tours

Morillo Beach Eco Resort ADVENTURE SPORTS
(☎6017-0965; www.morrillobeachresort.com; Playa Morillo; tours from US$45; ⊙hours vary) While big plans are in the works here for a coastal lodge and farm-to-table Mexican restaurant, for now this up-and-coming Colorado-owned enterprise offers stand-up paddleboarding tours in the mangroves, visits to nearby Parque Nacional Cerro Hoya, surf lessons, snorkeling on Isla Cebaco and cultural tours. Its base sits tucked against the mangroves, with prolific wildlife including endangered Azuero howler monkeys.

Sleeping

Villa Vento Surf HOSTEL $
(☎6151-8048; www.villaventohostels.com; Playa Morillo; dm/d US$15/40) Wavefront on a wild and remote beach, this surf hostel is a gigantic dose of paradise. However, the remote location and gnarly surf aren't for everyone. Sandy rooms are new and adequate, with a sprawling shaded deck with hammocks. BYO provisions and cook in a shared kitchen. There's few distractions but surf lessons (US$30), horse riding (US$25) and fishing (US$40).

It's a 2km walk from the main road. Requires a high-clearance vehicle for access. A taxi from Mariato is US$20.

Hotel El Sol BOUTIQUE HOTEL $
(☎6616-1632; www.ecoelsol.com; Morillo; d/ste US$60/120; ❄ 🛜 🏊) Run by an eccentric Brit with roots in Malaysia, this quirky, laidback lodging with permaculture farming is good value. Rooms feature private decks with driftwood furniture and there's a lovely pool adequate for laps. The owner also cooks good Asian and Mediterranean cuisine with advance notice (dinner from US$12) – karaoke optional. Breakfast with fresh bread is available early for surfers.

Meals are also available to the public.

Hotel Playa Reina HOTEL $
(☎6319-1770, 848-2013; www.hotelplayareina.com; Playa Reina, Mariato; dm/d without bathroom US$16/35, r US$35-65, ste US$95-115; P ❄ 🛜 🏊) Set up for surfers, this new hotel, the sister property to Hotel Santa Catalina (p145), has a little something for everyone, with rooms ranging from acceptable budget dormitories to comfortable suites with ocean views. With a sprawling thatched restaurant area and swimming pool, it lords over the waves of Playa Reina.

★ **Heliconia Bed & Breakfast** B&B $$
(☎ 6676-0220; www.hotelheliconiapanama.com; Palmilla; s/d incl breakfast US$55/85; P ❄ ☜ ≋) The Sunset Coast's anchor tenant, Heliconia Bed & Breakfast in Palmilla, on the main road just north of Malena, is an excellent retreat thoughtfully crafted by two extremely knowledgeable Dutch biologists, who also offer recommended area tours. Heliconia has three smart rooms set within 8 hectares of botanical gardens, a lovely lounge and terrace, and an above-ground pool.

El Nido del Tucán CABAÑAS $$
(The Toucan's Nest; ☎ 6430-0912, 6430-0987; www.elnidodeltucan.com; Playas Duarte & Morillo; s/d US$55/85; P ❄ ☜ ≋) This handsome property is located about 2km down a track from the main road to Morillo has a guesthouse with large bedroom and sitting room, fully equipped kitchen and good-sized terrace. Below it are two smaller *cabañas* with kitchenettes and balcony. All have views looking across the water out to Isla Cébaco.

There's a long, narrow pool on site and two beaches – Playas Duarte and Morillo – are within easy walking distance, just down the hill. The lovely Swiss owners couldn't be more welcoming.

★ **Punta Duarte Garden Inn** INN $$$
(☎ 6152-7817, 6645-4635; www.puntaduarte.com; Punta Duarte; r incl breakfast US$85-148; ❄ ☜ ≋) Brimming with style, this lovely inn offers a peaceful and inspired beach retreat. Off a wraparound veranda, there's five elegant, ample rooms with ocean views, playful styles and cool, original artwork. Some baths feature double showers and there's a Jacuzzi and pool on property. The German host Gabrielle provides a warm welcome. Meals are also available (US$8 to US$25).

It sits in a gated community on the point; the beach is accessible via two forest trails with capuchin monkeys.

★ **Camino del Sol Ecolodge** LODGE $$$
(☎ 6810-7122; www.caminodelsol.com.pa; Punta Duarte; d/bungalow incl breakfast US$155/220; P ❄ ☜ ≋) In a 35-hectare preserve, this very private lodge showcases fine modern design with drop-dead Pacific views and plenty of attitude. The owner from St Tropez is architect, host and cocktail-maker. Glass bungalows and large rooms feature king-sized four-poster beds, oceanfront terraces and Italian furnishings. There's also a delicious infinity pool and a long trail to the water.

Eating & Drinking

La Fondita PIZZA $
(Camino a Playa Reina s/n, Mariato; mains US$7-13; ⊙ noon-2:30pm & 5-10pm) On the way to Playa Reina, this tiny thatched restaurant serves up marinated octopus, lasagna and authentic pizza served on wooden boards. It's the creation of a cheerful Italian couple, Daniele and Liria. With espresso drinks.

La Chantin INTERNATIONAL $
(☎ 6506-4249, 6685-7862; www.facebook.com/estasenlachantin; Calle Zapotal s/n, Torio; mains US$5-12; ⊙ 6-10pm Wed-Sun) Run by a young Panamanian–French Canadian couple, this lively cafe with open decks and hammocks is the spot to be after sundown. A varied menu offers up portobello goat-cheese sandwiches, burritos, and watercress salad with strawberries. There's also refreshing juices and beer.

They can also point visitors to local farm tours.

★ **Palati Fini** ITALIAN $$
(☎ 6853-7064, 6423-7880; Calle Zapotal s/n, Torio; mains US$8-15; ⊙ noon-9:30pm Wed-Mon) One of the better restaurants on the Sunset Coast. The pastas at this open-air venue are tasty and substantial, with other dishes based on fresh seafood. The Genovese owners are best known for extraordinary pesto, made with basil grown on-site.

Cafe Julia CAFE
(Calle Zapotal s/n; mains US$3-6; ⊙ 8am-2pm Fri-Wed) In a cool hangar furnished with pallet sofas, this easygoing French-owned cafe is the perfect spot for a morning snack. There's espresso drinks in addition to homemade brownies, financiers and fondant. For savory options, check out the quiche or quesadillas.

Information

There's a branch of **Banco Nacional de Panamá** (☎ 999-8657; Av Central; ⊙ 8am-3pm Mon-Fri, 9am-noon Sat) with an ATM in Mariato.

Getting There & Around

Up to 10 buses a day link Santiago with Torio (US$5, 1½ hours), via Mariato, between 6am and 5pm. The buses at noon and 2pm carry on as far as Rusia de Quebra, where Centro AAPEQ (p151) is located.

Once you've arrived on the Sunset Coast, having your own transport is incredibly useful. There are two local taxis: **Taxi Chato** (☎ 6934-8387; Mariato) and **Taxi Luis** (☎ 6429-0521; Mariato).

Chiriquí Province

POP 451,230 / ELEV SEA LEVEL TO 3474M

Includes ➜

Best Places to Eat

- ➜ Retrogusto (p171)
- ➜ El Refugio La Brisa del Diablo (p180)
- ➜ Hotel Panamonte Restaurant (p171)
- ➜ Cerro Brujo (p176)
- ➜ Boquete Fish House (p171)
- ➜ Colibri (p171)

Best Places to Stay

- ➜ Lost & Found Hostel (p180)
- ➜ Finca Lérida (p169)
- ➜ Los Quetzales Cabins (p179)
- ➜ Bambuda Castle (p168)
- ➜ Bocas del Mar (p161)
- ➜ Haven (p168)

Why Go?

Chiriquí claims to have it all: Panama's tallest mountains, longest rivers and most fertile valleys. The province is also home to spectacular highland rainforests and the most productive agricultural and cattle-ranching regions in the country. As a result, *los chiricanos* (natives of Chiriquí) take a particular pride in their province and wave the provincial flag – in every sense – at the slightest opportunity.

It's also a land of immense beauty. On the coast, the pristine Golfo de Chiriquí boasts long sandy beaches and a rich diversity of marine life. The mist-covered mountains near the town of Boquete, a favorite of North American and European retirees, is a good base for adventures such as white-water rafting and hiking the flanks of Panama's highest point, Volcán Barú (3474m). Boquete is also the center of Panama's coffee industry, which means that a potent cup of shade-grown arabica is never more than a cafe away.

When to Go

Apr & May The best months to spot the resplendent quetzal nesting in highland destinations such as Parque Nacional Volcán Barú and Parque Internacional La Amistad. The annual orchid fair lights up Boquete in April.

Dec–Apr High season on the Pacific coast has little precipitation, making it the best time to hit highland trails that get muddy and damaged during the rainy season.

Jan, Feb & Mar Boquete's Feria de las Flores y del Café draws the crowds in January. La Concepción celebrates its patron's feast day in early February, and David holds the huge Feria Internacional de San José de David over 10 days in early March.

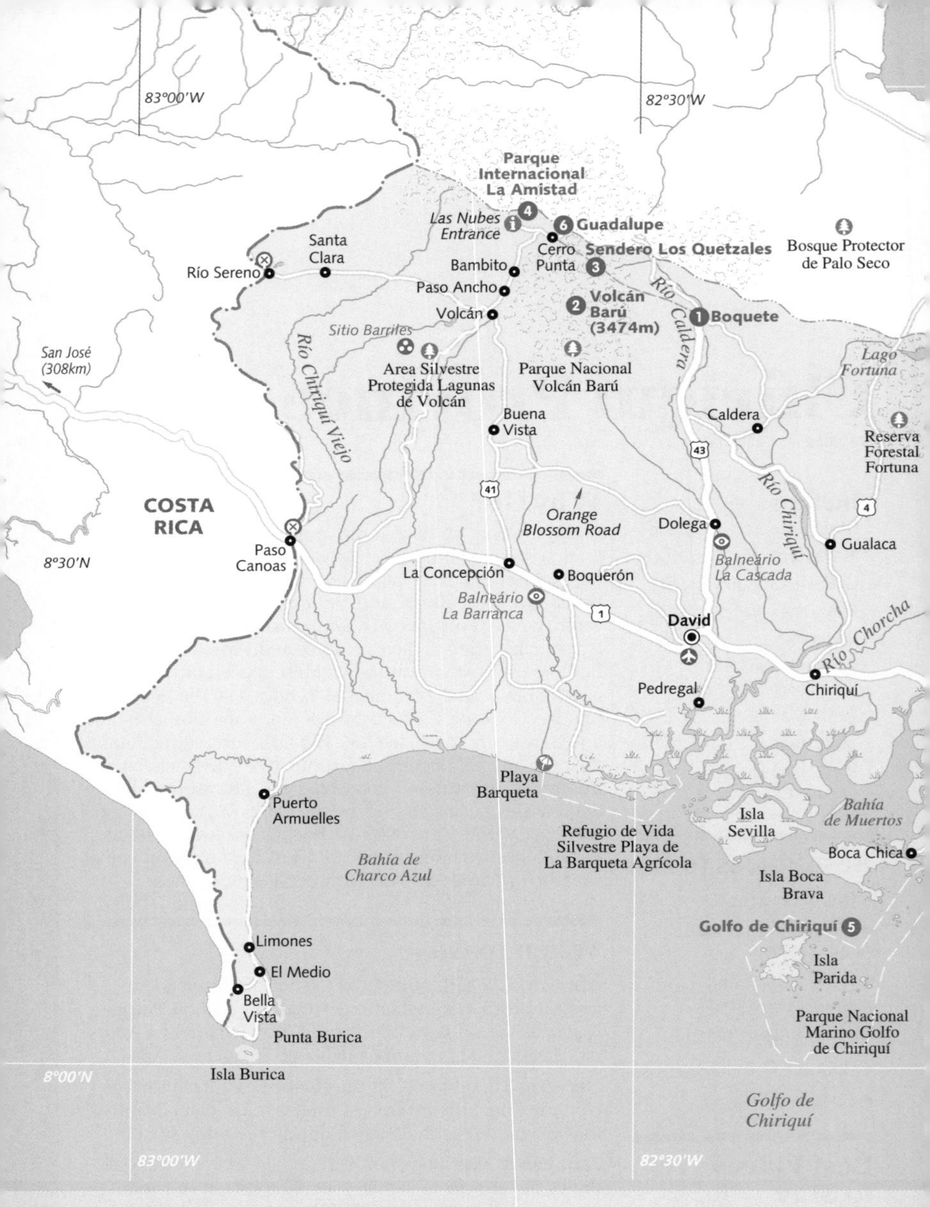

Chiriquí Province Highlights

1. **Boquete** (p164) Fueling up for highland adventures with local mountain-grown coffee in the town of eternal spring.

2. **Volcán Barú** (p173) Ascending for views of both the Pacific and Atlantic coastlines – provided the weather is clear.

3. **Sendero Los Quetzales** (p173) Hiking through cloud forests in search of the elusive quetzal.

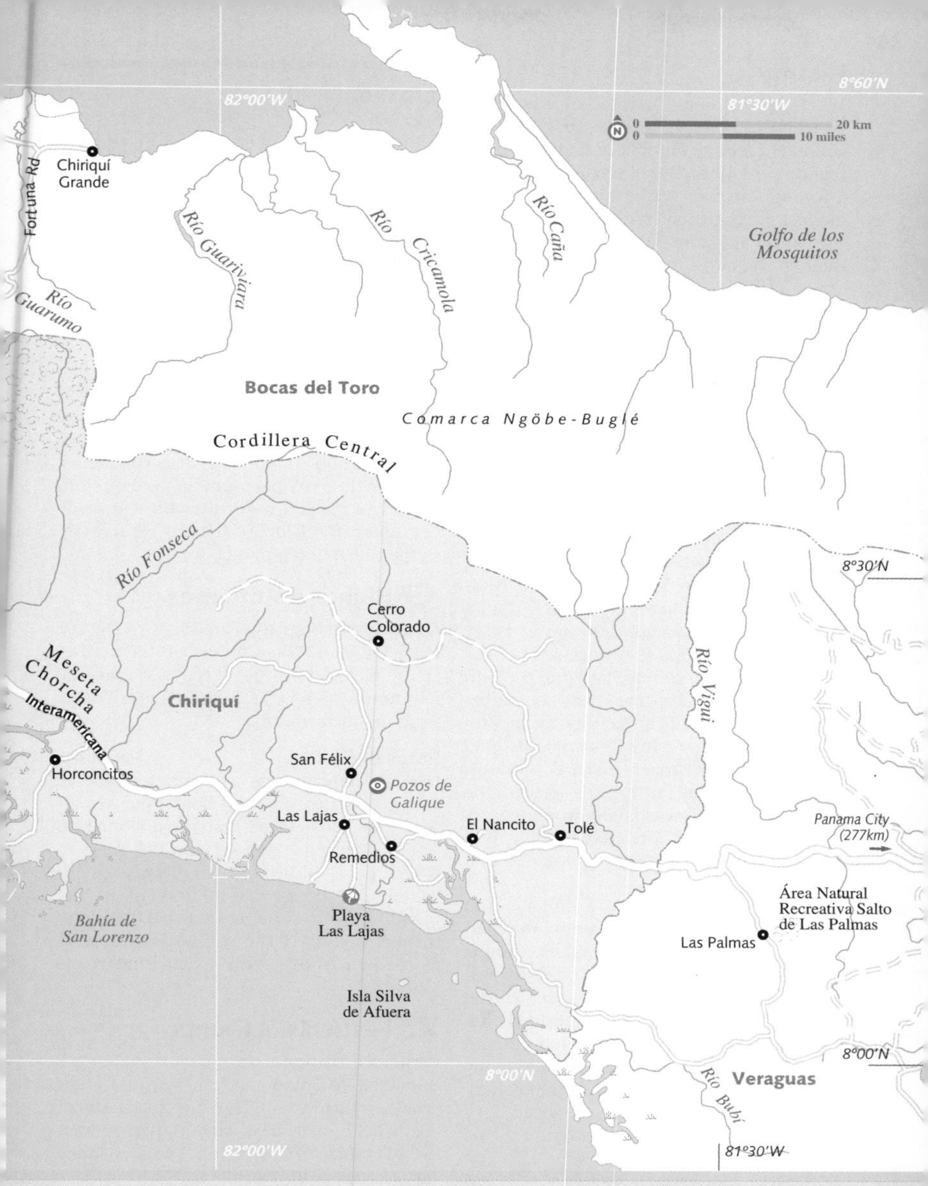

8°60'N
82°00'W
81°30'W
0 20 km
0 10 miles
Chiriquí Grande
Fortuna Rd
Río Guariviara
Río Cricamola
Río Caña
Golfo de los Mosquitos
Río Guarumo
Bocas del Toro
Comarca Ngöbe-Buglé
Cordillera Central
Río Fonseca
8°30'N
Cerro Colorado
Meseta Chorcha
Interamericana
Chiriquí
Río Viguí
Horconcitos
San Félix
Pozos de Galique
Las Lajas
El Nancito
Tolé
Panama City (277km)
Remedios
Área Natural Recreativa Salto de Las Palmas
Playa Las Lajas
Bahía de San Lorenzo
Las Palmas
Isla Silva de Afuera
8°00'N
Río Bubí
Veraguas
82°00'W
81°30'W

4 **Parque Internacional La Amistad** (p179) Wondering why you're the only one around in this pristine and bio-rich park.

5 **Golfo de Chiriquí** (p160) Island-hopping and exploring the clear blue seas of the national marine park on the 'other side' of Chiriquí.

6 **Guadalupe** (p178) Waking up surrounded by wilderness while staying in the cool jungle lodges near Cerro Punta.

History

When the Spaniards arrived in what is now Panama in the early 16th century, they encountered a large number of tribes living in relative isolation. Often separated by only a few kilometers, each group maintained a distinct language, culture and religion.

Spanish missionaries arrived and began their conversions. In the early 17th century, a group led by Padre Cristóbal Cacho Santillana rounded up more than 600 indigenous people from across the region and began recording a glossary of the most common words. He was able to identify six distinct languages.

Sadly, an epidemic of measles brought by the colonists swept through the towns and killed half of the study population. The survivors, having had enough of the Spaniards, their linguistic studies and their religion, took to the hills. Unfortunately, their fate was already sealed. Of the 10 distinct tribes, only the Ngöbe-Buglé survived. Today they are the most populous of Panama's seven indigenous groups, though their numbers are but a fraction of what they once were.

During the 17th century and into the 18th century, Chiriquí Province was the target of pirate attacks, much like the rest of Panama. It was just outside Remedios in 1680 that English buccaneer Richard Sawkins, attempting to lead an assault against the well-defended city, was fatally wounded. Six years later, English privateers from Honduras sacked the towns of Alanje and San Lorenzo.

In the 19th century, the climate and slopes of the Chiriquí highlands attracted farmers from North America and Europe who planted coffee and other crops as well as exploiting the forests for timber. The wave of immigration hasn't subsided. Recent arrivals are mainly foreign retirees and real-estate speculators, which has led many *chiricanos* to question who it is that actually owns the land they love so much.

LOWLANDS

Chiriquí has much to offer beyond its famed highland rainforests. The region's lowlands are home to Panama's second-largest city, David, as well as large stretches of striking Pacific coastline, a marine park and some lovely islands.

David

POP 144,860

Although it feels more like an overgrown country town, David is Panama's second-largest city and the capital of Chiriquí Province. It's more a center of agricultural industry than a cultural hub; you will be disappointed if you have museums, clubs and fine dining in mind. Yet with foreign capital flowing into Chiriquí, David is rapidly gaining wealth and importance, and is poised to boom.

For most travelers David is a pit stop on the way to surrounding destinations. Halfway between Panama City and San José (Costa Rica), David is an important transportation hub. If the road has you weary, slip into the slow pace, grab a *jugo de caña* (sugarcane juice) in downtown's Parque de Cervantes, the heart of the city, or day-trip to the beach or highlands.

Sights & Activities

Iglesia de la Sagrada Familia CATHEDRAL

(Av 3 Este s/n) The Church of the Sacred Heart, facing downtown's central Parque de Cervantes, has a bell tower and dates largely from the 19th century.

Pozos de Galique HOT SPRINGS

(www.explorasinfronteras.com/contacto/pozos-en-galique; Juay; 9am-4pm) Soak your travel-weary bones at three no-frills hot springs. The easy-to-miss turnoff for the road to the springs – note that it requires a 4WD vehicle to access – is 4km west of the turnoff for Playa Las Lajas. The 3.8km-long turnoff leading to the springs is 30m west of a small bridge with a sign that reads 'Galique.'

Festivals & Events

Feria Internacional de San José de David FERIA

(www.feriadedavid.com) This big international fair is held for 10 days each March; contact the ATP office (p159) for exact dates, as they vary from year to year.

Fiesta de La Concepción FERIA

A half-hour drive west of David, the town of La Concepción celebrates the feast day of its patron saint, La Virgen de la Candelaria, on February 2 or the following Saturday if it lands on a weekday.

David

Sleeping

★Bambu Hostel HOSTEL $
(☎730-2961; www.bambuhostel.com; Calle de la Virgencita; dm US$11-13, d with/without bathroom US$35/30; P ❄ 📶 🏊) This great chilled-out house is the creation of a friendly musician and former Brooklynite. There's air-conditioned dorms, decent private rooms and a thatched 'jungle house' on stilts out back, with beds draped in mosquito nets. You might see a coati roaming the sprawling garden, which has a swimming pool, a cheap beer bar and the requisite hammocks.

Hotel Puerta del Sol HOTEL $
(☎775-1662, 774-8422; www.hotelpuertadelsol.com; Av 3 Este; d/q US$50/72; P ❄ 📶) A very secure budget choice, this central hotel offers 86 tasteful tiled rooms with wood furnishings. Rooms are on the small side, but the setting is pleasant. Amenities include hot-water showers, cable TV and a full-service restaurant open daily till 10pm (Sunday lunch only, till 3pm).

David

Sights

1 Iglesia de la Sagrada Familia ... C3

Sleeping

2 Gran Hotel Nacional ... C3
3 Hotel Castilla ... C3
4 Hotel Ciudad de David ... D2
5 Hotel Puerta del Sol ... C3

Eating

6 Café Rincón Libanés ... B4
7 Java Juice ... A3
8 MultiCafe ... C3
9 Pho Palace ... A4
10 Restaurante El Fogón ... C2
11 Super 99 ... A3

Entertainment

12 Multicines Nacional ... C3

DAVID DAY TRIPS

Spice up your travels with these excursions:

➡ Take a soak in the Los Pozos de Caldera (p163) hot springs on the way to Boquete. Take a bus to the town of Caldera, hike along the dirt road for one hour and enjoy the springs.

➡ Learn to appreciate rum before you down a tumbler or two on a free tour of the **Carta Vieja Rum Factory** (772-7073; www.cartaviejapa.com; Alanje; by appointment) FREE on the outskirts of town.

➡ Swim with *chiricanos* at **Balneário La Barranca** (Bagala; 11am-6pm) FREE, a natural swimming pool with a bar-restaurant about 20km west of David. Hop on a Concepción-bound bus.

➡ Beat the David heat at the beach. Grab some friends and take a taxi to the lovely dark-sand Playa Barqueta (p160).

Hotel Castilla HOTEL $
(774-5260, 774-5236; www.hotelcastilladavid.com; cnr Calle A Norte & Av 3 Este; d/tr/ste US$53/74/77; P ❄ 📶) Professional and superclean, this hotel offers 69 cheerful tiled rooms with matching beds and desk sets in a vaguely art-deco style. Each room is equipped with hot-water shower, air-con and cable TV. There's an underground parking garage.

Hotel Ciudad de David BUSINESS HOTEL $$
(774-3333; www.hotelciudaddedavid.com; cnr Calle D Norte & Av 2 Este; d/ste incl breakfast from US$75/106; P ❄ @ 📶 ≋) David's flashiest hotel, the sleek 'City of David' has 103 tastefully furnished rooms with wooden floors, minibars and fully wired desks. Rooms 303 and 304 look onto the fabulous amoeba-shaped swimming pool; suite 305 has a balcony as well. There's a sauna, a fully equipped gym and a stylish bar-restaurant called – what else? – Stylo.

Gran Hotel Nacional HOTEL $$
(775-2222; www.hotelnacionalpanama.com; cnr Calle Central & Av 1 Este; d/ste US$95/135, d deluxe US$110; P ❄ 📶 ≋) David's largest hotel offers 119 modern yet fairly sterile rooms better suited to domestic businesspeople than travelers. But the hotel isn't short on amenities, and the on-site bar-restaurant, pizzeria, casino and six-screen cinema sweeten the deal. Some rooms, such as deluxe double room 140, look onto a leafy courtyard and large swimming pool – a plus in Panama's hottest city.

Eating

Super 99 SUPERMARKET
(cnr Calle F Sur & Av 4 Oeste; 24hr) Self-caterers can head to the Super 99, a large supermarket open 24 hours a day and convenient to the city's hostels.

Pho Palace VIETNAMESE $
(6352-3000; Calle F Sur s/n; mains US$6-12; 9am-10pm) A find for the area, this immaculate restaurant with screens, ambient lighting and flower arrangements serves authentic Hanoi cuisine. Big bowls of pho (noodle soup) and sweet-and-sour fish, plus more mainstream options like pineapple chicken and spring rolls. It's all well prepared, though service can be slow.

Polo PANAMANIAN $
(6406-9088; Calle de la Virgencita; mains US$4-8; 10am-11pm Mon-Sat) A longstanding neighborhood staple, this basic seafood restaurant (with a few pork dishes thrown in) does cheap and cheerful pretty well. The *ceviche* (citrus-cured seafood) is a cut above and the whole fried fish is the best (and probably cheapest) in town.

MultiCafe CAFETERIA $
(774-5133; cnr Calle A Norte & Av 2 Este; dishes US$3-6; 7am-7pm; ❄) A prime choice if you're looking for something cheap and filling while you're on the hoof downtown. This colorful cafeteria south of the landmark cathedral has trays of local beef, chicken and pasta dishes as well as salads. Good for a local breakfast too.

Java Juice HEALTH FOOD $
(730-3461; www.facebook.com/javajuice.ch; cnr Calle E Sur & Av 3 Oeste; mains US$3-5; 9:30am-10pm Mon-Sat, from 2pm Sun; 🖉) Fruit smoothies, salads and grilled burgers are the fare at this health-food cafe-restaurant with a US owner to the west of downtown. Good vegetarian selection, including a great green smoothie.

Café Rincón Libanés MIDDLE EASTERN **$$**
(☎730-3911, 774-2700; Calle F Sur; mains US$8-18; ⊙11am-11:30pm) This fairly authentic Lebanese restaurant southwest of downtown provides a welcome relief from a steady diet of rice and beans. Homemade hummus, tabbouleh, baba ghanoush and lamb kofta (meatballs) will make you wonder if you're in the Middle East. Try the homemade pink lemonade.

Restaurante El Fogón INTERNATIONAL **$$**
(☎775-7091; Av 2a Oeste; mains US$8-18; ⊙noon-10:30pm Mon-Sat, to 9pm Sun) This spacious red, yellow and orange eatery is a welcome oasis northwest of the center. Grilled meats and seafood are the standard main courses, and there are burgers and sandwiches for the less-than-ravenous. Checked tablecloths and fake foliage throughout. 'The Stove' is favorite with locals.

☆ Entertainment

Multicines Nacional CINEMA
(☎775-2222; www.hotelnacionalpanama.com; cnr Calle Central & Av 1 Este) This old-style movie theater at the Gran Hotel Nacional has six screens and is the perfect spot to catch up on all the 'latest' Hollywood films; the majority are in English with Spanish subtitles. It's also a way to beat David's oppressive heat in summer.

ℹ Information

The central branch of **Banco Nacional de Panamá** (☎774-6400; Calle B Norte; ⊙8am-3pm Mon-Fri, 9am-noon Sat) has an ATM and faces Parque de Cervantes.

ATP Office (☎775-2839; chiriqui@atp.gob.pa; Calle Central; ⊙8:30am-4:30pm Mon-Fri) Has information on David and Chiriquí Province.

Ministerio de Ambiente (fax 774-6671; Av Red Gray; ⊙8am-4pm Mon-Fri) Provides tourist information and advice, and camping permits for national parks. It's 4.5km south of David's center.

ℹ Getting There & Away

AIR

David's airport, **Aeropuerto Enrique Malek** (☎721-1072; David), is about 5km south of the center. There are no buses to the airport; take a taxi (US$5).

Air Panama (☎721-0841; www.flyairpanama.com; Aeropuerto Enrique Malek) and **Copa Airlines** (☎217-2672; www.copaair.com; Aeropuerto Enrique Malek) have daily 45-minute flights to and from Panama City, from US$90 one way. Air Panama also flies between David and Bocas del Toro town.

BUS

The Interamericana does not go through David but skirts around its western and northern sides. The David **bus terminal** (Av del Estudiante) is about 500m northeast of Parque de Cervantes. Most buses begin service around 6am.

Tracopa (☎775-0585; www.tracopacr.com) has direct buses between David and San José, Costa Rica (US$28, seven hours), from Monday through Friday at 7:30am and 3pm from the David bus terminal.

BUSES FROM DAVID

DESTINATION	FARE (US$)	DURATION	FREQUENCY (DAILY)
Boquete	1.75	1hr	every 20min to 9:30pm
Caldera	2.40	45min	hourly to 7:30pm
Cerro Punta	3.50	2¼hr	every 20min to 6pm
Changuinola	9.70	4½hr	half-hourly to 6:30pm
Guadalupe	3.50	2½hr	every 20min to 6pm
Horconcitos	2	45min	11am & 5pm
Las Lajas	5	1½hr	4
Panama City	18	7-8hr	every 45min 6:45am to 8pm
Paso Canoas	2.10	50min	every 15min to 9:30pm
Puerto Armuelles	4	2½hr	every 15min to 9pm
Río Sereno	5.10	2½hr	every 30min to 5pm
Santiago	9	3hr	hourly to 9pm
Volcán	3	1½hr	every 20min to 8pm

Getting Around

David has a complex network of local buses, but the easiest way to get around is by taxi; fares within the city are generally about US$2 to US$3.

All of the major car-rental companies have booths at the airport.

You can hire a taxi to Pedregal (US$4), Boquete (US$25), Volcán (US$35) and Playa Barqueta (US$30).

Playa Barqueta

This long black-sand **beach** 25km southwest of David is a popular weekend escape, though it remains quiet during the week.

Some 14km of the eastern beach falls under the jurisdiction of the **Refugio de Vida Silvestre Playa Barqueta Agricola** (6am-3pm), whose mangrove and scrub offer protection to four species of turtles. It's hatching season here from September to December. Contact the Ministerio de Ambiente office (p159) in David for information about visits.

Capping the western end of the beach is **Las Olas Resort** (772-3000; www.lasolasresort.com; d/ste from US$75/450; P). Its 48 terraced rooms and suites are decorated with soft, natural colors and feature sweeping ocean views. Facilities include bars and restaurants, an ocean-view pool, a spa and gym, and an equestrian center (note the decorative saddles in the lobby). Children stay and eat for free.

Getting There & Away

Two morning buses leave David for the 40-minute trip to Playa Barqueta, but it's easier to catch one of the frequent departures to Guarumal and then a taxi (US$6) from there. A taxi all the way from David will cost US$35. You should be able to negotiate a reasonable price if you need a ride back to David.

Golfo de Chiriquí

POP 440

The gem of the Chiriquí lowlands is the Golfo de Chiriquí, home to the **Parque Nacional Marino Golfo de Chiriquí**, a national marine park with an area of just over 147 sq km, protecting 25 islands, 19 coral reefs and abundant wildlife. The marine park also protects the 30-sq-km **Isla Boca Brava**, a lovely little island with hiking trails and beautiful outer beaches. It's home to howler monkeys, several types of nesting sea turtles and 280 recorded bird species. It is reached from the mainland village of Boca Chica. Resorts in the area offer a range of tours.

Visitors can enjoy surfing, kayaking the calm interior waters, snorkeling, watching wildlife under the rainforest canopy or fishing for big game.

GETTING TO COSTA RICA

The most heavily trafficked border crossing between Panama and Costa Rica is at **Paso Canoas** (open 7am to 7pm), 53.6km northwest of David on the Interamericana. Allow one to 1½ hours to get through the formalities on both sides. Buses from David depart frequently for the border (US$2.10, 50 minutes, every 15 minutes) from 4:30am. On the Costa Rican side of the border, you can catch regular buses to San José or other parts of the country.

The least trafficked crossing into Costa Rica is the border post at **Río Sereno** (open from 9am to 5pm Monday to Saturday, to 3pm Sunday), located 35km northwest of Volcán. Buses to the border depart from David and travel via La Concepción, Volcán and Santa Clara (US$5.10, 2½ hours, every half-hour). On the Costa Rican side of the border, you can take a 15-minute bus or taxi ride to San Vito, where you can catch buses to regional destinations.

From David, you can also taxi to Paso Canoas (US$30) or Río Sereno (US$60). Note that you will be asked for an onward ticket if you are entering Costa Rica. If you do not possess one, you can buy a round-trip bus ticket back to Panama. Also note that Costa Rica is one hour behind Panama.

If you require a visa, contact the **Costa Rican Consulate** (774-1923; www.embajadacostaricaenpanama.com; Calle B Norte & Av Primera, Torre del Banco Universal No 304; 9am-1pm Mon-Fri) in David.

Sleeping & Eating

Hotel Boca Brava HOTEL $

(☎6929-2996, 851-0017; www.hotelbocabrava.com; Isla Boca Brava, Boca Chica; s/d without bathroom US$35/40, d/ste with bathroom from US$50/75; ❄) An unexpected budget option on Isla Boca Brava, this hotel with 15 rooms, ranging from rustic to deluxe, is ideal for mingling with fellow travelers, though we have received some complaints from readers about the quality of the accommodations. Doubles are snug; the cheapest fan-cooled 'economy' doubles have shared bathroom.

At the other end of the spectrum are the delightful bay-view cottage (US$60) and two-bedroom suite (US$75) with air-conditioning. The eyrie-like bar and restaurant (mains US$5 to US$12) occupies a cool space on an overhanging deck with expansive water views. It's the perfect setting for a sundowner. The hotel can arrange excursions such as snorkeling, whale-watching and birdwatching.

Pacific Bay Resort LODGE $$

(☎6678-1000; www.pacificbayresort.org; s/d incl 3 meals US$75/125) This recommended all-inclusive eco resort catering to only 20 guests runs on wind and solar power. Linked by a garden path, each cottage houses six people and is themed to represent a region of Panama. There's access to local beaches and a great on-site restaurant. It also offers snorkeling tours to Isla Secas and island-hopping for picnics and swimming.

★ **Bocas del Mar** RESORT $$$

(☎6395-8757; www.bocasdelmar.com; Boca Chica; ste/superior incl breakfast US$295/379; P ❄ 📶 🏊) This elegant Belgian-owned resort on the mainland has 20 brilliant-white ultra-modern bungalows that offer the ultimate in comfort. Amenities range from two infinity pools and massage services to suites with private hot tubs. Rooms have handmade furniture, lovely artwork and windows with smoky glass. A full menu of excursions includes horse riding, kayaking, and fishing and snorkeling tours. Excellent restaurant and service.

Cala Mia Boutique Resort RESORT $$$

(☎851-0025, 6972-6954, USA 1-210-390-4259; www.calamiaresort.com; Isla Boca Brava, Boca Chica; ste incl breakfast US$189-239; ❄ 📶 🏊) Cala Mia on Isla Boca Brava offers luxurious ocean-front tranquility. Some 11 thatched bungalows have ample living spaces, handcrafted local furniture and their own deck with hammock. Two beaches – one with a bar – are just a stroll away, and a massage spa occupies its own islet, reached via suspension bridge. Organic three-course meals are served around a big community table.

Getting There & Away

To reach Boca Chica from David, take any of the Interamericana buses heading east to the Horconcitos turnoff (US$2, one hour). From there a van (US$3, 50 minutes) leaves four to five times daily for Boca Chica. At the Boca Chica dock, hire a water taxi (US$4 per person) to take you 200m to the Isla Boca Brava dock at Hotel Boca Brava.

If you drive your own vehicle, you can safely leave it near the village dock.

Playa Las Lajas

POP 1520

One of the longest beaches in Panama, 12km-long palm-fringed Playa Las Lajas seems to stretch forever. The beach gathers serious crowds at weekends, but during the week it often lies empty, so you can savor the glorious expanse all by yourself.

Ngöbe-Buglé people sell handicrafts in a wooden-walled structure 500m west of the turnoff to Playa Las Lajas, 76km east of David.

Tours

Cocaleca Tours TOUR

(☎6240-2705; www.cocalecatours.com; Las Lajas Beach Resort; ⊙hours vary) A great way to explore Las Lajas, you can go to mangroves, ride horses on the beach (US$30), visit a Ngöbe-Buglé community (US$45 per person), or check out petroglyphs in the hills. It's run by a Dutch-Panamanian couple with a passion for nature.

Sleeping & Eating

Nahual Eco Hostel HOSTEL $

(Hospedaje Ecológico Nahual; ☎6620-6431; www.nahualpanama.com; dm US$10, s/d with bathroom US$30/40, without bathroom US$15/25; P 📶) With *ranchos* (small house-like buildings) and attractive cabins, this fun, Italian-run place is the best bargain lodging in Las Lajas. It sits across the road from the beach in a leafy garden and is 100% chemical free. There are six rooms, including a dorm, and an open-air guest kitchen. The mostly vegan cafe serves organic food, homemade pasta and fish.

Casa Laguna B&B B&B $

(☎6896-0882; www.casalagunapanama.com; d incl breakfast US$45-65; P ❄ 📶 🏊) This small Italian-run B&B with just three rooms is a popular option for couples in Playa Las Lajas. There are open-air *ranchos* for relaxing in the main garden and that face a lagoon with mangrove in back; the beach is just 100m away. Immense breakfasts include yogurt, fruit and pancakes, and other meals are available upon request. The pool is above ground.

The only drawback is access. It's 2km from the main access road down a sandy track strewn with potholes.

Las Lajas Beach Resort RESORT $$

(☎6790-1972; www.laslajasbeachresort.com; Playa Las Lajas; d/ste US$99/132; P ❄ 📶 🏊) A lovely destination on the beach, with 14 impeccable, ample and cheery rooms and great service. We love the indigenous designs on the bedspreads and murals on the walls; room 12 features portraits of Panamanian greats. Guests can float in the pool or ocean, rent body boards (US$6) or consult the on-site agency, Cocaleca (p161), for great tours further afield.

The breezy, open-air restaurant facing the beach serves US-style breakfasts, big cheeseburgers and international fare (mains US$8 to US$14) daily till 9pm. Visitors who just want to use the pool can buy a day pass (US$13).

Naturalmente B&B $$

(☎727-0656, 6211-1787; www.naturalmentepanama.com; d incl breakfast US$65; P 📶 🏊) The three fan-cooled thatched cabins with little terraces at this delightful B&B accommodate between two and four people. It's at the northern end of Las Lajas town – not at the beach – but there's a small above-ground pool in the gardens. The Mediterranean restaurant (mains US$10 to US$13) with an Argentine chef is one of the best eateries on the gulf.

Finca Buena Vista B&B $$

(☎6814-8693; www.finca-buenavista-laslajas.com; d incl breakfast US$80; P ❄ 📶 🏊) On the outskirts of Las Lajas town, about 500m east, this German-run B&B has sweeping views and warm hospitality. Four spacious and well-appointed rooms feature private patios, small fridges and hot water. Patio-side breakfasts are outstanding. Rooms with lofts are ideal for families. Hosts are happy to arrange fishing, mangrove boat trips and excursions to the local indigenous community.

Chiricream ICE CREAM $

(☎6240-9463; cones US$3; ⏲2-9pm Thu-Tue) In Las Lajas town near the main plaza, you will swoon for this artisan gelato with flavors ranging from tropical fruits to tart yogurt and chocolate as rich as pudding. It's Italian-run, need we say more?

SURFING IN CHIRIQUÍ PROVINCE

Surfing in Chiriquí is less popular than in other provinces, due to the greater difficulty of access, but there is still great surf to be had. To go beyond the following suggestions, hire a local guide or tour operator.

Isla Silva de Afuera Remote island southeast of Playa Las Lajas, with a right and left break. The right: a big peak breaking over a shallow rock ledge at medium tide. Occasionally throws a big tube with steep drops and no wall. The left: breaks over a rock reef at medium tide. This spot catches almost every swell.

Morro Negrito Near the town of Morro Negrito, southeast of Isla Silva de Afuera near the Veraguas border. About five breaks, including a variety of lefts and rights with occasional tubes.

Playa Las Lajas (p161) Southeast of David. Beach-bottom break with rights and lefts but infrequent waves.

Playa Barqueta (p160) Southeast of David. Beach-bottom break with rights and lefts. Breaks at all tides, but medium to high tide is best.

Punta Burica Peninsula shared with Costa Rica. Four left points that break along the point for long, tubing rides. Catches any swell.

WORTH A TRIP

THE ROAD TO VERAGUAS PROVINCE

Heading to Veraguas Province, you can see some cool attractions, best accessed with your own wheels.

About 25km east of David, on the northern side of the Interamericana, the enormous **Meseta Chorcha** (Chorcha Plateau) beguiles photographers. From the west, you'll see a white streak running down its glistening granite face – it's actually an extremely tall but inaccessible waterfall. Awesome stuff.

About 20km east of Las Lajas, **Parque Arqueológico Petroglifo El Nancito** (El Nancito Petroglyph Archaeological Park; ☎727-0534; El Nancito; adult/child US$1/0.25; ⏲9am-5pm Mon-Sat) offers up mysterious rock carvings. Locals say that boulders were carved more than 1000 years ago, though no one really knows for sure. From the Interamericana, turn north onto the road to El Nancito. After 3.5km, when you reach the 'Museo' sign, turn left (west) and drive 100m until you come to rather large fenced-in boulders and the park's museum entrance. With public transportation, jump off any Interamericana bus at El Nancito, and then hike the 3.5km uphill to the boulders.

Soak your travel-weary bones at Pozos de Galique (p156), three no-frills hot springs. The easy-to-miss turnoff for the road to the springs – which requires a 4WD vehicle to access – is 4km west of the turnoff for Playa Las Lajas. The 3.8km-long turnoff leading to the springs is 30m west of a small bridge with a sign that reads 'Galique.'

Getting There & Away

From David, the Las Lajas turnoff is 76km east on the Interamericana. The town of Las Lajas is 3km south of the Interamericana and the beach a further 9km south.

To reach Las Lajas, take any bus from David (US$5, 90 minutes). You can take a taxi (US$5) to the beach from town.

David to Boquete

Interesting attractions line the way between David and Boquete, including hot springs, places to cool off in the summer heat and an archaeological site with some excellent petroglyphs.

Sights & Activities

La Piedra Pintada de Caldera ARCHAEOLOGICAL SITE
(Painted Rock Archaeological Park) FREE Some of the best examples of petroglyphs found in Panama can be seen in this park at Caldera, about 23km southeast of Boquete. It's located 400m down a marked trail about 1km past the police station on the right.

Los Pozos de Caldera HOT SPRINGS
(US$5; ⏲dawn-dusk) The area's most famous attraction, Los Pozos de Caldera are natural hot springs renowned for health-giving properties. The springs are located on private land near the town of Caldera, southeast of Boquete. Further on are newer springs called Los Pozos de Abuela (Grandmother's Hot Springs). You may have to make room at both for local indigenous women doing their laundry.

To get to the springs, take a bus or drive to the town of Caldera, which is 8km east of the David–Boquete road. From where the bus drops you off, continue to the end of town; here you'll see a sign indicating the turnoff to the springs. Turn right along this rugged dirt road, accessible by 4WD only. If you're walking it's about one hour from here. Continue along the road until you reach a suspension bridge. Cross it, and take the first left leading up the hill. After 100m you'll see a gate that marks the entrance to the property. Turning right after crossing the bridge will lead you to Los Pozos de Abuela.

If you get overheated in the springs, the pleasant Río Caldera is just a stone's throw away, and is an excellent spot to cool off. Tour agencies in Boquete offer day trips.

Balneário La Cascada SWIMMING
(Los Anastacios; US$3) Popular swimming spots take the edge off the heat. Balneario La Cascada, about 30 minutes north of David, has two waterfall-side swimming pools and a small bar. Take the bus on Calle F Sur in David to get here. It can get fairly crowded on weekends, though the atmosphere is always upbeat.

Sleeping

El Río Encantado Nature Resort RESORT **$$**
(☎6090-4951; www.rioencantado.com; Caldera; d US$85-95, q US$110-140; P ❄ 🛜 🏊) This remote resort idyllically located on 40 manicured hectares on the Río Caldera offers four comfortable self-catering cottages, as well as a wonderful treehouse (US$150) reached by winding steps (not for those with a fear of heights). There's fishing and swimming in the river and the Los Pozos de Caldera (p163) (hot springs) are 15 minutes away.

Getting There & Away

Having your own wheels is best for really exploring this area, though most places can be accessed (at least partially) via public transportation.

HIGHLANDS

The highland rainforests are the heart of Chiriquí Province. From the rugged mountains of Parque Internacional La Amistad and the misty hills of Boquete to the continental divide traversing the *cordillera* (mountain range), this is probably the only spot in Panama where you might need a sweater. While Panamanians relish the chill, you'll appreciate locals' laid-back hospitality and the astounding natural beauty throughout the region.

Boquete

POP 19,000

Boquete is known for its cool, fresh climate and pristine natural surroundings. Flowers, coffee, vegetables and citrus fruits flourish in its rich soil, and the friendliness of the locals seems to rub off on everyone who passes through. Boquete gained a deluge of expats after the American Association for Retired Persons (AARP) named it a top retirement spot. Until you see the gated communities and sprawling estates dotting the hillsides up close, though, you'd be hard-pressed to see what the fuss is about.

The surrounds, however, are another matter. Boquete is one of the country's top destinations for outdoor-lovers. It's a hub for hiking, climbing, rafting, visiting coffee farms, soaking in hot springs, studying Spanish or canopy touring. And, of course, there's nothing quite like a cup of locally grown coffee.

Sights

El Explorador GARDENS
(☎720-1989; www.facebook.com/ElExploradorBQT; Calle Jaramillo Alto; adult/child US$5/2; ⏲10am-6pm) Great for families, this private garden is located in a hilly area 3km northeast of the town center. You can walk to it in about 45 minutes. The 2 hectares of gardens are designed to look like something out of *Alice in Wonderland,* with no shortage of quirky eye-catching displays, including fanciful suspension bridges, koi ponds and playful sculptures.

Parque José Domingo Médica PARK
Boquete's central plaza has flowers, a fountain and a children's playground.

Activities

Adventure-hub Boquete has the lion's share of outfitters in the region, so it's not a stretch to book coastal trips such as sea kayaking or sportfishing here. Hostels and various agencies rent bicycles, scooters and ATVs (quad bikes), which are a good way to explore the charms of the surrounding hillsides.

Hiking

With its breathtaking vistas of mist-covered hills and nearby forests, Boquete is one of the most idyllic regions for hiking and walking. Several good paved roads lead out of town into the surrounding hills, passing coffee farms, fields, gardens and virgin forest.

Trails are mostly poorly marked, and seasonally affected by floods and landslides, which can change the routes. In the past there have also been security issues. For these reasons it's really best to hire local guides to explore the trails.

Although many visitors will be content with picturesque strolls along the river, the more ambitious can climb Volcán Barú (p174). There are several entrances to the Parque Nacional Volcán Barú, but the most accessible trail starts near Boquete.

It's possible to access the Sendero Los Quetzales (p173) from Boquete, though the trail is uphill from here; you'll have an easier time if you start hiking from Cerro Punta above Volcán. Landslides have affected the trail in the past. Ask locals about conditions before heading out.

Sendero El Pianista HIKING
(Pianist Trail) This day-hike wends its way through dairy land and into humid cloud forest. You need to wade across a small river after 200m, but then it's a steady, leisurely incline for 2km before you start to climb a steeper, narrow path. Using a guide is highly recommended.

The path leads deep into the forest, but you can turn back at any time. To access the trailhead from Boquete, head north on the right bank of the river and cross over two bridges. Immediately before the third bridge, about 4km out of town, a track leads off to the left between a couple of buildings. The trail is not especially difficult, but it isn't always well maintained. In April 2014 two Dutch nationals died while hiking here, though the cause of their deaths remains a mystery. Don't go alone and always let the people at your hostel or hotel know your plans.

Finca Lérida HIKING
(trail fee US$12) For a relaxed hike without orientation issues, this coffee farm with its adjoining forest is an excellent option. For the entrance fee you also get a trail map and water. At 5000ft, it's a significant jump in altitude above Boquete, so dress for cooler weather. You can also do a guided hike (US$55 for two to three hours).

Rafting

Adventure seekers shouldn't miss the excellent white-water rafting that's within a 1½-hour drive of Boquete. Ríos Chiriquí and Chiriquí Viejo both flow from the fertile hills of Volcán Barú, and are flanked by forest for much of their lengths. In some places, waterfalls can be seen at the edges of the rivers, and both rivers pass through narrow canyons with awesome, sheer rock walls.

The Río Chiriquí is most often run from May to December, while the Chiriquí Viejo is run the rest of the year. Rapids are III and III-plus, and tours last four to five hours.

When booking a trip, inquire if the outfitter uses a safety kayak for descents and if guides are certified in swift-water rescue. These should be minimum requirements for a safe trip.

Courses

Spanish by the River LANGUAGE
(☎720-3456; www.spanishatlocations.com; Entrada a Palmira) The sister school to the popular Spanish school in Bocas del Toro (p189) is located 5km south of Boquete near the turnoff to Palmira. Standard/intensive lessons cost US$225/300 for a one-week course. Discounts come with comprehensive packages and longer stays. Also offers homestays (US$22), simple dorms (US$14) and private rooms (US$24).

Habla Ya Language Center LANGUAGE
(☎730-8344; www.hablayapanama.com; Plaza Los Establos, Av Central; ⏰8am-6pm Mon-Fri, 9am-noon Sun) Habla Ya offers both group and private Spanish lessons. A week of group lessons (20 hours) starts at US$275. The language school is also well connected to local businesses, so students can take advantage of discounts on everything from accommodations to tours and participate in volunteer projects.

Tours

Coffee Adventures Tours BIRDWATCHING
(☎720-3852, 6634-4698; www.coffeeadventures.net; half-day tours per 2 people US$65) Dutch naturalist guides Terry and Hans are locally renowned as great birding and nature guides. They also offer hiking in the cloud forest, including Sendero Los Quetzales (US$175 per person) and visits to indigenous communities. They have lodgings in three lovely cottages in dense forest 3km southwest of the town center.

Finca Lérida Birdwatching Tour BIRDWATCHING
(☎720-1111, 720-2816; www.fincalerida.com; tours US$75; ⏰7:30am) Finca Lérida, located 9km northwest of Boquete, is a stunning coffee farm dating back to 1924. It's also considered one of the premier birdwatching spots in Panama, with hundreds of species spotted regularly. A birdwatching trip includes a knowledgeable guide, lunch and transportation.

The extensive grounds and forested trails here are prime habitat for the quetzal, a Central American symbol and the national bird of Guatemala. Nearly extinct there, it has found refuge in Chiriquí Province. The quetzals are most likely to be seen here between February and May.

Boquete Outdoor Adventures ADVENTURE
(☎6630-1453, 720-2284; www.boqueteoutdooradventures.com; Plaza Los Establos, Av Central; ⏰8am-7:30pm) This highly recommended outfitter run by veteran outdoorsman Jim Omer offers quality rafting trips (US$65 to

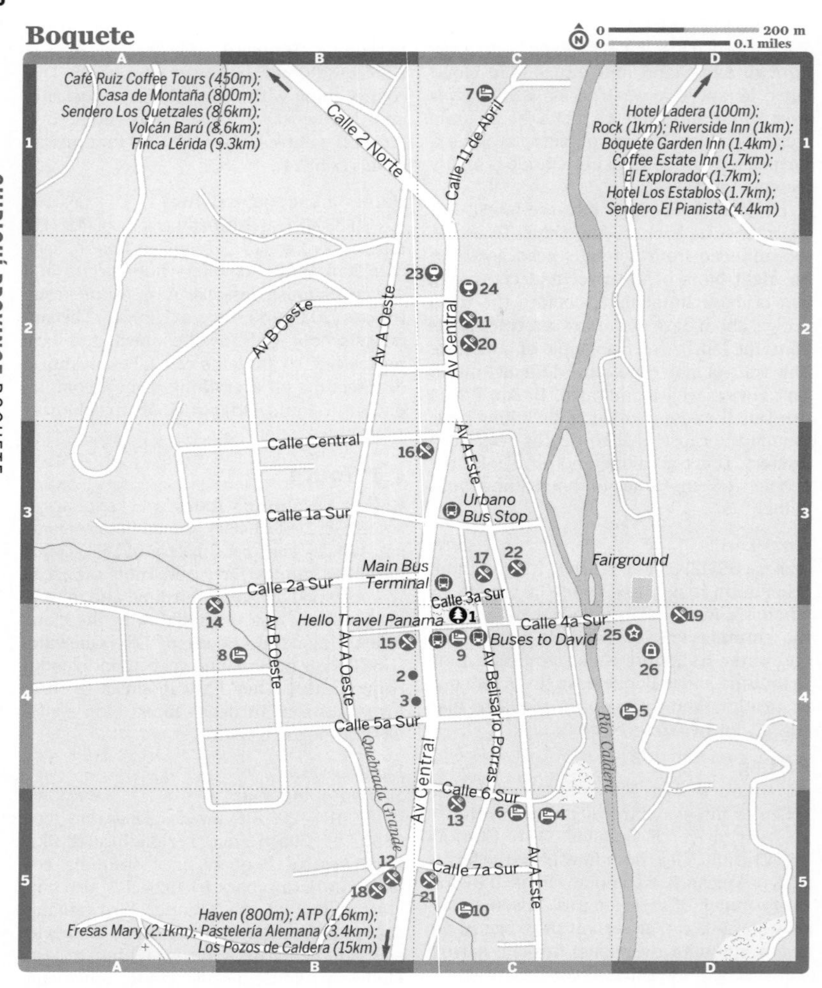

US$75) and tailored vacations that are ideal for families. Also offers cloud-forest hiking (US$35) and snorkeling by the coastal islands (US$75). Guides are bilingual and the company uses local service providers. Excellent source of information.

Cafes de la Luna Coffee Tour TOURS
(Finca Dos Jefes; ☎6677-7748; www.boquetecoffeetour.com; El Salto; tours US$30; ⊙tours 9am & 2pm) If you are looking to learn about small-scale organic coffee production, check out this extended tour of Finca Dos Jefes in the highlands above Boquete that includes roasting and tasting. In addition to guiding the tour, Californian coffee aficionado Richard Lipner is the brains behind the beans. The tour takes about 2½ hours.

Finca Lérida Coffee Tour TOURS
(☎720-1111; www.fincalerida.com; 2hr tours US$45; ⊙9:30am & 1:30pm) The coffee here won best in Panama in 2017. Tours of the estate are quite thorough, showing both the business side of a small farm and the process of production from coffee cherry to cup with regular and geisha varieties. Also covers the farm's transition to organic and sustainable practices, such as through composting and reduced water consumption.

Boquete

Sights
1 Parque José Domingo Médica C4

Activities, Courses & Tours
2 Boquete Mountain Safari B4
Boquete Outdoor Adventures .... (see 3)
Boquete Tree Trek .... (see 3)
3 Habla Ya Language Center C4

Sleeping
4 Downtown Suites C5
5 El Oasis D4
6 Garden by Refugio del Río C5
7 Hotel Panamonte C1
8 Isla Verde Hotel B4
9 Mamallena Boquete Hostel C4
10 Pensión Topas C5

Eating
11 APizza C2
Big Daddy's Grill .... (see 2)
12 Boquete Fish House B5
13 Café de Punto Encuentro C5
14 Colibri A4
15 El Sabrosón #3 .... B4
16 Gelateria La Ghiotta C3
Hotel Panamonte Restaurant .... (see 7)
17 Mercado Municipal C3
18 Mike's Global Grill B5
19 Pizzeria Ricos Little Italy D4
20 Retrogusto C2
21 Sugar & Spice C5
22 Supermercado Romero C3

Drinking & Nightlife
23 Boquete Brewing Company C2
24 Taboo C2

Entertainment
25 Boquete Community Playhouse D4

Shopping
26 Tuesday Market D4

Boquete Tree Trek ADVENTURE
(720-1635; www.boquetetreetrek.com; Plaza Los Establos, Av Central; canopy tours US$65; tours 8am, 10:30am & 1pm) Travelers love this four-hour canopy tour with 12 ziplines, 12 platforms and a rappel in secondary forest. Tours depart daily at 8am and 1pm. The lines pick up some serious speed, so consider going heavy on the handbrake. Its newest feature is a hanging bridge walk (US$30) crossing six bridges. Includes transportation from the center. It also offers coffee tours (US$30) at 8am and 1pm.

Boquete Mountain Safari DRIVING
(6627-8829, 730-9353; www.boquetesafaritours.typepad.com; Av Central; half-day 4WD tours US$25; 8am-6pm) Scenic back-country tours in open jeeps. Highlights of the cloud-forest safari include stops at coffee estates, basalt formations and waterfalls, or you can make a beeline for the Caldera hot springs. Also runs rafting tours (US$65), guided horseback riding ($45) in the Caldera hills, and rents scooters (US$25 per hour) and does ATV tours (US$50 per hour).

Café Ruíz Coffee Tours TOURS
(730-9575, 6672-3786; www.caferuiz-boquete.com; tours US$30; 9am & 1pm Mon-Sat) Located on the main road about 600m north of the town center, Café Ruíz is Panama's most famous coffee-grower, and now produces the award-winning geisha varietal. The three-hour tour includes transportation to a nearby coffee farm, a presentation on the history of coffee in Boquete, a tour of a roasting facility and a tasting session. Reservations required.

Festivals & Events

Feria de las Flores y del Café FERIA
(http://feriadeboquete.com; fairgrounds) The town's annual Flower & Coffee Fair is held for 10 days each January. While there's coffee in the name, it's strangely missing from exhibits, though you will find plenty of rum and children's carnival rides. Book accommodations well ahead.

Boquete Jazz & Blues Festival MUSIC
(www.boquetejazzandbluesfestival.com; fairgrounds) Local and international talent converges on Boquete for four days in February for the biggest annual music event in Chiriquí Province.

Feria de las Orquídeas FERIA
(fairgrounds) Showing more than 150 varieties, the orchid fair is held for 10 days every April. It's not all flowers: sundown brings rock concerts and dancing.

Sleeping

Garden by Refugio del Río HOSTEL $
(6676-5786, 720-1380; www.refugiodelrio.com; Av A Este; dm/d US$14/40;) The most stylish in-town hostel is this newcomer with huge

gardens, pallet furniture and sleek murals. Double rooms have old-fashioned charm. There's a guest kitchen, hammocks in the garden and pets that cozy the place up. With a Netflix projector and boardgames. It recycles.

Mamallena Boquete Hostel HOSTEL $
(730-8342, 6723-2014; www.mamallenaboquete.com; Av Central; dm US$14, d with/without bathroom US$38/33; P) Facing the central plaza, this turquoise ex-boardinghouse is backpacker central, complete with kitchen, laundry and free pancake breakfasts. For its huge capacity, it feels rather cozy. Three eight-bed dorms boast orthopedic mattresses, while 13 of the 16 private rooms have their own bathrooms. There's a sheltered patio area with grill. Service-oriented, it runs tours and shuttles to Bocas and Santa Catalina.

Pensión Topas GUESTHOUSE $
(720-1005; www.pensiontopas.com; Av Belisario Porras; s/d with bathroom US$29/42, without bathroom US$16/28; P) Built around a small organic garden, this blue-and-orange lodging run by an eccentric German features Tintin murals, a collection of a half-dozen motorbikes and eight tidy rooms. A shady outdoor patio provides ample shared space, and perks include a shared kitchen, a swimming pool and cable TV. The best rooms are on the 2nd floor of the outbuilding with a balcony.

★**Bambuda Castle** HOSTEL $$
(6873-8386; www.bambuda.net/boquete; El Santuario, Los Naranjos; dm US$14-16, d US$69-79;) Once upon a time, a Dutchman built this castle to pay homage to his beloved. Now it's a surreal fun center with an indoor swimming pool and Jacuzzi, on-site bar and gardens overlooking the hills. There's three dorm rooms, but the most sought-after lodgings are fiberglass hobbit holes out back, though budding Rapunzels could opt for the two-story tower.

The owners, Tom and Dan, are two Canadians from Alberta who aim to please. It's a US$3 taxi ride from the center.

★**Haven** BOUTIQUE HOTEL $$
(730-9345, 6491-5578; www.hotelboquete.com; Av A Oeste; d standard US$90-130, d deluxe US$110-150, ste US$150-200; P) This sleekly designed hotel and spa provides a very chic retreat. British-owned, it has eight rooms with cool space-saving designs, set amid verdant gardens. Water features, river stones and palms set the scene for relaxation. Amenities include a full gym and spa with sauna, yoga, steam room, an indoor pool, a natural health center and a Jacuzzi. Professional and service-oriented.

It's 2km south of the town center; watch for signs for the left-hand turn as you approach Boquete.

Tinamou Cottage Jungle Lodge COTTAGE $$
(6634-4698, 720-3852; www.coffeeadventures.net; d incl breakfast US$119-149) If you'd like to get away from it all but still be within striking distance of the town and its amenities, choose these lovely cottages on 9 hectares of dense forest, 3km southwest of Boquete. It's owned by Dutch naturalists who are well-known birding guides. Cottages are quite luxurious, with one or two bedrooms and kitchens, and breakfast comes in a basket.

Boquete Garden Inn INN $$
(720-2376; www.boquetegardeninn.com; Palo Alto; d incl breakfast US$99-135; P) On the edge of the Río Palo Alto, this garden inn with a dozen rooms in six red-mud cottages is run by a welcoming Briton. The grounds overflow with blossoming tropical flowerbeds, and birds abound (95 species spotted). Rooms – there are five types – with canopy beds are lovely and modern. Service stands out.

Lounging around the patio bar decorated with traditional Panamanian masks proves a fine cap on the day, especially from 6pm to 7pm when drinks are complimentary.

Casa de Montaña B&B $$
(730-9472; www.casademontana.com; Calle 2 Norte; d US$139; P @) Under new ownership, this B&B features six large, fan-cooled rooms with terrace or balcony. Special features include concierge service, memory-foam mattresses, a fridge, a microwave oven and a dehumidifier in each. Two of the rooms are adapted for guests with disabilities. It's just over 1km northwest of the center – a US$3 taxi ride. Kids 12 and up are welcome.

Also offers airport transfers to David (US$35).

Hotel Ladera HOTEL $$
(730-9000; www.hotel-ladera.com; Av Buenos Aires, Jaramillo Arriba; incl breakfast s US$99-120, d US$120-142; P) This upscale hotel along the the road leading to the Boquete hills features an appealing ultramodern style

and attentive staff at the front desk. The 20 rooms have mock-wood tiles and either an outdoor terrace or a small balcony; some larger rooms (eg room 17) feature two king-sized beds with wicker headboards. There's on-site dining as well as room service.

With weekend and weekday rates.

El Oasis HOTEL **$$**
(720-1586; www.oasisboquete.com; Av Buenos Aires; d incl breakfast US$90; P @) Although it's within walking distance, El Oasis is across the Río Caldera from Boquete proper and is a good deal quieter than staying in town; the river's just meters away. The 18 rooms and suites are immaculate, with an English garden theme and flat-screen TVs.

The restaurant was undergoing renovations at the time of research.

Coffee Estate Inn B&B **$$$**
(6821-6215; www.coffeeestateinn.com; Calle Jaramillo Arriba; studio US$139, incl breakfast cabins US$159-269; P) Surrounded by orange groves with private trails winding through gardens and forest, this stunning property is run by a Panamanian-Californian couple. Bungalows are in plantation style with kitchenettes, heated floors and private terraces with valley views. Newer additions are more retro-industrial chic, with huge decks and electric fireplaces. With cooked-to-order breakfasts and coffee from the on-site estate.

Call ahead, as the gate is not always staffed. Kids are welcome.

Hotel Panamonte HISTORIC HOTEL **$$$**
(720-1324; www.panamonte.com; Calle 11 de Abril; d/ste incl breakfast from US$250/310; P) This historic 21-room hotel dating from 1914 wins you over with its sprawling flower gardens, serene spaces, and handsome rooms and public areas. Choose between the original rooms, bursting with character, or new, larger terrace rooms outfitted as modern deluxe. Service is impeccable, and the restaurant (p171) is among Panama's best. The day spa is the perfect complement to a mountain getaway.

You can relax here, knowing that John Wayne, Ingrid Bergman and Richard Nixon did so too. It's located on a quiet road at the northern end of town just west of where the bridge washed away in 2008.

Riverside Inn INN **$$$**
(720-1076; www.riversideinnboquete.com; Av Buenos Aires, Palo Alto; d incl breakfast US$135-175; P) A casual stunner, this exclusive inn with six suites has a relaxed and intimate setting and an upscale restaurant called the Rock (p172). Living areas feature original artwork and a grand stone fireplace. Suites are expansive, with vaulted ceilings, soft cotton bedding and Jacuzzi baths. Though the setting is lovely, the flat riverside location lacks the mountain panoramas of other inns.

It's about 2km north of the town center on the way to the hills.

Isla Verde Hotel CABIN **$$$**
(720-2751, 720-2533; www.islaverdepanama.com; Av B Oeste; ste US$130-160, d cabins US$110-160; P @) Set in a large, lush garden with a small stream running through it, this delicious property offers different types of lodgings in 16 units – from *casitas* (cottages) to suites and two-story round cabins, all featuring luxuriant mattresses, vaulted ceilings, complete kitchens and roomy bathrooms. It's probably the best in-town retreat, with prompt service and even massages available (from US$60).

Accommodation is for two; each additional person is charged US$20 (kids US$10).

Hotel Los Establos BOUTIQUE HOTEL **$$$**
(720-2685; www.losestablospanama.com; Jaramillo Arriba; d/ste incl breakfast US$295/355; P @) These lavish quarters enveloped in manicured grounds and a coffee farm bear no trace of their past as erstwhile stables. Decor is elegant but a little fussy – heavy on brocade, carved mirrors, candelabras and gold highlights. The dozen rooms and suites have elegant furnishings and private terraces with views, some of Volcán Barú. With a restaurant and spa.

Located northeast of the center.

Downtown Suites HOTEL **$$$**
(790-9302, 6461-9134; www.downtownsuitesboquete.com; Av A Este; ste US$185-195; P) This design-oriented hotel features seven modern suites with living rooms and kitchenettes. It's all spick and span but way overpriced; luckily, there are huge low-season discounts. Perks include down duvets, flat-screen TVs with Netflix and safe boxes. Rooms look out on a small grass courtyard with a Jacuzzi. Dogs OK.

★ **Finca Lérida** HISTORIC HOTEL **$$$**
(720-1111; www.fincalerida.com; Alto Quielk; d/ste incl breakfast from US$175/270; P @) Famous for its coffee farm and birdwatching opportunities – it's one of the best places in

THE GEISHA COFFEE BEAN

During the 19th century, farmers from North America and Europe discovered that the cool climate and rich volcanic soil of Chiriquí were perfectly suited for the cultivation of coffee. Since dried beans are relatively nonperishable and thus easy to ship, coffee quickly surpassed other cash crops and became an important source of revenue for the area. Although less well known than the Costa Rican competition, Panamanian coffee is praised for its high caffeine content and acidic, multidimensional flavor.

In the early 1990s the collapse in the world quota cartel system dealt the industry a severe blow. Growers could no longer rely on a stable price for their harvest. In turn, a few growers switched tactics, planting quality varieties in smaller amounts, aiming at the gourmet market instead of the usual high-yield crops.

Selectivity paid off. The biggest coup was the emergence of geisha coffee on the world scene. After winning first place in multiple international competitions, geisha became a rock-star bean. Originally from Ethiopia (the birthplace of coffee), geisha is coveted for its light body, citrus and honey notes and jasmine-like aroma.

Geisha has been auctioned for up to US$260/kg and sold at Starbucks for US$7 a cup. You can also find it for sale online, but because it is grown in small quantities, it often sells out. While Boquete's Finca Esmeralda was the first to make good on geisha, it's now found at Café Ruiz (p172), Finca Lérida (p169) and a growing number of local estates.

the country to see quetzals – Finca Lérida also offers classic lodgings with 22 rooms, suites and cabins. Rooms feature comfortable beds with oversized fabric headboards, lovely wood details and espresso machines, each with a deck and outdoor seating for watching the hummingbirds. Suites feature Jacuzzis.

Breakfasts go over the top, with walnut pancakes, honey sausage and fresh juices. Guests and day-trippers (which are legion) can dine at the on-site restaurant, which features excellent salads made with local produce, and favorites such as smoked tomato soup and trout. There's also a gorgeous bar with a fireplace running on chilly cloud-forest days.

Eating

APizza PIZZA $
(☎720-2358; www.apizzapanama.com; Av Central s/n; mains US$6-10; ⏲3-10pm Tue-Fri, from noon Sat & Sun) Crisp, thin-crust Neapolitan pies are the simple stars of this casual eatery. They're made from local mozzarella, San Marzano tomatoes and flour imported from the home country. Local Italians say it's the best in town, and who are we to argue? Also has soups and gluten-free options.

Gelateria La Ghiotta ICE CREAM $
(☎6107-1465; cnr Av Central & Calle Central; cones US$2-4; ⏲11am-8pm Thu-Tue) Great selection of Italian ice cream at this central and very friendly little *gelateria*. Choose from 10 flavors, including *guanabana* (soursop), pineapple and coffee.

Pizzeria Ricos Little Italy PIZZA $
(☎6390-2415, 720-1291; opposite Calle 4a Sur; pizzas small US$7-10, large US$13-20; ⏲11am-9pm Tue-Sun) You can enjoy the real McCoy at this hole in-the-wall pizzeria with six tables. It's just across the bridge and facing the fairgrounds.

Mike's Global Grill INTERNATIONAL $
(☎6865-8873, 730-9360; www.mikesglobalgrill.com; Av Central Oeste; mains US$7-12; ⏲8am-10pm Mon-Thu, to 11pm Fri & Sat, 9am-10pm Sun) A real expat hub, this homesick restaurant is the lovechild of Mike and Heidi who met – where else? – at the South Pole. Indulging the wanderlust theme, dishes range from Asian fusion to American chili and British fish and chips. The ambience is chilled, with a long bar and sofas. Breakfast daily, and live music on weekends.

Sugar & Spice BAKERY, DELI $
(☎730-9376; cnr Av Central & Calle 7a Sur; breakfast & sandwiches US$4-7.50; ⏲8am-6pm Thu-Sat, Mon & Tue, to 4pm Sun) Throngs gather at this artisan bakery, a modest storefront with a couple of patio tables, for US-style sandwiches, organic salads and oh-so-good brownies. You can also take away fresh bread, including whole-grain and ciabatta, and cinnamon buns.

Café de Punto Encuentro CAFE $
(Olga's; 720-2123; Calle 6 Sur; mains US$3-7; 7am-1pm) In a converted carport and garden, this family-run eatery is a find. All guests are *mi amor* (my love) to the affectionate Olga, who cooks breakfast like nobody's business. The menu ranges from pancakes and bacon to Panamanian breakfasts (US$7) with bottomless cups of coffee. Expect to wait, but for this quality of home-cooked food, you won't mind.

Pastelería Alemana BAKERY $
(Via Boquete; pastries from US$3; 8am-noon Thu-Mon) On the main road 3km south of town, this German patisserie serves up decadent apple strudel and tortes, as well as authentic German breads.

Big Daddy's Grill SEAFOOD $
(6675-9887; Av Central; mains US$4-14; noon-9pm Tue-Sat, 9am-8pm Sun) A stalwart choice of gringo *boqueteños,* this friendly eatery serves the most enormous and satisfying fish tacos. The menu also includes chicken wings, lovely salads, margaritas rimmed with chili salt and (if you must) corn dogs. The backyard patio offers privacy and a better atmosphere (in both senses).

Fresas Mary DESSERTS $
(Calle Volcancito Principal; snacks US$3-5; 10am-7pm Tue-Sun) With strawberry and other fruit *batidos* (shakes) that will make you quake with pleasure, this cute cafe on the road to Volcán Barú makes a worthy stop.

El Sabrosón #3 CAFETERIA $
(720-2147; Av Central; mains US$3-6; 6:30am-10pm Mon-Fri, to 11pm Sat & Sun) Our favorite of the three branches of this much-loved local institution cooks up cheap and filling Panamanian cuisine served cafeteria-style, and has tables on a terrace overlooking the main drag. Although Boquete is rapidly being colonized by gringo-friendly boutique eateries, this is one local institution that remains true to its local roots.

Mercado Municipal MARKET $
(9am-1pm) Fresh produce is sold at this enclosed market on the northeastern corner of the central plaza.

Supermercado Romero SUPERMARKET $
(Av A Este; 24hr Nov-Feb, 7am-10pm Mar-Oct) One block east of the central plaza, this has Boquete's best selection of groceries. It's open round the clock in high season from November to February.

★**Retrogusto** ITALIAN $$
(720-2933; www.ilretrogusto.com; Av Central s/n; mains US$7-19; 5:30-10pm Tue-Sat, 11:30am-3pm & 5:30-9:30pm Sun) At this new Italian farm-to-table restaurant, it's a struggle not to order everything on the menu – it all looks and smells so good. But you can't go astray starting with stuffed mushrooms or an exuberant salad. Hormone-free beef, homemade pastas and bubbly artisanal pizzas with sourdough crust are all hits. Watch the action in the open kitchen. Service is attentive.

★**Boquete Fish House** SEAFOOD $$
(6918-7111, 6521-2120; www.facebook.com/BoqueteFishHouseRestaurant; Av Central; mains from US$16; noon-8pm Mon-Sat;) One of our favorite places in Boquete for great seafood is this fish house along the Quebrada Grande. It offers sea bass prepared in eight different ways – from the delightful version that's steamed and wrapped in lettuce leaves to good ol' fish and chips. There are wonderful veggie sides as well as meat and vegetarian choices.

Il Pianista ITALIAN $$
(720-2728; Palo Alto; mains US$12-17.50; noon-10pm Tue-Sun) This Italian restaurant and pizzeria has riverstone walls and just a few tables along one of Boquete's hillside roads. Sicilian Giovanni cooks while his Panamanian wife, Doris, serves. A bottle of wine and pizza or calzone make the perfect leisurely lunch, but don't come in a rush: service can be slow.

Local buses go past, or follow signs for Boquete Garden Inn; it's just above it.

★**Colibri** INTERNATIONAL $$$
(6379-1300; Calle 2a Sur; mains US$12-28; noon-9pm Tue-Sat, 11am-1pm Sun) Run by a warm Italian couple from Padua, this farm-to-table restaurant serves up fresh and delicious meals. The menu items are a real fusion between local and international, with gorgeous beef salad with passionfruit dressing, lobster from Boca Chica and local goat's cheese ice cream. There's also a good wine list and limoncello to cap the night.

★**Hotel Panamonte Restaurant** INTERNATIONAL $$$
(720-1327; www.panamonte.com; Calle 11 de Abril; mains US$18-28; noon-10pm) This sophisticated restaurant has a long-standing reputation. Chef Charlie Collins takes a modern

approach, exquisitely preparing everything from smoked pork chops with a rum glaze to fresh salad in blackberry vinaigrette and sublime lemon pie. While the powder-blue dining room is romantic, you may prefer a tiny table near the cracking hearth in the bar-lounge. Also ideal for cocktails and wine. Reserve ahead.

Rock INTERNATIONAL **$$$**
(☎6982-8876, 720-2516; www.therockboquete.com; Av Buenos Aires, Palo Alto; mains US$16-20; ⊙noon-9:30pm Wed-Mon) Bringing cosmopolitan dining to the highlands of Panama, this restaurant attached to the Riverside Inn (p169) does decent gourmet fare, though it can be hit-or-miss. The herbed octopus with coconut rice comes recommended and there's lovely pasta and meat dishes as well as well-informed service.

The restaurant can be a lively spot for a drink some evening; it has an extensive wine list and a full bar. Two-for-one cocktails are served from 6pm to 7pm on Mondays with live jazz.

Drinking & Nightlife

Boquete Brewing Company MICROBREWERY
(☎6494-4992; www.boquetebrewingcompany.com; Av Central; ⊙3-10pm Tue, Wed & Sun, to midnight Thu-Sat) With craft-beer bars all the rage in Panama these days, Boquete's contribution is more than hipster-friendly, with an outdoor patio with a food truck serving great pub grub. There's eight beers and two hard ciders on tap at any given time, and they range from the sublime (hard lemonade) to the ridiculous (watermelon ale). Cheers!

Taboo CLUB
(☎6245-8761; www.facebook.com/tabooboquete; ⊙8pm-midnight, to 2am Fri & Sat) Young people gather at this dim club for whatever nightlife they can grab in an ostensibly agricultural town, with occasional live rock and salsa.

Café Ruiz CAFE
(☎6672-3786, 720-1000; www.caferuiz-boquete.com; Calle 2 Norte; cakes US$3; ⊙8:30am-5:30pm Mon-Sat) The outdoor patio at Ruiz makes a good spot to sip a cappuccino and watch the mist move across the mountains. It's also the epicenter of Panama's famous coffee industry, so you can be sure that your brew has its origin in the surrounding hillsides.

Entertainment

Boquete Community Playhouse THEATER
(☎6362-0770; www.bcpeventscenter.org; Calle de la Feria; tickets US$15) Hosts local theater and special events like the Tuesday Market. Check with your hotel or the tourist office about current offerings.

Shopping

Tuesday Market MARKET
(www.bcpeventscenter.org; Boquete Community Playhouse, Calle de la Feria; ⊙9am-noon Tue) A weekly market at the local theater features arts and crafts, jewelry, organic produce and prepared foods.

Information

About 1.5km south of Boquete on the road to David, the large **ATP** (☎720-4060; chiriqui@atp.gob.pa; Hwy 43; ⊙9:30am-5:30pm) office sits atop a bluff overlooking the town. This is the place to go to pick up maps and obtain information on attractions in the area. There's a coffee shop on the ground floor and an exhibition upstairs detailing the history of the region (in Spanish only).

Banco Nacional de Panama (☎720-1328; Av Central; ⊙8am-3pm Mon-Fri, 9am-noon Sat) and **Global Bank** (☎720-2329; Av Central; ⊙8am-3pm Mon-Fri, 9am-noon Sat) both have an ATM.

Try **Centro Medico San Juan Bautista** (☎720-1881; Calle 2 Norte) for medical care.

Getting There & Away

The main bus terminal is on the main road near the main plaza. Buses to David (US$1.75, one hour) depart from the south side of Boquete's main plaza every 30 minutes from 5am to 6:30pm. From David they run from 6am to 9:30pm. Hourly buses run to the town of Caldera (US$2, 45 minutes).

Hello Travel Panama (www.hellotravelpanama.com; Mamallena Hostel) has shuttle vans linking Boquete with Bocas del Toro (US$30 including boat, four hours), stopping at the Lost & Found Hostel (p180), and Santa Catalina (US$35, five hours). You can also link to Puerto Viejo, Costa Rica (eight hours).

Getting Around

Boquete's small size lends itself to easy exploration. The *urbano* (local) buses that wind through the hills cost US$0.50. They depart on the main road one block north of the plaza. Taxis charge US$3 to US$6 for most places around town.

For scooter or bike rentals, check out local travel agencies and hostels. Cars can be rented at **Dollar** (☎721-1103; Plaza Los Establos, Av Central; ⏰8:30am-5pm), and are a great option to explore more of the local area.

Parque Nacional Volcán Barú

This 143-sq-km **national park** is home to Volcán Barú, Panama's only volcano and the dominant geographical feature of Chiriquí Province. Volcán Barú is no longer active, but it apparently once was, and counts not one but seven craters. At 3474m its summit, the highest point in Panama, affords views of both the Pacific and Caribbean coasts when clear.

The national park is also home to the Sendero Los Quetzales, one of the most scenic treks in the entire country. As its name implies, the trail is one of the best places in Central America to spot the rare resplendent quetzal, especially during the dry season (from February to May). However, even if the Maya bird of paradise fails to show, the park is home to more than 250 bird species as well as pumas, tapirs and the agouti paca, a large spotted rodent also called *conejo pintado* (painted rabbit).

Activities

★Sendero Los Quetzales HIKING
(trail fee US$3) One of Panama's most beautiful trails runs between Cerro Punta and Boquete, crisscrossing Río Caldera. You can hike from either direction, but west to east offers more downhill: the town of Cerro Punta is almost 1000m higher than Boquete. The 8km route takes between four and six hours. Getting to and from the trailhead takes another couple of hours either side (about 23km in total). A guide is recommended.

A 4WD taxi can take you to the trailhead on the Cerro Punta side for about US$35 per person; a *colectivo* (shared taxi) will cost US$6. Taxi drivers know the area as Respingo. Road conditions may be very poor due to landslides. The trail is approximately 10km from Cerro Punta, first by paved road (6km) and later dirt (3.5km). When you exit the trail, it's another 8km along the road to Boquete, though you may be able to catch a taxi along the road. In total, the hike is about 23km, so plan accordingly if you intend to walk the length of the trail.

Buses run from David to Cerro Punta (US$3.50, 2¼ hours); last departure is 6pm. Consider leaving your luggage at one of the hotels in David to save yourself the hassle of backtracking. Take only the bare essentials with you on the walk, and a little cash for a good meal and/or lodging when you arrive in Boquete.

Be aware that conditions can change any time, especially after heavy rain. There's talk that hiking the trail with a guide may become a requirement – in recent times many travelers have gotten lost on this stretch and the resources for rescue are practically nonexistent.

THE RESPLENDENT QUETZAL

The lore of the resplendent quetzal originated during the era of the Maya and the Aztecs, who worshipped a deity known as Quetzalcoatl (Plumed Serpent). This mythical figure was often depicted wearing a crown of male quetzal tail feathers and was believed to be responsible for bestowing corn upon humans.

A popular legend regarding the scarlet-red breast of the quetzal originated during the colonial period. In 1524 in the highlands of Guatemala, the Spanish conquistador Pedro de Alvarado defeated Tecun Uman, the last ruler of the Quiché people. As Uman lay dying, his spiritual guide, the quetzal, stained its breast with Uman's blood and then died of remorse. From that day on, all male quetzals bore a scarlet breast, and their song hasn't been heard since.

Today quetzals are regarded in Central America as a symbol of freedom, and it's commonly believed that they cannot survive if held in captivity. Birdwatchers from far and wide continue to brave the elements in Panama for the chance to see the most famous bird in Central America.

The best time to spot a quetzal is in April and May when they nest in the highlands and wait for their young to hatch. Look for their nests in rotted tree trunks that they carve out with their beaks.

Volcán Barú HIKING

Climbing Volcán Barú is a goal of many visitors seeking views from the summit of both the Pacific and the Caribbean coasts. It might not be worth it in poor weather, as the going is strenuous and rough, and there is little to see in cloud cover. You can enter the national park on the eastern (Boquete) and western (Volcán) sides of the volcano.

The eastern summit access from Boquete is the easier, but it involves a strenuous uphill hike along a 13.5km road that goes from the park entrance – about 8km northwest of the center of town – to the summit. The road is paved to the ranger station and several kilometers beyond. If you drive or taxi as far up as possible and then walk the rest of the way, it takes about five or six hours to reach the summit from the park gate; walking from town would take another two or three hours each way.

We recommended you hike at night, starting at 11pm or midnight and arriving at dawn to see the sunrise. But for this you'll need to hire a guide and be prepared for the cold. Another option is to spend the night. Camping will also allow you to be at the top during the morning, when the views are best.

The western access is just outside the town of Volcán, on the road to Cerro Punta. From this side, the views of the volcano are far more dynamic. The rugged 16.5km-long road into the park (requiring a 4WD vehicle) goes only a short way off the main road to the foot of the volcano. The view of the summit and the nearby peaks from this entrance are impressive, and there's a lovely loop trail that winds through secondary and virgin forest. The ascent takes 10 to 12 hours.

Sleeping

Parque Nacional Volcán Barú Camping CAMPGROUND $

(campsites US$5) Camping is possible in the park and on the trail to the summit from the Boquete side, along the Sendero Los Quetzales at a picnic spot called Mirador La Roca or at the ranger station at the entrance to the Sendero Los Quetzales on the Cerro Punta side.

Information

The best time to visit is during the dry season, especially early in the morning when wildlife is most active.

Be advised that overnight temperatures can drop below freezing, and it may be windy and cold during the day, particularly in the morning. Dress accordingly and bring a flashlight (torch).

Getting There & Away

The trailhead leading to the summit of Volcán Barú is best accessed from the town of Boquete, while the Sendero Los Quetzales is best approached from Cerro Punta. A taxi will cost US$35 and US$30 respectively.

Volcán

POP 12,720

Clinging to the southwest flank of towering Volcán Barú, Volcán has a pleasant feel and serves as a good base for eating and sleeping and as a springboard for excursions. If you want to see what Boquete was like back when it was just another town in the Chiriquí highlands, this may be the perfect stop for you.

Sights

Arte Cruz WORKSHOP

(☎6503-1128, 6622-1502; www.facebook.com/artecruzpanama/; ⏰8:30am-noon & 1:30-5:30pm Tue-Fri, from 9am Sat & Sun) FREE On the west side of Hwy 41, some 3.5km south of Volcán, you'll spot this workshop where master carver and artist José de la Cruz González makes and sells exquisite signs, sculptures and furniture in mahogany and other woods, as well as impressive etchings on crystal and glass. José trained in fine arts in Italy and Honduras, and his work has been commissioned by buyers worldwide. Visitors are treated to his entertaining demonstrations.

Área Silvestre Protegida Lagunas de Volcán NATIONAL PARK

Some 4km west of Volcán, this protected area encompasses the highest lake system (1240m) in Panama. The two picturesque lakes swell in the rainy season, with lush, virgin forest at their edges and Volcán Barú in the background. Surrounding woodlands are excellent sites for birdwatching.

To get to the lakes from downtown Volcán, turn west onto Calle El Valle and follow the signs. Buses don't run here, but you can take a taxi from Volcán for about US$6.

Sitio Barriles ARCHAEOLOGICAL SITE

(☎6575-1828; Barriles; donation US$5; ⏰8am-4pm) The pre-Columbian ruins at this site 6km west of Volcán along the Río Gariche date from between AD 300 and 900, when the settlement had as many as 1000 residents. The site is on the private Finca Campestre; the owners have a variety of artifacts on display in their yard and in a small, underwhelming museum. Not all of the artifacts were found on site. Guided tours of the collection and gardens are in both Spanish and English.

Barriles is named after several small stone 'barrels' found in the area. It is one of the few archaeological sites accessible to the public in Panama.

Tours

Janson Coffee Farm TOURS

(☎6867-3884; www.jansoncoffeefarm.com; ⌚9am-3pm) Tours of this very productive coffee farm, located about 3km west of Volcán on the way to the lakes, range from a one-hour overview (US$10) to a 2½-hour all-in tour (US$35) that includes tasting the expensive geisha coffee and touring the estate. Other activities include birdwatching and fishing tours, and horseback riding tours in dry season (December to February).

Highland Adventures ADVENTURE

(☎6685-1682; hlaaizpurua@hotmail.com; Av Central s/n) Activities run by local English-speaking guide Gonzalo Aizpurua include rainforest mountain-biking, birding or hiking in Parque Internacional La Amistad (US$150 for two people, including transportation) and guided climbs to the top of Volcán Barú (US$190 for two people, 10 to 12 hours). His shop is 1.5km after the police station on the road to Cerro Punta.

Sleeping

★ **Mount Totumas Cloud Forest** CABIN $$

(☎6963-5069; www.mounttotumas.com; r US$110-180, cabin US$130-180; @ 📶) This 162-hectare ecolodge lies 20km northwest of Volcán. At 1900m it's among the highest in Panama, and the cloud forest bordering Parque Internacional La Amistad is a nature-lover's dream. Nine trails over 50km lead to waterfalls and hot springs. Choose from a stylish main lodge, a trailside treehouse or cabins with full kitchens. All have hammock decks with views.

The cabins are off the grid, so hot water, electricity and internet comes via a micro-hydroplant. Guests can sign up for guided hikes to the top of Mt Totumas (2630m) and into La Amistad park. Transportation is available from Volcán (US$60 one way), located 70 minutes away by a rough road, or from Boquete and David (US$100). Otherwise guests will need a high-clearance 4WD. Services are more limited September to October.

Los Brezos HOTEL $$

(☎787-5687; www.losbrezosvolcan.com; Av 3a s/n; d/ste incl breakfast US$99/120; P ❄ 📶) The best option in the center of Volcán is this new hotel with lovely modern rooms decked out with minibars, safes and flat-screen TVs. The on-site restaurant has an international menu.

Hotel Dos Ríos HOTEL $$

(☎771-4271, 771-5555; www.dosrios.com.pa; Nueva California; d/ste incl breakfast US$94/116; P @ 📶) On Volcán's main road 500m northwest of the center, this friendly midrange hotel has 20 adequate rooms built around lush gardens and a gurgling stream with a little arched footbridge. We love the antique cash register in the lobby, and there's a decent restaurant, too. Choose room 108 for the views.

Las Plumas VILLA $$

(☎6527-3848, 771-5541; www.las-plumas.com; Paso Ancho; 2-/3-bedroom bungalows US$60/130; P 📶) Located about 10km northeast of Volcán en route to Cerro Punta, this friendly Dutch-owned property sits on 2.4 hectares of land on the edge of Paso Ancho village. The five fully equipped bungalows sleep two to six people and are beautifully furnished. Beds feature orthopedic mattresses. A massive hedge keeps it all secluded.

The main attractions here are the beauty of the surrounding forest, the gushing Río Chiriquí Viejo and the breathtaking mountain views. There's a minimum stay of two nights, with discounted weekly and monthly rates.

Eating

Black Mountain Cafe CAFE $

(☎787-5271; Calle Quinta Norte; mains US$2-10; ⌚8:30am-9pm Mon-Thu, to 9:30pm Fri-Sun; 📶) Serving its own delicious fresh-roasted coffee, this new Spanish cafe also does great pastries, with wine, Spanish tapas and dessert for later in the day. It also has fresh juices and sells homemade bread.

Cafe Volcán INTERNATIONAL $

(☎6637-4503; Av Central; mains US$6-11; ⏰9am-9pm) This charming cafe with a long breezy terrace overlooking Volcán's main thoroughfare has a menu with Panamanian specialties, and also choices such as Romanian steak that may seem odd until you learn that owner Morena hails from that part of the world. The local trout is particularly good. Unfortunately, it's open only sporadically.

Mana Restaurante PANAMANIAN $

(☎6461-2970, 771-4709; Calle 11 Este; mains US$5-12; ⏰11am-8pm) Not heavenly but certainly good, Mana offers an interesting menu that combines Panamanian favorites such as *tostadas* (toasted corn) and *gallo pinto* (blended rice and beans) with North American staples including hamburgers and chili, reflecting the owners' long-term residence there. A favorite with local expats.

★**Cerro Brujo** MEDITERRANEAN $$

(☎6669-9196; Brisas del Norte; mains US$9-18; ⏰1-3pm & 6-9pm Tue-Sun) A gourmet restaurant in a funky country house with garden seating. The chalkboard menu offers just three or four daily options. Gregarious owner-chef Patti Miranda's mouthwatering creations use organic and local ingredients only. Offerings might include a spectacular salad from the garden, a lamb stew to die for, mahi-mahi coated in sesame seeds and, for dessert, *tomate de palo* sorbet.

It's in the Brisas del Norte district 1km north of Av Central. Grab a taxi there or take the signed turnoff on the main road.

La Carbonera ITALIAN $$

(☎6449-7117, 6590-5639; mains US$8-14; ⏰noon-9pm Tue-Sun) A surprising find some 3km along the road heading northeast to Cerro Punta, this authentic Italian eatery serves excellent pasta and pizza as well as chicken breast in white wine and pork fillet with tomato relish. Portions are generous. It's a relaxed place with rather relaxed service too.

Shopping

Friday Market MARKET

(⏰9-11am Fri) Held behind Mana restaurant, this weekly farmers market is a great place to stock up on picnic items. Homemade hot sauces, aged goat cheese, baked goods and homemade sausages are some of the great offerings. Or stop by for the corn tamales alone.

Getting There & Away

Hwy 41, linking Volcán with La Concepción to the south, forks in the center of town: one arrow points left toward Río Sereno, on the Costa Rican border (35km); the other points right toward Cerro Punta (16km), the western entrance to the Sendero Los Quetzales.

Buses to David (US$3, 1½ hours) depart every 15 minutes from 5am to 7:30pm from the station next to the municipal market, 100m northeast of the police station on the road to Cerro Punta. There are also pickup-truck taxis parked by the Delta gasoline station near the Río Sereno–Cerro Punta fork in the road.

Santa Clara

POP 2640

Just over 30km from Volcán, on the highway to Río Sereno and the Costa Rican border, the village of Santa Clara at first appears to offer little more than a grocery store and a gas station. But it's home to **Finca Hartmann** (☎6450-1853; 2-/4-person cabins US$92/145; P), a working shade-grown coffee farm with accommodations situated in highland rainforest, where you'll find a rich variety of wildlife.

The birdwatching is simply superb, with more than 280 unique species in the area. Ardent conservationists, the Hartmanns have hosted a number of Smithsonian-affiliated scientists over the years.

The estate's five hiking trails pass through a variety of habitats ranging between 1300m and 2000m. Guests can go on birdwatching excursions and coffee tours. The coffee harvest season runs roughly from October to January.

The rustic amd handsomely constructed cabins occupy fantastic surroundings. The smaller one has a bedroom, a bathroom and a kitchen. The bigger lodge counts six guest rooms over two stories; a veranda encircling the top floor is accessed via outside staircase. There's hot water and drinking water but no electricity.

Getting There & Away

To reach here by public transportation, take the Río Sereno bus (US$5.10, 2½ hours) from David, via La Concepción and Volcán, and ask to be let out at the entrance to Finca Hartmann. It is located a few hundred meters past the gas station, on the right-hand side – look for the small sign. The estate is another 1km up a dirt track.

Bambito

POP 700

There's no shortage of tiny mountain towns and villages along the road to Cerro Punta and Parque Internacional La Amistad, but Bambito is a good place to stop if you want to spend the night or visit a working trout farm.

Activities

Truchas de Bambito FISHING

(US$5; 8am-5pm Mon-Fri, from 9am Sat & Sun) This rainbow-trout farm, where thousands of fish are raised in three pools fed by spring water, belongs to the Hotel Bambito opposite and is really all about catching your own lunch or dinner. Pay the admission, throw in your line (included) and within minutes (perhaps even seconds) you'll be reeling in a fish. It costs another US$5 to take your fish away with you.

Sleeping & Eating

★**Cielito Sur B&B** B&B $$

(6602-3008, 771-2038; www.cielitosur.com; Nueva Suiza; d incl breakfast US$105-115; P@) Just under 3.5km north of Bambito is this sweet highland retreat set in a garden of anthuriums and hummingbirds. Owned by a friendly Panamanian-American couple, it offers four spacious guest rooms named (and decorated) after indigenous tribes; some have kitchenettes. There's also a two-bedroom house with a large fireplace and a full kitchen.

From here a trail leads to a coffee plantation, the produce from which is served daily at the property. Lounge spaces abound both inside and out; the common lounge with fireplaces and a library is an oasis. You can also arrange canoeing, birdwatching and quetzal-trail transfers here.

Casa Grande Bambito Highlands RESORT $$

(771-5127; www.casagrandebambito.com; d/tr US$109/142; P@) Just north of Bambito along the Río Chiriquí Viejo, this 20-room resort set in the forest is ideal for families as it offers health-spa facilities, a pool and a list of outdoor activities as long as your arm. Rooms are in small individual cabins or a central low-level building; the wood-paneled restaurant with stained glass is a delight.

The friendly staff at the front desk can organize everything from horseback riding and tubing on the river to rock climbing.

Hotel Bambito Resort HOTEL $$

(771-4265, 771-4373; www.hotelbambito.com; d incl breakfast US$100; P@) This sprawling roadside hotel (a pool does not a resort make) has 45 rooms in both a main building and a stone-and-wood cabin. The grounds are quite attractive, the Truchas restaurant serves trout from the farm across the street, and it's a hop, skip and a jump to Parque Internacional La Amistad. Room 3222 has a king-size bed and a lovely balcony.

Dulces Caseros Alina ICE CREAM $

(6758-4705; www.facebook.com/DulcesCaserosAlina; snacks US$3; 10am-6pm Wed-Mon) This small shop sells fruit jam, candy, milkshakes and ice cream using the region's famous strawberries, which thrive at this altitude. Stock up on some goodies – especially if you're on your way to the Parque Internacional La Amistad. You'll find it about 1.5km north of the landmark Hotel Bambito.

Getting There & Away

Buses from David to Cerro Punta (US$3.50, 2¼ hours, every 20 minutes) pass through Bambito and can drop you off in the center.

Cerro Punta

POP 7750

Lying at 800m, this tranquil highland town is reminiscent of an alpine village. Here the region takes on an almost European look, with meticulously tended vegetable plots and chalet-like houses with steep-pitched roofs. It's unsurprising to learn that a Swiss colony was founded here many decades ago and the hamlet just south is called Nueva Suiza (New Switzerland).

Visitors come to Cerro Punta primarily during the dry season (from mid-December to April) to access the two nearby national parks: Volcán Barú and La Amistad. The town itself makes a charming stop, however, especially since the area is known for its succulent strawberries, available for much of the year at roadside stands.

On the main road, the friendly **Hotel Cerro Punta** (6546-7334, 771-2020; www.hotelcerropunta.com; r US$37; P) offers a row of 10 concrete rooms. They are a bit tired and beaten up but they overlook a grassy backyard, and the hot showers will be the last you'll see for a while if you're on your way to Volcán Barú or La Amistad national parks. Decent and good-value in-house restaurant.

THE NGÖBE-BUGLÉ

The Ngöbe-Buglé comprise two separate ethnolinguistic groups, the Ngöbe and the Buglé, though the distinction is minor, and both are commonly referred to in conjunction with one another. As Panama's largest indigenous community, the Ngöbe-Buglé number close to 200,000. Like the Guna indigenous people, the Ngöbe-Buglé retain their own *comarca* (autonomous region) with its own system of governance and economy while maintaining their language, representation in the Panamanian legislature and full voting rights.

The Ngöbe-Buglé are largely confined to the Chiriquí highlands, and predominantly survive on subsistence agriculture, much like their precolonial ancestors. Their social structure is based on a system of small villages comprised of *chozas* (thatched huts) with dirt floors. In the villages, men practice slash-and-burn agriculture in order to produce staple crops such as plantain, banana, corn, cassava and rice. During the coffee-harvest season, many of the younger men work as migrant laborers in the fields around Boquete, which generates a significant amount of income for the village.

In the villages, women are primarily responsible for raising the children; many also work as skilled artisans, and their crafts can fetch a high price. The two most common items produced by Ngöbe-Buglé women are the *chacara* (a woven bag of plant fibers that is meant to mimic the landscapes of the rainforest) and the *naguas* (a traditional dress of handsewn appliqué, worn by women and girls). Throughout Chiriquí Province, you can find both items for sale in traditional markets and shops.

Like other indigenous groups in Panama, the Ngöbe-Buglé struggle to maintain their cultural identity, especially as outside pressures continue to descend on the *comarca*. However, although the Ngöbe-Buglé are not as politically organized as the Guna, they are far greater in number, and they control large tracts of undeveloped land. As a result, the Ngöbe-Buglé have been more successful than other indigenous groups, such as the Emberá and Wounaan, in maintaining their cultural identity and resisting the drive to modernize.

Getting There & Away

Buses run from David to Cerro Punta (US$3.50, 2¼ hours, every 20 minutes), stopping at Volcán and Bambito along the way, and carrying on to Guadalupe. If you're coming from Costa Rica, catch this bus at the turnoff from the Interamericana at La Concepción.

If you're driving, the main road continues through Cerro Punta and ends at Guadalupe, 3km further on. Another road takes off to the left heading for the Las Nubes entrance to Parque Internacional La Amistad, just under 7km to the northwest.

Guadalupe

POP 8400

Situated about 3km north of Cerro Punta and at an elevation of 2200m, Guadalupe is the end of the road. It's a glorious area where you can stroll among meticulously tended farms and gardens. This little community is chock full of flowers, and the agricultural plots curling up on steep hillsides are straight out of a picture book. Wildlife abounds up in the hills.

Sights

The folks at the Los Quetzales Ecolodge & Spa can organize any number of activities and excursions, including guided trekking (US$40), horseback riding, birdwatching tours and bicycle rentals.

Around 500m from the center beyond the Los Quetzales Ecolodge & Spa, the **Finca Dracula** (771-2070; www.facebook.com fincadracula; adult/student US$10/3.50; 8am-4pm) contains one of Latin America's finest orchid collections, with some 2600 species cultivated here. The knowledgeable staff take great pride in showing off this impressive sanctuary on an included 45-minute tour run hourly.

Sleeping & Eating

Los Quetzales Ecolodge & Spa RESORT $$
(6671-2131, 771-2182; www.losquetzales.com; camping per person US$15, dm/d/ste incl breakfast from US$18/85/135, apt US$130;) Located in town, this large resort complex run by tourism pioneer Carlos Alfaro is a favorite among birdwatchers and hikers. Among the 21 rooms are dorms for men, for women

and families, and doubles and suites with vaulted ceilings, wood furnishings and private hot-water bathrooms. Most of the guests tend to congregate in the excellent restaurant, featuring a bar and cozy fireplace lounge.

Couples might want to splurge on one of the five cedar-walled suites with a romantic hewn-stone fireplace, private bathtub and balcony facing the forest; families can ask about the six-bedroom farmhouse (US$400) and other options in Bajo Grande, 3km to the southeast. All guests have access to a full-service spa and three hot tubs by the Río Chiriquí Viejo (all water on the premises is piped-in spring water). Also on the premises is an equestrian center with 10 horses and a private network of trails adjoining Parque Nacional Volcán Barú, which is less than an hour's walk away (transportation available).

EcoTreat CABIN **$$**
(☎6478-7014; www.ecotreat.com; d incl breakfast US$72, cabins US$225-350; P ❄ 📶) With just two tiny houses with adorable fittings, this Argentine lodging is a snug option. The on-site cafe serves good pub grub and there's a small tour agency on-site offering trips to Barriles, hot springs, Lagunas del Volcán and Volcán Barú. It also manages cabins inside Parque Internacional La Amistad for large groups, with hot water, electricity, BBQ and sauna.

★ **Los Quetzales Cabins** CABIN **$$$**
(☎6671-2131, 771-2182; www.losquetzales.com; dm US$30, 4-person cabins US$150-240; 📶) Have we died and gone to heaven? Sleep in one of six rustic retreats, or dormitories of between two and 10, tucked into the rainforest; your nose is practically in the canopy. The forested setting, with its darting hummingbirds, lookout balconies and trout ponds, is among the most spectacular in Panama. All cabins have electricity, hot showers and fireplaces (with wood supplied).

Bring your own food, make arrangements for a cook or groceries to be delivered, or eat in the ecolodge restaurant (open daily till 9:30pm). The cabins are between 1.5km and 2km from the ecolodge up a 4WD track; transportation is provided.

Getting There & Away

Buses run from David to Guadalupe (US$3.50, 2½ hours, every 20 minutes) via Volcán, Bambito and Cerro Punta.

Parque Internacional La Amistad (Las Nubes)

The 4000-sq-km **Parque Internacional La Amistad** (International Friendship Park; campsites US$10; ⌚8am-4pm), a favorite of hikers and naturalists alike, covers portions of both Chiriquí and Bocas del Toro Provinces. Although the lion's share of the park lies in the latter, the Chiriquí side, with its entrance at Las Nubes, is more accessible.

Activities

Sendero La Cascada HIKING
(Waterfall Trail) Starting at the Las Nubes ranger station, this 3.7km round-trip hike takes in three *miradores* (lookouts) as well as a 45m-high waterfall. At the time of research the stairs to the bathing pool were closed due to flood damage.

Sendero Panamá Verde HIKING
This is an easy and well-marked trail of less than a kilometer focusing on local flora. It's just beyond the Las Nubes park entrance.

Sendero El Retoño HIKING
(Shoot Trail) From the Las Nubes ranger station this moderately difficult trail loops a couple of kilometers through secondary forest, crosses a number of rustic bridges and winds through bamboo groves.

Sleeping

Las Nubes Ranger Station CABIN **$**
(☎775-3163, 774-6671; Las Nubes; dm US$15) This basic ranger station has a dormitory cabin with bunk beds. Due to its popularity among international school groups, reservations are advisable. Guests have kitchen access; stock up on provisions in Cerro Punta. Bring your own bedding; a mosquito net is a good idea. To reserve, call Ministerio de Ambiente (p159) in David or visit the Co-op Restaurant at the park entrance.

Information

Enter via the Las Nubes park office, 6km northwest of Cerro Punta. Camping permits (US$10 per person) are payable at the Las Nubes ranger station.

If you plan to spend much time at Las Nubes, be sure to bring a jacket or sweater. At 2280m above sea level, this area of the park has a cool climate; temperatures are usually around 75°F (24°C) in the daytime, but can drop as low as 38°F (3°C) at night.

Getting There & Away

The Las Nubes entrance is about 6km northwest from Cerro Punta; a sign on the main road in Cerro Punta marks the turnoff. A taxi should cost US$10.

The Fortuna Road

Hwy 4, also known as Fortuna Rd after the large artificial lake (Lago Fortuna) supplying much of Panama's hydroelectric power, crosses the continental divide as it wends its way over the Cordillera Central. Not only is it the only way to get from Chiriquí Province to Bocas del Toro Province (short of flying), but it is also where you'll find two of the most interesting places to stay in the province.

Sleeping & Eating

★Lost & Found Hostel HOSTEL $
(☎6432-8182; www.thelostandfoundhostel.com; Valle de la Mina; dm/d/tr without bathroom US$15/35/50; @ 📶) High in the cloud forest, this wondrous backpacker community is a short and steep hike rewarded with yawning mountain panoramas. There are four dorms (with eight to 16 bunks) and basic private rooms. Shared bathroom stalls are numerous and well maintained. The Canadian owners have plotted every detail, from fun treasure hunts to coffee tours and a viewing tower.

The kitchen is well stocked with basic provisions for sale, and you can also order tasty homestyle meals (breakfast US$4 to US$8, lunch US$5 to US$6, dinner US$6 to US$8). There's a mini-pub, a lounge and a movie-room loft, set well away from sleepers.

Activities are varied and well priced, and as many as three excursions depart each day. There's an eight-hour maze of trails through La Fortuna Forest Reserve that go as high as 2200m. Hikers can visit an impressive waterfall and visit an indigenous community. You can also tour the trails on horseback (US$40) and visit a local coffee producer (US$25). The hostel's mascot is Rocky, a resident kinkajou that cannot be released into the wild.

Given the isolation, it's necessary to call or email reservations 24 hours in advance. To reach here take the bus from David (US$4, one hour) and ask to be dropped off at Km42 near the large Lost & Found billboard. Follow the trail to the right of the provisions shop upward for about 20 minutes. You can also take a bus from Bocas del Toro Province, starting in Changuinola or Almirante (around US$7).

★El Refugio La Brisa del Diablo B&B $$
(☎6597-0296, 6852-3600; www.facebook.com/RefugioLaBrisaDelDiablo; Valle Hornito; incl breakfast d US$110-132, 6-person house from US$150; P 📶 🏊) Overlooking a coffee plantation with views of Boquete, Volcán Barú and the Pacific, this tiny B&B punches way above its weight. The main building is built of river stones and has two guest rooms. Both rooms are gorgeously decorated, boast firm mattresses and internet TV, and have a private terrace. Next door is a self-catering jungle house that sleeps six.

The in-house restaurant (three-course dinners US$35 to US$40) is a gourmet treat; order in advance. The French-Canadian owners could not be more welcoming and will help organize excursions to local hot springs and a coffee plantation. Ask for a map showing hikes in the area.

Getting There & Away

Buses from both David and from Changuinola or Almirante in Bocas del Toro Province run along Hwy 4 (Fortuna Rd) and stop at or near accommodations.

Hello Travel Panama (p172) shuttles going between Boquete and Bocas del Toro also stop here.

Bocas del Toro Province

POP 156,480 / ELEV SEA LEVEL TO 3336M

Includes ➡

Best Places to Eat

- ➡ El Último Refugio (p194)
- ➡ Firefly Restaurant (p206)
- ➡ Om Café (p193)
- ➡ Leaf Eaters Cafe (p200)
- ➡ Bibi's on the Beach (p200)
- ➡ Azul Restaurant (p194)

Best Places to Stay

- ➡ Tranquilo Bay (p204)
- ➡ Hummingbird (p198)
- ➡ Dolphin Bay Hideaway (p201)
- ➡ Casa Cayuco (p205)
- ➡ Hotel Bocas del Toro (p192)
- ➡ Mamallena (p190)

Why Go?

With its Caribbean islands dotting a shock of blue waters, Bocas del Toro is all that's tropical. This is Panama's principal tourist draw and it will no doubt provide some of your most memorable experiences. The archipelago consists of six densely forested islands, scores of uninhabited islets and the Parque Nacional Marino Isla Bastimentos, Panama's oldest marine park.

The longtime base of the Chiquita Banana company, the mainland boasts the Parque Internacional La Amistad, shared with Costa Rica. It's also home to diverse wildlife such as the elusive jaguar, traditional Ngöbe-Buglé settlements, and the Naso, one of few remaining American tribes with its own monarch.

Most visitors come for a hefty dose of sun and surf. Few are disappointed with the Bocas cocktail of water, fun and thatched luxury, but there's a lot more to what might be Panama's most beautiful corner.

When to Go

Dec–Mar, Jul & Aug The biggest swells for surfers to ride are from December to March, while green turtles can be found nesting on Isla Bastimentos in July and August.

Feb–Apr, Aug Dry conditions and calm seas mean the best visibility for snorkeling and diving, with better access to ocean caves. Turtle nesting is monitored for six months starting in February at Humedal de San San Pond Sak.

Nov Bocas breaks into mayhem for its anniversary celebration in mid-November, along with a plethora of feast days and public holidays. It's also a boom month for national tourism.

Bocas del Toro Province Highlights

1. **Archipiélago de Bocas del Toro** (p184) Whiling away the days, sipping coconut juice and snorkeling at laid-back resorts.
2. **Isla Bastimentos** (p202) Swimming through a bat cave or soaking up the sunny rays while lazing on pristine beaches.
3. **Bocas del Toro Town** (p185) Taking the party from boat bars to cocktail lounges in this lively town.
4. **Surfing the Caribbean** (p197) Surfing some of the best breaks you'll find in the Caribbean – beginners get their start at Playa Punch.
5. **Parque Internacional La Amistad** (p209) Exploring where the Naso people live under one of the world's last tribal monarchies.
6. **Humedal de San San Pond Sak** (p208) Spotting manatees and river otters while boating through the wetlands.

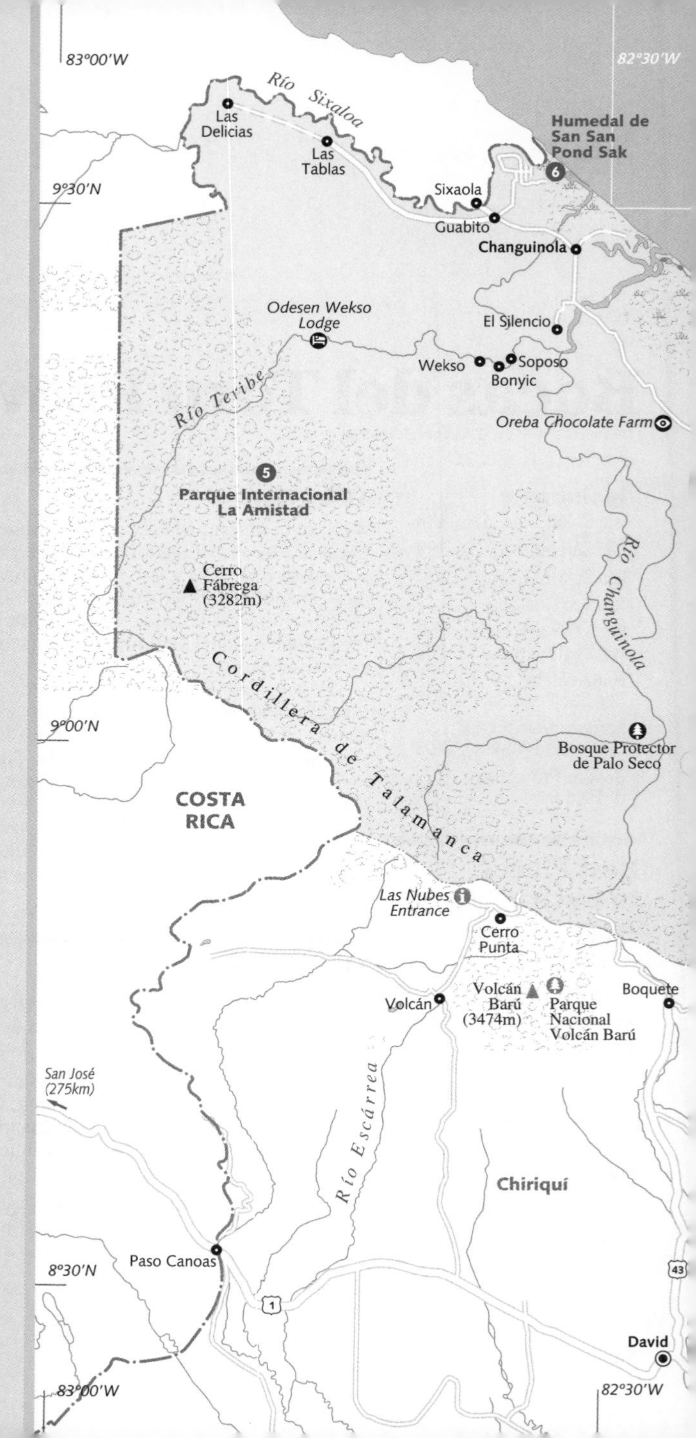

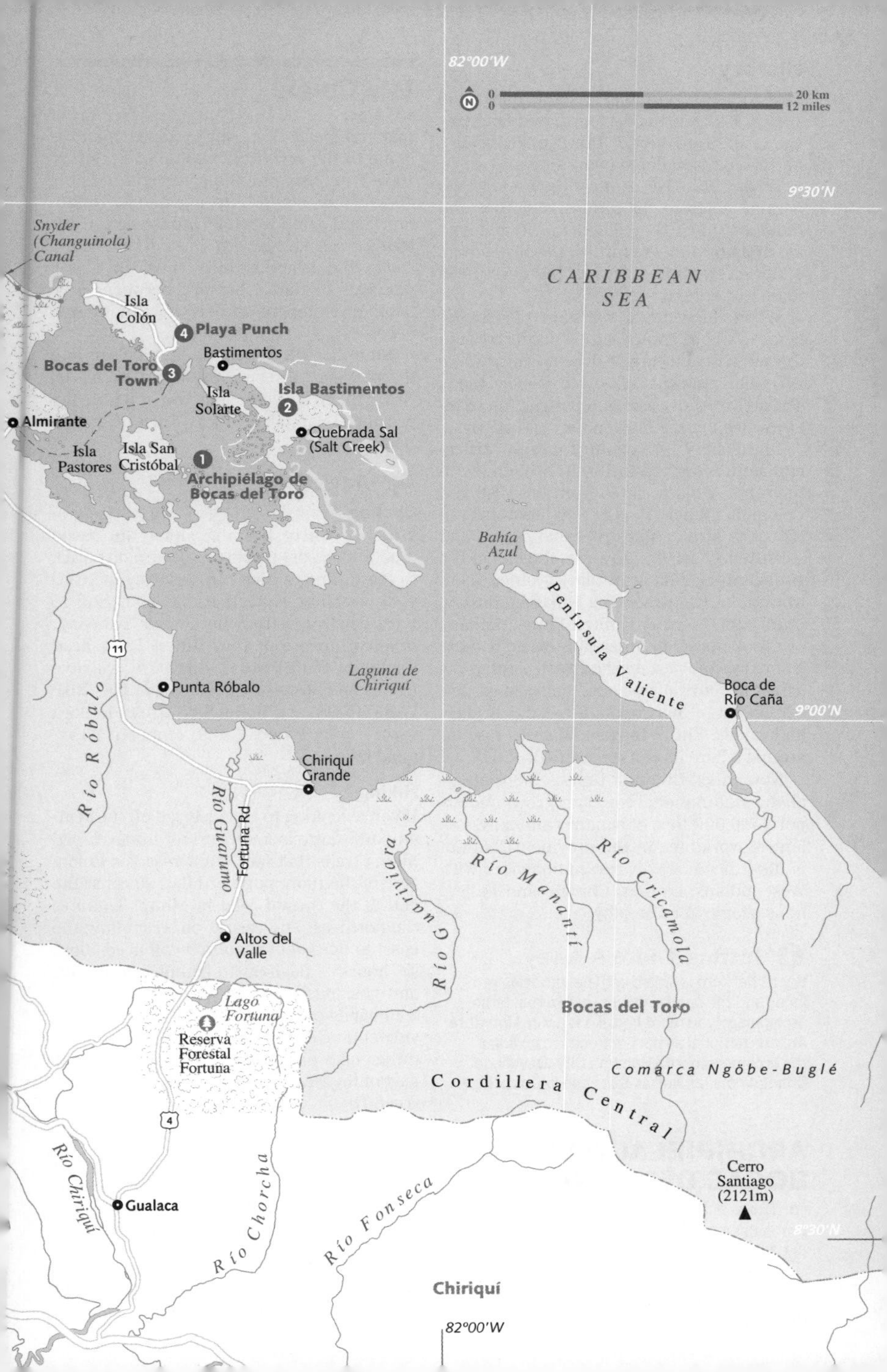

82°00'W
0 20 km
0 12 miles
9°30'N
Snyder (Changuinola) Canal
CARIBBEAN SEA
Isla Colón
4 Playa Punch
Bastimentos
Bocas del Toro Town 3
Isla Solarte
Isla Bastimentos 2
Almirante
Quebrada Sal (Salt Creek)
Isla Pastores
Isla San Cristóbal
1 Archipiélago de Bocas del Toro
Bahía Azul
Península Valiente
11
Laguna de Chiriquí
Punta Róbalo
Río Róbalo
Boca de Río Caña
9°00'N
Chiriquí Grande
Río Guarumo
Fortuna Rd
Río Guariviara
Río Mananti
Río Cricamola
Altos del Valle
Lago Fortuna
Reserva Forestal Fortuna
Bocas del Toro
Comarca Ngöbe-Buglé
Cordillera Central
4
Río Chiriquí
Gualaca
Río Chorcha
Río Fonseca
Cerro Santiago (2121m)
8°30'N
Chiriquí
82°00'W

History

Christopher Columbus visited Bocas del Toro in 1502, during his fourth and final voyage to the New World. Taken by its beauty, he affixed his name to many sites.

During the 17th century the archipelago became a haven for pirates repairing and building ships; they felled the forests and fed upon nesting sea turtles. Despite rumors of buried treasure, their loot has never been found (or at least reported).

When Huguenots (Protestants) fleeing religious wars in France settled on the coast in the late 17th and early 18th centuries, a Spanish militia was sent to Bocas to dislodge them. The arrival of diseases and destruction virtually wiped out the indigenous populations.

In the early 19th century, wealthy aristocrat settlers arrived in Bocas, bringing with them many black slaves from the USA and Colombia. When slavery was abolished in 1850, the former slaves became fishers and subsistence farmers. Towards the end of the 19th century, Jamaican blacks joined them to work in the burgeoning banana industry.

In 1899, however, United Fruit Company overtook the small American-owned banana company. As it established vast plantations across the entire peninsula it also constructed elaborate networks of roads, bridges and canals. Entire towns and cities rose up around where its workers settled.

Now called Chiquita Brands International, the multinational company grows and exports 750,000 tons of bananas annually. The largest workforce in the province, Chiquita is also the most diverse nationwide, with West Indians, Latinos, Chinese and indigenous people in its employ.

Getting There & Away

Bocas del Toro is linked with neighboring provinces and the capital by bus, but to reach the archipelago you must board a ferry in Almirante. An international airport at Bocas town links the archipelago with Panama City, David and Changuinola, as well as San José in Costa Rica.

ARCHIPIÉLAGO DE BOCAS DEL TORO

POP 13,000

For most travelers, the archipelago *is* Bocas del Toro. Caribbean clichés aside, there's no shortage of postcard-pretty beaches, emerald waters and swaying palms, and scads of things to see and do.

Isla Colón

POP 9000

The archipelago's most developed island is home to the provincial capital of Bocas del Toro. From the mid-1990s, foreign investors flooded the island, creating hotels, restaurants and condos while infrastructure for water, trash and sewage lagged far behind. Today the island, which runs on diesel, struggles to find a balance between satisfying development and serving community needs.

Note that the town, the archipelago and the province all share the name Bocas del Toro. To avoid confusion, we refer to the provincial capital as Bocas town or simply Bocas.

Activities

Cycling

Whether you're heading along the paved road to Boca del Drago or taking a dirt track to Playa Bluff, a bike can seriously increase your mobility. Note that the bike ride to Boca del Drago from Boca town is taxing; if you're unsure of your fitness level, head for Punta Bluff instead. Bikes are available from some hostels as well as from Ixa's Bike World (p188) and Bocas Bicis (p188) in Boca town. Flying Pirates (p188) rents out ATVs/quad bikes.

Hiking

If you're looking to seriously get off the beaten path, there is a network of undeveloped hiking trails that fans out across Isla Colón. One of the more popular hikes starts at the end of the coastal road in Mimbi Timbi to the northeast and carries on west along the coast to Boca del Drago. You will need about six hours of daylight to complete the hike, and you must carry in all your water. The trail winds past caves, caverns and plenty of vine-entangled jungle. A bike will help speed things up a bit, though you'll be carrying it part of the way, especially if it's been raining recently.

Kayaking

Sea kayaking is a great way to travel between islands. You will need to be wary of boat traffic, though, and the occasional swell. Some dive shops and hostels rent kayaks.

Birdwatching

While birdwatching on the islands isn't as good as on the mainland, it can still be rewarding. Particularly rare birds, or at least those not well known to Panama, have been recorded on the islands in recent years, including the red-fronted parrotlet, the chestnut-colored woodpecker, the purple martin and the black-cowled oriole.

Bocas del Toro Town

POP 7400

Colorful and full of Caribbean-style clapboard houses, Bocas del Toro (better known simply as Bocas town) was built by the United Fruit Company in the early 20th century. Today it is a relaxed community of West Indians, Latinos and resident gringos, with a friendly atmosphere that is contagious. It's an easy place to adapt to and even easier to linger in.

Bocas serves as a convenient base for exploring the archipelago; *taxis marinos* (water taxis) can whisk you away to remote beaches and snorkeling sites for just a few dollars. The real allure here, though, is simply to be able to slow down and soak up the Caribbean vibes.

Sights

Finca Los Monos Botanical Garden GARDENS

(Map p186; ☎757-9461, 6729-9943; www.bocasdeltorobotanicalgarden.com; garden/birdwatching tours US$15/25; ⏲garden tours 1pm Mon & 8:30am Fri, birdwatching tours 6:30am & 5pm on request) One of the joys of visiting Bocas is touring the 'Monkey Farm' botanical garden a couple of kilometers northwest of the center. Painstakingly carved out of 10 hectares of secondary rainforest over almost two decades, it contains hundreds of species of local and imported trees and ornamental plants, and is teeming with wildlife.

Co-owner and guide Lin Gillingham will point out howler and white-faced capuchin monkeys, sloths and various bird species. Tours, on Fridays and Mondays, must be booked in advance; garden tours depart regularly while birding tours are on demand.

La Gruta CAVE

(The Grotto; Map p186; Colonia Santeña; US$5; ⏲8am-6pm) If sun, sand and surf isn't your thing then consider a trip to this cave in Colonia Santeña, a small village of cattle farmers 7km northwest of Bocas town. Here you'll wade through waist-high water while trying not to disturb thousands of sleeping bats overhead. It's all over in about five minutes.

> **BAD WATER**
>
> Unlike most other places in Panama, the archipelago has tap water that's not safe to drink unless it is filtered. Bocas town has a water-treatment plant, but locals say the tap water is not to be trusted. It's certainly fine for brushing your teeth, but for drinking purchase bottled water or purify your own.

The cave entrance, marked by a small shrine to the Virgin Mary, is along a short trail on the right along the road to Boca del Drago.

A round-trip taxi should cost about US$20 or you can take the Boca del Drago bus (US$2.50).

Activities

Lil' Spa Shop SPA

(Map p190; ☎6591-3814; www.spashopbythesea.com; cnr Av H & Calle 7; ⏲10am-6pm) Should you need a bit of pampering after a hard day on the waves, this lovely oceanfront spa run by a gregarious New Yorker offers massage, reflexology and beauty treatments.

Bocas Yoga YOGA

(Map p190; www.bocasyoga.com; Calle 4; classes US$6) Geared to both locals and travelers, this hatha yoga studio run by the effervescent Laura makes a good break from the party scene. Offers daily classes in English.

Surfing

Bocas Surf School SURFING

(Map p190; ☎757-9057, 6852-5291; www.bocassurfschool.com; cnr Av H & Calle 5; half-/full-day courses US$59/89) This well-regarded school, conveniently located next to a small hostel, caters to beginner surfers with daily classes at 8:30am and 2:30pm. It also rents out boards for US$15 per day.

Mono Loco Surf School SURFING

(Map p190; ☎760-9877; http://monolocosurfschool.com; Calle 2; 3hr lessons US$50; ⏲9am-6pm) Recommended surf shop and school run by a group of serious surfing dudes. Also rents boards (half/full day US$15/20).

Diving & Snorkeling

Although experienced divers accustomed to crystal-clear Caribbean diving may be disappointed with the archipelago – nearly 40 rivers discharging silt into the seas around the archipelago reduce visibility dramatically – it still has much to offer. The islands'

Archipiélago de Bocas del Toro

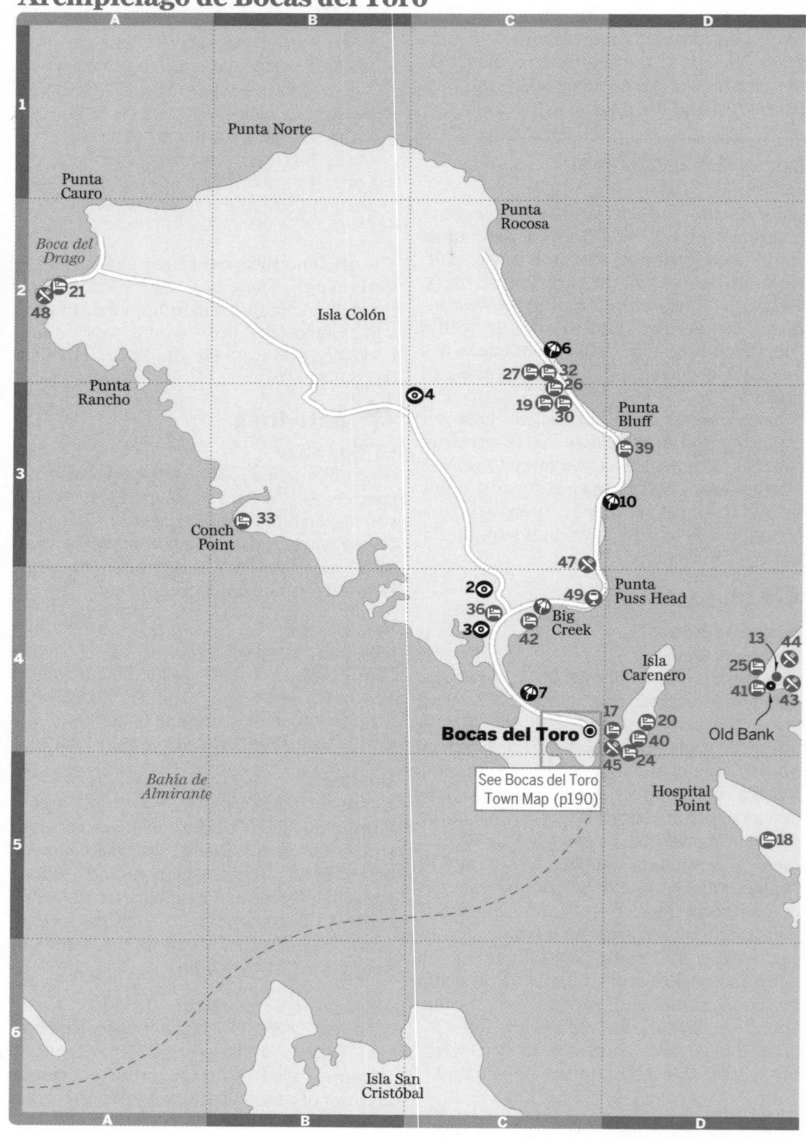

emerald-green waters are home to the usual assortment of tropical species and with a little luck you might see barracudas, stingrays, dolphins and nurse sharks. The better sites include **Dark Wood Reef**, northwest of Bastimentos; **Hospital Point**, a 15m wall off Cayo Nancy; and the base of the buoy near **Punta Juan**, north of Isla Cristóbal.

Two-tank dives cost around US$85; there are also dive certification courses. A number of reliable suppliers offer good-value snorkeling and diving trips out of Bocas.

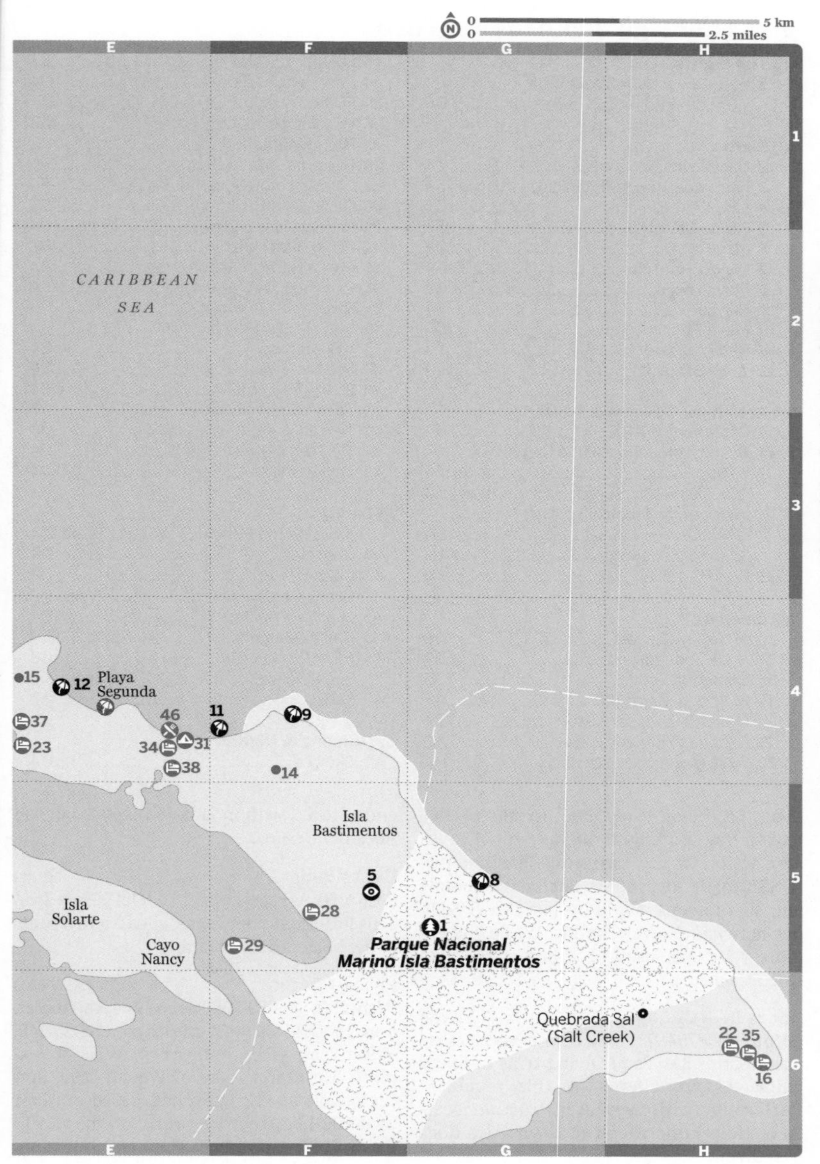

Panama Dive School DIVING
(Map p190; ☎6984-4745; Av H; ⊙8am-6:30pm) Guests give this PADI dive shop high marks. It offers two-tank dives (US$75), open-water certification (US$280) and snorkeling (US$20 for a half-day). If you are new to scuba diving, you can try it out on a discovery dive (US$100). It is also insured.

La Buga DIVING
(Map p190; ☎757-9534, 6781-0755; www.labugapanama.com; Calle 3; ⊙8am-8pm) A very well-regarded dive shop with a new approach

Archipiélago de Bocas del Toro

Top Sights
1 Parque Nacional Marino Isla Bastimentos ... G5

Sights
2 Castillo Inspíración ... C4
3 Finca Los Monos Botanical Garden ... C4
4 La Gruta ... C3
5 Nivida Bat Cave ... F5
6 Playa Bluff ... C2
7 Playa El Istmito ... C4
8 Playa Larga ... G5
9 Playa Polo ... F4
10 Playa Punch ... D3
11 Red Frog Beach ... F4
12 Wizard Beach ... E4

Activities, Courses & Tours
13 Bastimentos Alive ... D4
14 Bastimentos Sky Zipline Canopy Tour ... F4
Escuela de Mar Surf School ... (see 20)
Institute for Tropical Ecology & Conservation ... (see 21)
Scuba 6 Ecodiving ... (see 41)
15 Up in the Hill ... E4

Sleeping
16 Al Natural Resort ... H6
17 Aqua Lounge ... D4
18 Bambuda Lodge ... D5
19 Bluff Beach Retreat ... C3
20 Bocas Buccaneer Resort ... D4
21 Cabañas Estefany ... A2
22 Casa Cayuco ... H6
23 Eclypse del Mar ... E4
24 El Faro del Colibri ... D4
25 Firefly ... D4
26 Hummingbird ... C3
27 Island Plantation ... C2
28 La Loma ... F5
29 Los Secretos Guesthouse ... F5
30 Oasis Bluff Beach ... C3
31 Palmar Tent Lodge ... E4
32 Playa Bluff Hotel ... C2
33 Punta Caracol Acqua Lodge ... B3
34 Red Frog Bungalows ... E4
35 Residencia Al Natural ... H6
36 Sand Dollar Beach Bed & Breakfast ... C4
37 Sea Monkey ... E4
38 Selina Red Frog ... E4
39 Tesoro Escondido ... D3
40 Tierra Verde ... D4
41 Tío Tom's Guesthouse ... D4
42 Villa Paraiso ... C4

Eating
Bibi's on the Beach ... (see 20)
43 Chavela ... D4
44 Coco Hill ... D4
Firefly Restaurant ... (see 25)
45 Leaf Eaters Cafe ... D4
46 Nacho Mama's ... E4
47 Paki Point ... C3
Sea Monkey ... (see 37)
48 Yarisnori Restaurant ... A2

Drinking & Nightlife
49 Skully's ... C4

boat, La Buga leads two to three dive trips a day. Highlights include night dives and visits to the caves off Bastimentos (US$100). It also offers surfboard rentals and surf lessons, stand-up paddles (US$15 per hour) and kayak rentals. While you explore your options, grab a bite at the cute cafe attached.

Bocas Dive Center DIVING
(Map p190; ☎757-9737; www.bocasdivecenter.com; Calle 6 Sur; ⊙8am-8pm) Diving trips in many languages are offered by this reputable PADI center with five-star instruction located at the southern end of town. Also does free diving.

Cycling

Ixa's Bike World CYCLING
(Map p190; Av H; bikes per hr US$3, fat bikes per 24hr US$15; ⊙8am-6pm Mon-Sat) Repairs and rents out a wide selection of bicycles from a hole-in-the-wall workshop at the northern end of town, with mountain bikes to take on Boca del Drago.

Bocas Bicis CYCLING
(Map p190; Av E; per hr/day US$3/12; ⊙9am-7pm) This little stand between Calles 2 and 3 rents two-wheelers year-round.

Flying Pirates ADVENTURE SPORTS
(Map p190; ☎6689-5050; www.flyingpiratesbocas.com; cnr Calle 3 & Av C; half/full day US$110/140; ⊙9am-7pm) One of the best ways to explore Isla Colón is by ATV/quad bike, and the people at Flying Pirates, based on their own 600-hecatre *finca* (farm) on the way to Playa Bluff, can oblige. They rent out more than 30 of the fat-tired vehicles for use on or off-road, including 15km of trails on private land. The beach is off-limits.

You'll be transported to and from downtown Bocas. There's an information and booking truck in the center. Free beers and hot showers included after your day out.

Courses

Spanish by the Sea LANGUAGE
(Map p190; ☎757-9518, 6592-0775; www.spanishbythesea.com; Calle 4) A language school in a relaxed setting. Group lessons are US$360/450 per week for 20/30 hours. Has a branch in Boquete (p165).

Homestays can be arranged (from US$22 per night), or you can bunk down in clean and comfy dorms (US$14) or private rooms (US$24). Also organizes parties, dance classes and open lectures.

Habla Ya LANGUAGE
(Map p190; ☎757-7352; www.hablayapanama.com; cnr Av G & Calle 9 Sur; ⊗8am-5:30pm) This Spanish-language school, with branches in Boquete and Panama City, has a solid reputation. It offers a Spanish for Travelers course that lasts four hours and costs US$75. Classrooms are air-conditioned. Special rates available on lodging in its own dorms and in private rooms with host families.

Tours

The most popular tours in the area are all-day snorkeling trips, which are perfect for nondivers who want a taste of the area's rich marine life. A typical tour costs US$25 per person, and goes to Dolphin Bay, Cayo Crawl, Red Frog Beach (p202; US$5 entry) and Hospital Point.

A trip to the distant Cayos Zapatillas costs US$35, and includes lunch, beach time and a jungle hike on Cayo Zapatilla Sur.

Many 'tours' are really little more than boat transportation to a pretty spot. If you have your own snorkel gear (or if you rent it), you can also charter motor boats. Agree on a price before you go.

Dragon Tours BOATING
(Map p190; ☎6879-5506, 757-7010; www.facebook.com/Jadedragon9; Calle 3; per person incl lunch US$45; ⊗9am-5pm) This perennially popular charter company sails its purpose-built 19m catamaran complete with water slide to various islands on day trips. It usually rents to groups of 45 people, but if there's space individuals can get on a trip. Snorkeling and coolers filled with ice included.

Transparente Tours BOATING
(Map p190; ☎6700-2453, 757-7326; www.transparentetours.bocas.com; Calle 3; per person US$20-25; ⊗office 8am-9pm, tours 10am-4:30pm) This recommended tour operator provides guides, gear and drinks on boat excursions around the archipelago.

Anaboca TOURS
(La Asociación Natural Bocas Carey; Map p190; ☎6843-7244; www.anaboca.bocasdeltoro.org; Calle 3era; per person US$20) This nonprofit run by the local community addresses marine-turtle conservation. In season (April to August), certified guides offer nighttime tours to groups of eight or fewer to view turtle hatching on Playa Bluff. You can also arrange overnight community stays, a good idea if you are there to watch hatching in the wee hours.

The office is in an on-street stand.

Oreba Chocolate Tour TOURS
(☎6649-1457; www.oreba.bocasdeltoro.org; Río Oeste Arriba, mainland; per person US$35) This guided tour leaves Bocas and takes you around an organic chocolate farm, run by the indigenous Ngöbe-Buglé community, on the mainland near Almirante. Tour the farm, see tree sloths, sample chocolate – classified as some of the highest-grade cacao in the world – and enjoy a traditional lunch. Book direct or through Super Gourmet (p193).

The trip (two-person minimum) is guided in Spanish and English. The price does not include the boat trip from Bocas to Almirante (US$12 round trip).

Festivals & Events

Feria del Mar FERIA
The 'Sea Fair' is held on Playa El Istmito (p198), a few kilometers northwest of downtown Bocas, for a week in September.

Día de la Virgen del Carmen RELIGIOUS
Bocatoreños make a pilgrimage to the cave at La Gruta in the middle of the Isla Colón for Mass in honor of the Virgen del Carmen on the third Sunday in July.

Fundación de la Provincia de Bocas del Toro CULTURAL
(⊗Nov 16) Celebrating the foundation of the province in 1903, this is a day of parades and other events; it's a big affair, attracting people from all over the province.

Sleeping

Bocas town is a major tourist draw, though many people don't realize there is no town beach. Water shortage can be a problem, so it's recommended that you take short showers.

Bocas del Toro Town

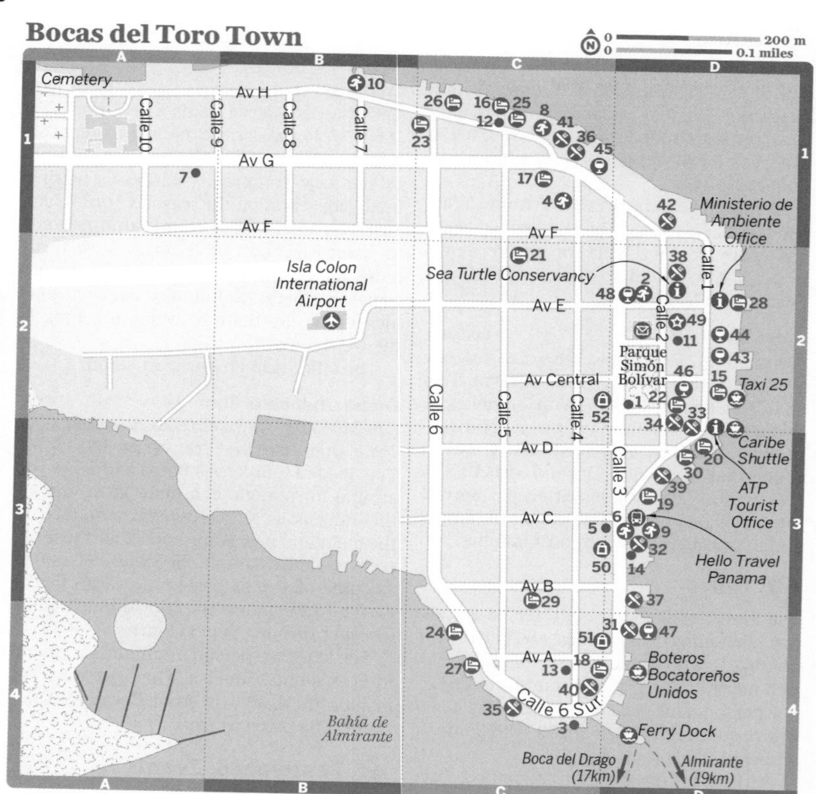

There are lodgings in a range of prices. Reservations are a good idea between December and April, and during national holidays (especially in November) and local festivals. Discounts available in low season.

★Mamallena HOSTEL $

(Map p190; ☎760-9934; www.mamallenabocas.com/bocas-del-toro; Av H; dm US$18, d US$45-60, q US$90; ❄☜) Our favorite hostel in Bocas town is this stylish new over-the-water option with tropical prints, palms and a wraparound bar with a pool table on the ocean deck. Big enough to meet folks but not industrial sized, it has regular happy-hour events and kayaking right off the dock (US$20 all day). The 14 rooms are all air-conditioned, some with balcony.

Surfari B&B B&B $

(Map p190; ☎760-8248; Av B s/n; ⌚s/d/apt US$32/35/45; ❄☜) This budget B&B is a good option for shoestring travelers. Rooms are simple but clean with plain concrete floors. There's a wonderful 3rd-story terrace with views and helpful management. With kitchen use.

Bocas Surf School & Hotel HOSTEL $

(Map p190; ☎757-9057, 6852-5291; http://bocassurfschool.com; cnr Av H & Calle 5; dm/d without bathroom US$20/50; ❄☜) It's not every day that your hostel has its own swim-off dock. This super-cute cottage at a celebrated surf school (p185) offers 10 solid bunks in two rooms, and two doubles – the one on the 1st floor is quite posh. There's a communal kitchen and a good food truck parked onsite. Nonsurfers can rent kayaks.

Hotel del Parque HOTEL $

(Map p190; ☎757-9008; www.hdelparque.webs.com; Calle 2; s/d US$45/50; ❄☜) A classic clapboard Caribbean house fronting the leafy main square, this tranquil place has lots of style but is within budget reach.

Bocas del Toro Town

Activities, Courses & Tours

1	Anaboca	D2
2	Bocas Bicis	D2
3	Bocas Dive Center	C4
	Bocas Surf School	(see 16)
4	Bocas Yoga	C1
5	Dragon Tours	D3
6	Flying Pirates	D3
7	Habla Ya	A1
8	Ixa's Bike World	C1
9	La Buga	D3
10	Lil' Spa Shop	B1
11	Mono Loco Surf School	D2
12	Panama Dive School	C1
13	Spanish by the Sea	C4
14	Transparente Tours	D3

Sleeping

15	Bocas Paradise Hotel	D2
16	Bocas Surf School & Hotel	C1
17	Casa Max	C1
18	Gran Hotel Bahía	C4
19	Hotel Bocas del Toro	D3
20	Hotel Bocas Town	D3
21	Hotel Cala Luna	C2
22	Hotel del Parque	D2
23	Hotel Lula's	C1
24	Hotel Olas	C4
25	Hotel Vista Mar	C1
26	Mamallena	C1
27	Residencial Dos Palmas	C4
28	Selina Hostel Bocas del Toro	D2
29	Surfari B&B	C3
30	Tropical Suites	D3

Eating

31	Azul Restaurant	D4
32	Buena Vista Bar & Grill	D3
33	Cafe del Mar	D2
34	El Chitré	D2
35	El Último Refugio	C4
36	La Casbah	C1
37	Om Café	D3
38	Panadería & Dulcería Alemana	D2
	Pizzeria Alberto	(see 21)
39	Raw	D3
40	Super Gourmet	C4
41	Sweet Love Bocas	C1
42	Tom's	D1

Drinking & Nightlife

43	Barco Hundido	D2
44	Bocas Brewery	D2
45	Bookstore Bar	C1
46	El Toro Loco	D2
47	La Iguana Surf Bar	D4
	Selina Bar	(see 28)
48	Tequila Republic	D2

Entertainment

49	Cine Cafe	D2

Shopping

50	Artesanía Bribrí	C3
51	Lido Isle	C4
52	Tropix Surfboards	C2

Eight ample rooms on two floors have big windows, cool concrete floors, hot showers and firm beds with crisp linens. The terraces provide views of the plaza and hammocks for naps. There is a compact guest kitchen.

Casa Max HOTEL **$**
(Map p190; 757-9120; casamax1@hotmail.com; Av G; r with fan/air-con US$25/45;) This sprawling pea-green Caribbean-style house has 15 brightly painted rooms, with wooden floors and somewhat dated bathrooms. The service isn't much to speak of, but dreamy balconies overlook the town and ocean. There's a large on-site restaurant serving international cuisine (separately run); and the location is very good, just up from the center and on the way to the beaches.

Residencial Dos Palmas HOTEL **$**
(Map p190; 757-9906; residencialdospalmas@yahoo.com; Calle 6 Sur; s/d US$35/40;) Boastfully '100% *bocatoreño,*' Dos Palmas offers eight basic wooden rooms with old-fashioned furnishings and bright turquoise walls. Run by Noviña, a matriarch at turns friendly or indifferent, it's not some cookie-cutter lodging, though some might find it a little stuffy. It sits above the water and boasts exceptional views of the bay from the back terrace. Don't miss sunset!

★ **Hotel Lula's** B&B **$$**
(Map p190; 757-9057; www.lulabb.com; cnr Av H & Calle 6; d/tr incl breakfast US$77/88; @) A place of porches and rocking chairs, this lovely B&B offers a stylish stay. Its eight rooms are immaculate, with orthopedic mattresses, and wooden ceilings and floors. The hosts, two affable firefighters from Atlanta, Georgia, give first-rate service, in addition to free big Southern breakfasts. Has filtered water and a well-stocked honor bar.

Selina Hostel Bocas del Toro HOSTEL **$$**
(Map p190; 202-7966; www.selinahostels.com; Calle 1; dm US$25-35, d with/without bathroom from US$100/80; @) This ever-expanding

hostel chain, which has properties in Panama City's Casco Viejo and on Playa Venao in Península de Azuero, has a mammoth turquoise 196-bed property on the waterfront with something for everybody. Choose from a rock-bottom bunk in a dorm with 12 beds to a deluxe double with balcony on the top floor (room 312 or 313).

You can swim in azure waters directly from the two-level waterfront deck, watch films in the video room, enjoy a drink at the open-air bar or order the meal of the day at the restaurant. There's also a common kitchen for guests' use. An in-house travel agency rents equipment and organizes excursions and there are water taxi departures to Red Frog Beach (p202).

Hotel Bocas Town HOTEL **$$**
(Map p190; ☎6750-5174, 757-7381; www.hotelbocastown.com; Calle 1; d incl breakfast US$88-132; ❄ 📶) This prim pastel hotel sits on the water next to the police station. It features 18 rooms with wicker furniture, facing the street or the sea. Among the latter, rooms 105 and 106 are choicest, with balconies and views across to Isla Carenero. The restaurant sports a huge waterfront deck and a bar with a large mural of rock musicians.

Gran Hotel Bahía HISTORIC HOTEL **$$**
(Map p190; ☎757-9626; www.ghbahia.com; cnr Av A & Calle 3; d incl breakfast US$83-99; ❄📶) This 1905 landmark was built by the United Fruit Company to receive visitors to its headquarters. Though it's not a standout, some careful restorations have revived its 18 rooms and original splendor and the service is congenial. Second-floor deluxe rooms (eg room 208) with wicker furniture, safe boxes and original oak floors are considerably bigger and brighter than their ground-floor counterparts.

Bocas Paradise Hotel INN **$$**
(Map p190; ☎757-9546, 6780-0063; www.bocasparadisehotel.com; Calle 1; d/ste from US$79/97; ❄📶) On the waterfront, this upmarket inn has 27 rooms with brocade bed covers, carved hardwood furniture and little balconies with wooden loungers. Installations are shiny and up to date; the bathrooms are quite spacious. Perks include kitchenettes with fridges and microwaves.

Hotel Cala Luna HOTEL **$$**
(Map p190; ☎757-9066; www.calalunabocas.com; Calle 5; s/d US$60/70; ❄@📶) Attached to the excellent Pizzeria Alberto , the Italian-owned Cala Luna was built with fine attention to detail. The hotel has features such as cathedral windows, tasteful wood details and eight crisp, functional rooms. There's a lovely lounge with tropical plants, and guests can watch planes coming in for a landing 30m above their heads from the rooftop lookouts.

Hotel Vista Mar B&B **$$**
(Map p190; ☎757-9198; www.hotelvistamar.net; cnr Av H & Calle 5; d/tr incl breakfast US$77/88; ❄ 📶) This pretty 14-room inn right on the water at the northern end of Bocas town offers rather good value. Standard rooms have town views, or splurge for a balcony facing the sea. The turquoise interiors and fish murals are cheery, and the terrace hammocks are begging to be swung. There's an attractive bar-restaurant.

Hotel Olas HOTEL **$$**
(Map p190; ☎757-9930, 6914-4556; www.hotelolas.com; Calle 6 Sur; s/d incl breakfast US$70/80; ❄@📶) Shining like a beacon from the southwestern tip of Bocas town, the three-story 'Waves' has 25 clean polished-wood rooms with electric hot-water showers, though rooms are rather small and pretty basic. The biggest draw here is the exceptional oceanfront lounge and restaurant. Offers tours and bicycle rentals through its travel agency, Olas Tours.

★**Hotel Bocas del Toro** INN **$$$**
(Map p190; ☎757-9018; www.hotelbocasdeltoro.com; Calle 2; d incl breakfast US$129-299; ❄@📶) Our favorite place to stay in Bocas town, this three-story waterfront inn has 11 spacious all-hardwood rooms with firm beds, luxurious linens and a warm decor; some have seafront balconies. Perks include concierge service and amenities such as Silico Creek coffee produced by a Ngöbe-Buglé community. There's a fun streetside bar and an excellent waterfront restaurant serving Panamanian classics.

Hotel Bocas del Toro is a member of APTSO, Panama's sustainable tourism alliance.

Punta Caracol Acqua Lodge CABIN **$$$**
(Map p186; ☎6612-1088, 757-9410; www.puntacaracol.com; r incl 2 meals US$485-535; @📶) A poster child for Caribbean luxury, Punta Caracol has nine exquisite cabins perched on a long pier over crystal waters. Two-story thatched cabins feature king-sized canopy beds, big skylight windows and soft lighting. There are solar panels and local renew-

able materials used in construction, and the long boardwalk leads over a reef to a 2km-long mangrove coast.

About 3km northwest of Bocas town and accessed only by boat, Punta Caracol is the ultimate in tranquillity. Nonguests can dine at the deck-side restaurant (mains from US$10 to US$25), which serves fresh seafood, tasty oversized cocktails and tropical style.

Tropical Suites HOTEL $$$
(Map p190; 757-9880; www.bocastropical.com; Calle 1; ste with town/sea views incl breakfast US$139/174;) Boasting a functional elevator, this all-suites hotel has modern comforts including Jacuzzi tubs, flat-screen TVs, hairdryers and room safes. Ample rooms easily fit three, and kitchens have rangetops and refrigerators. For the ultimate in seaside luxury, choose the Starfish suite, which has a balcony plus a porthole in the floor with a direct view into the briny deep.

Eating

Sweet Love Bocas CAFE $
(Map p190; Av H; snacks $3-11; 8am-1pm & 5-8pm Tue-Sun) For top-notch crepes that come savory (with coconut curry) or sweet (honey cream) and a broad selection of teas, try this bohemian cafe, popular with locals in the know. With bench seating and an artsy crafts shop attached, it's more tranquil than spots on the main strip. You can also try some homemade ginger soda.

Cafe del Mar CAFE $
(Map p190; 6212-8712; Calle 1; dishes US$6-9; 8am-10pm Tue-Sun;) For all-natural wraps, sandwiches and burgers served with homemade hot sauce, duck into this tiny eatery. There's also all-day breakfast, smoothies and juices, including a watermelon ginger cooler that's to die for. Preservatives are banned, and vegetarian choices are legion. Eat in or take-out. Great coffee too.

Super Gourmet SUPERMARKET $
(Map p190; 757-9357; www.supergourmetbocas.com; Calle 3; 9am-7pm Mon-Sat) This treasure trove of a grocery store stocks special treats such as natural grass-fed meats and coveted imported items. It also has a section of sustainable local gifts, which include local hot sauce, handmade soaps and outstanding local Bocas chocolate, as well as kosher foodstuffs. Vegetables arrive on Tuesday and Friday.

Pizzeria Alberto PIZZA $
(Map p190; 757-9066; Calle 5; pizzas US$8-14; 5-10pm Fri-Wed) Sardinian-run Alberto's is a favorite local haunt, where pizza with toppings such as artichokes, olives and Gorgonzola satisfies big appetites.

Tom's PANAMANIAN $
(Map p190; 6776-9280, 760-0290; Av G; mains US$5-10; 10:30am-5pm Mon-Sat) Locals of every stripe agree that Tom's is the spot for a tasty lunch of seafood or chicken paired with rice or fries (fixed menu US$6) that doesn't break the bank. Head upstairs in a concrete market building and you'll find it on a shaded 2nd-floor terrace overlooking the water. Great views!

Panadería & Dulcería Alemana BAKERY $
(Map p190; 757-9436; www.facebook.com/panaderia.dulceria.alemana; Calle 2; sandwiches US$3-5, dishes US$5-10; 7am-8pm Mon-Sat, 8am-4pm Sun) In addition to moist slabs of carrot cake and freshly baked wholegrain bread, this German bakery and patisserie also sells sandwiches, salads and pasta dishes.

El Chitré PANAMANIAN $
(Map p190; Calle 2; dishes US$3-5; 6:30am-8pm Mon-Sat) Patronized by locals and travelers alike, this no-frills cafeteria is the best spot in town for cheap but tasty grub. Soups are especially good.

★ **Om Café** INDIAN $$
(Map p190; 6127-0671; http://omcafebocas.com; Calle 3; mains US$9-19; 4-10pm Mon-Fri year-round, plus Sat Dec-Apr;) When you smell gorgeous aromas spilling out onto the sidewalk, you're at this welcoming Indian cafe serving classic curries, korma and thalis. Service can be slow, so pass the wait with an original cocktail, such as the Tipsy Turban (US$6), a dizzy mix of passionfruit or lime juice, rum and sugar. Good selection of vegetarian dishes.

La Casbah MEDITERRANEAN $$
(Map p190; 6477-4727; Av H; menu US$14, mains US$13-16; 6-10pm Tue-Sat) Locals and travelers love this Mediterranean restaurant serving up gazpacho, goat's cheese salad, and seafood and meat dishes such as tabbouleh couscous salad with chicken. The fish of the day comes in cream or white-wine sauce, and there's a nice veggie plate for noncarnivores.

★Azul Restaurant FUSION **$$**
(Map p190; ☎6531-5916; www.facebook.com/azulrestaurantbocas; Calle 3era s/n, 2nd fl; set menus US$20; ⊙6-10pm Tue-Sun; ☑) Come to Azul for excellent-value gourmet dining set on a lovely 2nd-floor balcony (there's also seating inside). There's no menu, just the option of a vegetarian or non-vegetarian (though heavy on seafood) set meal with six courses (including two desserts). Options range from sesame mango tuna tartare to beetroot carpaccio and squid-ink risotto. Impeccable service.

Raw ASIAN **$$**
(Map p190; ☎6938-8473; www.facebook.com/RawFusionBocas; Calle 1 s/n; mains US$12-15; ⊙3-10pm Tue-Sun) It's just a little plank restaurant on the water, but the Asian-fusion offerings are spot on. Sake accompanies fresh tofu spring rolls and amazing tuna tapas. The salads are wonderful, and service is friendly and attentive. At night candles are lit and the full bar, specializing in original martinis (from US$7) and cocktails, starts humming.

Buena Vista Bar & Grill AMERICAN **$$**
(Map p190; ☎757-9035; www.buenavistabocas.com; Calle 3; mains US$9-22; ⊙noon-10pm Wed-Mon) This long-established but peripatetic establishment has had a sleek revamp with leather wall booths and imposing beams. It serves burgers, tacos and wraps in town, and dinner ups the ante with a surf-and-turf menu. Run by a welcoming Panamanian-American couple; the fare won't blow your mind but it is a decent bite with swift service.

★El Último Refugio CARIBBEAN **$$$**
(Map p190; ☎6726-9851; www.ultimorefugio.com; Calle 6 Sur; mains US$14-20; ⊙6-10pm Mon-Sat) A favorite splurge for the Bocas locals, this mellow North American–run place on the edge of the sea does date night right. Caribbean and seafood dishes include red curry calamari and miso-crusted grouper on the chalkboard. Service is friendly and the tranquil location makes it a great spot for a quiet, romantic dinner. Reserve ahead.

Drinking & Nightlife

For its size, Bocas offers a surprisingly varied and lively nightlife, with bars and clubs along the waterfront or just a short water-taxi ride away on Isla Carenero.

One wildly popular party crawl is the three-island Filthy Fridays (www.filthyfridaybocas.com). Your ticket (US$35) includes boat rides, shots and temporary tattoos, but you're on your own with the hangover.

Selina Bar CLUB
(Map p190; ☎202-7966; www.selinahostels.com; Calle 1; ⊙7pm-midnight Sun-Thu, to 2am Fri & Sat) The bar at this landmark hostel is open daily, with happy hour between 7pm and 8pm, but most people make it here between 10pm and 2am on a Friday, when all the stops are pulled out and it's party time.

Tequila Republic BAR
(Map p190; ☎6912-5183, 6913-6333; www.facebook.com/tequilarepublicbar; Av E; ⊙2-11pm Mon-Sat) While you're still 3000km from Cancun, this lively bar with an island vibe offers more than a tequila fix, though you'll get that too. There's frosty *cerveza* and good cocktails in addition to great tacos and grass-fed burgers.

Bookstore Bar BAR
(Map p190; ☎6452-5905; Calle 2; ⊙noon-1am Mon-Sat, 5pm-12:30am Sun) Just what its name suggests: this cavernous spot sells both books and drinks, though most seem more interested in the latter. It's the best spot for live music in Bocas, with rock, salsa and punk on Tuesday and Saturday. Run by a couple of affable North Americans, it's a mecca for gringos at the start (and sometimes at the end) of an evening.

La Iguana Surf Bar CLUB
(Map p190; Calle 3; ⊙9:30pm-3am Sun-Wed, to 4am Thu-Sat) Kick off your crazy Bocas night at this popular surfer and skate bar on the waterfront. Start with a US$2 beer-tequila combo. You probably won't be in the mood for the dancing pole yet, though.

Barco Hundido BAR
(Map p190; Calle 1; ⊙8pm-midnight) At some point you'll probably find yourself at this open-air bar, affectionately known as the 'Wreck Deck' after the sunken banana boat that rests in the clear Caribbean waters in front. A short boardwalk extends from the bar to an island seating area that includes swings; perfect for stargazing.

Bocas Brewery BREWERY
(Map p190; ☎6347-5279; http://bocasbrewery.com; Calle 1, Barco Hundido; ⊙3-10pm) This smart little brewpub in the Barco Hundido complex has nine beers on tap, ranging from its

greatest hit Maracuya Wheat (with passionfruit) to IPAs and tropical red ale. Start out with a four-beer sampler.

El Toro Loco SPORTS BAR
(Map p190; 757-7011; www.facebook.com/toro.loco.121; Av Central; 11am-midnight) Expat-owned, this sports bar is the closest thing you'll find to Hooters in Bocas. Five different screens are aglow at the same time and there's occasional live music. Bottled beer only.

Entertainment

Cine Cafe CINEMA
(Map p190; 6549-4158; Calle 2; tickets US$7-8; 3-11pm) Great on a rainy afternoon or evening, Cine Cafe is a chilled (quite literally) spot that offers a wide-ranging selection of movies, comfortable beanbag seating and drinks with popcorn (natch) and some sweets.

Shopping

You'll find a selection of *molas* (colorful hand-stitched appliqué textiles) and a range of other handicrafts for sale by indigenous Guna people near central Parque Simón Bolívar.

Artesanía Bribrí ARTS & CRAFTS
(Map p190; 757-9020; Calle 3; 8am-7pm) This centrally located and heavily stocked shop sells hammocks, clothing and local handicrafts, such as jute bags made by indigenous Ngöbe-Buglé people, *molas* by Guna people and mats from the Darién.

Lido Isle CLOTHING
(Map p190; 6789-6337, 760-9981; Calle 3; 10am-7pm Mon-Sat) This upbeat boutique sells women's clothing designed by the Californian owner as well as original jewelry, bags and wallets.

Tropix Surfboards SPORTS & OUTDOORS
(Map p190; 757-9727; http://tropixsurf.tripod.com; Calle 3; 9am-7pm Mon-Sat) Sells custom-made surfboards and a few used ones as well. Also has a large selection of swimwear and other island apparel.

Information

DANGERS & ANNOYANCES

- The surf can be dangerous and there are frequent riptides – use caution when going out into the waves.
- The archipelago is generally a conservative place and local law bans men (and women) from walking the streets shirtless. Even if you are on your way to the beach, wear a shirt or you might be sent back to your hotel by the police.
- No matter what age you are, you will almost certainly be offered drugs for sale while walking the streets of downtown Bocas. Do not even think about it: Panama takes its drug laws very seriously indeed.

MEDICAL SERVICES

Bocas del Toro Hospital (757-9201; Av G; 24hr) is the island's only hospital and has a 24-hour emergency room. A new Taiwan-funded facility is under construction to the northwest.

MONEY

Banco Nacional de Panamá (758-3850; cnr Calle 4 & Av E; 8am-3pm Mon-Fri, 9am-2pm Sat) exchanges traveler's checks and has a 24-hour ATM.

POST

The **post office** (Map p190; Calle 3; 8am-3pm Mon-Fri, to 1pm Sat) is in the town hall overlooking Parque Simón Bolívar from the north.

TOURIST INFORMATION

Bocas.com (www.bocas.com) The official tourism website.

ATP Tourist Office (Autoridad de Turismo Panama; Map p190; 757-9642; bocasdeltoro@atp.gob.pa; Calle 1; 9am-4pm Mon-Fri) In a large government building next to the police station on the eastern waterfront.

Ministerio de Ambiente Office (Map p190; 758-6822, 757-9442; Calle 1; 9am-5pm Mon-Fri) Can answer questions about national parks or other protected areas.

Sea Turtle Conservancy (Map p190; 757-9186; www.conserveturtles.org; Calle 2; 9am-5pm Mon-Fri) World's oldest sea-turtle research and conservation organization has an information office in Bocas town.

Getting There & Around

All arrivals must pay US$3 tourist tax when arriving at any port in Bocas del Toro.

AIR

Air Panama (757-9841; www.airpanama.com) flies to Panama City (from US$123, one hour) twice daily, sometimes via Changuinola (US$63), as well as to David (US$85). Office at the **airport** (Map p190; 757-9208; Av E).

BOAT

If you don't fly into Bocas you'll have to take a water taxi (US$6) from Almirante on the mainland. On the waterfront, **Taxi 25** (Map p190;

757-9071; www.facebook.com/bocastaxi25; 6am-6pm) makes the half-hour trip between 6am and 6:30pm every 30 minutes.

Caribe Shuttle (Map p190; 757-7048; www.caribeshuttle.com; Calle 1) runs a combination boat-bus trip (US$33) to Puerto Viejo and Cahuita in Costa Rica three times daily. There's also an option to go on to San Jose (US$76). It provides a hotel pick-up, but you must reserve one day in advance.

Ferries to Almirante on the mainland and boats to Boca del Drago leave from the **ferry dock** (Map p190) at the southern end of Bocas del Toro town.

BUS

A cross-island bus goes to Boca del Drago (US$2.50, one hour) and another goes to Playa Bluff (US$3) from Parque Simón Bolívar, with departures between 7am and 7pm. It doubles as a school bus, so afternoon trips may be delayed.

SHUTTLE

Hello Travel Panama (Map p190; 757-7004; www.hellotravelpanama.com; Calle 3era s/n; 8:30am-8pm) offers reliable air-conditioned shuttle service (including boat) to Boquete (US$30, five hours) with a stop at Lost & Found Hostel (p180), and Puerto Viejo (US$33) or San Jose (US$76), Costa Rica.

WATER TAXIS

To reach nearby islands, you can hire boaters operating motorized boats and canoes along the waterfront. As a general rule, you should always sort out the rate beforehand, and clarify if it is for one way or round trip. Always pay on the return leg – this guarantees a pick-up – though most boaters will want some money up-front to buy petrol. Though rates vary, you will get a better deal if you speak Spanish, are with a group and arrange for a pick-up.

Boteros Bocatoreños Unidos (Map p190; 757-9760; Calle 3; 6:30am-11pm) runs to destinations including Isla Carenero (US$2), Isla Bastimentos and Isla Solarte (US$5) and Red Frog Beach (US$8). Scheduled boats leave for Almirante (US$6, 20 minutes) every half-hour. Staff are trained in safe boating and sustainable-tourism practices.

Boca del Drago

Located on Isla Colón's northwest coast, this sleepy beach is known for its huge number of starfish along Starfish Beach, a 15-minute walk around the bend. The addition of commercial stands and cabins as well as increased water-taxi traffic have taken their toll on the beach, however. There has been a lot of erosion and the starfish have moved much further offshore. Still, the calm and relaxed atmosphere here will draw beach bums aplenty. The swimming and snorkeling are good, and the lack of surge makes this one of the safest spots for swimming in the archipelago.

Sights & Activities

Castillo Inspiración LANDMARK
(Plastic Bottle Village; Map p186; 6917-1318; www.plasticbottlevillage-theline.com; Camino a Bocas del Drago; call ahead) French-Canadian Robert Bezeau crafted this four-story castle from 40,000 plastic bottles. The epitome of recycling, it's one of a kind and worth a good look. His mission is to educate the public about creative options for reuse of plastics. For now the interior is only open to the public for special events but there are plans in the works for a restaurant.

Institute for Tropical Ecology & Conservation VOLUNTEERING
(ITEC; Map p186; 6624-9246, 6853-2134; www.itec-edu.org) Boca del Drago is home to a branch of the Institute for Tropical Ecology & Conservation, a nonprofit education, research and conservation organization. The field station here offers field ecology courses to undergraduate and graduate students, provides facilities for tropical researchers, operates marine conservation programs and engages in community development. A water taxi from the beach will cost US$5.

Sleeping & Eating

Cabañas Estefany CABIN $
(Map p186; 6956-4525; www.facebook.com/cabinasturisticasestefany; dm/d US$15/44, 7-person cabin US$100;) Though a far cry from luxury, this 11-room complex is one of the few budget beach lodgings on Isla Colón. Its brightly painted wooden *cabañas* are bare-bones and bathrooms have cold-water showers. Secure a room with a fan as it can get quite buggy. The rooms on the 1st floor have balconies and ocean views.

Yarisnori Restaurant PANAMANIAN $$
(Map p186; 6615-5580; www.yarisnori.com; mains US$8-25; 9am-6pm Wed-Mon) Overlooking the water and with hammocks strung between the palms on the beach, this open-air restaurant is a local favorite, due in large part to the warm hospitality of owners Juany and Willy. Grab a table on the sand and feast on the catch of the day, served with

SURFING IN BOCAS

With beginner-friendly beach swells, ripping reef breaks and some seriously suicidal barrels, Bocas del Toro is emerging as an international surf destination. The following is a rundown of the major surfing spots in the archipelago.

If you don't have your own board, you can rent from Tropix Surfshop (p195) in Bocas town or from various accommodations on the outer islands, including Red Frog Bungalows (p205) on Isla Bastimentos.

Isla Colón

Beginner surfers looking for a bit of reef experience should check out Playa Punch (p198), which offers a good mix of lefts and rights. Although it can get heavy when big, Punch generally offers some of the kindest waves around.

Just past Punch en route to Playa Bluff is a popular reef break known as **Dumpers**. This left break can get up to 3m and should only be ridden by experienced surfers; wiping out on the reef here is dangerous. There is also an inner break known as **Inner Dumps**, which also breaks left but is more forgiving than its outer mate.

Be careful walking out on the reefs as they are sharp and full of sea urchins – don't go barefoot. If you wipe out and get cut up, be sure to properly disinfect your wounds. Be aware that seawater in the Caribbean does not help the healing process; the warm water temperature means the ocean is full of live bacteria.

The island's most infamous surf spot is Playa Bluff (p198), which throws out powerful barreling waves that break in shallow water along the beach and have a reputation for snapping boards (and occasionally bones). The waves close quickly, but the tubes here are truly awesome, especially when the swells are strong.

Isla Bastimentos

If you're looking for a solid beach break, both Wizard Beach (p203) and Red Frog Beach (p202) offer fairly constant sets of lefts and rights, perfect for beginners and intermediates. When the swells are in, however, Wizard occasionally throws out some huge barrels, though they tend to close up pretty quickly. **Silverbacks** is a fierce wave break between Isla Bastimentos and Isla Carenero that can reach peak heights of more than 5m during winter months.

Isla Carenero

Very experienced surfers may want to tackle **Silverbacks**, an enormous barreling right that breaks over a reef and can reach heights of more than 5m. On a good day, Silverbacks is a world-class break that wouldn't look out of place on Hawaii's North Shore. Silverbacks breaks off the coast, so you're going to need to hire a water taxi (from US$3) to get out there.

Two places suitable for beginners are **Old Man's**, which has an A-frame that breaks in the middle of a channel, and **Black Rock**, with a right suitable for beginners that also breaks in the middle of the channel with a sandy reef bottom.

beans and coconut rice. Their breakfast offering is also quite good.

Yarisnori also offers accommodations (double US$55) in three cramped rooms out the back looking out on some pretty gardens.

Getting There & Away

To get here from Bocas town, take a local bus (US$2.50) from Calle 3 near Parque Simón Bolívar, a water taxi (US$25 round trip) or a taxi (US$15 to US$20 one way).

Playa Bluff & Around

A string of beaches on Isla Colón's east coast can be reached by a road that skirts along the shore up from Bocas town. This has traditionally been the terrain of surfers (and turtles), but as more lodgings pop up, travelers are discovering this once-secluded option. Playa Bluff stretches for 5km all the way to Punta Rocosa. September through to March are sure months to enjoy the beach without worrying about the hatching turtles.

Sights

Playa Bluff BEACH

(Map p186) This lovely beach is pounded by intense waves. Though you wouldn't want to get into the water here without a board, the soft, yellow sand and palm-fringed shores are pristine. The beach is 8km from Bocas town, alongside the road after you round Punta Bluff. It serves as a nesting area for sea turtles from May to September.

Playa El Istmito BEACH

(Isthmus Beach; Map p186) Playa El Istmito, also called Playa La Cabaña, is the closest beach to Bocas town (2.5km away), but as it's on Bahía Sand Fly the *chitras* (sand flies) here have an itchy bite. This is not the most attractive beach and, unless you're walking, it's worth heading further north to **Sand Dollar Beach** or beyond.

Playa Punch BEACH

(Playa Paunch; Map p186) Further up the coast from Playa El Istmito and Sand Dollar Beach is Playa Punch (or Paunch), which is dangerous for swimming but good for surfing. It's about 5km from Bocas town.

Sleeping

Tesoro Escondido CABIN $

(Map p186; 6711-9594; www.tesoroescondido.info; Playa Paunch; d/tr from US$50/60, 2-/3-/4-person cabins US$95/120/135) Exuding a very homespun charm, this colorful seafront lodge with eight rooms, three thatched cottages and a suite works its magic. Mosaic tables and recycled-bottle construction in the showers lend a bohemian air; the hammock-strewn upstairs balcony is a treat; and rooms 7 and 8, accessed by a stepped tree trunk, are awesome.

Guests dine on fixed menus with fab desserts (best chocolate ever?). Snorkel gear is free to borrow and there are bicycles for rent. Note, it's relatively isolated, located on the right just before Playa Bluff, and has its own tiny private beach.

Oasis Bluff Beach B&B $$

(Map p186; WhatsApp 1-479-381-0096; www.oasisbluffbeach.com; Playa Bluff; d incl breakfast US$120;) This airy, modern and tasteful off-the-grid home is a wonderful British-run B&B. It's on a sprawling green lawn facing the water, with a long wraparound porch on the 2nd story. Guests can order excellent meals too. It's 20 minutes from Bocas town.

Sand Dollar Beach Bed & Breakfast B&B $$

(Map p186; 757-9671, 421-1324; www.sanddollarbeachbb.com; Sand Dollar Beach; d/ste incl breakfast from US$110/175;) Vaguely reminiscent of a US antebellum plantation, this B&B in a yellow clapboard manor about 3km west of Bocas town has four lovely rooms, a suite named after flowers and a separate apartment for families. The wraparound verandas on two floors give views of the beach across the road and are the ultimate in relaxation.

The surrounding gardens harbor monkeys, sloths and trails. Bicycles and snorkeling gear are available to guests.

Playa Bluff Hotel LODGE $$

(Map p186; 6871-6064; www.playablufflodge.com; d/tr incl breakfast from US$130/145;) Running on solar power, the 20 rooms at this Playa Bluff property are modern and Mediterranean in style, nestled into a rainforest location that includes lily ponds with caimans and huge trees with sloths. There's also a small pool, and jungle treks are available within the 23-hectare property. Kids and pets OK.

★**Hummingbird** B&B $$$

(Map p186; 6949-3694; www.thehummingbirdpanama.com; d incl breakfast US$175;) This lovely B&B on Playa Bluff boasts six rooms in a house and two bungalows constructed with gorgeous tropical hardwoods, with sensational balconies and louvered windows and doors that let in cool breezes. Open-plan bathrooms behind the bedrooms are tastefully designed. Grounds are planted as a botanical garden to attract butterflies and hummingbirds.

The on-site restaurant is an excellent choice, even for nonguests, with huge leafy salads and appetizing plates of seafood or burgers. Transfers from the airport are included with a three-night stay.

★**Island Plantation** BOUTIQUE HOTEL $$$

(Map p186; 6612-7798; www.islandplantationbocas.com; Playa Bluff; d/ste US$160/224; @) Reminiscent of an intimate resort in Bali, this boutique property has seven lovely rooms with private open-air showers in the garden, king-size four-poster beds, mosquito nets and hardwood balconies. The stunner is a two-bedroom suite featuring an enormous hardwood veranda. Guests can dine on the beach for lunch; there's a clay oven for excellent pizzas. Warm welcome, great service.

Villa Paraiso INN $$$
(Map p186; ☎6494-3042, 6552-2395; www.villaparaiso.info; Playa Tortuga; ste US$130-220; ❄📶🏊) With a waterfront location 2km from Bocas town, this family-orientated, California-style home offers three comfortable suites in a main building and annex. The construction is contemporary classic, with rooms surrounding two saltwater pools. Lodgings feature kitchenettes and a BBQ grill, and there are kayaks and bicycles to borrow.

Bluff Beach Retreat B&B $$$
(Map p186; ☎6677-8867; www.bluffbeachretreat.com; Playa Bluff; incl breakfast 2-/4-person cabins US$250/325, 9-person houses US$795; 📶🏊) This lush property facing Playa Bluff makes the perfect honeymoon getaway. One large home with a lap pool and two smaller cabins feature open-floor plans, lovely hardwood details, and slatted windows that keep out the sun and prevent the need for air-conditioning. Guests get the use of bicycles; it's also the site of yoga retreats. Three-night minimum stay.

You've also the option to ride horses at the Canadian owners' nearby citrus-fruit farm.

Eating & Drinking

Paki Point CAFE $$
(Map p186; ☎6948-6562; mains US$7-15; ⊙11am-6pm) This outdoor open-deck restaurant with graffiti art and full views of the beach serves pizzas and seafood with cold beers and margaritas. For cyclists making the arduous trip to Playa Bluff, it's a godsend. You can also rent surfboards.

Skully's PUB
(Map p186; ☎6689-5050; Playa Paunch; mains US$7-15; ⊙4-10pm) A waterfront tiki bar with good pub grub, this is a nice place to gather for sunsets and cocktails, and the burgers ain't bad either. It's a US$2 taxi ride from Bocas town.

Getting There & Away

A local bus (US$3) leaves every 40 minutes from Calle 3 near Parque Símon Bolívar in Bocas town. Expect to pay US$15 one way for a taxi to Playa Bluff. Prices fluctuate since the road is sometimes in a ruinous condition. A water taxi will cost US$7 per person.

Many people cycle this route. With a steady effort, it's about an hour one way from Bocas town to Playa Bluff, but be warned that the sun is unrelenting and it isn't a flat route. Take plenty of water and sunscreen. And there's the ATV/quad bike option...

Isla Carenero

POP 350

Slightly larger than a postage stamp, this tiny isle ringed by sand feels a notch more relaxed than the main island. It lies a few hundred meters southeast from Isla Colón and its close location makes it a go-to for a leisurely waterfront lunch or happy-hour action. Often overlooked, it takes its name from 'careening,' which in nautical talk means to lean a ship on one side for cleaning or repairing. In October 1502 Columbus' ships were careened and cleaned on this cay while the admiral recovered from a bellyache.

In recent times many hotels have been added, and nature isn't as wild here as it is on the more remote islands. Yet Carenero remains a nice alternative if you're seeking peace and quiet.

Activities

Escuela de Mar Surf School SURFING
(Map p186; ☎6981-2749, 757-7008; www.surfschoolpanama.com; ⊙9am-6pm) For quality surf classes (US$45 for three hours) or kayak rentals ($10 for three hours), stand-up paddles (US$30 for four hours) and boards, check out this Argentine-run surf school.

Sleeping

Aqua Lounge HOSTEL $
(Map p186; www.bocasaqualounge.info; dm/d without bathroom incl breakfast US$15/32; 📶🏊) Rough, rustic and grungy, this 12-room backpacker palace is a matchstick construction on the dock facing Bocas town. And guests just can't get enough – from the hugely popular US$1-a-bottle bar (open from 7am to midnight; party night is Friday) to the wraparound dock with swimming platform and swings.

Fan-cooled dorms have up to a dozen beds; choose the one with four on the upper floor. Wi-fi at the bar.

Tierra Verde HOTEL $$
(Map p186; ☎757-9903; www.hoteltierraverde.com; s/d incl breakfast US$65/75, ste US$150-175; ❄@📶) This family-run three-story hotel sits

back from the beach amid shady palms and flowers. Designed in a contemporary island style, there are six spacious all-wood rooms on two floors. The suite at the top allows in ample light. There's the option of airport pick-ups (US$10). Go for rooms 4 or 5 for ocean views.

Bocas Buccaneer Resort CABIN $$
(Map p186; 6902-8976, 757-9042; www.bocasbuccaneerresort.com; cabin/bungalow incl breakfast US$85/75;) Located on a lovely strip of sand, this low-key resort is really just a humble clutch of romantic cabins, a bungalow and an attractive all-wood suite. Elevated units have polished hardwood floors and walls, a thatched roof, a screened porch and a modern tiled bathroom with composting toilets. Bungalows fit three people.

El Faro del Colibri CABIN $$$
(Hummingbird Lighthouse; Map p186; 6791-0840, 757-7315; www.farodelcolibri.com; d incl breakfast from US$149;) Six canary-yellow cabins plus a 69-sq-meter mock lighthouse line a wooden dock. With individual swim-up decks and wood floors, they are lovely and considerably private. There are another four apartments in the main building. The buffet breakfast is sumptuous.

Eating

★Leaf Eaters Cafe VEGETARIAN $
(Map p186; 6675-1354; www.facebook.com/bocasleafeaters; dishes US$8-12; 11am-5pm Mon-Sat;) For excellent pescatarian, vegetarian and vegan lunches, head to this over-the-water restaurant on Isla Carenero. Start off with a cool cucumber-mint-coconut-watermelon shake. Quirky and flavorful offerings include 'hippie bowls' (brown rice with vegetables and dressing), grilled fish sandwiches with caramelized onions, blackened fish tacos and scrumptious shiitake burgers. Cheery decor and friendly atmosphere.

★Bibi's on the Beach SEAFOOD $$
(Map p186; 757-9137, 6981-2749; http://bocasbuccaneerresort.com/surfside-restaurant-and-bar; mains US$7-15; 9am-9pm) With great atmosphere, this over-the-water restaurant and surf outfitter makes tasty soups, killer *ceviche* (citrus-cured seafood), whole lobsters (US$27) and lightly fried fish. The service couldn't be friendlier and the sea views (and cocktails) will keep you lingering. Happy hour coincides with sundown: 4pm to 7pm.

It's in front of Bocas Buccaneer Resort.

Getting There & Away

Isla Carenero is a quick and easy US$2 boat ride from the waterfront in Bocas town. Oddly there is no public pier. Water taxis dock at the small marina on the tip of the island. From here, there is a track that leads to the little town and continues across the island. Exercise caution on the track, as there can be aggressive dogs around.

Isla Solarte

Isla Solarte (aka Cayo Nancy) is distinguished by Hospital Point, renowned among snorkelers for its 20m underwater wall. The island was named after the United Fruit Company hospital built here in 1900 to isolate victims of yellow fever and malaria. At the time, it was not known that these diseases were transmitted by mosquitoes. Although the hospital complex eventually included 16 buildings, it was abandoned after two decades of operation following the blight that killed all of United Fruit's banana trees here.

Sleeping & Eating

Bambuda Lodge RESORT $
(Map p186; 6765-4755, 6962-4644; www.bambuda.net; dm US$18, d US$69-99, d without bathroom US$59, d bungalows US$89, incl breakfast;) Run by two Calgary friends focused on fun and service, this destination hostel is set up in lush rainforest with fruit trees and trails, overlooking a coral reef. The attractive all-wood complex features a gorgeous swimming pool and an adrenaline-stoking 60m-long water slide plunging from hillside reception into the ocean. Water taxis provide transfers (US$5) from Bocas.

Bambuda has two fan-cooled dorms with 10 beds each and private rooms that include quite deluxe jungle bungalows. The open-air bar and dining room serves set meals (US$8 to US$12). If they're in season, there's mango, star fruit and custard apples for the picking, while 10km of trails fan out in several directions. Nonguests can get a pass (US$8) to use the facilities. There's snorkeling equipment as well kayaks and canoes sometimes available.

Getting There & Away

Isla Solarte is a quick and easy boat ride (US$4) from the waterfront in Bocas town, but lodgings on the far end are considerably more expensive to reach. If you want to snorkel at Hospital Point, either join an excursion or negotiate a price with a water taxi.

Isla San Cristóbal & Around

POP 450

A half-hour away from Bocas town and you're in another world among the Ngöbe-Buglé indigenous community on Isla San Cristóbal. These subsistence farmers and fishers have a strong sense of their cultural identity, though they live mostly in difficult circumstances. There are some community tourism initiatives in their communities. To the south, Dolphin Bay is famous for sightings of dolphin pods. Beyond there is a lodging on another nearby island and a mainland restaurant accessed by boat.

Tours

★Green Acres Chocolate Farm TOURS

(☎6716-4422; www.greenacreschocolatefarm.com; Cerro Bruja Peninsula; adult/child US$15/free; ⏲10am & 2pm Thu-Tue) Facing Dolphin Bay but actually on the mainland's Cerro Bruja peninsula, this chocolate farm sitting within 12 hectares of forested slopes is one of the largest in the archipelago that's open to the public. A two-hour tour led by North American owner Robert will take you seamlessly from cocoa pod to candy bar and leave no question unanswered.

The grounds are stunning and teeming with flora and fauna: hundreds of orchid species, green and black poison dart frogs, and golden silk orb-weaver spiders, whose high-tensile-strength webs may one day replace Kevlar.

Sleeping & Eating

★Dolphin Bay Hideaway LODGE $$$

(☎6886-4502; www.dolphinbayhideaway.com; Isla San Cristóbal; d incl 2 meals US$175-225; wi-fi) Located amid mangroves and gorgeous gardens, this ecolodge has five rooms on two levels, with a big wooden deck, docks with hammocks and both a lily pond and a pool. Rooms are colorful and well appointed, with canopy beds, mosquito nets and large fans. Two cabins complete the picture. North Americans Brian and Amy are delightful hosts and offer tours.

There is snorkeling equipment available as well as kayaks, canoes and stand-up paddleboards. Meals are eaten communally in the lovely dining room on the top level. A transfer from Bocas town costs US$30 one way.

Finca Vela LODGE $$$

(☎6809-5534; www.fincavela.com; Isla Pastores; d incl breakfast & transfers US$190, extra guest $40; wi-fi, pool) This stylish ecolodge run by a French family lets you leave the world behind. There's snorkeling right off the dock, where there's also a shady hammock hut and restored *cayucos* (dugout canoes) for guest use. Well-designed cabins show minimalist elegance. Take a golf cart uphill to the restaurant with a daily menu of local products cooked up by the French chef.

It's five minutes by boat to Almirante, and 30 minutes to Bocas town. Contact via WhatsApp as there's no signal on-site.

Rana Azul PIZZA $$

(☎6710-0395; Darkland; pizza US$8-16; ⏲3-8pm Fri, noon-5pm Sun) A real only-when-traveling experience, Rana Azul is a remote restaurant-pizzeria facing Dolphin Bay from the Bocas mainland. Hosts Joseph and Maria, arrived here some years back on their boat from Austria. There are other mains on the menu (eg gargantuan meat plates to share from US$22) but most come here for pizzas cooked in the wood-burning oven.

Getting There & Away

Getting to Isla San Cristóbal from Bocas town is not cheap. A water taxi will cost upwards of US$30.

OFF THE BEATEN TRACK

THE OTHER BOCAS

Tired of the crowds? Find adventure by hiring a boat to try out these excursions:

Cayo Crawl Get lost in these mangrove-dotted channels – also called Coral Cay – near Isla Bastimentos.

Cayo Swan Spot red-billed tropic birds and white-crowned pigeons in this cay near Isla de Los Pájaros, north of Isla Colón.

Cayos Zapatillas Set out for the pristine white-sand beaches and virgin forests on these two uninhabited islands southeast of Isla Bastimentos.

Dolphin Bay Spot dolphins frolicking at this densely populated breeding ground south of Isla San Cristóbal.

Isla Bastimentos

POP 1950

Although it's just a 10-minute boat ride from the town of Bocas del Toro, Isla Bastimentos is like a different world. Some travelers say this is their favorite island in their favorite part of Panama. The northwest coast of the island is home to palm-fringed beaches that serve as nesting grounds for sea turtles, while most of the northern and southern coasts consists of mangrove islands and coral reefs that lie within the boundaries of the Parque Nacional Marino Isla Bastimentos.

The main settlement on Bastimentos is Old Bank. It has a prominent West Indian population whose origins are in the banana industry. The island is also home to the Ngöbe-Buglé village of Quebrada Sal (Salt Creek).

Sights

Old Bank

Located on the western tip of the island, Old Bank (also called Bastimentos town) is a small enclave of 1500 residents of West Indian descent. Until the 1990s most of the adults in Old Bank traveled daily to Changuinola to work in banana fields; today, residents have taken to fishing or farming small plots. Some work in the burgeoning tourism industry.

Although Old Bank is very poor and devoid of any real sights, it has a pronounced Caribbean vibe, and it's a relaxing place to stroll around and soak up the atmosphere. It's also the best place in Bocas del Toro to hear Gali-Gali, a hybrid language of Jamaican English and Spanish with elements of the Guaymí language spoken by the Ngöbe-Buglé.

There are no roads, just a wide, concrete footpath lined on both sides with colorfully painted wooden houses.

Parque Nacional Marino Isla Bastimentos

Established in 1988, this 132-sq-km **marine park** (Map p186) was Panama's first. Protecting 130 islands of the Bocas del Toro archipelago, including the coral-fringed Cayos Zapatillas, and the wetlands in the center of Isla Bastimentos, the marine park is an important nature reserve for mangroves, monkeys, sloths, caimans, crocodiles and 28 species of amphibians and reptiles.

Get up-to-date park information from the ATP (p195) or Ministerio de Ambiente (p195) offices in Bocas del Toro town. To camp out anywhere in the park, you are required to first obtain a permit (US$10) from the latter.

Nivida Bat Cave CAVE

(Bahía Honda; Map p186; US$5) One of Bastimentos' most fascinating natural wonders, Nivida is a massive cavern with swarms of nectar bats and a subterranean lake. The cave lies within the borders of the Parque Nacional Marino Isla Bastimentos and half the fun is getting here. But it's next to impossible to do it on your own. An organized tour from Old Bank costs US$45 per person.

The tour involves a 25-minute boat ride from Old Bank to the channel entrance. You'll then spend a similar amount of time gliding though mangroves and lush vegetation. From the dock it's then a half-hour hike to the cave. Wear sturdy shoes or boots; you will be provided with headlamps at the cave entrance.

Around the Island

Red Frog Beach BEACH

(Map p186; US$5) Small but perfectly formed, Red Frog Beach is named after the *rana rojo* (strawberry poison-dart frog), an amphibian you're most unlikely to encounter here due to development, local kids trapping them to impress tourists, and a tidal wave of day-trippers in season. From Bocas town, water taxis (US$7) head to the public dock next to a small marina on the south side of the island, from where the beach is an easy 15-minute walk.

Playa Larga BEACH

(Long Beach; Map p186) This 6km-long beach on the southeast side of the island falls under the protection of the marine park. Hawksbill, leatherback and green sea turtles nest here from March to September. It's also good for surfing. To get here, you can follow the path past Red Frog Beach, but the best access is the one-hour walk with a guide from Salt Creek.

Playa Polo BEACH

(Map p186) Polo Beach wraps around a sheltered cove and is protected by a reef. It has good snorkeling. Can be reached by short hike from Red Frog Beach.

Wizard Beach BEACH

(Playa Primera; Map p186) The most beautiful beach on Isla Bastimentos is awash in powdery yellow sand and backed by thick vine-strewn jungle. It's connected to Old Bank via a wilderness path, which normally takes 20 minutes or so but can be virtually impassable after heavy rains. The path continues along the coast to Playa Segunda (Second Beach) and Red Frog Beach.

Quebrada Sal (Salt Creek)

The Ngöbe-Buglé village of Quebrada Sal (Salt Creek) is on the southeastern side of the island. Reached via a long canal cut through the mangrove forest, it is home to 750 people, 60-odd houses, an elementary school, a handicrafts store, a general store and a soccer field. The community largely depends on fishing and subsistence farming, travels mostly by canoe, and resides in wooden, thatched-roof huts without electricity or running water.

The Quebrada Sal is slowly modernizing and villagers are friendly and open to visitors, especially if you can speak Spanish. Water taxis can drop you off at the concrete dock near the entrance to the village where you'll need to pay a US$2 entry fee and sign the visitors' book.

If you have the time, it's worth hiring a local guide to walk with you along the roughly one-hour cross-island trail to Playa Larga (US$20 per person); shorter pelican- and caiman-spotting tours are also available, costing US$12 and US$7 respectively.

Activities & Tours

Scuba 6 Ecodiving DIVING

(Map p186; 6722-5245; www.scuba6ecodiving.com; Old Bank; 2-tank dive $95; 8am-8pm) A PADI five-star resort, this scuba-diving agency makes it a priority to educate about the marine environment and operates with a Leave No Trace ethic. Instructors speak English, Spanish and French and have Blue and Green Fin certifications. The office is located in Tío Tom's Guesthouse.

★Up in the Hill TOURS

(Map p186; 6570-8277, 6607-8962; www.upinthehill.com; Old Bank; 2hr tour & tasting US$25) It's worth the hot 20-minute haul up to this organic farm at the highest point on Isla Bastimentos to see a permaculture project with chocolate groves and many exotic fruits. Linger at the wonderful cafe serving all-day breakfast, chocolate with coconut milk and delectable baked goods. There's also coffee from Boquete, golden milk with fresh turmeric, and homemade hibiscus tea.

The on-site shop has its own lauded line of coconut-based natural body products. You can hang with the sloths and anteaters by staying over in one of two rustic two- to three-person cabins (US$70) with kitchens. To reach Up in the Hill, head right from the dock in Old Bank and go straight up the hill from the park.

Bastimentos Alive ADVENTURE

(Map p186; 6514-7961; www.bastimentosalive.com; Old Bank; trek incl lunch US$45; 8am-8pm Mon-Sat) Led by Tom, a young Dutchman, this well-regarded tour operator leads daily treks through the jungle, with stops at Red Frog Beach and lunch on Polo Beach. It also offers full-day excursions to Cayo Zapatilla for snorkeling, with lunch. Tours to Nivida bat cave and Laguna de Bastimentos are in the works. Trips depart from the Bastimentos Alive office.

Bastimentos Sky Zipline Canopy Tour ADVENTURE

(Map p186; 836-5501, 6987-8661; http://redfrogbeach.com/bocas-del-toro-zipline; per person US$55; 10am, 1pm & 3:30pm) Seven ziplines, a swaying sky bridge and a vertical rappel are highlights of this attraction, brought to you by a well-known Costa Rican zipline designer, in the hills just south of Red Frog Beach. Tours last two hours.

Festivals & Events

Día de Bastimentos FIESTA

(23 Nov) Bastimentos Day is celebrated with a huge parade in Old Bank and drumming demonstrations on the island.

Sleeping

Though most of the action is in Bocas del Toro town, the largely rustic digs in Old Bank offer a laid-back, Caribbean atmosphere. Lodgings outside of town, especially to the south, are mostly resorts, some quite high-end, and usually include transfers from Bocas town in their rates.

Tío Tom's Guesthouse GUESTHOUSE $

(Map p186; 6951-6615; www.tiotomsguesthouse.com; Old Bank; dm US$25-30, 2-person bungalow US$35;) This rickety wooden guesthouse perched over the sea has been offering cheap, clean and unfussy rooms for years. A highlight is the waterfront deck strewn with hammocks. There are rooms for two or three people and a separate bungalow; all have private bathrooms. The German owner offers pizza in the afternoons. Breakfast with farm eggs and fresh bread is extra.

There's also a dive school on-site with sustainable dive practices.

★Palmar Tent Lodge CAMPGROUND $$
(Map p186; ☎838-8552; www.palmartentlodge.com; Red Frog Beach; dm US$23, d/tr tents from US$90/110, 2-person bungalows from US$220) On the edge of the jungle and facing celebrated Red Frog Beach (p202), Palmar has introduced glamping to Bocas del Toro to unanimous acclaim. Accommodations are in solar-powered circular tents for two to three, with all the comforts (including large lock boxes for valuables), wooden dorms, or a luxurious two-story thatched 'jungalow' for two. Guests 12 years and up are welcome.

The huge open-sided restaurant-bar is the place to be most nights (and days, come to think of it). The fun and well-informed owners, two friends from Washington, DC, offer a laundry list of tours and excursions and there are yoga classes (US$6) twice daily onsite. Water-taxi shuttles, included with your reservation, link the lodge with Bocas town twice a day. No internet.

Eclypse del Mar CABIN $$
(Map p186; ☎6611-4581; www.eclypsedemar.com; Old Bank; d US$110, 4-person bungalows incl breakfast US$250-300; ⌚closed Jun; 📶) These stylish over-the-water bungalows offer a charming retreat right on the fringe of Old Bank. Their boardwalks lead straight into a mangrove reserve where you can spy on sloths and caimans. Each wooden house features canopy beds, cheerful pillows and even a floor window with fish flitting by. The onsite cafe serves seafood and good pub grub.

There's kayaks for guest use. Come and go via water taxi.

Firefly B&B $$
(Map p186; ☎6524-4809; www.thefireflybocasdeltoro.com; Old Bank; incl breakfast d US$120-140, bungalow US$175) With simple but sweet Caribbean style, these wood-slatted rooms facing rough surf offer an idyllic retreat on the far end of Old Bank. Doubles and two-person bungalows come in cheerful seafoam tones with canopy beds and fans. The onsite restaurant is a huge draw. With on-site yoga twice a week.

Los Secretos Guesthouse GUESTHOUSE $$
(Map p186; ☎6795-6355; https://lossecretosguesthouse.wordpress.com; western Isla Bastimentos; d US$130; ⌚closed Jun & Jul; ❄📶🏊) This pretty pink-and-green Caribbean-style home sits high on a forested hill. It's a hike up the stairs from the dock, but you'll find five rooms with hardwood floors, balconies and modern comforts. Run by Frenchman Xavier and his mother, the hotel has a good restaurant too, with healthy options. Two-night minimum.

The lovely swimming pool and *rancho* are located by the dock. There's snorkeling equipment and kayaks to use, and a complimentary half-hour guided tour of the surrounding forest, which is full of sloths, monkeys and birds. A water taxi costs US$10 one way from Bocas Town.

Selina Red Frog HOTEL $$
(Map p186; ☎800-7354; www.selina.com/red-frog; Red Frog; dm US$16, r US$79-119; ❄📶🏊) Located amid the foliage on the way to the beach, this chain budget resort manifests in Red Frog in a huge hotel, with options ranging from 11-bed dorms to standard rooms, easily upstaged by its all-wood deluxe upgrades with sliding glass doors and decks. Includes a beach bar, a swimming pool and a kitchen, and has activities such as surfing and yoga on offer.

★Tranquilo Bay RESORT $$$
(☎838-0021; www.tranquilobay.com; southern Isla Bastimentos; per person incl 3 meals & activities US$225; ❄@📶) 🍃 The oldest and most remote resort on Isla Bastimentos, this family-friendly North American–run lodge creates a fantastic environment for play and relaxation. Grounds feature nine comfortable cabins with orthopedic beds, fine linens and locally crafted hardwood furnishings. Tailored excursions run by biologist guides include wildlife-watching (there's a 63ft birdwatching tower and 200 species onsite). Also perfect for just beaching it.

Cabins either face the water or sit in the jungle. Guests dine at the main lodge (alcohol included; special diets catered for) with a wraparound porch and ocean views. The lodge composts, captures rainwater, uses a minimum of plastics and educates staff on water usage. Created on around 80 hectares of conservation land, Tranquilo Bay also works with local scientists and conservation agencies and does not print marketing material. Transportation is US$100 per person, round trip, with travel days on Wednesday and Saturday. Three-night minimum stay, with kids half-off.

★Casa Cayuco RESORT $$$
(Map p186; ☎USA 1-313-355-6692; www.casacayuco.com; southern Isla Bastimentos; s/d incl 3 meals & wine from US$235/305;) This beachfront retreat combines nature with modern conveniences. It's off-grid and jungle-chic, with sweeping views from lofty suites in the post-and-beam hardwood lodge, and jungle cabins by the water. *Table d'hote* meals (wine included) eaten on the dock are a big deal to the foodie owners from Detroit; lobsters and octopus come from nearby waters. There's also yoga retreats.

Kayaks and snorkel gear are included to explore the nearby reefs, mangroves and rivers. Guided excursions run extra but include unique offerings such as in-depth tours of the nearby indigenous village of Quebrada Sal (Salt Creek). The resort runs on solar power and collected rainwater. It's located on the white-sand beach of Punta Vieja, with some of the best tranquil swimming around. Minimum stay three nights. It's 30 minutes by boat to Bocas town; transfers are included.

★La Loma LODGE $$$
(Map p186; ☎6619-5364, 6592-5162; www.thejunglelodge.com; western Isla Bastimentos; r per person incl 3 meals & activities US$120-130) Integrated into a 23-hectare rainforest and its community, this 'jungle lodge and chocolate farm' offers tasteful stays to consistently rave reviews. The location is hidden in mangroves, accessed by boat. A steep hill leads past a rushing creek to four sedate, ultra-private cabins with hand-carved beds. Each has a propane-fuelled, rainwater-fed bathroom, a mosquito net and solar-powered energy system.

One cabin is by a rock pool; two are in the treetops (we love No 2 and its views). Meals include fresh-baked bread and organic vegetables grown on the farm. Two-hour tours are included in the price. Guests and nonguests can reserve a chocolate tour (US$15), farm-to-table lunch or dinner (US$15 to US$25) or take a chocolate cooking course. La Loma distributes a number of beautifully illustrated pamphlets to guide guests through the jungle and to help you appreciate its wildlife and medicinal plants.

It also works with volunteers to help teach English to local children.

Residencia Al Natural VILLA $$$
(Map p186; ☎757-9004; www.alnaturalresort.com; Punta Vieja; 1-/3-bedroom apt incl transfer & 3 meals US$400/600;) Fans of Al Natural Resort who prefer conventional lodgings can book spacious lofts in this gorgeous hardwood villa further down the beach. There's screens, air-conditioning and wi-fi, rarities in these parts, as well as decks and hammock areas. Guest can choose to participate in Al Natural's social life at will or add on tours. It's ideal for families.

Sea Monkey LODGE $$$
(Map p186; ☎6693-9168; www.seamonkeybocasdeltoro.com; Old Bank; d incl breakfast US$150-200;) Run by an American couple, the bungalows at this luxury B&B hover over the gin-clear water at the far end of Old Bank harbor. Enormous fan-cooled rooms accommodating three or four people sit 30m from shore, with hand-hewn king-sized beds, high-quality mattresses and fridges. A glass wall with private hammock decks beyond affords uninterrupted sea views.

Red Frog Bungalows CABIN $$$
(Map p186; ☎6539-5151; www.redfrogbungalows.com; Red Frog Beach; s/d incl 2 meals & transport from US$190/320;) Set in the sheltering jungle, the original Red Frog Beach (p202) resort has accommodation in a three-bedroom stilted house meters from the beach; two fabulous bungalows under palms imported from Bali; and a bizarre 'tentalow' – a colorful canvas safari tent with thatched roof. The clubhouse has a games room, a wide-screen TV, a library and a hot tub.

The owner leads surf tours (US$100 for two). On the clubhouse walls are broken boards owned (and broken) by visiting word-title holders Kelly Slater and Dusty Payne, among others. On the beach are *palalapas* – open-sided thatched lounging huts for guest use. Price includes transfers to and from Bocas del Toro airport.

Al Natural Resort RESORT $$$
(Map p186; ☎6576-8605, 757-9004; www.alnaturalresort.com; southern Isla Bastimentos; d incl 3 meals from US$220; closed Jun & Jul) This relaxed desert-island hideaway lends a bohemian twist to all-inclusive. If you love nature, it's sublime. Based on traditional Ngöbe-Buglé architecture, the seven driftwood-and-palm bungalows have an open design that delivers sea views – even from some toilets – and good swimming in tranquil waters. The hosts are uncommonly

gracious, and the meals (including wine) are well prepared by the Belgian owner Vincent.

The center of the action is the two-story restaurant and bar with a chilled-out upstairs game room. On-site, there's Bocas' only remotely located dive operator (two-tank dives US$120), and the resort loans kayaks to paddle out to choice snorkel spots. The fourth night is half-price and the seventh free. Militantly internet-free.

They also have an excellent small on-the-water lodging in Bocas town, ideal if you arrive too late to transfer.

Eating

Chavela SEAFOOD **$**

(Map p186; ☎6246-5193; www.facebook.com/barrestaurantechavela; Old Bank; mains US$4-12; ⏰6-10pm) In an attractive little lime-green shack at the bottom of the landmark Hostel Bastimentos, a Panamanian-American couple serve cheap-as-chips burgers but emphasize seafood in all its guises, from *ceviche de pulpo* (octopus cured in lime juice) and fish tacos to barracuda steak. Locals say it's the best eats in town.

Nacho Mama's TEX-MEX **$**

(Map p186; ☎6539-5151; Red Frog Beach; tacos US$5-7, with drink US$12; ⏰11am-5pm Tue-Sun) Pitched on the shifting sands of Red Frog Beach (p202), this one-hit wonder does a thriving business dispensing tacos with fish, shrimp, *ceviche* and chicken throughout the day. But never on a Monday. And never nachos.

★ **Firefly Restaurant** FUSION **$$**

(Map p186; ☎6524-4809; www.thefireflybocasdeltoro.com; Old Bank; mains US$8-15; ⏰5-9pm Wed-Mon; 🖉) A clutch of open-air tables facing rough surf, this reservation-only restaurant is the perfect sunset date. An American chef cooks up local and organic ingredients in Thai and Caribbean preparations. Think sweet chili calamari, coconut gnocchi and fresh seafood curries. The tapas menu allows you to sample a range of flavors.

If taking a water taxi, ask to be dropped off at Cholo's dock, a five-minute walk away.

Sea Monkey FUSION **$$**

(Map p186; ☎6693-9168; Old Bank; mains US$13-16; ⏰8am-11am & 5-10pm Mon-Sat) In a simple over-the-water clapboard house, this breezy little restaurant churns out wonderful plates of Asian beer fish and local patuk greens with handmade cocktails (from US$5). Perfect for a sundowner. Moreover, the end-of-the-pier location provides a bit of peace and quiet in raucous Old Bank.

Coco Hill VEGETARIAN **$$**

(Map p186; ☎6826-6485; Old Bank; dishes US$7.50-16; ⏰10am-10pm Wed-Mon; 🖉) Close to the island's highest point, Australian Michelle concocts some pretty exotic meatless dishes at her vegetarian, vegan and gluten-free restaurant and bar. Unfortunately it can be closed without warning and it's a long hike in. The blackboard menu changes daily. Cocktails are made with fresh fruit juices.

Information

In the past there have been reports of muggings on the trail between Old Bank and Red Frog Beach. After a rape and fatal attack in 2017, police have stepped up their presence and the area is considered safe. Still, travelers should not hike alone or go on any trail after dark. Carry only essentials such as a towel and water – never valuables.

Getting There & Away

A water taxi from Bocas to Old Bank costs US$5; US$8 to the public dock for Red Frog Beach. From Old Bank to Isla Solarte it's US$5. You'll pay from US$10 to US$25 one way to locations further south on the island from Old Bank.

MAINLAND

POP 143,480

The mainland jungles of Bocas del Toro Province teem with wildlife and are pocketed with remote indigenous villages – the contrast with the archipelago could not be greater. Here you'll also find the province's biggest towns and cities.

Almirante

POP 12,730

A clutch of stilted homes on the water, this unkempt village has seen better days, but it remains the springboard for the Archipiélago de Bocas del Toro, so it's always busy.

About 20km south of Almirante down a steep dirt track from the coastal highway, **La Escapada** (☎6618-6106; www.laescapada.net; Hwy 11, Km48.5; d incl breakfast US$120-140; 🅿❄) has four comfortable though sparse rooms with large screened porches. A deteriorating boardwalk though the mangroves leads to decks over the water and a restaurant with lovely views to Isla San Cristóbal. The welcoming owners from Florida, USA, can organize fishing and boating trips.

Getting There & Away

Taxi 25 (p195) runs a water shuttle to Bocas town (US$6, 30 minutes); a taxi between the bus terminal and the dock should cost no more than US$1.

An air-conditioned bus to Changuinola (US$1.45) leaves every 15 minutes between 6am and 8pm and takes 45 minutes. Taxis to Changuinola (from US$20) can be bargained, particularly if you start your walk from the dock to the bus terminal.

Changuinola

POP 42,000

Headquarters of the Chiriquí Land Company, the company that produces Chiquita bananas, Changuinola is a hot and rather dusty town surrounded by a sea of banana plantations. Although there is little reason to spend any time here, overland travelers linking to Costa Rica will have to pass through. Changuinola also serves as the access point for the Humedal de San San Pond Sak and the Parque Internacional La Amistad. Av 17 de Abril (also called Av Central) runs north to south and serves as the town's main artery.

Sights

Snyder (Changuinola) Canal CANAL

In 1903 a 12km-long canal connecting the Río Changuinola and Almirante Bay was dug parallel to the Caribbean shoreline to facilitate the barging of bananas from the fields of the Bocas del Toro archipelago to ships. Abandoned years ago, the 30m-wide channel is now an amazing spot to view wildlife. It's about 5km east of Changuinola (taxi one way US$3).

Sleeping & Eating

Hotel Plaza Changuinola HOTEL $

(758-6168; hotelplazachanguinola@gmail.com; r US$50;) This relatively modern hotel in a shopping plaza offers rooms with flat-screen TVs, though not all feature an exterior window. At least there's a variety of restaurant and supermarket options right there.

Hotel Alhambra HOTEL $

(758-9819; Av 17 de Abril; s/d US$33/38; P) This 33-room place above a shopping center is a good-value stay, though you can expect dated bathrooms with showers with a spigot and room-temperature water. Reception is on the 1st floor. It's right at the southern end of the main drag leading out of town.

Hotel Golden Sahara HOTEL $

(758-7908; hotelgolden_sahara@hotmail.com; Av 17 de Abril; s/d US$32/42;) This big family-run place has 28 rooms, but make sure to choose one in the back as those on the main street near the central bus station are noisy. Friendly place.

La Fortuna CHINESE $

(758-9395; Av 17 de Abril; mains US$8-13; 11:30am-10:30pm) Should you need a fix of rice and noodles, La Fortuna, diagonally opposite from the Urraca bus terminal, can oblige.

BUSES FROM CHANGUINOLA

DESTINATION	COST (US$)	DURATION (HR)	FREQUENCY (DAILY)
Almirante (with boat connections to Isla Colón)	1.45	¾	every 30min
Altos del Valle (Bosque Protector de Palo Seco)	7.25	2¼	every 30min
David	9.70	4¾	every 30min
El Silencio (Parque Internacional La Amistad)	1.25	½	every 20min
Guabito-Sixaola	1.25	½	every 30min
Las Tablas (Las Delicias)	2	1½	hourly
Panama City	29	12	7am
San José (Costa Rica)	16	6	10am

Restaurante Ebony CARIBBEAN $$
(☎6506-8402; Av 17 de Abril; mains US$10-16; ⊙noon-11pm) More expensive than your typical Changuinola restaurant, but loaded with atmosphere, this Afro-Caribbean restaurant at the southern end of the main street serves up creole dishes (shrimp with coconut, rice and peas, ackee and salt fish). Carved birds and portraits of black icons Malcolm X, Bob Marley and US president Barack Obama adorn the walls.

Information

Banco Nacional de Panamá (☎758-8136; Av 17 de Abri; ⊙8am-3pm Mon-Fri, 9am-noon Sat) has a branch with an ATM on the main street.

The **Ministerio de Ambiente office** (Ministerio de Ambiente de Panamá; ☎758-6603; Comunidad Suiche 4; ⊙8am-4pm Mon-Fri), west of Av 17 de Abril, should be able to provide information on national parks and some indigenous tourism projects in the province, though service is lax.

Getting There & Away

AIR

From Panama City, **Air Panama** (☎316-9088; www.airpanama.com) flies to Changuinola (US$136 one way) up to twice a day on weekdays and once daily on weekends. Taxis between the Changuinola airport and the center should cost about US$3.

BUS

Buses for Costa Rica leave from the terminal just south of the Delta gas station. Other buses depart from **Terminal Urraca** (☎758-8115) between 6am and 7pm.

TAXI

A taxi seating five people from Changuinola to the Costa Rican border at Guabito costs US$7.50 and takes about a half-hour.

Humedal de San San Pond Sak

If you want to get far from other travelers without a huge detour, check out these wetlands just 5km north of Changuinola. In an area of 160 sq km, you can find an incredible variety of tropical fauna. San San Pond Sak is best known for its turtle conservation, a worthwhile initiative to visit. But it's also home to sloths, river otters, monkeys, caimans, iguanas, sea turtles, poison-dart frogs and the elusive manatee.

Five-hour tours of the wetlands are arranged by **Aamvecona** (Association of Friends & Neighbors of the Coast & its Environment; ☎6679-7238; www.aamvecona.com), a conservation organization of mostly volunteers working in close conjunction with the Ministry of the Environment. Tours leave from the road bridge over the Río San San, 6km north of Changuinola. Get here on the bus bound for Guabito–Sixaola on the Costa Rican border. Tours are priced for groups of two.

There's a visitor center at the beach at the mouth of the Río San San that has displays on wildlife as well as a manatee-viewing area.

Although it's possible to visit the wetlands on a day trip from Changuinola, the best way to appreciate the area is to stay overnight. Located inside the park on a stunning wilderness beach is a rustic **house** (r per person US$10) on stilts, which has three simple rooms, cold-water showers, a flush toilet (fed by rainwater) and a cooking area.

Bring your own sleeping bag or blanket – bedding is not provided. Economical meals are available, or you can bring food and drink. You will also want to bring a mosquito net and bug spray, as the sand fleas and mosquitoes show no mercy.

GETTING TO COSTA RICA

The border post at Guabito–Sixaola (open 8am to 5pm), 16km northwest of Changuinola, is a less frequented crossing than others to and from Chiriquí Province, and most travelers find it hassle-free. Buses from Changuinola depart frequently for the border (US$1.25, 20 minutes, every half-hour) from 6am to 7pm. On the Costa Rican side of the border, you can catch regular buses on to Puerto Limón and San José, as well as regional destinations.

Note that you can be asked for an onward ticket if you are entering Costa Rica. If you do not possess one, it is acceptable to buy a round-trip bus ticket back to Panama. Also note that Costa Rica is one hour behind Panama.

TURTLE PATROL IN SAN SAN POND SAK

There are only eight sea-turtle species in the world and half of those can be found nesting in the Archipiélago de Bocas del Toro, primarily on the long beaches of the northern coast of Isla Bastimentos. The loggerheads appear from April or May, the leatherbacks in March and the hawksbills and greens from July to September.

Sea turtles leave the water only to lay their eggs. Two months after the eggs are laid, the hatchlings break loose from their shells, leave their sandy nests and enter the sea – if they are not stolen or first eaten by raccoons, birds or dogs.

Human predators and the encroachment of development may be their greatest obstacle. Throughout Panama, many communities still eat turtles and their eggs, greatly contributing to turtles' dwindling populations.

The community-based organization Aamvecona, based in the Humedal de San San Pond Sak, is working toward turtle preservation, with projects active between February and July. It accepts volunteers on turtle-nesting and hatching projects, and also offers nature tours.

Getting There & Away

Reach the Humedal de San San Pond Sak on the Guabito–Sixaola bus (US$1), which leaves every 30 minutes from Changuinola. A taxi can charge up to US$10.

Parque Internacional La Amistad (Wekso)

The 4000-sq-km Parque Internacional La Amistad was established jointly in 1988 by Panama and Costa Rica – hence its name of 'Friendship Park.' In 1990 it was declared a Unesco World Heritage Site and later became part of the greater Mesoamerican Biological Corridor. In Panama the park covers part of Chiriquí and Bocas del Toro Provinces, contains seven of the 12 classified life zones, and encompasses prolific endangered flora and fauna.

La Amistad is also home to three indigenous groups: the Naso (or Teribe), the Bribrí and the Ngöbe-Buglé. Although living traditional ways of life, these groups are dwindling fast under outside influences. In an effort to preserve their identity and provide income, the Naso created an ecological center at Wekso, the former site of the infamous US-run Pana-Jungla survival school. Today, more travelers are discovering the beauty of both the rugged wilderness of La Amistad and the Nasos' ancestral culture.

History

According to Spanish colonial records, the Naso were present in mainland Bocas del Toro when the first explorers arrived in the early 16th century. The Spaniards referred to the Naso as the Teribe, or the Tjër Di (Grandmother Water) in Naso, which is the guiding spirit that forms the backbone of their religious beliefs. The Spaniards gradually pushed the Naso off their lands, driving the population into exile in the highlands near the Costa Rican border.

Although the establishment of the modern Panamanian state has enabled the Naso to return to their ancestral home, their survival is threatened by the lack of their own *comarca* (autonomous region). This scenario contrasts with other Panamanian indigenous population groups such as the Guna, the Emberá, the Wounaan and the neighboring Ngöbe-Buglé. The plight of the Naso is amplified by the fact that the tremendous ecotourism potential in Parque Internacional La Amistad is at odds with a massive hydroelectric project planned in the region. Although proposals for establishing a *comarca* are on the table, in true Panamanian form, progress is being held up by bureaucracy.

The Naso population today is estimated at 3500, the majority of whom live in 11 communities along the Río Teribe and survive as subsistence farmers. Although they remained virtually autonomous for generations, the Naso have recently started losing their cultural self-sufficiency due to missionary activity, land encroachment and youth migration. Today, most Naso are bilingual (Naso and Spanish), wear Western-style clothing and practice some form of Christianity. However, strong elements of ancestral Naso culture remain, and they are one of the few remaining indigenous groups in the Americas to retain their traditional monarchy.

Sights

Before the US invasion of Panama in 1989, Wekso was named Pana-Jungla, and served as a US-run survival school that trained Panamanian and international troops in jungle warfare. Although it was disbanded in 1990 following the ousting of General Noriega, the **ruins** of the old structures remain scattered around the Wekso grounds. Highlights include the barracks, mess hall, chapel, armory and serpentarium.

Activities

Although most of Parque Internacional La Amistad is inaccessible, the park is home to a recorded 90 mammal species (including six cat species) and more than 450 bird species (including resplendent quetzals and harpy eagles).

Visitors can hire local guides for about US$30. A 3.5km loop trail at Wekso, for example, cuts through secondary and virgin rainforest, with good opportunities for wildlife-watching. You can also take a dip in the river, though be careful of the current. A network of trails links various Naso communities together, though it's best to tackle these with a guide.

For the more ambitious, from Wekso it's a five-hour hike into the Parque Internacional La Amistad. The Caribbean side of La Amistad is much less developed than the Pacific side. You will need to hire the services of local boaters and guides, and you must be completely self-sufficient. The terrain is extremely rugged; it's without hiking trails, and the river rages during the rainy season. If you're prepared for a serious trek, you're almost certain to have an adventure.

Sleeping & Eating

Permits to camp in the park are payable at the ranger station.

Posada Media Luna HOSTEL $
(☎6343-5496, Whats App 6874-4530; www.ocen.bocasdeltoro.org; Bonyic; per person US$18, 3 meals US$15) The welcome of this women's co-op could not be warmer. They have built a handsome wooden hostel in the village of Bonyic on the Río Teribe. Accommodations are basic but clean. Try traditional food with vegetarian options and bring drinking water. There are excellent tours to medicinal gardens, a waterfall, neighboring villages accessed by raft and Parque Internacional La Amistad (from US$30).

A stay here is well worth the effort and proceeds go to needed funding to help sustain the village. There are solar lights but no electricity. Tours, running from US$30, are priced for three participants. The hostel is run by run by OMUB (Organización de Mujeres Unidades de Bonyic), an association of indigenous women, whose Whats App contact is the very friendly and responsive Nilka.

Odesen Wekso Lodge CABIN $
(☎6695-6419, 6574-9874; www.odesen.bocasdeltoro.org; per person US$20, 3 meals US$14) Run by Odesen, the first Naso community organization based at Wekso, this guest lodge has a handful of very basic rooms, with a secure water supply, flush toilets and an outdoor shower. It's staffed by community members who prepare meals, lead guided jungle tours and can explain about Naso culture and history.

Guided walks are charged by group (US$20) with river transportation extra.

ADVENTURE IN NASO COUNTRY

On the border of Parque Internacional La Amistad and a proposed Naso *comarca* (autonomous region), **Soposo Rainforest Adventures** (☎6875-8125; www.soposo.com; Soposo; day tour per person US$90, 2-/3-day package incl lodging, meals & tours US$140/275) is a unique jungle lodging and sustainable tour operator, and a recommended step off the well-worn trail. Guests stay in stilted thatched huts, eat traditional foods and immerse themselves in Naso culture. Tours may include community visits, camping trips, birdwatching and manatee viewing.

The project, spearheaded by an ex–Peace Corps volunteer and her Naso husband, has been lauded by travelers. It was created to offer the Naso people an alternative income, bolster cultural self-esteem and protect natural resources in the face of a massive hydroelectric project, which is changing the nature of the area. A highlight is a three-day trip up the Río Teribe to the village of the Naso monarch.

From Changuinola, it's a 30-minute taxi ride to the village of El Silencio, from where there's river access to the lodging.

Information

Bocas del Toro Community Tourism Network (6480-5601; www.redtucombo.bocasdeltoro.org) can organize visits to Naso communities.

Contact Edwin to visit **Odesen** (Organization for the Sustainable Development of Naso Ecotourism; 6569-2844, 6574-9874, 6695-6419; www.odesen.bocasdeltoro.org) in Wekso by the Parque Internacional La Amistad. It's accessible only by boat.

Getting There & Away

The Naso communities at Wekso and Bonyik are upriver from the hamlet of El Silencio, connected by bus from Changuinola (US$1.25, 30 minutes, every 20 minutes). From El Silencio, take a bus that runs hourly to Bonyic (US$2) or a taxi (US$25). It's a short boat ride across the river to Wekso (US$2 to US$4).

In El Silencio you can opt to hire a six-person boat up the Río Teribe for around US$70 or a *balsa* (wooden raft, US$30) for the downstream return. You will pass hills blanketed with rainforest and intermittent waterfalls. The backdrop is the glorious Talamanca range and the jungle comes all the way down to the river water. After about 45 minutes on the river, a sign on the right bank announces your arrival at Wekso.

Las Delicias

Set in rainforest hills, the small indigenous community of Las Delicias lies along the Río Sixaola, 20km from the Costa Rican border crossing at Guabito. The community has shifted its income source from harvesting and logging to preservation and ecotourism. Visiting is one way you can make a positive contribution.

Attractions include waterfalls, abundant wildlife and impressive viewpoints over the Sixaola river valley and the Talamanca mountains. On a day trip, you can boat the Ríos Sixaola and Yorkín, hike through rainforest or go horseback riding.

Sleeping & Eating

Accommodation is undeveloped in these areas, and there's no electricity, so bring your own supplies, especially a water purifier, flashlight (torch), mosquito net and bug repellent. Prices are quite reasonable (from US$20 to US$30 per person).

El Guabo Cabins CABIN $

(6211-9856; per person US$20) These rustic cabins in El Guabo on the Río Yorkin are run by indigenous women who form a group called Alakolpa (Association of Women Protecting the Forest). There's a shower and toilet but no electricity. Hardy travelers can string up a hammock or pitch a tent at one of the *ranchos*.

Information

Make arrangements to visit Las Delicias through Changuinola's Ministerio de Ambiente (p208) office.

Getting There & Away

To reach the community, take a bus from Changuinola to Las Tablas (US$2, 1½ hours, hourly) and then a taxi to Las Delicias (US$10). You can also negotiate a price with one of the 4WD taxis in Changuinola. From here, boats ply the Ríos Sixaoloa and Yorkin.

Bosque Protector de Palo Seco

Set high up in the Talamanca range, the 1675-sq-km Bosque Protector de Palo Seco is a lush cloud forest home to monkeys, sloths, armadillos, butterflies, tarantulas and eyelash vipers. Birdwatching is superb – keep an eye out for rarities such as the lanceolated monklet, rufous-tailed jacamar, dull-mantled antbird and speckled tanager. The ashy-throated bush tanager is unique to this area.

The reserve was created in 1983 to serve as a conservation corridor linking La Fortuna Forest Reserve and Parque Internacional La Amistad.

Obtain information about current hiking conditions at the Ministerio de Ambiente station at the entrance. There are three trails in the park, each about 45 minutes in duration, allowing visitors the chance to get a taste of the region's natural wonders.

Getting There & Away

The entrance to the reserve and the Ministerio de Ambiente station is about 30km south of Chiriquí Grande on Hwy 4, the road over the continental divide to David (also called the Fortuna Rd).

From David, take any bus heading toward Changuinola. Ask to stop just before Altos del Valle and disembark at Km68.5, which is right by the Ministerio de Ambiente station. From Bosque Protector de Palo Seco, buses pass every 30 minutes heading north to Changuinola (US$7.25, 2¼ hours) or south to David (US$5, 2½ hours).

Colón Province

POP 285,430 / ELEV SEA LEVEL TO 979M

Includes ➡

Best Places to Eat

- El Bar de Pupy (p226)
- Restaurante Las Anclas (p223)
- El Fin del Mundo (p226)
- El Palenque (p224)

Best Places to Stay

- Meliá Panamá Canal (p218)
- La Morada de la Bruja (p223)
- Hotel Sister Moon (p226)
- Casa Congo (p223)
- Macondo Hostel (p225)

Why Go?

Colón Province is much, much more than its run-down capital. Think pristine beaches and lowland rainforests, colonial splendor and the modern engineering marvel of the Panama Canal. Portobelo, with its growing music and art scene, shows the best of the vibrant culture of the Congos, descendants of African slaves who have preserved the legacy of their ancestors, while the train trip between Panama City and Colón remains one of the greatest rail journeys in the Americas.

The region's incredible history encompasses the earliest European explorers. During the colonial era, these coastal cities ranked among the world's richest; their gold and silver stores enticed everyone from English privateer Sir Francis Drake to Admiral Edward Vernon. Today the fallen fortresses and cannons embedded in the coral reefs recall the fallen Spanish empire.

When to Go

Dec–Apr The dry season is a great time for snorkeling or diving for Caribbean treasure, as visibility is at its best. It's high season for lodging and beaches fill up.

Oct Pilgrims from all over Panama set out walking weeks ahead to attend the Black Christ Festival, an enormous event with masses and street celebrations held in October in Portobelo.

May–Jul The summer months of May through July are a relatively good time to visit, with some rain showers and off-season prices.

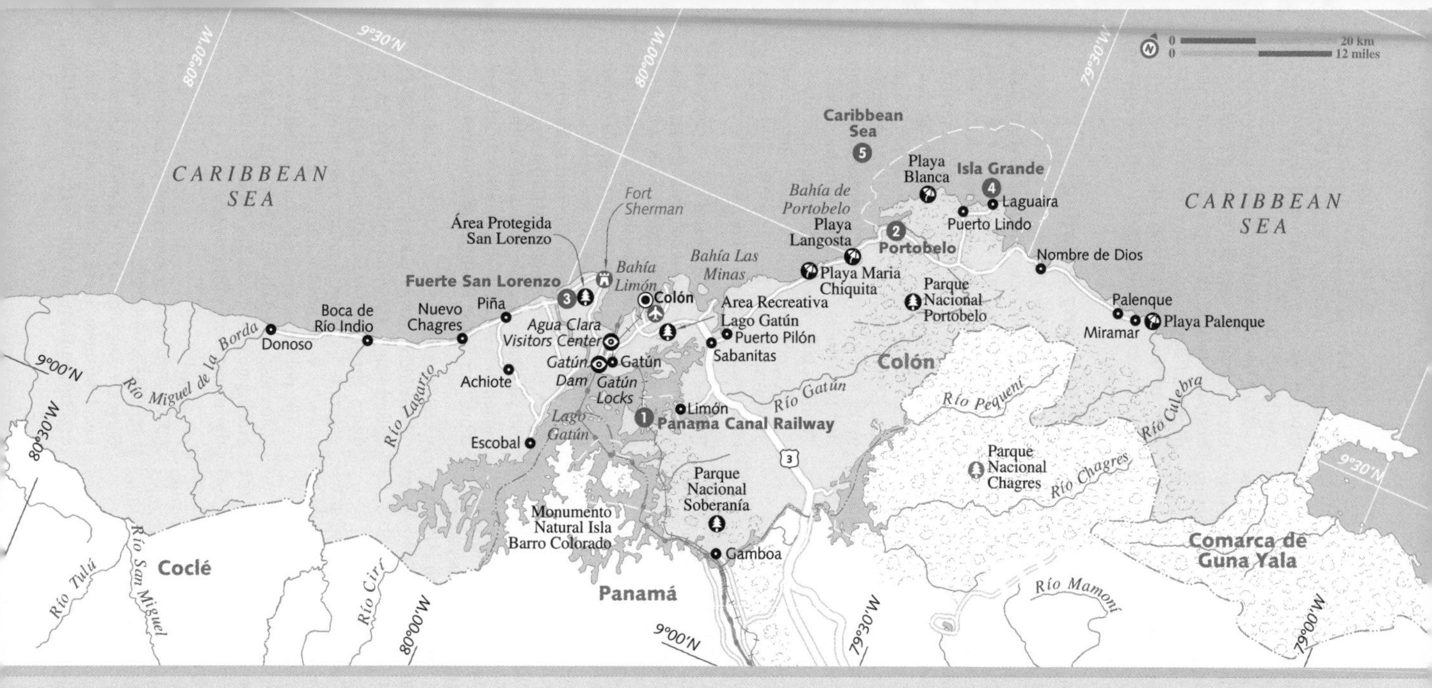

Colón Province Highlights

1 Panama Canal Railway (p215) Riding through lush vistas in a period carriage heading from Panama City to Colón along this historical railway.

2 Portobelo (p219) Exploring hallowed colonial ruins or finding festival frenzy in what was once the Caribbean's most important port.

3 Fuerte San Lorenzo (p217) Living out your *Pirates of the Caribbean* fantasy at this historic Spanish fortress that stands guard over the Caribbean.

4 Isla Grande (p225) Soaking up the natural beauty and laid-back vibe on a picture-perfect Caribbean island.

5 Caribbean Sea (p221) Finding sharks, cargo ships and military planes while scuba diving in the sea around Portobelo.

Colón

POP 29,640

With its colonial grandeur in decay and its neighborhoods marginalized, Colón is the city that Panama forgot, despite vigorous encouragement to attract Caribbean cruise ships. Before 1869 the railroad connecting Panama City and Colón was the only rapid transit in the continental western hemisphere. A last wheeze of prosperity was heard during the construction of the Panama Canal.

On the city's edge, the Zona Libre de Colón (Colón Free Zone) was created in 1948. It generates some US$6.5 billion in annual commerce, but little benefit seems to trickle down to local inhabitants. From up close, it's an island of materialism floating in a sea of unemployment and poverty.

Recent improvements in city safety are attributed to tighter gang control. There is also a much ballyhooed – but barely visible – urban restoration plan, kicked off in 2014. One major improvement: the Autopista Panamá–Colón is now a four-lane highway.

History

In 1850 the city of Colón (originally called Aspinwall after the Panama railway promoter) was established as the Caribbean terminus of the Panama Railroad. It became a boomtown, attracting Americans from the east coast who favored this 'shortcut' to California at the height of the gold rush. Even with sea voyages on the Atlantic and Pacific oceans and crossing the isthmus, this was considered a faster and safer journey than lumbering across the US mainland in wagons and facing hostile indigenous groups.

Following the completion of the US transcontinental railroad in 1869, Colón faded into obscurity just two decades after its founding.

At the peak of Colón's economic depression in 1881, the French arrived to build an inter-oceanic canal, but the city was burned to the ground four years later by a Colombian hoping to spark a revolution. In the years to follow, the city blossomed, and was entirely rebuilt in French colonial architectural style. Rivaling Panama City in beauty and wealth, this 'capital of the Canal Zone' offered a pleasant and highly profitable lifestyle at the time.

The French abandoned their efforts eight years later after huge monetary losses and the death of 22,000 workers from yellow fever and malaria. The USA seized the opportunity, reinventing Colón as a dormitory town as workers from around the world arrived by the boatload.

After the completion of the canal in 1914, unemployment caused Colón's economy to disintegrate and the city spiraled into the depths of depravity. Today much of the imprint of this colonial city can still be seen, but most of the buildings are on the verge of collapse.

Sleeping & Eating

New Washington Hotel HISTORIC HOTEL **$**

(☎441-7133; www.newwashingtonhotel.com; Calle lera, Paseo Washington; s/d US$49/50; P ❄ 📶 ≋) Looking out to the Caribbean from the northern end of Colón, the New Washington offers a pentimento or two of the glorious hostelry that opened in 1913 – stucco work, chandeliers, an impressive marble staircase in the lobby. From the 124 rooms, choose one that faces the sea or the pretty front gardens. There's a large pool and a bar-restaurant.

Check out the colorful stucco logo above the entrance with the slogan 'The land divided, the world united.' Those were the days.

Radisson Colón 200 Hotel HOTEL **$$**

(☎446-2000; www.radisson.com/colonpan; cnr Paseo Gorgas & Calle 13; d/ste US$129/169; P ❄ @ 📶 ≋) Really you could be anywhere, but this chain hotel offers the best digs in Colón, though service verges on the cavalier. The 102 rooms are comfortable and sufficiently stylish, with minibar and flat-screen TVs, and you can always let off steam with some laps in the pool. Big off-season discounts will more than halve the price of your room.

Cafe Lebanese LEBANESE **$$**

(☎431-1066; Paseo Gorgas; dishes US$8-18; ⏱11am-9pm) If Panamanian *ropa vieja* (spicy shredded beef) and *patacones* (fried plantains) are not floating your boat after a week or so, head for this friendly eatery in the port area for a fix of meze and *kofta* (Lebanese-style kebabs). The menu is in several languages, including Arabic; count on the authenticity of the dishes.

Arrecifes SEAFOOD **$$**

(☎441-9308; www.facbook.com/Restaurante-Arrecifes-239328576101580; cnr Calle 11 & Paseo Gorgas; mains US$10-20; ⏱11am-8pm Mon-Sat) Local business owners lunch at this nondescript building in the port area cooking

RIDE THE PANAMA CANAL RAILWAY

One of the best ways to fully appreciate the extent (and function) of the canal is to travel from Panama City to Colón along the historic **Panama Canal Railway** (☎317-6070; www.panarail.com; one way adult/child US$25/15; ⊙departure from Panama City 7:15am, return from Colón 5:15pm Mon-Fri). The rails fell into disrepair during the Noriega regime, but in 1998 the Panama government partnered with Kansas City Southern, an American-based railway holding company, to create the Panama Canal Railway Company (PCRC). The joint venture sought to re-establish the Atlantic–Pacific rail link and create a profitable alternative to the Panama Canal trade route. In 2001 PCRC also introduced a passenger service with a fully operational vintage train.

If you're looking to relive the golden age of railway travel, the vintage train features exotic wood paneling and blinds, carpeted interiors, open-air viewing decks and (sometimes) a glass-domed car. The hour-long ride parallels the canal, sometimes traversing thick rainforest.

While you're sipping a hot cup of coffee and admiring Panama's scenic interior, consider for a moment these train-spotting fun facts:

- Peaking at US$295 a share, the Panama Railroad was the highest-priced stock on the New York Stock Exchange in the mid-19th century.
- With a total construction bill of US$8 million, the Panama Railroad was, at the time, the most expensive railroad per kilometer ever built.
- Despite being only 76km long, the Panama Railroad required 304 bridges and culverts.
- During the first 12 years of its operations, the Panama Railroad carried over US$750 million in gold and silver and collected a quarter of 1% on each shipment.
- In 1913 the Panama Railroad hauled 2,916,657 passengers and transported 2,026,852 tons of freight across the isthmus, which was the heaviest per-kilometer traffic of any railroad in the world.
- An estimated 12,000 laborers died during the construction of the Panama Railroad, mainly from malaria and yellow fever.
- Disposing of the dead was such a problem that the Panama Railroad administration started pickling the bodies in barrels and selling them to medical schools, the proceeds of which were used to build a hospital in the Panama Canal Zone.

up good Caribbean dishes. Expect no frills and minimal views, just generous and tasty portions of *Criollo*-style seafood, stewed in onions, peppers and tomatoes, and whole fried snapper.

Shopping

Zona Libre MALL

(Duty-Free Zone; southeast Colón; ⊙8am-5pm Mon-Fri, hours vary Sat & Sun) Second in size only to Hong Kong's, Colón's free-trade zone is a huge fortresslike area of giant international stores selling items duty free. Most stores only deal in bulk merchandise and aren't set up to sell to individual tourists. To enter the Zona Libre, you'll need to present your passport at the security office.

Individual purchases are sent to Tocumen International Airport (p298) in Panama City, where they may be retrieved upon the visitor's departure. Hours vary depending on each store, with some open on weekends.

Colon 2000 MALL

(Paseo Gorgas; ⊙8am-5pm) This sterile shopping and entertainment sector geared toward cruise-ship travelers sits on the east side of Colón. Though lacking in any discernible Panamanian flavor, it is safe to peruse and features a good selection of restaurants and souvenir shops, as well as a casino.

Hours vary with each shop or restaurant.

Information

Away from the cruise port on the eastern side of the city and the bustling Zona Libre, Colón can be unsafe. Violent crime rates have lowered, but visitors should exercise caution when walking around, even during the day and in well-trafficked areas. Paseo de Washington, the renovated waterfront area to the north, should be safe to stroll along by day. Always travel by taxi at night.

The safest place to withdraw money is the Banco Nacional de Panamá's ATM in the Colón 2000 (p215) mall.

Getting There & Away

BUS

From Panama City's Albrook Bus Terminal (p300), express and regular buses for Colón depart every 30 minutes.

Colón's **bus terminal** (Terminal de Buses; cnr Calle Terminal & Av Bolívar) serves towns throughout Colón Province.

DESTINATION	COST (US$)	DURATION	FREQUENCY (DAILY)
Escobal (near Área Protegida San Lorenzo)	1.25	35min	hourly
Laguaira	3	2hr	half-hourly
Nombre de Dios	3.80	2½hr	hourly
Panama City	3.50	1-1½hr	half-hourly
Portobelo	1.60	1½hr	half-hourly

Note that if you are headed east of Colón from Panama City, these buses can be boarded at Sabanitas, the turnoff for Portobelo, thus avoiding a trip into Colón. Be aware that buses may be standing-room only, particularly on weekends, and Sabanitas is a bottleneck where traffic moves at a snail's pace.

TRAIN

One of the best ways to fully appreciate the canal's expanse (and function) is to travel from Panama City to Colón via the resurrected Panama Canal Railway (p215). Note that the Panama City terminus is actually in the town of Corazal, a 10-minute drive from the Albrook Bus Terminal.

Getting Around

While in Colón, it's not a good idea to walk around most neighborhoods. Fortunately, taxis congregate at the bus terminal, train station and the Zona Libre, and fares across the city are usually under US$2.

A round-trip taxi for three to four passengers runs around US$60 to Fuerte San Lorenzo (p218) and about US$20 to the Agua Clara Visitors Center, or US$30 if including the Gatún Dam in your visit to the Agua Clara Locks. From the terminal, the bus to Costa Abajo (US$1) will drop you off a couple of kilometers from the visitor center and dam.

Around Colón

Agua Clara Visitors Center VIEWPOINT
(☎276-8325; http://visitcanaldepanama.com/en/centro-de-visitantes-de-agua-clara; adult/child US$15/10; ⊙8am-4pm) This expansive observation center offers a panoramic view of the Panama Canal expansion, including the three-chambered Agua Clara Locks. Covered decks view Lago Gatún and the original Gatún Locks as well; there is also a theater with two videos in English, a cafe and gift shop. With no on-site museum, the focus here is really about getting a good look at the expansion. A short rainforest trail features sloths, howler monkeys and toucans.

Exhibits close at 4pm but visitors must enter by 3:15pm; a visit should take about one hour. To reach here from Colón, catch any bus to Costa Abajo and alight before crossing the canal. It's a 2.5km walk up the access road to your left. A taxi will cost about US$20, or US$30 if you want to include Gatún Dam.

Gatún Locks CANAL
(US$5; ⊙8am-4pm) The impressive Gatún Locks, 10km south of Colón, raise southbound ships 30m from Caribbean waters to Lago Gatún. Just the size of them is mind-boggling: three sets of double lock chambers stretch on for 3km. Each chamber could have accommodated the *Titanic* with room to spare. With the opening of the Agua Clara Visitors Center, the viewing stand opposite the control tower has unfortunately now been closed.

Workers poured a record-setting 1.82 million cu meters of concrete to construct the Gatún Locks. The concrete was brought from a giant mixing plant to the construction site by railroad cars that ran on a circular track. Huge buckets maneuvered by cranes carried the wet concrete from the railroad cars and poured it into enormous steel forms. Locomotives moved the forms into place. This protracted process continued virtually uninterrupted for four years until the locks were completed.

Once ships pass through the locks, they travel 37km to the Pedro Miguel Locks, which lower southbound ships 9.3m to Lago Miraflores, a small body of water between two sets of Pacific locks. Ships are then lowered to sea level at the Miraflores Locks (p76).

Gatún Dam LAKE

Constructed in 1908 to shore up the Río Chagres and create Lago Gatún, the Gatún Dam was once the world's largest earthen dam, while Lago Gatún was also the world's largest artificial body of water. Its creation submerged 262 sq km of jungle, entire villages that had been relocated and large sections of the Panama Canal Railway. Today, power generated by the dam drives all the electrical equipment operating the canal, including the locomotives that guide ships through the locks.

While the sight of the dam is impressive enough, if the concrete spillway is open you can watch millions of gallons of water rushing out. Before going, ask staff at the Agua Clara Visitors Center if the spillway is open.

If arriving by bus, take the turn left after passing the Gatún Locks and follow the road for approximately 2km.

Área Protegida San Lorenzo

Centered around the ruins of the Spanish colonial fortress of **Fuerte San Lorenzo**, the 120-sq-km Área Protegida San Lorenzo includes the former US military base of Fort Sherman as well as 12 different ecosystems, including mangroves, marshlands, semideciduous forests and humid rainforest. Since the departure of the US military in 1999, native fauna has slowly recolonized the area. Today it is a prime location for birdwatching, with some 436 species recorded.

As part of the Mesoamerican Biological Corridor, San Lorenzo protects and fosters species migration between the continents. Unfortunately, poachers, loggers and slash-and-burn farmers are threatening the reserve. Conservation and tourism may win out, however, due in part to the massive quantities of unexploded ordnance (dubbed UXOs) left in the area by the US military after their hasty exit from Panama. For decades, they used the jungles surrounding Fort Sherman for target practice and survival training.

History

After the destruction of Nombre de Dios by privateer Sir Francis Drake in 1572, the Spanish moved to fortify the Caribbean coast. Of principal concern was the Río Chagres, which flowed inland to the town of Venta de Cruces (near today's Gamboa), and then linked up with the trade route leading to the city of Panamá. In 1595, by order of Phillip II of Spain, Fuerte San Lorenzo was built into the side of a steep cliff near the mouth of the river. Fuerte San Lorenzo, Portobelo and Panamá, the 'three keys' of the Americas, became known as the strategic heart of the Spanish trade empire.

Fuerte San Lorenzo was under constant pirate attack. Indeed, Drake seized it less than a year after its completion. Although it recovered and was rebuilt with greater fortifications, San Lorenzo was again assaulted, this time by Sir Henry Morgan in 1671. Captain Morgan (of spiced-rum fame) succeeded in overpowering its guns and sailing up the Chagres. A few months later, Morgan burned Panamá to the ground, plundered its riches and sailed back to England with galleons laden with Spanish gold.

In 1680 a new fortification was built on the highest part of the cliff, but this was no match for British Admiral Edward 'Old Grog' Vernon, who destroyed San Lorenzo yet again in 1740. In 1761 the Spanish once again rebuilt San Lorenzo, though the decision to abandon the overland trade route in favor of sailing around Cape Horn meant that the fort didn't suffer renewed attacks. As a result, Fuerte San Lorenzo was abandoned by Spain in 1821 when Panama became independent. The fort was subsequently used as a Colombian prison, a post office for inbound English mail and a campsite for gold miners en route to California.

The US military built Fort Sherman in 1911 with the express purpose of defending the Atlantic side of the canal. Although changes in battle technology rendered the fortifications obsolete after WWII, the area surrounding the fort became an important jungle warfare training center. In 1963 these operations came under the responsibility of the US army's School of the Americas at nearby Fort Gulick, but five years later the so-called Jungle Operations Training Center became an independent entity. Fort Sherman subsequently became the main jungle operations school for the US army and was used as a training center for Vietnam-bound Special Forces.

On June 30, 1999, following the Torrijos–Carter treaties, Forts Sherman, Davis and Gulick, along with the territory now comprising the Área Protegida San Lorenzo, were transferred to Panamanian sovereignty.

Sights & Activities

Most travelers set their sights on the ruins of Fuerte San Lorenzo, but there are plenty of opportunities here for jungle exploration. The forests and swampland of the protected area are rich in birdlife and there's no shortage of mountainous trails and ponds fed by waterfalls to discover. You can also visit organic shade-grown coffee farms and hike to splendid lookouts with views of the protected area and the Río Chagres.

Centro El Tucán CULTURAL CENTER
(6261-6291, 6626-9790; www.centroeltucan.org; 9am-1pm & 3-6:30pm) The Área Protegida San Lorenzo is best explored with a guide, easily arranged at this community learning and visitor center, which lies on the edge of the reserve. Guides generally charge US$100 per group for a two-hour hike, though longer and more difficult treks can also be arranged. El Tucán also has an excellent documentation center on the flora and fauna of the reserve, human ecology and history. Hiking trails start 200m behind the center.

The Centro El Tucán is in the village of Achiote, 13km northwest of Escobal on Lago Gatún. It can be reached on buses from Colón (US$1.50, one hour) marked 'Costa Abajo,' but is best accessed by private vehicle.

Fuerte San Lorenzo FORT
(Fort San Lorenzo; www.sanlorenzo.org.pa; 8am-4pm) FREE Declared a Unesco World Heritage Site in 1980, Fuerte San Lorenzo is perched on the Río Chagres on a promontory west of the canal. Despite its violent history, much of San Lorenzo is well preserved, including the moat, cannons and vaulted chambers. The fort also commands a wide view of the river and bay far below, which was one of the reasons the Spanish chose to build here.

San Lorenzo was constructed of blocks of cut coral and armed with row upon row of cannons. If you inspect the cannons closely, you'll notice that some of them are actually British-made, dating from the time in the 17th century when Sir Francis Drake and his privateer brethren occupied the fort.

Sleeping

Centro El Tucán HOSTEL $
(6261-6291, 6626-9790; www.centroeltucan.org; dm/4-person cabaña US$12/50;) This community learning and visitor center on the edge of the reserve in the village of Achiote offers Hostelling International–supported accommodations in two dormitories with a dozen beds each and in two private *cabañas*, each with four beds.

Meliá Panamá Canal HISTORIC HOTEL $$
(470-1934; www.melia.com/melia-panama-canal; d from US$70;) Building 400 of the US army's notorious School of the Americas is now a giant resort hotel. The US$30 million property features 230 comfortable but somewhat dated guest rooms, a large outdoor pool complete with swim-up bar, and a formal restaurant offering stunning views of Lago Gatún. Service can be slow.

A range of hotel-organized tours include fishing trips as well as canal, Emberá village and Fuerte San Lorenzo visits.

SWEET DREAMS IN THE EX-DEN OF DICTATORS

The borders of the San Lorenzo protected area are home to Fuerte Espinar, which was known as Fort Gulick before the USA transferred it to Panama. Within this compound is the infamous Building 400, which was the onetime home of the School of the Americas.

Established in 1949, the School of the Americas trained more than 34,000 Latin American soldiers before moving to Fort Benning, Georgia, in 1984. The school was created to keep Latin America free of communism, which quickly translated into teaching Latin American soldiers how to thwart homegrown armed communist insurgencies.

The school graduated some of the worst human-rights violators of our time, including Argentine dictator Leopoldo Galtieri, who 'disappeared' thousands during Argentina's Dirty War of the 1970s, and El Salvador's Roberto D'Aubuisson, who led death squads that murdered Archbishop Oscar Romero and thousands of others during the 1980s.

In a bizarre twist, Building 400 is now a giant resort, Meliá Panamá Canal. Not too surprisingly, all evidence that the hotel has ever been anything but an upscale center for entertainment has gone.

In the past, overnight guests at Building 400 arrived via convoy or Blackhawk chopper. Today, it's recommended that you arrive via private vehicle; take the Centro Comercial Quatro Altos turnoff from the Autopista Panamá–Colón and follow signs for the hotel.

Orientation

Fuerte San Lorenzo and the Área Protegida San Lorenzo are located west of the city of Colón and northwest of Lago Gatún. The ruins of San Lorenzo are 9km southwest of Fort Sherman on the Caribbean coastal highway and lie along the northwestern boundary of the protected area. Although there is no official entrance to the reserve, there is a visitor center in the village of Achiote, along the northeastern edge of the reserve halfway between the coastal villages of Piña and Escobal.

Getting There & Away

There is no public transportation to Fuerte San Lorenzo (though buses from Colón marked 'Costa Abajo' will get you to parts of the reserve). As a result, this area is best explored by private vehicle or on tour from Panama City. It is, however, possible to take a taxi to Fuerte San Lorenzo from Colón (around US$70 round trip). Taxis are rare closer to the reserve.

If driving, go to the Gatún Locks and take the roll-on roll-off car ferry near the northern entrance. Once across follow the 'Fuerte San Lorenzo' signs, which lead for 12km to the entrance of the former Fort Sherman, where you'll be asked to show identification. Once you've done this, you'll be allowed to proceed the remaining 10km to Fuerte San Lorenzo.

Portobelo

POP 4600

This Caribbean fishing village is so laid-back and languorous, it's hard to imagine it was once the greatest Spanish port in Central America. Mules carried Peruvian gold and Oriental treasures to Panama City via the fortresses at Portobelo. Though English privateers destroyed them many times throughout their history, several of these atmospheric colonial fortresses still stand amid village homes.

Today Portobelo's residents scratch out a living by fishing, tending crops or raising livestock. Though economically depressed, Portobelo is experiencing something of a cultural revival, with renewed interest in Congo art, music (especially *punta,* better known abroad as reggaetón) and dancing. The town bursts to life every October 21 for the Festival del Cristo Negro (p222), one of the country's most vibrant and spiritual celebrations.

There are also nice nearby beaches, accessed by boat, and worthwhile diving and snorkeling.

History

Columbus named the settlement Puerto Bello (Beautiful Port) in 1502, when he stopped here on his fourth New World voyage. Over time, the name shortened to 'Portobelo.'

Portobelo consisted of no more than 10 houses when the celebrated Italian engineer Juan Bautista Antonelli arrived in 1586 on a mission to examine the defensibility of the Caribbean. After noting how well Portobelo's bay lent itself to defensive works, King Felipe II ordered that Nombre de Dios be abandoned and Portobelo colonized. However, it wasn't until after the former settlement was completely destroyed by Sir Francis Drake in 1596 that the transfer took place. Drake died of dysentery that year while anchored off Portobelo. He was buried at sea in full armor in a lead-lined coffin. Divers continue to search for it.

The city of San Felipe de Portobelo was founded in 1597 and for 200 years was subject to invasions at the hands of both English privateers and the Royal Navy. Portobelo was first attacked in 1602 by the English pirate William Parker, and the infamous Sir Henry Morgan sacked the city in 1671.

However, not all of the invasions were the product of superior tactics or numbers. In 1679 the crews of two English ships and one French vessel united in an attack on Portobelo. They landed 200 men at such a distance from the town that it took them three nights of marching to reach it. As they neared Portobelo, they were seen by a farmer, who ran ahead to sound the alarm, but the pirates followed so closely behind that the town had no time to prepare. Unaware of how small the buccaneer force was, all the inhabitants fled.

The pirates spent two days and nights in Portobelo, collecting booty in constant apprehension that the Spaniards would return in great numbers and attack them. However, the buccaneers got back to their ships unmolested and then distributed 160 pieces of eight to each man. At the time, one piece of eight would pay for a night's stay at the best inn in Seville.

Attacks on Portobelo continued unabated until the city was destroyed in 1739 during an attack led by Admiral Edward 'Old Grog' Vernon. Portobelo was rebuilt in 1751, but it never attained its former prominence and, in time, became a virtual ruin. Later, much of the outermost fortress was dismantled to build the Panama Canal and many of the

Portobelo

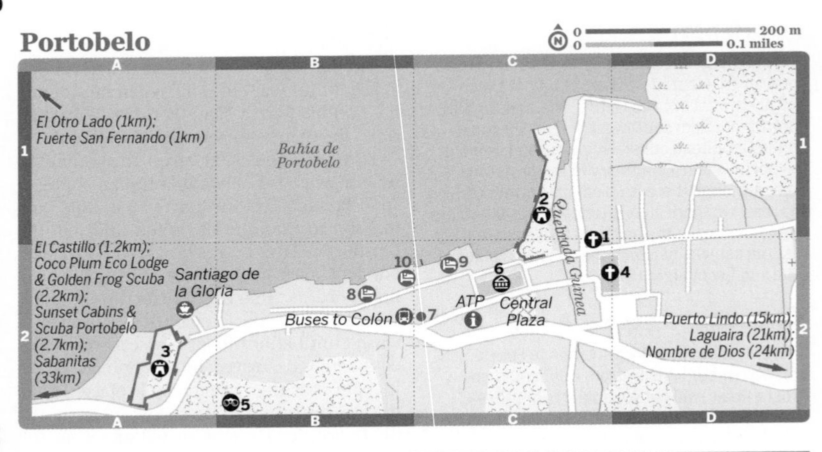

Portobelo

Sights
1 Capilla de San Juan de Dios C2
2 Fuerte San Jerónimo C1
3 Fuerte Santiago A2
4 Iglesia de San Felipe C2
5 Mirador Perú B2
6 Real Aduana de Portobelo C2

Activities, Courses & Tours
7 Agrupaciones de Congo C2
Las Delicias de Sole .... (see 10)

Sleeping
8 Casa Congo B2
9 Casa Rayo Verde C2
10 La Morada de la Bruja B2

Eating
El Palenque .... (see 8)

Shopping
Galería de Arte Casa Congo .... (see 8)
Taller Portobelo .... (see 10)

larger stones were used in the construction of the Gatún Locks. There are, however, still considerable parts of the colonial town and fortresses left, and today Portobelo is protected as a national park and as a Unesco World Heritage Site.

Sights

Playa Blanca BEACH

A 20-minute, US$45 return boat ride from Portobelo will bring you to this lovely white-sand beach on a tranquil cove surrounded by dense wilderness. It boasts some of the least disturbed reefs between Colón and the Archipiélago de San Blas, and its sheltered waters offer better visibility than beaches closer to Portobelo. There's a colorful reef in the center of the cove near the beach, as well as a second reef that sits in deeper waters about 100m offshore.

Capilla de San Juan de Dios CHURCH

(Chapel of St John of God) This small chapel is all that remains of a Catholic church dating back to 1589.

Real Aduana de Portobelo HISTORIC BUILDING

(US$5; 8am-4pm) Under renovation at the time of research, the handsome, two-story Royal Customs House of Portobelo was originally built in 1638 to serve as the *contaduría* (counting house) for the king's gold. Now the two main rooms house permanent exhibitions, including replicas of Spanish-colonial rifles, sketches of Portobelo's forts, 20th-century black-and-white photos of the town and a few dozen rusty cannonballs.

Iglesia de San Felipe CHURCH

(Church of St Philip) This Roman Catholic church dating from 1814 is home to Portobelo's famed Black Christ (p222); it's to the left of the main altar. The faithful attribute scores of miracles to the 1.5m-high statue found floating in the bay, and it's celebrated every October with the popular Festival del Christo Negro (p222). The church was the last structure built by the Spanish before they withdrew from Panama.

Parque Nacional Portobelo NATIONAL PARK
Located in and around Portobelo, this 360-sq-km park and Unesco World Heritage Site protects islands and coastal communities of coral reefs, mangroves and tropical forest. Ruined forts – including those named for San Fernando, San Jerónimo and Santiago – and the Perú lookout date from colonial times when gold and silver from throughout the Americas were brought here to be transported to Europe in Spanish galleons. At one time, all the Caribbean pirates lusted after the treasures of Portobelo.

Fuerte San Jerónimo, close to the center of Portobelo, was the largest fortress ever built to protect the bay. Some two dozen embrasures with 16 cannons face the mouth of the bay, some exactly where the Spanish troops left them in 1821, the year Panama declared its independence. Beyond the impressive gateway, there's the remains of the officers' quarters, barracks, guardroom and huge observation terrace over the water.

If you're short on time, San Jerónimo is the most complete of Portobelo's accessible forts and makes for the best visit.

Overlooking much of the bay is small but well-preserved watchtower **Mirador Perú**, which was built at the same time as Fuerte Santiago. There are steps carved into the hillside to reach the lookout, and the views of the coastline from here are expansive.

In 1601 **Fuerte San Felipe** and **Fuerte San Diego** were built near the mouth of the bay. They were destroyed by Admiral Vernon in 1739. Fuerte San Fernando was built over the ruins in 1760, with one battery of 14 cannons and one of six. American engineers dismantled much of the fort at the start of the 20th century, using the stones from the walls to create the breakwater protecting the northern end of the Panama Canal.

Approaching from the west, Portobelo's first fort is **Fuerte Santiago**. Built in 1753, some 14 years after Vernon's attack, some walls were 3m thick and made of cut coral blocks. Known to the Spaniards as 'reef rock,' coral was a popular building material since it's easily shaped, tough as granite yet light as pumice. Ruins include officers' quarters, artillery sheds, a sentry box, barracks, watchtowers and a half-dozen cannons.

Activities

Diving & Snorkeling

It's not Belize or the Bay Islands of Honduras, but if you're an avid scuba diver you'll have a good time here with no fewer than 16 major sites in nearby waters. Though the visibility can't compare to more traditional Caribbean diving destinations, the variety of underwater wrecks include a 34m-long cargo ship and a C-45 twin-engine plane. In addition to these, the waters around Portobelo are home to soft coral-laden walls, offshore reefs and rock gardens, some of which are also good for snorkeling. Dive centers have snorkel gear and information.

The good news is that you'll probably see several pelagic creatures including nurse sharks, black-tip reef sharks and eagle rays. The bad news is that you probably won't see them very well, especially if it has been raining. Generally speaking, you can expect about 10m of underwater visibility, but don't be surprised if it gets as low as 3m. Fortunately, scuba diving along this stretch of the Caribbean is fairly inexpensive.

Dive operators in Portobelo are located along the Sabanitas–Portobelo road, about 2km west of town. If you're planning to dive, it's best to phone ahead or make a reservation online.

Golden Frog Scuba DIVING
(☎6586-4838; www.goldenfrogscuba.com; 2-dive trip US$100; ⏲diving 9am-1:30pm) A PADI dive center run by English-speaking dive master Rey Sanchez at the Coco Plum Eco Lodge (p223). Excursions are made from a comfortable catamaran.

Scuba Portobelo DIVING
(☎6673-3681, 261-3841; www.scubapanama.com) Outfitter Scuba Portobelo offers all-inclusive scuba packages. It's located at Sunset Cabins (p222) on the left-hand side of the road into town.

Swimming

If you're looking for a day of fun in the sun, nearby Playa Blanca is a great day trip from Portobelo. Closer, you'll find the small cove beach **La Huerta** and **Puerto Francés**, which has a covered hammock hut and bathroom (arrange ahead of time for a key; local boat drivers know the caretakers).

Courses

Las Delicias de Sole COOKING
(☎6322-6215; www.lamoradadelabrujaportobelo.com/es/otros-servicios.html; per person US$50; ⏲8am-4pm) Wonderful cook Soledad prepares Afro-Caribbean cuisine like nobody's business. You can join her at La Morada de

la Bruja to learn some local techniques while preparing a meal to enjoy on-site. The menu varies according to what's fresh and available, but might include specialties like *fufu* (fish soup) or *tortillas changa* (thick tortillas made from fresh corn) grilled with maize and coconut.

Though the class is given in Spanish, guests can take home a recipe booklet in English. There's a three-person minimum.

Agrupaciones de Congo DANCING

(☎6693-5690; Casa Artesanal, Calle Principal; per person US$20; ⏲noon-2pm Fri, to 4pm Sat & Sun) This established local group preserves the long-standing tradition of Congo dancing. Manager Aristela Blandon gives tailored dance classes and provides a fascinating background on the slave history behind this unique tradition (in Spanish). Participants can also purchase a CD of original music. The base is a crafts store open only on weekends, but you can call to organise classes.

Festivals & Events

On the last Sunday of each month there is an Afro Mass with a town fair displaying local food and traditional crafts. Holy Week just before Easter is also an interesting time to be here.

Festival del Cristo Negro FIESTA

(Black Christ Festival) On October 21 annually, pilgrims from all over Panama arrive in Portobelo to participate in this festival, which honors a miraculous 1.5m-high statue of the Black Christ housed in the Iglesia de San Felipe (p220). After sunset, the statue is paraded through the streets, while pilgrims bedecked in purple robes and crowns of thorns dance and drink until the wee hours.

Festival de Diablos y Congos CULTURAL

(Festival of Devils & Congos; ⏲Feb/Mar) The most intriguing local party is this festival of rebellion and ridicule that mocks the colonial Spaniards. Participants assume the role of escaped slaves and take 'captives.' It's held two weeks after Carnaval, marking the start of Lent.

The tradition of the Congos dates from the slave-trading days when blacks escaped into the jungle and formed communities of exiles called *cimarrones*. As part of the tradition, a 'prisoner' is taken and a huge ransom demanded, though the prisoner is freed upon paying a token sum. The Congos perform before audiences dressed in outlandish outfits that include tattered clothes, hats that resemble crowns and wooden swords.

Should a wild and crazy group descend upon you and demand thousands of dollars as ransom, try not to freak out – they'll settle for a few coins.

Sleeping

There are plenty of choices for accommodations at all budget levels in Portobelo. In addition, local families may rent out spare rooms, particularly during festivals. Ask at the ATP (p224).

Sunset Cabins CABIN $

(☎261-3841, 448-2147; www.panamaportobelocabins.com; d/cabin US$55/75; P ❄) Nondivers are welcome at this seafront lodging run by Scuba Portobelo (p221). In a very reduced space, a bright structure has five motel-style doubles with balconies, electric showers and

THE LEGEND OF THE BLACK CHRIST

The Festival del Cristo Negro honors a statue of the 'Black Christ' that has had many miracles attributed to it. Normally housed in the Iglesia de San Felipe (p220), the statue's exact origins are a matter of speculation. All definitive church records were lost in the fire that followed Henry Morgan's sacking of Panamá in 1671, but there is no shortage of fanciful stories surrounding the origins of the statue.

One story has it that a ship bound for Cartagena in Colombia tried to leave Portobelo five times, but on each occasion a storm blew the ship back to the town's edge, nearly sinking it. The crew lightened their vessel by tossing a heavy box overboard. On their sixth attempt to sail out, the weather calmed, and they were able to go on their way. Several days later, local fishers found the discarded box floating off Portobelo and discovered the Black Christ inside.

A second story claims that the box was found floating at sea during a cholera epidemic. After being retrieved by local fishers, it was placed inside the Iglesia de San Felipe. Almost immediately the epidemic passed and the infected were cured. Or so the story goes...

air-con. The five cabins offer pocket-sized charm – best for a couple or a family with small children. For all-inclusive scuba packages, see the website.

El Castillo HOSTEL **$**
(☎6738-1561, 448-2244; www.castilloportobelo.com; dm/d without bathroom US$10/20; 📶) This seafront restaurant and hostel with one private room and dormitory accommodating up to 15 people does resemble a castle – one drawn by manga artist Miyazaki. Still, its French-speaking Vietnamese host Richard is welcoming and it has tumbledown charm. Rooms have mosquito nets and fans. The large sea-facing restaurant (mains US$12 to US$25) is open from 10am to 9pm.

The restaurant offers some appealing options for vegetarians as well as Thai curry and some Vietnamese dishes. El Castillo is 900m before Portobelo on the left-hand side.

★**La Morada de la Bruja** BOUTIQUE HOTEL **$$**
(The Witch's Abode; ☎6759-6987, 6008-6867; www.lamoradadelabrujaportobelo.com; r US$50-75, 4-person loft US$80, 2-bedroom house US$200-225; P ❄ 📶) This chill photographer's home has been adapted for guests but maintains a very personal touch. Three small apartments and two ample waterfront houses – all differently colored – sport artful decor and a grassy seafront perfect for lounging. The bright, open interiors showcase photography and local Congo art. We like Casa Turquesa facing the sea best.

There are also kayaks for rent and boat services for excursions to remote beaches. It is fine to cook here (rooms have fridges and microwaves) but prepared meals are available, and you can opt to take a Caribbean cooking course (p221). Transportation to Panama City can also be arranged.

★**Casa Congo** B&B **$$**
(☎202-0880, 6672-6620; http://casacongo.fundacionbp.org/es/houses-2/casa-congo; d US$80-100; 📶) Part of a foundation that supports local arts and culture, this attractive waterfront inn features three pleasant and bright rooms and an apartment decorated with Congo art. It also offers workshops with artists. It's mostly doubles with one apartment that accommodates four (US$20 per extra person).

Casa Rayo Verde GUESTHOUSE **$$**
(☎6672-6620, 202-0880; info.rayoverde@gmail.com; d/apt US$60/130; ❄ 📶) Run by a top-end resort across the bay, this attractive four-room guesthouse comes recommended by guests. The property faces the water, with four quaint rooms and an apartment with minifridges, private bathrooms and a shared terrace. Attention is lax – you're on your own here. The guesthouse helps fund culture and arts in the local community.

Coco Plum Eco Lodge HOTEL **$$**
(☎448-2309, 448-2102; www.facebook.com/CocoPlumPanama; s/d/tr/q US$55/65/80/90; P ❄) An attractive, motel-style lodging with eight rooms, the very friendly Coco Plum has been around for years. On the waterfront, the feel of the place is ocean kitsch, replete with nets, shells and pastels, but the effect is cozy. The attached Restaurante Las Anclas is popular with travelers. It's on the road into town on the left.

Golden Frog Scuba (p221) is also based here. Can provide boat service.

★**El Otro Lado** RESORT **$$$**
(☎202-0111; www.elotrolado.com.pa; Bahia Portobelo; cabins incl breakfast US$650, villas US$750-1400; ❄ 📶 🏊) 🍃 Awash in Caribbean style under a hush mountainside, this 'private retreat' (ie luxury resort) is laid-back and restful – don't expect beach parties. It's across the bay from Portobelo; that short distance keeps the Congo drumming at bay. Set around an infinity pool, four pastel cabins display exquisite, playful taste. The four large, art-filled villas sit tucked in the rainforest.

The grounds are enormous and interesting – the resort borders some of the Spanish ruins and was once the site of an American community brought to work on the Panama Canal. The housing has since been torn down, but some remnants of that time, including a dammed jungle reservoir, are fascinating. The dining room is an elaborate gazebo with glass walls and high-style Caribbean cooking (meals from US$70). Boats can taxi guests to remote beaches and fishing spots. The resort supports Fundación Bahía Portobelo, a community nonprofit promoting local art and culture.

Eating

Portobelo has several bakeries and *fondas* (cheap eateries) strung along the main road and plaza.

★**Restaurante Las Anclas** SEAFOOD **$$**
(The Anchors Restaurant; ☎448-2309, 448-2102; www.facebook.com/CocoPlumPanama; mains US$8-16) This popular bar-restaurant located

at the Coco Plum Eco Lodge serves fish and shellfish dishes with a Caribbean twist in a large sea-facing dining room. Try the octopus in coconut milk or the mixed seafood stew.

★**El Palenque** PANAMANIAN **$$**
(☎6106-4518, 202-0880; http://casacongo.fundacionbp.org/es/our-food; mains US$12-20; ⊙8am-10pm) Located at the Casa Congo, the best feature of this restaurant is its location. There's ample open-air seating overlooking the beautiful bay of Portobelo. Whole fried fish, *patacones* and coconut rice are prepared nicely, but the service can be woefully slow.

Shopping

★**Galería de Arte Casa Congo** ART
(☎6672-6620; http://casacongo.fundacionbp.org/es/foundation/gallery; Casa Congo; ⊙9am-5pm Mon-Fri, to 8pm Sat, 8am-5pm Sun) A wonderful gallery with museum-quality pieces made mainly by Afro-Caribbean craftspeople and artists. Helpful displays explain the cultural background of the groups represented, including Congo and indigenous cultures. It's not all high end though – you will also be able to find reasonably priced jewelry and souvenirs.

Taller Portobelo ART
(Portobelo Workshop; ☎6777-5022; ⊙9am-6pm) This artist-run studio is fascinating for art and culture buffs. Resident artist Gustavo can explain the historical and cultural significance of Congo art and will sell you some of his works. It's attached to the hotel La Morada de la Bruja (p223).

Orientation

Portobelo consists of about 15 square blocks beside a paved, two-lane road that intersects with the Panama City–Colón highway at the town of Sabanitas, 35km to the west. East of Portobelo, the road forks after 9km. The right branch of the road extends 14km further east to Nombre de Dios; the left branch extends 11km to the hamlet of Laguaira, where you can take a boat to Isla Grande.

Information

The **ATP** (☎448-2200; ⊙8am-4pm) just off the main road may test your Spanish skills. Many of the employees only speak Spanish with varying degrees of helpfulness about Portobelo, Colón Province and/or Panama. You'll find better service and more useful information at the local gas station.

Getting There & Away

Buses to Portobelo (US$1.60, 1½ hours, every 30 minutes) depart from Colón's Terminal de Buses from 4am to 6pm. Buses to Colón from Portobelo leave from a bus stop on the main road through town.

If traveling to Portobelo from Panama City you can avoid Colón by alighting from the Colón bus at the Supermercado Rey in Sabanitas, 10km before Colón. From there catch the bus to Portobelo (US$1.40, 1¼ hours).

Getting Around

Along the Sabanitas–Portobelo road you can flag down any bus headed in your direction. After about 6pm, there is no public transportation. Taxis can be scarce.

Leaving from Fuerte Santiago, co-op **Santiago de la Gloria** (☎448-2266) water taxi charges a two-person minimum of US$30 to Playa La

SURFING IN COLÓN PROVINCE

One of the least surfed provinces will make you a believer with its great unknown breaks.

Playa Maria Chiquita In front of Maria Chiquita village. Beach break with lefts and rights, but limited to big swell.

Isla Grande In front of Laguaira and best reached by water taxi. Reef bottom break with three peaks, rights and lefts.

Isla Mamei Southwest of Isla Grande, reached by boat or by paddling. Left-hand point break over shallow reef.

Playa Palenque In front of Cuango village, 50km east of Isla Grande. Beach break with rights and lefts; surfers seldom make it here.

Playa Grande (Mainland) East of Isla Grande. Beach break with some reef. Waves break left and right.

V-Land Near Devils Beach in Sherman, west of Colón. Unbelievable right-point reef break with great tubes when there's big swell and it's glassy.

Huerta, US$45 to Playa Blanca and US$40 to the beach at Puerto Francés; all fares are round trip. **Water Taxi Juan** (☎6008-6867) may offer better rates.

Puerto Lindo

Located 6km west of Laguaira, the springboard to Isla Grande, this snoozy village has a protected bay increasingly favored by sailboats voyaging to the San Blas archipelago or Cartagena in Colombia. Excursions to the nearby Isla Mamei take you to a beautiful beach and surrounding mangroves. If you are deciding between Mamei and Isla Grande, this may be a better choice, especially on crowded high-season weekends.

Sleeping & Eating

Visitors can eat at a basic cafe or *fonda,* or cook at their lodgings.

Hostel Wunderbar HOTEL **$**
(☎448-2426, 6700-7790; www.hostelwunderbar.com; d US$35-55, house US$150; P ❄) Run by German-Austrian Silvia and Guido, who traded their sailboat for a hotel (but called it a hostel), this breezy retreat with six rooms and a holiday villa sleeping up to eight has a relaxed setting. Mosaic tiles adorn the outdoor kitchen, and rooms have attractive, colorful decor; there's a tree house, too. The more expensive rooms have air-con. There are also sailing and canoe trips to the mangroves on offer.

Casa X B&B **$$**
(☎448-2507, 6689-6923; johan.ja.ka@live.com; s/d/q US$50/60/80; P ᯤ) Casa X is a less-inspiring place to stay, with three scruffy apartments sleeping up to four people. But it's right on the water, with a pleasant deck on which to lounge and stare out to sea.

The in-house restaurant serves *comida típica* (regional specialties; mains US$8 to US$12) and is open from 9am to 8:30pm.

Getting There & Away

Buses headed to Laguaira from Colón stop in Puerto Lindo (US$3, 1¾ hours).

Isla Grande

POP 1050

Palm trees and white-sand beaches form the backdrop to this lovely little island, just 15km from Portobelo. A popular getaway for folk fleeing the urban grind of Panama City, Isla Grande is an ideal setting for snorkeling, scuba diving or simply soaking up the island's relaxed vibe. There are no roads, just a footpath along the island's southern coast, backed by pastel-colored cottages. Many of the people living here are of African descent and are eking out a living from fishing and growing coconuts – you'll get a taste of both when you sample the local cuisine.

Owing to its location on Panama's northern Caribbean coast, Isla Grande gets a lot of rain year-round. Terms like 'rainy' and 'dry' seasons don't really apply here, though torrential showers are usually short-lived.

Activities

This 5km-long, 1.5km-wide island has two trails: one that loops the shoreline and another slippery cross-island trail. The lovely beaches on the northern side of the island can be reached by boat or on foot. The closest beach to civilization is on the west coast not far from the pier.

Some fine snorkeling and dive sites are within a 10-minute boat ride of the island. For diving, contact a Portobelo-based operator. Diving is restricted to between April and December, when seas are calmer. Boat taxis can also take you further afield to explore the mangroves east of Isla Grande or to go snorkeling off the coast of the nearby islets.

Festivals & Events

Isla Grande Carnaval CULTURAL
(⏲Feb-Mar) Isla Grande celebrates Carnaval in a rare way: women wear traditional *polleras* (festive dresses), while men wear ragged pants tied at the waist with old sea rope, and everyone dances to African-influenced Conga drums and songs. There are also satirical songs about current events and a lot of joking in the Caribbean calypso tradition.

La Virgen del Carmen FIESTA
The Virgen del Carmen, the island's patron, is honored with a land and sea procession, baptisms and Masses on July 16.

Sleeping

★**Macondo Hostel** HOSTEL **$**
(☎6102-6262; www.facebook.com/Macondo-Hostel-Isla-Grande-1541624226094296; dm/d/q US$15/35/45; ᯤ) Follow the signposted path a block inland to this agreeable, breezy, two-story

hostel set in a lush tropical garden. Five and eight bunks occupy two ample-sized dorms with fans. The three private rooms sleep two to four people. It's good value for budget travelers, with shady shared spaces and hammocks. It's relaxed but you'll be sure to party here too.

★Hotel Sister Moon CABAÑAS **$$**
(☎6948-1990; www.hotelsistermoon.com; d/tr with fan US$87/102, d with air-con US$120, day pass US$20;) Your best choice for island lodging is this lovely clutch of 11 hillside cabins surrounded by swaying palms and crashing waves. With no beach, guests sunbathe on attractive waterfront decks and swim in the pool. Perks include private balconies with hammocks; cabins 1 and 2 dangle right over the water. The in-house El Fin del Mundo restaurant is excellent.

Hotel Isla Grande CABAÑAS **$$**
(☎225-2798, in Colon 448-2019; d with/without view US$98/65, 4-person cabin US$110, day pass US$8-12) On the closest point to the mainland, this hotel boasts the only decent beach within reach of services. This explains its popularity, as rooms – while decent and clean – are overpriced. Without a website or email, phone reservations are necessary. Cabins lack kitchens but there's an on-site restaurant that's open from 8am to 5pm on weekdays and to 8pm on weekends.

Villas Brother Sun VILLA **$$$**
(☎6948-1990; www.hotelsistermoon.com; villas US$250-400;) Owned and operated by Hotel Sister Moon a short distance to the east, Brother Sun rents four luxurious villas sleeping between two and six people. They all have terraces gazing out to sea from above the footpath, fully equipped kitchens, air-conditioning and BBQ areas. One even has its own private swimming pool.

Eating

Many visitors bring a picnic lunch, though there's a handful of seaside restaurants lining the footpath.

El Muro SEAFOOD **$**
(☎6106-8382; mains US$8-12; ⏲8:30am-9pm) This little Venezuelan place, the first eatery on the water to the right as you begin walking along the footpath, serves fresher than fresh clam, lobster and crab dishes. It's very friendly and the staff are always welcoming.

★El Fin del Mundo SEAFOOD **$$$**
(☎6948-1990; www.hotelsistermoon.com; mains US$15-22; ⏲8am-8pm Mon-Fri, to 10pm Sat & Sun) Sister Moon's bar-restaurant is built right over the water. The menu features the island's famous coconut-infused seafood alongside high-end cocktails.

Island Gume SEAFOOD **$$$**
(☎6906-9306; mains US$8-25; ⏲9am-6pm Mon-Fri, to 9pm Sat & Sun) About halfway along the island footpath, this small Colombian-owned restaurant serves some of the best food on the island, though portions are a little too modest. Try the octopus *ceviche* and the shrimp sautéed in garlic and served with coconut rice. There's also fresh fish and cocktails (US$4 to US$5).

Drinking & Nightlife

Floating Rum Bar COCKTAIL BAR
(cocktails US$6; ⏲noon-late) Why would you nurse a cocktail by the sea when you can do the same *in* the sea? This floating bar is anchored off the footpath and accessible by complimentary *lancha* (small motorboat). There's BBQ food on offer and the bar boasts a Tarzan swing that will get you into the drink in no time.

El Bar de Pupy BAR
(☎6789-7433, 6503-7530; ⏲9am-9pm) This Rasta-reggae bar-restaurant, hosted by the eponymous local lad Pupy, reaches right into the sea. While the day (or evening) away, your feet planted in the sand, enjoying grilled chicken, octopus with onion and garlic, or fresh fish (mains US$12 to US$15). Great cocktails too.

Getting There & Away

Isla Grande is a 10-minute boat ride from Laguaira, a tiny coastal hamlet linked with Colón by frequent buses. Boats arrive at the Isla Grande dock just down from the Hotel Isla Grande.

Buses to Laguaira leave from the Colón bus terminal (US$3, 1½ hours). From Panama City, take a Colón-bound bus to Sabanitas and change buses next to the Supermercado Rey for Laguaira. Buses return from Laguaira at 8am, 9am and noon.

In Laguaira, boats at the dock go to the island (or beyond), departing when full from 8am to 7:30pm Monday to Friday, to 7pm on Saturday and to 5pm on Sunday. The trip costs US$5 per person; secure parking is US$6 per day.

Comarca de Guna Yala

POP 44,230 / ELEV SEA LEVEL TO 1160M

Includes ➡

Best Off-the-Beaten-Track Spots

➡ Cayos Holandeses & Los Grullos (p238)

➡ Cayos Limones & Chicheme (p236)

Best Places to Stay

➡ Cabañas Demar Achu (p238)

➡ Burbayar Lodge (p241)

➡ Yandup Island Lodge (p240)

➡ Pachamama Gypsy Lodge (p241)

➡ Cabañas Casso (p238)

Why Go?

With white sand and waving palms, the islands of the turquoise Archipiélago de San Blas of the Comarca de Guna Yala are a vision of paradise. This is home to the Guna people, the first indigenous group in Latin America to gain autonomy. Though they have had contact with Europeans since Columbus sailed these waters in 1502, clan identity and the traditional way of life remain paramount.

A decade ago the road to the port of Gardi (Cartí) was finished, making the region more accessible than ever. Still off the beaten track, this narrow, 373km-long strip on the Caribbean coast with 365 offshore islands stretches from the Golfo de San Blás to the Colombian border.

Community (ie populated) islands numbering four dozen are acre-sized cays packed with thatched huts, livestock and people. Visitors often prefer the more remote outer islands with fewer inhabitants. Some islands charge a landing/visitation fee.

When to Go

Dec–Apr During trade-wind season there's little rain. It can get hot in the thatched huts, but conditions are ideal for sailing, with winds from the north and northeast.

Oct Digir Dubu (Isla Tigre) communities celebrate traditional dance at the Nogagope, which brings communities together for a week of dancing as well as canoe races and an art fair.

May–Aug There's good visibility for snorkeling, though rainstorms are around and so are annoying *chitras* (sand flies). Thunderstorms mean it's not a preferable time to sail.

Comarca de Guna Yala Highlights

1 **The Guna** (p229) Interacting with the Guna, a fiercely independent people who maintain their traditions in a changing world.

2 **Sailing** (p231) Cruising white-sand cays, swimming in clear waters and soaking up the sunrise on a sailboat. Some trips now depart from Colón Province.

3 **Molas** (p233) Shopping the community islands for *molas*, traditional Guna textiles that have become the national handicraft of Panama.

4 **Cayos Holandeses** (p238) Snorkeling aquamarine waters through reefs and wrecks in the magical Cayos Holandeses.

5 **Boats to Colombia** (p236) Sleeping in hammocks on sandy beaches, eating the local catch and living the adventure of a four-day motorboat trip to Colombia.

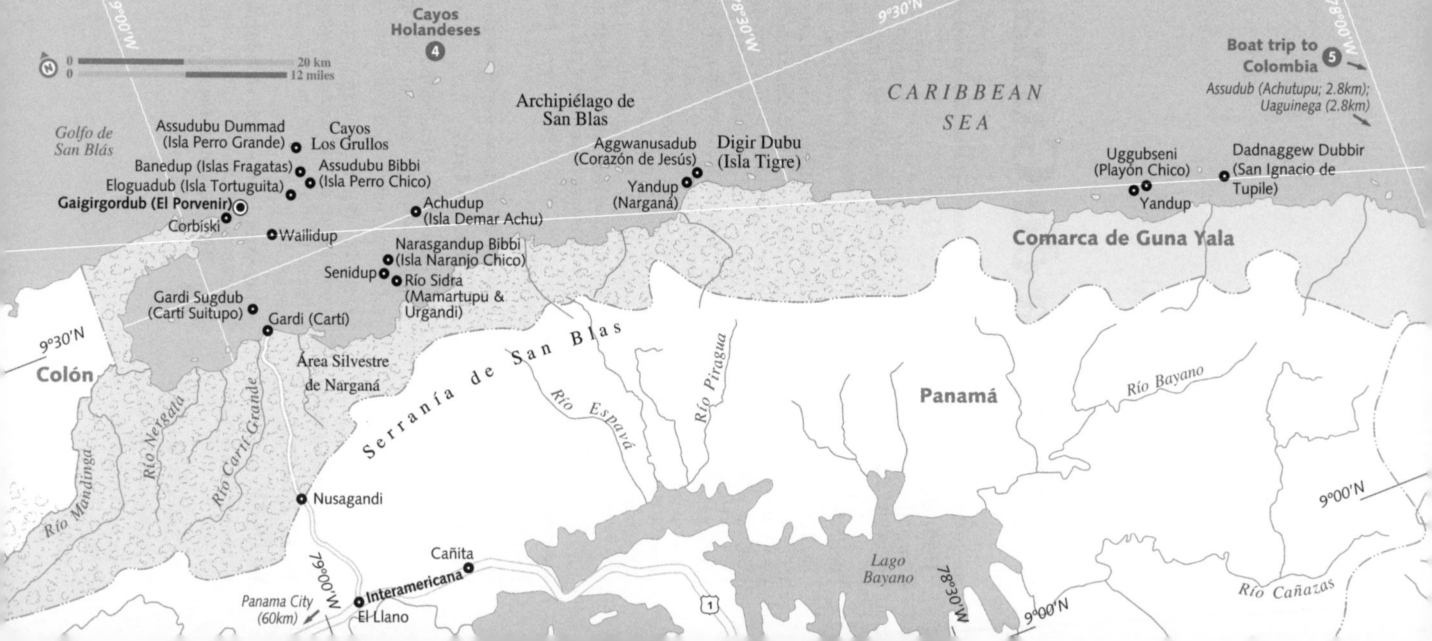

History

Although the Guna people have lived in eastern Panama for at least two centuries, scholars fiercely debate their origins. Language similarities with people who once lived several hundred kilometers to the west would indicate that the Guna migrated east. However, oral tradition has it that the Guna migrated to the San Blás islands from Colombia after the 16th century, following a series of devastating encounters with other tribes armed with poison-dart blowguns.

Regardless of the origins of the Guna, who called themselves the Dule, scholars agree that life on the islands is relatively new for them. Historians at the end of the 18th century wrote that the only people who visited the San Blás islands at that time were pirates and the odd Spanish explorer. However, the Guna flourished on the archipelago due to the abundance of seafood. They supplemented this with food crops grown on the mainland, including rice, yams, yucca, plantains, bananas and pineapples.

Today there are more than 44,000 Guna living in the *comarca,* with three-quarters living on the islands and the rest on tribal land along the coast; about 6000 Guna live elsewhere in Panama and Colombia. So communal are the island-dwelling Guna that they inhabit only 48 of the 365 cays; the rest are mostly left to coconut trees, sea turtles and iguanas.

Culture

The traditional Guna belief structure is based on three principal concepts: God, nature and the cosmos.

According to the Guna religion, the world was created by God, Baba Dummad, and the Great Mother, Nana Dummad, who continue to keep watch over everyone's daily actions. Although Guna shamans often look into the future and make minor divinations, everything in life is believed to be preordained by the divine couple Baba Nana. In fact, the Guna make great efforts in their daily lives to ensure that their actions follow the will of their divine parents, even though they do not know their fate.

The Guna identify strongly with nature, and their rich oral traditions are full of songs, hymns and prayers that recount the beauty and majesty of the wind, the land and the sea. To the Guna, people and nature are considered parts of the same entity and thus the rules of nature follow human life through its eight levels – from birth to

RESPONSIBLE TRAVEL IN GUNA YALA

When visiting the Comarca de Guna Yala, consider how your visit may affect the community. Tourism revenue can play a vital role in the development of the region, particularly if you are buying locally produced crafts or contracting the services of a Guna guide. However, Western interests have already caused irreversible damage to the region. Be aware of your surroundings and remain sensitive about your impact.

One look at the paradisiacal setting, the colorful flag and the distinctive Guna dress and you might feel transported into the pages of *National Geographic*. Don't snap that shutter just yet, though. If the Guna appear less than friendly – and they sometimes do – consider their predicament. When tourist boats arrive, the number of people on an already congested island can triple. Then, nearly two-thirds of the populace (the tourists) turn paparazzi on the other third (the Guna). It's an unsavory scene repeated again and again. To rein in the situation, the Guna usually charge fees for photographs taken of them as well as landing/visitation fees for each island. If you can't afford the photo fee or don't want to pay it, put your camera away and strike up a conversation instead.

Remain mindful of the way you dress. Guna men never go shirtless and Guna women dress conservatively, with their cleavage, their belly and most of their legs covered. Arriving in Guna villages in a bikini or shirtless might be interpreted as a sign of disrespect.

Trash is a huge problem on the more populous islands, and there is no effective plan for its management. For the Guna, the cost of removal to the mainland is too high, and there is no designated site or 'culture' of waste management, since all refuse was relatively innocuous until outside influence prevailed. You may see litter and piles of burning plastic. With no current solution to the issue, do what you can to pack out your own garbage, if necessary, and try to consume fresh products with minimal packaging – eg choose coconut water over packaged drinks.

death. The Guna love and admire nature, and they believe that true happiness is only experienced within its presence.

Guna cosmology is based on the doctrine that the knowledge of a concept allows the knower to manipulate the power of the concept. As a result, Guna myths and legends have both a literal and a symbolic meaning. For example, the story of the Ibeorgun, who descended to earth to teach the Guna what to eat and how to prepare it, how to choose their chiefs *(sailagan)*, build houses and brew *inna* (*chicha brava* in Spanish, a sugarcane-based home brew used in ceremonies), is often associated with most of the moral and ethical teachings of the Guna people.

Lifestyle

The cornerstone of the Guna political organization is the *onmagged nega* (community gathering house). Here, men gather nightly for heated discussions about local events, to make decisions about important problems and to listen to the advice of chiefs. Generally, each island has at least three chiefs and their authority is officially recognized by the Panamanian government. Every year, there are two general assemblies called by the Onmagged Dummad (Congreso General) for the representatives from all of the islands in the *comarca* at which major issues affecting the Guna are discussed.

Historically the Guna were matrilocal, meaning that when a man married, he would move into the household of his wife's parents and come under the control of his father-in-law. Today, this pattern is disappearing, and newlyweds usually set up house away from both parents. As recently as a generation ago, Guna households had an average size of seven to 12 people, but today households often comprise as few as five people.

The distinctive dress of the Guna is immediately recognizable no matter where you are in Panama. Most Guna women continue to dress as their ancestors did. Older women may be adorned with a black line painted from the forehead to the tip of the nose, with a thick gold ring worn through the septum. Colorful fabric is wrapped around the waist as a skirt, topped by a short-sleeved blouse covered in brilliantly colored *molas* (p233). The women wrap their legs, from ankle to knee, in long strands of tiny beadwork

GUNA LIVING 101

Lodging options in the *comarca* are vastly different from those on the mainland. Here, a spot in a thatched hut with a sand floor with three meals can cost anywhere between US$35 in a dormitory and US$170 in a luxury lodge per night. So, what's the difference?

Often it has more to do with access, ambience and organization than anything else. Densely populated community islands are more likely to have budget options, but they will not live up to your image of a remote tropical paradise at all. Resort islands with lodges generally have a bigger price tag, but they may not offer many opportunities to interact with locals. When planning, consider why you're visiting and ask yourself the following questions:

Space Does the island have shade? Privacy? Are there pleasant areas to swim or do you have to take a boat to reach swimming and snorkeling sites?

Access Is the island too remote, requiring expensive transfers to do anything?

Hospitality Have other travelers had good experiences here?

Water Is it potable? Consider bringing a filter.

Bathrooms Are there modern installations or does the toilet sit at the end of a dock?

Safety Do excursion boats have recently inspected life vests and good motors?

Lodgings generally include three meals (but not drinks), one outing per day (eg snorkeling or a community visit) and sometimes transportation to or from the airport or Gardi (Cartí) port, but do confirm ahead. Visits to other Guna islands may cost extra. It is always wise to bring snacks, insect repellent, a first-aid kit and a flashlight. Rates are generally lower from April to November.

When booking, remember that internet access is not prevalent here and any cell-phone number is only good until that phone accidentally falls into the ocean. But approach your hosts with good humor and patience, and they will probably reciprocate in spades.

(wini), forming colorful geometric patterns. A printed scarlet headscarf *(muswe)* and many necklaces, rings and bracelets complete the wardrobe. In sharp contrast to the elaborate women's wear, Guna men have adopted Western dress, including shorts, sleeveless shirts and sandals.

In recent years, Guna culture has come under growing threat of westernization, particularly as young Guna are drawn to Panama City in search of employment and increased opportunities. However, Guna culture has survived countless generations of foreign encroachment, and communities are just as committed to preserving their identity today as they were when the Spanish first arrived.

Economy

Until the late 1990s, the district's principal currency was the coconut but now the sale of *molas* is the *comarca*'s number-one revenue source. The Guna are coconut barons: a good year's harvest reaches over 30 million. Coconuts are bartered to Colombians, whose old wooden schooners can hold 50,000 to 80,000 of the coconuts. In return, the Colombians provide clothing, jars of coffee, vinegar, rice, sunglasses, canned milk, batteries, canned and dried soups and other goods.

In Colombia the coconuts are exported or turned into copra and used in the production of candy, gelatin capsules, cookies, shampoos and other products. Colombia has many processing plants for coconuts, but Panama, oddly, has none.

Shrewd businesspeople, the Guna regulate the price of coconuts on a yearly basis to prevent buyers from bargaining down individual sellers. Every year, Guna chiefs agree on one price for coconuts. A Guna found selling coconuts below or above price is severely punished by the community. By stabilizing the sale of coconuts and enforcing trade restrictions, the chiefs prevent price wars among the Guna.

In another protectionist move, Guna law prohibits outsiders from owning property in the district. A conscious move to ensure limitations on tourism in the region, the law also prevents foreigners from speculating in real estate and driving up living costs. Today, lodgings are 100% owned and managed by Guna families and are fairly uniform in offerings and quality.

Sleeping & Eating

Carefully selecting your accommodations on the islands is key, since their remoteness makes it difficult to change your mind. Camping on an uninhabited island isn't wise, because you run the risk of encountering drug traffickers in the night and being eaten alive by *chitras* (sand flies). The Guna do not allow the Panamanian coast guard or US antidrug vessels to operate in the archipelago, so the uninhabited islands are occasionally used by Colombian traffickers running cocaine up the coast.

Since there are almost no restaurants, each lodging provides meals for guests. They are usually seafood based, with lobster available at an extra cost. Quality varies, as some of the fishing stocks have been depleted, but there is always rice and a healthy supply of fresh coconuts. Always ask before taking a coconut – they are among the region's main sources of income.

Activities

Most lodgings offer complete packages, where a fixed price gets you a room, three meals a day and boat rides to neighboring islands for swimming, snorkeling and lounging on the beach. If you seek community life, you can also arrange visits to more populated islands.

Before swimming off the shores of a heavily populated island, consider that all waste goes here – unfiltered in most cases.

Snorkeling is good in places, but many coral reefs are badly damaged. You can often rent snorkeling equipment from hotels; serious snorkelers should bring their own gear.

Jaunts to hike the mainland jungles are arranged with a guide. Most travelers are content with simply soaking up the Caribbean sun.

Tours

San Blas Adventures BOATING

(☎6032-8498; http://sanblasadventures.com; 4-day trip US$445) More a tour and a holiday than mere transport, the popular San Blas Adventures four-day service takes travelers between Gardi (Cartí) and Capurganá just over the border in Colombia, visiting both inhabited and deserted islands, sleeping in hammocks under thatched lean-tos or in Guna communities, eating meals that verge on gourmet and swimming and snorkeling along the way.

A GUIDE TO THE GUNA LANGUAGE

Feeling a little tongue-tied? The following glossary will help you break the ice with the Guna. Note: the second entry in all listings is Spanish, and the third is Guna.

Getting Started

Yes.	Sí.	Elle.
No.	No.	Suli.
Thanks.	Gracias.	Dot nued.
Please.	Por favor.	Uis anga saed.
OK.	Esta bien.	Nued gudii o.
Good.	Bueno.	Nabir, nuedi.

Greetings

Hello.	Hola.	Na.
How are you?	¿Como esta usted?	Bede nued guddi?
Fine, thank you. And you?	Bien, gracias. ¿Y usted?	An nuedi. Bedina?
Fine.	Bien.	Nuedi.
What is your name?	¿Cual es su nombre?	Igi be nuga?
My name is...	Mi nombre es...	An nuga...
Nice to meet you.	Encantado.	An yeel itoe.
Goodbye.	Adiós.	Degi malo.
I had a good time.	Me divertí.	An yer ittosa.
I'll see you tomorrow.	Hasta manãna.	An banedse be dagoe.

Feelings

I'm hungry.	Tengo hambre.	An ugur itoe.
I'm thirsty.	Tengo sed.	An gobie.
I'm cold.	Tengo frío.	An dambe itoe.
I'm warm.	Tengo calor.	An uerba itoe.
I'm sleepy.	Estoy cansado.	An nue gapie.
I'm happy.	Estoy contento.	An yee ito dii.

Useful Expressions

How much does this cost?	¿Cuánto cuesta?	Qui mani?
I want to buy it.	Quiero comprarlo.	An bag-bie.
Do you speak English?	¿Habla inglés?	Be sumage mergi galla?
Speak slowly, please.	Hable despacio por favor.	Uis binna sunmage.
I don't understand.	No entiendo.	Agu ittoe.
I'm sorry.	Lo siento.	An oague.
Foreigner	Extranjero	Uaga

Food & Drink

Rice	Arroz	Oros
Bread	Pan	Madu
Fish	Pescado	Ua
Coconut	Coco	Goibir
Coffee	Café	Gabi

Travel is on a covered fiberglass boat with twin outboard engines, and the convivial crew is multilingual. There are regular set departures and the website features useful planning details. It's a good alternative to the sailboat crossing, avoiding cramped overnight quarters and rough seas.

Cacique Cruiser BOATING
(Map p56; ☎6111-4241; www.caciquecruiser.com; day trips US$150) A licensed and highly recommended tour agency specializing in daily trips and excursions to San Blás, from one to six days. Also offers trips between Panama and Colombia on highly rated boats. The company is a major contributor to the local economy and supporter of social and environmental programs.

Blue Sky Sailing BOATING
(☎6009-9042; www.blueskysailingsanblas.com) Charter sailing trips with a friendly and experienced American couple on their 52ft sailing boat *Blue Sky*. Includes kayaks, fishing gear and snorkel gear.

Pantalasa BOATING
(☎6075-8080; www.pantalasa.com) Charter sailing trips with an experienced Spanish couple offering personalized attention.

Mola Nega Adventures BOATING
(☎6884-0262, 6098-1874; www.molanegadventures.com) Run by an affable Guna named Lenin Vásquez, this outfit offers transfers from Panama City to Gardi (Cartí) as well as day trips (US$110) and overnights (US$165) in the archipelago.

Panama Travel Unlimited TOURS
(Map p48; ☎6676-5583, 6993-9919; http://panamatravelunlimited.com; Calle Primera Perejil, Casa 7-62, Panama City; ⏲9am-6pm Mon-Sat) Specializing in travel to Guna Yala, this small British-run agency in Panama City focuses on services for backpackers, including transportation, day tours, overnight packages and boats to Colombia. It's a good resource for comparing products. It also coordinates community volunteering through a nonprofit. Located at Mamallena hostel (p58) in Panama City.

Igua's Tours TOURS
(☎6791-6499; iguat28@yahoo.com) A reliable Guna naturalist guide speaking Spanish and English, Igua Jiménez leads tours into the rainforest of Área Silvestre de Narganá (p241) and has boat tours to nearby **Lago Bayano** and its caves, which could be combined with a visit to the reserve.

Kuna Yala Expeditions BOATING
(☎6530-4834, 6708-5254; eliasperezmartinez@yahoo.com) Local entrepreneur Elías Perez speaks English and offers day tours in covered *pangas* (small motorboats) with fast, two-stroke motors. Excursions include kayaking mangroves, a visit to the mainland cemetery and a hike, and snorkeling Cayos Holandeses.

Germain Perez TOURS
(☎6734-3454; www.cartihomestaykunayala.blogspot.com) Offers tours and activities, as well as transfers from Panama City to Gardi (Cartí) for US$25 per person.

Festivals & Events

Guna Revolution of 1925 CULTURAL
(⏲Feb 23-25) One of the biggest holidays here is the commemoration of the anniversary of the 1925 Guna Revolution. It marks the day when the Guna rebelled against the Panamanian police occupying the islands and expelled them from the *comarca* with support of US forces. Skirmishes are reenacted on land and sea throughout the archipelago, including on Digir Dubu (Isla Tigre) and Agligandi.

Shopping

Molas are the most famous of Panama's traditional handicrafts. Made of brightly colored squares of cotton fabric sewn together, the finished product reveals landscape scenes, birds, sea turtles, fish and beasts – often surrounded by mazelike geometric patterns. Traditional geometric designs are usually valued more than modern ones. Craftsmanship varies considerably. You can find *molas* on the islands (or, rather, the *mola* sellers will find you).

Mola work originated from the transfer of body-painting designs to cloth, particularly blouses. When the Panamanian government tried to modernize the Guna by prohibiting traditional dress, the *mola* emerged as a symbol of independence. Even when Guna schools were administered by Panamanian officials, girls wore special *molas* in school colors as a silent protest.

Today there is a wonderful sense of pride among Guna women regarding *molas*. In addition to being an integral part of the Guna culture, *molas* are unique to the *comarca*.

Molas are classified by differences in the technical process:

Abiniguat One color; refers to a single layer of color sewn onto a base layer.

Obagalet Two colors; refers to two layers sewn onto a base layer.

Mormaralet A few colors; refers to two or more layers sewn onto a base layer.

Morgonikat Many colors; refers to two or more layers sewn onto a base layer with additional filler layers, embroidery and/or appliqué.

The simplest *molas* are sold for upwards of US$10; elaborate designs are works of art valued at several hundred dollars.

Information

Flights in and out of the *comarca* are limited, so book as far in advance as possible. You should also reserve your hotels in advance, especially since all-in package deals are the norm here. There's no cash machine, so visit an ATM before reaching the islands. The closest one is at Chepo on the Interamericana, about 20km southwest of the El Llano turnoff.

From May through November temperatures are generally lower in the archipelago. When humidity sets in, life on the San Blás islands can cease to be paradisiacal. During January and February the trade winds arrive.

In the *comarca* it helps to have a good command of Spanish as few Guna outside the tourist centers speak English. In fact, many older Guna do not speak much Spanish. In more remote areas your guide or boat operator may have to do the talking for you. A few words of Guna will win you friends wherever you go.

The Guna are very particular about what *uagmala* (foreigners) do on their islands. As a result, tourists must register and pay a visitation fee (usually around US$3) on most islands. You're expected to pay regardless of whether you stay for a week or only a half-hour. On smaller, privately owned islands, you must seek out the owner, obtain permission to stay and pay a fee of around US$7 per person to camp.

Visitors are expected to pay to take photographs of the Guna people (around US$1 per subject or photo). If you want to take a photo, ask their permission first. You may not be required to pay for a photograph taken of an artisan from whom you buy crafts, but it depends on the person.

You need your passport to enter the region.

Getting There & Away

Until 2009, when a 47km-long road linking the Interamericana with the port of Gardi (Cartí) was finished, the only way to visit the Comarca de Guna Yala was by plane or private sailboat. Hired 4WD vehicles now make the trip from Panama City in about two hours and charge from US$25 one way. Visitors must show their passports and pay an entry fee (US$20) upon crossing the border into the *comarca* after the 18Km marker.

From the port of Gardi (Cartí), boat transportation can be arranged from the docks (US$2 usage fee) to the islands. Those staying on one of the far-flung islands have the option of flying into one of several remote landing strips scattered throughout the *comarca*.

AIR

Air Panama (316-9000; www.airpanama.com) has daily flights to Uggubseni (Playón Chico; p240) and Assudub (Achutupu; p241). There are also flights to **Ogobsucum (Ustupo)** three times a week and to **Puerto Obaldía** daily except Saturday. All flights depart from Albrook Airport in Panama City and take 30 minutes to an hour. Ticket prices vary according to the season and availability but average about US$80 one way.

Book as far in advance as possible, as demand far exceeds supply. Note that planes may stop at several islands in the archipelago, loading and unloading passengers or cargo before continuing on.

CAR

The El Llano–Gardi (Cartí) road is the only land route into the district. It connects the town of El Llano, on the Interamericana 72km east of Panama City, to the San Blás coastal hamlet and port of Gardi (Cartí).

It's best to take a shared 4WD with a powerful engine, a winch and good tires. Your Panama City hostel can easily transportation, as can Mola Nega Adventures (p233), Kuna Yala Expeditions (p233) and driver Germain Perez (p233).

BOAT

Sailboats travel to Colombia via the archipelago, but they tend to board in Puerto Lindo or Portobelo on the Caribbean coast in Colón Province these days. Lodgings in Panama City have more information about these privately run trips.

San Blas Adventures (p231) runs a four-day service between Gardi (Cartí) and Capurgana in Colombia.

Getting Around

Few islands in the archipelago are more than 10km from the district's mainland. All of the heavily inhabited islands are very close to the coast to permit access to agricultural areas and vital natural resources, such as water, firewood and construction materials. Also on the mainland are the giant trees from which the Guna make their chief mode of transportation – the *cayuco* (a dugout canoe made from a burned and hollowed-out trunk). There are 10 towns and two mountain villages on the mainland, all within 100m of the sea, though there are no restaurants or hotels in any of these places.

BOATS

Boats await the arrival of planes to shuttle people to their island destination (US$5 to US$80). If you want to travel by boat between island groups or explore some of the far-flung islets, you can either hire local guides at the docks or have your hotel make the arrangements. Inquire about your ride in advance if you don't like small craft (some go quite slowly).

In June 2018 the Congreso General Guna announced it would levy fines of US$5000 on yachts carrying tourists that sailed through Guna Yala waters. These 'floating hotels' have long been controversial. Some perceive them as unfair competition, but individual Guna who live in remote areas are often supportive, since the boats support locals by buying their produce and *molas*. We suggest you exercise caution when booking such sailing trips and be fully aware of what is legal and what is against Guna law.

Sailboats charge between US$150 and US$350 per person per day, including meals and some drinks, and they usually provide snorkeling gear. Costs like Guna island-visitation fees and boat transfers are not included.

Gardi (Cartí) Islands & Around

Gardi (Cartí) is the collective name for a group of islands and a small strip of coast near the road. If you've arrived in the *comarca* by 4WD, the coastal hamlet of Gardi (Cartí) will be your first port of call. The nearby islands are minutes away by boat.

Gardi (Cartí)

Most places on the Gardi (Cartí) Islands are in Gardi Sugdub (Cartí Suitupo), or 'Crab Island,' a mere 100m from the mainland and one of the most densely populated islands in the *comarca*: it feels as crowded as Manhattan at rush hour and is terribly polluted. But it can serve as a base for exploring nearby Ikodub (Isla Aguja), or 'Needle Island,' a picture-perfect retreat with lazy palms, golden sands and gentle surf.

Excursions cost from US$35.

The **Museo de la Cultura Guna** (Museum of Kuna Culture; 6967-0416; US$3; 8am-4pm) is stuffed with objects from everyday life as well as *molas* and religious artifacts, and it provides a good cultural and historical understanding of the Guna. A guided tour with curator Delfino Davies, who speaks some English, will elucidate everything from Guna coming-of-age rituals to funerary rites.

Catering to backpackers, **Cartí Homestay** (6734-3454, 6517-9850; www.cartihomestaykunayala.blogspot.com; r per person incl 3 meals & tour US$50; @) is the best place to meet young Guna, though the inflatable Jägermeister bottle in the corner might be a good indicator of the kind of cultural interactions you can expect. There are two very basic rooms with double beds and a six-bed dorm. The English-speaking hosts also have cabin lodgings on a more remote island.

A 20-minute boat ride from Gardi Sugdub (Cartí Suitupo) leads to **Cabañas Asseryaladub** (Isla Aroma; 6121-2050, 6757-5050; www.facebook.com/islaaroma; dm/r per person incl 3 meals & tour US$36/46). These 13 *cabañas* are popular with day-trippers and those not intending to venture too far afield. Most *cabañas* have three beds; a few sleep up to 10. A conch sounds breakfast (7am to 8am), lunch (noon to 1pm) and dinner (6pm to 7pm) daily. Food is wholesome but basic.

Getting There & Away

With the only road access, Gardi (Cartí) is the gateway to the archipelago. Most visitors come here by 4WD contracted via their lodgings or local agencies.

At the pier or on the river, motorboats transfer visitors to islands. Most trips are included with lodgings. Visitors must pay a port fee (US$2).

Corbiski

Corbiski is a populated community island with plenty of opportunities to interact with locals, especially at the local school. While it's a convenient launching point and just 10 minutes by boat from Gaigirgordub (El Porvenir), Corbiski is crowded and does not have great swimming or snorkeling off the island itself.

At **Bungalows Corbiski** (6530-4834, 6708-5254; eliasperezmartinez@yahoo.com; per person incl tour, meals & transfers US$85), five grey cabins, each with its own bathroom, sit right over the water; go for cabin 4 or 5. Snorkeling tours are included in the price. The affable owner, Elías Perez, provides boat services, so you can get around the islands easily. There's solar-powered electricity 24 hours a day.

Cayos Limones & Chicheme

A lovely island chain popular with yachts (there's a mooring close to a good scuba site), these cays are likely to draw visitors who are traveling by sailboat.

The fabulous sandbar **La Piscina** (Swimming Pool) is a popular swimming spot for day-trippers on any of the Cayos Limones.

Banedup (Islas Fragatas)

Sailboats moor alongside these two tiny private islets – Banedup Dummad (Isla Fragata Grande) and Banedup Bibbi (Isla Fragata Chica) – where you can stop by for seafood meals at **Restaurante Banedup** (☎6119-4743; Banedup Dummad; mains from US$8; ⌚8am-7pm) or **Kairbir Nega** (☎6119-4743; Banedup Bibbi; mains US$8-15; ⌚noon-4pm & 8pm-late).

Located near Banedup is Isla Perro Grande, a tiny island that provides nothing but **camping** (per person US$7) for adventurous souls with their own gear. To preserve the site, guests must pack out all trash and practice leave-no-trace ethics.

Getting There & Away

Sailboats mostly visit this area independently; otherwise you can transfer via motorboat from Gardi (Cartí) for US$35 to US$40 one way.

Wissudub Dummad (Isla Chicheme Grande)

About as far north as islands go in the Archipiélago de San Blas, Wissudub Dummad (Isla Chicheme Grande) is a popular anchorage point for boats arriving from and going to Colombia. The Wissudub is named after the tropical icaco fruit *(Chrysobalanus icaco)*, or cocoplum, which grows in abundance here.

Host Argelio Morales offers shady camping and six thatched **cabins** (☎6846-5217; argeliomorales2347@gmail.com; per person camping/dm/r incl 3 meals & transfer US$70/80/90) with electricity, plus one tour per day. As at other island destinations, trash is building up here – guests are required to pack out their own. Campers are supplied with tents and camping equipment; if you have your own, ask for a discount.

SAILING THE GUNA YALA TO COLOMBIA

If you're a backpacker or don't mind living like one in the name of adventure, consider this: small sailboats can take passengers to Colombia via the scenic Archipiélago de San Blas for the same price as a flight. But the trip may not be for everyone.

Potential guests should know that these boats are not official charters: passengers help out in exchange for cheap passage. But in exchange you usually get a few days of sun and sand in the San Blás, often with a snorkeling trip or two. The rough open-sea passage to Cartagena accounts for half the duration of the trip. Before you book, find out the following:

- Are accommodations a cabin or floor space?
- What is the size of the boat and the number of passengers?
- Is the boat equipped with adequate lifeboats and life vests for all passengers?
- Does it have adequate safety equipment and a functioning radio?
- Does the captain have a charter license?
- What are the meals like? (Some boats serve beans and rice three times a day.)

We have heard happy reports, but travelers have also complained about boats skimping on meals, overcrowding passengers or traveling despite bad weather in order to fit in more trips. Bring snacks and ask ahead whether the boat needs fresh groceries (hard to stock when boats spend extended periods in the islands). Do your research and check a boat or captain's references with hostels and other travelers before committing. If you are only traveling for the novelty of sailing, consider a trip that sticks to the Guna Yala.

The best place to inquire about scheduled departures is at any of the youth hostels in Panama City. A typical five-day backpacker sailing trip, including food and activities (but not island fees), costs around US$550. A much better alternative is the leisurely, four-day motorboat trip offered by San Blas Adventures (p231), which offers basic but very comfortable accommodations, food verging on gourmet and a convivial crew.

Eloguadub (Isla Tortuguita)

Hardly bigger than a handkerchief, this idyllic island is kept immaculate with a raked white-sand beach and limited visitation. It comes closest in the Cayos Limones to the idea of a 'paradise island.'

One way to fulfill your castaway fantasy is to **camp** (☎6030-3428, 6651-8858; www.sanblastourspanama.com; camping/cabin per person incl meals & transfers US$86/135) on this tiny isle run by one family. Tents and cushions are provided, and meals are well prepared. Some new cabins stand right over the water.

Also on the island is the fabulous **Restaurant Chef Blas** (☎6651-8858, 3030-3428; www.sanblastourspanama.com; dishes US$5-15; ⏲7-11am, noon-3pm & 6-7pm). At three long picnic tables under the palms, you can feast on lobster and fish with cabbage salad and *patacones* (plantains) on the side.

Wailidup

This picturesque island in the Cayos Limones has a sprawling sugar-like sand beach and dense forest. With ample mooring, it's a popular stop for sailboats and has a lot of fresh water. Come during the tradewind season to avoid *chitras* (sand flies).

On a beautiful spit of white sand, the **Guna Niskua Lodge** (☎6043-6327, 6715-2335; cabins per person incl meals & tour US$150, r with/without bathroom US$85/75) has six lovely high-ceilinged cabins on stilts sitting over the water, with shady decks and breezes. The cabins are considerably better than the four basic lodge rooms at the back of the beach. An attached restaurant with bar offers dishes of fresh octopus, fish, crab and lobster. It's connected to the island via a long wooden dock and patronized by yachties. Book ahead.

Boat transfers to Gardi (Cartí; US$40) are charged separately from lodging prices.

Assudubu Bibbi (Isla Perro Chico)

Small 'Little Dog Island' – not to be confused with nearby 'Big Dog Island' – is very popular with day-trippers because of its excellent snorkeling (there's a sunken cargo boat in the nearby channel).

Barco Hundido (☎6959-0866; www.facebook.com/islaperrobarcohundido; per person incl 3 meals & excursions r/cabañas US$75/50) is a restaurant (mains US$7 to US$15) that also has five thatched *cabañas* and six rather stuffy, wood-paneled rooms in an ugly concrete block. It can get very crowded here.

Transfers from Gardi (Cartí) are usually included in lodging. Otherwise, transportation will cost US$35 to US$40 each way.

Niadup (Isla Diablo)

Just a stone's throw from busy Assudubu Bibbi (Isla Perro Chico), this islet has sheltered swimming and a couple of decent places to stay that are somewhat off the beaten track.

Cabañas Niadub (☎6654-1467, 6967-0641; www.facebook.com/niadub; per person incl 3 meals camping/dm/cabaña US$30/40/50) is the better of the two island accommodations. It has nine cabins (including a lovely wooden one by its own little beach), two dorms sleeping seven to 12 people on air mattresses with sheets, and camping sites. All accommodations share large tiled-floored bathrooms. The restaurant (mains from US$8) is open for breakfast, lunch and dinner (till 8pm).

Cheaper **Cabañas Igwa Dad** (☎6020-1995; per person incl 3 meals dm/cabaña US$35/40) has eight basic *cabañas* and a cramped dormitory for up to 12 people.

Transfers to or from Gardi (Cartí) average US$30 each way.

Río Sidra (Mamartupu & Urgandi) & Western Islands

Río Sidra

Located 15km east of Gardi Sugdub (Cartí Suitupo), Río Sidra is a major settlement in the archipelago. It is in fact two islands – Mamartupu and Urgandi – joined together with landfill. From here it's a quick and easy boat ride to places like Narasgandup Bibbi (Isla Naranjo Chico), Achudup (Isla Demar Achu) and Senidup. It's also relatively close to the far-flung Cayos Los Grullos, Holandeses and Ordupuquip.

Río Sidra is extremely congested – the population hovers around 2000 – and the effects of westernization are more prevalent here than on other islands.

Local historian and master *mola*-maker **Lisa Harris** (☎6158-8590; per person US$25) offers a recommended walking tour (four people minimum) on the *comarca* mainland to a waterfall, focusing on birds, medicinal plants and Guna legends. Her *molas*, priced from US$30 to US$80, are widely acclaimed, and some are quite affordable. Any local can point you to her house, but try to make contact in advance.

Río Sidra's small dock isn't too far from the **airport** on the mainland, which currently only receives charter flights. Most visitors access the area from Gardi (Cartí), 15km west; boat trips cost from US$35.

Achudup (Isla Demar Achu)

Located northeast of Río Sidra (Mamartupu and Urgandi), this beautiful palm-forested island offers as accommodations both cabins and camping. Grounds are raked for debris and kept immaculate. Excursions include nearby Gorgidup (Isla Pelicano).

The excellent-value **Cabañas Demar Achu** (6806-5976, 6959-0866; camping/cabin per person incl 3 meals, transfers & tour US$55/80) has 20 cabins that are well spaced for privacy, and there are spacious concrete bathhouses, volleyball facilities and hammocks. Shady camping is also all-inclusive and well priced. Provides community visits to Río Sidra and snorkeling excursions.

Senidup

A tiny islet divided by a chain-link fence between two communities, this is a popular destination for backpackers, as it offers just about the cheapest lodging in the archipelago.

Franklin's Place (Cabañas Dubesenika; 6768-4075; www.facebook.com/pages/San-Blas-Isla-Franklin/401213326628331; dm/cabaña per person incl 3 meals US$31/50) is the best-known budget lodgings on the island. What is officially called Cabañas Dubesenika counts some 21 cane and wood cabins, five of which are dorms with five to 10 beds. It's a sprawling, friendly place with volleyball and basketball courts, electricity from 6pm to 10pm and a party atmosphere.

A thatched village of a dozen tourist cabins (half of them private), **Cabañas Senidup** (6945-4301; www.facebook.com/pages/Cabañas-Senidup/490060327776722; dm/cabaña per person incl 3 meals US$26/31) is a popular spot, even though its six dorms are a little crowded, with one sleeping 12 people. There's usually one English-speaking host on-site. Guests have access to beach games and volleyball, and free use of snorkel gear.

Transfers to Gardi (Cartí) are a bargain at US$20 round trip.

Narasgandup Bibbi (Isla Naranjo Chico)

Three kilometers northwest of Río Sidra (Mamartupu and Urgandi), this island is somewhere between a community and a resort island. It is populated, but it's also possible to find solitude.

Sleeping & Eating

There are several lodging options on the island with similar amenities. All provide boat transfers from Gardi (Cartí).

Cabañas Miro CABAÑAS **$**
(6951-8317; dm/r per person incl 3 meals US$35/50) For shoestringers who want nothing more than some thatch over their head and sand beneath their toes, this is the real deal. Accommodations are pretty basic in seven cabins – four private and three dormitories. There is little to do here, but dining at the big wood restaurant around the picnic table provides the perfect opportunity to mix with fellow travelers.

Transfers to Gardi (Cartí) are charged separately (US$20 one way).

★**Cabañas Casso** CABAÑAS **$$**
(Coco Loco; 6807-2768, 6151-7379; www.facebook.com/pg/sanblasfrontera; dm/r per person incl 3 meals & transfers US$30/70) Our favorite new place on Isla Naranjo Chico – which is also known as 'Coco Loco' – is small, with just four brightly painted cabins (one used as a dormitory with seven beds) that are perfectly formed and as upbeat as you'll find in the archipelago. Step outside your lodgings and you're halfway in the water.

Cabañas Naranjo Chico CABAÑAS **$$$**
(6686-7437, 6086-7716; www.sanblaskunayala.com; r/beach cabaña/stilt cabaña per person incl 3 meals, transfers & tours US$95/115/135) Six quiet cabins and a lovely swimming beach. Beachside cabins have sand floors; newer cabins set on stilts over the water are the most expensive. All have solar power. The Del Valle family are prompt with responses for reservations, which is rare in these parts. Prices drop to US$75/95/115 on the second night.

Cayos Los Grullos, Holandeses & Ordupuquip

The undisputed gems of the Archipiélago de San Blas are the Cayos Los Grullos, Holandeses and Ordupuquip, a triangle of three virtually uninhabited island chains that are separated by calm blue-green waters and surrounded by shallow reefs.

At the lower southwestern corner of the triangle are the Cayos Los Grullos (Crane Cays), a mere 10km northeast of Río Sidra. The northern tip of the triangle is formed by the Cayos Holandeses (Dutch Cays), while the Cayos Ordupuquip are located in the southeastern corner. Despite the lack of tourist facilities in the cays, yachties love to anchor near these islands, though it takes skill to keep your boat afloat here. The snorkeling in the Cayos Holandeses is astounding, though you'll see plenty of tropical fish and colorful reefs anywhere in the cays.

Getting There & Away

Most visitors come by sailboat on multiday tours. Depending on the distance between your hotel and the cays, motorboat transfers charge US$150 to US$200 round trip from Gardi (Cartí). The sea can get very rough out here, so make sure you have confidence in your captain and vessel, and ensure there are enough life jackets on board for everyone. And don't forget your snorkeling gear!

Aggwanusadub (Corazón de Jesús), Yandup (Narganá) & Central Islands

The densely populated islands of Aggwanusadub (Corazón de Jesús) and Yandup (Narganá), which are linked by a wooden footbridge, are of little interest to travelers, as they're the most westernized Guna communities in the *comarca*. Here Guna families inhabit cinderblock houses with tin roofs, wear Western clothing and hold all-island baseball tournaments. The people are friendly, and the visit makes an interesting contrast to some of the less developed islands. The islands are a springboard for Digir Dubu (Isla Tigre), oddly enough one of the most traditional islands in the archipelago.

The larger of the two islands, Yandup (Narganá) is on the south side of the bridge. It is home to the district's only courthouse and jail, so there are a lot of policemen on the island. If any ask for your passport, politely present it – that's their job. There's a mast here so wi-fi reception is good.

In 'downtown' Yandup (Narganá), the pink concrete **Hotel Noris** (☎6039-6842; s/d with fan US$10/20, air-con US$20/30; ❄) will do if you find yourself stuck waiting for a flight. Spotlessly clean, it has eight rooms, five of which are air-conditioned. Find the affable owner, Paco, at the pier.

Information

Banco Nacional de Panamá (⏰8am-3pm Mon-Fri, 9am-noon Sat) changes large bills. There is no ATM on the islands.

Getting There & Away

Charter flights from Panama City arrive at the Corazón de Jesús airstrip. There is currently no commercial service. Travel here by boat from Gardi (Cartí; one way US$20).

Digir Dubu (Isla Tigre)

Just a short boat ride from Aggwanusadub (Corazón de Jesús) and Yandup (Narganá), Digir Dubu (Isla Tigre) ranks among the most traditional islands in the Comarca de Guna Yala – though the whole island is lit by solar energy. With wide walkways separating homes, the island is tidy and uncrowded, which makes it easy to interact with local

WRECK REEF

Approximately 100m north of Cayos Holandeses is a spot known as Wreck Reef, which earned its name by snaring all kinds of vessels over the years. The reef's notoriety stems from the fact that it's fairly far offshore from the closest island, though the water south of the reef is barely 1m deep – the ocean floor north of the reef plunges 100m in half that distance. From a captain's perspective, this means that the ocean floor very quickly rises 100m to a dangerously shallow depth.

Over the years, many experienced sailors have died here, though these days it's mostly smugglers who meet their doom. In 1995 a smugglers' boat filled with TV sets slammed into the reef at night. Although the smugglers had hoped to skip out on import taxes by sailing from Colón's Zona Libre to Cartagena in Colombia, they instead helped local Guna communities catch up on their favorite Venezuelan soap operas without paying a cent.

A massive wreck is clearly visible at low tide offshore at Diadup (Isla Coco Bandera).

Guna. However, an island guide must accompany visitors; he/she will find you as soon as you get off the boat. The island is also home to some of the biggest festivals in the *comarca*. Traditional dances are performed free of charge, but visitors should offer a tip.

Festivals & Events

Feria de Isla Tigre DANCE
(Oct 10-15) This festival on Digir Dubu (Isla Tigre) celebrates the traditional Guna dance called Nogagope. The event is marked by communities from outlying islands converging on the island and dancing and competing for three days. The event is followed by a huge three-day festival that includes more dancing as well as various games and canoe races.

Sleeping

Cabañas Digir CABIN $
(6105-9581, 6099-2738; with/without bathroom s US$25/15, d US$35/25) The best feature here is the relaxed reception – guests have their own ample space but also get to see a fair amount of typical village life, with locals who seem more relaxed with travelers than elsewhere. Two cane-and-thatch *cabañas* have concrete floors, colorful hammocks and shared facilities; three more desirable ones are on stilts and closer to the beach.

The ocean here – on both sides of the complex – is crystal clear and fairly placid, so perfect for kayaking (from December to June) or snorkeling. Snorkel gear, meals (mains US$4.50 to US$7.50, lobster US$15) and transfers to Gardi (Cartí; US$30) are extra. The restaurant is open daily from 10am to 3pm and 6pm to 10pm.

Getting There & Away

Most guests arrive from Gardi (Cartí). A water taxi will cost US$30 one way.

Uggubseni (Playón Chico) & Eastern Islands

With regular air connections to Panama City, Uggubseni (Playón Chico) serves as a popular gateway to the eastern San Blás islands, especially since it's located near the archipelago's poshest accommodations on the tiny island of Yandup. If you're looking for more modestly priced accommodations, Playón Chico can provide; it also serves as a convenient jumping-off point for Dadnaggwe Dubbir (San Ignacio de Tupile).

While much of the island is covered by traditional dwellings, the main drag here is home to everything from missionaries and concrete churches to sundry shops and liquor stores. Although Uggubseni isn't set up to receive tourists, a quick stroll from the airstrip to the docks reveals the conflicting pressures shaping modern Guna life.

Domy's (6068-9985; per person US$10) is a three-bed dormitory on the 2nd floor of his wooden village house. Breakfast (only) is available for US$5 and tours can be arranged. It's located at the far end of the village from the main pier.

The island's only eatery, **Refresquería Sol** (6100-9255; mains US$3.50-5; 6am-10pm) is a hole-in-the-wall place not far from the pier. There'll be fish and seafood dishes on offer, as well as chicken and/or pork ones.

It's a 40-minute boat ride (US$20) from Uggubseni (Playón Chico), where the closest airport is located.

Yandup

Just five minutes by boat from Uggubseni, the islet of Yandup is home to the lovely **Yandup Island Lodge** (203-7762, 6682-9848; www.yandupisland.com; per person incl 3 meals & tours US$155-175) run by a very attentive Spanish and Guna family. Accommodations at this lodge are simple but comprise 10 lovely octagonal thatched-roof cabins with cold-water bathrooms; a half-dozen of the cabins sit right over the water. Light comes from solar panels and water from the mainland. The island's grassy grounds, palm shade and small but powder beach might be reason enough to just stay put.

Guests can be catered for with vegetarian meals at the large and breezy restaurant-bar, with more seating in a thatched *bohio* (hut) at the end of a very long pier. Tailored excursions include cultural visits as well as the usual snorkeling and hiking.

Air Panama (www.airpanama.com) flies daily to nearby **Uggubseni (Playón Chico) Airport** (US$80 one way). The lodge provides local boat transfers.

Assudub (Achutupu) & Uaguinega

With daily flights to Panama City, Assudub (Achutupu) – like Uggubseni to the west – serves as a popular gateway to the eastern San Blás islands.

Although the densely populated island isn't set up to receive overnight visitors, it's a popular day trip for visitors interested in seeing Guna village life. Of particular interest is the *onmagged nega,* the community gathering house at the center of the island, which often hosts important meetings, rituals and celebrations.

Getting There & Away

Air Panama (www.airpanama.com) flies daily to **Assudub (Achutupu) Airport** on the mainland from Panama City (one way US$80).

Uaguinega

Although it's a mere 100m from Assudub (Achutupu), the grassy isle of Uaguinega is a tiny and private refuge.

The **Hostal Guna** (☎6095-5309; d/r per person US$10/15) was once the upmarket Dolphin Lodge, although it's a decidedly low-budget affair now. The six cane-and-thatch cabins are collapsing into the sea, and a lackluster restaurant faces litter-plagued Assudub.

Air Panama (www.airpanama.com) flies daily to Assudub (Achutupu) Airport on the mainland from Panama City (one way US$80). Hostal Guna charges US$10 for a five-minute boat transfer from there.

The Road to Gardi (Cartí)

A 47km-long road links the Interamericana at El Llano with the port of Gardi (Cartí), the gateway to the Archipiélago de San Blas and its 365 offshore islands. While most travelers will be making a beeline in search of their own tropical island paradise, there are options for tarrying along the way.

Visitors must show their passports and pay an entry fee (US$20) upon crossing the border into the Comarca de Guna Yala after the 18Km marker.

Sights

Área Silvestre de Narganá WILDLIFE RESERVE
(www.miambiente.gob.pa; US$20) With excellent birdwatching and good rainforest trails, the 994-sq-km Área Silvestre de Narganá is a wildlife reserve of species-rich primary forest ideally explored with a naturalist guide. It was created by the Guna indigenous community in 1987 primarily to try to keep away squatters. Access the reserve via the Interamericana, going via Chepo, and turning onto the road to Gardi (Cartí) at the El Llano turnoff. Go by sturdy 4WD with plenty of clearance.

This is the best place in Panama to spot the speckled antshrike, the black-headed ant thrush and the black-crowned antpitta.

Guided tours of the reserve are available through Panama City tour agencies, and Guna guide Igua Jiménez' Igua's Tours (p233).

Sleeping

Pachamama Gypsy Lodge HOSTEL $
(☎6622-0479, 6761-9958; www.facebook.com/pachamamapanamaontheroadtosanblas; camping/dm/apt/cabin per person US$10/13/15/20) This eccentric place at the 11Km marker is where to head if you want to chill in the clouds. Set on 32 hectares of forest with a dozen waterfalls and a network of well-marked trails, it has five colorful cabins with little balconies, eight 'semi-private apartments' (bunk beds, shared bathroom) and two dormitories with up to six beds.

Mostly organic vegetarian meals – including a lot of mushrooms – are available from US$5. Day/overnight trips (US$60/75) on offer to the San Blás islands include meals. It's a fun and relaxing place to stay run by an affable French-Mexican couple.

Burbayar Lodge LODGE $$$
(☎269-9415; www.burbayar.com; 2-night package per person incl 3 meals, transfers & tours US$375) A work in progress during our visit, this somewhat shabby-chic lodge at the 15Km marker, run by Ancon Expeditions (p302), has five comfortable and good-sized cabins – ask for the one on the hilltop with 360-degree views of the surrounding rainforest. The jungle is the main reason for staying here; it is teeming with birds and other wildlife.

It is not exactly roughing it, but creature comforts are limited to cold-water showers and generator-powered electricity (from 6pm to 10pm only at the moment). Meals are served *table d'hôte*-style in the breezy open kitchen. Birdwatching trips and excursions to Lago Bayano also available.

Getting There & Away

Hired 4WD vehicles make the trip from Panama City in about two hours and charge from US$25 one way; ask at your hotel or hostel. They can drop you off at either of the two places to stay along the road to Gardi (Cartí). Alternatively take any bus headed for the Darién from Panama City and ask to be dropped off at El Llano (US$3.50). The lodges will pick you up from the Interamericana.

Darién Province

POP 55,753 / ELEV SEA LEVEL TO 2280M

Includes ➡

Best Places to Eat

- Canopy Camp (p248)
- Playa Muerto Community Lodging (p254)
- Hija del Conde (p247)
- Mi Niña Nidia (p249)

Best Places to Stay

- Canopy Camp (p248)
- Punta Patiño Lodge (p252)
- Pijibasal Community Tourism (p250)
- Hospedaje Sobia Kiru (p249)
- Tropic Star Lodge (p254)

Why Go?

One of the world's richest biomes is the 5790-sq-km Parque Nacional Darién, where the primeval meets the present with scenery nearly unaltered from one million years ago. Even today in the Darién, the Emberá and Wounaan people maintain many of their traditional practices and retain generations-old knowledge of the rainforest. Much of the Darién has remained untouched because of its volatile reputation.

The road to Yaviza – the most accessible part of the province – has scenes of habitat destruction. Cruising the waterways and hiking trails are the only ways to explore the slow-paced interior of Darién and the Pacific coast, where Emberá, Wounaan and Afro-Panamanians coexist.

The region's issues are complex. Police and military checkpoints are not infrequent because of drug trafficking. The Darién is not for everyone, but with careful planning and the right destinations, it offers opportunities for intrepid travelers to discover something truly wild.

When to Go

Dec–mid-Apr The premium months for sportfishing in the Pacific. Overall the ideal time to visit Darién, with drier trails and easier and more reliable transportation.

May, Oct–Nov With rivers running high and heavy rainfall, these months are generally the most difficult time to visit the region.

Oct–Feb Marine turtle hatching on the Pacific coast.

Darién Province Highlights

1. **Reserva Natural Punta Patiño** (p252) Searching for capybara while exploring this lush jungle reserve on the edge of the Golfo de San Miguel.
2. **Rancho Frío** (p251) Hiking along the spectacular jungle trails surrounding Rancho Frío, a ranger station on the edge of Parque Nacional Darién.
3. **Playa Muerto** (p254) Looking for harpy eagles and interacting with the Emberá people in this far-flung Pacific coast village.
4. **Canopy Camp** (p248) Enjoying the spectacular birdwatching and the lush setting of this ecolodge south of Metetí.
5. **Río Sambú** (p252) Traveling the wide, molten-chocolate river through spectacular jungle and mangroves to a remote Emberá settlement.

History

Living within the boundaries of the Darién, the group commonly known as the Chocóes emigrated from Colombia's Chocó region long ago. Anthropologists divide the indigenous people here into two groups – the Emberá and the Wounaan – though, language apart, the groups' cultural features are identical. Both groups prefer to be thought of as two separate peoples though.

Before the introduction of guns, the Emberá and Wounaan were experts with the *boroquera* (blowgun), using darts tipped with lethal toxins from poisonous frogs and bullet ants. Many scholars believe these groups forced the Guna out of the Darién and into the coastal area and islands they now inhabit.

The Emberá and Wounaan are known for their incredibly fine dugout canoes. Known as *piraguas,* they have shallow bottoms that are ideal for use in the dry season when rivers run low. The Panama Canal Authority has long employed Emberá and Wounaan craftspeople to make the *piraguas* used to reach the upper parts of the canal's watershed. At the same time, as late as the 1990s, the US Air Force solicited Emberá and Wounaan help with jungle living. Many of them trained US astronauts and pilots at Fort Sherman, near Colón, in tropical-wilderness survival.

Today the majority of the nearly 10,000 Emberá and Wounaan in Panama (another 6000 or so are in Colombia) live deep in the rainforests of the Darién, particularly along the Ríos Sambú, Jaqué, Chico, Tuquesa, Membrillo, Tuira, Yapé and Tucutí.

Culture

The Emberá and Wounaan live on subsistence agriculture supplemented by limited fishing and poultry raising. Historically both groups were more reliant on slash-and-burn agriculture and hunting, which are practices now restricted in the national park. Commercial rice and maize plantations offer work for seasonal migrant laborers.

The Emberá and Wounaan are also exceptional woodcarvers and basket weavers. Boas, frogs and birds were traditionally carved from dark reddish-brown cocobolo hardwood, and now tiny animal figurines are also made from tagua nuts. The women (especially the Wounaan) produce some of the finest baskets in Latin America. Woven from palm fibers, each requires months of intensive labor. These products fetch a high market price and provide a much-needed secondary income for most communities.

Built on stilts 3m to 4m off the ground, Emberá and Wounaan homes are extremely well suited to the rainforest. Flooring uses thin but strong strips of plentiful palm bark, and the vaulted design protects occupants and food from ground pests and swelling rivers. Medicinal plants and edible vegetables and roots are grown below. Many homes are thatched and open-sided for breezes, with barbecues and mud ovens.

Western clothing is replacing traditional attire, except among older women. Traditionally they wore only a skirt but they are increasingly donning bras and shirts. Many wear traditional jewelry, especially wide silver bracelets and silver-coin necklaces. They also stain their bodies with purplish-black designs made with juice from the *jagua* fruit. The henna-like dye is believed to have health-giving properties and wards off insects.

Like the Guna, the Emberá and Wounaan have a strong measure of political autonomy, though this is under threat by increasing external pressures. These include encroachment by *interioranos* (interior people), the

RESPONSIBLE TRAVEL IN THE DARIÉN

Travelers should carefully consider the impact they might have if they visit Emberá and Wounaan communities in the Darién. Unlike Guna Yala, the Darién sees few foreign visitors. Yet the Emberá and Wounaan are very hospitable.

Make an effort to respect the sensibilities of your hosts. Although some women still go topless, these are fairly conservative societies. Most villagers are happy to pose for a photo, but you should always ask first. Photos of communities sent back in thanks (via a guide) are treasured.

Instead of giving out candy or coins to village children, consider buying dictionaries, Spanish-language books and much-needed stationery supplies to donate to local schools.

Tourism has a long way to go in the region, which is one reason that a visit to an Emberá or Wounaan village is so refreshing. Visitors must work together with locals to promote cultural preservation.

'Hispano-Indians' that make up the vast majority of the Panamanian population from Los Santos and Chiriquí provinces, and habitat destruction by loggers, accelerated in recent years due to the paving of the Interamericana. Missionaries, particularly evangelicals, have almost entirely eliminated the traditional religious values of both groups. Youth move to the cities for their employment prospects, or work for drug traffickers as mules, both of which have prompted fears that the Emberá and Wounaan cultures are under serious threat.

Tours

The Darién is the only part of Panama where a guide is necessary, and it is obligatory in the national park. You can hire Spanish-speaking guides locally for about US$25 to US$35 per day, but transportation costs will be very expensive. Tour operators can take care of all arrangements without a language barrier, teach you about the incredible local ecology, cook for you and humor you when you have blisters. Another option is to go with an independent naturalist guide.

★ Jungle Treks ADVENTURE
(☎6438-3130; www.jungletreks.com) Run by veteran naturalist Rick Morales, this recommended outfitter specializes in boutique, expedition-style travel for groups of six or more. Destinations include the interior and Pacific coast. Check the website for set dates. Custom trips have a three-day minimum.

Ancon Expeditions TOURS
(☎Panama City 269-9415; www.anconexpeditions.com) Ancon travels to its own private lodge in Punta Patiño on the Pacific coast and further afield. Special programs for birdwatchers and hikers are outstanding. Excellent English.

Ecotour Darién TOURS
(☎6510-6838, 6736-1607; www.ecotourdarien.com; Santa Fé) Smaller and more flexible than other operators, this is one of the very few agencies leading tours in the Darién that is actually based in the province. Everything from a one-day trip to La Palma to five days visiting Sambú and Playa Muerto is available. Some English spoken.

Information

Information on the Darién quickly goes out of date. Always seek updates, ideally from a guide who leads frequent trips to the area or lives there.

KNOW BEFORE YOU GO

To visit the Parque Nacional Darién (p250) you must pay lodging fees before you go. Call the Ministerio de Ambiente (p70) in Panama City for the direct-deposit account number for the 'Cuenta de Vida Silvestre' at BNP (Banco Nacional de Panamá). Visit any branch, but be sure to keep your receipt to show at the Sede Administrativa Parque Nacional Darién (p249) in Yaviza, where you must stop to register (note: it's open only on weekdays until 4pm). If you somehow forget, the closest BNP branch to Yaviza is in Metetí (p248).

Note that in order to travel in the area you must write to **Senafront** (Servicio Nacional de Fronteras; ☎Panama City 527-1000; www.senafront.gob.pa; Las Cumbres; ⏰8am-4pm Mon-Fri) in Panama City ahead of time, in Spanish, with details of your itinerary and carry a half-dozen photocopies of the letter (and the same number of copies of your passport) with you as it will be examined at checkpoints. The office can also suggest local guides.

In Yaviza, the Sede Administrativa Parque Nacional Darién (p249) can provide some information on the park and potentially help you find guides (usually rangers with days off). Travelers must register here to visit the park and check in with the police before heading out into the jungle. There are also a half-dozen checkpoints along the road to Yaviza beginning at Chepo and at all ports.

Panama City's Instituto Geográfico Nacional (p294) sells topographical maps for some regions of the Darién.

DANGERS & ANNOYANCES

The greatest hazard in the Darién is the difficult environment. Trails, when they exist at all, are often poorly defined and are rarely marked. Many large rivers that form the backbone of the Darién transportation network create their own hazards. Any help at all, let alone medical assistance, is very far away. If you get lost, you are almost certainly done for. To minimize these risks, it's recommended that you explore the Darién either as part of an organized tour or with the help of a qualified guide.

Dengue and malaria are risks. Consult your doctor before you go about necessary medication, and cover up as much as possible, especially at dusk. Areas of the Parque Nacional Darién are prime territory for the deadly fer-de-lance snake. The chances of getting a snakebite are remote, but do be careful and always wear boots on treks. Although they don't carry Lyme disease, ticks are widespread. Bring tweezers and a few books of matches to ensure you're able to remove the entire tick if it's burrowed well into your skin.

In May 2017 the US State Department lifted its warning about visiting remote areas of the Darién off the Interamericana, including the entire Parque Nacional Darién. It does, however, continue to advise on security, choosing safe transportation, health issues and documentation.

Although the no-go zones in the Darién are well removed from the traditional tourist destinations, their dangers cannot be underestimated. Drug traffickers who utilize these jungle routes don't appreciate encountering travelers. In the past, former Colombian guerrillas or runaways took refuge here. Missionaries and travelers alike have been kidnapped and killed in the southern area of the Darién.

The areas between Boca de Cupe and Colombia, the traditional path through the Darién Gap, remain particularly treacherous. As there's only minimal police or military presence here, you're on your own if trouble arises.

Despite all this, most parts of the Darién can be visited in total safety.

Getting There & Away

The Interamericana terminates 285km from Panama City in the frontier town of Yaviza, and the vast wilderness region of the Darién lies beyond. The highway starts again 150km further on in Colombia. This break between Central and South America is known as the Darién Gap – literally the end of the road.

There are buses every hour from Albrook Bus Terminal (p300) in Panama City to Yaviza (US$16, 4½ hours). Be sure to tell the bus driver your destination if getting off along the way.

Getting Around

In the vast jungles of Darién Province, rivers are often the only means of travel, with *pangas* or *canoas* (long canoes; mostly motorized) providing the transportation.

Boats depart Puerto Quimba, near the Interamericana city of Metetí, for La Palma and from Yaviza for interior destinations such as El Real. In La Palma, you can hire motorized boats to Sambú. From El Real, travelers can access Pijibasal or Parque Nacional Darién via land transportation.

THE ROAD TO YAVIZA

The Interamericana runs from Panamá Province along the spine of Darién Province, with Yaviza literally at the end of the road. Police checkpoints are frequent along this road, so have your passport (and five photocopies of it) ready and be prepared to discuss your travel plans.

Lago Bayano

Heading toward the Darién on the Interamericana there are some excellent attractions within an easy day's drive from Panama City, including Lago Bayano. It was formed when the Río Bayano was dammed in 1976, thus creating the second-largest source of power in Panama after Lago Gatún. The lake (admission US$2), which takes its name from Bayano, the man who led the largest slave revolt in 16th-century Panama, is a great destination for boating, birdwatching and, to the south, caving. The area has little development and lots of waterbirds, including the largest heron in Panama. It is also where you'll find sizable Emberá and Wounaan indigenous communities, whose homeland, the mainland Comarca Guna de Madugandi, is north of the lake.

Sights & Activities

Bayano Caves CAVE

(Cuevas Bayano; www.facebook.com/pages/Bayano-Caves/139611959391512) On the south side of Lago Bayano, the Bayano Caves are a fun adventure. Cavers wade up Río Tigre though a sculpted Paleolithic cavern that is 850m long and full of bats and amphibians. Depending on water levels, it might be necessary to swim. Exploring the cave requires round-trip boat transportation, a guide, headlamps and helmets. Contact Igua's Tours in Panama City or local operators Bayano Tour or Panama Caves for the full package.

Bayano Tour CAVING

(☎6744-5300, 6959-6833; orteganoy@hotmail.com; boat tour for up to 5 people US$60) Noy Ortega runs tours of the Bayano Caves from his house on the west side of the bridge spanning Lago Bayano. Including a visit to the canyon and impressive rock walls that enclose the entrance to the Río Tigre costs US$70 and a visit to an Emberá village US$90. He also rents one-/two-person kayaks for US$5/10 per hour.

Panama Caves CAVING

(☎6674-1135; http://panamacaves.com/en) This established local tour agency near the Bayano Caves can organise tours.

Igua's Tours TOURS
(☎6791-6499; iguat28@yahoo.com) A recommended English-speaking Guna naturalist guide, the Panama City–based Igua Jimenez leads boat tours to Lago Bayano with visits to the caves, indigenous communities and surrounding rainforest.

Sleeping

★**Hija del Conde** AGROTURISMO $$
(☎296-7576, 6679-7731; www.hotelhijadelconde.com; Chepo; d/tr US$60/90;) Should you want to pause for a spell while traveling to the Darién, you could do a lot worse than this homey 30-room hotel outside Chepo in the middle of a working farm, with cows and pigs, and horses to ride. There's a curious viewing tower, a fishing pond, a three-part pool and a decent restaurant (mains US$10 to US$15).

Getting There & Away

Half-hourly buses linking Panama City with Yaviza will drop you off at Chepo or Lago Bayano (US$6, two hours).

Getting There & Away

From Panama City to Yaviza it's 285km. The last stop with decent services before Darién Province is Tortí (US$7, two hours), 155km from Panama City. Police checkpoints are more frequent from here onward. Always stop at the checkpoints; note that your papers – passport and five photocopies, letter to Senafront (p245) and driver's license if driving – may be reviewed.

Ipetí & Around

Some 45km southeast of Lago Bayano is the town (or towns) of Ipetí: Ipetí Choco, Ipetí Guna and Ipetí Colono. Each is occupied by a different cultural group (Emberá, Guna and *interiorano,* or 'Latino').

It's worth stopping in Ipetí Choco to visit the thatched **Casa Cultural** (Cultural House; ☎6763-5048, 6760-3227) on stilts. Here you'll find some two-dozen women artisans who will sell you their magnificent woven baskets and masks, cocobolo walking sticks and small animals carved from tagua nuts. You can also have a traditional *jagua* body painting done for a few dollars. This henna-like plant extract leaves a temporary tattoo for up to two weeks.

Twelve kilometers past Ipetí is the village of Tortí, a useful stop with restaurants, a police station, a health clinic and a two restaurants. The **Hotel Portal Avicar** (☎6746-0051; http://hotelportalavicar.com-panama.com/en; Interamericana s/n; s/d/tr/f US$38/44/55/60;) is a peach-colored blockhouse on the Interamericana that conceals a lovely garden with coconut palms, banana trees, and hummingbirds feasting on sugar water. It has 15 attractive rooms with terraces and hammock. The vine-covered terrace restaurant (open 6am to 9pm) serves traditional country-style dishes (mains US$7 to US$16).

After Tortí, police checkpoints are more frequent. Always stop at the checkpoints and ensure that your paperwork (passport, five photocopies, letter to Senafront, driver's license) is in order.

GETTING TO COLOMBIA

The Interamericana stops at the town of Yaviza and reappears 150km further on, far beyond the Colombian border. Overland crossings through the Darién Gap on foot are not recommended and are, in fact, illegal. The only way to reach South America is to fly directly to the city of your choice, to fly with Air Panama (p298) to Puerto Obaldía on Panama's Caribbean coast and cross over to Capurganá in Colombia, or to take a sailing excursion or a motorboat trip such as that offered by San Blas Adventures (p231).

Puerto Lara

POP 300

8km south of the Interamericana and 12km south of Santa Fé, the small but well-organized community of Puerto Lara (also known as Boca de Lara) offers a unique opportunity to view the Wounaan, a more elusive indigenous group than the Emberá. Though both groups are celebrated for their basket-weaving and tagua-seed carving, the Wounaan are generally viewed as the better *artesanos* and you'll find plenty of delightful crafts for sale. Activities on hand include boating, fishing, hiking and birdwatching.

Sleeping

Camp Laurel Wounaan CABAÑAS $
(☎6695-9364, 6874-0957; www.puertolara.com; s/d US$15/25) This mini 'village' on a grassy slope right by the Río Lara has 10 thatched huts that accommodate two people each

and a central pavilion used as a common area. There's dancing and artisan displays (US$15); meals are US$5 extra.

Puerto Lara Community Accommodations CABAÑAS $
(☎6691-3008; www.puertolara.com; s/d US$20/25) Right in the center of the village, this open-sided lodge giving on to the main road has a half-dozen basic rooms and a shared toilet. Activities on offer include fishing (US$10), hiking, birdwatching (US$10) and traditional dancing (US$50).

Information

Caja de Ahorros (⏱9am-3pm Mon-Fri, to noon Sat) National Savings Bank branch in nearby Santa Fé; has an ATM.

Getting There & Away

From Panama City, buses to Santa Fé (US$8, three hours) depart every hour or so. From here take a *colectivo* (US$1) to Puerto Lara.

Metetí

POP 7980

Located 1km southeast of a police checkpoint, Metetí is the Darién's fastest-growing locality, with the best infrastructure in the region. The surroundings are being quickly deforested, though at least one interesting ecolodge can be found on the outskirts. Travelers generally come to reach La Palma and interior Darién via a scenic boat ride.

Sleeping & Eating

For last-minute purchases there is a good-sized grocery store.

Hotel Felicidad HOTEL $
(☎299-6544; www.hotelfelicidad.com; d/tr US$25/35; P ❄ 📶) Bleach-scented with clean concrete rooms, this place has friendly service and flowery gardens. When choosing from among the 29 rooms, avoid the ones without an outside window as they tend to be musty.

★ **Canopy Camp** LODGE $$$
(☎Panama City 264-5720; 7-night package high/low season US$3180/2125; P 📶) Catering to serious birdwatchers, this ecocamp sits in the Reserva Hidrológica Filo del Tallo, a verdant secondary rainforest. Eight spacious, multiroom safari tents with wooden decks are outfitted with comfortable beds, screens, electricity and fans. Each thatched lodging is extremely private, with freestanding bathrooms equipped with open-air hot-water showers that bring the forest and its wildlife that much closer.

Guiding is top-notch, with dedicated naturalists and an on-site 1550m-long trail. For birdwatchers, a trip to the Darién is a chance to glimpse a harpy eagle or a crested eagle, in addition to poison-dart frogs, golden-headed manakins and barred puffbirds.

Sitting on 40 hectares of forest with orange, papaya, banana and soursop trees and 2km down a rough road from the Interamericana, the lodge is made sustainable by such initiatives as solar panels, wastewater treatment and composting.

In low season, lodging may be open to passers-by. The communal area/lounge has wi-fi and a library replete with Darién titles. Visitors mostly come on four- to seven-day packages that include meals, guiding and transfers from Panama City. It's between kilometer markers 247 and 248.

Restaurante Doña Lala PANAMANIAN $
(☎6722-8022, 299-6601; Camino a Puerto Quimba; mains US$9-12; ⏱6am-9pm) Cheap and cheerful, this spotless cafeteria-style restaurant is usually packed with locals. Breakfasts like shredded beef and eggs are popular. Lunch options (around US$4) include stewed chicken, grilled meat, rice and plantains. There's lots of fish and seafood at night. It's 800m inland from the Interamericana on the way to Puerto Quimba.

Information

BNP (Banco Nacional de Panamá; ☎299-6125; Interamericana s/n; ⏱8am-3pm Mon-Fri, 9am-noon Sat) Along the Interamericana north of town opposite the police station. Has an ATM.

Getting There & Away

From Panama City, buses to Yaviza stop in Metetí (US$10, three hours) about every hour.

For boats to La Palma or Sambú, take the turnoff for Puerto Quimba, a port on the Río Iglesias. A passenger pickup shuttles between Metetí and Puerto Quimba every 30 minutes from 6am until 9pm (US$2) or take a taxi (US$10). The 20km-long paved road between Metetí and Puerto Quimba is excellent.

From Puerto Quimba, boats to La Palma (US$3.50, 20 minutes) leave when full between 5:30am and 5pm. A one-way charter may also be an option. Passengers must register at the police checkpoint next to the ticket counter.

Boats seating up to 18 passengers also go to Sambú (US$22, 2¾ hours) daily.

Yaviza

POP 4400

Part bazaar and part bizarre, this concrete village is literally at the end of the road. Here the Interamericana grinds to a halt after 12,580km from Alaska, and beyond lies the famous Darién Gap, the no-man's-land between Panama and Colombia. Rough edged and misshapen, it's hardly a destination in its own right, but for travelers it's an essential check-in stop for entry to Parque Nacional Darién.

Sights

Fuerte de San Gerónimo FORT

(Fort of St Geronimo) Yaviza's only real 'sight' (apart from the wobbly **footbridge** spanning the Río Chucunaque), the ruined Fort of St Geronimo, built by the Spanish to keep pirates (and buccaneers and privateers and corsairs) at bay looks out at the confluence of the Ríos Chico and Chucunaque southeast of the center.

Sleeping & Eating

Hospedaje Sobia Kiru HOTEL $

(6150-5449, 299-4409; leticiapitti0311@gmail.com; d US$25; P ❄) A two-story turquoise house with 24 spick-and-span rooms and powerful air-conditioning, the 'Good Heart Inn' is on a side street running up from the port, next to the Cable Onda office. Manager Leticia Pitti Lewis extends a very warm welcome.

Ya Darien GUESTHOUSE $

(6653-0074; d US$25; ❄) This slightly grubby guesthouse located down from the port has 16 frayed but tidy rooms with cold-water showers. The best of the seven rooms upstairs are Nos 1 and 5 between the small balcony.

★ **Mi Niña Nidia** PANAMANIAN $

(My Daughter Nidia; mains US$3-5; 6am-8pm) We might visit this place for the name alone, but its eyrie-like position above the main street and overlooking the port is a major draw (as is a quick breakfast before the boat to El Real sets sail).

Information

Those heading to Parque Nacional Darién must stop here to register at the **Sede Administrativa Parque Nacional Darién** (299-4495; Interamericana, Ministerio de Ambiente Bldg; 8am-4pm Mon-Fri) and check in with the police before heading into the jungle.

THE LAST ROADLESS PLACE: DARIÉN GAP

Since the first Interamericana Congress met in Buenos Aires in 1925, the nations of the Americas have been dedicated to the completion of a great hemispheric road system. Today only 106km of unfinished business prevents that system from being realized – the so-called **Darién Gap**. This defiant stretch of wilderness, which separates the continents of North and South America, is the sole barrier in the way of an otherwise unbroken 30,600km highway winding from Circle City, Alaska, to Puerto Montt in Chile.

Constructing this missing bit of highway would increase trade and travel options. Colombia's civil war got in the way for years, and during that time the Darién Gap was both buffer zone and safe haven for rogue factors. Today drug trafficking in the region has become the greatest issue. But there is still a lobby for a unified Panamerican highway, called the Interamericana here.

Detractors, many of them Panamanians, cite the cost of excavating rugged terrain, the threat of foot-and-mouth and other diseases spreading to North America and the still-delicate issue of security. Every year the national border service, Senafront (p245), seizes hundreds of kilos of drugs making their way through the region from Colombia. Human traffickers also transport migrants heading to North America via this ungovernable expanse.

Road building provides a quick conduit for resource extraction, and thus a road through the Darién Gap would likely spur the deforestation of one of the world's finest remaining tropical rainforests, precipitating devastating habitat loss for its unique flora and fauna. A cultural shift in remote communities would inevitably follow.

Currently Panama's mostly paved Interamericana highway traverses deforested cattle country to end at the town of Yaviza in Darién Province. The road, marked by many police checkpoints, frequently deteriorates due to weather and heavy use by trucks.

Getting There & Away

Buses from Panama City go to Yaviza (US$16, 4½ hours) at least every hour every day.

Public boats to El Real go sporadically when full (US$5) from the ferry pier. The cost of a private boat charter to El Real (US$60 to US$90 one way) depends on the motor size and the price of fuel at the time.

PARQUE NACIONAL DARIÉN

Parque Nacional Darién is the most ecologically diverse land-based national park in all of Central America. Although it's often overshadowed by oft-repeated security concerns in the province, there is no doubt that it is the crown jewel of Panama's national parks, mostly sought after by specialists like biologists and botanists.

El Real

POP 1180

Riverside El Real (official name: El Real de Santa María) dates from the conquistador days when it was merely a fort beside the Río Tuira. The settlement prevented pirates from sailing upriver to plunder Santa María, where gold from the Cana mines was stored. Today El Real is one of the largest towns in the Darién, though it's still very much a backwater. It's not an unattractive place, with a few hints of its colonial past, including a 16th-century Spanish cannon in the main square.

El Real is the last sizable settlement before Parque Nacional Darién. Those heading up to Rancho Frío or Pijibasal should either hire a local guide or join a tour – the Ministerio de Ambiente won't let you proceed unescorted. Before arriving, send a letter of intent to Senafront (p245) and contact the Panama City office of the Ministerio de Ambiente (p70) to pay for lodging in the park. See p245 for more information.

The best place for a meal is **Fonda Doña Lola** (meals US$3-5; 7am-8pm), a cheap eatery serving rice and meat dishes with fried plantains. It's in the center of El Real near the church.

Getting There & Away

Piraguas (long canoes) ferry passengers down the Río Chucunaque in Yaviza to the port of Mercadeo; the center of El Real is a 15-minute walk from the jetty. When your boat arrives at Mercadeo, register at the Senafront stand in front of the boat landing.

Pickup trucks transfer passengers via Pirre Uno to Pijibasal (US$30), a 1½-hour hike from Rancho Frío, the entry point to Parque Nacional Darién.

Pijibasal

POP 160

Tourism is relatively new to this welcoming Emberá indigenous village adjacent to Parque Nacional Darién, but it is well worth visiting if you are in the vicinity. On the banks of the Río Pirre, the village consists of about 15 thatched huts raised on stilts around a large 'green.' Come with insect repellent and boots.

Villagers sell traditional crafts, like baskets and masks, and will paint you with *jagua* 'ink' (US$1.50); these traditional 'tattoos' are considered a form of insect repellent and wash off after a few weeks. As part of a visit you can participate in a number of activities like birdwatching or day trips to the national park with a local Emberá guide (US$35).

Activities

Pijibasal is an excellent base for Parque Nacional Darién as you can walk to the entrance along a paved road in 15 minutes. Rancho Frío is an easy 1½-hour hike away. To reach the fabulous **Cascada del Río Perresénico**, a wonderful waterfall the agile can slide down, takes 45 minutes. There are also several trails to 1435m-tall **Cerro Pirre**.

Sleeping & Eating

★**Community Tourism** HOMESTAY $
(6771-7388, 6907-3716; www.facebook.com/people/Pijibasal-Darien/100009774465964; per person US$15) Visitors can stay in the village in one of two open-sided thatched huts with mosquito nets, foam mattresses and bed linens. There's a total 10 beds, a concrete bathroom with cold-water shower and solar-powered electricity for a couple of hours in the evening. Meals (US$5) such as chicken or fish with rice and fruit are taken in a communal hut.

Getting There & Away

Pijibasal is 12km from Mercadeo/El Real, where you can arrange a transfer in the back of a pickup (US$30 one way). In the rainy season (April to November), it may be possible to transfer via the Río Pirre for about the same price.

Rancho Frío

Some 17km south of El Real, as the lemon-spectacled tanager flies, is the Rancho Frío sector of Parque Nacional Darién. It's home to Station VIII (sometimes called Pirre Station, not to be confused with the station at the top of Cerro Pirre near Cana). Rare bird species here include the crimson-bellied woodpecker, the white-fronted nunbird and the striped woodhaunter.

The excellent trail network includes a two-day trek to Cerro Pirre ridge and a one-hour walk through jungle to cascades; the Cascada del Río Perresénico is about a half-hour away on foot. Neither should be attempted without a guide as they are unmarked – if you get lost out here you're finished.

Sleeping & Eating

At Rancho Frío (or Station VIII along the trail), there is a very basic two-story **dormitory lodge** (per person US$15) with a total of 14 bunk beds accommodating 28 visitors. There is also a shady **campsite** (per person US$6). Electricity is run off batteries and its use is very limited (when available).

Visitors must bring their own food and purified water. Cooking fuel is scarce, so let the rangers do the cooking (about US$15 a day for the service, if available, is appropriate). Try the *zapote* (sapodilla) fruit growing in front of the lodge – its fleshy orange meat has the taste and texture of mango.

Getting There & Away

Rancho Frío is 17km from Mercadeo/El Real and can be reached by hiking (four hours), or a combination of boating and hiking or 4WD transportation (from US$30). It's a 1½-hour hike from Pijibasal. For those hiking, the trails offer minimal indications; it's imperative to go with a guide.

INTERIOR DARIÉN

Leaving the pavement behind, you enter the untamed wilderness of indigenous villages, forest-lined rivers and vast forest reserves teeming with plant and animal life.

La Palma

POP 6000

The provincial capital of Darién Province, La Palma is a one-street town located where the wide Río Tuira meets the Golfo de San Miguel. Pastel-colored houses on stilts lord it over the muddy waterfront, a scene abuzz with commerce and bars.

Most travelers pass through La Palma in order to take a boat ride to somewhere else, such as the nature reserve and lodge at Reserva Natural Punta Patiño or the Emberá village of Sambú up the muddy river of that name. If you have time, check out the ruins of 18th-century Spanish **Fuerte San Lorenzo**, five minutes away by boat (US$15).

Every facility of interest to travelers is located on Calle Principal, the main street, which is just over the boat pier. There's a bank, a hospital and a police station, as well as three hotels, bars, restaurants and provisions stores.

Sleeping & Eating

Pensión Tuira PENSION $
(299-6316; Calle Principal; d US$25-35;) Our favorite of the La Palma trio, this guesthouse has 18 so-so rooms, but the greatest attraction is the fabulous terrace with expansive views of the gulf. Room 13 just off the terrace is the best choice, though the smaller room 17 is also a decent option. Air-conditioning costs US$5 extra.

Hotel Biaquirú Bagará HOTEL $
(299-6224; Calle Principal; d with/without bathroom US$25/15;) Simple and sweet, Hotel Biaquirú Bagará has hardwood decks, wicker furniture and firm beds above street level. Five of the 13 rooms share a bathroom, while the rest have their own and are air-conditioned. Choose room 13 for its great terrace with views and own rocking chair.

La Paila del Pueblo HOTEL $
(299-6490; Calle Principal; s/d US$10/15;) The waterfront La Paila del Pueblo has thin walls and mattresses, and 10 none-too-salubrious rooms but good sea views. Staff here can arrange visits to the Emberá community at Mogué.

Restaurante La Paila del Pueblo PANAMANIAN $
(Calle Principal; mains US$2.50-4; 6am-10:30pm) This simple place offers inexpensive meals (think soup or meat with rice) in a waterfront setting.

★**Lola Grill** PANAMANIAN $$
(6721-8632; Calle Principal; mains US$8-15; 7am-8pm Mon-Sat) Drop in to this clean and cheerful cafe for a serve of shrimp or

fish *criollo*-style (with a flavorful sauce) in addition to grilled meats. Always a warm welcome. It's located up a flight of steps from the main street.

Information

There's a branch of the **Banco Nacional de Panamá** (299-6230; Calle Principal; 8:30am-3pm Mon-Fri, 9am-noon Sat) with an ATM at the northern end of Calle Principal.

Getting There & Away

Boats from Puerto Quimba (US$3.50, 20 minutes), the springboard for La Palma, leave when full, passing by between 5:30am and 5pm. Puerto Quimba has buses to Metetí, from where other buses head north for Panama City or south to Yaviza.

Chartering a private boat and guide will cost between US$120 and US$300 per day, gas included.

Reserva Natural Punta Patiño

On the southern shore of the Golfo de San Miguel, 25km from La Palma, is this private 263-sq-km wildlife reserve owned by Ancon and managed by the organization's for-profit arm, Ancon Expeditions. It contains species-rich primary and secondary forest and is one of the best places in the country to spot a harpy eagle, Panama's national bird. Even if the big bird proves elusive, there's a good chance of seeing everything from three-toed sloths and capybaras, the world's largest rodents, to pumas.

The only way to reach the reserve is by boat or plane. Landing on the tiny strip of oceanside grass that's called a runway is definitely part of the experience.

Sleeping

★Punta Patiño Lodge LODGE $$$
(in Panama City 269-9415; www.anconexpeditions.com; 3-night package incl guide, meals & lodging per person US$950;) Perched on a ridge in a gorgeous nature reserve, these 10 gaily painted wooden cabins have air-conditioning and private cold-water showers, but the decor is forgettable, worn and tired. Staff are extremely attentive and meals well prepared; views from the dining area are breathtaking. Activities include guided nature hikes, night tours, boating the mangroves and swimming from a black-sand beach.

Getting There & Away

The Ancon Expeditions (p245) tour includes the round-trip airfare between Panama City and Punta Patiño Airport, lodging, food and activities including a trip up the Río Mogué to the Emberá village of Mogué and a naturalist-guided hike to a harpy eagle's nest.

Independent travelers can hire boats in La Palma to reach Punta Patiño for about US$450. Contact Ancon Expeditions to reserve a cabin.

Mogué

Mogué is an Emberá village on the banks of the Río Mogué, east of Punta Patiño and south of La Palma. Villagers here are keen to show off their culture and lifestyles and are adept at finding harpy-eagle nests in the surrounding jungle. Though Mogué is set up for tourism, it remains a traditional village, seeing fewer visitors than Emberá villages in Panamá Province and Guna villages in the Comarca de Guna Yala.

Everything done for the benefit of tourists certainly has a price tag; the community has reportedly started charging visitors US$50 per person and a local guide is US$20.

Visitors may sleep in a tent in the *casa comunal* (US$10) or string up a jungle hammock (bring your own). A private outhouse and cold shower are unlocked when tour groups arrive. Although the village sounds are part of the whole experience, light sleepers may want to bring earplugs.

Meals (US$5) are hearty portions of rice, beans, meat and plantains – tasty and filling.

Getting There & Away

Several outfitters and guides offer overnight excursions to Mogué. It might be possible to catch a local boat from La Palma (US$15 one way). In the future, there may be access via a paved road; enquire at the boat pier in La Palma.

Río Sambú

The mouth of the wide and very brown **Río Sambú** is two hours by boat southwest of La Palma. Fortitude is a must, but a trip up the Sambú offers a true *Heart of Darkness*–style adventure. The gateway to the dozen indigenous communities here is Sambú and its sister settlement, Puerto Indio.

You can camp in a tent, sleep in a jungle hammock or arrange to sleep on the floor of an Emberá or Wounaan family home. If you can speak Spanish, finding a host family for the night won't be difficult.

Getting There & Away

A *panga* (small motorboat) from Puerto Quimba (US$22, 2¾ hours) goes to Sambú daily at around 6am, with one stop in La Palma. Beyond that you will need to hire another guide and a separate, smaller *piragua* (long canoe) to navigate the narrow, shallow sections upriver. In rainy season, the river is navigable by *piragua* all the way to Pavarandó, the most inland of the indigenous communities on the Sambú.

Sambú

POP 950

Riverside Sambú (sometimes appearing as Boca de Sábalo on maps) is an interesting stop, populated by Emberá, Wounaan, *interioranos* (or mestizos) and *cimarrones* (the ancestors of African slaves who escaped and settled in the jungle). Quite built up and populous by Darién standards, it makes a good springboard for visiting riverside indigenous communities further upstream and absorbing the slow jungle pace.

Sights & Activities

Puerto Indio VILLAGE

From Sambú, visitors can cross the **Río Sábalo Bridge** to the twin village of Puerto Indio (with permission from the Emberá and Wounaan) and visit petroglyphs or mangrove forests. The village stands in stark contrast to 'built-up' Sambú, with thatched houses on stilts surrounding a large grassy football pitch.

Bayamón VILLAGE

This Emberá village south of Sambú is worth visiting. Get here by public bus (US$1), which runs along the paved road leading south from town between 6am and 8pm.

Lupicinio Zarco TOURS

(☎6870-8528) Local guide Lupicinio Zarco, who lives near the Sambú Hause hotel, leads hiking excursions to Bocaca Verano, a lagoon with crocodiles and prolific birdlife, in the dry season.

Sleeping & Eating

Sambú Hause GUESTHOUSE $

(☎6672-9452; www.sambuhausedarienpanama.com; s/d US$10/20) Orthographically challenged Sambú Hause is an attractive yellow-and-turquoise thatched clapboard run by friendly Maria. Cozy but simple, it has two rooms with shared bathroom and one with its own facilities and air-conditioning. There's a lovely breezy terrace with barbecue. Cultural tours can be arranged here.

Villa Fiesta GUESTHOUSE $

(☎6792-9493,6712-0250; ricardosambu76@yahoo.com; d US$25; ❄) This very central guesthouse atop a general store counts four simple but large rooms, two with air-con, two with fans and all with cold-water bathrooms. The shared terrace looks out to the underused airport. Host Emberá *cacique* (local leader) Ricardo Cabrera speaks fluent *americano* and is a treasure trove of local information.

Brytnie PANAMANIAN $

(mains US$3-6; ⏱7:30am-8pm) Pretty much the only game in town, this tiny place with two tables serves up acceptable fish, chicken and pork dishes with the inevitable *patacones* (fried plantains). Cold beer and a warm welcome.

Getting There & Away

At the time of research, there were only charter flights flying in and out of Sambú Airport. A panga (small motorboat) from Puerto Quimba (US$22, 2¾ hours) goes to Sambú's boat pier daily at around 6am, making a brief stop in La Palma. It returns between 4pm and 4:30pm.

PACIFIC COAST

With rough surf, jungle rivers and deep wilderness, the Pacific coast of the Darién is barely a destination, save for adventurers and hard-core deep-sea fishers. There is little here in terms of infrastructure, but it is a fascinating area that merits preservation and a visit – if you have the time, money and fortitude.

Jaqué & Around

POP 3000

On a pretty coastline pounded by waves, Jaqué is a sleepy, rather unattractive village with no road access. Concrete paths run down the middle of streets and there's a diverse population of Emberá, Wounaan and *cimarrones* (descendants of escaped slaves that set up communities in the Darién jungle). Marine turtles come to nest here seasonally and volunteers can get involved during the seasonal *arribadas* (arrivals).

TURTLE VOLUNTEERING

From mid-July through December, throngs of marine turtles make a pilgrimage to this wild coast to lay their eggs where they were born. The presence of avid predators – including humans – is threatening this natural cycle and turtle populations have been dwindling.

The **Grupo de Conservación de Tortugas de Jaqué** (Colegio de la Tierra; ☎264-6266, 6047-2373; www.colegiodelatierra.org), a grassroots organization made up of concerned Jaqué residents, has been able to save tens of thousands of turtle hatchlings in recent years. The group has spent the last decade patrolling beaches and releasing hatchlings, a daily task that takes place both late at night and in the dawn hours. Now it is looking for help.

The five species found along this coast are the olive ridley, the endangered greenback, the endangered hawksbill, the endangered leatherback and the critically endangered Kemp's ridley. Volunteers patrol the beach, transfer eggs to a safe nursery until their hatching and help in their release. From October to February hundreds of turtles are released in the dawn hours. It's a magnificent task to take part in and a wonderful experience.

October marks the height of the season. In low season, volunteers can assist with community outreach or work with mangrove reforestation along the Río Jaqué.

The group provides dorm accommodations including three meals for around US$35.

A large Senafront (border control) presence flags the town's relative proximity to the Colombian border, 40km to the southeast, though there is no official border crossing here. Check in with Senafront upon arrival and departure; it's in a large concrete building near the river port.

Boat driver **Ovedio Cardenas** (☎6124-8123; 1hr boat ride US$45) speaks Spanish and can take visitors upstream to see Bioquera, a Wounaan village where you can purchase tagua carvings and handmade baskets. Available mostly weekends.

On the beach, **Marie Village** (☎6003-8468; per person incl breakfast US$20) has cute cabins with kitchenette. They're the best digs in town, though they're a good 10-minute walk to the center. Dinner is available with advance notice.

If money is no object, the **Tropic Star Lodge** (☎in USA 800-682-3424; www.tropicstar.com; Bahía Piña; 3-day/4-night nonfishing/fishing package per person from US$2490/3570; ❄@≋) overlooking Bahía Piña offers one of Panama's best experiences for fishing enthusiasts. Packages include lodging, all meals and the use of a boat with captain. Tropic Star arranges charter flights (for an extra fee) to and from Panama City.

Getting There & Away

Air Panama no longer has scheduled flights between Panama City and Jaqué. The only reliable way to reach Jaqué is via chartered transport, though you might be able to catch a ride in a boat from La Palma (around US$50 per person, three to five hours).

Playa Muerto

POP 180

Easily the most remote and exciting place you'll visit in Panama, this coastal settlement with the less-than-enticing name of 'Dead Beach' is well worth a visit for up-close views of a genuine Emberá community, unspeakably beautiful and unspoiled beaches, and long hikes through streams and up hills that will almost certainly reward you with a glimpse of a harpy eagle. But it's not a destination for everyone, requiring a long, uncomfortable and expensive boat ride or an arduous two-day trek through the jungle from Sambú to get to.

Sleeping

Community Lodging HOSTEL $
(☎6672-7663, 6510-6838; hostel lodgings per person US$15) This raised *casa comunal* with thatched roof due east of the police station provides mattresses on the floor under mosquito netting or hammocks for sleeping in. Shared toilets and showers are below. There's a total lack of privacy here, but the Emberá women dressed (in fact, undressed from the waist up) in traditional garb are friendly. Excellent meals served here.

Getting There & Away

The only reliable way to reach Playa Muerto is via chartered transport from La Palma (from US$700 round-trip, four hours), though you might be able to catch a ride in a public boat from the boat pier there (around US$50 per person, three to five hours).

Understand Panama

Panama Today

After Panama cut the ribbon on one of the world's most ambitious transportation projects, the mood is mixed. Will the Panama Canal expansion turn out to be a sound investment? The country is already in the hole for its recent spending spree. Though modernity rules, dig a little and you will find that challenges persist for the underserved population of indigenous groups and the rural poor. Working through conflicting ambitions of conservation and growth, this is a country at the crossroads.

Best on Film

Hands of Stone (2016; dir. Jonathan Jakubowicz) Biopic of boxing legend Roberto Durán, with Robert De Niro.
Quantum of Solace (2008; dir. Marc Forster) Agent 007 is out for revenge, with scenes filmed in Casco Viejo.
The Tailor of Panama (2001; dir. John Boorman) A reluctant spy lets loose.

Best in Print

Getting to Know the General (Graham Greene; 1984) A portrait of General Omar Torrijos by his longtime friend.
Empire of Blue Water (Stephen Talty; 2008) An intriguing pirate history and a *New York Times* bestseller.
Panama (Carlos Ledson Miller; 2007) Explores the turmoil of the Noriega years with snapshots of history.
Confessions of an Economic Hitman (John Perkins; 2005) Investigates the shadowy world of overseas business.

Best Food Websites

Degusta (www.degustapanama.com) Website and app with diner-based reviews and photos.
Restaurant Week (http://restaurant.week.com.pa) Restaurants showcase their offerings each September with tastings and deals.
Andres Madrigal (www.andresmadrigal.com) Site of a prominent Panama City chef.

The Expanding Canal

Consistently one of the fastest-growing economies in Latin America, Panama owes much of its prosperity to the Panama Canal. In the last century, the canal has cast the isthmus as the western hub of global commerce. Each year, more than four million containers traverse it, their hulls filled with everything from bananas to oil, lumber and shiny new cars. You may have never visited Panama, but it is quite likely that both the fruit in your juice and the accessories in your pocket once did.

One of the world's largest transportation projects, the Panama Canal's US$17 billion expansion has doubled the capacity and tripled the traffic in the canal by digging deeper to accommodate bigger vessels and adding a third lane. Before the expansion, the canal hauled in US$2 billion annually.

A financial boon for Panama, the expanded Panama Canal was first projected to reach completion on the heels of the canal's 100-year anniversary. Thanks to a series of setbacks, however, the project was completed nearly two years later, with the first ship, a giant Chinese container ship, passing through its locks in June 2016.

As of early 2019, the Panama Canal expansion has reportedly exceeded expectations in both total tonnage and traffic. Transit times have also decreased from three and a half hours to two and a half hours. The success of the wider locks have, according to Esteban G. Saenz, former vice president for transit business at the Panama Canal Authority, via *The American Journal of Transportation,* sparked discussions of a possible fourth lock.

Sitting on Green Riches

Although the canal has defined Panama for the last century, it's what lies just beyond this engineering marvel that could define the next 100 years. A third of the country is set aside as protected areas and national parks, and the culture and customs of Panama's indigenous populations remain largely intact. Yet visitor numbers are nowhere near those of neighboring Costa Rica. Many assume that Panama is all about its capital and commerce. But while Panama races toward rapid-fire development, the resources it has always had (and often neglected) have started to attract attention.

Panama's intriguing history, which includes the voyages of Columbus and the plunders of 17th-century pirates, may be its main intact treasure. One of the most biodiverse places in the world, the country is a refuge for an incredible array of species. Its first-rate nature destinations range from lush, untapped rainforests to solitary beaches and uninhabited isles.

Is it packaged and tourist ready? Not exactly. Yet many travelers will find that that's precisely its charm.

Building a New World

There is a sharp contrast between Panama's urban and rural counterparts. Panama City is all sparkling skyscrapers, cement mixers and scaffolds, yet an hour outside of the capital, indigenous Emberá paddle dugout canoes. The modern and ancient somehow coexist, but each year there is friction at their boundaries.

The reduction in poverty levels has slowed, and Panama still has the fifth-worst income distribution in Latin America. Many provincial residents have relocated to Panama City in search of opportunity. City dwellers blame the most recent influx for increasing traffic, pollution and crime. Yet, with record low unemployment and robust foreign investment, Panama has remained dogged in its attempts to unlock its potential. It's also very good at putting its best foot forward. Stroll through the renovated historic Castro Viejo or drive the ultra-modern coastal beltway and you might think all is right with the world.

There is hope that the country's investments in infrastructure will pay off. But with US$20 billion in national debt, many Panamanians are weary of the national 'spend now, pay later' approach. More and more, citizens have been protesting about the privatization of public resources, high-level corruption and unchecked development.

Yet growth continues on the horizon. Panama restored diplomatic ties with China in 2017 and was brought into China's global Belt and Road Initiative. The new trade partnership, which comes with the promise of a bullet train, is expected to infuse billions of dollars of Chinese investment in Panamanian infrastructure in the next 20 years.

Other upgrades include a new cruise port slated for the Amador Causeway in 2020 and the expansion of Tocumen International Airport, expected for the 2019 papal visit. And just like that, this country of 4 million residents bets the farm and steps into the big league.

POPULATION: **4.1 MILLION**

AREA: **75,417 SQ KM**

GDP: **US$62 BILLION**

GDP GROWTH: **5.8%**

UNEMPLOYMENT: **4.7%**

INFLATION: **0.7%**

if Panama were 100 people

65 would be mestizo
12 would be indigenous
9 would be of African descent
7 would be of European descent
7 would be of mixed African and Spanish descent

belief systems

(% of population)

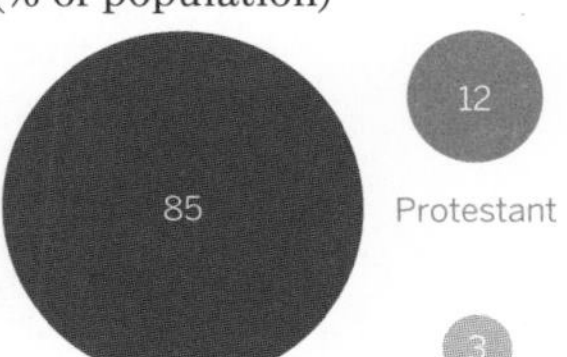

population per sq km

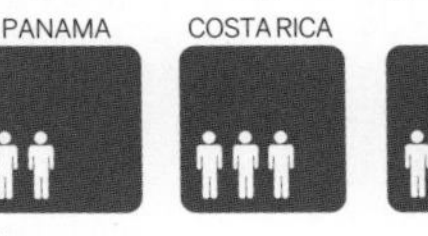

≈ 30 people

History

The waistline of the Americas, Panama has played a strategic role in the history of the western hemisphere, from hosting the biological exchange of species to witnessing clashes between cultures. Once an overland trade route linking ancient Peru and Mexico, post–Colombian conquest Panama became the conduit for exported Inca treasures. Set amid two oceans, transit is a longtime theme here. As the Panama Railroad once brought prospectors to the California gold rush, the Panama Canal has become the roaring engine of global commerce.

Lost Panama

The coastlines and rainforests of Panama have been inhabited by humans for at least 10,000 years, and it's estimated that several dozen indigenous groups, including the Guna, the Ngöbe-Buglé, the Emberá, the Wounaan and the Naso were living on the isthmus prior to the Spanish arrival. However, the tragedy of Panama is that, despite its rich cultural history, there are virtually no physical remains of these great civilizations.

Old Panama and Castilla Del Oro, by CLG Anderson, is a narrative history of the Spanish discovery, conquest and settlement of Panama as well as the early efforts to build a canal.

Unlike the massive pyramid complexes found throughout Latin America, the ancient towns and cities of Panama vanished in the jungles, never to be seen by the eyes of the modern world. However, tales of lost cities still survive in the oral histories of Panama's indigenous communities, and there is hope among Panamanian archaeologists that a great discovery may yet be made.

What is known is that early inhabitants were part of an trading zone that extended as far south as Peru and as far north as Mexico. Archaeologists have uncovered exquisite gold ornaments and unusual life-size stone statues of human figures as well as distinctive types of pottery.

Panama's first peoples also lived beside both oceans, and fished in mangrove swamps, estuaries and coral reefs. Given the tremendous impact that fishing has had on the lives of isthmians, it seems only fitting that the country's name is derived from an indigenous word meaning 'abundance of fish.'

TIMELINE

11,000 BC

The first humans occupy what is now Panama, and their populations quickly flourish thanks to the rich resources found along both the Pacific and Atlantic coastlines.

2500 BC

Panama is home to some of the first pottery-making villages in the Americas, including those of the Monagrillo culture, dating from 2500 to 1700 BC.

100 BC

Panama becomes part of an extensive trade network of gold and other goods that involves many disparate civilizations and extends from Mesoamerica to the Andes.

New World Order

In 1501 the discovery of Panama by Spanish explorer Rodrigo de Bastidas marked the beginning of the age of conquest and colonization in the isthmus. However, it was his first mate, Vasco Núñez de Balboa, who was to be immortalized in the history books, following his discovery of the Pacific Ocean 12 years later.

On his fourth and final voyage to the New World in 1502, Christopher Columbus went ashore in present-day Costa Rica and returned from the encounter claiming to have seen 'more gold in two days than in four years in Spain.' Although his attempts to establish a colony at the mouth of the Río Belén failed due to fierce local resistance, Columbus petitioned the Spanish Crown to have himself appointed governor of Veraguas, the stretch of shoreline from Honduras to Panama.

Following Columbus' death in 1506, King Ferdinand appointed Diego de Nicuesa to settle the newly claimed land. In 1510 Nicuesa followed Columbus' lead and once again tried to establish a Spanish colony at Río Belén. However, local resistance was once again enough to beat back Spanish occupation, and Nicuesa was forced to flee the area. Leading a small fleet with 280 starving men aboard, the weary explorer looked upon a protected bay 23km east of present-day Portobelo and exclaimed: *'¡Paremos aquí, en nombre de Dios!'* ('Let us stop here, in the name of God!'). Thus was named the town of Nombre de Dios, one of the first Spanish settlements in the continental New World.

Much to the disappointment of Columbus' conquistador heirs, gold was not abundant in Panama. Add tropical diseases, inhospitable terrain and less than welcoming natives to the mix, and it's easy to see why Nombre de Dios failed several times during its early years. However, a bright moment in Spanish exploration came in 1513 when Vasco Núñez de Balboa heard rumors about a large sea and a wealthy, gold-producing civilization across the mountains of the isthmus – almost certainly, these rumors referred to the Inca empire of Peru. Driven by equal parts ambition and greed, Balboa scaled the continental divide, and on September 26, 1513, he became the first European to set eyes on the Pacific Ocean. Keeping up with the European fashion of the day, Balboa immediately claimed the ocean and all the lands it touched for the king of Spain.

The famous crossing of the isthmus included 1000 indigenous slaves and 190 Spaniards, including Francisco Pizarro, who would later conquer Peru.

The Sack of Panamá: Sir Henry Morgan's Adventures on the Spanish Main, by Peter Earle, details the Welsh pirate's looting of Panamá in 1671.

The Empire Expands

In 1519 a cruel and vindictive Spaniard named Pedro Arias de Ávila (or Pedrarias, as many of his contemporaries called him) founded the city of Panamá on the Pacific side, near where Panama City stands today. The governor is best remembered for such acts as ordering the beheading of Balboa in 1517 on a trumped-up charge of treason, as well as ordering

1501

Spaniard Rodrigo de Bastidas becomes the first European to see Panama; Christopher Columbus arrives a year later and explores Bocas, coastal Veraguas and Portobelo.

1506

Christopher Colombus dies and Diego de Nicuesa is appointed to settle the territory known as Veraguas.

1513

Searching for a city of gold, Vasco Núñez de Balboa leads a grueling overland expedition and is the first European explorer to see the Pacific Ocean.

1519

Pedro Arias de Ávila (Pedrarias) founds the city of Panamá, which becomes a major transit point for gold plundered from Peru, packed overland to the Pacific coast and transferred by galleon to Spain.

murderous attacks against the indigenous population, whom he roasted alive or fed to dogs when the opportunity arose.

Despite his less than admirable humanitarian record, Pedrarias established Panamá as an important Spanish settlement, a commercial center and a base for further exploration, including the conquest of Peru. From Panamá, vast riches including Peruvian gold and Oriental spices were transported across the isthmus by foot to the town of Venta de Cruces, and then by boat to Nombre de Dios via the Río Chagres. Vestiges of this famous trade route, which was known as the Sendero Las Cruces (Las Cruces Trail), can still be found throughout Panama.

Panama: Four Hundred Years of Dreams and Cruelty, by David A Howarth, chronicles the history of the isthmus from Balboa's 1513 exploration through to 1964, with scintillating tales of conquistadors and buccaneers.

As the Spaniards profited from the wealth of plundered civilizations, the world – especially the English privateers lurking in coastal waters – began to notice the prospering colony. In 1572 Sir Francis Drake destroyed Nombre de Dios and set sail for England with a galleon laden with Spanish gold. It was also during this expedition that Drake climbed a high tree in the mountains, thus becoming the first Englishman to set eyes on the Pacific.

Hoping to stave off further ransacking and pillaging, the Spanish built large stone fortresses at Portobelo and Fuerte San Lorenzo. However, these fortifications weren't enough to stop the Welsh buccaneer Sir Henry Morgan from overpowering Fuerte San Lorenzo and sailing up the Río Chagres in 1671. After crossing the length of the isthmus, Morgan destroyed the city of Panamá, made off with its entire treasure and arrived back on the Caribbean coast with 200 mules loaded with loot.

After Panamá burnt to the ground, the Spanish rebuilt the city a few years later on a cape several kilometers west of its original site. The ruins of the old settlement, now known as Panamá Viejo, as well as the colonial

SALVAGING SUNKEN GALLEONS

During the period of colonization between the 16th and 18th centuries, Spanish galleons left home carrying goods to the colonies and returned laden with gold and silver mined in Colombia, Peru and Mexico. During these years, literally thousands of ships – not only Spanish but also English, French, Dutch and pirate, and those carrying African slaves – foundered, overcome by pirates or hurricanes, in the green-blue waters of the Caribbean.

On many occasions great storms wiped out entire fleets, resulting in a tremendous loss of lives and cargo. The frequency of shipwrecks spurred the Spaniards to organize operations to recover sunken cargo. By the 17th century, Spain maintained salvage flotillas in the ports of Portobelo, Havana and Veracruz. These fleets awaited news of shipwrecks and then proceeded immediately to the wreck sites, where the Spaniards used Caribbean and Bahamian divers, and later African slaves, to scour sunken vessels and the sea floor around them.

1671

Henry Morgan overpowers Fuerte San Lorenzo, sails up the Chagres and sacks the city of Panamá. After a crushing defeat, a new walled city is built in present-day Casco Viejo.

1698

A Scottish trading colony established in the Darién fails and plunges Scotland into economic depression. The financial losses heavily influence the union of Scotland with England in 1707.

1739

Following numerous pirate attacks, Spain finally abandons the short but perilous trans-isthmian trade route in favor of sailing all the way around Cape Horn in South America.

1821

Liberator Simón Bolívar leads the northern swath of South America to independence from Spain, and Panama joins the newly formed union of Gran Colombia.

city of Casco Viejo, are both located within the city limits of present-day Panama City.

British privateering didn't cease with the destruction of Panamá. In 1739 the final nail was hammered into the Spanish coffin when Admiral Edward Vernon destroyed the fortress of Portobelo. Humiliated by their defeat and robbed of one of their greatest defenses, the Spanish abandoned the Panamanian crossing in favor of sailing the long way around Cape Horn to the western coast of South America.

Heat, starvation and botfly infestations were just some of the challenges troops faced in the US Army's disastrous 1854 Darién expedition, chronicled by Todd Balf in *The Darkest Jungle.*

The Empire Ends

Spain's costly Peninsular War with France from 1808 to 1814 – and the political turmoil, unrest and power vacuums that the conflict caused – led Spain to lose all its colonial possessions in the first third of the 19th century.

Panama gained independence from Spanish rule in 1821 and immediately joined Gran Colombia, a confederation of Colombia, Bolivia, Ecuador, Peru and Venezuela – a united Latin American nation that had long been the dream of Simón Bolívar. However, internal disputes led to the formal abolition of Gran Colombia in 1831, though fledgling Panama retained its status as a province of Colombia.

Birth of a Nation

Panama's future forever changed from the moment that the world's major powers learned that the isthmus of Panama was the narrowest point between the Atlantic and Pacific Oceans. In 1846 Colombia signed a treaty permitting the USA to construct a railway across the isthmus; it also granted it free transit and the right to protect the railway with military force. At the height of the California gold rush in 1849, tens of thousands of people traveled from the east coast of the USA to the west coast via Panama in order to avoid hostile Native Americans living in the central states. Colombia and Panama grew wealthy from the railway, and talks of an inter-oceanic canal across Central America began.

Mountains were moved and thousands perished in the process. *Panama Fever,* by Matthew Parker, makes real the magnitude of building the Panama Canal, documenting the imperial vision and the backbreaking work of the laborers from the West Indies.

The idea of a canal across the isthmus was first raised in 1524 when Charles V of Spain ordered that a survey be undertaken to determine the feasibility of constructing such a waterway. In 1878, however, it was the French who received a contract from Colombia to build a canal. Still basking in the warm glory of the recently constructed Suez Canal in Egypt, French builder Ferdinand Marie de Lesseps brought his crew to Panama in 1881. Much like Napoleon before him, de Lesseps severely underestimated the task at hand, and over 22,000 workers died from yellow fever and malaria in less than a decade. By 1889, insurmountable construction problems and financial mismanagement had driven the company bankrupt.

1855

An estimated 12,000 laborers die, particularly from malaria and yellow fever, while building the Panama Railroad. Despite being only 76km long, the railroad requires 304 bridges and culverts.

1878

The French are granted the right to build a canal though Panama. After malaria and yellow fever claim over 22,000 lives, the French declare bankruptcy and abandon the project.

1902

US president Theodore Roosevelt convinces the US Congress to take control of the abandoned French canal project. Colombia is in the midst of the Thousand Days' War.

1912

Isla de Coiba becomes a penal colony infamous for its brutality. (Closed in 2004, it now operates as a national park renowned for its biodiversity.)

The USA saw the French failure as a lucrative business opportunity that was ripe for the taking. Although it had been scouting locations for a canal in Nicaragua, the USA pressured the French to sell them their concessions. In 1903 de Lesseps' chief engineer, Philippe Bunau-Varilla, agreed to the sale, though the Colombian government promptly refused to accede to it.

At one time the Panama Railroad was the highest-priced stock on the New York Stock Exchange, at US$295 a share.

In what would be the first of a series of American interventions in Panama, Bunau-Varilla approached the US government to back Panama if it declared its independence from Colombia. On November 3, 1903, a revolutionary junta declared Panama independent, and the US government immediately recognized the sovereignty of the country. Although Colombia sent troops by sea to try to regain control of the province, US battleships prevented them from reaching land. Colombia did not recognize Panama as a legitimately separate nation until 1921, when the USA paid Colombia US$25 million in 'compensation.'

Growing Pains

Following independence, Bunau-Varilla was appointed Panamanian ambassador to the USA and his first act in office paved the way for future American interventions in the region. Hoping to profit from the sale of the canal concessions to the USA, Bunau-Varilla arrived in Washington, DC, before Panama could assemble a delegation. On November 18, Bunau-Varilla and US secretary of state John Hay signed the Hay–Bunau-Varilla Treaty, which gave the USA far more than had been offered in the original treaty. In addition to owning concessions to the canal, the USA was also granted 'sovereign rights in perpetuity over the Canal Zone,' an area extending 8km on either side of the canal, and a broad right of intervention in Panamanian affairs.

Despite opposition from the tardy Panamanian delegation as well as lingering questions about the treaty's legality, the treaty was ratified, ushering in an era of friction between the USA and Panama. Construction began again on the canal in 1904, and despite disease, landslides and harsh weather, the world's greatest engineering marvel was completed in only a decade. The first ship sailed through the canal on August 15, 1914.

The Panama Railroad (www.panamarailroad.org) website contains photographs, historical information and fascinating travelogues, including one written by Mark Twain in 1868.

In the years following the completion of the canal, the US military repeatedly intervened in the country's political affairs. In response to growing Panamanian disenchantment with these interventions, the Hay–Bunau-Varilla Treaty was replaced in 1936 by the Hull–Alfaro Treaty. The USA relinquished its rights to use its troops outside the Canal Zone and to seize land for canal purposes, and the annual sum paid to Panama for use of the Canal Zone was raised. However, increased sovereignty was not enough to stem the growing tide of Panamanian

1914

The Panama Canal is finally completed after a decade of monumental effort, thanks to the work of 75,000 laborers, many thousands of whom perish during the construction.

1964

The riots of January 9 (Martyrs' Day) escalate tensions between Panama and the USA over occupation rights of the Canal Zone. Twenty Panamanian rioters are killed and more than 500 are wounded.

1968

The Panamanian army overthrows president-elect Arnulfo Arias after just 11 days in office. Exploiting the power gap, General Omar Torrijos becomes Panama's leader.

1977

The Torrijos–Carter Treaty is signed, allowing for the complete transfer of the canal and 14 US army bases from the USA to Panama by 1999.

opposition to US occupation. Anti-US sentiment reached boiling point in 1964 during a student protest that left 27 Panamanians dead and 500 injured. Today the event is commemorated as Día de Los Mártires (National Martyrs' Day).

As US influence waned, the Panamanian army grew more powerful. In 1968 the Guardia Nacional deposed the elected president and took control of the government. Soon after, the constitution was suspended, the national assembly was dissolved and the press was censored, while the Guardia's General Omar Torrijos emerged as the new leader. Torrijos' record is spotty. Though he plunged the country into debt as a result of a massive public-works program, Torrijos was successful in pressuring US president Jimmy Carter into ceding control of the canal to Panama. The Torrijos–Carter Treaty guaranteed full Panamanian control of the canal as of December 31, 1999, as well as a complete withdrawal of US military forces.

For all things canal related visit www.pancanal.com, the official site, with historical information, photographs and even webcams of the canal in action.

The Rise & Fall of Noriega

Still feeling triumphant from the recently signed treaty, Panama was unprepared for the sudden death of Torrijos in a plane crash in 1981. Two years later, Colonel Manuel Antonio Noriega seized the Guardia Nacional, promoted himself to general and made himself the de facto ruler of Panama. Noriega, a former head of Panama's secret police, a former CIA operative and a graduate of the School of the Americas, quickly began to consolidate his power. He enlarged the Guardia Nacional, significantly expanded its authority and renamed it the Panama Defense Forces. He also created a paramilitary 'Dignity Battalion' in every city, town and village, its members armed and ready to inform on any of their neighbors if they showed less than complete loyalty to the Noriega regime.

Things went from bad to worse in early 1987 when Noriega became the center of an international scandal. He was publicly accused of involvement in drug trafficking with Colombian cartels, murdering his opponents and rigging elections. Many Panamanians demanded Noriega's dismissal, protesting with general strikes and street demonstrations that resulted in violent clashes with the Panama Defense Forces. In February 1988 Panamanian president Eric Arturo Delvalle attempted to dismiss Noriega, though the general held on to the reins of power, deposing Delvalle and forcing him to flee Panama. Noriega subsequently appointed a substitute president who was more sympathetic to his cause.

The US Army's School of the Americas, previously based in Panama, trained some of the worst human-rights abusers in Latin America – including Manuel Noriega.

Noriega's regime became an international embarrassment. In March 1988 the USA imposed economic sanctions against Panama, ending a preferential trade agreement, freezing Panamanian assets in US banks and refusing to pay canal fees. A few days after the sanctions were imposed, an unsuccessful military coup prompted Noriega to step up

1980

Panamanian boxer Roberto Durán beats Sugar Ray Leonard for the world welterweight championship.

1983

Following General Torrijos' death in a plane crash in 1981, former CIA operative Manuel Noriega rises to power and ushers in an era of repression.

1988

US president Ronald Reagan invokes the International Emergency Economic Powers Act, freezing Panamanian government assets in US banks and prohibiting payments by American businesses to the Noriega regime.

1989

The US invades Panama and extradites Noriega to Miami, where he is later convicted on charges of conspiracy and drug trafficking. He is incarcerated until September 2007.

violent repression of his critics. After Noriega's candidate failed to win the presidential election in May 1989, the general declared the election null and void. Meanwhile, Guillermo Endara, the winning candidate, and his two vice-presidential running mates were badly beaten by some of Noriega's paramilitary Dignity Battalions, and the entire bloody scene was captured by a TV crew and broadcast internationally. A second failed coup in October 1989 was followed by even more repressive measures.

The Path Between the Seas by acclaimed historian David McCullough makes vivid the mammoth undertaking of creating the Panama Canal.

On December 15, 1989, Noriega's legislature declared him president and his first official act of office was to declare war on the USA. The following day, an unarmed US marine dressed in civilian clothes was killed by Panamanian soldiers while exiting a restaurant in Panama City.

The US reaction was swift and unrelenting. In the first hour of December 20, 1989, Panama City was attacked by aircraft, tanks and 26,000 US troops in 'Operation Just Cause,' though the US media often labeled it 'Operation "Just 'cuz."' Although the stated intention of the invasion was to bring Noriega to justice and create a democracy, it left more than 2000 civilians dead and tens of thousands homeless, and destroyed entire tracts of Panama City.

On Christmas Day, the fifth day of the invasion, Noriega claimed asylum in the Vatican embassy. US forces surrounded the embassy and pressured the Vatican to release him, as entering the embassy would be considered an act of war against the tiny country. However, the USA memorably used that psychological tactic beloved of disgruntled teenagers, namely bombarding the embassy with blaring rock music (Van Halen and Metallica were among the selections). The embassy was also surrounded by mobs of angry Panamanians calling for the ousting of Noriega.

After 10 days of psychological warfare, the chief of the Vatican embassy persuaded Noriega to give himself up by threatening to cancel his asylum. Noriega surrendered to US forces on January 3 and was flown immediately to Miami, where he was convicted of conspiracy to manufacture and distribute cocaine. After his US prison sentence ended in 2007, he was extradited to Paris in April 2010. A retrial found Noriega guilty and sentenced him to seven years in prison, but he was conditionally released in order to serve 20 years in Panama, starting in December 2011, where he was incarcerated until his death on May 29, 2017.

Spanish readers and history buffs should pick up *El Caballo de Oro* by Juan David Morgan, a novel about the building of the Panama Railroad in the quest for California gold.

Modern Woes

After Noriega's forced removal, Guillermo Endara, the legitimate winner of the 1989 election, was sworn in as president, and Panama attempted to put itself back together. The country's economy was in a shambles, and its capital had suffered damage not only from the invasion itself but also from the widespread looting that followed. Corruption scandals and

1994

Ernesto Pérez Balladares is sworn in as president after an internationally monitored election campaign. Balladares emphasizes his party's populist Torrijos roots rather than its former association with Noriega.

1999

Mireya Moscoso is elected Panama's first female president. The USA ends nearly a century of occupation by closing all of its military bases and turning over control of the canal.

2006

Seventy-eight per cent of Panamanian voters cast a 'yes' ballot in support of an expanded canal that could double its capacity.

2010

After Noriega finishes his US prison sentence, France indicts him on charges of money laundering, but before he can serve his seven-year term, he is extradited by Panama to serve a 20-year sentence there.

internal fighting were rampant during both the Endara administration as well as the ensuing Balladares administration.

In 1999 Mireya Moscoso took office and became Panama's first female leader. Moscoso's ambitious plans for reform were not realized. As Panama celebrated its centenary in 2003, unemployment rose to 18%. Moscoso was accused of wasteful spending – as parts of the country went without food, she paid US$10 million to bring the Miss Universe pageant to Panama.

Moscoso was followed by Martín Torrijos, who implemented a number of fiscal reforms, including an overhaul of the nation's social-security system. His proposal to expand the Panama Canal was overwhelmingly approved in a national referendum on October 22, 2006.

A Panama of Scandals

On May 3, 2009, Panama bucked the Latin American leftist trend by electing conservative supermarket magnate Ricardo Martinelli president. Part of the conservative Democratic Change (CD) party, Martinelli was a pro-business choice who created an investment boom by slashing trade barriers and red tape. During his tenure, ambitious public projects like Central America's first subway system became the order of the day and Panama's 8% growth rate sparkled as the best in Latin America.

Eventually the honeymoon ended and the success story turned part pulp fiction, part political thriller. Martinelli's former vice president and dark-horse opposition leader Juan Carlos Varela was elected president in 2014 on promises to play by the book and implement constitutional checks and balances. Martinelli faced charges of corruption in a US$45 million program to feed poor schoolchildren. There was also a wire-tapping scandal involving political foes. Remember those colossal infrastructure projects? Some US$1.2 billion of contracts have come under scrutiny and some project directors with government contracts have been arrested. Martinelli fled to Miami via private jet to a luxury condo that was made famous in the film *Scarface*. US marshals arrested him on June 12, 2017, putting him into a Miami federal detention center. He was extradited to Panama in June 2018 to face wire-tapping charges.

Adding to Panama's woes, an anonymous source leaked over 11.5 million documents from the Panamanian law form Mossack Fonseca in 2015. Known as the Panama Papers, they detailed financial information of worldwide leaders and public figures revealing corruption on a colossal scale. Mossack Fonseca had created shell companies which helped international entities and individuals evade international sanctions, commit fraud and evade taxes. Though the law firm shut down in 2018, the fallout from the papers still continues.

Learn how one company's tropical meddling created a model for capitalism in *Bananas: How the United Fruit Company Shaped the World* by Peter Chapman.

2014

Opposition leader Juan Carlos Varela is elected president on the back of promises to tame corruption; previous president Ricardo Martinelli flees to Miami where he is eventually detained in relation to various charges.

2015

The Panama Papers are leaked from Panamanian law firm Mossack Fonseca, exposing the dubious financial practices of wealthy public figures worldwide.

2016

Panama inaugurates the US$17 billion canal expansion on June 26, tripling container traffic to meet the growing needs of international shipping.

May 2017

Noriega dies aged 83 following ongoing complications from an operation to remove a brain tumour in March of the same year.

The Panamanian Way of Life

At the crossroads of the Americas, the narrow isthmus of Panama bridges not only two continents but also two vastly different paradigms of Panamanian culture and society. Roughly one hour from the gleaming skyscrapers of Panama City, you can find an indigenous family paddling a dugout canoe. Sharp contradictions simply coexist in Panama. But when they clash it raises the question: what exactly is the Panamanian national character?

The National Psyche

Panamanian identity is in many ways elusive. Perhaps it's only natural given the many years that Panama has been the object of another country's meddling. From the US-backed independence of 1903 to the strong-armed removal of Noriega in 1989 – with half-a-dozen other interventions in between – the USA has left a strong legacy in the country.

Nearly every Panamanian has a relative or at least an acquaintance living in the USA, and parts of the country seem swept up in mall fever, with architectural inspiration straight out of North America. Panamanians (or at least the ones who can afford to) deck themselves out in US clothes, buy US-made cars and take their fashion tips straight from Madison Ave.

Others are quite reticent to embrace the culture from the north. Indigenous groups like the Emberá and Guna struggle to keep their traditions alive as more and more of their youth are lured into the Western lifestyles of the city. On the Península de Azuero, where there is a rich Spanish cultural heritage exemplified by traditional festivals, dress and customs, villagers raise the same concerns about the future of their youth.

Given the clash between old and new, it's surprising the country isn't suffering from a serious case of cognitive dissonance. However, the exceptionally tolerant Panamanian character weathers many contradictions – the old and the new, the grave disparity between rich and poor, and the stunning natural environment and its rapid destruction.

Much of the famous Panamanian tolerance begins in the family, which is the cornerstone of society and plays a role in nearly every aspect of a person's life. Whether among Guna sisters or Panama City's elite, everyone looks after each other. Favors are graciously accepted, promptly returned and never forgotten.

This mutual concern extends from the family into the community, and at times the whole country can seem like one giant extended community. In the political arena, the same names appear time and again, as nepotism is the norm rather than the exception. Unfortunately, this goes hand-in-hand with Panama's most persistent problem: corruption.

Panamanians view their leaders' fiscal and moral transgressions with disgust, and they are far from being in the dark about issues. Yet they accept things with patience and an almost fatalistic attitude. Outsiders sometimes view this as a kind of passivity, but it's all just another aspect of the complicated Panamanian psyche.

Lifestyle

In spite of the skyscrapers and gleaming restaurants lining the wealthier districts of Panama City, 23% of the country's population lives in poverty. It's a grim figure, though it actually represents an improvement from a decade ago, when a third of the population lived below the poverty line. Panama is chipping away at the problem, but improvement might not be fast enough for its residents. Indigenous people make up a growing proportion of Panama's poor, while other rural populations have improved their income with urban migration. Almost 67% of the population is now urban. Those hardest hit by poverty tend to be in the least populated provinces: Darién, Bocas del Toro, Veraguas, Los Santos and Colón.

Formal marriage is rare outside the middle and upper classes. Some estimate that 60% of children are born to short-term unions.

In the Emberá and Wounaan villages of the Darién, traditional living patterns persist much as they have for hundreds of years. The communities are typically made up of 30 to 40 *bohíos* (thatched-roof, stilted, open-sided dwellings), and they survive by means of subsistence agriculture, hunting, fishing and pastoralism. However, existence can be extremely difficult in these frontier villages – life expectancy is about 10 years below the national average and the majority of Emberá and Wounaan communities lack access to clean water and basic sanitation.

Today Panamanian office workers who earn minimum wage make an average of US$2.85 per hour. For the *campesinos* (farmers), life is hard. A subsistence farmer in the interior earns far below the national average of US$14,900 per year. Rural dwellings might consist of a simple cinder-block building, with a roof and four walls and perhaps a porch. Families have few possessions and every member assists with working the land or contributing to the household.

The middle and upper classes largely reside in Panama City environs, enjoying a level of comfort similar to their economic brethren in Europe and the USA. They live in large homes or apartments, have a maid, a car or two and, for the lucky few, a second home on the beach or in the mountains. Cell phones are *de rigueur*. Vacations are often enjoyed outside of the country in Europe or the USA. Most middle-class adults can speak some English and their children usually attend English-speaking schools.

Celebrations, weddings and family gatherings are a social outlet for rich and poor alike, and those with relatives in positions of power – nominal or otherwise – don't hesitate to turn to them for support.

Population

The majority of Panamanians (65%) are *mestizo,* which is generally a mix of indigenous and Spanish descent. In truth, many non-black immigrants are also thrown into this category, including a sizable Chinese population – some people estimate that as much as 10% of the population is of Chinese ancestry. There are several other large groups: about 9% of Panamanians are of African descent, 7% of European descent, 7%

RESPONSIBLE TRAVEL

Traveling sensitively in Panama means being mindful of the environment around you. Try to patronize locally owned businesses and small businesses, and spend your money where it will go directly to the people working for it.

Don't support businesses that keep exotic pets. It's an offense to keep a parrot, toucan or macaw in a cage. In some restaurants you may see endangered species on the menu; avoid *tortuga* (sea turtle), *huevos de tortuga* (turtle eggs), *cazón* (shark), *conejo pintado* (paca), *ñeque* (agouti) and *venado* (deer).

of mixed African and Spanish descent, and 12% are indigenous. Generally, black Panamanians are mostly descendants of English-speaking West Indians, such as Jamaicans and Trinidadians, who were originally brought to Panama as laborers.

Indigenous Groups

Of the several dozen native tribes that inhabited Panama when the Spanish arrived, only seven now remain. While indigenous culture is much more vibrant and present than in neighboring countries, an inordinately high percentage of the indigenous population live in poverty. In the *comarcas* (autonomous regions), illiteracy runs between 10% and 30%. Access to health care and education is a serious issue.

Smaller indigenous populations include the Bokotá, who inhabit Bocas del Toro Province, and the Bribrí, found in Costa Rica and in Panama along the Talamanca reserve. Both of these groups maintain their own language and culture, but their numbers and political influence are less than for the larger groups.

The Ngöbe-Buglé

Panama's largest indigenous group is the Ngöbe-Buglé (pronounced Nobay Boo-glAY), who number around 156,000 and occupy a *comarca* that spans the Chiriquí, Veraguas and Bocas del Toro Provinces. Similarly to the Guna, the Ngöbe-Buglé enjoy a high degree of political autonomy and have been successful in managing their lands and protecting their cultural identity. Unlike the Emberá and the Wounaan, the highland Ngöbe-Buglé have largely resisted outside cultural interventions, primarily because their communities are scattered among huge tracts of undeveloped land. In recent years, their young people have been increasingly heading to the cities for work, and missionaries have made numerous inroads in their attempt to convert the indigenous population to Christianity. Religion aside, the Ngöbe-Buglé continue to live much as they have always done by relying almost exclusively on subsistence agriculture.

The Guna

Perhaps the most well-known group in the West, due to their distinctive dress, is the Guna, who inhabit the Archipiélago de San Blas and run their native lands as a *comarca*. Regarded as having one of the largest degrees of autonomy in Latin America, the Guna are fiercely protective of their independence and routinely introduce new legislation to protect their lands from foreign cultural invasion. In recent years, this has resulted in barring foreigners from owning property in the *comarca,* imposing restrictions on tourism in San Blás and introducing standard fees for visitation, photography and video throughout the region. This tenacity has proved successful, as one of the highlights of visiting San Blás is witnessing firsthand the vibrancy of the Guna's unique culture.

Molas are beautiful, elaborate patches of embroidery. To learn about the culture, history and sewing of world-famous Guna *molas,* visit www.molasfrompanama.com.

In 2011 the Panamanian government recognized the Guna wish to change the official spelling of their name from Kuna to Guna, and also changed the spelling of Kuna Yala to Guna Yala, as the hard 'k' sound does not exist in the Guna language.

Emberá & Wounaan

The Emberá and Wounaan inhabit the jungle of the eastern Panamá Province and the Darién, and although the groups distinguish themselves from one another, the difference is more linguistic than cultural. Historically, both groups have eked out a living on the edges of the jungles through hunting, fishing, subsistence farming and rearing livestock, though rapid deforestation has reduced the extent of their traditional lands. Today the majority of Emberá and Wounaan inhabit the edges of the Darién and live on the fringes of the destruction wrought by loggers, farmers and ranchers. Narcotrafficking through the region from Colombia has further compromised their situation. An increasing number of communities are turning to tourism for survival, particularly in the Canal Zone, where traditional lifestyles are no longer feasible. There are also Emberá refugees from Colombia, who fled heavy fighting in the Chaco region by the thousands in early 2004.

A People Who Would Not Kneel: Panama, the United States and the San Blás Kuna by James Howe describes the struggles the Guna underwent in order to gain the independence they enjoy today.

The Naso

The Naso (Teribe) inhabit mainland Bocas del Toro and are largely confined to the Panamanian side of the binational Parque Internacional La Amistad. Unlike other indigenous population groups, the Naso do not have an independent *comarca* of their own, which has resulted in the rapid destruction of their cultural sovereignty in recent years. Another blow for them is the tremendous tourism potential of the international park, which has prevented the Panamanian government from coming to their aid. Today traditional villages are rapidly disappearing throughout the region and only a few thousand Naso remain. However, in an effort to ensure their cultural survival, a few villages have banded together to create an ecological center near the Wekso entrance to the park, which aims to draw more visitors to the region and employ more Naso as tourist guides.

Sports

Owing to the legacy of US occupation, baseball is the preferred pastime in Panama. This is indeed a rarity in Latin America, where *fútbol* (soccer) is normally the national craze.

A dozen Panamanian players currently play pro ball in the USA. Mariano Rivera is a former record-setting Panamanian pitcher for the New York Yankees. Carlos Lee from Aguadulce was an outfielder for the Miami Marlins. Carlos Ruiz from Chiriquí was a catcher for the Philadelphia Phillies. Batting champ Rod Carew, another Panamanian star, was inducted into the Hall of Fame in 1991.

Boxing is another popular spectator sport and a source of pride to Panamanians (and Latin Americans) ever since Roberto Durán, a Panama City native and boxing legend, won the world championship lightweight title in 1972. He went on to become the world champion in the welterweight (1980), light middleweight (1983) and super middleweight (1989) categories.

Multiculturalism

Panama has a rich mix of cultures, with immigrants from around the globe as well as a diverse indigenous population. Shortly after the Spanish arrived, slaves were brought from Africa to work in Panama's mines and perform grunt labor in the colony. Slaves that escaped set up communities in the Darién jungle, where their *cimarrones* (descendents) still live today. Subsequent waves of immigration coincided with the construction of both the Panama Railroad in 1850 and the Panama Canal – the French effort in the late 1800s and the American completion in the early 1900s. During these times, thousands of workers were brought to Panama from the West Indies, particularly Jamaica and Trinidad.

Workers also came from the East Indies and from China to labor – and many to die – on these massive projects. The majority of the Chinese settled in Panama City, and today you can see two Chinatowns (one is near Casco Viejo, the other is in El Dorado). There are two daily Chinese newspapers and even a private school for Chinese. The term for Chinese Panamanians is 'Once' (pronounced '*awn*-say').

Move over, Brooklyn: there are now 29 coworking stations in Panama City, where creative professionals convene with wi-fi and a comfortable shared space.

Mixed-race offspring – and mixed marriages – are increasingly common. Among the East Indian community, Hindus complain that their culture is disappearing: where once it was common for young men to return to India to find a bride, this is no longer the case. This intermixing of races happens across the nation, although indigenous groups and whites – representing each end of the economic scale – are least likely to marry outside of their group.

Although Panama is a much more racially tolerant society than many other Latin American countries, there is distrust among groups, particularly between indigenous groups and *mestizos*. This stems largely from *mestizo* land grabs – by loggers, ranchers and settlers – that have pushed indigenous communities off their lands. Indigenous communities also view the government as corrupt and largely indifferent to their plight – and to some extent, they are correct.

Class distinctions also persist. While politicians from the president on down take pride in mingling with the public and maintaining some semblance of a classless society, the *rabiblancos* (whites) control the majority of the wealth and have nearly all the power.

Class divisions and racism exist in Panama. Generally, members of a certain class marry only members of that same class. And at the Union Club (*the* social club of Panama City), memberships are rarely given to people with dark skin.

Media

Panama has a number of daily newspapers, ranging from sensationalist rags to astute independents. However, in Panama City the most popular form of mass media is television. Mainstream broadcast views tend to represent business and the oligarchy, which is for the most part what urban viewers want to hear.

Outside the capital, however, radio is the most important medium. There are approximately 90 radio stations on the dial, though most Panamanians have two or three favorites – morning talk shows are particularly popular and represent a wide range of viewpoints.

The Martinelli government took media criticism hard, even pursuing imprisonment and fines for journalists for 'offending the honor' of a public figure. This is a legacy of Noriega, who used such laws to suppress the voices of critics. International human-rights and press-advocacy organizations have decried Panama as supporting one of the most repressive regimes in the Americas because of the various 'gag laws' that bureaucrats can use to stifle opposition.

In the current media environment, underfunding is an issue. There's a lamentable lack of investigative reporting and broad-spectrum coverage on controversial issues. Still, many young Panamanians in particular have turned to the web to inform and be informed. For an alternative, Spanish-language view on national issues, interesting sites include www.kaosenlared.net and the environment-focused www.ciampanama.org. For perspectives in English, check out www.thepanamanews.com and www.latinamericanpost.com.

Check out the *Panama Digest* (www.thepanamadigest.com) for 'unfiltered' lifestyle, tourism, crime, development and environment news in English.

Religion

Religion in Panama can best be observed by walking the streets of the capital. Among the scores of Catholic churches, you'll find breezy Anglican churches filled with worshippers from the West Indies, synagogues, mosques, a shiny Greek Orthodox church, an impressive Hindu temple and a surreal Baha'i House of Worship (the headquarters for Latin America).

Freedom of religion is constitutionally guaranteed in Panama, although the preeminence of Roman Catholicism is also officially recognized, with 85% of the population describing themselves as Catholic. Schoolchildren have the option to study theology, though it is not compulsory. Protestant denominations largely account for the remaining 15% of the population; although a recognizable population of Muslims and Baha'i also exists, and approximately 3000 Jews (many of them recent immigrants from Israel), 24,000 Buddhists and 9000 Hindus also live in Panama.

The various indigenous tribes of Panama have their own belief systems, although these are fading quickly due to the influence of Christian missionaries. As in other parts of Latin America, the evangelical movement is spreading like wildfire.

Although Catholics are the majority, only about 20% of them attend church regularly. The religious orders aren't particularly strong in Panama either – only about 25% of Catholic clergy are Panamanian, while the rest are foreign missionaries.

Just outside Panama City, the City of Knowledge (Ciudad del Saber; http://ciudaddelsaber.org) is a sustainable city and a campus for international nonprofits. Learn more about this unique spot on its website.

Women in Panama

Women enjoy more opportunities in Panama than they do in most other Latin American countries. Panama even had a female president, Mireya Moscoso, whose term ended in 2004. At the forefront of the country's political arena is the PNF (Feminist National Party), which was founded in 1923 and is one of the oldest feminist parties in Latin America. Historically, the PNF has been strongly critical of the male-dominated government and has secured numerous social reforms for women and children. In 1941 the PNF helped women secure the right to vote, while in 1981 it helped ratify the law that eliminated all forms of discrimination against women. The Family Code, adopted in 1995, upholds the equal rights of women and abolished discriminatory clauses in the code of 1917.

In spite of these advances, women still face many obstacles in Panamanian society. Machismo and gross stereotypes are more prevalent in rural areas than in urban ones, but even in the cities women have to face lower wages and sexual harassment, and they are nearly twice as likely to be unemployed. Although women make up nearly half the workforce, they remain underrepresented in positions of power and in public service, with 18% representation in parliament.

Overall, women are having fewer children and are having them later in life. Many postpone motherhood to enter the workplace – a pattern that also exists in Europe and the USA. Panama has a growing number of single mothers, particularly in the lower income bracket. This problem is compounded by the facts that women have no right to an abortion (it's illegal in Panama) and the teenage-pregnancy rate is high. The average age for women to marry in Panama is 22; at the same time, they are expected to work and help support the household.

In indigenous communities, women face many hardships, including poor access to health care and a low level of prenatal care. Prevailing stereotypes also mean that girls are less likely to attend school – among indigenous populations, more than half of women are illiterate, compared to one-third of men. Women also enter motherhood much earlier than their *mestizo* counterparts and bear more children.

Music

While Panamanians may have an inordinate degree of affection for '80s rock, there is far more diversity at work in this small country – it helps to have a population of many cultures. From West Indian calypso to jazz, salsa, electronica, reggaetón and rock 'n' roll, music is always drifting out of taxis and apartment windows and into your experience.

Salsa

With blaring brass horns, the swish of skirts and pulsing rhythms, salsa music is the very air one breathes in the Latin Caribbean. And Panama is home to the biggest icon of them all: renowned salsa singer Rubén Blades. Raised in Panama City, Blades has had several international hits, has appeared in a few motion pictures and once even ran for president – he finished third.

Salsa has traditionally been the most popular music in Panama, but live salsa has become harder to come by, given the current popularity of reggaetón (known here as *plena*).

El Salsero: Rubén Blades

Salsa singer, songwriter, lawyer, actor and politician Rubén Blades was born on July 16, 1948, and raised in a middle-class neighborhood in Panama City. As a songwriter, Blades is revered for bringing lyrical sophistication to salsa and creating intelligent dance music. His 1978 hit 'Pedro Navaja' still remains the biggest-selling single in salsa history. Today his music continues to be incredibly popular in Panama, throughout Latin America and in the West. After a failed attempt at the Panamanian presidency in 1994, Blades served as the minister for tourism under President Martín Torrijos.

A case study in Panamanian versatility, Blades also personifies the love-hate relationship between Panama and the USA. Blades inherited musical talent from his mother, a Cuban immigrant who played the piano and sang on the radio, and his father, a police detective who played the bongos. Inspired by doo-wop singing, Blades began singing North American music in his early teens. However, the political upheaval in Panama during the mid-1960s made Blades increasingly patriotic. For a brief period he refused to sing in any language other than Spanish.

Blades has not shied away from politically charged lyrics. In 1980 he became embroiled in controversy over his song 'Tiburon,' which used a shark metaphor to describe American political and military intervention in the Caribbean. It was eventually banned on Miami radio. In the '80s Blades experimented with a fusion of Latin, rock, reggae and Caribbean music while simultaneously completing a masters degree in international law at Harvard University and breaking into Hollywood.

The same year he formed Los Seis de Solar, Blades got his first acting role in the film *The Last Fight* (1983). Blades' character, a singer-turned-boxer, seeks to win a championship against a fighter portrayed by real-life world-champion boxer Salvador Sánchez. In the years to follow, Blades appeared in a string of movies, including *The Milagro Beanfield War* (1988), *The Two Jakes* (1990), *Mo' Better Blues* (1990), *The Devil's Own* (1997) and *Cradle Will Rock* (1999). However, his most memorable performances were in Paul Simon's Broadway musical *The Capeman* (1997) and in the cult movie *Once Upon a Time in Mexico* (2003). The 2017 film *Yo no me llamo Rubén Blades* (Rubén Blades is not My Name) looks at his lasting legacy.

After a mediocre stint in national politics as minister for tourism, Blades returned to the music scene, rapping with Puerto Rican sensation Calle 13 in 'La Perla,' just to keep it real. But perhaps he hasn't quite recovered from the political bug. Last we heard, he was considering running for president of Panama in 2019.

For a heads-up on new Latin music beyond the mainstream, including Panamanian artists, check out the weekly US-based radio program *Alt.Latino* (www.npr.org/sections/altlatino).

Jazz

Jazz came to Panama from the US and found a welcoming home: it can be heard in several Panamanian clubs. Composer Danilo Pérez is widely acclaimed by American and European jazz critics. He has recorded with many greats from around the world and now serves on the faculty of the Berklee College of Music in Boston (USA).

Reggaetón & Beyond

Reggaetón, also known as *punta,* permeates all social levels in Panama. Like rap, reggaetón spread from the urban poor to conquer all social strata, though at its heart it's a youth trend. Key artists include Danger Man, who died in gang violence; balladeer Eddie Lover; and the artist known as Flex, who has also been very successful in Mexico. Alt-cool Los Rakas is popular – check out their addictive version of Rubén Blades' 'Camaleon.' From Colón, Kafu Banton is a popular reggae star.

Rock 'n' roll, in both English and Spanish, is played on most Panamanian FM radio stations, and some decent bands play it in Panama City clubs. For classic rock, Los Rabanes is considered Panama's most well-known sound. For alt-music sounds, check out SHOKED, cult favorite Señor Loop and jazz-influenced Luci and the Soul Brokers.

Folk

Attend any Azuero festival and you will see Panamanian *típico* (folkloric music) alive and thriving. In *típico* the accordion is dominant. The style is well represented by Dorindo Cárdenas, the late Victorio Vergara (whose band lives on as Nenito Vargas y los Plumas Negras) and the popular brother-sister pair of Samy and Sandra Sandoval.

Arts

Panamanian art reflects the country's stunning ethnic mix, with indigenous, African and Latin influences informing a diversity ranging from delicate carvings of wood and tagua nut to flamboyant costumes and extraordinary lace dresses. These treasures are found in the depths of the Darién or in dusty villages of the Península de Azuero, where artisans pursue traditions that have been handed down over many generations. Panama's talented photographers, painters and writers are also reinventing understandings of this tropical crossroads.

The Written Word

Often inward-looking, Panamanian literature has not carved much of a presence in international circles.

Several of the country's best novelists wrote around the mid-20th century. *El Ahogado* (The Drowned Man), a 1937 novel by Tristán Solarte (the pen name of Guillermo Sánchez Borbón, a well-known poet, novelist and journalist), ingeniously blends elements of the detective, gothic and psychological genres, along with a famous local myth. *El Desván* (In the Garret), a 1954 novel by Ramón H Jurado, explores the emotional limits of the human condition. *Gamboa Road Gang* (1960), by Joaquín Beleño, is the best work of fiction about the political and social events surrounding the Panama Canal.

Inauguración de La Fe (Inauguration of La Fe) by Consuelo Tomás is a collection of tales depicting the idiosyncrasies of the popular neighborhoods of Panama City.

Fiction writer (and half-Panamanian) Cristina Henríquez offers insight into Panamanian identity from a sometimes displaced point of view. Her 2010 novel *The World in Half* was followed in 2014 by *The Book of Unknown Americans,* a love story that weaves in the experiences of diverse Latin immigrants to the USA.

American RM Koster has written about Panama as his adopted home for decades. Reissued in 2013, his cult classic *The Prince* portrays an imaginary Central American country; it's the first in a still-unfolding magical-realism trilogy.

Current authors to look for include poet and novelist Giovanna Benedetti, historical novelist Gloria Guardia and folk novelist Rosa María Britton.

Panama in Film

Though Panama has served as the backdrop for several Hollywood films (for example, *The Tailor of Panama* and *Quantum of Solace*), the country is just beginning to produce its own commercial features. The first released in Panama was 2009's *Chance,* a tropical comedy about class shenanigans, told through the adventures of two maids and the upper-class family they work for. The 2016 film *Salsipudes* tells the story of man returning to his childhood barrio after years in the US.

Burwa dii Ebo (The Wind and the Water), directed by Vero Bollow and the Igar Yala Collective, was an official Sundance Film Festival selection in 2008. A narrative drama with social undercurrents, the story follows an indigenous Guna teenager who moves to Panama City from the Caribbean islands of his homeland. The movie has won numerous international awards.

The 1992 documentary *The Panama Deception* recounts the events that led up to the US removal of Noriega, including his previous collaboration with the CIA. Seeing this movie is a must to understand the complications and nuances of US–Panama relations. Also worthwhile, *Curundú* is a 2011 documentary by Ana Endara Mislov that shows the artistic vision of a charming photographer hoodlum trying to chronicle neighborhood life in this tough Panama City slum.

For the beat on current cultural events and contemporary Panamanian authors, check out the Spanish-language website www.escritorespanama.com.

The first Panamanian film submitted for the Best Foreign Language Oscar, *Invasión* is a 2014 documentary written and directed by Abner Benaim about the 1989 US invasion. It was followed by *Caja 25* (Box 25), a 2015 Panamanian documentary directed by Mercedes Arias and Delfina Vidal about letters written by the men building the Panama Canal. In 2018, the film *Diciembres,* about the aftermath of the US military invasion, debuted at the IFFP (International Film Festival of Panama) to much acclaim.

Action thriller *Contraband* is a 2012 film directed by Baltasar Kormákur, starring Mark Wahlberg and Kate Beckinsale. The 2016 *Hands of Stone* is a biopic about boxer Roberto Durán, starring Édgar Ramírez and Robert De Niro. Much of the film was shot in Panama. A chronicle of salsa legend turned politician Rubén Blades, *Yo no me llamo Rubén Blades* (Rubén Blades is not My Name) debuted in 2017.

Made by Hand

Panama's indigenous groups produce high-quality woodcarvings, textiles, ceramics, masks and other handicrafts. The Latin folk tradition from the Penínusula de Azuero – *polleras* (elaborate traditional outfits of Spanish origin), masks and leather sandals – is also worth noting.

The Wounaan and Emberá people in the Darién create carvings of jungle wildlife from cocobolo, a handsome tropical hardwood, and tiny figurines from the ivory-colored tagua nut.

However, the Emberá and Wounaan are most renowned for producing beautiful woven baskets of incredibly high quality. There are two types: the utilitarian and the decorative. The utilitarian baskets are made primarily from the chunga palm but can contain bits of other plants, vines, bark and leaves. They are usually woven, using various plaiting techniques, from single plant strips of coarse texture and great strength, and are rarely dyed. These baskets are often used for carrying seeds or harvesting crops.

The decorative baskets are much more refined, usually featuring many colors, and are created from materials of the nahuala bush and the chunga palm. The dyes are 100% natural and are extracted from fruits, leaves, roots and bark. Typical motifs are of butterflies, frogs, toucans, trees and parrots. The baskets are similar in quality to the renowned early-20th-century Chemehuevi Indian baskets of California. You can buy baskets at any of the markets.

Michel Perrin's *Magnificent Molas: The Art of the Kuna Indian* contains photographs of 300 fabric works of art. Perrin describes the vivid relationship between Guna art and culture.

Ocú and Penonomé people produce superior Panama hats.

Polleras are handmade in Guararé and other villages in Las Tablas and Los Santos Provinces. Also available on the Península de Azuero are handcrafted festival masks from Villa de Los Santos and Parita.

Huacas are golden objects made on the isthmus centuries before the Spanish conquest. They were placed with indigenous leaders at the time of burial, intended to accompany and protect their souls on the voyage to the other world. Most took the form of a warrior, crocodile, jaguar, frog or condor. You can purchase exact (solid-gold) and near-exact (gold-plated) reproductions of these palm-sized objects.

Because of their proximity to mineral-rich Colombia and Brazil, the jewelry stores here often have high-quality gems at excellent prices. Buyers beware: there are many fake gems on the world market, as well as many flawed gems that have been altered to appear more valuable than they really are.

Molas

The Guna of the Comarca de Guna Yala are known worldwide for their *molas* (the blouse panels used by women in their traditional dress). Also sold as crafts, *molas* symbolize the identity of the Guna people to outsiders, and their colorful and elaborate designs often depict sea turtles, birds and fish.

Molas are as ubiquitous as soccer shirts in Panama. A traditional *mola* is made of brightly colored squares of cotton fabric laid atop one another. Cuts are made through the layers, forming basic designs. The layers are then sewn together with tiny, evenly spaced stitches to hold the design in place. Beware of industrially made rip-offs (flip them over to check for uniform stitching).

Mola means 'blouse' in Guna, and Guna women make *molas* in thematically matching but never identical pairs. A pair will comprise the front and back of a blouse. The most traditional colors are black, maroon and orange, while the most traditional designs are abstract and geometric. These days *molas* can feature anything from cartoonish animals to Christmas themes, but the most valued ones are classically designed.

Regardless of the design, the very best *molas* should always have the following characteristics:

- Stitches closely match the color of the cloth they are set against.
- Stitches are very fine and neatly spaced.
- Stitches are pulled evenly and with enough tension to be barely visible.
- Curves are cut smoothly and the sewing follows the curves of the cut.
- Outline strips are uniform in width, with no frayed edges.

Painting

Panama has internationally recognized artists, even though it is all too difficult for them to establish a public presence in their own country. There is promise in endeavors like the Museo de Arte Contemporáneo (p46), but there is almost no government support for museums or training. Yet art is far from dead: graffiti murals, small-scale expositions and cooperatives work hard to close the gap.

Trained in France, Roberto Lewis (1874–1949) became the first prominent figure in Panama's art scene. He painted portraits of the nation's leaders and allegorical images to decorate public buildings. Among his most notable works are those in the Palacio de las Garzas (p50) in Panama City. In 1913 Lewis became the director of Panama's first art academy, where he and his successor, Humberto Ivaldi (1909–47), educated a generation of artists.

Among the school's students were Juan Manuel Cedeño and Isaac Benítez, as well as the painters who would come to the fore in the 1950s and '60s. This group includes Alfredo Sinclair, Guillermo Trujillo, Eudoro Silvera and others. More recent artists include Olga Sinclair and Brooke Alfaro. Most of these artists are still active, with occasional shows at local galleries.

The largest Panamanian art exposition – the Bienal de Arte – is held every two years at the MAC in Panama City.

CONGO RENIASSANCE

Started by the descendants of escaped slaves, Congo art tells the story of contemporary Portobelo by recounting their self-liberation. The movement started after the US invasion of Panama. Arturo Lindsay, a native Panamanian, artist and professor at Spelman College, and photographer Sandra Eleta created Taller Portobelo (p224), an artists' workshop for a community in the throes of hardship. It was art as salvation, and it worked. Lindsay describes Congo as contemporary art with folk elements. Extremely expressive, with color and textures such as beads or broken mirror shards, Congo paintings are often self-portraits. Painted *bastones* (walking sticks) represent those used by slaves to escape to freedom into the mountains and ward off pursuing Spaniards and forest predators.

Congo art has evolved and matured since its initial period, and artists have found the stability that is so hard to come by through commissions and gallery showings. In annual exchanges with visiting US artists, the groups collaborate on earthworks, sustainable architecture and biodegradable installations in addition to painting.

Portobelo is the best place to buy paintings direct, but you can also find Congo art in Panama City at Karavan (p68). Look for work by Yaneca Esquina, the movement's best-known artist.

Photography

Panama has several gifted photographers, including Iraida Icaza, Stuart Warner and Sandra Eleta. Icaza's abstract art is bold and innovative, made with photographic equipment. After living in Tokyo for many years, she now resides in New York. Warner, who has spent much of his life in Asia, the Middle East, Europe and the USA, captures the human spirit in beautiful landscapes and portraits.

Producing stunning and thought-provoking work, Sandra Eleta is among the most important photographers in Latin America. Particularly lauded are her portraits of the black inhabitants of Panama's Caribbean coast (particularly those of Portobelo, where she resides part of the year). She also founded the Panama City gallery Karavan, featuring Guna and Congo art.

Land & Wildlife

Imagine a country slightly bigger than Ireland with 21 times more plant species per square kilometer than Brazil. Panama is gaining fame for its vast tropical forests, hundreds of pristine islands and astounding biodiversity. The country is also home to an incredible variety of landscapes. In the span of a week, you can hike through highland cloud forests and verdant jungles and take a dip in both the Caribbean Sea and the Pacific Ocean.

The Land

Panama is both the narrowest and the southernmost country in Central America. The long S-shaped isthmus borders Costa Rica in the west and Colombia in the east. Its northern Caribbean coastline measures 1160km, compared to a 1690km Pacific coastline in the south, and its total land area is 78,056 sq km.

Panama is just 50km wide at its leanest point, yet it separates two great oceans. The Panama Canal, which is about 80km long, effectively divides the country into eastern and western regions. Panama's two mountain ranges run along its spine in both the east and the west. Volcán Barú is the country's highest point and only volcano.

Like all of the Central American countries, Panama has large, flat coastal lowlands with huge banana plantations. There are about 480 rivers in Panama and 1518 islands near its shores. The two main island groups are the San Blás and Bocas del Toro archipelagos on the Caribbean side, but most of the islands are on the Pacific side. Even the Panama Canal has islands, including Isla Barro Colorado, which has a world-famous tropical-rainforest research station.

Wildlife

Panama's biodiversity is staggering: the country is home to 220 mammal species, 226 species of reptile, 164 amphibian species and 125 animal species found nowhere else in the world. Panama also boasts 978 avian species, which is the largest number in Central America.

Although Panama is still largely undiscovered, more and more visitors are drawn to its remarkable wildlife. Panama's rainforests are home to countless creatures, from agoutis scurrying across the canopy floor to jaguars prowling the forests. In the sea, shallow coral-reef beds support countless varieties of tropical fish, while hammerheads and manta rays roam deeper waters. In the air, nearly a thousand avian species make Panama one of the top birdwatching destinations in the world.

The country's rich biodiversity owes a great deal to its geological history. Around 65 million years ago, North and South America were joined by a land bridge not unlike what exists today. Around 50 million years ago, the continents split apart and remained separate for millions of years.

During this time, unique evolutionary landscapes were created on both continents. South America experienced an astonishing diversification of many species. The land soon gave rise to many bird families (toucans and hummingbirds included), unique neotropical rodents (agoutis and capybaras) and groups such as iguanas, poison-dart frogs and basilisks. In North America, which collided repeatedly with Eurasia, animal species that had no relatives in South America (horses, deer, raccoons, squirrels and mice) flourished.

The momentous event that would change natural history for both continents occurred around three million years ago when the land bridge of Panama arose. Species from both continents mingled: northern animals went south and southern animals went north. In the lush forests and wetlands along the isthmus, the great variety of plant species created ideal conditions for nourishing wildlife.

Today the interchange of species between North and South America is limited to winged migrations, an annual event that can be breathtaking to behold.

A Neotropical Companion, by John Kricher, is an excellent book for learning about ecology, evolutionary theory and biodiversity in the New World tropics.

Land & Marine Mammals

Panama's many species of primate include white-faced capuchins, squirrel monkeys, spider monkeys and howler monkeys. Some fascinating varieties, like the Geoffroy's tamarin, are found nowhere else in Central America. These tiny, gregarious monkeys can live in groups of up to 40 in lowland forest, and many weigh less than 600g. They're identified by their whistles and chirps, mottled black-and-brown fur, white chests and diminutive stature. Spot them in Parque Natural Metropolitano, Monumento Nacional Isla Barro Colorado and the Darién.

Big cats prowl the jungles of Panama. Although you'd be extremely fortunate to catch even a glimpse of one, their prints are easy to come across. Jaguars, pumas, ocelots, jaguarundis and margays are all found on the isthmus. The jaguar is the largest cat in the Americas, needing large tracts of land in order to survive. Without sufficient space, the big cats gradually exhaust their food supply (which numbers 85 hunted species) and perish. They are excellent swimmers and climbers and at times are spotted resting on sunny riverbanks.

Panama's offshore waters host a fascinating assortment of creatures. Reefs found off both coasts support a plethora of tropical fish, and visitors to the national marine parks might spot humpback whales, reef sharks, bottlenose dolphins, and killer or sperm whales. Underwater, hammerheads, whale sharks, blacktip and whitetip sharks and occasionally tiger sharks also visit.

Emergent Ecologies by Eben Kirksey (2015) examines how chance encounters, historical gaffes and parasitic invasions have shaped ecological communities, with examples from Panama.

One of Panama's biggest coastal draws is the sea turtle. Of the world's seven species, five can be seen in Panama at various times throughout the year. All sea turtles evolved from terrestrial species and the most important stage of their survival happens on land when they come to nest. Although you'll need a bit of luck and a lot of patience, the experience of seeing hatchlings emerge is unparalleled.

Arribadas (arrivals) are rare events that occur when thousands of female sea turtles flood the beach to lay their eggs. This happens occasionally on Isla de Cañas when 40,000 to 50,000 olive ridleys come to nest at a single time. It mostly happens in the wet season (usually September to October) during the first and last quarter of the moon.

OBSESSION FOR OCELOTS

Ocelots are nocturnal, elusive and native to Panama. When researchers and wildlife photographers had trouble capturing these cats in Panama's dense rainforest, they turned not to science but to Calvin Klein. Christian Ziegler, a photographer working on assignment for *National Geographic,* heard a claim from the San Diego Zoo about perfume, so he bought Calvin Klein's Obsession in a duty-free shop. The scent, which contains pheromones that appeal to both humans and animals, was sprayed on a tree.

The result? The ocelots rubbed up against bark doused in the scent. But, according to Ziegler, the attraction (not unlike many a hormonal drive) proved fleeting.

Birds

Birdwatchers consider Panama to be one of the world's best birdwatching sites. Quetzals, macaws, amazons, parrots and toucans all have sizable populations here, as do many species of tanager and raptor. Right outside Panama City hundreds of species have been spotted along the famous 17km-long Pipeline Rd in Parque Nacional Soberanía.

One of the most sought-after birds is the harpy eagle, the national bird of Panama. With a 2m wingspan and a weight of up to 12kg, this raptor is the world's most powerful bird of prey and a truly awesome sight. It's recognizable by its huge size, its broad, black chest band with white underneath, its piercing yellow eyes and its prominent, regal crest. The harpy's powerful claws can carry off howler monkeys and capuchins, and it also hunts sloths, coatis, anteaters and just about anything that moves. It's best spotted in the Parque Nacional Darién around Reserva Natural Punta Patiño.

Monkey's Bridge: Mysteries of Evolution in Central America, by David Rains Wallace, tells of the colorful evolutionary unfolding of fauna and flora on the isthmus, beginning three million years ago and ending in the present.

The elusive, emerald-green quetzal lives in habitats throughout Central America, but Panama is one of the best places to see it. The male has an elongated wing covert (train) and a scarlet breast and belly, while females have duller plumage. Parque Nacional Volcán Barú is a top spot for sightings, as is Parque Internacional La Amistad. Quetzals are best spotted in the breeding season, from March to June, when males grow their spectacular trains and start calling for mates.

Panama's geographical position also makes it a crossroads for migratory birds. Out of the country's 950 bird species, 122 occur only as long-distance migrants (ie they don't breed in Panama). From August to December, North American raptors migrate south into Central America by the millions – at times, there are so many birds that they make a black streak across the sky. The canopy tower in Panama's Parque Nacional Soberanía is a particularly good vantage point for watching this migration.

In Bocas del Toro, keep an eye out for kettling hawk migrations – October is the best month to see them in large numbers. The migration of turkey vultures over the islands in early March and again in October is another striking sight. These big, black-bodied, red-necked birds can streak the sky and are able to soar for long periods without a single flap as they migrate between southern Canada and Tierra del Fuego.

SEA-TURTLE NESTING

TURTLE	NESTING SEASON	PEAK	HOT SPOTS
green	May-Oct (Caribbean)	Aug-Oct (Caribbean)	Isla Bastimentos
	Jun-Dec (Pacific)	no peak	Humedal de San San Pond Sak
hawksbill	Apr-Oct (Caribbean)	Jun & Jul (Caribbean)	Isla Bastimentos
	Apr-Nov (Pacific)	Jun & Jul (Pacific)	Humedal de San San Pond Sak
leatherback	Mar-Jul (Caribbean)	Apr & May (Caribbean)	Isla Bastimentos
	Oct-Mar (Pacific)	Nov-Jan (Pacific)	Humedal de San San Pond Sak
loggerhead	May-Sep (Caribbean)	no peak	Isla Bastimentos
	Apr-Sep (Pacific)		Humedal de San San Pond Sak
olive ridley	year-round (Pacific)	Jun-Nov (Pacific)	Isla de Cañas

FINDING NEW SPECIES

In a country known for its biodiversity, the disappearance of species is unsettling on many levels. But there may be even greater concern over species not yet identified, particularly in light of rapid habitat destruction. We may never understand their roles in local ecosystems or potential contributions toward scientific research. In recent years, scientists have made these findings:

Bush dog *(Speothos venaticus)* Rare and nocturnal. A foot tall, it resembles a small pig and keeps company in aggressive packs in the tropical forests of Central and South America. Its habitat, near the borders, is threatened by clear cutting.

Poison-dart frog *(Andinobates geminisae)* Found in Colón Province. Tiny and orange, it's no bigger than a fingernail. Habitat loss is a serious concern as it only exists in a very reduced area.

River dolphin *(Isthminia panamensis)* Now extinct, it lived some six million years ago. As whales and dolphins evolved from terrestrial to marine mammals, these river dolphins represent a reversal, as the species turned inland to freshwater ecosystems.

Endangered Species

There are 388 threatened species in Panama. Among the animals appearing on the 'red list' for Panama are the jaguar, the spectacled bear, the Central American tapir, the American crocodile, all five species of sea turtle that nest on Panamanian beaches, and dozens of birds, including several eagle species and the military and scarlet macaw.

Laws meant to curb illegal hunting are widely ignored due to lack of enforcement. For example, keeping a parrot, toucan or macaw in a cage is a fineable offense in Panama. Nonetheless, it's common to see them in cages, even in some public venues.

You can help reduce the threat to Panama's endangered species. If you see caged animals at a hotel, complain to the manager, take your business elsewhere and report the crime to APPC (www.appcpanama.org), a conservation nonprofit organization with experience in wild-animal rescue.

Plants

Humid, tropical rainforest is the dominant vegetation in the canal area, along the Caribbean coast and in most of the eastern half of the country – Parque Nacional Darién protects much of Panama's largest tropical rainforest. Other vegetation zones include dry tropical rainforest and grassland on the Pacific coast, cloud forest in the highlands, alpine vegetation on the highest peaks and mangrove forest on both coasts and around many islands. Among the flora, Panama has over 10,000 species of plant, including approximately 1200 orchid species, 675 fern species and 1500 species of tree.

A Field Guide to the Orchids of Costa Rica and Panama, by Robert Dressler, has 240 photos, and almost as many drawings, of orchids within its 274 pages.

National Parks

Today Panama has around 40 national parks and officially protected areas, and about 33% of the country's total land is set aside for conservation. In many of the national parks and protected areas there are mestizo and indigenous villages. In some scenarios these communities help protect and maintain the park.

Headquartered in Panama City, the Ministerio de Ambiente (Autoridad Nacional del Ambiente; Panama's national environmental authority; www.miambiente.gob.pa) runs Panama's parks. Panama recently decided to make entry to national parks free, with the exception of Parque Nacional Coiba. Visitors still must register upon entry. Permits to camp or stay at a ranger station can generally be obtained at a regional office or ranger station within the park.

In Panama City, the 265-hectare Parque Natural Metropolitano protects vast expanses of tropical semideciduous forest within the city limits.

Find out about upcoming seminars and recent publications about tropical ecology and biodiversity topics on the Smithsonian Tropical Research Institute website (www.stri.org).

A short distance from the capital in Panamá Province, Parque Nacional Soberanía is a birdwatcher's paradise where, in a single day, you can see hundreds of species. Lush rainforest also abounds on the nearby biological reserve of Monumento Natural Isla Barro Colorado, where scientists study the area's rich biodiversity. Also close to Panama City is the historical Fuerte San Lorenzo.

The lovely Parque Nacional Omar Torrijos is in Coclé Province. It remains largely overlooked since access is difficult, requiring a good 4WD or at least an hour's walk to reach the entrance. It offers prime birdwatching and the possibility of viewing both the Atlantic and the Pacific Oceans.

In Azuero, the Refugio de Vida Silvestre Cenegón del Mangle is a mangrove forest and wildlife refuge that's a prime nesting ground for herons and other birdlife. It also contains a series of pools said to have therapeutic properties.

Although the province of Los Santos has no national parks, there is an attractive wildlife refuge and a protected area frequented by nesting sea turtles. The Refugio de Vida Silvestre Isla Iguana near Pedasí offers snorkeling, and occasional sightings of humpback whales. Nearby, Isla de Cañas is a major nesting site for olive ridley sea turtles.

In Veraguas, Parque Nacional Coiba is one of the largest marine parks in the world. It contains Panama's largest island, the 493-sq-km Isla de Coiba, which is regarded by scientists as a biodiversity hot spot. Also in Veraguas, the 32,577-hectare Parque Nacional Cerro Hoya protects some of the last remaining patches of dry tropical forest on the Península de Azuero. The newest national park is Parque Nacional Santa Fé, around Santa Fé.

In Chiriquí Province, Parque Nacional Marino Golfo de Chiriquí is an impressive 14,740-hectare marine park with 25 islands and numerous coral reefs. The aquatic life here is astounding. In the highlands, Parque Nacional Volcán Barú surrounds Panama's only volcano, a fine destination for hikers and birdwatchers. Volcán Barú (3474m) is Panama's highest peak. Chiriquí also has part of the binational Parque Internacional La Amistad. Although largely unexplored, La Amistad offers several excellent day hikes, and local indigenous guides lead overnight excursions.

In the Archipiélago de Bocas del Toro, Parque Nacional Marino Isla Bastimentos protects various areas of the archipelago and is an important nature reserve for many species of Caribbean wildlife. Turtles nest on its beaches and its abundant marine life makes for great snorkeling and diving. On the mainland is the other sector of Panama's share of the binational Parque Internacional La Amistad. Wekso, as this sector of the park is called, is home to several indigenous groups, pristine rainforest and abundant wildlife. Near the border with Chiriquí Province, the Bosque Protector de Palo Seco contains several hiking trails through lush cloud forest high in the Talamanca range.

TRADING DEBT FOR FOREST

Conservationists are rethinking how to keep valuable resources in countries whose national debt represents a more pressing public concern. Nonprofits are purchasing national debts and using later payments toward forest-protection programs. The USA, with the involvement of the Nature Conservancy (www.nature.org), has forgiven US$21 million in debt-for-nature swaps in Panama. This is good news, though a downturn in the trend has been attributed to the high cost of commercial debt in secondary markets.

Panama's crown jewel is the Parque Nacional Darién, which boasts 576,000 hectares of wildlife-rich rainforest. The heart of this Unesco World Heritage Site is Cana, a former mining valley that is now regarded as one of the best birdwatching spots in the world. Unfortunately, at the time of writing, authorization was closed for visits to this area. The Darién is also home to the Reserva Natural Punta Patiño, a 26,315-hectare wildlife reserve on the southern shore of the Golfo de San Miguel. This private reserve is one of the best places in the country to see the harpy eagle.

Environmental Issues

Panama faces grave environmental threats at the hands of loggers, miners, developers and indifferent or corrupt government agencies, who apparently don't understand that the country's finest gem – its natural beauty – is rapidly disappearing.

According to the Centro de Incidencia Ambiental, 33% of Panama's land is set aside for conservation – more than any other Central American country. Panama's forests also contain the greatest number of species of all the New World countries north of Colombia.

The principal threat to Panama's ecology is deforestation, which is an issue throughout the country, most notably in the Darién. In addition, the balance between conservation and development is tipping in favor of the latter, particularly in tourist hot spots like the Península de Azuero and Bocas del Toro.

Panama's national parks are staffed by few rangers. Although their areas of coverage are colossal, many rangers aren't given patrol vehicles or radios. In Parque Nacional Darién, for instance, there are usually no more than 20 rangers (generally unarmed and poorly paid) assigned to protect 576,000 hectares – an area larger than some countries. Meanwhile, illegal hunting, settling and logging take place inside parks. Unless drastic measures are taken, it may not be long before many of the country's protected areas are nothing more than national parks on paper.

In recent years, increased foreign investment, coupled with the desire to improve tourist infrastructure, has threatened several of Panama's most pristine ecosystems. Development projects such as dams and mines are allowed to proceed without meaningful environmental-impact assessments. This green-light approach to divvying up environmental resources has stirred the utmost concern in conservation circles.

Deforestation

Panama's loses 1% of its primary forest every year. Illegal logging now accounts for nearly half of Panama's timber industry, according to a 2015 report by the Ministerio de Ambiente. Most of this wood is sourced in the Darién, one of the richest biomes on the planet. Just over three decades ago, the region north of Yaviza – the town where the Interamericana ends – was covered with virgin forest. Unfortunately, everything changed when the highway was extended from Chepo to Yaviza.

The loggers initially sought big trees within easy reach, felling all the giants near the highway and trampling young trees with their machinery. Once the giant trees were gone, the loggers cut roads perpendicular to the highway, which led into tall stands of hardwoods. After those stands were removed, more roads were cut and yet more stands were leveled.

Tropical rainforests cover just 7% of the earth's surface but account for 50% of the world's biodiversity.

Right behind the loggers were thousands of settlers looking to eke out a living by turning the trampled vegetation left by the loggers into cropland. With the mature trees gone, all that was required to create cropland was an ax and a match. After some crackling, sizzling and a lot

THE VALUE OF RAINFORESTS

Why get serious about saving the rainforest? Even though they may be far from our daily experience, rainforests and their survival affect every one of us in more ways than we realize.

Carbon Sink Effect

As developing nations modernize, global carbon emissions are on the rise, and evidence of the greenhouse effect can already be seen across the planet.

One of the best defenses humans have against rising carbon-dioxide levels is the tropical rainforest. Rainforests limit the greenhouse effect of global warming by storing carbon, which reduces the amount of carbon dioxide in the atmosphere. With fewer densely wooded sub-canopy trees, the ability of tropical rainforests to act as a carbon sink is in jeopardy. The deforestation of Latin America can impact desertification as far away as the Sahel in Africa. This reality eventually affects us all.

Bioprospecting

Scientific research in Panama could have long-lasting implications for rainforest conservation around the globe. With cooperation from universities and pharmaceutical companies, Smithsonian Tropical Research Institute scientists are scouring the rainforest for compounds that may one day become new treatments for disease or useful in agriculture. The results place a great deal of importance on the rainforest's biodiversity. With important findings already established, bioprospecting could help unlock the mysteries of the rainforest and consequently preserve them through funding. Ultimately, this would make conservation both the end and the means.

Intrinsic Value

Panama's vegetation was originally almost all forest, though much of this has been cleared in recent generations to create pastures and agricultural land. Countless flora and fauna species have been wiped out. Beyond the plants and animals that actually inhabit the forests, deforestation also threatens the traditional cultures of the Emberá and Wounaan, who have lived in the rainforest for generations. But the effects do not stop there. Migratory animals also pass through the forests annually, such as bats, butterflies and birds. A simple argument for saving the rainforest is simply that its intrinsic value is enough to warrant increased conservation efforts.

of smoke, subsistence farmers had fields for planting. All of this is not only legal but actively encouraged by Panamanian law.

However, the story doesn't end here. In a healthy rainforest ecosystem, huge, exposed tree roots prevent heavy rains from washing away the thin layer of nutrient-rich topsoil. But a big storm over a denuded area will quickly carry the topsoil into rivers and out to sea, leaving only the nutrient-deficient lower clay soil where the vibrant jungle once stood. In the space of only two to three years, the soil in the Darién could no longer support a decent harvest and little more than grass grew on it. Since cattle eat grass, the ranchers stepped in and bought fields that frustrated farmers could no longer use.

Today, with the Interamericana paved to Yaviza, the succession of loggers, farmers and ranchers keeps growing, although now loggers must further explore secondary roads to find trees. The farmers are still a step behind the loggers, unintentional nomads employing the slash-and-burn method so widespread in the developing world. And everywhere the settler-farmers go, ranchers move in behind them.

Mining

Today roughly 26% of Panama is mined or under mining concessions, prompting concerns of contaminated water sources, and the destruction of forest and human habitats. In 2013 mining activity rose by a quarter, and that's just the beginning, according to CAMIPA (Cámara Minera de

Panamá), which estimates that Panama is sitting on some US$200 billion in mineral reserves.

In spite of objections by prominent environmental groups, the government has approved and expedited large-scale mining projects, most notably a US$6.2 billion project – an investment greater than the initial Panama Canal expansion – to extract gold and copper. In 2018, the Cobre Panama Project in Colón inaugurated with the expectation of extracting 320,000 tons of copper per year, which would be roughly 4% of the country's GDP.

In 2004 Panama, Costa Rica, Colombia and Ecuador created the Eastern Pacific Marine Biological Corridor to preserve the area's ecosystems.

A major victory for community interests was the 2012 passing of Law 415, which prohibits extraction in indigenous territories and requires their approval for hydroelectric projects. The change came after a shutdown of Ngöbe-Buglé community protests in February 2012 left two protesters dead.

Yet protests persist, as most of the gold and copper reserves lie within indigenous lands. Panama is looking at reforming the mining industry in order to keep the peace, but environmentalists and rural residents worry that reform will not provide sufficient protection for communities and the environment.

For more information on mining issues, contact Centro de Incidencia Ambiental (p286).

Dams

Dams have become an epidemic in Panama, where proposals have been submitted for almost every river in the country. One of the most alarming is the US$50 million hydroelectric-dam project on Naso tribal territory. The Río Bonyic project threatens the settlement, the water supply and nearby Unesco World Heritage Site Parque Internacional La Amistad. In addition to drawing international opposition, the dam has divided the tribe and deposed its king, who acted in favor of the dam without the approval of his assembly. These controversies resulted in the Inter-American Development Bank removing its funding, though construction on the dam went through, impeded by indigenous protests that periodically cut off the access road. Another highly controversial dam on the Changuinola River (Chan-75) displaced several Ngöbe-Buglé communities and created schisms within the native community.

In 2015, the Ministerio de Ambiente imposed a US$1.2 million fine on hydroelectric companies building a controversial dam in Chiriqui Province known as the Barro Blanco project. The companies were charged with illegally discharging material into the river, affecting a nearby Ngöbe-Buglé community.

Development

As Panama City grows, even conservation sites are coming under threat. After a long tussle with developers, Bahía de Panamá was finally returned to being a wildlife-refuge site in 2015. The bay came under threat in 2012 when the government removed its protected status to make way for urban and resort development, including hotels and golf courses. Although the protected-area status has been restored, widespread destruction of the area's mangrove forests continues.

The passage of a ship through the entire Panama Canal requires approximately 52 million gallons of water.

As a Ramsar wetland site, it's crucial to the hemisphere as it hosts more than two million shorebirds in their annual migrations and provides numerous ecosystem services. The mangrove forests around Panama Bay provide vital nursery grounds for fish and shellfish, a natural filter for sewage, and a buffer zone protecting the city from storms. The Panama Audubon Society (p286) is leading campaigns crucial in its protection and recuperation.

ENVIRONMENTAL ORGANIZATIONS

Though there is little public sensitivity about environmental issues in Panama, a number of organizations strive to protect the environment and biodiversity.

ANCON (☎314-0060; www.ancon.org; 157 Quarry Heights Rd, Ancon, Panama City; ⏰9am-5pm Mon-Fri) Founded in 1985 by academic and business leaders, it has played a major role in the creation of national parks and on many occasions has spurred the government into action.

Audubon Society (Map p48; ☎232-5977; www.audubonpanama.org; Casa No 2006-B, Llanos de Curundú, Curundú, Panama City; ⏰7am-3pm Mon-Fri) Promoting birds in Panama for more than 35 years, with more than 20 birdwatching field trips every year. Find upcoming events online.

Centro de Incidencia Ambiental (CIAM; ☎236-0866; www.ciampanama.org; Calle Thays de Ponds, Edificio Ojil, Piso 2, Oficina 3, Panama City; ⏰8:30am-4:30pm Mon-Fri) Promotes environmental advocacy through grassroots campaigns.

Fundación Albatros Media (☎317-3450; www.albatrosmedia.com) Creates quality environmental documentaries on Panama.

Fundación Avifauna Eugene Eisenmann (☎306-3133; www.avifauna.org.pa) Promotes the preservation of tropical forest to support Panama's astounding diversity of birdlife. Created the Panama Rainforest Discovery Center on Pipeline Rd.

Fundación Mar Viva (☎317-4350; www.marviva.net) Patrols protected marine areas in Costa Rica and Panama with the goal of ending illegal fishing and replenishing marine life. Also promotes conservation and the sustainable use of marine resources.

Nature Conservancy (www.nature.org) Prominent international conservation agency working extensively in the areas of Bocas del Toro, the Península de Azuero, the upper Chagres and the Darién Biosphere Reserve.

The Martinelli administration expanded the coastal highway known as Cinta Costera into the sea to wrap around the historic neighborhood of Casco Viejo, a Unesco World Heritage Site. With a price tag of US$189 million, the completed project has done little to mitigate the traffic problems it sought to address, as entry and entrance points miss the bottleneck traffic areas. It has also damaged the aesthetic values of the Casco. Within Casco Viejo, large-scale gentrification has largely displaced the local community.

Isla de Coiba

One of the hottest environmental topics in Panama is the future of Isla de Coiba. This rainforest-covered island and Unesco World Heritage Site is set in one of the largest marine parks on the planet – scientists often compare Coiba to the Galápagos Islands. Yet, with paltry funding, it is far from the Galápagos standard. A lack of funding also hinders patrols in combating illegal fishing activity.

Owing to the presence of a penal colony, this island and its surrounding waters remained long untouched, but now that the prison has been phased out, developers and members of the government see glorious tourism possibilities for this ecological gem. There are concerns that big development plans would destroy the fragile ecosystem.

The unregulated presence of cruise ships has caused disturbing situations, with sometimes as many as 200 tourists visiting the tiny snorkeling island of Granito de Oro – a number that is outrageously unsustainable. In 2015 a 200-passenger cruise ship ran aground in Coiba. Little is being done to preserve the penal colony as a historic site; unfortunately, it is deteriorating rapidly.

Survival Guide

Directory A–Z

Accessible Travel

Panama is not wheelchair friendly, though high-end hotels provide some accessible rooms. There are parking spaces for people with mobility issues and some oversized bathroom stalls. Outside the capital, adequate infrastructure is lacking.

Download Lonely Planet's free Accessible Travel guides from http://lptravel.to/AccessibleTravel.

Accommodations

Book accommodations two to six months ahead for Semana Santa ('Holy Week'; the week preceding Easter), the November festivals and the week between Christmas and New Year. Most lodgings require reservations in high season.

Hotels In abundance in the midrange and high-end categories.

B&Bs A midrange phenomenon most common in the capital as well as Boquete and Bocas del Toro.

Hostels Cheap and becoming more common in Panama, ranging from quiet budget digs to party central.

Lodges Range from rustic to high end, found mostly in the highlands.

BOOK YOUR STAY ONLINE

For more accommodations reviews by Lonely Planet authors, check out http://lonelyplanet.com/panama/hotels. You'll find independent reviews, as well as recommendations on the best places to stay. Best of all, you can book online.

SLEEPING PRICE RANGES

The following price ranges refer to a double room with bathroom in high season. Unless otherwise stated, tax is included in the price.

$ less than US$60

$$ US$60–130

$$$ more than US$130

Activities

Panama has scores of ways to spend a sun-drenched afternoon, from hiking through lush rainforest to snorkeling coral reefs. Diving, surfing, birdwatching, fishing and island-hopping are just a few of Panama's star attractions. See p34 for more information.

Children

Panama is a family oriented culture and is generally very accommodating to travelers with children. The same can't be said of many businesses owned by expats, who very clearly state the age requirements of their guests.

Most of Panama is quite safe to travel with children, though dengue fever and, less so, malaria are present in some limited areas. Bring good insect repellent and light long-sleeved tops and long pants.

A number of tours, some low intensity, are an enjoyable way for you and your children to see Panama's lush environment. Look for agencies with tailored family outings.

For more ideas about making the most of your family travels, look for Lonely Planet's *Travel with Children*.

Practicalities

High chairs in restaurants are a rarity in Panama, but safety seats in rental cars are available on request. For diapers (nappies), creams and other supplies, stock up in Panama City. Generally speaking, the supermarkets are excellent in Panama, and you can find just about any product you'd find in the USA in them.

Climate

Bocas Del Toro

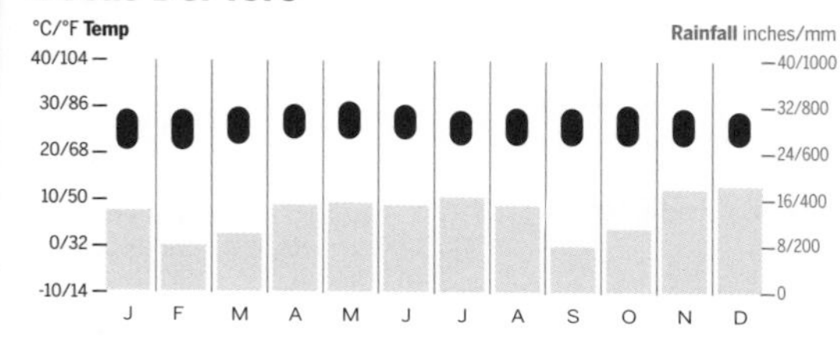

David

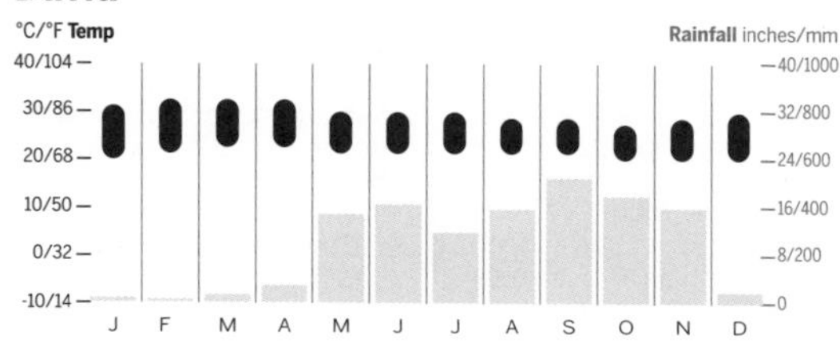

Panama City

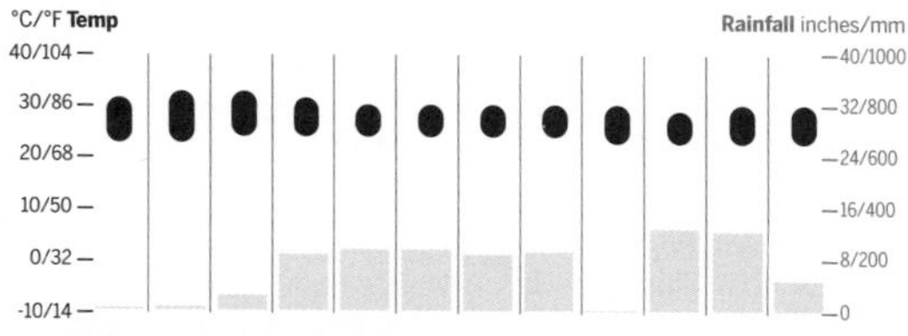

Electricity

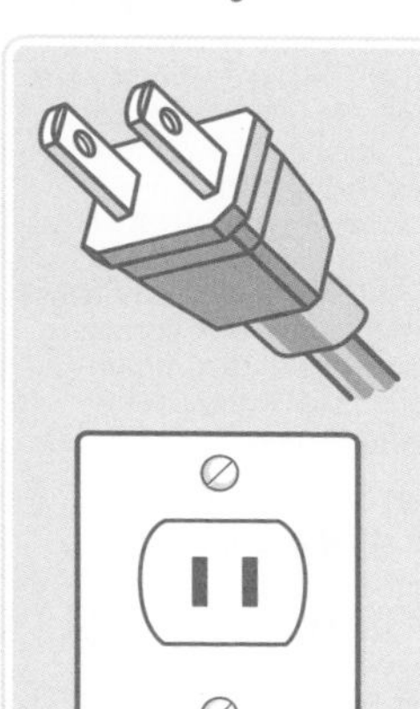
Type A
110V/60Hz

Type B
110V/60Hz

The electrical current is 110V, 60Hz in Panama. Plugs are two pronged, as in the US and Canada, though occasionally you'll see one with an extra prong for grounding/earthing.

Embassies & Consulates

More than 50 countries have *embajadas* (embassies) or *consulados* (consulates) in Panama City. With the exception of those of the USA and France, most of these embassies are located in the Marbella district of Panama City.

Ireland, Australia and New Zealand have no embassies or consulates in Panama. In all three cases, refer to the relevant nation's legation in Mexico.

Canadian Embassy (☎294-2500; www.canadainternational.gc.ca/panama; Piso 11, Tower A, Torre de las Americas, Punta Pacifica; ⏱8:30am-1pm Mon-Fri)

Colombian Embassy (☎392-5893; http://panama.consulado.gov.co; 1st fl, Condominio Posada del Rey, Vía Italia, Punta Paitilla; ⏱7:30am-1:30pm Mon-Fri)

Costa Rican Embassy (☎6521-4665, 264-2980; www.embajadacostaricaenpanama.com; 30th fl, Edificio Bisca, cnr Aquilino de la Guardia & Av Balboa, Bella Vista; ⏱9am-1pm Mon-Fri)

Costa Rican Consulate (☎774-1923; www.embajadacostaricaenpanama.com; Calle B Norte & Av Primera, Torre del Banco Universal No 304; ⏱9am-1pm Mon-Fri)

Dutch Consulate (☎280-6650; www.paisesbajosmundial.nl/paises/panama; No 23, 23rd fl, Tower 1000, Calle Hanono Missri, Punta Paitilla; ⏱9am-noon Mon-Fri)

French Embassy (☎211-6200; www.ambafrance-pa.org; Plaza de Francia, Las Bóvedas, Casco Viejo; ⏱8:30-11:30am Mon-Fri)

German Embassy (☎263-7733; www.panama.diplo.de; Piso PH,

PRACTICALITIES

Weights & Measures Panama uses the metric system, but occasionally weights and distances are given in pounds and miles.

Smoking Since 2005, smoking has been prohibited in all indoor public places, indoor workplaces and on public transportation; in 2013 Panama banned all advertising, promotion and sponsorship of tobacco products.

World Trade Center, Calle 53 Este, Marbella; ⌚9am-noon Mon-Fri)

UK Embassy (☎297-6550; www.gov.uk/government/world/panama; 4th fl, Humbolt Tower, Calle 53 Este, Marbella; ⌚7:30am-4:30pm Mon-Thu, to 12:30pm Fri)

US Embassy (☎317-5000; https://pa.usembassy.gov/; Av Demetrio Basillo Lakas 783, Clayton; ⌚8am-5:30pm Mon-Thu, to noon Fri)

Food

Panama has a wide range of dining options, from world-class contemporary restaurants in Panama City and a few provincial capitals, to humble roadside grills found everywhere and food stalls attached to markets serving cheap local specialties. In Panama City there's an excellent range of restaurants, but outside the capital and major tourist attractions, there is much less variety.

Panama's national dish is *sancocho*, a kind of chicken and vegetable stew. *Ropa vieja* (literally 'old clothes'), a spicy shredded-beef combination served over rice, is another common dish.

EATING PRICE RANGES

The following price ranges refer to a meal.

$ less than US$12

$$ US$12–18

$$$ more than US$18

Rice – grown on dry land – is Panama's staple food. Green salads are hard to come by outside the capital, but tropical fruit is abundant.

Meat figures prominently in the Panamanian diet. In addition to staples such as *bistec* (steak) and *carne asado* (roast meat), you'll encounter specialties such as *carimañola* (a yucca roll filled with chopped meat and then deep-fried). Common snacks include the *empanada* (a fried turnover filled with ground meat) and the *tamale* (ground corn filled with spices and chicken or pork, wrapped in banana leaves and boiled).

One breakfast staple is *tortillas de maíz*. Unlike those found in Mexico and Guatemala, Panamanian tortillas are much thicker – essentially deep-fried cornmeal cakes. They go quite nicely with eggs or roast meat. *Hojaldras* (deep-fried dough served hot and covered with sugar) are served at breakfast and available at snack bars.

At *almuerzo* (lunch), many Panamanians opt for simple *comida corriente*, the meal of the working class. This is an inexpensive set meal of beef, chicken or fish served alongside *arroz* (rice), *frijoles* (black beans), *patacones*, twice-fried green *plátanos* (plantains), chopped cabbage and maybe an egg or an avocado.

Seafood is abundant. On the Caribbean coast and islands, everyday foods include shrimp, Caribbean king crab, octopus, lobster and fish such as *corvina* (sea bass). Along the Caribbean coast, dishes have a West Indian influence. Seafood is often mixed with coconut milk; coconut rice and coconut bread are also Caribbean treats.

You may see people pushing carts and selling *raspados* (cones filled with shaved ice topped with fruit syrup and sweetened condensed milk).

Health

There are no required vaccinations for Panama, but among those recommended are yellow fever, typhoid, rabies, and hepatitis A and B. See your doctor well ahead, since most vaccines don't produce immunity until at least two weeks after being given. Request an International Certificate of Vaccination (aka the yellow booklet); it's mandatory for countries that require proof of yellow-fever vaccination.

Tap water is generally drinkable in Panama, except in Bocas del Toro and the Comarca de Guna Yala. Visitors who have recently arrived may want to start with bottled water and minimal amounts of tap water.

A superb book called *International Travel and Health*, revised annually and available online at no cost, is published by the World Health Organization (www.who.int/ith). Another website of general interest is MD Travel Health (www.mdtravelhealth.com), with complete travel-health recommendations for every country, updated daily.

Before You Go

HEALTH INSURANCE

You should have travel insurance that covers the cost of an emergency flight home, should you develop a life-threatening condition. You may prefer a policy that pays doctors or hospitals directly rather than you having to pay on the spot and claim later. If you have to claim later, ensure that you keep all documentation. Check that the policy covers ambulances.

MEDICAL CHECKLIST

- Acetaminophen (Tylenol) or aspirin
- Adhesive or paper tape
- Antibacterial ointment (eg Bactroban) for cuts and abrasions
- Antibiotics
- Antidiarrheal drugs (eg loperamide)
- Antihistamines (for hay fever and allergic reactions)
- Anti-inflammatory drugs (eg ibuprofen)
- Bandages, gauze, gauze rolls
- DEET-containing insect repellent for the skin
- Malaria pills (recommended for the Darién)
- Oral rehydration salts
- Permethrin-containing insect spray for clothing, tents and bed nets
- Pocket knife
- Scissors, safety pins, tweezers
- Steroid cream or cortisone (for poison ivy and other allergic rashes)
- Sunblock
- Syringes and sterile needles
- Thermometer

In Panama

Good medical care is widely available in Panama City and also David – it's even sought after, with the cities doing brisk business in medical tourism – though it's limited elsewhere. Most doctors and hospitals expect cash payment, regardless of whether you have travel health insurance.

Infectious Diseases

CHIKUGUNYA

Chikungunya is a virus transmitted by mosquitoes. Common symptoms include fever and joint pain, though sufferers may experience headache, muscle pain, joint swelling or rash. Since there is no vaccine or treatment, travelers should prevent mosquito bites by using insect repellent, wearing long sleeves and pants, and staying indoors. Consult www.cdc.gov for up-to-date information.

DENGUE FEVER

A viral infection, dengue fever (aka 'breakbone' fever) is transmitted by mosquitoes breeding in standing water. It is especially common in densely populated, urban environments. Flu-like symptoms include fever, muscle aches, joint pains, headaches, nausea and vomiting, often followed by a rash. Most cases resolve in a few days. Take analgesics such as acetaminophen/paracetamol (Tylenol) and drink plenty of fluids. Severe cases may require hospitalization. In recent times, Panama has reported cases nationally.

HEPATITIS A

The vaccine for hepatitis A is extremely safe and highly effective. The second most common travel-related infection (after traveler's diarrhea), it's a viral infection of the liver that is usually acquired by ingestion of contaminated water, food or ice. Symptoms include fever, malaise, jaundice, nausea, vomiting and abdominal pain. Most cases resolve without complications, though hepatitis A occasionally causes severe liver damage. There is no treatment.

HEPATITIS B

Hepatitis B is a liver infection usually acquired by sexual contact or by exposure to infected blood, generally through blood transfusions or contaminated needles. The hepatitis B vaccine is safe and highly effective. A total of three injections is necessary to establish full immunity.

LEISHMANIASIS

Leishmaniasis occurs in rural and forested areas throughout Panama, especially the eastern and south-central regions. The disease causes slow-growing ulcers on the body, but the infection may become generalized, especially in those with HIV. Leishmaniasis is transmitted by sand flies. To protect yourself, follow the same precautions as for mosquitoes, with finer-size mesh on mosquito netting (at least 18 holes to the linear inch).

LEPTOSPIROSIS

Leptospirosis is acquired by exposure to water contaminated by the urine of infected animals. The greatest risk occurs at times of flooding, when sewage overflow may contaminate water sources. Initial symptoms resemble a

TAP WATER

Tap water in Panama City *is* safe to drink, as is the water in most other parts of the country. However, you're better off buying bottled water or purifying your own water in the provinces of Bocas del Toro and Guna Yala.

If you have the means, vigorous boiling for one minute is the most effective method of water purification. Another option is to disinfect water with iodine pills, or add 2% tincture of iodine to one quart or liter of water (five drops to clear water, 10 drops to cloudy water) and let stand for 30 minutes. If the water is cold, longer periods may be required.

RECOMMENDED VACCINATIONS

VACCINE	RECOMMENDED FOR	DOSAGE	POSSIBLE SIDE EFFECTS
hepatitis A	all travelers	1 dose before trip; booster 6-12 months later	soreness at injection site, headaches, body aches
typhoid	all travelers	4 capsules by mouth, 1 taken every other day	abdominal pain, nausea, rash
yellow fever	all travelers	1 dose lasts 10 years	headaches, body aches; severe reactions are rare
hepatitis B	long-term travelers in close contact with the local population	3 doses over 6-month period	soreness at injection site, low-grade fever
rabies	travelers who may have contact with animals and may not have access to medical care	3 doses over 3- to 4-week period	soreness at injection site, headaches, body aches
tetanus/ diphtheria	all travelers who haven't had a booster within 10 years	1 dose lasts 10 years	soreness at injection site
measles	travelers born after 1956 who have only had one measles vaccination	1 dose	fever, rash, joint pains, allergic reaction
chickenpox	travelers who've never had chickenpox	2 doses 1 month apart	fever, mild case of chickenpox

mild flu and usually subside in a few days, but a minority of cases are complicated by jaundice or meningitis. Minimize your risk by staying out of bodies of fresh water that may be contaminated by animal urine.

MALARIA

Malaria is transmitted by mosquito bites, usually between dusk and dawn. High-spiking fevers may be accompanied by chills, sweats, headache, body aches, weakness, vomiting or diarrhea. Severe cases may lead to seizures, confusion, coma and death.

Malaria pills are recommended for rural areas in the provinces east of the Panama Canal and Ngöbe-Buglé Comarca. There have been rare cases in the provinces of Bocas del Toro, Colón and Veraguas.

Protecting yourself against mosquito bites is the best prevention. If you develop a fever after returning home, see a physician, as malaria symptoms may not occur for up to six months after being bitten.

RABIES

In Panama, rabies is transmitted mainly by vampire bats. If you are bitten by any animal, thoroughly wash the wound and visit a doctor to determine whether further treatment is necessary. A vaccine is recommended if you will be in wild areas, since Panama does not carry the immunoglobulin that bite victims without the vaccine need right away (getting it involves an urgent flight out).

TRAVELER'S DIARRHEA

To prevent traveler's diarrhea, avoid untreated tap water, eat fresh fruits or vegetables that are cooked or peeled, and be highly selective when eating food from street vendors.

If you do develop diarrhea, drink plenty of fluids, preferably an oral rehydration solution containing lots of salt and sugar. A few loose stools don't require treatment, but if you start having more than four or five stools a day, you should start taking an antibiotic (usually a quinolone drug) and an antidiarrheal agent (such as loperamide). If diarrhea is bloody or persists for more than 72 hours, or is accompanied by fever, shaking chills or severe abdominal pain, seek medical attention.

TYPHOID

Typhoid is caused by ingestion of food or water contaminated by *Salmonella typhi;* fever occurs in virtually all cases. Other symptoms may include headache, malaise, muscle aches, dizziness, loss of appetite, nausea and abdominal pain. Either diarrhea or constipation may occur. Possible complications include intestinal perforation or bleeding, confusion, delirium and, rarely, coma.

The vaccine is usually given orally but is also available as an injection. The treatment drug is usually a quinolone antibiotic such asciprofloxacin (Cipro) or levofloxacin (Levaquin).

YELLOW FEVER

A life-threatening viral infection, yellow fever is transmitted by mosquitoes in forested areas. Flu-like symptoms include fever, chills, headache, muscle aches, backache, loss of appetite, nausea and vomiting. Some patients enter a second, toxic phase, which can lead to death.

Vaccination is recommended for travelers visiting Chepo, Darién and mainland Guna Yala.

ZIKA

Zika virus spreads through the bite of an infected *Aedes* species mosquito. Common symptoms include fever, rash, joint pain and conjunctivitis. Most victims experience mild illness with symptoms that last for several days to a week. Since zika may cause brain damage to infants in utero, pregnant women should be mindful of the country-wide risk. The virus may also be sexually transmitted by an infected partner. Since there is no vaccine or treatment, travelers should prevent mosquito bites by using insect repellent, wearing long sleeves and pants, and staying indoors. Consult www.cdc.gov for up-to-date information.

Insurance

- Prior to your trip, sign up for a travel-insurance policy to cover theft, loss and medical problems.
- Read the fine print. Some policies specifically exclude dangerous activities, which can include scuba diving, motorcycling and even trekking.
- Look into policies that pay doctors or hospitals directly instead of requiring a payment on the spot and a subsequent claim.
- If you have to claim later, ensure you keep all documentation.
- Check that the policy covers ambulances or an emergency flight home.
- Worldwide travel insurance is available at www.lonelyplanet.com/travel-insurance. You can buy, extend and claim online anytime – even if you're already on the road.

Internet Access

Public wi-fi access is increasingly common in bus terminals, plazas, libraries and restaurants. Hotels and hostels in more tourist-oriented areas have wi-fi and some computer terminals for use; the Guna Yala and Darién regions are generally exceptions. If desperate, visit the local school – it's often possible to pick up a signal outside.

Legal Matters

You are legally required to carry identification at all times in Panama. This should be an ID with a photograph, preferably a passport. Although this may seem like an inconvenience, police officers reserve the right to request documentation from tourists at all times, and several readers have been forced to spend the night in prison for failure to produce proper ID.

It is illegal for women and men to walk around topless, even if you are on your way to the beach. This rule is strictly enforced in Bocas del Toro town on Isla Colón, and you can expect to be stopped on the streets by police officers if you don't cover up. You are never allowed to enter government buildings dressed in shorts.

In Panama you are presumed guilty until found innocent. If you are accused of a serious crime, you will be taken to jail, where you will likely spend several months before your case goes before a judge. Some simple but valuable advice: stay away from people who commit crimes. For example, you can expect to go to jail if discovered in a car found to contain illegal drugs, even if they aren't yours.

In Panama the penalties for the possession of even small amounts of illegal drugs are much stricter than in Europe, the USA and Australia. Defendants can often spend years in prison before they are brought to trial and, if convicted (as is usually the case), can expect sentences of several more years. Most lawyers won't accept drug cases because the outcome is fairly certain: conviction.

If you are jailed, your embassy will offer only limited assistance. This may include a visit from an embassy staff member to make sure your human rights have not been violated, letting your family know where you are and putting you in contact with a lawyer (whom you must pay for yourself). Embassy officials will not bail you out.

LGBTIQ+ Travelers

Panamanians are more out than ever, though this openness is much more prevalent in Panama City than anywhere else. You will probably meet more openly gay locals here than in other parts of Central America, though the culture is generally discreet.

Gay marriages are still not legal in Panama, but many think this may change relatively soon. According to locals, discrimination is more prevalent against lesbians than gay men.

Maps

Outside of Panama City, maps are hard to come by.

Canada-based **International Travel Maps** (☎Canada 604-273-1400; www.itmb.com; 12300 Bridgeport Road, Richmond, BC, Canada V6V 1J5) publishes an excellent 1:300,000 color map of Panama (US$11.95) showing the geographical features, cities, towns, national parks, airports and roads of Panama. Maps are available for purchase online.

At **Instituto Geográfico Nacional** (Tommy Guardia; Map p48; ☎236-2444; http://ignpanama.anati.gob.pa; La Cresta; ⊙8am-4pm Mon-Fri) in Panama City, you can buy topographical maps of selected cities and regions. Various free tourist publications distributed in Panama also have maps, though hiking maps are rarely available at national-park ranger stations.

Money

ATMs are readily available except in the most isolated places. Credit cards are widely accepted at restaurants and upscale hotels but may be problematic elsewhere.

For more information, see p19.

Opening Hours

Opening hours vary throughout the year. The following are high-season hours.

Banks 8am–3pm Monday to Friday, 9am–noon Saturday

Bars and clubs Bars from 9pm; clubs 11pm–3am or 4am

Government offices 8am–4pm Monday to Friday

Malls and shops 10am–9pm or 10pm

Offices 8am–noon and 1:30–5pm Monday to Friday

Restaurants 7–10am, noon–3pm and 6–10pm (later in Panama City); often closed Sunday

Supermarkets 8am–9pm; some open 24 hours

Photography

Panamanians may be relaxed about having their photo taken, but it is always best to ask before doing so. General landscape scenes that include locals are usually fine. Flash equipment is forbidden in Panama's churches and museums.

In general, indigenous people should not be photographed without their permission; in the Comarca de Guna Yala, photographing locals is considered rude. Those who will pose may attach a price tag – usually US$1 per photo.

Those honing their skills should consult *Lonely Planet's Guide to Travel Photography*.

Post

Correos Panamá (www.correospanama.gob.pa) operates Panama's mail service; check its website for locations. In theory, airmail to the USA takes five to 10 days; to Europe and Australia, 10 days. Panama has neither vending machines for stamps nor drop-off boxes for mail. You may be able to buy stamps and send mail from an upscale hotel to avoid going to the post office and standing in line. To mail packages, bring all packing materials yourself.

Public Holidays

Días feriados (national holidays) are taken very seriously in Panama, and banks, public offices and many stores close. Public transportation tends to be tight on all holidays and the days immediately preceding or following them – book tickets in advance.

There is no bus service at all on the Thursday afternoon and Friday before Easter, and many businesses are closed for the entire *Semana Santa* (Holy Week; the week before Easter). From Thursday to Easter Sunday, all bars are closed, and alcohol sales are prohibited. Beach hotels are usually booked several weeks in advance for Semana Santa, though a limited choice of rooms is often available.

The week between Christmas and New Year, along with the first week of the year, tends to serve as an unofficial holiday. In addition, various towns have celebrations for their own particular days throughout the year. These other holidays and special events are not official holidays, and businesses remain open.

Most national holidays are celebrated on Monday to create long weekends. When holidays fall on a Thursday or Friday, they are celebrated on the following Monday; holidays that happen to fall on Tuesday or Wednesday are usually celebrated the prior Monday.

New Year's Day (Año Nuevo) January 1

Martyrs' Day (Día de los Mártires) January 9

Good Friday (Viernes Santo) March/April

Labor Day (Día del Trabajo) May 1

Founding of Old Panama (Aniversario de Panamá La Vieja; Panama City only) August 15

Independence Day (Día de la Independencia) November 3

First Call for Independence (Primer Grito de la Independencia) November 10

Independence from Spain (Independencia de Panamá de España) November 28

Mothers Day (Día de la Madre) December 8

Christmas Day (Día de la Navidad) December 25

Safe Travel

- Crime is a problem in parts of Panama City, though the city's better districts are safer than in many other capitals.
- The city of Colón has a high rate of street crime, so consult hotel staff on areas to avoid.
- When traveling in Darién Province, always register with Senafront (border control) before traveling and go with a guide.
- There have been cases of drug trafficking on boats traveling the Caribbean from Colombia north to Panama.

Hiking

Though it's tropical, Panama's weather runs the gamut from hot to cold, and hiking is not always easy here. Always ask local outfitters or rangers about trail conditions before heading out, and ensure you go adequately prepared. Carry plenty of water, even on short journeys, and always bring food, matches and adequate clothing – jungles *do* get quite a bit colder at night, particularly at higher elevations.

Hikers have been known to get lost in rainforests, even seemingly user-friendly ones such as Parque Nacional Volcán Barú and the Sendero Los Quetzales. Landslides, storms and vegetation growth can make trails difficult to follow. In some cases, even access roads can deteriorate enough for transport to leave you a few kilometers before your intended drop-off point. This is just the reality of the jungle, and there is no official rescue organization to help you here. If you are heading out without a guide, make your plans known at your hotel or hostel and tell them the number of days you expect to be gone.

Never walk in unmarked rainforest; if there's no trail going in, you can assume that there won't be one when you decide to turn around and come back out. Always plan your transportation in advance – know where and when the last bus will pass your terminus, or arrange for a taxi pick-up with a responsible, recommended transporter.

Swimming

Unfortunately, drownings occur every year in Panamanian waters, about 80% of them caused by rip currents. A rip is a strong current that pulls the swimmer out to sea. It occurs when two currents that move parallel to the shore meet, causing the opposing waters to choose the path of least resistance, which is the path out to sea.

See p38 for what to do if you get caught in a riptide.

Police

Police corruption is not as big a problem in Panama as it is in some other Latin American countries. However, it's not unheard of for a police officer to stop a motorist for no obvious reason, invent a violation, and levy a fine to be paid on the spot. Showing confusion will sometimes fluster the officer into letting you go, though don't expect much leniency if the police are traveling in pairs. If there has been a violation, suggest you go to the police station to pay.

Some cities in Panama have tourist police – a division created to deal specifically with travelers. Identifiable by armbands on their uniform, officers in this division may be more helpful but it is unlikely.

Thefts & Muggings

Tourist-oriented crime is generally not common in Panama, but it can and does happen.

- Be smart – avoid carrying all your money in one place and avoid entering areas that appear unsafe. If you look like you don't have anything of value on you, you're less likely to interest a mugger.
- Ask your hotel about spots to avoid, and stay where it's well lit and populated.
- Victims of any crime should get a police report as soon as possible. This is a requirement for any insurance claim, although it is unlikely that the police will be able to recover the property. Non-Spanish speakers can ask their embassy for help.
- Panama has a long history of business-related crime, particularly with regard to real estate. If you want to make local investments, make sure you check them out *thoroughly*. If a deal seems too good to be true, it almost certainly will be.

Telephone

Panama's country code is ☎507. To call Panama from abroad, dial the international access code (usually 00 but 011 in the USA) then ☎507 (Panama's country code) and the seven-digit (landline) or eight-digit (cell/mobile) Panamanian telephone number. There are no local area codes in Panama.

Pay phones have been replaced with internet calling services. If you are traveling for an extended period, it may be useful to get a SIM card (US$5) if you have an unlocked cell phone. Otherwise, kiosks in malls and most *chinitos* (Chinese-run convenience stores) sell pay-per-use phones from US$20, and many come with minutes loaded. Having a phone can be invaluable for last-minute reservations or directions, especially since some lodgings are unresponsive to emails.

Cell Phones

Local SIM cards can be used in unlocked phones. Choose your carrier (eg Más Móvil, Digicel, Movistar) carefully, as only certain operators have coverage in the San Blás Islands and Darién Province.

International Calls

Travelers wishing to make international calls can do so via public wi-fi connection. Some cafes provide headphones for internet calls.

Connecting to an international operator from a landline is easy. To connect with a local international operator, simply dial ☎106. For an international operator in the USA, dial ☎109 (AT&T). To reach a Costa Rican operator, dial ☎107; for a Colombian operator, dial ☎116.

Time

Panama observes Eastern Standard Time (GMT/UTC minus five hours). From late October to early April, Panama's clocks coincide with Eastern Standard Time (EST). The rest of the year the country is one hour behind EST as Panama does not observe daylight-saving time.

Toilets

Most bathrooms have signs requesting users to place used toilet paper in trash bins instead of flushing it because the narrow piping may clog up.

Be advised that in parts of Guna Yala and Bocas del Toro, whatever you flush goes straight out to sea. While you certainly can't stop nature from calling, be sure not to flush anything else that doesn't belong in the water.

Public toilets are found mainly in bus terminals, airports and restaurants. In Spanish, restrooms are called *baños* and are often marked *caballeros* (gentlemen) and *damas* (ladies). Outside the cities, toilet paper is not always provided in public toilets, so consider carrying a personal supply or at least some tissues.

Tourist Information

Autoridad de Turismo Panamá (ATP; Panama Tourism Authority; Map p60; ☎526-7000; www.visitpanama.com; 29th fl, Edificio Bisca, cnr Av Balboa & Aquilino de la Guardia, Bella Vista; ⊙8:30am-3pm Mon-Fri) is the national tourism agency. Outside the flagship Panama City office, ATP runs offices in Bocas del Toro, Boquete, David, Paso Canoas, Portobelo, Santiago, El Valle and Pedasí. There are smaller information counters in both **Tocumen International Airport** (☎238-2700; www.tocumenpanama.aero; Av Domingo Díaz, Panama City; ⊙24hr) and **Albrook domestic airport** (Aeropuerto Marcos A Gelabert; ☎501-9272; Av Canfield, Albrook).

ATP has a few useful maps and brochures but often has a problem keeping enough in stock for distribution to tourists. Most offices are staffed with people who speak only Spanish. A few employees really try to help, but the majority are just passing the time. As a general rule, you will get more useful information if you have specific questions.

Visas

Visitors from most European countries as well as the USA, Canada, Australia, New Zealand and South Africa get a 90-day stamp in their passport upon entering Panama.

After 90 days have passed, visas can be extended at *migración* (immigration) offices. Travelers entering Panama overland will probably be asked to show an onward ticket and potentially proof of sufficient funds (US$500) or a credit card.

Citizens from certain other countries will need to obtain a visa, available at Panamanian embassies or consulates. Contact the one nearest you or call **Migración y Naturalización** (Immigration Office; ☎507-1800; www.migracion.gob.pa; cnr Av Cuba & Calle 28 Este, Calidonia; ⊙8am-4pm Mon-Fri) in Panama City.

Onward Tickets

Travelers officially need onward tickets before they are allowed to enter Panama. This requirement is not often checked at **Tocumen International Airport** (☎238-2700; www.tocumenpanama.aero; Av Domingo Díaz, Panama City; ⊙24hr), but travelers arriving by land should anticipate a need to show an onward ticket.

If you're heading to Colombia, Venezuela or another South American country from Panama, you may need an onward or round-trip ticket before you will be allowed entry into that country or even allowed to board the plane if you're flying. A quick check with the appropriate embassy – easy to do online – will tell you whether the country that you're heading to has an onward-ticket requirement.

Extensions

Visas are good for 90 days. To extend your stay, you'll have to go to a **Migración y Naturalización** (Immigration Office; ☎507-1800; www.migracion.gob.pa; cnr Av Cuba & Calle 28 Este, Calidonia; ⊙8am-4pm Mon-Fri) office in Panama City, David or Chitré. You must bring your passport and photocopies of the page with your personal information and of the stamp of your most recent entry to Panama. You must also bring two passport-size photos, an onward air or bus ticket and a letter to the director stating your reasons for wishing to extend your visit. You must have proof of funds (US$500) for the remainder of your stay (a credit card will suffice). You will have to fill out a *prórroga de turista* (tourist extension) and pay a fee. You will then be issued a plastic photo-ID card. Go early in the day as the whole process takes about two hours.

If you have extended your time, you will also need to obtain a *permiso de salida* (exit permit) to leave the country. For this, bring your passport and a *paz y salvo* (a certificate stating you don't owe any back taxes) to the immigration office. *Paz y salvos* are issued at Ministerios de Economia y Finanzas, found in towns with immigration offices; obtaining one simply requires that you bring in your passport, fill out a form and pay a fee of about US$1.

These documents can be obtained in Panama City at the Migración y Naturalización and the **Ministerio de Economia y Finanzas, Dirección de Ingresos** (DGI; ☎507-7985; www.dgi.gob.pa; cnr Via España & Calle 52 Este, Campo Alegre; ⏰8:30am-4:30pm Mon-Fri).

Volunteering

Volunteering opportunities are few in Panama, so potential volunteers should look for programs run by reputable, well-known NGOs such as the **Grupo de Conservación de Tortugas de Jaqué** (Colegio de la Tierra; ☎264-6266, 6047-2373; www.colegiodelatierra.org) in Darién. Many of the expat-run hostels employ volunteers on a casual basis in exchange for room and board.

Women Travelers

Female travelers usually find Panama safe. A minority of Panamanian men may make flirtatious comments, hiss, honk their horn or stare, even if you're accompanied. The best response is to follow the lead of Panamanian women: give these men a wide berth, ignore their comments and look away.

While locals might get away with skimpy, stretchy clothing, travelers will naturally attract less attention with a more conservative approach. In the interior, dress is more formal, with skirts and nice sandals the norm. It is not legal to go topless, even in beach towns – for both men and women.

Women traveling solo will get more attention than those traveling in pairs or groups. Although assault and rape of foreign travelers is rare, it may be dangerous to take drinks from strangers in bars, walk alone in isolated places, or hitchhike.

If you are taking a long-distance bus, sit next to a woman or a family if you are nervous about being approached. Be picky about your taxis: though shared taxis (between unknown parties) are common, avoid those with more than one man. If the driver tries to pick up another fare, you can offer to pay more to travel alone.

Work

It's difficult for foreigners to find work in Panama. The government prefers to give jobs to Panamanians, and labor laws reflect this sentiment (eg Uber drivers must be Panamanian citizens). Foreigners legally employed in Panama generally have their own businesses, possess skills not found in Panama, or work for companies that have special agreements with the Panamanian government.

Transportation

GETTING THERE & AWAY

Panama is well served by a number of airlines. It can be reached overland from Costa Rica by bus and Colombia by boat. Flights, cars and tours can be booked online at lonelyplanet.com/bookings.

Entering the Country

Passengers entering Panama by air are less scrutinized than those crossing by land. Upon arrival, most travelers will have to fill out a tourist card.

The most popular overland crossing is from Costa Rica at Paso Canoas. You may be asked to show an onward ticket – a return bus ticket to Costa Rica will suffice. Other land crossings include the low-key border at Sixaola/Guabito and the seldom-used Río Sereno. To and from Colombia by boat, the crossing is at Capurganá.

Passports

Every visitor needs a valid passport and an onward ticket to enter Panama, but further requirements vary by nationality and change occasionally. Anyone planning a trip to Panama is well advised to check online to obtain the latest information on entry requirements. Ticketing agents of airlines that fly to Panama and tour operators can often provide this information.

In the event that you lose your passport while in Panama, you'll need proof of when you entered the country to be able to leave. That proof, strangely enough, does not come from an immigration office but from the airline you flew in on. You need to go to the airline's main office in Panama City and request a certification of your entry date *(certificación de vuelo)*. There's no charge, but you'll likely be asked to come back the next day to pick it up. When you leave the country, along with your new passport (obtained from your embassy in Panama City), you'll present your *certificación de vuelo* to an immigration agent.

Air

At present Panama has three active commercial international airports:

Tocumen International Airport (☎238-2700; www.tocumenpanama.aero; Av Domingo Díaz, Panama City; ⏲24hr)

Aeropuerto Enrique Malek (☎721-1072; David)

Panamá Pacífico International Airport Located 12km southwest of Panama City. Viva Air Colombia airline began using this small airport, the former US Howard Air Force Base, in 2014.

Airlines with international flights to Panama include the following:

Air Panama (☎316-9000; www.airpanama.com; Albrook Airport)

Air France (☎800-226-0080, 800-992-3932; www.airfrance.com; Via Tocumen, Aeropuerto Internacional de Tocumen)

American Airlines (☎264-8999; www.aa.com; Calle 50, Plaza New York, 2nd fl; ⏲8:30am-6pm Mon-Fri, 9am-1pm Sat)

Avianca (☎206-8222; www.avianca.com; Calle 50; ⏲9am-5:30pm Mon-Fri, to 12:30pm Sat)

Copa Airlines (☎217-2672; www.copaair.com; Av Central s/n, Casco Viejo; ⏲8am-6pm Mon-Fri, 9am-1pm Sat)

Delta Airlines (☎214-8118; www.delta.com; Calle Punta Darien, Torre las Americas ground fl, Punta Pacífica; ⏲8am-5pm Mon-Fri, to noon Sat)

Iberia (☎836-7001; www.iberia.com; Av Balboa & Calle 43, ground fl, Edificio BAC; ⏲9am-4pm Mon-Fri)

KLM (☎800-226-0080; www.klm.com; Vía Tocumen, Aeropuerto Internacional de Tocumen)

Land

Many travelers arrive in Panama by bus from Costa Rica. It's recommended that you get to the border early in order to ensure that you don't miss onward transportation on the other side. There are no roads into Colombia, and travelers are strongly discouraged from crossing overland due to the instability of the border region, but sea crossings are possible.

Border Crossings

There are three border crossings between Costa Rica and Panama. Most travelers cross at Paso Canoas (gateway: David). Note that Panama is always one hour ahead of Costa Rica.

To enter Panama from Costa Rica, you'll need a passport and an onward ticket. Some nationalities may require a visa.

You can also be asked for an onward ticket if you are entering Costa Rica. If you do not possess one, it is acceptable to buy a return bus ticket back to Panama.

PASO CANOAS

The most heavily trafficked border crossing to and from Costa Rica is at Paso Canoas (open 7am to 7pm, Panama time), 55km northwest of David on the Interamericana. Tips:

- The best place to spend the night before crossing is David.
- Ensure that you have both entry and exit stamps in your passport.
- Allow one to 1½ hours for the formalities on both sides. Buses from David depart frequently for the border (US$2.10, 50 minutes, every 15 minutes) from 4am until 9:30pm.
- On the Costa Rican side, you can catch regular buses to San José or other parts of the country.
- From David, there are also taxis to Paso Canoas (US$35).

SIXAOLA & GUABITO

The Caribbean border post at Guabito/Sixaola (open 8am to 5pm, Panama time), 15km northwest of Changuinola, sees less traffic than Paso Canoas on the Pacific side, though most travelers find it hassle-free. Buses from Changuinola depart frequently for the border (US$1.25, 30 minutes, every half-hour) from 5:30am to 7pm. On the Costa Rican side of the border, you can catch regular buses on to Puerto Limón and San José, as well as regional destinations.

RÍO SERENO

The least used crossing into Costa Rica is the border post at Río Sereno (open 8am to 5pm Monday to Saturday, to 3pm Sunday, Panama time), located 40km northwest of Volcán. Buses to the border depart from David and travel via La Concepción, Volcán and Santa Clara (US$5.10, 2½ hours, every half-hour till

DRIVING TO PANAMA FROM NORTH AMERICA

Lonely Planet's reader-tested tips for the cross-continental drive:

Think it through Driving yourself through Central America is *not* a cheap option. Advantages include greater comfort and flexibility, but you *will* spend more than you expect on gas, insurance and fees.

Drive defensively Few cars use turn signals, pedestrians cross highways – things are different here. Driving in Panama is not for the faint of heart – be smart and stay safe.

Go mainstream Toyotas, Hondas and Nissans are extremely popular in Central America, which makes them substantially easier to service or sell, though you may not recover your initial expenditure.

Get insurance in the USA or Canada beforehand For full coverage, though, Panama requires its own insurance.

Learn to service your car Mechanics charge much more in Panama than in other Central American countries.

Be prepared Bring along a good tool kit, an (empty) emergency gas canister, plenty of emergency food and water, and industrial-strength duct tape. A spare tire is obligatory, especially if you'll be traveling over rough terrain.

Know the law Panamanian law requires that all vehicles be fitted with a catalytic converter.

Nationalize your car It costs approximately 20% to 25% of the vehicle's value in taxation, but it's required if you want to sell it. Since any damage reduces value, don't make repairs until afterwards.

Advertise your wares Try online expat forums or take out a classified in *La Prensa* newspaper on Sunday, when the majority of car buyers are looking.

CLIMATE CHANGE & TRAVEL

Every form of transport that relies on carbon-based fuel generates CO_2, the main cause of human-induced climate change. Modern travel is dependent on airplanes, which might use less fuel per kilometer per person than most cars but travel much greater distances. The altitude at which aircraft emit gases (including CO_2) and particles also contributes to their climate change impact. Many websites offer 'carbon calculators' that allow people to estimate the carbon emissions generated by their journey and, for those who wish to do so, to offset the impact of the greenhouse gases emitted with contributions to portfolios of climate-friendly initiatives throughout the world. Lonely Planet offsets the carbon footprint of all staff and author travel.

5pm). On the Costa Rican side of the border, you can take a 15-minute bus or taxi ride to San Vito, where you can catch buses to regional destinations.

Bus

At all three border crossings, you can take a local bus up to the border on either side, cross over, board another local bus and continue on your way. Be aware that the last buses leave the border crossings at Guabito and Río Sereno at 7pm and 5pm, respectively; the last bus leaves Paso Canoas for Panama City at 9:30pm.

Two companies, **Expreso Panama** (Map p48; ☎314-6837; www.expresopanama.com; Albrook Bus Terminal, Office 13-14) and **Tica Bus** (Map p48; ☎314-6385; www.ticabus.com; Albrook Bus Terminal, Stand 32), operate daily *directo* (direct) buses between San José (Costa Rica) and Panama City, departing from **Albrook Bus Terminal** (Gran Terminal; Map p48; ☎303-3030; www.grantnt.com; Albrook; ⌚24hr). Both recommend making reservations a few days in advance.

Sea

It's possible to cross to Colombia by sea, which makes for a very enjoyable passage. Expensive multiday sailboat voyages depart from Colón Province, while most motorboat trips depart from Cartí in the Comarca de Guna Yala.

GETTING AROUND

As most Panamanians use public transportation, it's reasonably priced and connections are frequent.

Air

Panama's domestic destinations are served by **Air Panama** (☎316-9000; www.airpanama.com; Albrook Airport) and **Copa Airlines** (☎217-2672; www.copaair.com; Av Central s/n, Casco Viejo; ⌚8am-6pm Mon-Fri, 9am-1pm Sat). Domestic flights depart Panama City from **Albrook Airport** (Aeropuerto Marcos A Gelabert; ☎501-9272; Av Canfield, Albrook). Located near the Costa Rican border, David's **Aeropuerto Enrique Malek** (☎721-1072; David) frequently handles flights to and from San José.

Book ahead in high season, when demand for flights to destinations like Bocas and the Comarca de Guna Yala exceeds availability.

Bicycle

If you can get over the heat, you can cycle through Panama easily enough, with lodgings within a day's ride away. Cycling within larger Panamanian cities – particularly Panama City – is not for the faint of heart. Roads tend to be narrow, and people drive aggressively. Also, frequent rains reduce motorists' visibility and tire grip.

The best places for cyclists in Panama City are the coastal routes of the Cinta Costera (a dedicated bike lane from downtown and around Casco Viejo) and the Causeway. Weekend cyclist groups often go out to Gamboa via a shady but narrow road.

Outside the cities, Panama's Interamericana boasts the best quality in Central America, although sections have an extremely narrow shoulder. Roads in many of the provinces (especially in Veraguas and Colón) are in poor shape – plan accordingly and bring lots of spare parts.

Boat

Boats are the chief means of transportation in several areas of Panama, particularly in Darién Province, the Archipiélago de Las Perlas, and the San Blás and Bocas del Toro island chains.

From Panama City, there are regular ferries from the Causeway to Isla Taboga and Isla Contadora. Panama City is also the jumping-off point for partial and full Panama Canal transits.

If you're planning an excursion to Isla de Coiba and the national marine park, the best way to reach the island is through an organized boat tour. Local fishers also ply the waters off the coast of Veraguas, though this is a riskier proposition as the seas can get really rough.

The tourist mecca of Bocas del Toro town on Isla Colón is accessible from Almirante by frequent water taxis.

Colombian and Guna merchant boats carry cargo and passengers along the San Blás coast between Colón and Puerto Obaldía, stopping at up to 48 of the islands to load and unload passengers and cargo. However, these boats are often dangerously overloaded. Taking passage on a sailboat, or the four-day motorboat service to Colombia, is a wiser option.

Since there aren't many roads in the eastern part of Darién Province, boat travel is often the only way to get from one town to another, especially during the rainy season. The boat of choice here is the *piragua* (long canoe), carved from the trunk of a giant ceiba tree. The shallow hulls of these boats allow them to ride the many rivers that comprise the traditional transportation network of eastern Panama. Many are motorized.

Bus

You can take a bus to just about any community in Panama that is accessible by road. Some of the buses are full-size Mercedes Benzes equipped with air-con, movie screens and reclining seats. These top-of-the-line buses generally cruise long stretches of highway.

Most common are small Toyota Coaster buses, affectionately called *chivas*. Use these to visit towns on the Península de Azuero and along the Interamericana.

Panama City has just about finished phasing out its *diablos rojos* (red devils) for modern, safe, air-conditioned buses on the Metrobus system. Riders can obtain swipe cards at Albrook Bus Terminal or main bus stops. Official bus stops are used, and the transportation is air-conditioned.

Car & Motorcycle

Signs can be confusing or wholly absent in Panama. There are many poor secondary roads, and even paved roads can sometimes resemble a lunar landscape.

Some tips:

- On all primary roads (including the Interamericana) the speed limit is 80km/h; on secondary roads it's 60km/h or less.
- Drivers should carry their passport and driver's license.
- If there's an accident, do not move the vehicles (even if they're blocking traffic) until after the police have arrived and made a report. It's also essential for insurance claims.
- Oncoming cars with flashing headlights often indicate that there is a problem or a police speed trap ahead. Slow down immediately. Piles of branches placed on the road's edge often signal a broken-down vehicle.

Rental

Due to the low cost and ready availability of buses and taxis, it isn't necessary to rent a vehicle in Panama unless you intend to go off the beaten track. Some beach areas have notoriously poor roads. There are car-rental agencies in major cities such as Panama City and David. Many also operate out of Tocumen International Airport.

To rent a vehicle in Panama, you must be 25 years of age or older and present a passport and driver's license – if you are over 21 and can present a valid credit card, some agencies will waive the age requirement. Even with an international agency, you are usually renting through their subsidiaries and will not get any support from them outside Panama.

Prices for rentals in Panama run from as low as US$20 per day for an economy car up to US$100 per day for a *cuatro por cuatro* (4WD). When you rent, carefully inspect the car for minor dents and scratches, missing radio antennae, hubcaps and the presence of a spare tire. Damage *must* be noted on your rental agreement; otherwise you may be charged for it when you return the car.

There have been many reports of theft from rental cars. You should never leave valuables in an unattended car, and you should remove all luggage from the trunk when you're checking into a hotel overnight – most hotels provide parking areas for cars.

Hitchhiking

Hitching is not common at all in Panama; most people travel by bus, and visitors would do best to follow suit. In any case, hitching is never entirely safe in any country and we don't recommend it. Travelers who hitch should understand that they are taking a small but potentially serious risk.

Local Transportation

The efficient Metrobus system covers Panama City and its outskirts, but services can be difficult to figure out. Panamanians are usually friendly, including bus drivers; they'll often be able to tell you where to wait for a particular bus if you ask in Spanish (few bus drivers speak English). Panama City's El Metro subway is fast and convenient but has a limited route. In general, taxis are cheap and can save a lot of time and hassle.

Subway

Panama City's mostly underground transportation system is known as **El Metro** (☎504-7200; www.elmetrodepanama.com; fare US$0.35-1.35; ⏰5am-11pm Mon-Fri, to 10pm Sat, 7am-10pm Sun). The one line (at present) runs west–east from Albrook and then north to San Isidra; a second line between Albrook and the City of Knowledge is on the way. The main terminal is across from **Albrook Bus Terminal** (Gran Terminal; Map p48; ☎303-3030; www.grantnt.com; Albrook; ⏰24hr). Fares are paid with the same swipe card used for the Metrobus system.

Taxis & Ride-sharing

Taxis are cheap and plentiful, though not all drivers have a good grasp of locations and directions.

Some tips:

➡ Before even getting into a taxi, state your destination and settle on a fare. Panamanian taxis don't have meters, but there are standard fares between Panama City's neighborhoods.

➡ Get informed. Ask the staff at your accommodations for the typical rates between city sectors; these usually go up after dark.

➡ Taxis can be scarce late at night and around the holidays. At these times, it's best to call for a radio taxi.

➡ More expensive 'sedan' taxis operate from upscale hotels. They charge double what you'd pay a hailed cab.

➡ Consider using Uber; it's reliable and cheap, and the drivers are helpful and friendly.

Tours

Panama's tourism industry is still young, though the number of tour operators is growing rapidly. While increasingly navigable for the independent traveler, Panama does have special conditions (complex logistics, limited public access and big wilderness) that make contracting a tour operator a good option. Some top attractions, including the Darién and Coiba, are all but inaccessible without a guide.

Prices vary depending on the services you require and whether you are prepared to join a group. It's increasingly common for hostels to provide their own budget tours for guests.

Ancon Expeditions (Map p60; ☎269-9415; www.anconexpeditions.com; Edificio Dorado, 2nd fl, Calle 49a Este, El Cangrejo; ⏰9am-5pm Mon-Fri, to 1pm Sat) Ancon offers quality service and employs some of the country's best nature guides, many with decades of experience and speaking multiple languages. Regular departures cover destinations throughout Panama. Ancon is also active in conservation.

EcoCircuitos (☎315-1488; www.ecocircuitos.com; Albrook Plaza, 2nd fl, No 31, Ancón) A great outfitter offering a range of tailored tours throughout the country, including wildlife-watching, adventure tourism, community tourism and beach destinations. It is a member of **APTSO** (Asociación Panameño de Turismo Sostenible; http://aptso.org), Panama's sustainable-tourism alliance. Excellent English spoken.

Isthmian Adventures (Map p139; ☎6429-8163; www.isthmianadventures.com; Terminal de Bus, local 3; ⏰8am-4pm Mon-Fri) A reputable outfitter offering a variety of private tours around Panama, as well as day trips from Panama City. Options include walking, birding, family tours and multisport activities. English is spoken. Also a member of APTSO.

Jungle Treks (☎6438-3130; www.jungletreks.com) Started by a bilingual naturalist guide, Jungle Treks runs a number of unique, recommended expeditions. Destinations include the Darién, the Chiriquí highlands, Veraguas and the canal watershed. Trips can be custom made but require six participants and a three-day minimum.

Scubapanama (☎261-3841; www.scubapanama.com; Calle 52c Oeste, Vista Hermosa; ⏰8am-6pm Mon-Fri, to 4pm Sat) The country's oldest dive operator, offering a variety of trips throughout the country.

Yala Tours (☎232-0215, 6641-6676; www.yalatourspanama.com) This recommended small outfitter specializes in nature travel and indigenous culture, with day trips to Parque Nacional Soberanía and Emberá village visits. It's swiss-run, and multiple languages are spoken.

Train

The country's only rail line is the historic Panama Railroad, which runs from Panama City to Colón. The **Panama Canal Railway** (☎317-6070; www.panarail.com; one way adult/child US$25/15; ⏰departure from Panama City 7:15am, return from Colón 5:15pm Mon-Fri) offers daily passenger service on a fully operational vintage train. Aimed at tourists looking to relive the heyday of luxury rail travel, the hour-long ride runs parallel to the canal and at times traverses thick jungle and rainforest.

Language

Spanish is the national language of Panama (see also p232 for the basics of the Guna language, spoken in the Comarca de Guna Yala). Latin American Spanish pronunciation is easy, as there's a clear and consistent relationship between what you see written and how it's pronounced. Also, most sounds have equivalents in English.

Note that kh is a throaty sound (like the 'ch' in the Scottish *loch*), v and b are like a soft English 'v' (between a 'v' and a 'b'), and r is strongly rolled. There are also some variations in spoken Spanish across Latin America, the most notable being the pronunciation of the letters *ll* and *y*. In our pronunciation guides they are represented with y because they are pronounced as the 'y' in 'yes' in most of Latin America. Note, however, that in some parts of the continent they sound like the 'lli' in 'million'. Read our colored pronunciation guides as if they were English, and you'll be understood. The stressed syllables are indicated with italics in our pronunciation guides.

The polite form is used in this chapter; where both polite and informal options are given, they are indicated by the abbreviations 'pol' and 'inf'. Where necessary, both masculine and feminine forms of words are included, separated by a slash and with the masculine form first, eg *perdido/a* (m/f).

BASICS

Hello.	*Hola.*	o·la
Goodbye.	*Adiós.*	a·*dyos*

WANT MORE?

For in-depth language information and handy phrases, check out Lonely Planet's *Latin American Spanish Phrasebook*. You'll find it at **shop.lonelyplanet.com**, or you can buy Lonely Planet's iPhone phrasebooks at the Apple App Store.

How are you?	*¿Qué tal?*	ke tal
Fine, thanks.	*Bien, gracias.*	byen *gra*·syas
Excuse me.	*Perdón.*	per·*don*
Sorry.	*Lo siento.*	lo *syen*·to
Please.	*Por favor.*	por fa·*vor*
Thank you.	*Gracias.*	*gra*·syas
You are welcome.	*De nada.*	de *na*·da
Yes./No.	*Sí./No.*	see/no

My name is ...
Me llamo ... — me *ya*·mo ...

What's your name?
¿Cómo se llama Usted? — *ko*·mo se *ya*·ma oo·*ste* (pol)
¿Cómo te llamas? — *ko*·mo te *ya*·mas (inf)

Do you speak English?
¿Habla inglés? — *a*·bla een·*gles* (pol)
¿Hablas inglés? — *a*·blas een·*gles* (inf)

I don't understand.
Yo no entiendo. — yo no en·*tyen*·do

ACCOMMODATIONS

I'd like a single/double room.
Quisiera una habitación individual/doble. — kee·*sye*·ra *oo*·na a·bee·ta·*syon* een·dee·vee·*dwal*/*do*·ble

How much is it per night/person?
¿Cuánto cuesta por noche/persona? — *kwan*·to *kwes*·ta por *no*·che/per·*so*·na

Does it include breakfast?
¿Incluye el desayuno? — een·*kloo*·ye el de·sa·*yoo*·no

campsite	*terreno de cámping*	te·*re*·no de *kam*·peeng
guesthouse	*pensión*	pen·*syon*
hotel	*hotel*	o·*tel*
youth hostel	*albergue juvenil*	al·*ber*·ge khoo·ve·*neel*

Signs

Abierto	Open
Cerrado	Closed
Entrada	Entrance
Hombres/Varones	Men
Mujeres/Damas	Women
Prohibido	Prohibited
Salida	Exit
Servicios/Baños	Toilets

air-con	*aire acondicionado*	*ai*·re a·kon·dee·syo·*na*·do
bathroom	*baño*	*ba*·nyo
bed	*cama*	*ka*·ma
window	*ventana*	ven·*ta*·na

DIRECTIONS

Where's ...?
¿Dónde está ...? — *don*·de es·*ta* ...

What's the address?
¿Cuál es la dirección? — kwal es la dee·rek·*syon*

Could you please write it down?
¿Puede escribirlo, por favor? — *pwe*·de es·kree·*beer*·lo por fa·*vor*

Can you show me (on the map)?
¿Me lo puede indicar (en el mapa)? — me lo *pwe*·de een·dee·*kar* (en el *ma*·pa)

at the corner	*en la esquina*	en la es·*kee*·na
at the traffic lights	*en el semáforo*	en el se·*ma*·fo·ro
behind ...	*detrás de ...*	de·*tras* de ...
in front of ...	*enfrente de ...*	en·*fren*·te de ...
left	*izquierda*	ees·*kyer*·da
next to ...	*al lado de ...*	al *la*·do de ...
opposite ...	*frente a ...*	*fren*·te a ...
right	*derecha*	de·*re*·cha
straight ahead	*todo recto*	*to*·do *rek*·to

EATING & DRINKING

Can I see the menu, please?
¿Puedo ver el menú, por favor? — *pwe*·do ver el me·*noo* por fa·*vor*

What would you recommend?
¿Qué recomienda? — ke re·ko·*myen*·da

Do you have vegetarian food?
¿Tienen comida vegetariana? — *tye*·nen ko·*mee*·da ve·khe·ta·*rya*·na

I don't eat (red meat).
No como (carne roja). — no *ko*·mo (*kar*·ne *ro*·kha)

That was delicious!
¡Estaba buenísimo! — es·*ta*·ba bwe·*nee*·see·mo

Cheers!
¡Salud! — sa·*loo*

The bill, please.
La cuenta, por favor. — la *kwen*·ta por fa·*vor*

I'd like a table for ...	*Quisiera una mesa para ...*	kee·*sye*·ra *oo*·na *me*·sa *pa*·ra ...
(eight) o'clock	*las (ocho)*	las (*o*·cho)
(two) people	*(dos) personas*	(dos) per·*so*·nas

Key Words

bottle	*botella*	bo·*te*·ya
breakfast	*desayuno*	de·sa·*yoo*·no
(too) cold	*(muy) frío*	(mooy) *free*·o
dinner	*cena*	*se*·na
fork	*tenedor*	te·ne·*dor*
glass	*vaso*	*va*·so
hot (warm)	*caliente*	kal·*yen*·te
knife	*cuchillo*	koo·*chee*·yo
lunch	*comida*	ko·*mee*·da
plate	*plato*	*pla*·to
restaurant	*restaurante*	res·tow·*ran*·te
spoon	*cuchara*	koo·*cha*·ra
with/without	*sin/con*	seen/kon

Meat & Fish

beef	*carne de vaca*	*kar*·ne de *va*·ka
chicken	*pollo*	*po*·yo
duck	*pato*	*pa*·to
lamb	*cordero*	kor·*de*·ro
pork	*cerdo*	*ser*·do
prawn	*langostino*	lan·gos·*tee*·no
salmon	*salmón*	sal·*mon*
seafood	*mariscos*	ma·*rees*·kos
tuna	*atún*	a·*toon*
turkey	*pavo*	*pa*·vo
veal	*ternera*	ter·*ne*·ra

Fruit & Vegetables

apple	*manzana*	man·*sa*·na
apricot	*albaricoque*	al·ba·ree·*ko*·ke
banana	*plátano*	*pla*·ta·no
beans	*judías*	khoo·*dee*·as
cabbage	*col*	kol

capsicum	*pimiento*	pee·*myen*·to
carrot	*zanahoria*	sa·na·*o*·rya
cherry	*cereza*	se·*re*·sa
corn	*maíz*	ma·*ees*
cucumber	*pepino*	pe·*pee*·no
grape	*uvas*	*oo*·vas
lemon	*limón*	lee·*mon*
lettuce	*lechuga*	le·*choo*·ga
mushroom	*champiñón*	cham·pee·*nyon*
nuts	*nueces*	*nwe*·ses
onion	*cebolla*	se·*bo*·ya
orange	*naranja*	na·*ran*·kha
peach	*melocotón*	me·lo·ko·*ton*
peas	*guisantes*	gee·*san*·tes
pineapple	*piña*	*pee*·nya
plum	*ciruela*	seer·*we*·la
potato	*patata*	pa·*ta*·ta
spinach	*espinacas*	es·pee·*na*·kas
strawberry	*fresa*	*fre*·sa
tomato	*tomate*	to·*ma*·te
watermelon	*sandía*	san·*dee*·a

Other

bread	*pan*	pan
cheese	*queso*	*ke*·so
egg	*huevo*	*we*·vo
honey	*miel*	myel

SPANISH IN PANAMA

Here's a rundown on some of the local expressions and colorful colloquialisms you may hear while traveling in Panama.

salve – street slang for *propina*, or tip

tongo – street slang for 'cop'

hota – street slang for 'police car'

diablo rojo – literally 'red devil'; refers to public buses

¡Bien cuidado! – 'Well taken care of!'; often used by a street person asking for a tip for taking care of your car (in parking lots at restaurants, cinemas, bars)

una pinta/fría – literally, 'one pint' or 'a cold one'; means 'a beer'

Dame una fría. – Give me a cold one (a beer)

guaro – hard liquor

chupata – an all-out drinking party

vuelve loco con vaca – literally 'makes crazy with cow'; refers to drinking *seco* and milk

buena leche – literally 'good milk'; means 'good luck'

salado/a (m/f) – literally 'salty'; refers to someone who is having bad luck

Me estoy comiendo un cable. – literally 'I'm eating a cable'; means 'I'm down on my luck'

Eso está bien pretty. – refers to something nice

¡Eso está pretty pretty! – refers to something supernice

¡Entonces laopé! – Hey, dude!

¡Juega vivo! – Be alert! (look out for your best interests)

¡Ayala bestia! – Holy cow!

¡Chuleta! – common expression similar to 'Holy cow!'

enantes – just now

Voy por fuera. – I'm leaving right now

Pa' lante. – Let's go now

Nos pillamos. – We'll see each other later

pelao/pelaito – common expression for a child

chombo/a (m/f) – an acceptable reference to a black person of Antillean descent

¡Pifioso! – a show-off, or something that looks cool

Tas buena, mami. – You're looking good, mama

racataca/meña – both terms refer to women who wear lots of gold jewelry and are perceived as lacking class

mangajo/a (m/f) – someone who is filthy

ladilla – literally 'crab louse'; refers to an annoying person

Eres un comemierda. – said to a pretentious person

rabiblanco/a (m/f) – literally 'white-tipped'; pejorative reference to a member of the socio-economic elite; comes from *paloma rabíblano* (white-tipped dove), a bird that walks with its head held high and its chest thrust out in a seemingly pretentious way

yeye – refers to kids and adults who pretend to be rich (eg by wearing fancy clothes and maybe driving a fancy car) but who in reality are living well beyond their means for as long as they can

vaina – common word used for 'thing,' as in *Pásame esa vaina* (Pass me that thing)

nueve letras – literally 'nine letters'; refers to Seco Herrerano, the national drink

jam	*mermelada*	mer·me·*la*·da
pepper	*pimienta*	pee·*myen*·ta
rice	*arroz*	a·*ros*
salad	*ensalada*	en·sa·*la*·da
salt	*sal*	sal
soup	*sopa*	*so*·pa
sugar	*azúcar*	a·*soo*·kar

Drinks

beer	*cerveza*	ser·*ve*·sa
coffee	*café*	ka·*fe*
(orange) juice	*zumo (de naranja)*	*soo*·mo (de na·*ran*·kha)
milk	*leche*	*le*·che
red wine	*vino tinto*	*vee*·no *teen*·to
tea	*té*	te
(mineral) water	*agua (mineral)*	*a*·gwa (mee·ne·*ral*)
white wine	*vino blanco*	*vee*·no *blan*·ko

EMERGENCIES

Help!	*¡Socorro!*	so·*ko*·ro
Go away!	*¡Vete!*	*ve*·te

Call ...!	*¡Llame a ...!*	*ya*·me a ...
a doctor	*un médico*	oon *me*·dee·ko
the police	*la policía*	la po·lee·*see*·a

I'm lost.
Estoy perdido/a. es·*toy* per·*dee*·do/a (m/f)

I'm ill.
Estoy enfermo/a. es·*toy* en·*fer*·mo/a (m/f)

I'm allergic to (antibiotics).
Soy alérgico/a a (los antibióticos). soy a·*ler*·khee·ko/a a (los an·tee·*byo*·tee·kos) (m/f)

Where are the toilets?
¿Dónde están los baños? *don*·de es·*tan* los *ba*·nyos

Question Words

How?	*¿Cómo?*	*ko*·mo
What?	*¿Qué?*	ke
When?	*¿Cuándo?*	*kwan*·do
Where?	*¿Dónde?*	*don*·de
Which?	*¿Cuál?* (sg) *¿Cuáles?* (pl)	kwal *kwa*·les
Who?	*¿Quién?*	kyen
Why?	*¿Por qué?*	por ke

SHOPPING & SERVICES

I'd like to buy ...
Quisiera comprar ... kee·*sye*·ra kom·*prar* ...

I'm just looking.
Sólo estoy mirando. *so*·lo es·*toy* mee·*ran*·do

Can I look at it?
¿Puedo verlo? *pwe*·do *ver*·lo

I don't like it.
No me gusta. no me *goos*·ta

How much is it?
¿Cuánto cuesta? *kwan*·to *kwes*·ta

That's too expensive.
Es muy caro. es mooy *ka*·ro

Can you lower the price?
¿Podría bajar un poco el precio? po·*dree*·a ba·*khar* oon *po*·ko el *pre*·syo

There's a mistake in the bill.
Hay un error en la cuenta. ai oon e·*ror* en la *kwen*·ta

ATM	*cajero automático*	ka·*khe*·ro ow·to·*ma*·tee·ko
credit card	*tarjeta de crédito*	tar·*khe*·ta de *kre*·dee·to
internet cafe	*cibercafé*	see·ber·ka·*fe*
market	*mercado*	mer·*ka*·do
post office	*correos*	ko·*re*·os
tourist office	*oficina de turismo*	o·fee·*see*·na de too·*rees*·mo

TIME & DATES

What time is it?	*¿Qué hora es?*	ke *o*·ra es
It's (10) o'clock.	*Son (las diez).*	son (las dyes)
It's half past (one).	*Es (la una) y media.*	es (la *oo*·na) ee *me*·dya

morning	*mañana*	ma·*nya*·na
afternoon	*tarde*	*tar*·de
evening	*noche*	*no*·che
yesterday	*ayer*	a·*yer*
today	*hoy*	oy
tomorrow	*mañana*	ma·*nya*·na

Monday	*lunes*	*loo*·nes
Tuesday	*martes*	*mar*·tes
Wednesday	*miércoles*	*myer*·ko·les
Thursday	*jueves*	*khwe*·ves
Friday	*viernes*	*vyer*·nes
Saturday	*sábado*	*sa*·ba·do
Sunday	*domingo*	do·*meen*·go

Numbers

1	*uno*	*oo*·no
2	*dos*	dos
3	*tres*	tres
4	*cuatro*	*kwa*·tro
5	*cinco*	*seen*·ko
6	*seis*	seys
7	*siete*	*sye*·te
8	*ocho*	o·cho
9	*nueve*	*nwe*·ve
10	*diez*	dyes
20	*veinte*	*veyn*·te
30	*treinta*	*treyn*·ta
40	*cuarenta*	kwa·*ren*·ta
50	*cincuenta*	seen·*kwen*·ta
60	*sesenta*	se·*sen*·ta
70	*setenta*	se·*ten*·ta
80	*ochenta*	o·*chen*·ta
90	*noventa*	no·*ven*·ta
100	*cien*	syen
1000	*mil*	meel

January	*enero*	e·*ne*·ro
February	*febrero*	fe·*bre*·ro
March	*marzo*	*mar*·so
April	*abril*	a·*breel*
May	*mayo*	*ma*·yo
June	*junio*	*khoon*·yo
July	*julio*	*khool*·yo
August	*agosto*	a·*gos*·to
September	*septiembre*	sep·*tyem*·bre
October	*octubre*	ok·*too*·bre
November	*noviembre*	no·*vyem*·bre
December	*diciembre*	dee·*syem*·bre

TRANSPORTATION

boat	*barco*	*bar*·ko
bus	*autobús*	ow·to·*boos*
plane	*avión*	a·*vyon*
train	*tren*	tren

... ticket	*billete de ...*	bee·*ye*·te de ...
1st-class	*primera clase*	pree·*me*·ra *kla*·se
2nd-class	*segunda clase*	se·*goon*·da *kla*·se
one-way	*ida*	*ee*·da
return	*ida y vuelta*	*ee*·da ee *vwel*·ta

first	*primero*	pree·*me*·ro
last	*último*	*ool*·tee·mo
next	*próximo*	*prok*·see·mo

bus stop	*parada de autobuses*	pa·*ra*·da de ow·to·*boo*·ses
cancelled	*cancelado*	kan·se·*la*·do
delayed	*retrasado*	re·tra·*sa*·do
ticket office	*taquilla*	ta·*kee*·ya
timetable	*horario*	o·*ra*·ryo
train station	*estación de trenes*	es·ta·*syon* de *tre*·nes

I want to go to ...
Quisiera ir a ... — kee·*sye*·ra eer a ...

Does it stop at ...?
¿Para en ...? — *pa*·ra en ...

What stop is this?
¿Cuál es esta parada? — kwal es *es*·ta pa·*ra*·da

What time does it arrive/leave?
¿A qué hora llega/sale? — a ke *o*·ra *ye*·ga/*sa*·le

Please tell me when we get to ...
¿Puede avisarme cuando lleguemos a ...? — *pwe*·de a·vee·*sar*·me *kwan*·do ye·*ge*·mos a ...

I want to get off here.
Quiero bajarme aquí. — *kye*·ro ba·*khar*·me a·*kee*

I'd like to hire a ...	*Quisiera alquilar ...*	kee·*sye*·ra al·kee·*lar* ...
bicycle	*una bicicleta*	*oo*·na bee·see·*kle*·ta
car	*un coche*	oon *ko*·che
motorcycle	*una moto*	*oo*·na *mo*·to

helmet	*casco*	*kas*·ko
mechanic	*mecánico*	me·*ka*·nee·ko
petrol/gas	*gasolina*	ga·so·*lee*·na
service station	*gasolinera*	ga·so·lee·*ne*·ra

Is this the road to ...?
¿Se va a ... por esta carretera? — se va a ... por es·ta ka·re·*te*·ra

(How long) Can I park here?
¿(Cuánto tiempo) Puedo aparcar aquí? — (*kwan*·to *tyem*·po) *pwe*·do a·par·*kar* a·*kee*

The car has broken down (at ...).
El coche se ha averiado (en ...). — el *ko*·che se a a·ve·*rya*·do (en ...)

I have a flat tyre.
Tengo un pinchazo. — *ten*·go oon peen·*cha*·so

I've run out of petrol.
Me he quedado sin gasolina. — me e ke·*da*·do seen ga·so·*lee*·na

GLOSSARY

For terms for food, drinks and other culinary vocabulary, see p304. For additional terms and information about the Spanish language, see the Language chapter on p303. This glossary contains some words in Guna (G) – for more on their language, see p232.

ANAM – Autoridad Nacional de Ambiente; former name for Panama's national environmental agency

ANCON – Asociación Nacional para la Conservación de la Naturaleza; National Association for the Conservation of Nature, Panama's leading private environmental organization

árbol – tree

artesanía – handicrafts

bahía – bay

balboa – the basic unit of Panamanian currency

baño(s) – restroom(s)

biblioteca – library

bocas – savory side dishes or appetizers

bohío – see rancho

boleto – ticket; for bus, museum etc

bolitas de carne – a snack of mildly spicy meatballs

boroquera – blowgun once used by the Emberá and Wounaan Indians

bote – motorized canoe

caballero(s) – gentleman (gentlemen)

cabaña – cabin

cacique – Guna tribal leader

calle – street

campesino/a – rural resident; peasant

carretera – highway

casa de cambio – money-exchange house

cascada – see chorro

catedral – cathedral

cayuco – dugout canoe

centavos – cent(s); 100 centavos equal one US dollar (or one Panamanian balboa)

cerro – hill

certificación de vuelo – certification of entry date into Panama

cerveza – beer

ceviche – marinated raw fish or shellfish

chévere – cool (slang)

chichas – heavily sweetened, fresh fruit drinks

chitra – sand fly

chiva – a rural bus, often a 28-seat Toyota coaster bus

chocosano (G) – storm that comes from the east

chorro – waterfall

cielo – the sky; the heavens

cine – cinema

ciudad – city

cocina – kitchen

cocobolo – a handsome tropical hardwood; used for carving life-sized images of snakes, parrots, toucans and other jungle wildlife

comarca – district

comida corriente – a set meal of rice, beans, plantains and a piece of meat or fish

conejo pintado – raccoon-like animal abundant in Parque Nacional Volcán Barú

cordillera – mountain range

corredor de aduana – customs broker

corvine – a flavorful white fish; Panama's most popular fish dish

cuatro por cuatro – 4WD vehicle

cuidado – caution

Cuna – See Guna

dama(s) – lady (ladies)

directo – direct bus

día feriado (días feriados) – national holiday(s)

edificio – building

Emberá – indigenous group living in Darién Province

empanada – corn turnover filled with ground meat, chicken, cheese or sweet fruit

feria – festival

fiesta – party

finca – farm

floresta – forest

frontera – border

fuerte – fort

Gali-Gali – the distinct Creole language of Bocas del Toro Province; it combines elements of English, Spanish and Guaymí

galón (galones) – gallon(s); fluid measure of 3.79L

gringo/a – tourist; especially a North American tourist

gruta – cave

guacamayo – macaw

Guna – the 70,000-strong indigenous tribe living in the Comarca de Guna Yala

habano – Havana cigar

haras – stable (for horses)

hombre – man

hormiga – ant

hospedaje – guesthouse

huaca(s) – golden object(s); made on the Panamanian isthmus in the pre-Columbian era and buried with Indians

huevo(s) – egg(s)

iglesia – church

Interamericana – the Pan-American Hwy; the nearly continuous highway running from Alaska to Chile (it breaks at the Darién Gap)

invierno – winter

IPAT – Instituto Panameño de Turismo; national tourism agency
isla – island

kilometraje – mileage
Kuna – see Guna

lago – lake
lancha – motorboat
lavamático/lavandería – laundromat
librería – bookstore
llanta – tire
llantería – tire repair shop
lleno – full
lluvia – rain
loro – parrot

manglar – mangrove
mariposa – butterfly
mercado – market
Merki (G) – American
mestizo/a – person of mixed indigenous and Spanish ancestry
metate – flat stone platform; used by Panama's pre-Columbian Indians to grind corn
migración – immigration
Migración y Naturalización – Immigration and Naturalization office
mirador – lookout point
molas (G) – colorful hand-stitched appliqué textiles made by Guna women
mono – monkey
montaña – mountain
muelle – pier
mujer(es) – woman (women)
museo – museum

Naso – an indigenous group scattered throughout the Bocas del Toro Province; also called the Teribe
Ngöbe-Buglé – an indigenous tribe located largely in Chiriquí Province

ola(s) – wave(s)

pájaro – bird
palapa – thatched, palm leaf–roofed shelter with open sides
panadería – bakery
parada (de autobús) – bus stop
Patois – a local dialect on the islands of Boca del Toro; a blend of English, Spanish and Gali-Gali
penca – palm tree leaves
permiso de salida – exit permit
pescador – fisherman
pescar – to fish
pipa – coconut water, served straight from the husk
piragua – canoe carved from a tree trunk
playa – beach
polleras – the intricate, lacy, Spanish-influenced dresses of the Península de Azuero; the national dress of Panama for festive occasions
pozo(s) – spring(s)
preservativo(s) – condom(s)
prohibido – prohibited; forbidden
prórroga de turista – a permit that resembles a driver's license, complete with photo; it allows you to stay in Panama for longer than the 90 days permitted for tourists
propina – tip; gratuity
protector solar – sunscreen lotion
puente – bridge
puerto – port
punta – point
puro – cigar

quebrada – stream

rana – frog
rana dorada – golden frog
rancho – a thatched-roof hut
raspados – shaved ice flavored with fruit juice
regalo – gift; present
río – river
seco – an alcoholic drink made from sugarcane
selva – jungle
Semana Santa – Holy Week; preceding Easter
sendero – trail
serpiente – snake
serranía – mountain range
sol – sun
supermercado – supermarket

tabla – surfboard
tagua – an ivory-colored nut that is carved into tiny figurines
tajadas – ripe plantains sliced lengthwise and fried
taller – workshop
tamales – spiced ground corn with chicken or pork, boiled in banana leaves
tarjeta(s) – plastic phonecard(s)
tarjeta de circulación – vehicle control certificate
tasajo – dried meat cooked with vegetables
taxi marino – water taxi
tigre – jaguar
típico – typical; traditional Panamanian folk music
tortilla de maíz – a thick, fried cornmeal tortilla
tortuga – sea turtle
trucha – trout

urbano – local (as in buses)

valle – valley
verano – summer
viajero – traveler
viento – wind
volcán – volcano

waga (G) – tourist
Wounaan – indigenous group living in Darién Province

Behind the Scenes

SEND US YOUR FEEDBACK

We love to hear from travelers – your comments keep us on our toes and help make our books better. Our well-traveled team reads every word on what you loved or loathed about this book. Although we cannot reply individually to your submissions, we always guarantee that your feedback goes straight to the appropriate authors, in time for the next edition. Each person who sends us information is thanked in the next edition – the most useful submissions are rewarded with a selection of digital PDF chapters.

Visit **lonelyplanet.com/contact** to submit your updates and suggestions or to ask for help. Our award-winning website also features inspirational travel stories, news and discussions.

Note: We may edit, reproduce and incorporate your comments in Lonely Planet products such as guidebooks, websites and digital products, so let us know if you don't want your comments reproduced or your name acknowledged. For a copy of our privacy policy visit lonelyplanet.com/privacy.

OUR READERS

Many thanks to the travelers who used the last edition and wrote to us with helpful hints, useful advice and interesting anecdotes:

Allen Hale, Camilo Consuegra, Christin Moser, Johan Claus, Jon Hanna, Joost Smekens, Leen Cuypers, Manuela Arigoni, Mike Vitiello, Mulle Harbort, Robin Vermoesen, Sharon Reeves, Susan Cohen, Wendy Girard

WRITER THANKS

Steve Fallon

Muchísimas gracias to the folk who offered assistance, ideas and/or hospitality along the way, including fellow traveller/guide Juan José Calvache in the Darién, Reggie & Cherie Flagg in Panama City, and the boys on the boats in the San Blás islands – Adam Riley, Fabio Carino and Brett Dickey. *Y a mi querido Panamá – ¡el país que unió las dos mitades del mundo!* (And to my dear Panama – the country that united the world's two halves!) As always, my share is dedicated to my now spouse, Michael Rothschild.

Carolyn McCarthy

Many thanks go out to the Bethels for accompanying me on part of my journey and for Daniel and Marta for providing some much needed refuge. I am also grateful to Rick Morales, Beatriz Schmidt, Annie Young and Carla Rankin for sharing their insights and contacts. Many others provided assistance in the form of homemade hot sauce, police intervention and karaoke. Lastly, my thanks to the isthmus for offering up one more great, sparkling adventure. *¡Hasta la próxima!*

ACKNOWLEDGEMENTS

Climate map data adapted from Peel MC, Finlayson BL & McMahon TA (2007) 'Updated World Map of the Köppen-Geiger Climate Classification'; *Hydrology and Earth System Sciences*, 11, 1633–44.

Cover photograph: three-toed sloth mother and young, Isla Barro Colorado, Christian Ziegler/Getty ©

THIS BOOK

This 8th edition of Lonely Planet's *Panama* guidebook was curated by Regis St Louis, and researched and written by Steve Fallon and Carolyn McCarthy. The previous edition was also written by Steve and Carolyn. This guidebook was produced by the following:

Destination Editor Alicia Johnson

Senior Product Editor Saralinda Turner

Regional Senior Cartographer Corey Hutchison

Product Editor Vicky Smith

Book Designer Aomi Ito

Cartographer Anthony Phelan

Assisting Editors Michelle Bennett, Andrea Dobbin, Bruce Evans, Gabrielle Innes, Kate James

Assisting Book Designer Jessica Rose

Cover Researcher Naomi Parker

Thanks to Bailey Freeman, Sandie Kestell, Amy Lynch

Index

Map Pages **000**
Photo Pages **000**

E

Map Pages **000**
Photo Pages **000**

F

G

H

V

W

Y

Z

Map Legend

Sights
- Beach
- Bird Sanctuary
- Buddhist
- Castle/Palace
- Christian
- Confucian
- Hindu
- Islamic
- Jain
- Jewish
- Monument
- Museum/Gallery/Historic Building
- Ruin
- Shinto
- Sikh
- Taoist
- Winery/Vineyard
- Zoo/Wildlife Sanctuary
- Other Sight

Activities, Courses & Tours
- Bodysurfing
- Diving
- Canoeing/Kayaking
- Course/Tour
- Sento Hot Baths/Onsen
- Skiing
- Snorkeling
- Surfing
- Swimming/Pool
- Walking
- Windsurfing
- Other Activity

Sleeping
- Sleeping
- Camping
- Hut/Shelter

Eating
- Eating

Drinking & Nightlife
- Drinking & Nightlife
- Cafe

Entertainment
- Entertainment

Shopping
- Shopping

Information
- Bank
- Embassy/Consulate
- Hospital/Medical
- Internet
- Police
- Post Office
- Telephone
- Toilet
- Tourist Information
- Other Information

Geographic
- Beach
- Gate
- Hut/Shelter
- Lighthouse
- Lookout
- Mountain/Volcano
- Oasis
- Park
- Pass
- Picnic Area
- Waterfall

Population
- Capital (National)
- Capital (State/Province)
- City/Large Town
- Town/Village

Transport
- Airport
- Border crossing
- Bus
- Cable car/Funicular
- Cycling
- Ferry
- Metro station
- Monorail
- Parking
- Petrol station
- Subway/Subte station
- Taxi
- Train station/Railway
- Tram
- Underground station
- Other Transport

Routes
- Tollway
- Freeway
- Primary
- Secondary
- Tertiary
- Lane
- Unsealed road
- Road under construction
- Plaza/Mall
- Steps
- Tunnel
- Pedestrian overpass
- Walking Tour
- Walking Tour detour
- Path/Walking Trail

Boundaries
- International
- State/Province
- Disputed
- Regional/Suburb
- Marine Park
- Cliff
- Wall

Hydrography
- River, Creek
- Intermittent River
- Canal
- Water
- Dry/Salt/Intermittent Lake
- Reef

Areas
- Airport/Runway
- Beach/Desert
- Cemetery (Christian)
- Cemetery (Other)
- Glacier
- Mudflat
- Park/Forest
- Sight (Building)
- Sportsground
- Swamp/Mangrove

Note: Not all symbols displayed above appear on the maps in this book

OUR STORY

A beat-up old car, a few dollars in the pocket and a sense of adventure. In 1972 that's all Tony and Maureen Wheeler needed for the trip of a lifetime – across Europe and Asia overland to Australia. It took several months, and at the end – broke but inspired – they sat at their kitchen table writing and stapling together their first travel guide, *Across Asia on the Cheap*. Within a week they'd sold 1500 copies. Lonely Planet was born.

Today, Lonely Planet has offices in Franklin, London, Melbourne, Oakland, Dublin, Beijing and Delhi, with more than 600 staff and writers. We share Tony's belief that 'a great guidebook should do three things: inform, educate and amuse'.

OUR WRITERS

Regis St Louis

Regis grew up in a small town in the American Midwest – the kind of place that fuels big dreams of travel – and he developed an early fascination with foreign dialects and world cultures. He spent his formative years learning Russian and a handful of Romance languages, which served him well on journeys across much of the globe. Regis has contributed to more than 50 Lonely Planet titles, covering destinations across six continents. His travels have taken him from the mountains of Kamchatka to remote island villages in Melanesia, and to many grand urban landscapes. When not on the road, he lives in New Orleans. Follow him on www.instagram.com/regisstlouis.

Steve Fallon Panamá Province, Coclé Province, Península de Azuero, Colón Province, Comarca de Guna Yala, Darién Province

A native of Boston, Massachusetts, Steve graduated from Georgetown University with a Bachelor of Science in modern languages. After working for several years for an American daily newspaper and earning a master's degree in journalism, his fascination with the 'new' Asia led him to Hong Kong, where he lived for over a dozen years, working for a variety of media and running his own travel bookshop. Steve lived in Budapest for three years before moving to London in 1994. He has written or contributed to more than 100 Lonely Planet titles. Steve is a qualified London Blue Badge Tourist Guide. Visit his website on www.steveslondon.com.

Carolyn McCarthy Panama City, Veraguas Province, Chiriquí Province, Bocas del Toro Province

Carolyn specializes in travel, culture and adventure in the Americas. She has written for *National Geographic, Outside, BBC Magazine, Sierra Magazine, Boston Globe* and other publications. A former Fulbright fellow and Banff Mountain Grant recipient, she has documented life in the most remote corners of Latin America. Carolyn has contributed to more than 40 guidebooks and anthologies for Lonely Planet, including the *Colorado, USA, Argentina, Chile, Trekking in the Patagonian Andes, Peru* and USA National Parks guides. For more information, visit www.carolyn mccarthy.org or follow her Instagram travels @mccarthyoffmap.

Published by Lonely Planet Global Limited
CRN 554153
8th edition – Jul 2019
ISBN 978 1 78657 491 6

10 9 8 7 6 5 4 3 2 1
Printed in China